T0178609

Lecture Notes in Computer Science

Lecture Notes in Artificial Intelligence   **13500**

Founding Editor

Jörg Siekmann

Series Editors

Randy Goebel, *University of Alberta, Edmonton, Canada*
Wolfgang Wahlster, *DFKI, Berlin, Germany*
Zhi-Hua Zhou, *Nanjing University, Nanjing, China*

The series Lecture Notes in Artificial Intelligence (LNAI) was established in 1988 as a topical subseries of LNCS devoted to artificial intelligence.

The series publishes state-of-the-art research results at a high level. As with the LNCS mother series, the mission of the series is to serve the international R & D community by providing an invaluable service, mainly focused on the publication of conference and workshop proceedings and postproceedings.

Mohamed Chetouani · Virginia Dignum ·
Paul Lukowicz · Carles Sierra

Editors

Human-Centered Artificial Intelligence

Advanced Lectures

 Springer

Editors
Mohamed Chetouani ⓘ
Sorbonne University
Paris, France

Virginia Dignum ⓘ
Umeå University
Umeå, Sweden

Paul Lukowicz ⓘ
German Research Centre for Artificial
Inteligence
Kaiserslautern, Germany

Carles Sierra ⓘ
Artificial Intelligence Research Institute
(IIIA-CSIC)
Bellaterra, Spain

ISSN 0302-9743   ISSN 1611-3349 (electronic)
Lecture Notes in Computer Science
Lecture Notes in Artificial Intelligence
ISBN 978-3-031-24348-6   ISBN 978-3-031-24349-3 (eBook)
https://doi.org/10.1007/978-3-031-24349-3

LNCS Sublibrary: SL7 – Artificial Intelligence

This Springer imprint is published by the registered company Springer Nature Switzerland AG
The registered company address is: Gewerbestrasse 11, 6330 Cham, Switzerland

Preface

The notion of human-centered AI increasingly dominates the public AI debate. It postulates the development and use of AI beneficial to humans on both individual and social level. As a discipline, human-centered AI (HCAI) aims to create AI systems that collaborate with humans, enhancing human capabilities and empowering humans to achieve their goals. That is, the focus amplify and augment rather than displace human abilities.

HCAI seeks to preserve human control in a way that ensures artificial intelligence meets our needs while also operating transparently, delivering equitable outcomes, and respecting human rights and ethical standards. Design methods that enable representation of and adherence to values such as privacy protection, autonomy (human in control), and non-discrimination are core to HCAI.

These are themes closely connected to some of the most fundamental challenges of AI. This volume provides a first comprehensive set of lecture notes on HCAI, developed for the European Advanced Course on AI (ACAI 2021). The chapters focus on issues related to the interface between AI and human-computer interaction (HCI), computational social science, and complexity science, as well as ethics and legal issues, with the objective to provide readers the basic knowledge needed to design, implement, operate and research the next generation of human-centric AI systems that enhance human capabilities and cooperate with humans on both the individual and the social level.

The present volume includes extended and improved lecture notes from ACAI 2021 courses, the following topics that are central to the understanding of the broad research field of human-centered AI. The topics also constitute the learning objectives of this volume:

- **Learning and Reasoning with Human in the Loop**: Learning, reasoning, and planning are interactive processes involving close synergistic collaboration between AI system(s) and user(s) within a dynamic, possibly open-ended real-world environment. Key gaps in knowledge and technology that must be addressed toward this vision include combining symbolic and sub-symbolic learning, explainability, translating a broad, vague notion of "fairness" into concrete algorithmic representations, continuous and incremental learning, compositionality of models and ways to adequately quantify and communicate model uncertainty.
- **Multimodal Perception**: Human interaction and human collaboration depend on the ability to understand the situation and reliably assign meanings to events and actions. People infer such meanings either directly from subtle cues in behavior, emotions, and nonverbal communications or indirectly from the context and background knowledge. This requires not only the ability to sense subtle behavior, and emotional and social cues but an ability to automatically acquire and apply background knowledge to provide context. The acquisition must be automatic because such background knowledge is far too complex to be hand-coded. Research on artificial systems with such abilities requires a strong foundation for the perception of humans, human actions,

and human environments. This foundation builds on recent advances in multimodal perception and modelling sensory, spatiotemporal, and conceptual phenomena.

- **Representations and Modeling**: Perception is the association of external stimuli to an internal model. Perception and modelling are inseparable. Human ability to correctly perceive and interpret complex situations, even when given limited and/or noisy input, is inherently linked to a deep, differentiated, understanding based on the human experience. A new generation of complex modelling approaches is needed to address this key challenge of human-centered AI including hybrid representations that combine symbolic, compositional approaches with statistical and latent representations. Such hybrid representations will allow the benefits of data-driven learning to be combined with knowledge representations that are more compatible with the way humans view and reason about the world around them.

- **Human-Computer Interaction (HCI)**: Beyond considering the human in the loop, the goal of human-AI is to study and develop methods for combined human-machine intelligence, where AI and humans work in cooperation and collaboration. This includes principled approaches to support the synergy of human and artificial intelligence, enabling humans to continue doing what they are good at but also be in control when making decisions. It has been proposed that AI research and development should follow three objectives: (i) to technically reflect the depth characterized by human intelligence; (ii) improve human capabilities rather than replace them; and (iii) focus on AI's impact on humans. There has also been a call for the HCI community to play an increasing role in realizing this vision, by providing their expertise in the following: human-machine integration/teaming, UI modelling and HCI design, transference of psychological theories, enhancement of existing methods, and development of HCI design standards.

- **Social AI**: As increasingly complex socio-technical systems emerge, consisting of many (explicitly or implicitly) interacting people and intelligent and autonomous systems, AI acquires an important societal dimension. A key observation is that a crowd of (interacting) intelligent individuals is not necessarily an intelligent crowd. Aggregated network and societal effects of AI and their (positive or negative) impacts on society are not sufficiently discussed in the public and not sufficiently addressed by AI research, despite the striking importance of understanding and predicting the aggregated outcomes of socio-technical AI-based systems and related complex social processes, as well as how to avoid their harmful effects. Such effects are a source of a whole new set of explainability, accountability, and trustworthiness issues, even assuming that we can solve those problems for an individual machine-learning-based AI system.

- **Societal, Legal and Ethical Impact of AI**: Every AI system should operate within an ethical and social framework in understandable, verifiable and justifiable ways. Such systems must in any case operate within the bounds of the rule of law, incorporating fundamental rights protection into the AI infrastructure. Theory and methods are needed for the responsible design of AI systems as well as to evaluate and measure the "maturity" of systems in terms of compliance with legal, ethical and societal principles. This is not merely a matter of articulating legal and ethical requirements but involves robustness, and social and interactivity design. Concerning the ethical and legal design of AI systems, we clarify the difference between legal and ethical concerns, as well as their interaction and ethical and legal scholars work side by side to develop both legal protection by design and value-sensitive design approaches.

ACAI School

The 18th European Advanced Course on AI (ACAI) took place in Berlin during October 11–15, 2021. It was organized by the European project Humane AI Net[1], in collaboration with EURAI[2], the European AI Association. Over 60 students participated in person in Berlin, while another 50 joined the school remotely. Most participants were PhD students, but also MSc students and postdocs attended ACAI 2021.

The school included 23 tutorials on different topics. The ACAI chairs invited senior members for HumanE AI Net and other EU AI networks to develop a tutorial in specific topics. The proposals were evaluated by the ACAI chairs in collaboration with HumanE AI Net scientific coordination team. After school, the lecturers were invited to submit a chapter, which were again reviewed by chairs, HumanE AI Net scientific coordination team as well as reviewers.

Next to the tutorials, the school also included invited talks by Yvonne Rogers, Kate Crawford, Yoshua Bengio and Ben Shneiderman, student poster presentations, and a mentorship program

Summary of Contributions

The themes of the volume cover topics on human-centered machine learning, explainable AI, ethics, law, argumentation and social simulation.

The contributions include learning objectives, a reading list and various resources (e.g., links to source codes).

The first section, *Introduction to Human-centered AI*, presents the main definitions and concepts covered in this volume.

The second section, *Human-centered Machine Learning*, includes several chapters on machine learning ranging from basic concepts of neural networks to interactive learning. This section also describes modern approaches such as transformers in natural language processing, speech processing, vision and multi-modal processing.

The third section, *Explainable AI*, deals with both technical and philosophical concepts. The section includes a conceptual overview of computational cognitive vision together with practical demonstrations.

The fourth section, *ethics, law and society AI*, introduces main concepts of Ethics and Law. This section also discusses ethics in communication.

The fifth section, *Argumentation*, focuses on concepts of arguments and attacks. The concepts are illustrated with several concrete examples in cognitive technologies of learning and explainable inference or decision making.

---

[1] https://www.humane-ai.eu/.

[2] https://www.eurai.org/.

The last section, *Social Simulation*, deals with agent-based social simulations that are used to investigate complex phenomena within social systems. The chapters show how they could be designed, evaluated and employed by decision makers.

September 2022

Mohamed Chetouani
Virginia Dignum
Paul Lukowicz
Carles Sierra

Organization

General Chairs

Virginia Dignum   Umeå University, Sweden
Paul Lukowicz   German Research Center for Artificial
     Intelligence, Germany

Publication Chair

Mohamed Chetouani   Sorbonne University, France

Publicity Chair

Davor Orlic   Knowledge 4 All Foundation, UK

Organization Chairs

Tatyana Sarayeva   Umeå University, Sweden
Carlos Sierra   Artificial Intelligence Research Institute, Spain

Reviewers

Bettina Fazzinga   DICES, University of Calabria, Italy
Antonis Kakas   University of Cyprus, Cyprus
Andreas Theodorou   Umeå University, Sweden
Clàudia Figueras   Stockholm University, Sweden
Marija Slavkovik   University of Bergen, Norway
Stefan Buijsman   TU Delft, The Netherlands
Leila Methnani   Umeå University, Sweden
Frank Dignum   Umeå University, Sweden
Adam Dahlgren   Umeå University, Sweden

Contents

Ethics, Law and Society AI

Argumentation

Social Simulation

Introduction to Human-Centered AI

The Advanced Course on Human-Centered AI: Learning Objectives

Mohamed Chetouani[1]([✉])[iD], Virginia Dignum[2][iD], Paul Lukowicz[3][iD], and Carles Sierra[4][iD]

[1] Sorbonne University, Paris, France
mohamed.chetouani@sorbonne-universite.fr
[2] Umeå University, Umeå, Sweden
virginia@cs.umu.se
[3] German Research Center for Artificial Intelligence (DFKI), Kaiserslautern, Germany
paul.lukowicz@dfki.de
[4] Artificial Intelligence Research Institute (IIIA-CSIC), Barcelona, Spain
sierra@iiia.csic.es

Abstract. Human-centered AI mobilizes several disciplines such as AI, human-machine interaction, philosophy, ethics, law and social sciences. In such a context, being introduced to the basic concepts of Human-centered AI is challenging. In this chapter, we describe the learning objectives of the Advanced Course on AI organized in 2021 with a focus on Human-centered AI.

Keywords: Machine Learning · Explainable AI · Ethics · Law · Argumentation · Social simulation

1 Introduction

There is broad agreement on a high level definition of "Human Centered AI" as AI that is "beneficial to humans and society". There is much less agreement on translating that broad vision into specific lower level technological requirements and scientific research questions. This is on one hand due to the fact that the notions of being beneficial to humans and society differ from stakeholder to stakeholder (and between cultures). On the other hand it is difficult (if not impossible) to come up with a 1:1 complete and consistent translation between a notion of "being beneficial" defined on a policy level and concrete technical properties of an AI system.

This work has received funding from European Union's Horizon 2020 ICT-48 research and innovation actions under grant agreement No 952026 (HumanE-AI-Net)). The ACAI school has also received support from EurAI.

M. Chetouani et al. (Eds.): ACAI 2021, LNAI 13500, pp. 3–7, 2023.
https://doi.org/10.1007/978-3-031-24349-3_1

The HumanE-AI-Net project[1] brings together leading European research centres, universities and industrial enterprises into a network of centres of excellence to conduct fundamental and applied research on Human-centered AI. In particular, to develop robust, trustworthy AI systems that can 'understand' humans, the challenge is to adapt to complex real-world environments and interact appropriately in complex social settings.

The Advanced Course on AI (ACAI) is a specialized course in Artificial Intelligence sponsored by the European Association on AI (EurAI)[2] in odd-numbered years. The theme of the 2021 ACAI School was Human-centered AI.

Within ACAI 2021 (Advanced course on AI), researchers from the HumanE-AI-Net consortium as well as invited speaker gave lectures related to the state of the art in Human-centered AI, focusing not just on narrow AI questions but emphasizing issues related to the interface between AI and Human-Computer Interaction (HCI), Computational Social Science (and Complexity Science) as well as ethics and legal issue.

This volume provides the reader with the basic knowledge needed to design, implement, operate and research the next generation of Human-centered AI systems that are focused on enhancing Human capabilities and optimally cooperating with humans on both the individual and the social level.

The volume gathers researchers from different backgrounds such as AI, human-machine interaction, philosophy, ethics, law and social sciences. A first chapter, from Luc Steels, is dedicated to the introduction and discussion of conceptual foundations. Then, a series of chapters are proposed to the reader focusing on specific scientific themes:

- Human-centered Machine Learning
- Explainable AI
- Ethics, Law and Society
- Argumentation
- Social Simulation

In the following, we describe the specific *Learning Objectives* of these chapters.

2 Specific Learning Objectives

2.1 Human-Centered Machine Learning

The first theme deals with machine learning from basic concepts to modern approaches using deep learning and interactive machine learning. Seven chapters are proposed.

Three chapters from James Crowley introduce neural networks, generative networks, autoencoders and convolutional neural networks. The first chapter describes fundamental concepts of deep-learning that are described and used

---

[1] https://www.humane-ai.eu.
[2] https://www.eurai.org.

in later chapters. The second one covers fundamental concepts from information theory as well as applications such as Variational Autoencoders (VAEs) and Generative Adversarial Networks (GANs). The last chapter reviews popular architectures that have played a key role in the emergence of Deep Learning as an enabling technology for Artificial Intelligence.

Three other chapters focus on Transformers, which is a model relying entirely on the attention mechanism. Transformers brought significant improvements in performance on several machine learning tasks. In a chapter dedicated to Natural Language Processing, François Yvon presents different facets of the Transformer architecture. He also discusses limitations. In the chapter Vision and Multimodal Transformers from Camille Guinaudeau, the reader will learn more about the historical approaches for computer vision, namely convolutions and self-attention. The learning objectives are also (i) to understand the adaptation of the Transformers architecture to deal with the visual data peculiarities; and (ii) grasp the functioning principles of recent work applying Transformers architecture to multimodal tasks and data. The last chapter, from Marc Evrard, provides a short history of the evolution of automatic speech recognition systems and shows how Transformers impacted the speech processing domain.

The last chapter of the Human-centered Machine Learning theme deals with Interactive Robot Learning. In this chapter, Mohamed Chetouani overviews methods and models of the research domain. The learning objectives are the following: (i) Understand human teaching strategies; (ii) Gain knowledge about learning from feedback, demonstrations and instructions; (iii) Explore ongoing works on how human teaching biases could be modeled; and (iv) Discover applications of interactive robot learning.

2.2   Explainable AI

This second theme addresses the challenge of Explainable AI with three chapters from different disciplines such as computer science and social sciences.

The first chapter from Gionnatati et al. provides a reasoned introduction to the work of Explainable AI (XAI) to date and surveys the literature focusing on symbolic AI-related approaches. The authors motivate the needs of XAI in real-world and large-scale applications while presenting state-of-the-art techniques and best practices and discussing the many open challenges.

The second chapter from Stefan Buijsman provides another view and highlights accounts of explanation in philosophy that might inform what those technical tools should ultimately deliver. The learning objectives there are (i) Awareness of the recent arguments against the need for explanations of machine learning algorithms; (ii) Ability to discuss the merits of these arguments; and (iii) Knowledge of the main accounts of explanation in the philosophical literature.

The last chapter of this theme is from Mehul Bhatt and Jakob Suchan. The chapter presents general methods for the processing and semantic interpretation of dynamic visuospatial imagery with a particular emphasis on the ability to abstract, learn, and reason with cognitively rooted structured characterisations of commonsense knowledge pertaining to space and motion. The chapter provides a practical or operational view of visuospatial commonsense reasoning and learning through five complementary examples (including source codes).

2.3 Ethics, Law and Society

The third theme focuses on Ethics, Law and Society with five chapters.

Boella and Mori propose in the first chapter an introduction to Ethics and AI. The learning objectives are (i) to have a glimpse about what is Ethics; (ii) to understand that Ethics evolves over time, also as a result of the emergence of new technologies; and (iii) to acquire the width of the impact of AI on Ethics.

The second chapter is an introduction to Law. Hildebrandt and De Bois provide insights on what law does, how it operates and why it matters. The chapter (i) provides a better understanding of the inner workings of the law; (ii) Identifies nonsensical headlines about the law as such (similar to tech headlines); (iii) offers a taste of EU legislation that co-defines the global marketplace for AI systems (Brussels Effect: EU exporting rules and standards); and enables reasoning about the content of the law (the interpretation of legal conditions when deciding on legal effect).

The third chapter from Marija Slavkovik is primarily intended for students of computer science and artificial intelligence (AI) who are interested in how to establish what ethical impact the research and products they develop have on individuals and society. The aim is to gain knowledge and familiarity with ethical principles of interest to AI problems such as Accountability, Transparency, Explainability, Interpretability, Fairness, and Privacy. Among the learning objectives of this chapter, we have the ability to discern between ethically motivated computation properties of an AI system and the extent to which an AI system satisfies an ethical principle.

The chapter of Methnani et al. presents ongoing research in the field of Responsible AI and explores numerous methods of operationalising AI ethics. The learning objectives of this chapter are: (i) Understand core concepts and misconceptions related to Responsible AI (RAI); (ii) Gain knowledge about ongoing policy initiatives around AI; (iii) Develop a practical grasp of why and how RAI is applied; and (iv) Explore ongoing research in the theme of RAI.

In the last chapter, Carme Torras and Luís G. Ludescher address how science and science fiction can inspire each other and how science fiction can be used as an educational tool in teaching ethics of AI and robotics. The chapter includes sections containing the questions asked by the audience during the tutorial as well as the provided answers.

2.4 Argumentation

In the first chapter, Fazzinga and Mellema focus on abstract argumentation and probabilistic abstract argumentation. In particular, they provide the reader with a proper knowledge of how dialogues and disputes are modeled as abstract argumentation graphs and how analysts reason over them.

The second chapter from Dietz et al. examines the role of Computational Argumentation at the theoretical and practical level of Human-centered AI.

2.5   Social Simulation

The last theme of this volume is dedicated to agent-based social simulations that are used to investigate complex phenomena within social systems.

The first chapter from Fabian et al. introduces agent-based social simulation (ABSS) models and methods. The learning objectives are: (i) to describe and relate the principles of ABSS, including fundamental ABSS approaches and techniques as well as applications of ABSS to real-world problems; (ii) to conduct and analyze experiments using an existing ABSS model and a well-established ABSS simulator (NetLogo); (iii) to identify and relate the key cognitive components in advanced ABSS models, to explain the main reasons for using cognitive models, and to identify the need for such models on a real-world problem; (iv) to explain and specify how an existing agent architecture in an ABSS model can be extended for facilitating the investigation of new policies; (v) to explain how using ABSS for policy making alters the ABSS-making activities and to relate these activities to concrete deliverables; (vi) to analytically discover the origin of a complex emerging phenomena, based on extensive raw multidimensional ABSS output.

The last chapter from Pedreschi et al. discusses the social dimension of Artificial Intelligence in terms of how AI technologies can support or affect emerging social challenges. The learning objectives of this tutorial are (i) understand and approach the emergent properties of real networks as well as their possible harmful effects on society; (ii) leverage agent-based models to understand phenomena where human behavior plays a key role; and (iii) familiarize with the previously illustrated concepts through python libraries and tailored notebooks.

Conceptual Foundations
of Human-Centric AI

Luc Steels[1,2]([⊠]) (ID)

[1] Barcelona Supercomputing Center, Barcelona, Spain
[2] Venice International University, Venice, Italy
`steels@arti.vub.ac.be`

Abstract. This tutorial does not focus on specific techniques or applications but on the conceptual foundations of human-centric AI. It discusses a number of fundamental questions: What is needed to make AI more human-centered or 'humane'? Why do we need to combine reactive and deliberative intelligence for human-centric AI? What is the nature of meaning and understanding in human intelligence? Why is emulating understanding in artificial systems necessary but hard? What is the role of narratives in understanding? What are some of the open issues for realizing human-centric AI capable of narrative-based understanding?

Keywords: Meaning · Understanding · Human-centric AI · Meaningful AI · Narrative · Conceptual foundations of AI

Learning objectives

1. Learn the distinction between reactive and deliberative intelligence and why we need both for human-centric AI.
2. Realize why emulating understanding in AI systems is hard and what can be done to cope with its difficulties.
3. Find out the role of multi-layered models and narratives in understanding.
4. Learn about the breakthroughs that are needed to reach narrative-based understanding.

---

1 Introduction

Despite the success in performance of data-driven AI, it also exhibits 'weird' behavior, because it lacks the capacity to understand and exercise deliberative

The writing of this paper was funded by the EU Pathfinder Project MUHAI on 'Meaning and Understanding in Human-centric AI' (EU grant 951846 to the Venice International University) and by the 'HumaneAI-Net' EU Coordination Project (EU grant 952026 to the Universitat Pompeu Fabra in Barcelona).

M. Chetouani et al. (Eds.): ACAI 2021, LNAI 13500, pp. 8–35, 2023.
https://doi.org/10.1007/978-3-031-24349-3_2

intelligence. You can consider this weird behavior humorous [46] but when it happens with applications that are operating in the real world and have real-life consequences, weird AI behavior becomes dangerous and unethical, for example, when an AI system recommends children to execute life-threatening challenges[1] or is making technocratic social decisions that are unfair and cause hardship for those undergoing those decisions.[2]

In reaction to a growing number of such incidents, there have been calls for the development of 'human-centric' or 'humane' AI. As suggested by Nowak, Lukowicz and Horodecki:

"Human-centric AI focuses on collaborating with humans, enhancing human capabilities, and empowering humans to better achieve their goals" [34].

Human-centric AI has become a focal point of current research and development, particularly in Europe, where the EU Commission's strategy on AI and the AI strategies of many EU member states call for AI that shows human agency and oversight, technical robustness and safety, privacy and data governance, transparency, care for diversity, non-discrimination and fairness, focus on societal and environmental well-being, and accountability [63].

Research in human-centric AI calls for a change in focus compared to the machine-centered AI typified by data-driven statistical machine learning:

- Human-centric AI systems are asked to be aware of the *goals and intentions* of their users and base their own goals and dialog on *meanings* rather than on statistical patterns of past behavior only, even if statistical patterns can play a very important role as well.
- Human goals and values should always take precedence. Respect for human autonomy should be built into the system by design, leading to qualities such as *fairness and respect.*
- Human-centric AI systems should be able to explain their reasoning and learning strategies so that the *decisions are understandable by humans.* Only by emphasizing human understandability will human-centric AI achieve proper *explainability* and *transparency.*
- Human-centric AI systems should not only learn by observation or theorizing about reality but also by *taking advice* from humans, as suggested in John McCarthy's original 1958 proposal of the Advice Taker [27].
- Human-centric AI should be able to use *natural communication*, i.e. communication primarily based on human language, not only by mimicking language syntax but, more importantly, using the rich semantics of natural languages,

---

[1] In december 2021 the chatbot ALEXA by Amazon recommended a 10 year old to 'plug in a phone charger about halfway into a wall outlet, then touch a penny to the exposed prongs'.

[2] In 2020 a scandal known as the 'toeslagenaffaire' (benefit scandal) hit the Dutch political world forcing a fall of the government. Due to excessive zeal of the tax agency controlling the allocation of child benefits and the use of machine learning on social data (which were supposed to be private) many families were pushed into poverty and experienced devastating legal difficulties.

augmented with multi-modal communication channels. This is needed to support explainability, and *accountability*.

– Human-centric AI systems should have the capacity of *self-reflection* which can be achieved by a meta-level architecture that is able to track decision-making and intervene by catching failures and repairing them. By extension, the architecture should support the construction of a theory of mind of other agents, i.e. how they see the world, what their motivations and intentions are, and what knowledge they are using or lacking. Only through this capacity can AI achieve intelligent cooperation and adequate explicability, and learn efficiently through cultural transmission.

– Finally, human-centric AI systems should reflect the *ethical and moral standards* that are also expected from humans or organisations in our society, particularly for supporting tasks that are close to human activity and interest.

All of these objectives point in the direction of meaningful AI, i.e. AI where meaningful distinctions are used to build rich models of problem situations and where deliberative reasoning complements reactive behavior. The desired properties of human-centric AI are all very difficult to achieve and certainly far beyond the state of the art. They will not appear by decree. Most importantly they require going towards a hybrid form of intelligence that combines reactive and deliberative AI [31].

Two arguments have been raised *against* the hypothesis that meaning, understanding and deliberative intelligence are necessary for advancing AI and its applications. The first argument is that big data and statistical training is sufficient to approximate human intelligence for most application areas of (economic) value. The limitations of reactive AI that are increasingly becoming apparent, namely the lack of robustness, a weak capacity to come up with human-understandable explanations and the difficulty to deal with novel situations and outliers, suggest that this argument is not true, or at least not true for many domains of human interest.

But there is a second counter-argument, namely that even though a deliberative form of intelligence would be beneficial, particularly for human-centric AI, it is an impossible target because the required knowledge is not available and cannot be acquired by machines. Proponents of this argument point to earlier research in AI on understanding and deliberation in the 1970s and 1980s. Although this work lead to an earlier strong wave of AI applications (namely expert systems in the 1990s and the semantic web in the 2000s) they argue this research has stalled once it was realized that understanding requires a massive amount of encyclopedic knowledge, fine-grained accurate language processing based on in-depth grammars, and the ability to categorize perceived reality in terms of the ontologies required for rich models.

However, the situation has changed compared to decades ago. Not only are there now more powerful symbolic learning strategies, we also have very large knowledge bases in the form of knowledge graphs that provide some of the needed encyclopedic background knowledge [1]. They have been made possible by the large-scale collective efforts to feed information to various open encyclopedic resources such as Wikipedia, and by AI-based 'crawlers' that scavange the web for information. These knowledge graphs are still expanding at a rapid pace.

Moreover thanks to advances in fine-grained precision language processing, particularly for computational construction grammar, we can now go significantly beyond the coarse-grained surface analysis that is common in statistical NLP and analyze sentences from a semantic and pragmatic point of view [53]. In addition, techniques for grounding situation models in real world sensory-motor data have made significant advances as well mainly due to advances in data-driven approaches to perception [58].

Nevertheless, a huge amount of work remains to be done to complement existing data-driven AI with the capacity for understanding and deliberation. The work consists partly in expanding greatly the knowledge sources already available today (knowledge graphs, fine-grained grammars, etc.) but also in researching novel architectures and learning strategies for emulating the process of understanding.

Summarizing:

Human-centric AI systems are asked to be aware of the goals and intentions of their users, exhibit fairness and respect, explain their decisions in human terms, take human advice, use natural communication, can self-reflect and follow ethical and moral standards. All this requires going beyond data-driven reactive AI and integrating the capacity to understand in a human-like narrative way, be sensitive to context, and perform deliberative reasoning in addition to reacting quickly with ready-made stimulus-response associations.

The rest of this paper unpicks the various concepts used in this summary.

2   What is the Distinction Between Reactive and Deliberative Intelligence?

Try to complete the sentence:

(1) Frank cannot come because his wife has tested positive for ...

Most people (and data-driven AI systems) would not hesitate for one second and complete this sentence automatically and quickly with the word 'covid' or a synonym of that word. Kahneman [22] categorises this as a *reactive* form of intelligence, which he calls system 1. It is *fast thinking* - if we could even call this thinking. It is automatic, effortless and without awareness. A fast response is possible when there is an associative memory that directly relates stimuli with responses and these stimulus-response patterns can be acquired by sufficient exposure to examples and an induction algorithm. In this case, the fast response is possible because the word 'covid' has been appearing a lot in this specific textual context (n-grams) and we (or an AI system) have acquired the statistical frequency of the n-gram 'tested positive for covid'. A decade ago the word 'AIDS' or 'Ebola' would have been more frequent in this n-gram.

Whereas reactive intelligence is found in all animals (and some would argue also in plants), human intelligence is unique because it can operate not only in a reactive but also in a deliberative mode (Kahneman's system 2). A *deliberative* mode of intelligence is classified as *slow thinking* because it takes more time and more effort. A deliberative mode is based on making a rich model of the situation that enables the formation and consideration of different hypotheses. The model should be grounded in the facts known about the situation but also in previous experiences of similar situations. In a deliberative mode we become aware of our reasoning, can verbalize the argumentation, and explain to others why we are thinking in a particular way. We learn in a constructivist fashion by creatively generating, testing and adapting theories and by cultural transmission through language and education.

Using a deliberative mode we can also complete the sentence above but now based on a model that contains not only the stated facts (for example that Frank has a wife and that she tested positive) but also inferences based on common sense knowledge (for example that a husband and a wife typically live together and hence have a lot of exposure to each other's infections) as well as specific knowledge (for example about what rules hold during the covid pandemic in a particular country).

Here are some more facts a rich model for sentence (1) could include:

- Frank was supposed to come to a meeting.
- Covid is an infectious disease
- There is a covid pandemic.
- Covid can be tested.
- A person infected has to stay in quarantine.
- Quarantine means you have to stay home.
- If you have been in contact with an infected person you have to go in quarantine yourself.
- A husband and wife typically live together and hence have a lot of exposure to each other.
- Frank's wife is a high risk contact for Frank.

Given these facts and additional world knowledge, it is possible to answer questions like 'If only Frank's wife has tested positive, why is he himself not able to come to the meeting?' 'Does Frank also have to be tested?', and counterfactual questions like 'Suppose that the meeting alluded to is in Australia and Frank has been spending the last month there without his wife who stayed in the Netherlands, would Frank still not be allowed to come?' The model also supports the formulation of specific hypotheses, such as 'Frank's wife was probably tested recently for Covid' or general hypotheses, such as 'Where Frank lives, people who have had contact with a positive person are supposed to receive a message to quarantine'.

A rich model gives *insight* into the problem situation and shows paths to problem solutions. It not only helps in question-answering, problem solving or decision making. It also prevents inappropriate predictions. Consider for example sentence (2):

(2) Soon after her marriage, Lise was even more happy because she tested positive for ...

Completion with the word 'pregnancy' is now more appropriate despite the higher frequency of the n-gram 'tested positive for Covid'. Understanding this sentence and providing the most sensible completion requires knowing and inferring facts such as: marriage is typically the beginning of forming a family, getting children requires getting pregnant, pregnancy can be tested, a positive test for pregnancy makes you happy if you want children, testing positive for Covid does not make you happy.

Summarizing:

> **Reactive intelligence rests on associations between stimulus patterns and responses. Deliberative intelligence rests on making rich models and using reasoning and inference to find a solution.**

3 Are Reactive and Deliberative Intelligence both Needed for AI?

Recent advances in AI have shown that neural networks trained on sufficient amounts of data are able to emulate reactive intelligence and reach unexpected high levels of performance. The training is typically carried out through a prediction task. For example, a large corpus of language texts is assembled and the network is trained to predict the next word in a sentence in this corpus, [10] or a large set of images is assembled and labeled and the network is trained to predict which label should be assigned to an image [39]. Due to the capacity of neural networks to generalize, the prediction is not just based on a simple recall but can handle variations in the input, as long as they stay within the statistical distribution found in the training data.

We call AI systems that emulate reactive intelligence *reactive AI*. Reactive AI is not the exclusive province of neural networks. The earlier rule-based expert systems from the 1970s and 80s mostly tried to solve expert problems by recognizing patterns and finding solutions as fast as possible by the application of heuristic rules [13]. A lot of the work in behavior-based robotics in the early 1990s also attempted to come to grips with reactive intelligence, but now by the construction of dynamical systems that establish direct connections between sensing and actuating without sophisticated world models [57].

On the other hand research in deliberative intelligence was the focal point of earlier AI research that emphasized the construction of symbolic (i.e. non-numerical) models, logical inference procedures, the design and implementation of ontologies, the gathering and implementation of large amounts of domain knowledge, symbolic and constructivist learning strategies, and fine-grained precision language processing based on grammars [19]. This research has also lead to impressive demonstrations ranging from mathematical theorem provers to expert systems supporting the configuration of complex equipment.

However, it has also become clear that there is no 'magic bullet' to obtain deliberative intelligence. Currently available techniques for artificial deliberative intelligence or *deliberative AI*, such as answer-set programming, constraint solving or logic programming, are powerful but they require that a problem is first exhaustively stated in a logical form and that all needed knowledge is expressed in carefully formalized axioms. Only in that case can the inference machine go to work.

It is precisely this first step, namely to define, formalize and structure the problem and the relevant world knowledge, that requires the process we call understanding. Certainly, understanding rests on vast amounts of knowledge and considerable ingenuity and effort is needed to sufficiently catch up and keep up with human competence. This makes deliberative AI not economically viable in many circumstances. But that does not mean that deliberative intelligence is not an integral component of human intelligence nor that deliberative AI is for ever out of reach. It is simply crucial in a wide range of applications that society expects from AI.

The Achilles' heel of achieving reactive AI based on statistical induction is the need for a large amount of representative high quality data, which often is not available or not available in a clean enough form to be reliable. The Achilles' heel of deliberative AI is the need for large amounts of knowledge, which may not exist or cannot be verbalized by human experts. The cooperation between the two modes of intelligence can potentially overcome both limitations and lead us to the next wave of AI.

Already many reactive AI systems are trained using the outcome of deliberative intelligence and they fall back on deliberative intelligence when there are no ready-made solution patterns available yet. This approach was first demonstrated by Arthur Samuel in 1959 [42] for the game of checkers but underlies also the success of AlphaGo and other AI systems for board games. At the same time many systems using deliberative intelligence rely on reactive intelligence to tackle larger scale problems, restrict search, provide fast access to very large knowledge bases or deal with grounding issues.

So it is a safe bet that the future lies in a combination of reactive and deliberative AI, even for sensory-motor intelligence. This combination is called *hybrid AI* (although that is also used for AI systems that work closely with humans) or also *composite* or *integrated* AI.

Summarizing:

Human intelligence relies both on reactive and deliberative intelligence and so should AI. Reactive intelligence can bring fast solutions to subproblems and agents can therefore solve more challenging problems. On the other hand deliberative intelligence can solve problems where no ready-made solution is available by exploiting domain knowledge and problems where solutions to subproblems have to be combined in novel ways.

4   What is Understanding?

Where do the rich models needed for deliberative intelligence come from? They are based on language input, data, images and sounds, actions and their effect, as well as contextual knowledge, memory of past episodes, mental simulation, and inference based on semantic memory. The process of constructing a model that integrates all these different sources of information in the service of making the rich models needed for deliberative intelligence is what we call *understanding* (Fig. 1). It requires reactive intelligence: for grounding the model in sensory data through feature detection and pattern recognition, for the fast access to possibly relevant information and for the acquisition and application of heuristics to decide which hypothesis deserves to be prioritized. The construction of a rich model also requires deliberative intelligence to fill in gaps through inference based on world knowledge and using fine-grained analysis of linguistic, visual or other kinds of input.

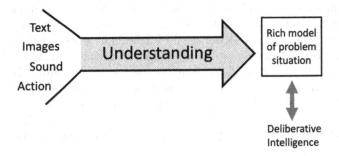

Fig. 1. Understanding constructs a rich model for use by deliberative intelligence from multi-modal sources (text, image, sound, action) by combining the outcome of a variety of knowledge sources.

Here is an example to clarify further the notion of understanding. Consider the image in Fig. 2 (left) (adapted from [56]). This is from a poster that used to be employed in French and Belgian schools to teach children about daily life and to learn how to talk about it. We instantly recognize that this is a scene from a restaurant, using cues like the dress and activities of the waiter and waitress, or the fact that people are sitting at different tables in the room. Data-driven image recognition algorithms are able to segment and identify some of the people and objects in the scene and in some cases label them with a fair degree of accuracy, see Fig. 2 (right).

But these algorithms do not understand the picture in the way we would commonly use the term understanding. Understanding requires a lot more than segmentation and labeling. For example, when asked whether a person is missing at the table on the right, we could all come up with a straightforward answer: Yes there is a person missing, because there is an empty chair, a plate and cutlery on the table section in front of the chair, and a napkin hanging over the chair. So there must have been a third person sitting there, probably the mother of the

Fig. 2. Left: Didactic image of a scene in a restaurant. Right: Image segmentation identifying regions that contain people (based on Google's Cloud Vision API).

child also sitting at the table. Moreover nobody has a lot of difficulty to imagine where the mother went. There is a door marked 'lavabo' (meaning 'toilet' in French) and it is quite plausible that she went to the toilet while waiting for the meal to arrive. Any human viewer would furthermore guess without hesitation why the child is showing his plate to the waitress arriving with the food and why the person to the left of the child (from our perspective) is probably the father looking contently at the child. We could go on further completing the description, for example, ask why the cat at the feet of the waitress looks eagerly at the food, observe that the food contains chicken with potatoes, notice that it looks windy outside, that the vegetation suggests some place in the south of France, and so on.

Clearly these interpretations rely heavily on inferences reflecting knowledge about restaurants, families, needs and desires, roles played by people in restaurants (waiter, waitress, bar tender, cashier, customer). These inferences are not only necessary to properly interpret the visual image in Fig. 1 but also to answer questions such as 'Who is the waitress?', 'Why is she approaching the table?', 'Where is the missing person at the table?', 'Who will get food first?', We can also make predictions and reconstructions, for example, that the waitress will reach the table, put the food on the table, cut the chicken into pieces, and put them on the different plates, or that the mother of the child will come back from the toilet, sit down again at the table, and start eating herself.

Summarizing:

Understanding is the process of constructing a meaningful model of a situation and linking this model to background knowledge, memory of similar past situations and factual observations. The model needs to be sufficiently detailed to support deliberative intelligence in tasks like answering questions, giving explanations for these answers, generating hypotheses, seeking more evidence, handling counterfactuals, inferring a plan of action and making predictions in a deliberative way.

5   What are Meanings?

The definition of understanding given earlier emphasizes that a model must be 'meaningful', but what does that mean? The concept of meaning is notoriously difficult to define and it has many facets. For the present purpose, let us adopt a definition articulated by philosophers Sperber and Wilson [50]: A model consists of descriptions and the building blocks of these descriptions are *distinctions*, also commonly called categorisations or concepts. We say that a model is meaningful if the distinctions it uses are <u>relevant</u> to the interaction between the agent making the model and the environment, in other words if the descriptions making up the model are critical for the tasks and contexts the agent has to cope with.

For example, the distinction between red and green is meaningful in the context of traffic because red means you should stop and green means you can advance. The exact choice for which region in the spectrum represents red or green is not critical - and its perception would vary with the ambient light and the context anyway. The spectral value is even culturally determined so that in some countries the green traffic light looks rather blue[3] or the orange traffic light amber or yellow. This example makes the point that a perceptual category exploits a regularity in the environment but is not entirely dependent on it and consequently human perceptual categories are not derivable from statistical induction over examples only.

Here is a second example: The distinction between adult and non-adult is meaningful in the context of law because it refers to the moment at which one acquires full capacities and responsibilities under the law. The age is usually defined as 18 years, but that can differ between countries (in Scotland it is 16 years) and purposes (like obtaining a driver's licence which may be allowed earlier). Moreover, in many countries (like Belgium) you can also be classified as adult (in the sense of gaining full legal capacity) if you are a parent or have gotten married *before* 18 years. The meaning of adult is therefore rooted in interactions between the agent and the environment, which now includes other agents and legal institutions and customs. This example makes again the point that human distinctions cannot be learned empirically from observations because the data simply does not contain the necessary information. As Wittgenstein said: Meaningful distinctions are imposed on reality, shared through conventions and procedures, and defined and transmitted through language.

It is not only that the distinctions used in meaningful models must be relevant, also the way the context is segmented into different entities must be relevant. Which entities are included in a model depends on the task and the context for which the model is intended. For example, a sequence of events may be considered as a single episode to be described as a whole or as different

---

[3] For example, in Japan the green light looks more blueish because until a century ago Japanese did not have a basic color word for green, only for blue ("ao") and green was considered a shade of ao. Contemporary Japanese has a word for green, "midori", but the traffic light is still called "ao". As a compromise to abide by international regulations but not deviate too much from language custom, traffic lights in Japan are a greenish shade of blue rather than prototypical green.

episodes, depending on the purposes of the model and the available data. How we decompose an object into its subcomponents depends on whether we have to recognize the object or to dismantle and repair it.

Although data-driven statistical AI applications are responsible for the recent headlines in AI, there are indications that the distinctions these applications acquire and use are not meaningful in a human sense. This leads to a lack of robustness and difficulty to provide human-understandable explanations.

Consider image recognition. Although on benchmarks like digit recognition very high scores are reached, adversarial examples show that for *natural* image recognition, segmentation and labeling, there is an important lack of robustness (one pixel can be enough to derail the recognition process), gross misclassification when an object is not exactly in a setting similar to that used in the training set or the object is slightly altered or its orientation shifted [60]. These limitations show that the acquired statistical models are sensitive to image features and categorisations which are to some extent adequate for a prediction task but only very indirectly related to the way humans visually identify and categorize objects for other tasks - including tasks which require recognizing objects in a way human intelligence would find natural.

Or consider language processing. BERT, a state-of-the-art statistical language model trained with a 300Mi word corpus and a neural bi-directional encoder transformer algorithm, correctly completes "A robin is a ..." with the word "bird", based on statistical frequency, but if you ask for the completion of "A robin is not a ..." it also answers "bird" for the same reason [41]. A human observer cannot help but conclude that BERT does not understand what the sentence is about and is therefore unreliable. BERT has been trained for language prediction but that task is not the same as that of language understanding or language production in communication tasks, which is after all what language is for. The observed success of BERT is due to the use of statistical short-cuts rather than actual understanding. This observed lack of robustness in performance will not improve with more data or with a better induction algorithm because it is due to fundamental epistemological limitations of empirically derived knowledge [35] and the fact that often the analyses which have to be learned are not observable. For example, we cannot expect that the semantic aspects of language grammars can be learned purely based on data of possible language forms [5]. To claim that BERT, or similar systems such as GPT-3 which are trained on sentence completion, understand language is confusing the issues and creates unrealistic expectations for the general public.

Coming up with explanations based on statistical models trained in prediction tasks has proven to be a headache as well. There is a large amount of research going on at the moment and many approaches are being tried: [32] Translating the decision making by a statistical black box model into another more comprehensive but still numerical model (for example decision trees); illustrating which features have been used in decision making by highlighting the areas of the input (for example in an image) that played a role; etc. This is all helpful but is only a stopgap to avoid constructing the kind of meaningful explanations that humans are able to provide and expect, i.e. explanations that explicate the background knowledge and the reasoning steps how a conclusion was reached in terms of rich models composed in human-understandable concepts, in other words using distinctions that overlap with those humans find relevant to their own experiences [33].

Summarizing:

We say that a model is meaningful if the entities described in the model and the distinctions (categories) and entities being used to form descriptions are <u>relevant</u> to the interaction between the agent and the environment in a specific set of tasks and domains. We call AI based on meaningful models Meaningful AI.

6   Why is Understanding Hard?

Many problem situations in which humans find themselves have properties that make it very hard to solve them with reactive intelligence alone. But these properties also make it hard to construct the models needed for deliberative intelligence, even though that is the only way to find and justify solutions in many cases. These properties include: indeterminacy, ambiguity, uncertainty, combinatorial complexity and the characteristics of open worlds.

- *Underspecification* arises when the situation or the problem definition does not contain enough information to find a solution. The missing information must be inferred based on prior knowledge.
- *Incompleteness* arises when there is so much knowledge involved in a domain that it cannot all be formalized or foreseen. This is known as the frame problem in AI [28]. The default cases can be described but all the exceptions cannot.
- *Ambiguity* arises when the same signal or sign can have many possible interpretations. The interpretation valid in the specific problem context must then be inferred by examining the consequences of the different possibilities. This is for example the case in parsing and interpreting human language where every word or phrase typically has more than one meaning or function.
- *Uncertainty* arises when facts can only be established approximately, for example because they are based on a measurement that gives only an approximation to what is to be measured or because facts were derived through induction and the data was incomplete or polluted. Medical diagnosis is a typical example of a domain where uncertainty is rampant because not everything can be measured accurately and detailed information of the behavior of a disease is often not available.
- *Combinatorial complexity* arises as a consequence of underspecification, ambiguity, incompleteness and uncertainty and when solution steps need to be chained. In those cases you need to construct a search space to explore different hypotheses and this space can grow exponentially. Board games, such as chess, are the prototypical example of combinatorial complexity, but this

issue is equally present in virtually all applications of AI, for example in syntactic and semantic analyis of natural language sentences or in the design of systems where many different components have to be chosen and put together to achieve a particular function.

– *Open worlds* arise when problem situations come up that are significantly different from anything seen before, i.e. not only variations within known statistical boundaries or new facts that deviate from templates derived from earlier facts. This issue is the norm for socio-economic applications or applications which involve living systems. It is also the case for handling natural language where novel sounds, words, phrases, constructions and pragmatic interaction patterns may appear, sometimes at a rapid pace.

Certainly, there are domains where the world is closed and the basic rules do not change. There are no ambiguous inputs, full knowledge is available of the situation, and the combinatorics can be worked out and computed in advance or sufficiently tamed with powerful heuristics to guide the search. A board game like checkers and most other adversarial games are examples of this. The rules of checkers are fixed, the board positions are totally determined and observable without ambiguity and the search space is large but computable. Recent progress in game playing (for chess, Go, and other games) is due to massive increases in computer power so that many more games can be tried and heuristics for navigating much bigger search spaces can be learned than before.

On the other hand there are plenty of domains of high human interest where these issues are very much present. These are the domains that cannot be solved in an algorithmic way and have therefore been traditionally the core research target of AI. They require that the AI system understands.

All the above issues were identified from the very beginning of the field in the 1950s, for example, in the work of Herbert Simon on bounded rationality [47], the work of John McCarthy on non-monotic reasoning to cope with incompleteness and open worlds [27], or the development of various probability calculi for uncertainty and inductive inference by Ray Solomonoff and many others [48]. To illustrate the issues further, I briefly introduce an example from the domain of common sense problem solving which has received considerable attention in recent AI research, namely cooking recipes [4].

Nothing seems to be more straightforward than preparing a dish from a recipe, except when you start cooking, and then it often turns out to be hard. I am not referring to all the skill required to handle food but of reading and understanding the recipe, in other words making a sufficiently rich model of the food preparation process so that concrete cooking actions can be undertaken. Part of the problem is to figure out what items and actions the descriptions in the recipe refer to, which objects are involved in each action, and what the parameters of actions are, such as how long something needs to be cooked. Often you also need to come up with alternative solutions to reach the same (implicit) goals.

Consider for example a recipe for preparing *Linguine con lenticchie e pancetta* (Linguine pasta with lentils and pancetta)[4]. The recipe starts with a list of the ingredients and some initial preparations:

200 g small brown lentils from Umbria.
Two tablespoons of extra virgin olive oil.
125 g Pancetta cut into small strips.
400 g of linguine, etc.

The first challenge is already to find these ingredients or decide on alternatives depending on their availability in your kitchen or in local shops. Although Umbria is renowned for lentils, other regions, like Puy in the Auvergne in France, produce excellent lentils as well. The pancetta can be replaced by bacon, the linguine by pappardelle. Notice that generating and selecting these alternatives already rests on significant knowledge of the different types of cooking ingredients and their functions in a recipe. For example, the pancetta can be replaced by bacon because they are both salt-cured pork belly salume, the linguine by pappardelle because they are both long dried pasta.

The first line of the recipe says: 'Place the lentils in a pan and add enough water to cover them with a layer of 5 cm'. Some of the words in this sentence are ambiguous. For example 'pan' means here a cooking pan but the word can also refer to the action of taking a wider view with a camera. 'Cover' means here 'to put something over something else' but it can also mean 'the object with which you cover something', 'to deal with a subject', 'the outside of a book', 'a place to go hiding'. We have such powerful context-sensitive parsing mechanisms that we do not even notice these ambiguities.

Then there is underspecification. The recipe talks about 'a pan' assuming there is such an object available in the context. 'Them' is presumably refering to the lentils. The water has to be added but to what - presumably to the pan. The recipe does not specify the exact quantity of water to be added but describes instead the end state ('until there is a layer of 5 cm'.).

The next line says 'Add salt and put the lid on the pan.' The salt is not mentioned in the ingredients but assumed to be present by default. Neither does the recipe specify what kind of salt should be added; regular kitchen salt, sea salt, Himalayan black salt? 'Add salt', yes - but to what? How much salt? 'The lid', but which lid? The lid has not been mentioned yet but because a pan has been mentioned and pans have lids, we know that it must be the lid of a pan. But which pan? Presumably the one mentioned in the first line of the recipe.

Clearly, a recipe is not like a computer program which is fully determinate and unambiguous. Understanding the recipe so that you can cook the dish, requires disambiguating, contextualizing and grounding the objects mentioned in order to resolve ambiguities and handle underspecification and incompleteness as much as needed. Doing this requires a significant amount of background knowledge but also the ability to build models of reality based on sensori-motor input, perform

---

[4] Werle, L. (2009) La Cucina della Mamma. Allegrio, Olen (BE), p. 22.

mental simulation of actions, and link the referents of descriptions in the recipe to the model.

The cooking domain is representative of a much larger set of domains with similar properties such as instructions for putting together IKEA furniture, manuals for installing and operating equipment, office procedures, legal procedures, instructions for a field trip in the forest. And there are many more domains where the same issues arise. Here are two more examples: making sense of events and medical or technical diagnosis.

All of us are constantly trying to understand the connections between events, both at a personal level and at a historical and political level, and there are scientific fields such as history, criminology, anthropology or journalism that are specialized in trying to piece together what has happened from bits and pieces of indeterminate, ambiguous and uncertain information and structure them into a coherent whole. This is another class of task challenges where the construction of rich models is central even though the 'true' sequence of events is often impossible to reconstruct, particularly for turbulent historical events, such as a coup d'état or a revolution. The efforts at the moment by a special parliamentary commission to document and understand the attack on the United States Capitol on January 6, 2021 shows how difficult the exercise is, even for recent events. In the case of events further in the past this reconstruction often has to happen from accounts that are only partly true due to lack of knowledge or because the available accounts warp the facts to convey particular viewpoints to serve certain agendas.

Here is another example: Medical or technical diagnosis. Both rest on a set of inputs that need to be puzzled together into a coherent model of a disease or a malfunction, which is sufficiently detailed to allow treatment or repair. The inputs are almost always incomplete. It may be possible to perform additional measurements but these measurements typically still yield uncertain outcomes and they may be too expensive or risky to perform. Knowledge about many diseases or causes of faults is often incomplete and continously evolving, not only because knowledge advances thanks to science but also because diseases themselves may change as the biological organisms that cause them (viruses and bacteria) change. The Covid pandemic that exploded world wide in 2021 is a contemporary example, where the medical profession as well as politicians and the public are visibly trying to cope with the changing nature of a virus and the unpredictable effect of rules to contain the pandemic. Here we see the process of understanding in action. It is another example domain showing not only why understanding is central to human intelligence, but also why it is hard.

Summarizing:

Understanding is hard in many tasks of human interest because of the indeterminacy, ambiguity and uncertainty of inputs and available knowledge. In addition, there may be rampant combinatorial complexity if different hypotheses have to be explored, and we may need to cope with novel situations due to the fact that the real world is open and in constant flux.

The issues listed here are experienced by humans and by machines alike. But human intelligence has distinct advantages: We collect throughout life a massive amount information that is relevant for our interactions with the world and others. We have all the necessary subsystems ranging from sensory-motor intelligence, language processing, mental simulation, semantic and episodic memory and learning to meta-level reflection and affective response generation 'under one roof' and we seamlessly integrate all these capacities in the service of solving hard problems. All of this is truely astounding and an enormous challenge to emulate in artificial systems. The argument, sometimes heard these days, that 'Artificial General Intelligence' surpassing human intelligence is just around the corner [61], underestimates human intelligence and/or overestimates the true state of the art in AI. Mastering understanding is the hard problem of AI and achieving it will require considerable breakthroughs and concerted effort.

7   Rich Models Have Multiple Layers and Perspectives

Let us now turn to the kind of models that area required for deliberative intelligence. I mentioned earlier that they have to be 'rich'. What should we mean by that? The first way in which deliberative models are rich is because they typically have several layers and describe situations from many different perspectives.

For example, understanding a recipe up to a point where you can execute it requires models at four layers:

- A *Linguistic description* is formulated in natural language and used to communicate among people. An example is the recipe text as found in a cook book. Linguistic descriptions are typically vague and highly underspecified and require a lot of knowledge, including knowledge of the language, to decode. For example, the cookbook may say 'add a handful of herbs' leaving it open which herbs to add or how much herbs constitute a handful [3].
- *Symbolic models* describe the situation in qualitative terms but in a computational form. Symbolic models are already more precise but still leave a lot of the exact parameters for concrete action open. They already support inference, including qualitative simulation, when the model is expanded with defaults, contextual and background knowledge [16].
- *Analog models* describe the situation in quantitative terms. They approach realistic conditions but are not necessarily identical to an actual situation in the world. Analog models support quantitative simulation, for example, using a physics simulator as used in computer games to simulate the execution of a recipe [4]. Sensors can be embedded in the simulation in order to answer questions about the course of an action that cannot be handled by symbolic models [9].
- *Perceptual models* are directly grounded in real world perceptual or proprioceptive data and therefore maintain continuous contact with reality. The raw data needs to be processed considerably to eliminate noise, callibration errors, intermittent sensor failure, etc. Various inferences can already be performed

directly on perceptual models, such as Kalman filters which predict what the world is going to look like at the next instant of time [51].

One of the main challenges in building understanding systems is to maintain intimate dependencies between these different models, namely to couple data from the perceptual models to the analog model so that the analog model becomes more realistic, to couple categorisations from perceptual or analog models to the symbolic models so that these models are grounded, and to couple the symbolic model to the language description. Conversely, the language description informs the symbolic model which constrains the analog model and provides expectations or completions of the perceptual model. AI systems that establish these dependencies during the life-time of objects are known as *digital twins*. They are considered the basis for future smart manufacturing, system maintenance, retail, medical care, and many other fields [?].

A perspective highlights a situation from a particular point of view. For example, architectural design requires a layout perspective, a functional and spatial perspective, a user perspective, perspectives for electrical systems, plumbing systems, etc. Maintaining the dependencies between these different viewpoints is another challenge for rich models, often handled using methods of constraint propagation and consistency checking.

Summarizing:

The rich models used for deliberative intelligence are multi-layered (linguistic, symbolic, analog, and perceptual) and describe situations from multiple perspectives.

8 Human Models Often Take the Form of Narratives

The models needed for deliberative intelligence studied by human-oriented and social disciplines (psychology, anthropology, economics, linguistics, semiotics, sociology, medicine, social neuroscience to name just these) are also rich in another sense. They take the form of *narratives*. A narrative is a way to structure experiences [6,62]. It identifies the relevant events connected principally by temporal and causal links, further enhanced with spatial, logical, analogical, hierarchical and other relations. A narrative identifies the actors and entities and the roles they play in events and the relevant properties of the events. It includes insights into the broader context and the motivations, deliberations and intentions of the actors.

The more a domain is related to human issues, the more narratives also include a moral viewpoint on the events and an ideological framing [18]. So a narrative combines a set of seemingly disconnected facts and episodes into a coherent structure in which the relationships between events and facts, the relevance of the events, as well as their moral and ethical framings are made explicit in order to explain and justify actions or convince others of a particular viewpoint.

Narrative intelligence is the ability to come up with narratives, either based on observations of reality or on semiotic representations of narratives (texts, novels, drawings, movies) created by others. Narrative intelligence exploits general facts in *semantic memory* to fill in details, sensory-motor data stored in *episodic-procedural memory* to ground narratives into reality, *mental simulation* to imagine how situations in the world will unfold visually, and memory of past narratives, often called *narrative memory* - or *autobiographic or personal memory* if the narratives are about making sense of your personal life. In human intelligence these different types of memory are personal, based on your history of interactions with the world and others. Today knowledge graphs and other semantic resources are assumed to be universal, but we must expect that future meaningful AI systems have their own 'personal' dynamic memories which they have acquired through their own interactions with the world and other agents. They will undoubtly have their own opinions or ways of framing reality that may differ from that of other AI systems or from humans [56].

Narratologists make a distinction between three levels of narratives: [2]

(i) There is the set of facts that the narrative is about. This is called the *fabula*. These facts may be objective data directly obtained by sensing the environment or qualitative descriptions without being colored by a particular viewpoint.

(ii) There is the *plot* which is the viewpoint, organisation and framing imposed on the fabula, partly in order to make a convincing narration.[5]

(iii) There is the *narration* of the narrative, in the form of a text or another medium, for example as a documentary film, a theatre piece, a painting, an opera.[6]

Narrations use *signs*, which brings us on the terrain of semiotics [11]. A sign is an association between a *signifier* (its form appearance) and a *signification* (its meaning) as governed by a *code*. The signifiers are constructed from material components (sounds, lines, colors, gestures, marks). Furthermore narrations abide by larger scale narrative structures classified and studied in the field of narratology.

Elements at the three levels of a narrative are intricately linked with each other. For example, a real world person in the fabula becomes a character in the plot and is presented by particular signifiers in the narration, such as a proper name, a specific dress, perhaps a melodic theme in an opera. Creating these linkages between levels is an important part of the understanding process and narrations have to contain enough cues to make these links detectable by readers or viewers.

---

[5] It is also common, particularly in earlier narratological research, to conflate fabula and plot, in which case the two terms become interchangable and there are only two levels.

[6] Somewhat confusingly, a narration is also often called a narrative (cf. narrativo in Spanish), whereas here it refers to both the facts and the plot on the one hand and their narration on the other hand.

The *narration* of a narrative by a narrator consists in gathering facts from observations or from collected data, selecting key facts, and organising them in terms of a plot, including the introduction of a viewpoint and framing of the facts, and then translating the story into a text or other form of semiotic representation by choosing signs that introduce the elements of the plot. Conversely, an interpreter has to recognize and decode the signs, connect their various significations into a coherent representation, reconstruct from the plot the narrative and the underlying facts, and ground these facts into observed data. The interpreter also has to fit the reconstructed narrative into his or her past experience stored in a personal dynamic memory. Each of these processes is in itself extraordinarily complex. Understanding how they work and operationalizing them are the core technical challenge for the advancement of meaningful AI.

Clearly narratives have different purposes and characteristics and each narrative is a point in a continuum along many different dimensions. One important dimension is the *veracity dimension*, where on one side we find non-fictional narratives considered (or claimed) to be true in the sense of conform to reality. Such narratives are called *theories* and their construction or reconstruction is based on strategies intended to guarantee veracity. These are the kinds of narratives that scientists, doctors or lawyers strive to construct and communicate accurately or that everybody constructs when dealing with reality, as in interpreting cooking recipes.

At the other end of the veracity dimension we find *fictional narratives*. They have ingredients based on reality but they do not pretend to be verifiably conform to reality. They may include fictional characters and events, exaggerations, unproven causal relations, rearrangements of the temporal order of events, etc. These changes are all in the interest of making the narrative more compelling and hence more effective in convincing others of a particular viewpoint and ensuring that the narrative spreads faster in the population. Fictional or semi-fictional narratives arise spontaneously if not enough facts are known but people still try to make sense of what happens to have some degree of prediction and control.

There are still other dimensions of narratives as summarized in the following table. Rationality refers to the role of logic in the narrative and the sobriety with which the narrative is told, i.e. how much rhetorical devices are used.

Dimension	Definition	High	Low
Veracity	Relation to reality	Truthful	Suggestive
Rationality	Argumentation basis	Logic and utility maximization	Compatibility with values and fit with prior experience
Sobriety	Persuasion style	Close to facts and logic	Amplified and selective expression of facts

The human propensity for creating narratives and adopting, modifying and communicating them as narrations is particularly well illustrated with the discourse on the Covid pandemic and vaccination campaigns. Because there is a general lack of understanding and an ongoing change in the nature of the covid virus, we see that scientific theories need to adapt constantly to new insights, observations, the behavior of variants and the behavior of populations (keeping distance, masks, etc.). But we also see a wealth of spontaneous semi-fictional narratives, some of them taking the form of conspiracy theories or fake news stories, narrated through memes on social media, that are actually harmful for those believing them and hamper gaining collective control over the pandemic.

The various disciplines that use the concept of a narrative provide important insights into the nature of narratives and the functioning of narrative intelligence that are very useful to advance the state of the art in understanding. These disciplines have also produced many case studies and challenges for concrete AI experiments which suggest new application areas for AI. Let me just give two examples.

Economics and sociology use the term 'narrative' in two ways, either for the narratives that people develop about economic and social phenomena, like inequality, or for the scientific models of these processes, in which case we speak about socio-economic theories. Scientific socio-economic theories strive for high veracity and typically treat humans as rational economic agents. 'Folk' economic narratives are often low on the veracity and rationality scale, but they can nevertheless have an important impact on socio-economic behavior. Identifying folk socio-economic narratives and studying their impact on the real economy is the primary topic in the recently emerging field of narrative economics [45] which includes studies of the strategic use of narratives in order to advance economical agendas as is common in advertising or negotiation. There is also the emerging field of narrative sociology [21], which focuses on how narratives shape social movements and social identity. It has similar concerns and approaches as narrative economics but focuses on social behaviors. Narrative sociology has strong interactions with social psychology and social neuroscience where the study of narratives and particularly narrative pathologies (leading to the construction and belief in conspiracy theories or radicalization) plays a growing role [64].

In *medicine* there is a similar dichotomy between non-expert narratives and scientific theories. Patients spontaneously construct narratives to come to grips with the symptoms and evolution of their disease. Although many doctors do not feel the need to encourage or influence these narratives, there is a field called narrative medicine which sees the construction of such narratives (in a co-construction between doctor and patient) as a path to healing or maintaining health, complementary to natural science-based treatments [7, 49]. Narrative medicine encourages close (attentive) reading of texts, authentic discourse and reflective writing with an emphasis on personal reflections on facts.

Knowledge-based medical AI is concerned with the natural science-based approach to the study of diseases and treatments. In that field medical narratives are making headway as well in order to support search and hypothesis generation

[24]. The notion of narrative is more narrow here than in the social sciences and humanities and the term theory is often considered more appropriate. The narratives now focus almost exclusively on temporal and causal relations and recurring explanation patterns. Veracity and rational argumentation are primary and a moral stance and rhetoric to express this stance does not play a role.

Summarizing:

Narratives play a central role in understanding because they are the frameworks that provide the structures underlying the kind of rich models humans make. These frameworks are imposed on experience in order to bring out the relations between events and entities playing a role in them, formulate a moral stance, justify our actions and decisions, remember new experiences in terms of past ones, put experiences into a broader context, and communicate experiences and our views on them to others.

There was already a flurry of research activity in AI on narratives between the mid nineteen-sixties and late nineteen-seventies. One of the first ideas that came up is the notion of a *semantic network*, as first proposed by Quillian [37], which blossomed into the knowledge graphs that we have today. Another notion is that of a *schema* or *frame*, as first proposed by Minsky [30], or *script*, as proposed and worked out by Schank and colleagues [44]. A frame is a set of questions to be asked about a particular situation with constraints, defaults and strategies to find answers. The classical example is a restaurant frame that structures the experience of entering a restaurant.

Schank also triggered the first AI research into dynamic semantic and episodic memory and how they play a crucial role in understanding [43]. These ideas developed further in memory-based or case-based AI applications [23]. Frames and scripts have underpinned a large number of earlier experimental AI systems for story understanding and story generation and for expert systems not based on rules but on solving cases by analogy with earlier cases. They also lead to some remarkable early demonstrations of language understanding capacities in the 1970s, such as Winograd's SHRDLU system, dubbed a system that could understand natural language, [65] and the HEARSAY speech understanding system that worked on spoken language [38]. Later in the 1980s we also saw the first attempts to build encyclopedic knowledge bases, of which CYC [25] was the most important representative.

Interest in narratives waned somewhat in the late 1990s as the attention of AI shifted to behavior-based robotics, neural networks, and the semantic web. Moreover it was realized that incorporating narratives as the core of AI was going to be a daunting task. The broad humanistic scope that characterized AI in its first four decades began to shrink with a focus on narrowly defined problems with measurable performance under economic pressures. But the past decade we have seen renewed attention in AI research to narratives [15, 17, 26, 29, 40, 66]. Efforts now incorporate also data-driven AI methods to learn aspects of narrative intelligence, such as the reconstruction of timelines or characters [20]. Still, it is early days and many problems remain unsolved.

9   Open Issues for Understanding

Clearly the integration of narratives in the understanding process by AI systems is very challenging, partly because of the many different components and skills that are needed (sensori-motor input, language, semantic memory, mental simulation, episodic memory) (see Fig. 3) and partly because they all need to be integrated.

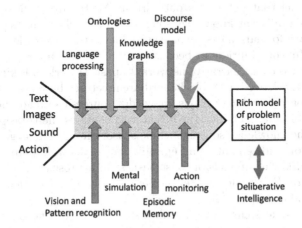

Fig. 3. Understanding calls upon a variety of knowledge sources and uses itself the partially constructed rich model. The knowledge sources use both reactive and deliberative AI.

What are some of the main priority problems we should focus on today? Given space limitations, I cannot do more here than list three directions in which further work is going on or needed - this is of course in addition to further advancing the state of the art for each of the knowledge sources.

1. *Computational represention of narratives*: It is obvious that we need a datastructure that captures all the information about a narrative and its narration. This datastructure must represent the facts in the fabula, the way the facts are selected, framed and organized as a story, and the intermediary structures that are being built to produce or comprehend a narration. Clearly this datastructure takes the form of a network, similar to a knowledge graph, but with much more information and meta-information. I will call it a *narrative network*. A narrative network is transient in the sense that it grows and changes as more information comes in during the construction or interpretation process. It has to be able to represent different hypotheses given the ambiguity and underspecification of inputs and the uncertainties associated with facts or inferences. It should support the exploration of multiple hypotheses and adapt to progressive insight or changes, both in the inputs and in the available knowledge sources.

There have been plenty of experiments and technical advances, for example for dealing with uncertainty or dealing with the exploration of multiple hypotheses, but the big challenge here is to create a comprehensive design and, if possible, standardize it so that many people can collaborate as has happened with ontologies. Work on narrative annotation tools and formal ontologies for ontologies already go in this direction [14, 29, 36].

2. *Cognitive architecture* Many different knowledge sources contribute to the build up of a narrative network and we certainly need to go beyond a strict pipeline model that dominates data-driven AI, towards a flexible architecture in which different knowledge sources can contribute at any time, either because new information has become available, so that a knowledge source can make a useful contribution, or because they are called in a top-down manner to expand areas of the narrative network. In past AI work, this kind of flexibility was often achieved with blackboard architectures based on the metaphor of a blackboard on which various knowledge sources can read and write [12]. In the case of understanding, the blackboard contains the transient narrative network. The knowledge sources include sensory input, language input, mental simulation and semantic and episodic memory. Blackboard architectures have resonated with models of consciousness in neuroscience, specifically the Global Neural Workspace Model by Bernard Baars and refined by Stanislas DeHaene and colleagues [8].

A blackboard-like architecture is a first step but we will need much more:

- First of all, we need ways in which the understanding system can *measure progress*: (i) how far ambiguity, incompleteness, underspecification and incompleteness is being reduced, (ii) how information has become integrated, meaning in how far network fragments could be connected to each other and how connections between different levels of the narrative (the fabula, story, and narration) could be established, and (iii) how far the distance towards a satisfactory narrative closure could be bridged. Narrative closure happens when the key questions for which the narrative is being developed have been answered.

- Second, these measures should be input to an *attention mechanism* that decides where further effort should go: Should more resources be applied for analyzing and interpretating certain inputs? Which nodes in the network are to be expanded preferentially? What additional inputs might profitably be sought? Should a knowledge graph be consulted? How many extra resources should be put into visual processing? It is unavoidable that the degree of understanding of a narration will sometimes decrease because new input enters that is not compatible with what was seen before or new facts are supplied by semantic memory that create a cognitive dissonance with the narrative network built so far.

- Third, there needs to be a *meta-level* that plays three crucial roles: (a) It should monitor progress and avoid catastrophic failure by catching fail states in components (in the same way an operating system catches an error in running applications and possibly repairs them to avoid that the whole system collapses). (b) It should govern learning processes, such as the process by which a narrative is stored in episodic memory to deal with similar situations in the future. (c) It should include a value system that monitors decision-making (and subsequent real-world action) to make it compatible with a moral framework that is compatible with human values in order to realize a form of *value-aware AI.*

3. *Other paths to learning:* Current AI applications focus on a narrow set of learning mechanisms but we need to become adventurous (again) and explore other learning strategies. I just list two possible paths for further exploration:

   (a) It was argued in Sect. 5 on meaning that the distinctions (categories or concepts) used in AI systems should be meaningful with respect to tasks and contexts and that an exclusive focus on prediction does not yield the kind of distinctions that humans find natural or fit with other tasks than prediction. So we need to find new frameworks for learning. In the case of language, one such framework are language games [59]. Language games are played by two agents selected out of a population of agents, possibly including humans. They have a communicative task, such as drawing attention to an object in their shared world-setting or giving instructions to carry out a certain action and should use some form of language to do so. However, the agents should start without a shared language system or a shared ontology of distinctions and build that up as part of becoming successful in playing games. This approach has now been followed for dozens of domains (color, space, time, action, etc.) [54] and for many different aspects of language [55]. It shows that categories need not be formed by induction over a large dataset only but can be learned in an incremental fashion and relevant for the task of communication.

   (b) The coupling of reactive and deliberative intelligence provides new avenues. For example, we could explore more constructivist (or abductive) approaches to learning domain knowledge for deliberative intelligence. A constructivist approach suggests that the learner is able to partially solve problems and then examine what domain knowledge is missing in order to complete the solution. Or the learner solves a problem but gets feedback whether the derived solution is adequate. If not, constructivist learning analyses in which way domain knowledge can be changed and repair it [52].

10   Conclusions

This paper briefly explored some of the conceptual foundations of human-centric AI, arguing that AI needs to come to grips with meaning and understanding in order to address the many demands and expectations for human-centric AI. Understanding is defined as the process of building up a rich model of the problem situation from which solutions and explanations can be derived by deliberative intelligence. The models made by human intelligence most often take the form of narratives with scientific models being a special case.

The state of the art in AI is not yet up to a level where the integration of narratives has become practical enough to be routinely applied. There are some very serious challenges for many areas of AI, including language processing, computer vision, knowledge representation, mental simulation, memory, learning and cognitive architecture. But with a clear vision where we need to go, we can look forward for a new jump forward in AI and perhaps a subsequent new wave of meaningful, human-centric AI.

Further reading

1. Melanie Mitchell (2019) Artificial Intelligence. A guide for thinking humans. Farrar, Strauss and Giroux, New York.
2. Luc Steels and Manfred Hild (2012) Language Grounding in Robots. Springer Verlag, New York.
3. Daniel Nyga, Subhro Roy, Rohan Paul, Daehyung Park, Mihai Pomarlan, Michael Beetz, and Nicholas Roy (2018) Grounding Robot Plans from Natural Language Instructions with Incomplete World Knowledge. In 2nd Conference on Robot Learning (CoRL 2018), Zurich, Switzerland, 2018. http://proceedings.mlr.press/v87/nyga18a/nyga18a.pdf
4. Steels, L. (ed.) (2022) Foundations for Meaning and Understanding in Human-centric AI. Zenodo, Cern, Geneva. Open Access: https://zenodo.org/record/6666820#.YtQNRsFBzw8

Acknowledgement. The author thanks Oscar Vilarroya (IMIM and UAB Barcelona) and Lise Stork (Vrije Universiteit Amsterdam) for valuable comments on the paper and Inès Blin (Sony CSL Paris) for introducing another didactic example of narrative-based understanding during the tutorial presentation at ACAI in Berlin (not included in this paper). The author is also indebted to many discussions with members of the MUHAI consortium: the team from the Free University of Brussels VUB AI Lab (Paul Van Eecke) and University of Namur (Katrien Beuls), the team of Frank van Harmelen at the Free University of Amsterdam (VUA), the team of Remi van Trijp and the Sony Computer Science Laboratory in Paris and the team of Robert Porzel at the University of Bremen, Computer Science Department.

References

1. Antoniou, G., Harmelen, F.V.: A Semantic Web Primer. The MIT Presss, Cambridge (2008)
2. Bal, M., Boheemen, C.V.: Narratology: Introduction to the Theory of Narrative. University of Toronto Press, Toronto (1997)
3. Barnes, J.: The Pedant in the Kitchen. Atlantic Books (2004)
4. Beetz, M., et al.: Cognition-enabled autonomous robot control for the realization of home chore task intelligence. Proc. IEEE **100**(8), 2454–2471 (2012)

5. Bender, E., Koller, A.: Climbing towards NLU: on meaning, form, and understanding in the age of data. In: Proceedings Annual Meeting of Association for Computational Linguistics Conference, pp. 5185–A5198. Association for Computational Linguistics (2020)
6. Bruner, J.: The narrative construction of reality. Crit. Inq. **18**(1), 1–21 (1991)
7. Charon, R., et al.: The Principles and Practice of Narrative Medicine. Oxford University Press, Oxford (2017)
8. De Haene, S., Changeux, J.P., Naccache, L.: The global neuronal workspace model of conscious access: from neuronal architectures to clinical applications. Res. Perspect. Neurosci. **18**, 55–84 (2011)
9. Decuyper, J.C., Keymeulen, D., Steels, L.: A hybrid architecture for modeling liquid behavior. In: Glasgow, J., Narayanan, N., Chandrasekaran, B. (eds.) Diagrammatic Reasoning. AAAI Press, Menlo Park (1995)
10. Devlin, J., Chang, M.W., Lee, K., Toutanova, K.: BERT: pre-training of deep bidirectional transformers for language understanding. In: NAACL-HLT (1), pp. 4171–4186. Association for Computational Linguistics (2019)
11. Eco, U.: Trattato di semiotica generale. La nave di Teseo, Milano (1975)
12. Englemore, R., Morgan, T.: Addison-Wesley, New York (1988)
13. Feigenbaum, E.: The art of artificial intelligence: themes and case studies of knowledge engineering. In: Proceedings of the Fifth International Joint Conference on Artificial Intelligence, pp. 1014–1029. IJCAI (1977)
14. Finlayson, M.: The story workbench: an extensible semi-automatic text annotation tool. In: AAAI Conference on Artificial Intelligence and Interactive Digital Entertainment, vol. WS-11-18 (2011)
15. Finlayson, M.: A survey of corpora in computational and cognitive narrative science. Sprache und Datenverarbeitung (Int. J. Lang. Data Process.) **37**(1–2), 113–141 (2013)
16. Forbus, K.: Qualitative physics: past, present and future. In: Exploring Artificial Intelligence, pp. 239–296. Elsevier (1988)
17. Gervás, P., Concepción, E., León, C., Méndez, G., Delatorre, P.: The long path to narrative generation. IBM J. Res. Dev. **63**(1), 1–8 (2019)
18. Goffman, E.: Frame Analysis: An Essay on the Organization of Experience. Harper and Row, New York (1974)
19. van Harmelen, F., Lifschitz, V., Porter, B. (eds.): Handbook of Knowledge Representation. Elsevier, Amsterdam (2007)
20. Hovy, D., Fan, J., Gliozzo, A., Patwardhan, S., Welty, C.: When did that happen? - linking events and relations to timestamps. In: Proceedings of the 13th Conference of the European Chapter of the Association for Computational Linguistics, pp. 185–193. Association for Computational Linguistics (2012)
21. Irvine, L., Pierce, J., Zussman, R. (eds.): Narrative Sociology. Vanderbilt University Press, Nashville (2019)
22. Kahneman, D.: Thinking Fast and Slow. Farrar, Strauss and Giroux, New York (2011)
23. Kolodner, J.: An introduction to case-based reasoning. Artif. Intell. Rev. **6**, 3–34 (1992)
24. Kroll, H., Nagel, D., Balke, W.-T.: Modeling narrative structures in logical overlays on top of knowledge repositories. In: Dobbie, G., Frank, U., Kappel, G., Liddle, S.W., Mayr, H.C. (eds.) ER 2020. LNCS, vol. 12400, pp. 250–260. Springer, Cham (2020). https://doi.org/10.1007/978-3-030-62522-1_18
25. Lenat, D.: Cyc: A large-scale investment in knowledge infrastructure. Comm. of the ACMs **38**(11), 33–38 (1995)

26. Mateas, M., Sengers, P.: Narrative Intelligence. John Benjamins Publishing (2003)
27. McCarthy, J.: Programs with common sense. In: Symposium on Mechanization of Thought Processes. National Physical Laboratory, Teddington (1958)
28. McCarthy, J., Hayes, P.: Some philosophical problems from the standpoint of artificial intelligence. In: Michie, D., Meltzer, B. (eds.) Machine Intelligence, vol. 4, pp. 463–502. Edinburgh University Press (1969)
29. Meghini, C., Bartalesi, V., Metilli, D.: Representing narratives in digital libraries: the narrative ontology. Semant. Web **18**, 1–24 (2021)
30. Minsky, M.: A framework of representing knowledge. In: Winston, P. (ed.) The Psychology of Computer Vision. McGraw-Hill, New York (1975)
31. Mitchell, M.: Artificial Intelligence. A Guide for Thinking Humans. Farrar, Strauss and Giroux, New York (2019)
32. Mohseni, S., Zarei, N., Ragan, E.: A multidisciplinary survey and framework for design and evaluation of explainable AI systems. ACM Trans. Interact. Intell. Syst. **1**(1) (2021)
33. Moore, J., Swartout., W.: Explanation in expert systems: a survey. ISI Research Reports, ISI, Marina del Rey (1988)
34. Nowak, A., Lukowicz, P., Horodecki, P.: Assessing artificial intelligence for humanity: will AI be the our biggest ever advance? or the biggest threat. IEEE Technol. Soc. Mag. **37**(4), 26–34 (2018)
35. Pearl, J., Mackenzie, D.: The Book of Why. The New Science of Cause and Effect. Penguin Books, London (2019)
36. Porzel, R.: On formalizing narratives. In: CAOS 2021: 5th workshop on Cognition and Ontologies. CEUR Workshop Proceedings, Bolzano (2021)
37. Quillian, R.: Semantic memory. In: Minsky, M. (ed.) Semantic Information Processing, chap. 4, pp. 227–270. The MIT Press, Cambridge (1968)
38. Reddy, R., Erman, L., Fennell, R., Lowerre, B., Neely, R.: The hearsay speech understanding system. J. Acoust. Soc. Am. **55**, 409 (1974)
39. Redmon, J., Divvala, S., Girshick, R., Farhadi, A.: You only look once: unified, real-time object detection (2016)
40. Riedl, M.O.: Computational narrative intelligence: a human-centered goal for artificial intelligence. In: CHI 2016 Workshop on Human-Centered Machine Learning (2016)
41. Riedl, M.O.: What BERT is not: lessons from a new suite of psycholinguistic diagnostics for language models. Trans. Assoc. Comput. Linguist. **8**, 34–49 (2020)
42. Samuel, A.: Some studies in machine learning using the game of checkers. IBM J. Res. Dev. **3**(3), 210–229 (1959)
43. Schank, R.: Dynamic Memory: A Theory of Reminding and Learning in Computers and People. Cambridge University Press, Cambridge (1990)
44. Schank, R.: Abelson: Scripts, Plans, Goals, and Understanding: An Inquiry into Human Knowledge Structures. L. Erlbaum, Hillsdale (1977)
45. Schiller, R.: Narrative Economics. How Stories Go Viral and Drive Major Economic Events. Princeton University Press, Princeton (2019)
46. Shane, J.: You Look Like a Thing and I Love You: How Artificial Intelligence Works and Why It's Making the World a Weirder Place. Little Brown and Company, New York (2021)
47. Simon, H.: The Sciences of the Artificial. The MIT Press, Cambridge (1969)
48. Solomonoff, R.: A formal theory of inductive inference. Inf. Control **7**(1), 1–22 (1965)
49. Sools, A., Tromp, T., Mooren, J.: Mapping letters from the future: exploring narrative processes of imagining the future. J. Health Psychol. **20**(3), 350–364 (2015)

50. Sperber, D., Wilson, D.: Relevance: Communication and Cognition. Wiley-Blackwell, London (1969)
51. Spranger, M., Loetzsch, M., Steels, L.: A perceptual system for language game experiments. In: Steels, L., Hild, M. (eds.) Language Grounding in Robots, pp. 89–110. Springer, Boston (2012). https://doi.org/10.1007/978-1-4614-3064-3_5
52. Steels, L.: Constructivist development of grounded construction grammars. In: Proceedings Annual Meeting of Association for Computational Linguistics Conference, pp. 9–16. Association for Computational Linguistics (2004)
53. Steels, L.: Computational Issues in Fluid Construction Grammar. Lecture Notes in Computer Science, vol. 7249. Springer, Berlin (2012). https://doi.org/10.1007/978-3-642-34120-5
54. Steels, L.: Experiments in Cultural Language Evolution. John Benjamins Pub., Amsterdam (2012)
55. Steels, L.: Agent-based models for the emergence and evolution of grammar. Phil. Trans. R. Soc. B. **371**, 20150447 (2016)
56. Steels, L.: Personal dynamic memories are necessary to deal with meaning and understanding in human-centric AI. In: Saffiotti, A, L.S., Lukowicz, P. (eds.) Proceedings of the First International Workshop on New Foundations for Human-Centered AI (NeHuAI) Co-located with 24th European Conference on Artificial Intelligence, vol. Vol-2659. CEUR Workshop Proceedings (2020)
57. Steels, L., Brooks, R.: The 'Artificial Life' Route to 'Artificial Intelligence'. Building Situated Embodied Agents, Lawrence Erlbaum Ass., New Haven (1994)
58. Steels, L., Hild, M.: Language Grounding in Robots. Springer, New York (2012). https://doi.org/10.1007/978-1-4614-3064-3
59. Steels, L.: The origins of ontologies and communication conventions in multi-agent systems. Auton. Agent. Multi-Agent Syst. **1**, 169–194 (1998)
60. Szegedy, C., et al.: Intriguing properties of neural networks. In: International Conference on Learning Representations, pp. 159–166. Springer (2014)
61. Tegmark, M.: Life 3.0: Being Human in the Age of Artificial Intelligence. Knopff, New York (2017)
62. Vilarroya, O.: Somos lo que nos contamos. Cómo los relatos construyen el mundo en que vivimos. Editorial Planeta, Barcelona (2019)
63. Von der Leyen, U., et al.: White paper on artificial intelligence. EU Commission reports (2020)
64. Willems, R., Nastase, S., Milivojevic, B.: Narratives for neuroscience. Trends Neurosci. **44**(5), 271–273 (2020)
65. Winograd, T.: Understanding Natural Language. Academic Press, New York (1976)
66. Winston, P.: The strong story hypothesis and the directed perception hypothesis. In: 2011 AAAI Fall symposium, AAAI Press, Menlo Park (2011)

Human-Centered Machine Learning

Machine Learning with Neural Networks

James L. Crowley$^{(\boxtimes)}$

Institut Polytechnique de Grenoble, Univ. Grenoble Alpes, Grenoble, France
James.Crowley@univ-grenoble-alpes.fr
http://crowley-coutaz.fr/jlc/jlc.html

Abstract. Artificial neural networks provide a distributed computing technology that can be trained to approximate any computable function, and have enabled substantial advances in areas such as computer vision, robotics, speech recognition and natural language processing. This chapter provides an introduction to Artificial Neural Networks, with a review of the early history of perceptron learning. It presents a mathematical notation for multi-layer neural networks and shows how such networks can be iteratively trained by back-propagation of errors using labeled training data. It derives the back-propagation algorithm as a distributed form of gradient descent that can be scaled to train arbitrarily large networks given sufficient data and computing power.

Learning Objectives: This chapter provides an introduction to the training and use of Artificial Neural Networks, and prepares students to understand fundamental concepts of deep-learning that are described and used in later chapters.

Keywords: Machine learning · Perceptrons · Artificial neural networks · Gradient descent · Back-propagation

Glossary of Symbols

x_d	A feature. An observed or measured value.
$\vec{X}$	A vector of D features.
D	The number of dimensions for the vector $\vec{X}$
y	A dependent variable to be estimated.
$a = f(\vec{X}; \vec{\omega}, b)$	A model that predicts an activation a from a vector $\vec{X}$.
$\vec{w}, b$	The parameters of the model $f(\vec{X}; \vec{\omega}, b)$.
$\{\vec{X}_m\} \{y_m\}$	A set of training samples with indicator values.
$\vec{X}_m$	A feature vector from a training set.
y_m	An indicator or target value for $\vec{X}_m$.
M	The number of training samples in the set $\{\vec{X}_m\}$.
$a_m = f(\vec{X}_m; \vec{\omega}, b)$	The output activation for a training sample, $\vec{X}_m$.
$\delta_m^{out} = a_m - y_m$	The error from using $\vec{\omega}$ and b to compute y_m from $\vec{X}_m$.
$C(\vec{X}_m, y_m; \vec{\omega}, b)$	The cost (or loss) for computing a_m from $\vec{X}_m$ using $(\vec{\omega}, b)$.
$\vec{\nabla} C(\vec{X}_m, y_m; \vec{\omega}, b)$	The gradient (vector derivative) of the cost.
L	The number of layers in a neural network.
l	An index for the lth layer in a network $1 \leq l \leq L$.

© Springer Nature Switzerland AG 2023
M. Chetouani et al. (Eds.): ACAI 2021, LNAI 13500, pp. 39–54, 2023.
https://doi.org/10.1007/978-3-031-24349-3_3

$a_j^{(l)}$ The activation output of the jth neuron of the lth layer.

$w_{ij}^{(l)}$ The weight from unit i of layer $l–1$ to the unit j of layer l.

$b_j^{(l)}$ The bias for unit j of layer l.

η A variable learning rate. Typically very small (0.01).

$\delta_{j,m}^{(l)}$ Error for the jth neuron of layer l, from sample $\vec{X}_m$.

$\Delta w_{ij,m}^{(l)} = -a_i^{(l-1)}\delta_{j,m}^{(l)}$ Update for the weight from unit i of layer $l–1$ to the unit j layer l.

$\Delta b_{j,m}^{(l)} = -\delta_{j,m}^{(l)}$ Update for bias for unit j of layer l.

1   Machine Learning

Machine learning explores the study and construction of algorithms that can learn from and make predictions about data. The term machine learning was coined in 1959 by Arthur Samuel, a pioneer in the field of computer gaming and inventor of the first computer program capable of learning to play checkers. Machine Learning is now seen as a core enabling technology for artificial intelligence.

Many of the foundational techniques for machine learning were originally developed in the late 19th and early 20th for problems of detecting signals for telegraph and radio communications. Throughout much of the 20th century, the science of machine learning was primarily concerned with recognizing patterns in data. For example, a key reference was the 1973 text-book by Duda and Hart named "Pattern Recognition and Scene Analysis" [1]. However, as the scientific study of machine learning has matured, and as computing and data have become increasingly available, it has become clear that, given enough data and computing, machine learning can be used to learn to imitate any computable function. In particular, machine learning and can be used to learn to control machines, to interact with humans with natural language, and to imitate intelligent behavior. Much of this progress has been due to the emergence of a technology for training artificial neural networks.

Over the last 50 years, artificial neural networks have emerged as a key enabling technology for machine learning. Such networks are composed of layers of identical units, each computing a weighted sum of inputs followed by a non-linear activation function. Such networks are computed as a form of Single-Instruction-Multiple-Data (SIMD) parallel algorithm, and thus can be scaled using parallel computers to arbitrarily large numbers of trainable parameters. The parameters can be learned from training data by a parallel form of gradient descent referred to as back propagation. Back propagation is also a SIMD algorithm. Thus both network computation (forward propagation) and network training (backward propagation) can be implemented using the highly parallel Graphical Processing Units (GPUs) now found in many personal computers, tablets and cell phones.

Many machine learning techniques, including neural networks, were originally developed for pattern recognition. In this case, the classic approach is to use a set of training data $\{\vec{X}_m\}$ to learn the parameters for a model that can compute a vector of activation functions $\vec{a}(\vec{X})$. A decision function, $d\left(\vec{a}\left(\vec{X}_m\right)\right)$, is then used to select a pattern label from a predefined set of possible labels. The full model has the form $f(\vec{X}_m) = d\left(\vec{a}\left(\vec{X}_m\right)\right) = \hat{y}_m$ where $\hat{y}_m$ is a predicted value for the target label, y_m.

For signal generation, a generator function $g\left(\vec{a}\left(\vec{X}\right)\right)$ can be designed (or trained) to approximate (or imitate) a desired output function such as a word, text, sound, image or video. In this case, the full model is $f(\vec{X}_m) = g\left(\vec{a}\left(\vec{X}_m\right)\right) = \vec{Y}_m$ where $\hat{Y}_m$ is a prediction of the desired output for $\vec{X}_m$. During learning, a cost function, $C(-)$, is used to evaluate the quality of the category label or generated signal. The learning process involves adjusting the parameters of the model in order to minimize this cost function, computed from the difference between the actual and desired function.

A variety of techniques have been developed to learn the function $f(\vec{X})$.

Supervised Learning. Most classical methods for machine learning learn to estimate a function from a set of training data with known ground truth labels. The data set is composed of M independent examples, $\{X_m\}$, for which target values $\{y_m\}$ are known. Having a target value for each training sample makes it much easier to estimate the function. Examples of popular techniques include K-nearest neighbors [1], Support Vector Machines [2], and Bayesian Estimation [3].

Semi-supervised Learning. A number of hybrid algorithms exist that initiate learning from a labeled training set and then extend the learning with unlabeled data, using the initial algorithm to generate synthetic labels for new data [4].

Unsupervised Learning. Unsupervised Learning techniques learn the function without a labeled training set. Most unsupervised learning algorithms are based on clustering techniques that associate data based on statistical properties. Examples include K-nearest neighbors, and Expectation-Maximization [5].

Reinforcement Learning. Reinforcement learning refers to techniques were a system learns through interaction with an environment. While originally developed for training robots to interact with the world, reinforcement learning combined with deep learning has recently produced systems that outperform humans at games such as Go or Chess. Deep reinforcement learning uses training with realistic simulators adapted through additional training with a target domain by transfer learning [6].

Transfer Learning. With transfer learning a system is first trained using supervised learning with a very large general-purpose data set or simulator, and then refined through additional training in a target domain. Transfer learning has provided a very useful method for overcoming the need for very large training data sets for most modern machine learning techniques based on Neural networks. [7].

Self-supervised Learning. Self-supervised learning learns to reconstruct missing data and to predict associated data from examples. Two classic self-supervised techniques are masked-token replacement and next-token prediction. With Self-Supervised learning, indicator variables are not needed. The data set is its own ground truth. Self-supervised learning makes it possible to pretrain a general purpose system with a very large collection unlabeled training data, followed by transfer learning using supervised learning or reinforcement learning to specialize for a particular problem [8].

2 Perceptrons

The Perceptron is an incremental learning algorithm for linear classifiers. The perceptron was first proposed by Warren McCullough and Walter Pitts in 1943 as a possible universal computational model [9]. In 1957 Frank Rosenblatt at Cornell University, constructed a Perceptron as a room-sized analog computer and demonstrated it for the popular press [10]. Rosenblatt claimed that the Perceptron was "the embryo of an electronic computer that would someday be able to walk, talk, see, write, reproduce itself and be conscious of its existence." Journalists called it the electronic brain. The obvious limitations of the perceptron led serious scientists to denounce such claims as fantasy.

The perceptron is an on-line learning algorithm that learns a linear decision boundary (hyper-plane) for separable training data. As an "on-line" learning algorithm, new training samples can be used at any time to update the recognition algorithm. The Perceptron algorithm uses errors in classifying the training data to iteratively update the hyper-plane decision boundary. Updates may be repeated until no errors exist. However, if the training data cannot be separated by a linear surface, the learning algorithm will not converge, and must be stopped after a certain number of iterations.

Assume a training set of M observations $\{\vec{X}_m\}$ of vectors composed of D components (features), with indicators variables, $\{y_m\}$ where $y_m = \{-1, +1\}$. The indicator variable, y_m, indicates the class label for a sample, $\vec{X}_m$. For a binary pattern detection,

$y_m = +1$ for examples of the target class (class 1)
$y_m = -1$ for all others (class 2)

The Perceptron will learn the coefficients, $\vec{w}$, b for a linear boundary such that for all training data, $\vec{X}_m$,

$$f(\vec{X}_m) = \begin{cases} 1 & \text{if } \vec{w}^T \vec{X}_m + b \geq 0 \\ -1 & \text{if } \vec{w}^T \vec{X}_m + b < 0 \end{cases} \tag{1}$$

Note that $\vec{w}^T \vec{X}_m + b \geq 0$ is the same as $\vec{w}^T \vec{X}_m \geq -b$. Thus b can be considered as a threshold on the product: $\vec{w}^T \vec{X}_m$.

A training sample is correctly classified if:

$$y_m \cdot \left(\vec{w}^T \vec{X}_m + b \right) \geq 0 \tag{2}$$

The algorithm requires a learning rate, η, typically set to a very small number such as $\eta = 10^{-3}$. Lack of a theory for how to set the learning rate, or even an explanation for why such a small learning rate was required was a frequent criticism. In 1969, Marvin Minsky and Seymour Papert at MIT published a monography entitled "Perceptrons", that claimed to document the fundamental limitations of the perceptron approach [11]. Notably, they observed that a linear classifier could not be constructed to perform an Exclusive OR (XOR) function. Ironically, in their final chapter, they noted that while this is true for a single perceptron, it is not true for multi-layer perceptrons. However, they argued that a multi-layer perceptron would require excessively expensive computations, exceeding what was reasonable for computers at the time.

A more fundamental criticism was that if the data was not separable, then the Perceptron would not converge, and learning would continue as an infinite loop. Thus it was necessary to set a limit for the number of iterations.

3 Artificial Neural Networks

In the 1970s, frustrations with the limits of Artificial Intelligence based on Symbolic Logic led a small community of researchers to explore the use of multi-layer perceptrons for recognizing patterns. As noted above, many of the problems described by Minsky and Papert could be solved with multilayer networks. For example, around this time, Fukushima demonstrated a mult-layered network for the interpretation of handwritten characters known as the Cognitron [12]. It was soon recognized that a perceptron could be generalised to non-separable training data by replacing the "hard" discontinuous decision function with a soft, differentiable "activation function", making it possible to train a perceptron with the classic gradient descent algorithm.

In 1975, Paul Werbos reformulated gradient descent as a distributed algorithm referred to as "Back-propagation" [13]. Back-propagation implements gradient descent as a backwards flow of "correction energy" mirroring the forward flow of activation energy computed by a multi-layer network of perceptrons. Back-propagation made it possible to train and operate arbitrarily large layered networks using SIMD (single-instruction-multiple-data) parallel computing. Multi-layer perceptrons were increasingly referred to as "Artificial Neural Networks".

Artificial Neural Networks are computational structures composed a network of "neural" units. Each neural unit is composed of a weighted sum of inputs, followed by a non-linear decision function.

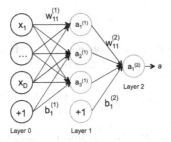

Fig. 1. A fully connected two-layer neural network, with 3 units in the hidden layer (layer 1) and a single unit in the output layer (layer 2). The input vector is composed of the D components of a feature vector, $\vec{X}$, plus a constant term that provides a trainable bias for each unit.

During the 1980's, neural networks went through a period of popularity with researchers showing that networks could be trained to provide simple solutions to problems such as recognizing handwritten characters, recognizing spoken words, and steering a car on a highway. However, the resulting systems were fragile and difficult to duplicate. The popularity of Artificial Neural Networks was overtaken by more mathematically sound approaches for statistical pattern recognition based on Bayesian learning [1, 3].

These methods were, in turn, overtaken by techniques such as support vector machines and kernel methods [2].

The Artificial Neuron. The simplest possible neural network is composed of a single neuron (Fig. 2).

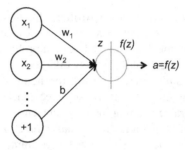

Fig. 2. A single neural unit. On the left side, z is the weighted sum of the coefficients of the input vector, $\vec{X}$ plus a bias. This is used to compute a non-linear activation, $a = f(z)$ shown on the right.

A "neuron" is a computational unit that integrates information from a vector of features, $\vec{X}$, to compute an activation, a.

The neuron is composed of a weighted sum of input values

$$z = w_1 x_1 + w_2 x_2 + \ldots + w_D x_D + b = \vec{w}^T \vec{X} + b \tag{3}$$

followed by a non-linear activation function, $f(z)$.

$$a = f(z) \tag{4}$$

A classic non-linear decision function is the hyperbolic tangent. This function provides a soft, differentiable, decision surface between +1 and +1, shown in Fig. 3.

$$f(z) = \tanh(z) = \frac{e^z - e^{-z}}{e^z + e^{-z}} \tag{5}$$

The hyperbolic tangent can be used to define a simple decision function:

$$\text{if } f(\vec{w}^T \vec{X} + b) \geq 0 \text{ then } P \text{ else } N \tag{6}$$

Most importantly, the hyperbolic tangent has a simple derivative function, making it possible to use gradient descent to train the unit. The derivative of the hyperbolic tangent is:

$$\frac{\partial \tanh(z)}{\partial z} = 1 - \tanh^2(z) \tag{7}$$

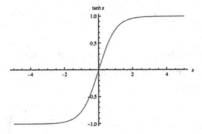

Fig. 3. The hyperbolic tangent is a soft decision function ranging from −1 to 1.

3.1 Gradient Descent

Gradient descent is a first-order iterative optimization algorithm for finding the local minimum of a differentiable function. Gradient descent is generally attributed to Augustin-Louis Cauchy, who first suggested it in 1847, and has long been a popular algorithm for estimating parameters for a large variety of models.

The gradient of a scalar-valued differentiable function of several variables, $f(\vec{X})$ is a vector of derivatives:

$$\vec{\nabla}f(\vec{X}) = \frac{\partial f(\vec{X})}{\partial \vec{X}} = \begin{pmatrix} \frac{\partial f(\vec{X})}{\partial x_1} \\ \frac{\partial f(\vec{X})}{\partial x_2} \\ \vdots \\ \frac{\partial f(\vec{X})}{\partial x_D} \end{pmatrix} \tag{8}$$

The gradient of the function $f(\vec{X})$ tells the direction and rate of change for the greatest slope of the function at the point $\vec{X}$. The direction of the gradient is the direction of greatest slope at that point. The magnitude of the gradient is the slope at that point. Following the direction of greatest change provides an iterative algorithm that leads to a local minimum of the function.

Interestingly, the components of the gradient of a function with respect to its parameters tells how much to correct each parameter to move towards the minimum. Subtracting the components of the gradient from the parameters of the function moves the function toward a local minimum. To use this to determine the parameters for a perceptron (or neural unit), we must introduce the notion of cost (or loss) for an error for that function, and then use the gradient to correct the parameters of the function until the cost reaches a minimum.

Cost (Loss) Function. A cost or loss function represent the cost of making an error when classifying or processing data. Assume a training sample $\vec{X}$ with ground truth y and a network function $a = f(\vec{X}; \vec{w}, b)$ with network parameters $\vec{w}$ and b. The error for a function is $\delta = a - y$. We can compute a cost for this error as 1/2 the square of the error.

$$C(\vec{X}, y; \vec{\omega}, b) = \frac{1}{2}(a - y)^2 \tag{9}$$

where the term 1/2 has been included to simplify the algebra when working with the derivative.

The gradient of the cost indicates how sensitive the cost is to each parameter of the network and can be used to determine how much to correct the parameter to minimize errors, as shown in Eq. 10 (Fig. 4).

$$\vec{\nabla}C(\vec{X}, y; \vec{\omega}, b) = \frac{\partial C(\vec{X}, y; \vec{\omega}, b)}{\partial(\vec{w}, b)} = \begin{pmatrix} \frac{\partial C(\vec{X}, y; \vec{\omega}, b)}{\partial w_1} \\ \vdots \\ \frac{\partial C(\vec{X}, y; \vec{\omega}, b)}{\partial w_D} \\ \frac{\partial C(\vec{X}, y; \vec{\omega}, b)}{\partial b} \end{pmatrix} = \begin{pmatrix} \Delta w_1 \\ \vdots \\ \Delta w_D \\ \Delta b \end{pmatrix} \tag{10}$$

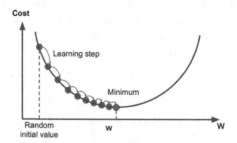

Fig. 4. Descending a gradient to the local minimum.

However, the gradient of the function depends on the point at which the function is evaluated. Real data tend to contain random variations (generally referred to as noise). As a result, while the ensemble of gradients will point in a general direction that improves the network, individual data points generally yield gradients that point in different directions. These random effects are minimized by multiplying the correction by a small learning rate, and using multiple passes through the training data to slowly converge towards a global minimum.

The derivative of the cost with respect to each parameter can be evaluated by using the chain rule. For example, suppose that we have a single neural unit composed of D inputs. The unit will have D weights indexed with the letter d, where $1 \leq d \leq D$. The contribution of the weight, w_d, to this error is given by the derivative of the cost with respect w_d. This can be evaluated by the chain rule, working back from the cost with respect to the activation, a, the derivative of the activation, a, with respect to the linear sum, z, and the derivative of the linear sum, z, with respect to w_d, as shown in Eq. 11.

$$\Delta w_d = \frac{\partial C(\vec{X}, \vec{\omega}, b)}{\partial w_d} = \frac{\partial C(\vec{X}, \vec{\omega}, b)}{\partial a} \cdot \frac{\partial a}{\partial z} \cdot \frac{\partial z}{\partial w_d} \tag{11}$$

The network can be improved by subtracting a fraction of gradient from each of the network parameters. Because the training data typically contains un-modelled phenomena, the correction is weighted by a (very small) learning rate "η" to stabilize learning, as shown in Eq. 12.

$$\vec{w}^{(i)} = \vec{w}^{(i-1)} - \eta \Delta \vec{w} \text{ and } b^{(i)} = b^{(i-1)} - \eta \Delta b \tag{12}$$

Typical values for η are from $\eta = 0.01$ to $\eta = 0.001$ and are often determined dynamically be an optimization algorithm. The superscripts *(i)* and *(i−1)* refer to successive iterations for the values of $\vec{w}$ and b.

The optimum network parameters are the parameters that provide the smallest cost or loss. To determine the best parameters, the network is iteratively refined by subtracting a small fraction of the gradient from the parameters. Ideally, at the optimum parameters, both the loss and the gradient would be zero. This can occur when training a network to approximate a mathematical function or a logic circuit from examples of uncorrupted outputs. However, this is almost never the case for real data, because of the intrinsic variations of samples within the data. As a result, if you evaluate gradient descent by hand with real world data samples, do not expect to easily see a path to convergence. Arriving at an optimum typically requires many passes through the training data, where each pass is referred to as an "epoch". Gradient descent may require many epochs to reach an optimal (minimum loss) model.

Feature Scaling. For a training set $\{\vec{X}_m\}$ of M training samples with D values, if the individual features do not have a similar range of values, than features with a larger range of values will dominate the gradient resulting in non-optimal convergence. One way to assure sure that features have similar ranges is to normalize the range of each feature with respect to the entire training set. For example, the range for each feature can be normalized by subtracting the minimum for that feature from the training data and dividing by the range, as shown in Eq. 13.

$$\forall_{m=1}^{M} : x'_{dm} := \frac{x_{dm} - min(x_d)}{max(x_d) - min(x_d)} \tag{13}$$

This has the effect of mapping a highly elongated cloud of training data into a sphere, as shown in Fig. 5. Ideally this will lead to a spherical cost function with the minimum at the center.

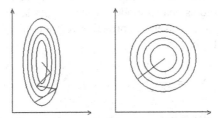

Fig. 5. Feature scaling improves gradient descent by projecting the data to a space where features have a similar range if values. This reduces the effects of small variations in the gradient.

Note that the 2-D surface shown in Fig. 5 is an idealized representation that portrays only two parameters, for example w, b for a single neural unit with a scalar input x. The actual cost surfaces are hyper-dimensional and not easy to visualize.

Local Minima. Gradient descent assumes that the loss function is convex. However, the loss function depends on real data with un-modeled phenomena (noise). Variations in the training samples can create a non-convex loss with local minima (Fig. 6).

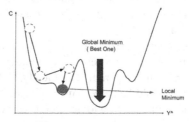

Fig. 6. Variations in the training samples can create a non-convex loss with local minima.

In most networks, the gradient has many parameters, and the cost function is evaluated in a very high dimensional space. It is helpful to see the data as a hyper-dimensional cloud descending (flowing over) a complex hyper-dimensional surface, as shown in Fig. 7.

Fig. 7. The data can be seen as a hyper-dimensional cloud descending (flowing over) a complex hyper-dimensional surface. (Drawing recovered from the internet - Source unknown)

Batch Mode: A popular technique to reduce the random variations of corrections is to average the gradients from many samples, and then correct the network with this average. This is referred to as "batch mode". The training data is divided into "folds" composed of M samples, and an average correction vector is computed from the average of the gradients of the M samples.

$$\Delta \vec{w} = \frac{1}{M} \sum_{m=1}^{M} \Delta \vec{w}_m = \frac{1}{M} \sum_{m=1}^{M} \vec{\nabla} C_m \qquad (14)$$

The model is then updated with the average gradient, using a learning rate "η" to stabilize learning as described above.

$$\vec{w}^{(i)} = \vec{w}^{(i-1)} - \eta \Delta \vec{w} \qquad (15)$$

While batch mode tends to be more efficient than updating the network with each sample, it is more likely to learning that is stuck in a local minimum. This likelihood can be reduced using stochastic gradient descent.

Stochastic Gradient Descent. With Stochastic gradient descent, individual training samples are randomly selected and used to update the model. This will send the model in random directions that eventually flow to the global minima. While much less efficient than batch mode, this is less likely to become stuck in local minima.

3.2 Multilayer Neural Networks

Artificial Neural Networks are typically composed of multiple layers of neural units, where each each neural unit is composed of a weighted sum of inputs, followed by a non-linear decision function. Such structures are often referred to as multi-layer perceptrons, abbeviated as MLP. For example, Fig. 1 shows a 2-layer network with 3 hidden units at layer $l = 1$ and a single output unit at level $l = 2$.

We will use the following notation to describe MLPs:

L	The number of layers (Layers of non-linear activations).
l	The layer index. l ranges from 0 (input layer) to L (output layer).
$N(l)$	The number of units in layer l. $N^{(0)} = D$
$\vec{a}^{(0)} = \vec{X}$	is the input layer. For each component $a_i^{(0)} = x_d$
$a_j^{(l)}$	The activation output of the jth neuron of the lth layer.
$w_{ij}^{(l)}$	The weight from the unit i of layer l-1 for the unit j of layer l.
$b_j^{(l)}$	The bias term for j^{th} unit of the lth layer.
$f(z)$	A non-linear activation function, such as a sigmoid, relu or tanh.

Note that all parameters carry a superscript, referring to their layer. For example: $a_1^{(2)}$ is the activation output of the first neuron of the second layer. $w_{13}^{(2)}$ is the weight for neuron 1 from the first level to neuron 3 in the second layer. The network in Fig. 1 would be described by:

$$a_1^{(1)} = f(w_{11}^{(1)}x_1 + w_{21}^{(1)}x_2 + w_{31}^{(1)}x_3 + b_1^{(1)})$$

$$a_2^{(1)} = f(w_{12}^{(1)}x_1 + w_{22}^{(1)}x_2 + w_{32}^{(1)}x_3 + b_2^{(1)})$$

$$a_3^{(1)} = f(w_{13}^{(1)}x_1 + w_{23}^{(1)}x_2 + w_{33}^{(1)}x_3 + b_3^{(1)})$$

$$a_1^{(2)} = f(w_{11}^{(2)}a_1^{(1)} + w_{21}^{(2)}a_2^{(1)} + w_{31}^{(2)}a_3^{(1)} + b_1^{(2)}) \tag{16}$$

This can be generalized to multiple layers. For example, Fig. 8 shows a 3-layer network, with an output vector $\vec{a}^{(3)}$ at layer 3 composed of 2 units.

In general, unit j at layer l is computed as shown in Eq. 17, illustrated by Fig. 9.

$$a_j^{(l)} = f\left(\sum_{i=1}^{N^{(l-1)}} w_{ij}^{(l)} a_i^{(l-1)} + b_j^{(l)}\right) \tag{17}$$

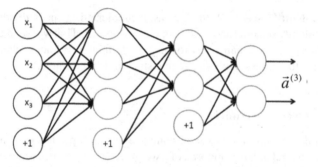

Fig. 8. A three layer network with an output vector of size $N^{(3)} = 2$ at level 3.

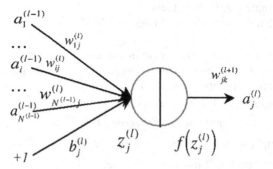

Fig. 9. The jth unit at layer l.

3.3 Activation Functions

Neural units are composed of a weighted sum of inputs followed by a non-linear activation function. The activation function must have a first derivative, so that the network can be trained using gradient descent.

For binary problems, the hard decision surface of the original perceptron is easily replaced with is the hyperbolic tangent (Fig. 10):

$$f(z) = \tanh(z) = \frac{e^z - e^{-z}}{e^z + e^{-z}}$$

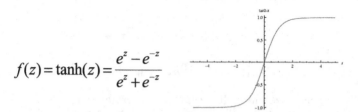

Fig. 10. The hyperbolic Tangent activation function

The derivative for the hyperbolic tangent is:

$$\frac{\partial \tanh(z)}{\partial z} = \frac{1}{cosh^2(z)} = sech^2(z) \tag{18}$$

A popular choice for activation function is the logistic sigmoid function. The logistic function is also known as the S-shaped curve or sigmoid curve and is widely used to model saturation phenomena in fields such as biology, chemistry, and economics (Fig. 11).

$$f(z) = \sigma(z) = \frac{1}{1+e^{-z}}$$

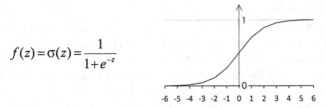

Fig. 11. The sigmoid function, $\sigma(z)$.

The sigmoid has a simple derivative function

$$\frac{\partial \sigma(z)}{\partial z} = \sigma(z)(1 - \sigma(z)) \tag{19}$$

Because the output of the sigmoid varies from 0 to 1, the sigmoid is easily generalized for multi-class problems, using the Softmax activation function.

$$f(z_k) = \frac{e^{z_k}}{\sum_{k=1}^{K} e^{z_k}} \tag{20}$$

The softmax function takes as input a vector $\vec{z}$ of K real numbers, and normalizes it into a distribution consisting of vector of K values that sum to 1. The result of a softmax sums to 1, and can be interpreted as a probability distribution indicating the likelihood of each component. Softmax is widely used as the output activation function for networks with multiclass outputs.

The rectified linear function is popular for intermediate levels in deep networks because of its trivial derivative (Fig. 12):

$$ReLu(z) = \max(0, z)$$

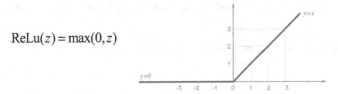

Fig. 12. The rectified linear (ReLu) activation function.

For $z \leq 0$, the derivative is 0. For $z > 0$ the derivative is 1. Many other activations have been proposed, for a variety of uses.

3.4 Backpropagation as Distributed Gradient Descent

As stated above, the weights and biases for a multi-layer network can be computed using the back-propagation algorithm. Back-propagation is a distributed algorithm for computing gradient descent and can thus be scaled to extremely large networks composed of billions of parameters, provided sufficient computing and training data are available. The back propagation algorithm can be directly derived from the gradient using the chain rule. Back-propagation propagates error terms back through the layers, using the weights and activations of units to determine the component of the gradient for each parameter.

As a form of gradient descent, back-propagation determines the correction factors to adjust the network the weights $w_{ij}^{(l)}$ and biases $b_j^{(l)}$ so as to minimize an error function between the network output $\vec{a}_m^L$ and the target value $\vec{y}_m$ for the M training samples $\{\vec{X}_m\}$, $\{\vec{y}_m\}$. Each input sample is input to the network to compute an output activation, $\vec{a}_m^L$. This can be referred to as forward propagation. An error term is then computed from the difference of $\vec{a}_m^L$ with the target vector, $\vec{y}_m$. This error is propagated back through the network to determine the correction vector for each parameter.

To keep things simple, let us consider the case of a two class network with a single unit, so that δ_m^{out}, a_m, and y_m are scalars. The results are easily generalized to vectors for multi-class networks with multiple layers. For a single neuron, at the output layer, the "error" for each training sample is the error resulting from using a_m as a value for y_m.

$$\delta_m^{out} = (a_m - y_m) \tag{21}$$

The error term δ_m^{out} is the total error for the whole network for sample m. This error is used to compute an error term for the weights that activate the neuron: δ_m. As shown in Fig. 13.

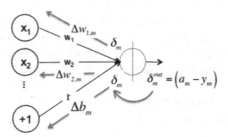

Fig. 13. The error term is propagated back through each unit to adjust the weights and biases.

The error term for the input activations is given Eq. 22:

$$\delta_m = \frac{\partial f(z)}{\partial z} \delta_m^{out} \tag{22}$$

This correction is then used to determine a correction term for the weights:

$$\Delta w_{d,m} = x_d \delta_m \tag{23}$$

$$\Delta b_m = \delta_m \tag{24}$$

Back propagation can be easily generalized for multiple neurons at multiple layers ($l = 1$ to L) with multiple outputs ($k = 1$ to K). In this case, both the network output activation and the indicator variable would be vectors with k components, with one component for each class, giving an error vector, $\vec{\delta}_m^{out}$ as shown in Eq. 25.

$$\vec{\delta}_m^{out} = \left(\vec{a}_m^{(out)} - \vec{y}_m\right) \text{ with k components: } \delta_{k,m}^{out} = \left(a_{k,m}^{(out)} - y_{k,m}\right) \tag{25}$$

The error term for unit k at layer L is:

$$\delta_{k,m}^{(L)} = \frac{\partial f(z_k^{(L)})}{\partial z} \delta_m^{out} \tag{26}$$

For the hidden units in layers $l < L$ the error $\delta_j^{(l)}$ is based on a weighted average of the error terms for $\delta_k^{(l+1)}$.

$$\delta_{j,m}^{(l)} = \frac{\partial f(z_j^{(l)})}{\partial z_j^{(l)}} \sum_{k=1}^{N^{l+1}} w_{jk}^{(l+1)} \delta_{k,m}^{(l+1)} \tag{27}$$

An error term, $\delta_j^{(l)}$ is computed for each unit j in layer l and projected back to layer $l-1$ using the sum of errors times the corresponding weights times the derivative of the activation function. This error term tells how much the activation of unit j was responsible for differences between the output activation vector of the network $\vec{a}_m^{(L)}$ and the target vector $\vec{y}_m$. This error term can then used to correct the weights and bias terms leading from layer j to layer i.

$$\Delta w_{ij,m}^{(l)} = a_i^{(l-1)} \delta_{j,m}^{(l)} \tag{28}$$

$$\Delta b_{j,m}^{(l)} = \delta_{j,m}^{(l)} \tag{29}$$

Note that the corrections $\Delta w_{ij,m}^{(l)}$ and $\Delta b_{j,m}^{(l)}$ are NOT applied until after the error has propagated all the way back to layer $l = 1$, and that when $l = 1$, $a_i^{(0)} = x_i$.

For "batch learning", the corrections terms, $\Delta w_{ji,m}^{(l)}$ and $\Delta b_{j,m}^{(l)}$ are averaged over M samples of the training data and then only an average correction is applied to the weights.

$$\Delta w_{ij}^{(l)} = \frac{1}{M} \sum_{m=1}^{M} \Delta w_{ij,m}^{(l)}$$
$$\Delta b_{j}^{(l)} = \frac{1}{M} \sum_{m=1}^{M} \Delta b_{j,m}^{(l)} \tag{30}$$

then

$$w_{ij}^{(l)} \leftarrow w_{ij}^{(l)} - \eta \cdot \Delta w_{ij}^{(l)}$$
$$b_{j}^{(l)} \leftarrow b_{j}^{(l)} - \eta \cdot \Delta b_{j}^{(l)} \tag{31}$$

where η is the learning rate.

Back-propagation is a parallel algorithm to compute a correction term for each network parameter from the gradient of the loss function. A common problem with gradient descent is that the loss function can have local minimum. This problem can be minimized by regularization. A popular regularization technique for back propagation is to use "momentum"

$$w_{ij}^{(l)} \leftarrow w_{ij}^{(l)} - \eta \cdot \Delta w_{ij}^{(l)} + \mu \cdot w_{ij}^{(l)}$$
$$b_j^{(l)} \leftarrow b_j^{(l)} - \eta \cdot \Delta b_j^{(l)} + \mu \cdot b_j^{(l)}$$
$$(32)$$

where the terms $\mu \cdot w_j^{(l)}$ and $\mu \cdot b_j^{(l)}$ serves to stabilize the estimation.

References

1. Duda, R.O., Hart, P.E.: Pattern Classification and Scene Analysis. Wiley, New York (1973)
2. Cristianini, N., Shawe-Taylor, J.: An Introduction to Support Vector Machines and Other Kernel-Based Learning Methods. Cambridge university press, Cambridge (2000)
3. Bishop, C.M., Nasrabadi, N.M.: Pattern Recognition and Machine Learning. Springer, New York (2006). https://doi.org/10.1007/978-0-387-45528-0
4. van Engelen, J.E., Hoos, H.H.: A survey on semi-supervised learning. Mach. Learn. **109**(2), 373–440 (2019). https://doi.org/10.1007/s10994-019-05855-6
5. Dempster, A.P., Laird, N.M., Rubin, D.B.: Maximum likelihood from incomplete data via the EM algorithm. J. Roy. Stat. Soc.: Ser. B (Methodol.) **39**(1), 1–22 (1977)
6. Sutton, R.S., Barto, A.G.: Reinforcement learning. J. Cogn. Neurosci. **11**(1), 126–134 (1999)
7. Weiss, K., Khoshgoftaar, T.M., Wang, D.: A survey of transfer learning. J. Big Data **3**(9) (2016)
8. Devlin, J., Chang, M.W., Lee, K., Toutanova, K.: Bert: pre-training of deep bidirectional transformers for language understanding (2018). arXiv preprint arXiv:1810.04805
9. McCulloch, W.S., Pitts, W.: A logical calculus of the ideas immanent in nervous activity. Bull. Math. Biophys. **5**(4), 115–133 (1943)
10. Rosenblatt, F.: The Perceptron: a probabilistic model for information storage and organization in the brain. Psychol. Rev. **65**(6), 386–408 (1958)
11. Minsky, M., Papert, S.: Perceptrons: An Introduction to Computational Geometry. MIT Press, Cambridge (1969)
12. Fukushima, K.: Cognitron: a self-organizing multilayered neural network. Biol. Cybern. **20**, 121–136 (1975)
13. Werbos, P.J.: Backpropagation through time: what it does and how to do it. Proc. IEEE **78**(10), 1550–1560 (1990)

Generative Networks and the AutoEncoder

James L. Crowley[(✉)]

Institut Polytechnique de Grenoble, Université Grenoble Alpes, Grenoble, France
James.Crowley@univ-grenoble-alpes.fr
http://crowley-coutaz.fr/jlc/jlc.html

Abstract. Neural networks were invented to classify signals. However, networks can also be used to generate signals. This chapter introduces generative networks, and shows that discriminative networks can be combined with generative networks to produce an autoencoder. Autoencoders can be trained with self-supervised learning to provide a compact code for signals. This code can be used to reconstruct clean copies of noisy signals. With a simple modification to the loss function using information theory, an autoencoder can be used for unsupervised discovery of categories in data, providing the basis for self-supervised learning that is at the heart of Transformers. To explain this modification, this chapter reviews basic concepts from information theory including entropy, cross entropy and the Kullback-Leiblier (KL) divergence. The chapter concludes with brief presentations of Variational Autoencoders (VAEs) and Generative Adversarial Networks (GANs).

Learning Objectives: This chapter provides students with an introduction to generative neural networks and autoencoders, covering fundamental concepts from information theory as well as well as applications such as Variational Autoencoders (VAEs) and Generative Adversarial Networks (GANs). Mastering the material in this chapter will enable students to understand how a neural network can be trained to generate signals, and how an auto-encoder can be used for unsupervised and self-supervised learning. Students will acquire an understanding of fundamental concepts from information theory such as entropy and sparsity. Students will be able to explain how generative networks can be combined with discriminative networks to construct generative adversarial networks.

Keywords: Generative Networks · Autoencoders · Entropy · Kulback-Leibler divergence · Variational Autoencoders (VAEs) · Generative Adversarial Networks (GANs)

1 Generative Networks

Neural networks were originally invented to recognize categories of phenomena in signals. For recognition, a network is trained to map a feature vector, $\vec{X}$, into a predicted category label, $\hat{y}$, taken from a discrete set of possible categories.[1] Such networks are called discriminative networks.

---

[1] The predicted category label is displayed with a "hat" symbol to distinguish it as an estimation that may vary from the true label, y.

© Springer Nature Switzerland AG 2023
M. Chetouani et al. (Eds.): ACAI 2021, LNAI 13500, pp. 55–66, 2023.
https://doi.org/10.1007/978-3-031-24349-3_4

$$\vec{X} \longrightarrow \boxed{D(\vec{X})} \longrightarrow \hat{y}$$

Fig. 1. A discriminative network maps a feature vector, $\vec{X}$, into a predicted category label, $\hat{y}$.

In principle, with enough data and computing, networks can be trained to estimate any computable function. In particular, networks can be trained to generate a typical feature vector from a category label. This is called a generative network. With sufficient data and computing, generative networks can be trained to generate realistic imitations for any signal including image, sounds, video, and motor commands for coordinated robot motions.

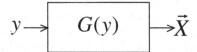

$$y \longrightarrow \boxed{G(y)} \longrightarrow \vec{X}$$

Fig. 2. A generative network maps a category label to a typical feature vector.

A discriminative network can be paired with a generative network to create an autoencoder. The autoencoder maps an input vector onto a compact code vector. This code vector can then be used to generate a clean copy of the signal, as shown in Fig. 2. When trained with a least squares loss function, as described in chapter 1, the autoencoder represents a signal with the largest principal values that would be found by eigenspace analysis of the training data. Augmenting the least-squares loss function with an information theoretic measure of sparsity enables the autoencoder to learn a minimal set of independent components that can be used to provide an abstract representation for a data set.

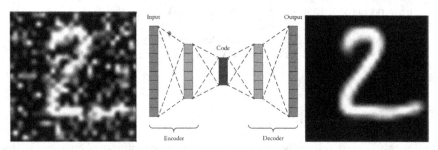

Fig. 3. An autoencoder combines a disciminative encoder with a generative decoder to create a clean (denoised) copy of a signal.

2   The AutoEncoder

An autoencoder is an unsupervised learning algorithm that uses back-propagation to learning a sparse set of features for describing a set of data. In the early days of perceptron learning, the autoencoder was used to compensate for a lack of labeled training data required to develop the back-propagation algorithm for computing gradient descent [1]. With the autoencoder, the data is its own ground truth! The autoencoder was gradually recognized as a powerful technique for self-supervised learning [2].

Rather than learn to estimate a target class label, y, the auto-encoder learns to reconstruct an approximation, $\hat{X}$, for an input vector $\vec{X}$ using a minimum size code vector. The autoencoder is trained to preserve the forms that are common to all of the training data while ignoring random variations (noise). The hidden units provide a code vector that is said to represent the latent energy (or information) in the signal.

Let $\hat{X}$ be the reconstructed version for a signal, $\vec{X}$. The error from using the reconstructed version to replace the signal is the difference between the input and ouput. The square of this error can be used as a loss function, $C(-)$ to learn a set of network parameters[2], $\vec{w}$, using gradient descent, as shown in Eq. 1.

$$C(\vec{X}, \vec{w}) = (\hat{X} - \vec{X})^2 \tag{1}$$

When computed with a loss function based on the least-squares error, the autoencoder converges to a code vector that captures a maximum quantity of signal energy from the training set for any given size of code vector. The theoretical minimum for such an encoding is provided by the eigenvectors of the training set. Thus, when computed with least squares error, the autoencoder provides an approximation for the principal components of the training data that express the largest energy. The addition of an information theoretic term for sparsity can force the auto-encoder to learn independent components of the data set, providing a minimal abstract representation for the data.

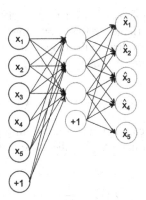

Fig. 4. A 2-layer autoencoder with an input vector of $D = 5$, and code vector of $N = 3$.

---

[2] In the following, we will simplify the notation by including the bias term, b, as a component of the network parameters, $\vec{w}$.

Consider a two-layer autoencoder for a signal composed of D elements as shown in Fig. 4. The first (hidden) layer, referred to as layer 1, is composed of N hidden units that provide a code vector, such that N is smaller than D. The second layer, referred to as layer 2, is composed of D units that use this code vector to generate a clean copy of the input signal. Each of the N hidden code units is fed by D input signals plus a bias. Using the notation from Chapter 3, these $D \cdot (N + 1)$ parameters are $\{w_{ij}^{(1)}, b_j^{(1)}\}$. The $N(D + 1)$ weights and biases the second layer (layer 2) are $\{w_{jk}^{(2)}, b_k^{(2)}\}$.

By training with the least-squares error between the signal and its reconstruction, the network learns to provide an approximate copy $\hat{X}$ of the input signals, $\vec{X}$ using the N coefficients of the hidden code vector. The code vector provides a lossy encoding for $\vec{X}$. Training the network with a least-squares loss function trains the network to learn minimal set of features that approximates a form of eigenspace coding of the training data, as explained above. The weights and biases of each neural unit (the receptive fields) define an orthogonal basis space that can be used for a minimum energy reconstruction of input signals. However, the energy for any input pattern is typically spread over many of the coefficients of a code vector. For pattern recognition, what we would like is to learn a set of independent categories for the data, such that any input data vector would be reflected by a concentration of energy in only one of the hidden units, with the other hidden units nearly zero. In this way, the hidden units provide a form of "one-hot coding" for the categories in the training data. This can be done by training the autoencoder with a cost function that includes an additional term that forces the coefficients to be unique for each data sample. This additional cost term is referred to as "sparsity", represented by the symbol, ρ. Defining the loss function for sparsity requires some background from information theory.

3   Background from Information Theory

3.1   Entropy

The entropy of a random variable is the average level of "information", "surprise", or "uncertainty" inherent in the variable's possible outcomes. Consider a set of M random integers, $\{X_m\}$, with N possible values in the range 1 to N. We can count the frequency of occurrence for each value with table of N cells, $h(x)$. This is commonly referred to as a histogram.

$$\forall m = 1, M \; : \; h(X_m) \leftarrow h(X_m) + 1 \tag{2}$$

From this training set we can compute a probability distribution that tells us the probability that any random variable X_m has the value x. This is written as $P(X_m = x)$ or more simply as $P(x)$.

$$P(x) = \frac{1}{M} h(x) \tag{3}$$

The information about the set $\{X_m\}$ provided by the observation that a sample X_m has value x, is measured with the formula:

$$I(x) = -log_2(P(x)) \tag{4}$$

This is the formal definition of information used in information theory. In physics, the practice is to use logarithms of base 10. In informatics and computer science we generally prefer base 2 because a base 2 logarithm measures information in binary digits, referred to as bits. The information content in bits tells us the minimum number of base 2 (binary) digits that would be needed to encode the data in the training set. The negative sign assures that the number is always positive or zero, as the log of a number less than 1 is negative.

Information expresses the number of bits needed to encode and transmit the value for an event. Low probability events are surprising and convey more information. High probability events are unsurprising and convey less information. For example, consider the case where X has $N = 2$ values and the histogram has a uniform distribution, $P(x) = 0.5$.

$$I(x) = -\log_2(P(x)) = -\log_2\left(2^{-1}\right) = 1 \tag{5}$$

The information from a sample X_m is 1 bit. If X_m had 8 possible values then, all equally likely, then $P(X_m = x) = 1/8 = 2^{-3}$ and the information is 3 bits.

3.2 Computing Entropy

For a set of M observations, the entropy is the expected value from the information from the observations. The entropy of a distribution measures the surprise (or information) obtained from the observation of a sample in the distribution. For a distribution $P(x)$ of features with N possible values, the entropy is

$$H(X) = -\sum_{x=1}^{N} P(x)\log_2(P(x)) \tag{6}$$

For example, for tossing a coin, there are two possible outcomes ($N = 2$). The probability of each outcome is $P(x) = 1/2$. This is the situation of maximum entropy

$$H(X) = -\sum_{x=1}^{2} \frac{1}{2}\log_2\left(\frac{1}{2}\right) = 1 \tag{7}$$

This is the most uncertain case. In the case where $N = 4$ values, the entropy is 2 bits. It would require 2 bits to communicate an observation. In the general case, there are N possible values for X, and all values are equally likely, then

$$H(X) = -\sum_{x=1}^{N} \frac{1}{N}\log_2\left(\frac{1}{N}\right) = -\log_2\left(\frac{1}{N}\right) \tag{8}$$

On the other hand, consider when the distribution is a Dirac function, where all samples X_m have the same value, x_o.

$$P(x) = \delta(x - x_o) = \begin{cases} 1 & \text{if } x = x_o \\ 0 & \text{otherwise} \end{cases} \tag{9}$$

In this case, there is no surprise (no information) in the observation that $X_m = x_o$ and the entropy will be zero. For any distribution, Entropy measures the non-uniformity of the distribution (Fig. 5).

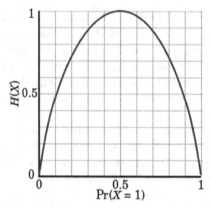

Fig. 5. Entropy measures the non-uniformity of a distribution. A uniform distribution, where all samples are equally likely, has an entropy of 1. (Image from [3], copied from wikipedia[3]).

3.3 Cross Entropy

Cross-entropy is a measure of the difference between two probability distributions. Cross-entropy can be thought of as the total entropy between two distributions and is a measure of the difference (or lack of similarity) of the two distributions. Perfectly matching distributions have a cross entropy of 0.

Cross-entropy loss is commonly used to measure the performance of a classification model whose output is a probability between 0 and 1, as with the sigmoid or soft-max. Cross-entropy loss increases as the predicted probability diverges from the actual label. So predicting a probability of .012 when the actual observation label is 1 would be bad and result in a high value for the log of the cross-entropy. A perfect model would have a log-loss of 0 (Fig. 6).

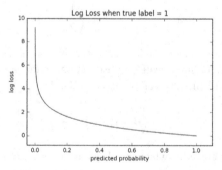

Fig. 6. Cross entry measures the difference of two distributions. Copied from "read the docs"[4]

---

[3] *Wikipedia, The Free Encyclopedia*, s.v. "Entropy (information theory)," (accessed August 20, 2022), https://en.wikipedia.org/w/index.php?title=Entropy_(information_theory)&oldid= 1101826646

[4] https://docs.readthedocs.io/en/stable/privacy-policy.html.

Binary Cross-entropy loss is useful for training binary classifiers with the sigmoid activation function. Categorical Cross-Entropy is used to train a multi-class network where softmax activation is used to output a probability distribution, $P(a)$, over a set of output activations for K classes.

3.4 Binary Cross Entropy

For binary classification, a network has a single activation output, $a^{(out)}$:

$$a^{(out)} = f(z^{(L)}) = \frac{1}{1 + e^{-z^{(L)}}} = \frac{e^{z^{(L)}}}{e^{z^{(L)}} + 1} \tag{10}$$

For a target variable of y, the binary cross entropy is

$$H(a^{(out)}, y) = y\log(a^{(out)}) + (1 - y)\log(1 - a^{(out)}) \tag{11}$$

3.5 Categorical Cross Entropy Loss

For a network with a vector of K activation outputs, $a_k^{(out)}$ with indicator vector y_k, each target class, $k = 1,...,K$, contributes to the cost (or loss) function used for gradient descent. This is represented by using a softmax activation function where the activation energy for each component, a_k, is

$$a_k = f(z^k) = \frac{e^{z^k}}{\sum_{k=1}^{K} e^{z^k}} \tag{12}$$

This results in a categorical cross entropy of

$$H(\vec{a}^{(out)}, \vec{y}) = -\sum_{k=1}^{K} y_k\log(a_k^{(out)}) \tag{13}$$

When the indicators variables are encoded with one-hot encoding (1 for the true class, zero for all others), only the positive class where $y_k = 1$ is included in the cost function. All of the other $K-1$ activations are multiplied by 0. In this case:

$$H(\vec{a}^{(out)}, \vec{y}) = \frac{e^{z^k}}{\sum_{k=1}^{K} e^{z^k}} \tag{14}$$

where z_k is the linear sum of weighted activations. The derivative for the positive activations is

$$\frac{\partial a_k}{\partial z_k} = \frac{\partial f(z_k)}{\partial z_k} = \frac{\partial}{\partial z_k}\left(-\log\left(\frac{e^{z^k}}{\sum_{k=1}^{K} e^{z^k}}\right)\right) = \frac{e^{z^k}}{\sum_{k=1}^{K} e^{z^k}} - 1 \tag{15}$$

The derivative for the negative class activations is:

$$\frac{\partial a_k}{\partial z_k} = \frac{e^{z^k}}{\sum_{k=1}^{K} e^{z^k}} \tag{16}$$

3.6 The Kullback-Leibler Divergence

The Kullback-Leibler (KL) divergence, $D_{KL}(P\|Q)$ also known as the relative entropy of Q with respect to P, measures the divergence between two probability distributions, $P(n)$ and $Q(n)$.

$$D_{KL}(P\|Q) = \sum_{x=1}^{N} P(x) \log\left(\frac{P(x)}{Q(x)}\right) \tag{17}$$

The KL divergence can be used to define cross entropy as

$$H(P, Q) = H(P) + D_{KL}(P\|Q) \tag{18}$$

The KL divergence can also be used to measure the divergence between a constant and a distribution. For example, KL divergence can provide a measure of the distance between a target activation energy, a, and a distribution of activation energy for a set of n units, a_n.

The KL divergence between a target activation, a, and a distribution of N activations, a_n, is:

$$D_{KL}(a\|a_n) = \sum_{n=1}^{N} a \cdot \log\left(\frac{a}{a_n}\right) \tag{19}$$

Adding the KL divergence to the loss function for the input layer of an autoencoder forces the autoencoder to learn a sparse code vector resembling a one-hot coding vector for the independent categories of a training set, as explained below.

3.7 Sparsity

Sparsity measures the average activation energy for the N hidden units of an autoencoder from a batch of M samples. During training with M training samples, the Kullback-Leibler (KL) divergence can be used to compare the sparsity of the activation values for the N hidden (latent) code variables to a target value, ρ. Including a target for sparsity in the loss function during batch training constrains the network parameters to converge toward a configuration that concentrates activation to a single unit for each training sample. This forces the autoencoder to learn a code vector where each latent unit represents one of independent components of the training data. The independent components are assumed to represent independent categories of phenomena in the training set.

Consider a simple 2-layer autoencoder that learns to reconstruct data from a training set $\{\vec{X}_m\}$ of M training samples of dimension D features. Assume a code vector, $\vec{a}$, of N $<< D$ latent variables, a_n. For any input vector $\vec{X}$, the N coefficients of the code vector, $\vec{a}$, are computed by

$$a_n = f\left(\sum_{d=1}^{D} w_{dn}^{(1)} x_d + b_n^{(1)}\right) \tag{20}$$

where $f(-)$ is a non-linear activation function, such as sigmoid or RELU. The sparsity for this vector is the average activation energy:

$$\rho = \frac{1}{N} \sum_{n=1}^{N} a_n \qquad (21)$$

The D components of the output vector, $\hat{X}$, are computed as

$$\hat{x}_d = f\left(\sum_{n=1}^{N} w_{nd}^{(2)} a_n + b_d^{(2)} \right) \qquad (22)$$

The least squares cost for using $\hat{X}_m$ as an estimate for $\vec{X}_m$ is:

$$C(\vec{X}_m; \vec{w}) = \frac{1}{2}(\hat{X}_m - \vec{X}_m)^2 \qquad (23)$$

where $\vec{w}$ represents the network parameters including the bias terms as explained above in Eq. 1. The average least squares loss for a training set $\{\vec{X}_m\}$ of M training samples is

$$C(\{\vec{X}_m\}; \vec{w}) = \frac{1}{2} \sum_{m=1}^{M} (\hat{X}_m - \vec{X}_m)^2 \qquad (24)$$

The auto-encoder can be trained to minimize the sparsity by addition of a loss term that uses the KL divergence to measure the difference between a target sparsity, ρ, and the vector of sparsities from the training data, $\hat{\rho}_n$.

$$C(\{\vec{X}_m\}; \vec{w}) = \frac{1}{2} \sum_{m=1}^{M} (\hat{X}_m - \vec{X}_m)^2 + \beta \sum_{n=1}^{N} D_{KL}(\rho \| \hat{\rho}_n) \qquad (25)$$

where ρ is a target value for sparsity, typically close to zero, and β controls the importance of sparsity. Computing the cost requires a pass through the M training samples to compute the sparsity for the training data, and thus requires batch learning.

The auto-encoder forces the hidden units to become approximately independent, representing hidden, or latent, information in the data set. Incorporating KL divergence into back propagation requires adding the derivative of the KL divergence to the average error term used to compute backpropagation. Recall that when computed with least-squares error, the output error for m^{th} training sample is;

$$\vec{\delta}_m^{out} = \left(\hat{X}_m - \vec{X}_m \right) \qquad (26)$$

The average error term for a batch of M samples is

$$\vec{\delta}^{out} = \sum_{m=1}^{M} \left(\hat{X}_m - \vec{X}_m \right) \qquad (27)$$

This output error is used to compute the error energy for updating weights and biases with backpropagation, as explained in Sect. 1. For example the error term for the D individual output units is

$$\vec{\delta}_d^{(2)} = \vec{\delta}^{(out)} \frac{\partial f\,(z_d^{(2)})}{\partial z_d^{(2)}} \tag{28}$$

where $f()$ is the non-linear activation function, typically a sigmoid for the autoencoder. The error energy for the discriminative layer is:

$$\vec{\delta}_n^{(1)} = \frac{\partial f\,(z_n^{(2)})}{\partial z_n^{(2)}} \sum_{d=1}^{D} w_{dn}^{(2)} \vec{\delta}_d^{(2)} \tag{29}$$

The discriminator can be trained to learn a sparse code by adding a penalty term based on the KL divergence of the activation energies of the code vector to the error energy at level 1 as shown in Eq. 30.

$$\delta_n^{(1)} = \frac{\partial f\,(z_n^{(2)})}{\partial z_n^{(2)}} \sum_{d=1}^{D} w_{dn}^{(2)} \delta_d^{(2)} + \beta \left(-\frac{\rho}{\hat{\rho}_n} + \frac{1-\rho}{1-\hat{\rho}_n} \right) \tag{30}$$

where ρ is the target sparsity, and $\hat{\rho}_n$ is the sparsity (average activation energy) of the nth hidden unit for the training set of M samples. The error energy computed with Eq. 30 is then used to update the weights and biases of the hidden units at level 1, as discussed in in the previous chapter.

4   Variational Autoencoders

The output of an auto-encoder can be used to drive a decoder to produce a filtered version of the encoded data or of another training set. However, the output from an auto-encoder is discrete. We can adapt an auto-encoder to generate a nearly continuous output by replacing the code with a probabilistic code represented by a mean and variance. This is called a Variational Autoencoder (VAE) [4]. VAEs combine a discriminative network with a generative network. VAEs can be used to generate "deep fake" videos as well as realistic rendering of audio, video or movements.

Neural networks can be seen as learning a joint probability density function $P(\vec{X}, Y)$ that associates that associates a continuous random vector, $\vec{X}$, with a discrete random category, Y. A discriminative model gives a conditional probability distribution $P(Y|\vec{X})$. A generative model gives a conditional probability $P(\vec{X}|Y)$. Driving the conditional probability $P(\vec{X}|Y)$ with a probability distribution $P(Y)$ can be used to generate a signal that varies smoothly between learned outputs (Fig. 7).

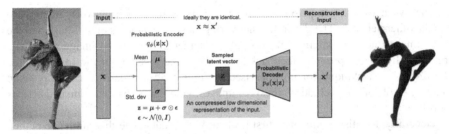

Fig. 7. A Variational autoencoder generates an animated output based on the motion patterns of an input. (Image from Lilian Weng[5])

Normally, for an autoencoder, the latent vector is a one-hot encoded binary vector $\vec{Z}$ with k binary values. The VAE learns a probabilistic encoder that provides a mean and variance in this latent space, $\vec{Z}$. The probabilistic decoder is trained to generate a target output $\vec{Y}_m$ for the latent encoding for each training sample $\vec{X}_m$. Driving this decoder with the smoothly varying probability distribution leads to a smoothly varying output, $\hat{Y}$.

5 Generative Adversarial Networks

It is possible to put a discriminative network together with a generative network and have them train each other. This is called a Generative Adversarial Network (GAN) [5–7]. A Generative Adversarial Network places a generative network in competition with a Discriminative network (Fig. 8).

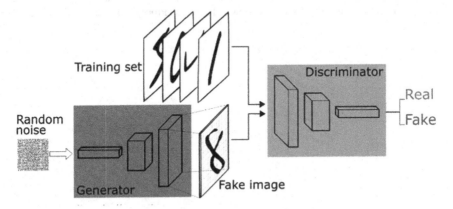

Fig. 8. A Generative Adversarial Network combines a Discriminative network with a genrative network. (Image from Thalles Silva[6])

---

[5] https://lilianweng.github.io/posts/2018-08-12-vae/

[6] https://www.freecodecamp.org/news/an-intuitive-introduction-to-generative-adversarial-net works-gans-7a2264a81394.

The two networks compete in a zero-sum game, where each network attempts to fool the other network. The generative network generates examples of an image and the discriminative network attempts to recognize whether the generated image is realistic or not. Each network provides feedback to the other, and together they train each other. The result is a technique for unsupervised learning that can learn to create realistic patterns. Applications include synthesis of images, video, speech or coordinated actions for robots.

Generally, the discriminator is first trained on real data. The discriminator is then frozen and used to train the generator. The generator is trained by using random inputs to generate fake outputs. Feedback from the discriminator drives gradient ascent by back propagation. When the generator is sufficiently trained, the two networks are put in competition.

References

1. Ackley, D.H., Hinton, G.E., Sejnowski, T.J.: A learning algorithm for boltzmann machines. Cogn. Sci. **9**, 147–168 (1985)
2. Hinton, G.E., Zemel, R.: Autoencoders, minimum description length and Helmholtz free energy. Adv. Neural Inf. Process. Syst. **6** (1993)
3. Cover, T.M., Thomas, J.A.: Elements of Information Theory. Wiley Inc., New York (1991)
4. Kingma, D.P., Welling, M.: Auto-encoding variational Bayes (2013). arXiv preprint arXiv: 1312.6114
5. Goodfellow, I., et al.: Generative adversarial nets. Adv. Neural Inf. Process. Syst. **27** (2014)
6. Creswell, A., et al.: Generative adversarial networks: an overview. Langr and Bok, GANs in Action: Deep learning with Generative Adversarial Networks (2019)
7. Creswell, A., White, T., Dumoulin, V., Arulkumaran, K., Sengupta, B., Bharath, A.A.: Generative adversarial networks: an overview. IEEE Signal Process. Mag. **35**(1), 53–65 (2018)

Convolutional Neural Networks

James L. Crowley[✉]

Institut Polytechnique de Grenoble, Université Grenoble Alpes, Grenoble, France
James.Crowley@univ-grenoble-alpes.fr
http://crowley-coutaz.fr/jlc/jlc.html

Abstract. This chapter presents Convolutional Neural Networks (CNNs). The chapter begins with a review of the convolution equation, and a description of the original LeNet series of CNN architectures. It then traces the emergence of Convolutional Networks as a key enabling technology for Computer Vision resulting from the publication of AlexNet at the 2012 ImageNet Large Scale Image Recognition Challenge. This is followed by a description of the VGG architecture and the YOLO Single Shot Detection network for Image Object Detection.

Learning Objectives: This chapter presents Convolutional Neural Networks, with a summary of the history, fundamental theory, and a review of popular architectures that have played a key role in the emergence of Deep Learning as an enabling technology for Artificial Intelligence. After reading this chapter, students will be able to understand the basic principles of convolutional neural networks and how such networks can be used to detect patterns in signals. Students will understand the meaning and significance of network hyper-parameters, and be able to select among the commonly used architectures such as VGG and YOLO to solve problems in pattern analysis and signal detection in audio, visual and other forms of multidimensional signals.

Keywords: Convolutional Neural Networks (CNNs) · Hyper-parameters · CNN architectures · LeNet · AlexNet · VGG · You Only Look Once (YOLO)

1 Convolutional Neural Networks

During the second wave of popularity of Neural Networks in the 1980s, researchers began experimenting with networks for computer vision and speech recognition. Direct application of neural networks in these domains required training networks with an excessively large number of parameters, greatly exceeding the memory and computing power of available computers. For example, direct recognition of the 44 English phonemes (speech elements) in a speech signal required a network capable of processing an audio signal composed of *1600* samples. A fully connected two layer network with 1600 hidden units in the first layer and 44 output units in the second layer would have more than *2.5* Million trainable parameters, while typical computer memory address spaces in this period were less than 1 Million bytes. In the case of computer vision, the situation was even more extreme. A typical digital image at that time was sampled at 512 × 512 rows and columns, represented by 2^{18} (or 256 K) 8-bit grayscale pixels. Training

© Springer Nature Switzerland AG 2023
M. Chetouani et al. (Eds.): ACAI 2021, LNAI 13500, pp. 67–80, 2023.
https://doi.org/10.1007/978-3-031-24349-3_5

a fully connected 2-layer perceptron to recognize a large set of objects in an image was not a serious proposition.

Inspiration for a solution was provided by neuroscience. In the early 1960s, David Hubel and Torsten Wiesel [1] fixed a cat's head in a rig and probed the visual cortex with electrodes while scanning patterns of light on a screen, as shown in Fig. 1. They found that individual cells in the visual cortex responded to specific patterns of light at specific locations and sized. They referred to these patterns as receptive fields. By systematic probing, they found that the visual cortex of the cat is composed of layers of retinotopic maps that respond to patterns of spots, bars, and edges at a narrow range of positions, sizes and orientations. Subsequent research showed that the receptive fields could be modeled as local filters for spatial frequency patterns at different spatial frequency bands and orientation. As they moved through the visual cortex, Hubel and Weisel found that these patterns were combined to form more complex patterns, such as corners and crosses. These more complex patterns were named "complex" receptive field.

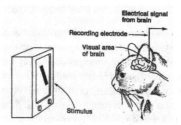

Fig. 1. David Hubel and Torsten Wiesel probed the visual cortex of a cat with electrodes and found layers of cells that responded to local patterns of stimulation. (Image widely used on the internet - source unknown)

Inspired by these results (and the subsequent Nobel Prize of Hubel and Weisel), computer vision researchers explored the use of image descriptions using convolution with Finite Impulse Response digital filters based on mathematical models of receptive fields [2, 3] including Gaussian derivatives and Gabor Functions [4]. Researchers in Machine learning speculated that it would be better to learn the weights for such filters with back-propagation. This would eventually lead to a new form of neural network known as a convolutional neural network. To properly understand such networks it can be worthwhile to review some basics from digital signal processing.

1.1 Convolution

Convolution describes the response of a linear time-invariant system to an input stimulus or driving function. An example of convolution is provided by shouting into a tunnel. The tunnel can be modeled as a shift invariant acoustic function that describe the multiple paths that sound waves of the shout may follow through the tunnel, with different lengths and different durations. The sound at the far end of the tunnel will be composed of multiple superimposed copies of the shout arriving at different times. An observer at the far end of the tunnel will hear a sonically blurred version of the shout. In addition, some vocal frequencies may resonate in the tunnel and dominant the sound at the far end, while other frequencies may be attenuated by interference. The effect is described mathematically as a convolution as shown in Eq. 1, where $s(t)$ is the waveform of a sound, $f(t)$ is a characteristic impulse response that describes the possible paths of the sound through the tunnel, and u is a dummy variable used for integration.

$$(s * f)(t) = \int_{-\infty}^{\infty} s(t - u)f(u)du \tag{1}$$

A copy of the waveform for the sound, $s(u)$, is placed at each time, t, and then multiplied by the characteristic impulse response of the tunnel, $f(u)$. For each time step, the resulting products are integrated and the result is placed in the output signal at position t. The result is a distorted version of the sound.

Computer science students generally find this operation easier to visualize and understand when expressed using sampled digitized signals. Let $s(n)$ represent a sampled copy of the sound and $f(n)$ represent the linear shift invariant system created by the tunnel. In order to compute the convolution it is necessary for at least one of the signals to have a finite duration. Let N represent the duration of the shorter of the two signal $s(n)$ and $f(n)$. The discrete convolution equation is written as

$$(s * f)(n) = \sum_{m=0}^{N-1} s(n - m)f(m) \tag{2}$$

A copy of the sound $s(-)$, is placed at each time, n, and then scaled by the value of system, $f(n)$. For each value of n, the products are summed and the result is placed in the output signal. This is exactly the equation for convolution with a Finite Impulse Response (FIR) digital filter, $f(n)$ composed of N coefficients with a digital signal, $s(n)$. Both multiplication and convolution are commutative, and so the order of the signals does not matter. In the engineering literature, convolution is commonly written as shown in Eq. 3.

$$f(n) * s(n) = \sum_{m=0}^{N-1} f(m)s(n - m) \tag{3}$$

Note that the operator "*" is exclusively reserved to represent convolution. This operator should never be used for multiplication in a context involving convolution.

For image processing, the image and filter are generally finite 2D signals with a positions defined over a range from 1 to N. For an image $P(x, y)$ with the horizontal and vertical axes noted as x and y, the 2D convolution of an $N \times N$ filter $f(x, y)$ would be written:

$$(f * P)(x, y) = \sum_{v=1}^{N} \sum_{u=1}^{N} f(u, v)P(x - u, y - v) \tag{4}$$

This operation can be seen as sliding the 2D filter, $f(x, y)$ over the image and at each position, multiplying the weights of the filter $f(u, v)$ by the pixels of the image, summing the product and placing this at the position *(x, y)*. Any image positions less than 1 or greater than the size of the image are taken as zero. The use of $x - u$ and $y - v$ rather than $y + u$ and $x + v$ flips the filter around the zero position, resulting in a mirror image of the filter. This is a mathematical convenience to assure that convolution is equivalent to multiplication in the Fourier domain, and has no relevance to Convolutional Neural Networks. In the machine learning literature, it is not unusual to see authors neglect this detail and write $y + u$ and $x + v$.

In the 1980s, researchers in machine learning asked if such filters could not be learned using back-propagation[1]. It was observed that learning perceptrons for small local windows greatly reduces the number of parameters to learn, while greatly increasing the availability of training data. Training a single perceptron to provide a binary classification for 512×512 image would require learning 2^{18} parameters and each image would provide only one training sample for a binary decision. Alternatively, training a perceptron for an 8 by 8 receptive field would require learning only 257 parameters, and each 512×512 image could provide up to 2^{18} examples of local neighborhoods to use as training samples. This makes it practical to learn many layers of local perceptrons with several perceptrons at each level, much like the visual cortex of cats or humans. Such a network could be used to recognize many different classes of visual patterns.

The dominant paradigm in computer vision at the time (and until well after 2000) was that receptive fields should be designed as digital filters with well-defined mathematical properties for bandwidth and invariance to scale or rotation. However, one area where image processing with neural networks did show promise was in reading handwritten digits for mail sorting and check processing.

1.2 Early Convolutional Neural Networks: LeNet

In the early 1990s, the US National Institute of Standards and Technology (NIST) published a data set of digitized images of handwritten digits collected during the 1980 US census and issued a research challenge for recognizing handwritten digits using this data set. Such a technology could potentially be used to build machines for labor intensive tasks such as sorting mail and processing checks. A team of researchers at AT&T led by Yann Lecun began experimenting with neural networks architectures for this task. The team proposed a family of neural network architectures, referred to as LeNet, composed of multiple layers of receptive fields using a number of insights inspired by techniques used in image processing and computer vision [5]. A typical example of a LeNet architecture is shown in Fig. 2.

The first insight was to process the image as a set of 5×5 overlapping windows. Training a perceptron to process a 5×5 window requires learning only 26 parameters. Processing every position in the image with the same perceptron greatly increases the amount of data available for training, as each position of the image provides a training sample. Processing an image in this way is referred to as a "sliding window" detector. For a perceptron, the linear part of the perceptron is equivalent to convolving a digital filter with the image. This was referred to as a convolutional neural network (Fig. 3).

---

[1] Private discussion between the author and Geoff Hinton at CMU in 1982 or 1983.

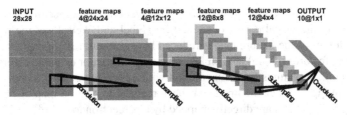

Fig. 2. An early LeNet architecture for recognizing handwritten digits on checks and postal codes. Image copied from [5].

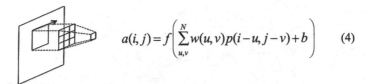

$$a(i,j) = f\left(\sum_{u,v}^{N} w(u,v)p(i-u,j-v)+b\right) \qquad (4)$$

Fig. 3. A convolutional network processes a stream of 2-D overlapping windows. In equation 4, $p(i, j)$ is a 2D input layer, $w(u, v)$ is an $N \times N$ learned receptive field, b is a learned bias, $f(-)$ is a non-linear activation function as discussed in the chapter on training neural networks with back-propagation [6], and $a(i, j)$ is the resulting output layer.

A second insight was to use several neural units in parallel to describe each window, as seen with the retinotopic maps observed in the visual cortex of the cat by Hubel and Weisel. This lead to a map of features for each pixel with the number of features referred to as the depth of the feature map. Figure 2 show that the first layer of LeNet-1 has a depth of 4 (Fig. 4).

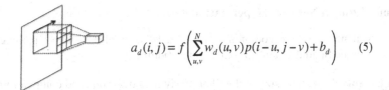

$$a_d(i,j) = f\left(\sum_{u,v}^{N} w_d(u,v)p(i-u,j-v)+b_d\right) \qquad (5)$$

Fig. 4. A convolutional network processes each window in parallel with D receptive fields, resulting in vector of D feature values $\vec{a}(i, j)$ for each image position (i, j). Equation 5 generalizes equation 4 by replacing a single learned receptive field, $w(i, j)$, with a vector of D learned receptive fields, $w_d(i, j)$ generating a vector of d output layers, $a_d(i, j)$.

A third insight was to reduce the resolution of each layer by resampling and then processing the resulting resampled feature map with another convolutional network. For example the second layer of LeNet-1 was produced by subsampling the feature map of first level using a sample distance of 2, and then processing the result with convolution by another set of 4 perceptrons trained with back-propagation. This resampling operation was referred to as "pooling" and had the effect of increasing the effective size of the receptive field at the second level, in a manner that is similar to the image pyramids used for computer vision at the time, and to the layers of larger receptive fields found in the deeper in the visual cortex of the cat by Hubel and Weisel. As the number of rows and columns of the feature map is reduced by successive resampling (or pooling), the number of features (depth) at each layer was increased. For example layers 3 and 4 of LeNet-1 contain features from convolution with 12 receptive fields (depth = 12), as can be seen in Fig. 2. Once the image has been reduced to a 5×5 map of 16 features, the resulting 400 features are directly mapped by a perceptron to one of the 10 possible output class labels.

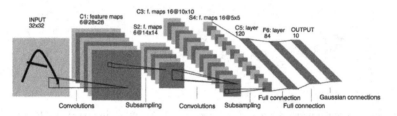

Fig. 5. The LeNet-5 architecture presented at the 1997 IEEE CVPR [7].

The AT&T team experimented with several such architectures. The LeNet-5 architecture, shown in Fig. 5, was found to provide the best recognition rates for the NIST dataset of hand-written digits and was used to construct a commercially successful system for processing checks.

In order to describe the architectures for convolutional networks such as LeNet, we need to define some of the common "hyper-parameters" that are used to define convolutional networks.

1.3 Convolutional Network Hyper-parameters

Convolutional networks are commonly specified by a number of hyper-parameters. These include the Spatial Extent, Depth, Stride, Padding and Pooling:

Spatial Extent: This is the size of the filter. Early networks followed computer vision theory and used 11×11 or 9×9 filters. Experimentation has shown that 3×3 filters can work well with multi-layer networks.

Depth: This is the number D of receptive fields for each position in the feature map. For a color image, the first layer depth at layer 0 would be $D = 3$. If described with 32 image descriptors, the depth would be $D = 32$ at layer 1. Some networks will use N × N × D receptive fields, including $1 \times 1 \times D$.

Stride: Stride is the step size, S, between window positions. By default, stride is generally set to 1, but for larger windows, it is possible define larger step sizes.

Zero-Padding: Size of region at the border of the feature map that is filled with zeros in order to preserve the image size (typically N).

Pooling: Pooling is a form of down-sampling that partitions the image into non-overlapping regions and computes a representative value for each region. An example of 2 × 2 max pooling is shown in Fig. 6. The feature map is partitioned into small non-overlapping rectangles, typically of size 2 × 2 or 4 × 4, and a single value it determined for each rectangle. The most common pooling operators are average and max. Median is also sometimes used. The earliest architectures used average pooling, where the neighborhood is replaced with the average value of the samples, creating a form of multi-resolution pyramid. Max pooling has generally been found to provide slightly better performance.

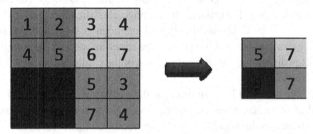

Fig. 6. Max pooling replaces an N × N window of features with the largest feature value in the window. For example the 2 × 2 red square in the upper left corner is replaced by the largest of the 4 values in the square (5). (Color figure online)

1.4 The LeNet-5 Architecture

LeNet-5 is composed of multiple repetitions of 3 operations: Convolution, Pooling, and Non-linearity. The system uses convolution of receptive fields of size 5 × 5 with a stride of 1, no zero padding and a depth of 6. Six receptive fields are learned for each pixel in the first layer. Using 5 × 5 filters without zero padding reduces the input window of 32 × 32 pixels to a layer of composed of 6 sets of 28 × 28 units. A sigmoid activation function was used for the activation function. Pooling was performed as a spatial averaging over 2x2 windows giving a second layer of 6 × 14 × 14. The output was then convolved with sixteen 5 × 5 receptive fields, yielding a layer with 16 × 10 × 10 units. Average pooling over 2 × 2 windows reduced this to a layer of 16 × 5 × 5 units. These were then fed to two fully connected layers and then smoothed with a Gaussian filter to produce 10 output units, one for each possible digit.

Despite the experimental and commercial success of LeNet, the approach was largely ignored by the computer vision community, which was more concerned at that time with multi-camera geometry and Bayesian approaches to recognition. The situation began to change in the early 2000's, driven by the availability of GPUs, and planetary scale data, made possible by the continued exponential growth of the World Wide Web, and the emergence of challenge-based research in computer vision. During this period, computer vision and machine learning were increasingly organized around open competitions for performance evaluation for well-defined tasks using publically available benchmark data-sets.

Many of the insights of LeNet-5 continued to be relevant as more training data, and additional computing power enabled larger and deeper networks, as they allowed more effective performance for a given amount of training data and parameters.

2   Classic CNN Architectures

The emergence of the internet and the world-wide web made it possible to assemble large collections of training data with ground truth labels, and to issue global challenges for computer vision techniques for tasks such as image classification and object detection. Many of the most famous CNN architectures have been designed to compete in these large-scale image challenges, and the size of the input image and the number of output categories are often determined by the parameters of the challenge for which the network was designed.

Several key data sets that have influenced the evolution of the domain. Perhaps the most influential of these has been ImageNet. ImageNet is an image database organized according to the nouns in the WordNet hierarchy compiled for research in Linguistics. In 2006, Fei-Fei Li began working on the idea for ImageNet based on the idea of providing image examples for each word in WordNet, eventually using Amazon Mechanical Turk to help with assigning WordNet words to images. The ImageNet data set was first presented as a poster at the 2009 Conference on Computer Vision and Pattern Recognition (CVPR) in Florida and later published in the Journal of Vision [8].

In 2010 Li joined with the European PASCAL Visual Object Class (POC) challenge team to create a joint research challenge on several visual recognition tasks. The resulting annual competition is known as the ImageNet Large Scale Visual Recognition Challenge (ILSVRC). The ILSVRC uses a list of 1000 image categories or classes, including 90 of the 120 dog breeds classified by the full ImageNet schema. In 2010 and 2011, a good score for the ILSVRC top-5 classification error rate was 25%.

Winning teams during the first years used statistical recognition techniques such as Support Vector Machines (SVM) combined with image features such as Scale Invariant Feature Transform (SIFT) and Histogram of Oriented Gradients (HoG). However, in 2012, Alex Krizhevsky won the competition with a deep convolutional neural net inspired by LeNet-5 called AlexNet, as shown in Fig. 7. AlexNet achieved an error rate of 16% (accuracy of 84%). This dramatic quantitative improvement marked the start of the rapid shift to techniques based on Deep Learning using Neural Networks by the computer vision community. By 2014, more than fifty institutions participated in the ILSVRC, almost exclusively with different forms of Network Architectures. In 2017, 29 of 38 competing teams demonstrated error rates less than 5% (better than 95% accuracy). Many state-of-the-art object detection networks now pre-train on ImageNet and then rely on transfer learning to adapt the learned recognition system to a specific domain.

Images classification
Top 5 error at ILSVRC 2012

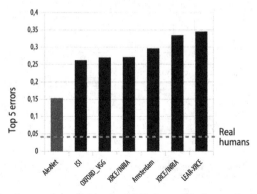

Fig. 7. Error rates for the top 5 entries in the 2012 ImageNet Large Scale Visual Recognition Challenge (ILSVRC) [9]

2.1 AlexNet

AlexNet [10], is a deeper and larger variation of LeNet5, using two parallel tracks of 5 convolutional layer followed by 3 fully connected layer. The initial receptive field is 11 × 11 with a stride (sample distance) of 4, followed by 48 parallel 5 × 5 receptive fields. Innovations in AlexNet include:

1. The use of ReLU avtivation instead of sigmoid or tanh: ReLU provided a 6 times speed up with no loss of accuracy, allowing more training for the same cost in computation.
2. DropOut: A technique called "dropout" randomly chose units that are temporarily removed during learning. This was found to prevent over-fitting to training data.
3. Overlap pooling: Max pooling was performed with overlapping windows (Fig. 8).

The AlexNet architecture is composed of 5 convolutional layers followed by 3 fully connected layers. ReLU activation is used after each convolution and in each fully connected layer. The input image size of 224 × 224 is dictated by the number of layers in the architecture.

Source code for AlexNet can be found in PyTorch[2]. The network has 62.3 million parameters, and needs 1.1 billion computations in a forward pass. The convolution layers account for 6% of all the parameters, and consume 95% of the computation. The network is commonly trained in 90 epochs, with a learning rate 0.01, momentum 0.9 and weight decay 0.0005. The learning rate is divided by 10 once the accuracy reaches a plateau.

---

[2] An open source machine learning framework available at https://pytorch.org/.

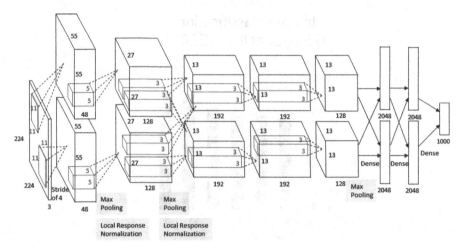

Fig. 8. The AlexNet architecture [10]. Image copied from https://medium.com/coinmonks/paper-review-of-alexnet-caffenet-winner-in-ilsvrc-2012-image-classification-b93598314160

2.2 VGG-16 - Visual Geometry Group 16 Layer Architecture

In 2014, Karen Simonyan and Andrew Zisserman of the Visual Geometry Group at the Univ of Oxford demonstrated a series of networks referred to as VGG [11], shown in Fig. 9. An important innovation in VGG was the use of many small (3×3) convolutional receptive fields. VGG also introduced the idea of a 1×1 convolutional filter, using a perceptron to reduce the number of features (depth) at each image position. For a layer with a depth of D receptive fields, a 1×1 convolution performs a weighted sum of the D features, followed by non-linear activation using ReLU activation.

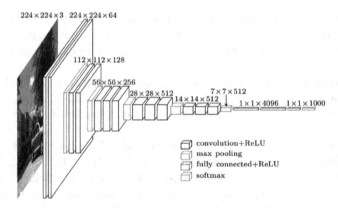

Fig. 9. The VGG-16 architecture.

VGG uses a stack of 18 convolutional layers in which decreases in resolution provided by pooling are accompanied by increases in depth. The final $7 \times 7 \times 512$ convolutional layer is followed by three Fully-Connected layers: the first two have 4096 channels while the third fully connected layer outputs a probability distribution for each of the 1000 classes of the ILSVR Challenge using a soft-max activation function. All except the last output layer use Relu activation.

2.3   YOLO: You Only Look Once

YOLO [12] poses object detection as a single regression problem that estimates bounding box coordinates and class probabilities at the same time directly from image pixels. This is known as a Single Shot Network (SSD). A single convolutional network simultaneously predicts multiple bounding boxes and class probabilities for each box in a single evaluation. The result is a unified architecture for detection and classification that is very fast (Fig. 10).

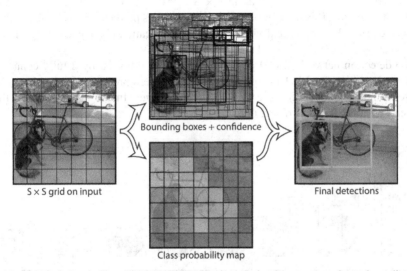

Fig. 10. You Only Look Once (YOLO). The Yolo network simultaneously estimate bounding box coordinates and class probabilities for objects. Image copied from [12].

The input image is divided into an S × S grid of cells. Each grid cell predicts B bounding boxes as well as C class probabilities. The bounding box prediction has 5 components: (x, y, w, h, confidence). The (x, y) coordinates represent the center of the predicted bounding box, relative to the grid cell location. Width and height (w, h) are predicted relative to the entire image. Both the (x, y) coordinates and the window size (w, h) are normalized to a range of [0,1]. Predictions for bounding boxes centered outside the range [0, 1] are ignored. If the predicted object center (x, y) coordinates are not within the grid cell, then object is ignored by that cell (Fig. 11).

Each grid cell predicts C class conditional probabilities $P(Class_i \mid Object)$. These are conditioned on the grid cell containing an object. Only one set of class probabilities are predicted per grid cell, regardless of the number of boxes. The scores encode the probability of a member of class i appearing in a box, and how well the box fits the object. If no object exists in a cell, the confidence score should be zero. Otherwise the

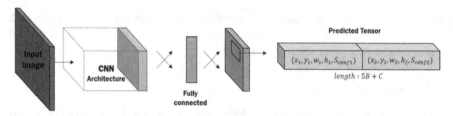

Fig. 11. Yolo uses a CNN architecture followed by a fully connected layer to simultaneously bounding boxes and classes for objects. Image copied from [13].

confidence score should equal the intersection over union (IOU) between the predicted box and the ground truth.

These predictions are encoded as an $S \times S \times (5B + C)$ tensor. Where $S \times S$ is the number of grid cells, B is the number of Bounding Boxes predicted and C is the number of image classes. For the Pascal visual Object Classification challenge, $S = 7$, $B = 2$ and $C = 20$ yielding a $7 \times 7 \times 30$ tensor.

The detection network has 24 convolutional layers followed by 2 fully connected layers as shown in Fig. 12. The convolutional layers were pretrained on the ImageNet data-set at half the resolution (224 by 224 input image). Image resolution was then doubled to (448×448) for detection.

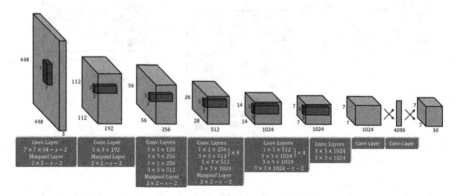

Fig. 12. YOLO is composed of 24 convolutional layers followed by 2 fully connected layers. (from: http://datahacker.rs/how-to-peform-yolo-object-detection-using-keras/)

2.4 YOLO-9000 (YOLOv2)

In 2017, the YOLO team published performance evaluation results and source code for a new version of YOLO referred to as Yolo9000. Yolo9000 employed a number of innovations, including ideas that had emerged in the machine learning literature the previous year. At low resolutions YOLO9000 operates as a cheap, fairly accurate detector. At 288x288 it runs at more than 90 FPS. This makes it ideal for smaller GPUs, high frame rate video, or multiple video streams. At high resolution the network is competitive with

Fig. 13. Typical output from YOLO-9000 [14].

the state of the art giving 78.6 mAP on VOC 2007 while still operating above real-time speeds (Fig. 13).

3 Conclusions

Convolutional neural networks are now a well established technology for analysis of multidimensional signals with applications in computer vision, recommender systems, image classification, image segmentation, medical image analysis, natural language processing, brain–computer interfaces, financial time series and many other areas. New architectures for deep convolutional networks appear regularly addressing applications in an ever expanding repertoire of domains.

Much of the progress of recent years has been obtained by training networks at ever-increasing depths, leveraging the growing availability of computing power provided by application specific integrated circuits and related technologies, and made possible by the availability of very large data set of annotated data. However, much of this work relied on supervised learning, and the need for annotated data has hindered development in some application domains.

Recently transformers, based on stacked layers of encoders and decoders with processing driven by self-attention, have begun to supplant convolutional neural networks in many areas, by improving performance while decreasing computational requirements. In addition, transformers can be trained by self-supervised learning, using data as its own ground truth, and eliminating the need for annotated training data as described in the chapter on Natural Language Processing with Transformers and Attention [15]. None-the-less, Convolutional networks remain an established tool with many practical applications.

References

1. Hubel, D.H., Wiesel, T.N.: Receptive fields and functional architecture of monkey striate cortex. J. Physiol. **195**(1), 215–243 (1968)
2. Rosenfeld, A.: Picture Processing by Computer. Academic Press, Cambridge (1969)
3. Duda, R.O., Hart, P.E.: Picture Processing and Scene Analysis. Wiley, New York (1973)
4. Zucker, S.W., Hummel, R.A.: Receptive Fields and the Reconstruction of Visual Information. New York University, Courant Institute of Mathematical Sciences (1985)
5. LeCun, Y., et al.: Comparison of learning algorithms for handwritten digit recognition. In: International Conference on Artificial Neural Networks, vol. 60, pp. 53–60 (1995)

6. Crowley, J.L.: Machine learning with neural networks. In: Chetouani, M., Dignum, V., Lukowicz, P., Sierra, C. (eds.) Advanced Course on Human-Centered AI. Lecture Notes in Artificial Intelligence (LNAI), vol. 13500, pp. 39–54. Springer, Cham (2022)

7. Bottou, L., Bengio, Y., LeCun, Y.: Global training of document processing systems using graph transformer networks. In: Proceedings of IEEE Computer Society Conference on Computer Vision and Pattern Recognition, CVPR 1997, San Juan, Porto Rico, pp. 489–494. IEEE (1997)

8. Fei-Fei, L., Deng, J., Li, K.: ImageNet: Constructing a large-scale image database. J. Vis. **9**(8), 1037 (2009)

9. Deng, J., Berg, A., Satheesh, S., Su, H., Khosla, A., Fei-Fei, L.: ILSVRC-2012 (2012)

10. Krizhevsky, A., Sutskever, I., Hinton, G.E.: ImageNet classification with deep convolutional neural networks. In: Advances in Neural Information Processing Systems, vol. 25 (2012)

11. Simonyan, K., Zisserman, A.: Very deep convolutional networks for large-scale image recognition. arXiv preprint arXiv:1409.1556 (2014)

12. Redmon, J., Divvala, S., Girshick, R., Farhadi, A.: You only look once: unified, real-time object detection. In: Proceedings of the IEEE Conference on Computer Vision and Pattern Recognition, CVPR 2016, pp. 779–788. IEEE (2016)

13. Kim, J., Cho, J.: Exploring a multimodal mixture-of-YOLOs framework for advanced real-time object detection. Appl. Sci. **10**(2), 612 (2020)

14. Redmon, J., Farhadi, A.: YOLO9000: better, faster, stronger. In: Proceedings of the IEEE Conference on Computer Vision and Pattern Recognition, pp. 7263–7271 (2017)

15. Yvon, F.: Natural language processing with transformers and attention. In: Chetouani, M., Dignum, V., Lukowicz, P., Sierra, C. (eds.) Advanced Course on Human-Centered AI. Lecture Notes in Artificial Intelligence (LNAI). vol. 13500, pp. 81–105. Springer, Cham (2022)

Transformers in Natural Language Processing

François Yvon$^{(\boxtimes)}$ (iD)

Université Paris-Saclay, CNRS, LISN, rue John von Neuman, 91 403 Orsay, France
`francois.yvon@limsi.fr`

Abstract. This chapter presents an overview of the state-of-the-art in natural language processing, exploring one specific computational architecture, the Transformer model, which plays a central role in a wide range of applications. This architecture condenses many advances in neural learning methods and can be exploited in many ways: to learn representations for linguistic entities; to generate coherent utterances and answer questions; to perform utterance transformations, a major application being machine translation. These different facets of the architecture will be successively presented, which will also allow us to discuss its limitations.

Keywords: Natural language processing · Machine learning · Language models · Neural machine translation

1 Introduction

Language technologies are prominent among the applications of Artificial Intelligence (AI) and are now reaching the general public. They are essential for an effective access to textual information available on the Web or in large document databases; they enable for new forms of interaction with the machine, either by voice or by means of writing aids; they help to communicate with other humans, for example through machine translation systems; in a more underground way, these algorithms structure, organize, filter, select, transform and make possible the management of the myriads of texts and audio recordings that circulate continuously on the Web or on social networks.

These technologies are gradually becoming more efficient for ever-increasing and varied uses. Their progress is the result of a combination of several factors: on the one hand, the development of sophisticated machine learning algorithms capable of taking advantage of the high performance computing devices; on the other hand, the possibility to access vast amounts of textual data, whether annotated or not, to feed the training process. Among the algorithms for text processing, neural algorithms and, in particular, the **Transformer** architecture are nowadays at the forefront. Transformers have become central to carry out three types of computations that, until then, required dedicated architectures: first, text mining and information retrieval algorithms, which benefit from the richness of the **internal representations** calculated by this model; second,

© Springer Nature Switzerland AG 2023
M. Chetouani et al. (Eds.): ACAI 2021, LNAI 13500, pp. 81–105, 2023.
https://doi.org/10.1007/978-3-031-24349-3_6

linguistic analysis algorithms, which can take advantage of the Transformers' ability to integrate and model very long-distance dependencies; finally, **text generation algorithms**, which use this model primarily for their predictive ability. If we add that this same architecture is also suitable for the processing of oral or even multimodal data, and that it allows efficient calculations on a very large scale, we can better understand why this model has become the modern workhorse of computational linguists.

This chapter proposes a gentle introduction to the Transformer architecture, adopting an historical perspective, so as to highlight how this model inherits from and extends previous machine learning approaches to Natural Language Processing. We start in Sect. 2 with an introduction to discrete statistical language models, before moving on to feed forward and recurrent neural architectures, enabling us to introduce important concepts such as lexical embeddings and attention. Section 3 then presents the Transformer architecture in details, and showcases its main applications: representation extraction on the one hand, language generation on the other hand. The last section is devoted to multilingual extensions of this model, which will make its genericity and wide applicability more obvious. We conclude in Sect. 5 by introducing the reader to the main limitations of this models and motivate some directions for future research. After studying this chapter, the reader should be in a position to understand why this architecture has been so successful for language modeling, and get a better grasp at the multiple extensions and developments that are happening in other domains such as audio processing or computer vision.

2   Writing Machines: Language Models

2.1   The Simplest Model

Let us consider starting a basic task of language processing: spam filtering. Its probabilistic treatment involves three steps:

1. the collection of a representative set of emails, containing a set D_{ok} of acceptable emails (hams) and a set D_{ko} of unwanted emails (spams);
2. the construction of a numerical representation for texts. A very simple representation encodes each email d as a large binary vector $\mathbf{h}$ in $\{0,1\}^{|V|}$, with V a predefined vocabulary. For each component, $h_w = 1$ if word w appears in the email, 0 otherwise. These representations (so-called "bag-of-words") are inherently sparse, since most of the components of this vector are null;
3. learning a probabilistic model $P(OK|d) \propto \exp \sum_w \theta_w h_w$,[1] which evaluates the likelihood that a mail is acceptable. The parameter vector $\boldsymbol{\theta}$ weights the contribution of each individual word to the final decision. The estimation of

---

[1] The notation $P(u|x) \propto \exp f(\theta, x)$ means that the conditional probability of event u given x is *proportional to* the logit $\exp f(\theta, x)$. $P(u|x)$ is obtained by normalizing this term, that is dividing by the summation over all possible outcomes $\sum_{u'} f(\theta, x)$.

$\boldsymbol{\theta}$ is realized by maximizing the log-likelihood of the training data, according to:

$$\ell(\boldsymbol{\theta}) = \sum_{d \in D_{\mathrm{ok}}} \log P(\mathrm{OK}|d) + \sum_{d \in D_{\mathrm{ko}}} \log(1 - P(\mathrm{OK}|d)).$$

This "historical" model is ubiquitous in modern natural language processing: multi-class routing and classification of documents, "sentiment" or opinion analysis (classes correspond to the polarity of the text), textual entailment, aimed at deciding whether a sentence logically implies another sentence, etc. It already highlights three essential concepts of the statistical approach that has become **dominant** since the 1990s to address NLP problems: (a) the computation of numerical representations (here binary representations) to encode linguistic entities and their properties; (b) the use of these representations in probabilistic models evaluating discrete decisions (here: to classify an email in one of the two possible classes); (c) the estimation of model parameters using annotated data (here: correct and incorrect emails). As we will see, the most recent developments in the field continue to rely on these concepts, using neural networks to learn incomparably more sophisticated representations and models than the one outlined above.

2.2 Word Order

Filtering emails is a simple task: useful representations for this task can disregard the order of word, and more broadly, the structure of the document. However, these representations ignore one of the essential properties of texts, namely their organization in a linear sequence of units. **Language models** are probabilistic models designed to take into account this sequentiality. We use $\mathbf{w} = w_1 \ldots w_T$ to denote a discrete sequence including T units (words) denoted w_t. In a n-gram language model, the probability of this sequence is written as:

$$\begin{aligned} P(w_1 \ldots w_T) &= \prod_{t=1}^{T} P(w_t|w_1 \ldots w_{t-1}) \\ &= \prod_{t=1}^{T} P(w_t|w_{t-n+1} \ldots w_{t-1}). \end{aligned} \quad (1)$$

The first line breaks down the probability of the sequence as a product of conditional distributions; the second makes this decomposition tractable by assuming *locality of dependencies* within the sequence. Formally, this means that the probability of occurrence of unit w_t is independent from the past units, given the context composed of the previous $n - 1$ words. The corresponding conditional distributions are discrete probabilities that parameterize the model; the bulk of these parameters will be denoted $\boldsymbol{\theta}$. Assuming that the vocabulary V is finite and known, these parameters are in finite numbers. Conceptually, this model is identical to the previous one: it assigns each "document" (here reduced to the few words preceding the current position) to a "class" (here, one word among all possible words). Effective estimation procedures for the n-gram model are based on counts of occurrences in large corpora, and the resulting parameters estimates take the following form for a trigram model ($n = 2$):

$$\forall u, v, w \in V : P(w|uv) = \frac{n(uvw)}{\sum_{w' \in V} n(uvw')}, \tag{2}$$

where $n(uvw)$ is the number of occurrences of the sequence uvw in a training corpus.

The two basic assumptions of the n-grams model (local dependencies, finite vocabulary) are linguistically naive. On the one hand, there are many examples of dependencies between distant words. These dependencies can be syntactic as in "*the decisions of my branch manager are effective*", where the plural agreement is between "*decisions*" and "*are*", separated by four words; they can be semantic, as in "*the judges of the European Court of Justice have decided...*", where "*decided*" can be predicted as a typical action carried out by judges; or even discursive, thematic or stylistic. There are, on the other hand, multiple arguments that oppose the idea of a finite vocabulary: we return to this issue in Sect. 2.4.

Despite their simplicity, language models are useful for a wide range of applications. First, they can be used as automatic *text generators*: it suffices to repeatedly use Eq. (1), sampling at each step the next word conditioned on the previously generated tokens. Second, these models make it possible *to compare several sequences* in order to select the most plausible one, which often will also be the most grammatically correct one. Such decisions are useful for a spell checker, which must choose the best correction; or for a machine translation system, to select the most correct translation hypothesis, etc. Third, they are useful for *comparing languages*: if a language model is trained with French texts and another one with Italian texts, comparing the probabilities of a sentence for these two models provides a way to decide the most likely language of that text. It can also be used for other types of linguistic sequences: sequences of sounds, letters, or even sequences of utterance to model discourse dependencies.

Initially developped for speech processing applications [38,39], language models have quickly became basic tools for the statistical processing of languages and have given rise to countless developments, notably including improvements in their estimation procedures. Pure count-base estimators (Eq. (2))) are in fact not appropriate to model the probability of very rare events. When using vocabularies of several tens of thousands of units, the vast majority of three word sequences are never observed, and using counts yields zero estimates for most parameters. Smoothing methods aim to improve these estimates, for instance by using word clusters. A review of these developments is in [68]; generalizations of the n-gram based on Markov models or stochastic grammars are in [17]; recent introductions to these techniques can be found in various NLP textbooks [26,41,54].

2.3   Neural Models: Smoothing the Context Space

Feedforward Language Models. The next word prediction task implemented in language models is fundamentally a classification task: [9] propose to implement it using the *feedforward network*) of Fig. 1 (corresponding to a four-gram model, n = 3).

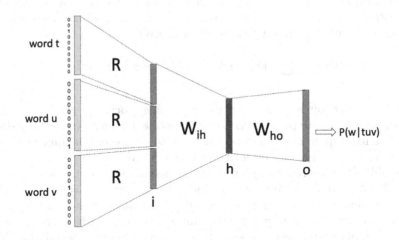

Fig. 1. A multi-layer feedforward network implementing a 4-gram model

The network computing $P(w|tuv)$ inputs the three vectors $\mathbf{t}, \mathbf{u}, \mathbf{v}$ in $\{0,1\}^{|V|}$, where words t, u, and v are replaced by binary vectors whose only non-zero component is the word index in the vocabulary (*one*-hot-encoding). The following computations are then performed:

$$\begin{aligned}
\mathbf{i} &= [\mathbf{R}; \mathbf{R}; \mathbf{R}], \text{ with } \mathbf{R} \in \mathbb{R}^{3\,V| \times d_{\mathrm{md}}} \\
\mathbf{h} &= \phi(\mathbf{W_{ih}i} + \mathbf{b_{ih}}), \text{ with } \mathbf{W}_{ih} \in \mathbb{R}^{3d_{\mathrm{md}} \times d_{\mathrm{md}}} \text{ et } \mathbf{b}_{ih} \in \mathbb{R}^{d_{\mathrm{md}}} \\
\mathbf{o} &= \mathbf{W}_{ho}\mathbf{h} + \mathbf{b_{ho}}, \text{ with } \mathbf{W_{ho}} \in \mathbb{R}^{d_{\mathrm{md}} \times |V|} \text{ and } \mathbf{b}_{ho} \in \mathbb{R}^{|V|} \\
P(w|tuv) &= \text{softmax}(\mathbf{o})_w, \text{ with } \text{softmax}(\mathbf{x})_t = \frac{\exp(x_t)}{\sum_{t'} \exp(x_{t'})}
\end{aligned} \qquad (3)$$

These four steps respectively correspond to:

1. the computation of *dense numerical representations*, via the matrix $\mathbf{R}$, which projects each input vector into a d_{md} dimensional space, with $d_{\mathrm{md}} \ll |V|$;
2. the introduction of a "nonlinearity", via the function $\phi()$, the hyperbolic tangent function (tanh) in the original implementation;
3. the calculation of non-normalized logits for each of the words that can follow the context tuv, obtained by comparing the output of the hidden layer $\mathbf{h}$ with the lexical output representations $\mathbf{W}_{ho}$
4. the normalization of these scores via the softmax operator, which outputs a probability vector.

Training such models requires to use numerical optimisation methods that adjust parameters in $\theta = \{\mathbf{R}, \mathbf{W_{ih}}, \mathbf{b_{ih}}, \mathbf{W_{ho}}, \mathbf{b_{ho}}\}$ so as to make more likely the associations between contexts and words observed in a large corpus. Formally, for each sequence $[t, u, v, w]$ in the training corpus, one wish that the quantity $\log P(w|tuv) = o_w - \log \sum_{w'} \exp o_{w'}$ will be as large as possible. This leads to maximizing (in θ) the following *cross-entropy* criterion:

$$\ell(\theta) = \sum_{[t,u,v,w]} \log P(w|tuv) = o_w - \log \sum_{w'} \exp o_{w'}. \tag{4}$$

This optimization is typically performed using stochastic gradient descent methods, which update parameters based on gradient values. Note that training again does not require any annotation and can be carried out on huge quantities of texts, as long as they can be segmented into "words".

The shift from discrete models to continuous space representations is computationally intensive, because computing the softmax operator involves a sum over a large vocabulary. Practical solutions are proposed and evaluated in [45,69]; we discuss them in Sect. 2.4. However, this shift has proven decisive to improve the quality of applications such as speech recognition or machine translation. This is because two quantities are learned simultaneously:

- a numerical representation $\mathbf{h}$ summarising the context made of several previous words into a low-dimensional vector, from which the conditional distribution of successor words is calculated. This ability to compute numerical representations of the prediction context is assimilated to the *encoding function* of the neural network.
- a lexical embedding of the vocabulary V into $\mathbb{R}^{d_{md}}$ through matrix $\mathbf{R}$. This embedding has remarkable properties; in particular, words that share many contexts, which are often semantically related words or words of the same morphological family, tend to get close in the embedding space. The use of these embeddings as generic lexical representations [20] has become widespread with the development of rapid and effective methods for calculating them [11,58].

Recurrent Neural Networks as Language Models. The previous model shares with the n-gram model the use of a context restricted to neighbouring $n-1$ words. The use of *recurrent networks* [27] makes it possible to overcome this limitation and to compute terms such as $P(w_{t+1}|w_1 \ldots w_t)$ without resorting to locality assumptions. The strength of this approach and its superiority over the feedforward model are highlighted in [59], who present a network capable of taking into account an unbounded context. It contains the same two components as before, namely: (a) dense numerical representations for lexical units computed by the matrix $\mathbf{R}$; (b) a context encoding function defined here recursively by $\phi()$, which again denotes a non-linear function:

$$\begin{aligned}
\mathbf{h_t} &= \phi(\mathbf{W_{h'h}h_{t-1}} + \mathbf{Rw_t} + \mathbf{b_h}) \\
&= \phi(\mathbf{W_{h'h}}\phi(\mathbf{W_{h'h}h_{t-2}} + \mathbf{Rw_{t-1}} + \mathbf{b_h}) + \mathbf{Rw_t} + \mathbf{b_h}).
\end{aligned} \tag{5}$$

As before, the final step will project the internal representation $\mathbf{h}_t$ to yield the conditional output distribution associated with context $w_{\leq t} = w_1 \ldots w_t$ according to $P(w|w_{\leq t}) = P(w|\mathbf{h_t}) = \text{softmax}(\mathbf{W}_{ho}\mathbf{h_t} + \mathbf{b_o})$. Parameters of the recurrent network $\{\boldsymbol{\theta} = \mathbf{R}, \mathbf{W_{h'h}}, \mathbf{W_{ho}}, \mathbf{b_h}, \mathbf{b_o}\}$ are trained by maximizing the cross-entropy loss function.

Unfolding the recursion (second line of Eq. (5)) makes the functional relationship between $\mathbf{h}_t$ and words $\mathbf{w}_t$ and $\mathbf{w}_{t-1}$, then, by recurrence, with all previous words. This also highlights that the influence of words decreases with their distance to the current position. It also highlights a computational difficulty associated to the direct computation of the gradient (by the rules of derivation of compound functions), which gives rise to numerical instabilities that make learning delicate. Remedies, which involve the use of more complex dependencies between $\mathbf{h}_t$ and $\mathbf{h}_{t-1}$ are proposed by [19,36]. They realize the full potential of these networks, which are then able to partly capture dependencies between distant words - such as the one observed in English between verb and subject, which must agree in number and person regardless of their distance in the sentence (see [50] for a study of such phenomena). Their expressiveness as a computational model is analyzed in [57].

In practice, however, the recursive formulation of the computation of latent representations poses a major problem, as it requires each sequence to be processed word by word from left to right in the order of their appearance. It is impossible to build $\mathbf{h_t}$ without having previously computed $\mathbf{h_{t-1}}$, which itself requires $\mathbf{h_{t-2}}$ etc.; such models are said to be *auto-regressive*. As a result, it is not possible to parallelize the computation of the objective function (Eq. (4))), which significantly slows down the training process.

Recurrent Models as "Pure" Representations: ELMo. Among the many extensions of these models, the most remarkable is their use as "pure" encoders. Let us first note again that learning such language models does not require annotation and can therefore be carried out on very large text corpora. Assuming that the parameters are known, a recurrent network transforms a string of words $w_1 \ldots w_T$ into a sequence of vectors $\mathbf{h}_1 \ldots \mathbf{h}_T$. The same process can be performed by running the sequence backwards, from w_T down to w_1, yielding another vector sequence $\tilde{\mathbf{h}}_1 \ldots \tilde{\mathbf{h}}_T$. Concatenating the two representations for word w_t yields $[\mathbf{h}_t; \tilde{\mathbf{h}}_t]$, which encodes w_t in a *bidirectional context* integrating both previous and subsequent words. It also turns out that $[\tilde{\mathbf{h}}_1; \mathbf{h_T}]$ is a very good way to represent the whole variable-length sentence $w_1 \ldots w_T$ into a *fixed-size vector*. This vector can then be used to compare sentences or to make predictions about their polarity or their meaning. It finally appears that stacking bi-directional recurrent layers, where $[\mathbf{h}_t; \tilde{\mathbf{h}}_t]$ are used as the input of a new layer, will deliver *deeper and better representations*. These principles are used to construct the ELMo model [60] model, one of the first to highlight the richness of these deep contextual representations, which can serve as a beneficial plug-and-play pre-processing module for any application dealing with linguistic sequences.

Consider, for instance, the task of textual entailment, which consists of deciding whether sentence w_P logically entails sentence w_C. For this task, we need to predict a Yes/No answer given the two input sentences, yielding a model $P(\text{Yes} \,|\, w_P, w_C)$. A possible approach encodes each sentence into a single vector (respectively $\text{ELMo}(w_P)$ and $\text{ELMo}(w_C)$) that are then concatenated and used in a log-linear model according to: $P(\text{Yes} \,|\, w_P, w_C) \propto \exp(\mathbf{W}[\text{ELMo}(w_P); \text{ELMo}(w_C)] + \mathbf{b})$, where matrix $\mathbf{W}$ and vector $\mathbf{b}$ are the model parameters. By *pre-training* the parameters of the ELMo model, then by fine-tuning those of the textual entailment model, it becomes possible to achieve very good performance even when the train data of the textual entailment model is limited.

2.4   Defining the Vocabulary

We left open the question of the support of probability distributions represented by Eqs. (1) and (3). They presuppose the existence of a finite inventory V of discrete units. To model sequences of letters, sounds or syllables, this hypothesis is easy to defend. For sequences of words, it no longer makes sense, as no corpus, however large, can exhaust the word formation processes, not to mention borrowings from other languages, and extra-lexical (names, numbers, acronyms) whose occurrences must also be modelled. This issue has long been a source of difficulty for language models and has justified to take into account very large vocabularies, despite the associated computational problems.

A better trade-off is achieved by *abandoning the notion of word* and segmenting texts into sub-lexical units, by means of processes that are themselves optimized over large corpora to take frequencies of occurrences into account. Frequent words are thus preserved in their integrity, while the rarest words are split into subwords, if necessary reduced to mere sequences of letters. This makes it possible to manipulate medium-size vocabularies (containing tens of thousands of units), while at the same time preserving the ability to compute the probability of arbitrary sequences (possibly including unknown words, made of the concatenation of known subwords). The best known-algorithms for learning such vocabularies are the Byte Pair Encoding (BPE) algorithm [31,70] and the unigram algorithm [22,44].

Example segmentations realized by these algorithms are in Fig. 2.

_tous _les _êtres _humains _n aissent _libres _et _ég aux _en _dign ité _et _en _droits . _Ils _sont _dou és _de _raison _et _de _conscience _et _doivent _agir _les _uns _envers _les _autres _dans _un _esprit _de _fra tern ité .

_all _human _b e ings _a re _bor n _fre e _and _e qu al _in _dign ity _and _ri gh ts .

_alle _M ens ch en _sin d _fre i _un d _g le ich _an _W ü r de _un d _Re ch ten _g eb or en .

Fig. 2. Sub-lexical unit segmentation of the beginning of the French, English and German versions of the Universal Declaration of Human Rights. The vocabulary contains 10,000 units, character '_' identifies word-initial units. With this segmentation model optimized on French texts, only rare words (such as 'dignité', 'fraternité') are segmented. It is also used to segment, *with the same alphabet*, texts written in other languages, here sentences in English and German.

3   The Transformer Model

3.1   Attention, a Fundamental Mechanism

Having established all the necessary basic concepts of LMs, we now turn to the Transformer model, which relies on a more generic and powerful model to encode the context of each decision.

Encoding the Context. The main idea of the Transformer model of [77] is to make the representation of word w_t depend on all preceding words according to $\mathbf{h}_t = \phi(\mathbf{w}_1 \ldots \mathbf{w}_t)$, while at the same time removing the recurrence of the computation of $\phi()$ so as to be able to parallelize it. In the Transformer model, this computation is achieved by stacking L layers. Each layer l recombines the representations from the previous layer $\mathbf{h}_1^{(l-1)} \ldots \mathbf{h}_t^{(l-1)}$ to construct outputs $\mathbf{h}_1^{(l)} \ldots \mathbf{h}_t^{(l)}$ through elementary operations: linear projections, linear combinations, vector concatenation, plus feedforward networks. The recursion of the recurrent model is thus replaced by a *stack of layers, each having a global scope*. The result remains the same as for other language models: a numerical vector representation of the context that summarises all the previous words, based on which one can predicts the next word in the sequence. Figure 3 illustrates the context encodings computed by these various architectures.

Formally, each layer in a Transformer is parameterized by a set of K *attention heads* and by a multi-layer feedforward model. Each attention head is parameterized by three projection matrices $\mathbf{Q}, \mathbf{K}, \mathbf{V}$ in $\mathbb{R}^{d_{\mathrm{md}} \times d_{\mathrm{kv}}}$ and performs the following computations to derive $\mathbf{h}_t^{(l)}$ from the outputs of the previous layer $\{\mathbf{h}_s^{(l-1)}, s = 1 \ldots t\}$. For the kth head in layer l:

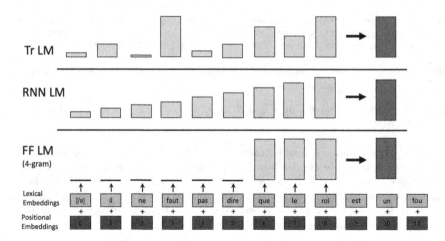

Fig. 3. The encodings of the left context computed by various language models: n-gram feedforward models (FF LM) encode only a small context; Recurrent models (RNNs) assume that close words are more important than remote words; Transformer models (Tr LM) process all the context words on an equal footing.

$$
\begin{aligned}
(6.q) \ \text{Query} \qquad & \mathbf{q_t}^{(k,l)} = \mathbf{Q}^{(k,l)}\mathbf{h_t}^{(l-1)} \quad (\in \mathbb{R}^{d_{kv}}) \\
(6.k) \ \text{Keys} \qquad & \mathbf{k_s}^{(k,l)} = \mathbf{K}^{(k,l)}\mathbf{h_s}^{(l-1)}, \forall s \le t \quad (\in \mathbb{R}^{d_{kv}}) \\
(6.v) \ \text{Values} \qquad & \mathbf{v_s}^{(k,l)} = \mathbf{V}^{(k,l)}\mathbf{h_s}^{(l-1)}, \forall s \le t \quad (\in \mathbb{R}^{d_{kv}}) \\
(6.a) \ \text{Attention} \qquad & \alpha_s^{(k,l)} = \text{softmax}(\tfrac{1}{\sqrt{d_{kv}}}, \mathbf{o_t})_s, \forall s \le t \quad (\in [0,1]) \\
& \text{avec } o_{ts} = \mathbf{q_t}^{(k,l)^T}\mathbf{k_s}^{(k,l)}, \forall s \le t \\
(6.o) \ \text{Output} \qquad & \mathbf{g_t}^{(k,l)} = \sum_{s \le t} \alpha_s^{(k,l)}\mathbf{v_s}^{(k,l)} \quad (\in \mathbb{R}^{d_{kv}})
\end{aligned}
\tag{6}
$$

The first three steps compute d_{kv}-dimensional projections of their input, respectively called *query*, *key* and *value*. The dot product o_{ts} computes a similarity between the query at position t and the keys at all positions before t (included). These similarities are normalized by the softmax operator, which transforms them into *attention coefficients* in $[0,1]$. The last step linearly combines the values to generate the output vector.

Each layer comprising several heads, it remains to aggregate their results. Two elementary operations come into play. The first is a transform made by a multi-layer perceptron according to:

$$
\begin{cases}
\mathbf{f}_t^{(l)} = \phi(\mathbf{W}_{if}^{(l)}\mathbf{g}_t^{(l)} + \mathbf{b_{if}}) \in \mathbb{R}^{d_{ff}}, \text{ with } \phi() \text{ a non-linear function.} \\
\mathbf{h}_t^{(l)} = \mathbf{W}_{fo}\mathbf{f}_t^{(l)} + \mathbf{b_{fo}} \in \mathbb{R}^{d_{md}}.
\end{cases}
\tag{7}
$$

The input $\mathbf{g}_t^{(l)}$ of this perceptron is the concatenation of the outputs of the K heads, to which we add the output of the previous layer: $\mathbf{g}_t^{(l)} = [\mathbf{g}_t^{(1,l)}; \ldots; \mathbf{g}_t^{(K,l)}] + \mathbf{h}_t^{(l-1)}$. Adding the output of the previous layer serves several purposes: (a) to provide gradients with a direct path from the higher layers to the lower layers; (b) to ensure that $\mathbf{h_t}^{(l-1)}$ and $\mathbf{h_t}^{(l)}$ remain close, and that each word thus retains its singularities, regardless of the influence of its context. One consequence is that both terms must have the same dimensions, which implies $K \times d_{\text{kv}} = d_{\text{md}}$. A typical implementation of this forward propagation step projects $\mathbf{g}_t^{(l)}$ via $\mathbf{W_{if}}^{(l)}$ into a d_{ff}-dimensional vector, with $d_{\text{ff}} \gg d_{\text{md}}$, for instance $d_{\text{ff}} = 4d_{\text{md}}$; the non-linearity of the hidden layer uses function $\phi() = \text{ReLU}$ (for *Rectified Linear Unit*).

The second basic operation normalizes the outputs, so that input and output vectors will remain commensurable throughout the layers. At a high level, each layer simply recombines the current representation at position t so as to incorporate the influence of the preceding words. Unlike the recurrent model, where the influence of the context words is computed in a left-to-right manner, in this model no position is privileged, and each attention head, in each layer, can select the positions that are the most significant for the current position, via the attention coefficients $\boldsymbol{\alpha}$.

Limiting Conditions: Layers 0 and L. We still have to describe the inputs and outputs of this system. For the input $\mathbf{h}_1^{(0)}$, one can choose to use either one-hot representations (see Sect. 2.3) or non-contextual representations computed by the skip-gram model [58]. However, lexical representations alone are not sufficient. In fact, equations ((6).[q–v]) do not distinguish between indices, whether close to or distant from the current position t. This illustrates the potential of Transformers to take into account non-local dependencies better than recurrent networks. However, it is useful to introduce the notion of position in the sequence, for example by encoding each index with s a d_{md}-dimensional vector $\mathbf{p}_s$, which is added to the lexical embedding. This *positional encoding* is either learned or computed by a deterministic function defined in [77] as:

$$\begin{cases} p_s[2i] = \sin(t/10000^{2i/d}) \\ p_s[2i+1] = \cos(t/10000^{2i/d}) \end{cases}$$

The output of the last layer $\mathbf{h}_t^{(L)}$ is used to compute the probability of the next word at position $t+1$ and involves the same steps as for the standard neuronal model (Eq. (3)): a linear transformation in a $|V|$-dimensional space to obtain logits, that are then normalized into a probability distribution.

3.2   Causal Transformer as Pure Language Models

The presentation above expresses the computation of $h_t^{(l)}$ as a sequential operation: $\mathbf{h}_1^{(l)}, l = 1 \ldots L$ are first computed, then $\mathbf{h}_2^{(l)}, l = 1 \ldots L$ in the context of $\mathbf{h}_1^{(l)}, l = 1 \ldots L$, etc. This is the most natural and computationally effective method for language models, since the representation of each word is computed only once. This model is dubbed as *self-attentional* (since the context consists of the previous words in the same sequence) and *causal* (the representation of each word only depends on the previous words). It is used for instance in the GPT-* architectures [14,64]. A non-causal variant recomputes all representations at each time steps, i.e. first $\mathbf{h}_1^{(l)}, l = 1 \ldots L$, then $\{\mathbf{h}_1^{(l)}, \mathbf{h}_2^{(l)}, l = 1 \ldots L\}$: this means, for instance, that the representation $h_1^{(l)}$ will change over time, integrating the context of words to its right as they are revealed. This variant, sometimes called *prefix language model*, is more computationally involved, but seems to yield better results [65].

Like other LMs, these architectures generate texts from left to right, by sampling at time step t the next word w_t according to $P(w_t|\mathbf{h}_{t-1})$. Trained on very large corpora, they generate texts that are often grammatically correct, or even show a form of global consistency. This suggests that Transformers are able to model dependencies between distant words in the same sentence or even in different sentences (when the context is sufficiently large). It is also possible to begin a text and let the model continue the generation. This form of text initialization is dubbed "prompting", where the prompt denotes the user-selected prefix. It turns out that with a proper choice of these "prompts", a language model can perform multiple tasks: when the prompt is composed of a text and comprehension questions, the model generate the answers, when prompted with a sentence in French, the model generates the translation into English, etc. It is possible, at the cost of a short learning stage, or by prompting with a handful of examples, to improve this behavior [64]. Owing to these remarkable properties, some of which are still poorly understood, large language models nowadays constitute a basic building block to address a large number of language processing tasks.

3.3   Transformers as Representations: Bert and Its Clones

As with recurrent models, the use of Transformers as pure contextualized representation extractors has proved to be extremely powerful and effective. Originally proposed in [23], the BERT model is mostly a *non-sequential and non-causal* Transformer. This means that the update formulas of Eq. (6) simultaneously apply to all positions in the input sequence via matrix calculations, and that the contextual representations of each word integrate both its left and right contexts. Learning such model is typically performed by optimizing the reconstruction of a noised input: in its basic form, noising simply randomly hides (masks) some tokens w_t, which the model then seeks to recover based on the representation $h_t^{(L)}$. By maximizing the log-probability of original text, it becomes possible to estimate model parameters (see Fig. 5) (Fig. 4).

As for other language models, this learning process does not require any annotation and can be performed on very large corpora. BERT thus provides contextualised "pre-trained" lexical representations that can be used as input to any automatic processing system [23,52]. Other methods for constructing denoising tasks have also been studied [65]: masking groups of words, parts

Prompt	Automatic Generation
In a shocking finding, scientist discovered a herd of unicorns living in a remote, previously unexplored valley, in the Andes Mountains. Even more surprising to the researchers was the fact that the unicorns spoke perfect English.	The scientist named the population, after their distinctive horn, Ovid's Unicorn. These four-horned, silver-white unicorns were previously unknown to science. Now, after almost two centuries, the mystery of what sparked this odd phenomenon is finally solved.
Article: Amina Ali Qassim is sitting with her youngest grandchild on her lap, wiping away tears with her headscarf. Only a few months old, this is the baby girl whose ears she desperately tried to cover the night the aerial bombardment started. She lay awake, she says, in a village mosque on the Yemeni island of Birim, counting explosions as the baby cried. It could have been worse though. They could have still been in their house when the first missile landed. "Our neighbor shouted to my husband 'you have to leave, they're coming.' And we just ran. As soon as we left the house, the first missile fell right by it and then a second on it. It burned everything to the ground," Qassim tells us (...) DL;TR	Yemen is in the middle of a civil war. Saudi Arabia is leading the coalition bombing campaign. It's been bombing Yemen for more than two months now.
Question: George wants to warm his hands quickly by rubbing them. Which skin surface will produce the most heat? Answer:	dry palms
The Gold Coast Hotel & Casino is a hotel and casino located in Paradise, Nevada. This locals' casino is owned and operated by Boyd Gaming. The Gold Coast is located one mile (~ 1.6km) west of the Las Vegas Strip on West Flamingo Road. It is located across the street from the Palms Casino Resort and the Rio All Suite Hotel and Casino. Question: The Gold Coast is a budget-friendly casino. True, False, or Neither?	Neither

Fig. 4. Prompting a language model. By varying the prompt, the same model can be used to perform multiple tasks. From top to bottom, language generation is used to write the continuation of a prompted text, to write a summary, to answer a question, to check the implication between two sentences, etc. Examples are from [14,64]

Input   Tous les êtres humains [MASK] libres et égaux en dignité et en droits. [MASK] sont doués de raison et de conscience et doivent [MASK] les uns envers les autres dans un esprit de [MASK].

Output   Tous les êtres humains **naissent** libres et égaux en dignité et en droits. **Ils** sont doués de raison et de conscience et doivent **agir** les uns envers les autres dans un esprit de **fraternité**.

Fig. 5. Learning the BERT model with random masking. The model parameters are trained to maximize the probability of recovering the hidden tokens (bold on the figure).

of words, deleting and permuting words, etc. Due to their performance, these models have quickly become central in NLP [71] and were quickly adapted to multiple languages, such as French [46,55], German [16], Dutch [78], Spanish [15], etc. Versions adapted to specialized textual genres such as patents [47], scientific texts [5], tweets [4] or even sub-domains such as medicine [48] or nuclear physics [37] have also developed. A rich literature also studies the empirical behaviour of Transformers, trying in particular to analyze the internal representations $\{h_t^l, t = 1 \ldots T, l = 1 \ldots L\}$ in relationship to linguistic concepts; or use attention matrices as a source of explanation of the system's decisions. A recent bibliographical survey of this "Bertological" literature has no less than 110 references [67].

3.4   Computational Costs of Transformer-ing

As Transformer based models take a central role in natural language processing, it becomes necessary to take a closer look at the computations performed by these algorithms and to better assess their cost, in a context where the carbon footprint of Artificial Intelligence algorithms is also becoming a concern [35, 73]. A first observation is that, unlike recurring networks, the computations of Transformers are easy to parallelize. In particular, computing the output representation of a word requires knowledge of its neighboring words, but not of their deep output representations. These output representations can then all be computed simultaneously by implementing Eq. (6) with operations. Table 1 provides indications regarding the size and number of parameters for some recent models.

Table 1. Measuring the size of Transformer models. The number of parameters used for lexical (L) and internal (I) representations are counted separately. Notations k, m, b respectively denote thousands, millions and billions of units.

$|V|$	T	K	L	d_{md}	d_{kv}	d_{ff}	Params (L)	Params (I)
32k	512	8	6	512	64	2048	32,8 m	49,9 m
32k	512	12	12	768	64	3072	49,2 m	127 m
32k	512	16	24	1024	64	4096	65,5 m	342 m
32k	512	32	24	1024	128	16384	65,5 m	2,38 b
32k	512	128	24	1024	128	65536	65,5 m	28,7 b

A last important dimension for complexity calculations is the sequences length T, which determines the overall dimension at the input and output of each layer ($T \times d_{md}$). Sequences typically contains several hundreds of words or even more (2048 for GPT-3). During training, it is necessary to keep the values of all layers in memory, as they are needed to compute the gradient. To speed up calculations, batches of B sequences are processed simultaneously, yielding tensors of dimension $B \times T \times d_{md}$, whose manipulations are optimized on GPU cards.

The computational complexity of the Transformer operations is dominated by the evaluation of attention matrices in Eq. (6). This computation is linear in d_{md}, but quadratic in T: for each of the T positions, the similarity with all the other positions need to be computed, in order to derive the attentions weights α, then the T output values vectors. To reduce this complexity, several directions are considered in the literature. It is first possible to restrict the computation of attention weight to a neighborhood $N(t)$ of w_t, by imposing words outside $N(t)$ to have null weights ($\alpha_t(s) = 0, \forall s \notin N(t)$); note that these words still influence w_t indirectly by influencing its neighbours (or the neighbors of its neighbors) across the multiple computations layers. By choosing neighborhoods $N(t)$ of fixed size S, with S much smaller than T, the attention computation becomes linear in T. There are several other ways to define $N(t)$, using syntactic dependencies, or using random subsets of indices: what matters is that for almost every word, $|N(t)|$ is small and, that for a few positions, $N(t)$ encompasses the whole sequence. Other approaches to speed up these computations focus on effective approximations of dot products (Eq. (6)a). A recent survey of effective implementations of the Transformer model is in [75]; some methods aimed to reduce the memory footprint are presented in [66]. Since the amount of training data continues to increase the performance for many tasks [42], developing larger models is likely to remain an active area of research [29], posing formidable computational challenges both for learning and inference.

3.5   Transformers: A Flexible Architecture

The language models implemented in Transformer architectures combine all the advantages of neuronal architectures: they can learn both predictive models capable of taking into account long-range dependencies and rich contextual representations for atomic units, which can be pre-trained and then used for multiple language processing tasks. They result in effective implementations [79], and have also been adapted for other types of structured data: acoustic sequences for speech modelling [2], images for artificial vision [63], and even image sequences [74]. Like other neural language models, their behavior remains difficult to control: while some regularities are almost perfectly learned, others are learned only approximately, and it is difficult to predict or understand the reasons for these failures.

4   Towards Multilingualism

4.1   Neural Machine Translation: Conditional Text Generation

A Simple Encoder-Decoder Model. The Transformer model presented above as a language model is initially introduced for machine translation (MT) [77]. This application formally corresponds to the generation (in a "target language") of a sentence $\mathbf{e}$ translating the input "source" sentence $\mathbf{f}$. Viewed as a probabilistic decision, this problem corresponds to finding:

$$\mathbf{e}^* = \mathrm{argmax}_{\mathbf{e}}\, P(\mathbf{e}|\mathbf{f}) = \mathrm{argmax}_{\mathbf{e}} \prod_t P(e_t|\mathbf{f}, \mathbf{e}_{<t}). \tag{8}$$

This formalization again requires to define a probability distribution over a set of sentences (see Eq. (1)), except that this distribution is conditioned by the input sentence $\mathbf{f}$. The Transformer model computes such a distribution by extending the neural encoder-decoder architectures proposed for MT in [3,18]. These architectures rely on two computation steps:

(a) the computation of a numerical representation (encoding) for $\mathbf{f}$ taking the form of a sequence of numerical vectors $\mathbf{s}_1, \ldots, \mathbf{s}_J$;
(b) the iterative decoding of the translation, by choosing at each step the most likely next word e_t given the source encoding $[\mathbf{g}_1^{(l)}, \ldots, \mathbf{g}_I^{(l)}], l = 1 \ldots L$ as well as the previous target words $\mathbf{e}_{<t}$, encoded as previously as $[\mathbf{h}_1^{(l)}, \ldots, \mathbf{h}_{t-1}^{(l)}], l = 1 \ldots L$.

The first neural MT systems perform these two steps using recurrent networks (Sect. 2.3). In a Transformer-based architecture, step (a) is performed by a non-causal encoder (Sect. 3.3) and step (b) is performed by a causal decoder (Sect. 3.2). During this stage, it is necessary to integrate the double dependency in $\mathbf{f}$ and $\mathbf{e}_{<t}$, since the prediction of the next target word is influenced by these two sequences (see Eq. (8)). This is implemented by the addition of an additional *cross-attentional sublayer* within the decoder. The corresponding computations are similar to those of Eq. (6), using $\mathbf{h}_t^{(l)} \ldots \mathbf{h}_t^{(l)}$ for the query, and $\mathbf{g}_1^{(L)}, \ldots, \mathbf{g}_J^{(L)}$ for keys and values. In this way, the context vector of each target word integrates not only the target prefix, but also all the words in the source phrase, represented at the last layer (L) of the encoder. As before, the last layer vector of the decoder is projected into a $|V|$—dimensional space, then normalized through the softmax function to provide the desired output distribution $P(\mathbf{e}_t|\mathbf{f}, \mathbf{e}_{<t})$.

Difficulties of Machine Translation

Learning from Parallel Corpora. The learning of conditional models is similar to the learning of language models and consists of optimizing the log-probability of the training sequences, which decomposes into a sum of terms as in Eq. (4). This computation requires both words from the source and the target sentences, which are aligned in large *parallel corpora* matching sentences with their translation. Such resources are now publicly available en masse from resource distribution agencies such as ELDA or the Linguistic Data Consortium. A variety of parallel corpora can be found specialized websites such as OPUS [76].

Machine Translation is Difficult. Once training (which can take days, depending on the amount of available parallel data) is complete, the Transformer is ready to translate. Translation is performed incrementally, word by word, in a greedy manner and poses the same difficult problems as the unconditional generation of texts. It appears, on the one hand, that choosing at each time step the best next word is a risky strategy, since each past error might yield incorrect or simply unusual internal representations, which in turn can cause more errors. This problem is known as the *exposure bias problem* [8] and requires to use of more sophisticated search strategies, such as beam search, to compute the argmax (Eq. (8)). An alternative decoding strategy simultaneously predicts all the target words in parallel, which dramatically speeds up decoding. However, global constraints on the relative positions of words must apply to ensure that the target sentence remains well-formed [32].

Two additional difficulties are directly related to the machine translation problem: in MT, it is necessary to *translate the entire source phase* (each word only once), *without introducing any additional information*. However, these two constraints are not explicitly formulated in Eq. (8): to ensure that the length of the target sentence matches that of the source, and effectively translates all input words, the search algorithm must include additional heuristics: [40] presents the most commonly used ones.

4.2   Multilingual Representations, Multilingual Translations

An additional benefits of numeric representations is that they represent words of different languages in a unified manner. It is then possible, assuming a shared units directory for all languages, to use the same encoders and decoders to process multiple languages. The easiest way to proceed is to implement the same learning procedure as for BERT (Sect. 3.3), inputting sentences in *multiple languages* into the system: this approach is used for mBERT [23] and XLM [21].

Such approaches readily deliver *multilingual contextual representations* that bring together, in the same vector space, units (words, sentences) that are mutual translations. Learning multilingual representations thus makes parallel sentences in multiple languages almost indistinguishable (for the neural network). This enables to transfer processing models and applications from a resource-rich language into languages for which resources do not exist. Let us take the example of a sentiment analysis system, which aims to associate textual comments on a merchant site with satisfaction scores, and assume that we have annotated training examples for language A, but not for language B. Learning to predict the numerical score from *multilingual representations of texts in language A* makes us also able to predict the note of texts in language B *without ever having observed any training example associating a text in language B with its evaluation* (see Fig. 6).

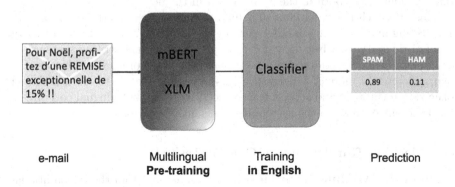

Fig. 6. A multilingual architecture for spam filtering. The second step uses multilingual pre-trained representations which enable to transfer knowledge across languages: French spam mails can then be identify even though the classifier has never seen any French example.

Learning multilingual representations is therefore a major challenge to broaden the spectrum of languages covered by language technologies. Many approaches have also been proposed to train non-contextual multilingual representations, or to adapt existing representations to a specialized domain. A recent survey of these methods is in [72].

Note finally, that the encoder-decoder architecture can also be used to compute *monolingual representations*: this is again achieved by inputting noisy texts into the encoder, that the decode will then have to recover. All that is needed is the definition of the noising operations used to generate parallel artificial data: masking one or several words, replacing a word with a similar word, changing the order of words are typical noising operations. BART, introduced by [49], has the benefits of a faster learning than BERT (more words are noised in the encoder). With an additional fine fine-tuning stage, BART can also be used as a generation model, as the decoder is non-causal: a possible application there is automatic summarization. Finally, like BERT, BART can be trained multilingually, simultaneously computing multilingual representations and machine translation.

4.3   One Model to Translate Them All

Multilingual translation combines the approaches described in the previous sections: the use of an encoder-decoder architecture, with conditional generation of texts; the use of sentence pairs combining input and output for multiple language pairs. This idea, originally proposed in [30,34] and recently used on a large scale in [1,28] opens new perspectives: (a) operationally it means that we just need one single system to handle all translations between N languages, where $O(N^2)$ where previously required; (b) it also enable to compute translations between languages for which no data is observed (again through cross-lingual transfer, which happens here both in the encoder and in the decoder).

This approach is not without difficulty, in particular from the point of view of collecting and balancing parallel learning data, as well as supporting a variety of linguistic systems, which may, for example, use different writing systems, or manipulate divergent underlying structures at the levels of word or phrases. For such multilingual models, a necessary pre-processing step is to learn a shared tokenization (in word and subwords, see Sect. 2.4) using multilingual corpora, so that all input-outputs in the system use the same vocabulary.

4.4   Machine Translation as a Generic Task

Generalizing Machine Translation. The transition from the unconditional model (Sect. 3) to the the conditional model (Sect. 4.1) outlines the flexibility of numerical representations manipulated by neural networks: by adding a cross-attention mechanism between two Transformers, it is possible to encode two word sequences in a single vector $\mathbf{h}$, from which the next word is generated. This technique enables to encode "generalized" contexts, to model more complex tasks or scenarios. It is for instance possible to handle *multi-source translation scenarios*, corresponding to the generation of a target sentence from several two sentences $\mathbf{f_1}$ and $\mathbf{f_2}$. In such setting, the distribution $P(\mathbf{e}|\mathbf{f_1}, \mathbf{f_2})$ can be obtained by computing the cross-lingual based on a concatenation of the two source encodings. Another illustration of this flexibility is document-level translation, which aims to integrate long-distance dependencies beyond the sentence level. This might be needed to handle pronominal references, as when computing the translation of *"This bike is broken. It needs a fix."* from English into French. For this example, the generation of the correct subject pronoun for the second sentence (*"il"* ou *"elle"*) requires knowledge of the translation of *"bike"* in the previous sentence: (*"vélo"* will imply a masculine subject, *"bicyclette"* a feminine one). By encoding contexts made of several previous sentences, such difficulties can be addressed [56].

Monolingual and Multimodal Machine Translation. Machine translation is an extreme example of a sequence transduction task, corresponding to a language change, while preserving the global meaning. Similar problems appear in a large number of monolingual tasks: for example, grammar correction can be viewed as a "translation" between a noisy sentence and its correction, a framework that also includes spelling normalization (to turn short texts into standard English). Simplification, paraphrase generation, style transfer (e.g from a formal style to more relaxed style), automatic summarization [51] are other instances of these monolingual translations: assuming the availability of pairs (input, output) to learn the parameters, it will be possible to use Transformer architectures.

The encoder-decoder architecture is also generalized in other ways. By considering pairs associating voice recordings with their transcription, it is possible to apply the same techniques for automatic speech recognition [24,33,43]; or even, when recordings and transcripts are in different languages, to directly translate the speech into foreign text [10]. Similar approaches consider the recognition of patterns in images [25] or the generation of descriptions from images [53]. The application of the Transformers to these other modalities is only starting and is expected to develop, both to learn generation models and to train multimodal representations. An introduction to these exciting developments is presented in this volume in M. Evrard's chapter on *Transformer in Automatic Speech Recognition* and C. Guinaudeau's chapter on *Vision and Multi-modal Transformers*.

4.5 Summary

The Transformer architecture readily generalizes to the conditional generation framework, with an interdependent encoder and decoder, an approach that has quickly become the de facto standard for neural machine translation. When fed with inputs and outputs in multiple languages, this architecture learns multilingual representations that can be used for cross-lingual transfer in many applications. By analogy with the translation task, the same approach model can be used for many monolingual tasks as well as for tasks involving other modalities (speech, image, video).

5 Conclusion

The Transformer architecture, both in its unconditional (Sect. 3) and in its conditional (Sect. 4) versions has quickly emerged as a critical component of all language processing tools and has often led to considerable improvements of the performance of these systems. This architecture generates contextual representations from vast amounts of raw data; these representations are useful for a wide range of applications, and also enable to transfer learned knowledge between tasks, domains and languages. This provides an operational response to the lack of annotated data that would be necessary to carry out supervised learning in many contexts. It is also used to learn word generation models capable of producing coherent texts, and, at the cost of elementary reformulations, to handle a large number of related tasks: sentiment analysis, textual implication, question answering, summarization, translation, etc. Multilingual and multimodal extensions of these architectures make it possible to build models from heterogeneous data, further opening the range of possible applications. Finally, Transformers define a shared conceptual framework for many communities of researchers and developers, facilitating interdisciplinary exchanges and accelerating the dissemination of effective implementations and sharing of models [12].

Have Transformer "solved natural language processing"? Several limitations of these models are highlighted in recent papers, suggesting many avenues for future research. A first limitation is that these models do not incorporate any linguistic knowledge (regarding the structure of words and phrases), which makes them unsuitable for reproducing the systematic behaviour that is expected when dealing with regular phenomena, such as grammatical agreement, or co-reference phenomena. Although possible, the integration of linguistic knowledge runs against the increase in training data and in the number of languages taken into account, and is not very actively researched. Similarly, the world knowledge injected into Transformers is restricted to whatever occurs in the training texts. Although these models are capable of memorizing and restoring many of these factual knowledge, they remain incomplete and their learning is uncertain and non-systematic [62]: it thus seems inappropriate to think that they help us progress towards deep language understanding [7]. For this, the combination of statistical models with knowledge graphs seems to be a promising research direction [13,61].

Another limitation of these architectures is that their "black box" behaviour, which creates multiple problems when these systems are run on a very large scale. In particular, it is extremely hard to explain the decisions made, as they ultimately result from the particular dynamics of model training, and from the nature of the training data. As shown on many occasions [6], these models in particular tend to amplify the biases present in the data, and may, for example, generate uncontrolled statements of a sexist or racist nature. The apparent consistency of automatically generated texts is also misleading, and may fool users into endowing these systems with a form of understanding they do not actually possess. These weaknesses are shared with all probabilistic models, which are constrained in their performance by the limitations of the training data, which are often too rare, incomplete, or biased, and result in systems that may be incomplete and inconsistent.

References

1. Aharoni, R., Johnson, M., Firat, O.: Massively multilingual neural machine translation. In: Proceedings of the 2019 Conference of the North American Chapter of the Association for Computational Linguistics: Human Language Technologies, Volume 1 (Long and Short Papers), pp. 3874–3884. Association for Computational Linguistics, Minneapolis (2019). https://doi.org/10.18653/v1/N19-1388
2. Baevski, A., Zhou, Y., Mohamed, A., Auli, M.: Wav2vec 2.0: a framework for self-supervised learning of speech representations. In: Larochelle, H., Ranzato, M., Hadsell, R., Balcan, M.F., Lin, H. (eds.) Advances in Neural Information Processing Systems, vol. 33, pp. 12449–12460. Curran Associates, Inc. (2020)
3. Bahdanau, D., Cho, K., Bengio, Y.: Neural machine translation by jointly learning to align and translate. In: Proceedings of the first International Conference on Learning Representations. ICLR, San Diego (2015)
4. Barbieri, F., Camacho-Collados, J., Espinosa Anke, L., Neves, L.: TweetEval: unified benchmark and comparative evaluation for tweet classification. In: Findings of the Association for Computational Linguistics: EMNLP 2020, pp. 1644–1650. Association for Computational Linguistics (2020). https://doi.org/10.18653/v1/2020.findings-emnlp.148
5. Beltagy, I., Lo, K., Cohan, A.: SciBERT: a pretrained language model for scientific text. In: Proceedings of the 2019 Conference on Empirical Methods in Natural Language Processing and the 9th International Joint Conference on Natural Language Processing (EMNLP-IJCNLP), pp. 3615–3620. Association for Computational Linguistics, Hong Kong (2019). https://doi.org/10.18653/v1/D19-1371
6. Bender, E.M., Gebru, T., McMillan-Major, A., Shmitchell, S.: On the dangers of stochastic parrots: can language models be too big? In: Proceedings of the 2021 ACM Conference on Fairness, Accountability, and Transparency, FAccT 2021, pp. 610–623. Association for Computing Machinery, New York (2021). https://doi.org/10.1145/3442188.3445922
7. Bender, E.M., Koller, A.: Climbing towards NLU: on meaning, form, and understanding in the age of data. In: Proceedings of the 58th Annual Meeting of the Association for Computational Linguistics, pp. 5185–5198. Association for Computational Linguistics (2020). https://doi.org/10.18653/v1/2020.acl-main.463
8. Bengio, S., Vinyals, O., Jaitly, N., Shazeer, N.: Scheduled sampling for sequence prediction with recurrent neural networks. In: Cortes, C., Lawrence, N., Lee, D., Sugiyama, M., Garnett, R. (eds.) Advances in Neural Information Processing Systems, vol. 28. Curran Associates, Inc. (2015)
9. Bengio, Y., Ducharme, R., Vincent, P., Janvin, C.: A neural probabilistic language model. J. Mach. Learn. Res. **3**, 1137–1155 (2003)
10. Bérard, A., Pietquin, O., Besacier, L., Servan, C.: Listen and translate: a proof of concept for end-to-end speech-to-text translation. In: NIPS Workshop on End-to-End Learning for Speech and Audio Processing, Barcelona, Spain (2016)
11. Bojanowski, P., Grave, E., Joulin, A., Mikolov, T.: Enriching word vectors with subword information. arXiv preprint arXiv:1607.04606 (2016)
12. Bommasani, R., et al.: On the opportunities and risks of foundation models. arXiv preprint arXiv:2108.07258 (2021)
13. Bosselut, A., Rashkin, H., Sap, M., Malaviya, C., Celikyilmaz, A., Choi, Y.: COMET: commonsense transformers for automatic knowledge graph construction. In: Proceedings of the 57th Annual Meeting of the Association for Computational Linguistics, pp. 4762–4779. Association for Computational Linguistics, Florence (2019). https://doi.org/10.18653/v1/P19-1470

14. Brown, T.B., et al.: Language models are few-shot learners (2020)
15. Cañete, J., Chaperon, G., Fuentes, R., Ho, J.H., Kang, H., Pérez, J.: Spanish pre-trained BERT model and evaluation data. In: PML4DC at ICLR 2020 (2020)
16. Chan, B., Schweter, S., Möller, T.: German's next language model. In: Proceedings of the 28th International Conference on Computational Linguistics, pp. 6788–6796. International Committee on Computational Linguistics, Barcelona (2020). https://doi.org/10.18653/v1/2020.coling-main.598
17. Charniak, E.: Statistical Language Learning. The MIT Press, Cambridge (1993)
18. Cho, K., et al.: Learning phrase representations using RNN encoder-decoder for statistical machine translation. In: Proceedings of the 2014 Conference on Empirical Methods in Natural Language Processing (EMNLP), pp. 1724–1734. Association for Computational Linguistics, Doha (2014)
19. Cho, K., van Merriënboer, B., Bahdanau, D., Bengio, Y.: On the properties of neural machine translation: encoder-decoder approaches. In: Proceedings of SSST-8, Eighth Workshop on Syntax, Semantics and Structure in Statistical Translation, pp. 103–111. Association for Computational Linguistics, Doha (2014). https://doi.org/10.3115/v1/W14-4012
20. Collobert, R., Weston, J., Bottou, L., Karlen, M., Kavukcuoglu, K., Kuksa, P.: Natural language processing (almost) from scratch. J. Mach. Learn. Res. **12**(Aug), 2493–2537 (2011)
21. Conneau, A., Lample, G.: Cross-lingual language model pretraining. In: Wallach, H., Larochelle, H., Beygelzimer, A., d'Alché-Buc, F., Fox, E., Garnett, R. (eds.) Advances in Neural Information Processing Systems, vol. 32. Curran Associates, Inc. (2019)
22. Deligne, S., Bimbot, F.: Language modeling by variable length sequences: theoretical formulation and evaluation of multigrams. In: 1995 International Conference onAcoustics, Speech, and Signal Processing, ICASSP-95, vol. 1, pp. 169–172. IEEE (1995)
23. Devlin, J., Chang, M.W., Lee, K., Toutanova, K.: BERT: pre-training of deep bidirectional transformers for language understanding. In: Proceedings of the 2019 Conference of the North American Chapter of the Association for Computational Linguistics: Human Language Technologies, Volume 1 (Long and Short Papers), pp. 4171–4186. Association for Computational Linguistics, Minneapolis (2019)
24. Dong, L., Xu, S., Xu, B.: Speech-transformer: a no-recurrence sequence-to-sequence model for speech recognition. In: 2018 IEEE International Conference on Acoustics, Speech and Signal Processing (ICASSP), pp. 5884–5888. IEEE (2018)
25. Dosovitskiy, A., et al.: An image is worth 16×16 words: transformers for image recognition at scale. In: International Conference on Learning Representations (2021)
26. Eisenstein, J.: Natural Language Processing. The MIT Press, Cambridge (2019)
27. Elman, J.L.: Finding structure in time. Cogn. Sci. **14**(2), 179–211 (1990). https://doi.org/10.1207/s15516709cog1402_1
28. Fan, A., et al.: Beyond English-centric multilingual machine translation. J. Mach. Learn. Res. **22**(107), 1–48 (2021)
29. Fedus, W., Zoph, B., Shazeer, N.: Switch transformers: scaling to trillion parameter models with simple and efficient sparsity (2021)
30. Firat, O., Cho, K., Bengio, Y.: Multi-way, multilingual neural machine translation with a shared attention mechanism. In: Proceedings of the 2016 Conference of the North American Chapter of the Association for Computational Linguistics: Human Language Technologies, pp. 866–875. Association for Computational Linguistics (2016). https://doi.org/10.18653/v1/N16-1101

31. Gage, P.: A new algorithm for data compression. Comput. Users J. **12**(2), 23–38 (1994)
32. Gu, J., Bradbury, J., Xiong, C., Li, V.O.K., Socher, R.: Non-autoregressive neural machine translation. In: Proceedings of the International Conference on Representation Learning, ICLR 2018 (2018)
33. Gulati, A., et al.: Conformer: convolution-augmented transformer for speech recognition. In: Proceedings of the Interspeech 2020, pp. 5036–5040 (2020)
34. Ha, T.H., Niehues, J., Waibel, A.: Toward multilingual neural machine translation with universal encoder and decoder. In: Proceedings of the 13th International Workshop on Spoken Language Translation, IWSLT 2016, Vancouver, Canada (2016)
35. Henderson, P., Hu, J., Romoff, J., Brunskill, E., Jurafsky, D., Pineau, J.: Towards the systematic reporting of the energy and carbon footprints of machine learning. J. Mach. Learn. Res. **21**(248), 1–43 (2020)
36. Hochreiter, S., Schmidhuber, J.: Long short-term memory. Neural Comput. **9**(8), 1735–1780 (1997). https://doi.org/10.1162/neco.1997.9.8.1735
37. Jain, A., Ganesamoorty, M.: NukeBERT: a pre-trained language model for low resource nuclear domain. CoRR abs/2003.13821 (2020)
38. Jelinek, F.: Statistical Methods for Speech Recognition. The MIT Press, Cambridge (1997)
39. Jelinek, F., Mercer, M.: Interpolated estimation of Markov source parameters from sparse data. In: Proceedings of the Workshop on Pattern Recognition in Practice, pp. 381–397. Amsterdam (1980)
40. Johnson, M., et al.: Google's multilingual neural machine translation system: enabling zero-shot translation. Trans. Assoc. Comput. Linguist. **5**, 339–351 (2017)
41. Jurafsky, D., Martin, J.H.: Speech and Language Processing, 3éme édition, 2018 edn. Prentice Hall (2000)
42. Kaplan, J., et al.: Scaling laws for neural language models (2020)
43. Karita, S., Soplin, N.E.Y., Watanabe, S., Delcroix, M., Ogawa, A., Nakatani, T.: Improving transformer-based end-to-end speech recognition with connectionist temporal classification and language model integration. In: Proceedings of the Interspeech 2019, pp. 1408–1412 (2019)
44. Kudo, T.: Subword regularization: improving neural network translation models with multiple subword candidates. In: Proceedings of the 56th Annual Meeting of the Association for Computational Linguistics (Volume 1: Long Papers), pp. 66–75. Association for Computational Linguistics, Melbourne (2018). https://doi.org/10.18653/v1/P18-1007
45. Le, H.S., Oparin, I., Allauzen, A., Gauvain, J.L., Yvon, F.: Structured output layer neural network language model. In: Proceedings of IEEE International Conference on Acoustic, Speech and Signal Processing, Prague, Czech Republic, pp. 5524–5527 (2011)
46. Le, H., et al.: FlauBERT: unsupervised language model pre-training for french. In: LREC. Marseille, France (2020)
47. Lee, J.S., Hsiang, J.: Patent classification by fine-tuning BERT language model. World Patent Inf. **61**, 101965 (2020). https://doi.org/10.1016/j.wpi.2020.101965
48. Lee, J., et al.: BioBERT: a pre-trained biomedical language representation model for biomedical text mining. Bioinform. (Oxford Engl.) **36**(4), 1234–1240 (2020). https://doi.org/10.1093/bioinformatics/btz682
49. Lewis, M., et al.: BART: denoising sequence-to-sequence pre-training for natural language generation, translation, and comprehension. In: Proceedings of the 58th

Annual Meeting of the Association for Computational Linguistics, pp. 7871–7880. Association for Computational Linguistics (2020). https://doi.org/10.18653/v1/2020.acl-main.703

50. Linzen, T., Dupoux, E., Goldberg, Y.: Assessing the ability of LSTMs to learn syntax-sensitive dependencies. Trans. Assoc. Comput. Linguist. **4**, 521–535 (2016)

51. Liu, P.J., et al.: Generating Wikipedia by summarizing long sequences. CoRR abs/1801.10198 (2018)

52. Liu, Y., et al.: RoBERTa: a robustly optimized BERT pretraining approach. CoRR abs/1907.11692 (2019)

53. Lu, J., Batra, D., Parikh, D., Lee, S.: ViLBERT: pretraining task-agnostic visiolinguistic representations for vision-and-language tasks. In: Wallach, H., Larochelle, H., Beygelzimer, A., d'Alché-Buc, F., Fox, E., Garnett, R. (eds.) Advances in Neural Information Processing Systems, vol. 32. Curran Associates, Inc. (2019)

54. Manning, C.D., Schütze, H.: Foundations of Statistical Natural Language Processing. The MIT Press, Cambridge (1999)

55. Martin, L., et al.: CamemBERT: a tasty french language model. In: ACL 2020–58th Annual Meeting of the Association for Computational Linguistics. Seattle/Virtual, United States (2020). https://doi.org/10.18653/v1/2020.acl-main.645

56. Maruf, S., Saleh, F., Haffari, G.: A survey on document-level neural machine translation: Methods and evaluation. ACM Comput. Surv. **54**(2) (2021). https://doi.org/10.1145/3441691

57. Merrill, W., Weiss, G., Goldberg, Y., Schwartz, R., Smith, N.A., Yahav, E.: A formal hierarchy of RNN architectures. In: Proceedings of the 58th Annual Meeting of the Association for Computational Linguistics, pp. 443–459. Association for Computational Linguistics (2020). https://doi.org/10.18653/v1/2020.acl-main.43

58. Mikolov, T., Chen, K., Corrado, G., Dean, J.: Efficient estimation of word representations in vector space. In: Proceedings of the International Conference on Representation Learning. ICLR (2013)

59. Mikolov, T., Karafiát, M., Burget, L., Černocký, J., Khudanpur, S.: Recurrent neural network based language model. In: Proceedings of the 11th Annual Conference of the International Speech Communication Association (Interspeech 2010), pp. 1045–1048. International Speech Communication Association (2010)

60. Peters, M., et al.: Deep contextualized word representations. In: Proceedings of the 2018 Conference of the North American Chapter of the Association for Computational Linguistics: Human Language Technologies, Volume 1 (Long Papers), pp. 2227–2237. Association for Computational Linguistics, New Orleans (2018)

61. Peters, M.E., et al.: Knowledge enhanced contextual word representations. In: Proceedings of the 2019 Conference on Empirical Methods in Natural Language Processing and the 9th International Joint Conference on Natural Language Processing (EMNLP-IJCNLP), pp. 43–54. Association for Computational Linguistics, Hong Kong (2019). https://doi.org/10.18653/v1/D19-1005

62. Petroni, F., et al.: Language models as knowledge bases? In: Proceedings of the 2019 Conference on Empirical Methods in Natural Language Processing and the 9th International Joint Conference on Natural Language Processing (EMNLP-IJCNLP), pp. 2463–2473. Association for Computational Linguistics, Hong Kong (2019). https://doi.org/10.18653/v1/D19-1250

63. Qi, D., Su, L., Song, J., Cui, E., Bharti, T., Sacheti, A.: ImageBERT: cross-modal pre-training with large-scale weak-supervised image-text data (2020)

64. Radford, A., Wu, J., Child, R., Luan, D., Amodei, D., Sutskever, I.: Language models are unsupervised multitask learners. Technical report, OpenAI (2019)

65. Raffel, C., et al.: Exploring the limits of transfer learning with a unified text-to-text transformer. J. Mach. Learn. Res. **21**(140), 1–67 (2020)

66. Rajbhandari, S., Rasley, J., Ruwase, O., He, Y.: ZeRO: memory optimizations toward training trillion parameter models. In: SC20: International Conference for High Performance Computing, Networking, Storage and Analysis, pp. 1–16 (2020). https://doi.org/10.1109/SC41405.2020.00024

67. Rogers, A., Kovaleva, O., Rumshisky, A.: A primer in BERTology: what we know about how BERT works. Trans. Assoc. Comput. Linguist. **8**, 842–866 (2020)

68. Rosenfeld, R.: Two decades of statistical language modeling: where do we go from here?? Proc. IEEE **88**(8), 1270–1278 (2000). https://doi.org/10.1109/5.880083

69. Schwenk, H.: Continuous space language models. Comput. Speech Lang. **21**(3), 492–518 (2007)

70. Sennrich, R., Haddow, B., Birch, A.: Neural machine translation of rare words with subword units. In: Proceedings of the 54th Annual Meeting of the Association for Computational Linguistics (Volume 1: Long Papers), Berlin, Germany, pp. 1715–1725 (2016). https://doi.org/10.18653/v1/P16-1162

71. Smith, N.A.: Contextual word representations: putting words into computers. Commun. ACM **63**(6), 66–74 (2020). https://doi.org/10.1145/3347145

72. Søgaard, A., Vulic, I., Ruder, S., Faruqui, M.: Cross-lingual word embeddings. In: Synthesis Lectures on Human Language Technologies. Morgan & Claypool Publishers (2019). https://doi.org/10.2200/S00920ED2V01Y201904HLT042

73. Strubell, E., Ganesh, A., McCallum, A.: Energy and policy considerations for deep learning in NLP. In: Proceedings of the 57th Annual Meeting of the Association for Computational Linguistics, pp. 3645–3650. Association for Computational Linguistics, Florence (2019). https://doi.org/10.18653/v1/P19-1355

74. Sun, C., Myers, A., Vondrick, C., Murphy, K., Schmid, C.: VideoBERT: a joint model for video and language representation learning. In: 2019 IEEE/CVF International Conference on Computer Vision (ICCV), pp. 7463–7472 (2019). https://doi.org/10.1109/ICCV.2019.00756

75. Tay, Y., Dehghani, M., Bahri, D., Metzler, D.: Efficient transformers: a survey (2020)

76. Tiedemann, J.: Parallel data, tools and interfaces in opus. In: Choukri, K., et al. (eds.) Proceedings of the Eight International Conference on Language Resources and Evaluation (LREC 2012). European Language Resources Association (ELRA), Istanbul (2012)

77. Vaswani, A., et al.: Attention is all you need. In: Guyon, I., et al. (eds.) Advances in Neural Information Processing Systems, vol. 30, pp. 5998–6008. Curran Associates, Inc. (2017)

78. de Vries, W., van Cranenburgh, A., Bisazza, A., Caselli, T., van Noord, G., Nissim, M.: Bertje: a dutch BERT model. CoRR abs/1912.09582 (2019)

79. Wolf, T., et al.: Transformers: state-of-the-art natural language processing. In: Proceedings of the 2020 Conference on Empirical Methods in Natural Language Processing: System Demonstrations, pp. 38–45. Association for Computational Linguistics (2020). https://doi.org/10.18653/v1/2020.emnlp-demos.6

Vision and Multi-modal Transformers

Camille Guinaudeau[⊠][ID]

University Paris-Saclay, CNRS - LISN, 91400 Orsay, France
`camille.guinaudeau@lisn.upsaclay.fr`

Abstract. Transformers that rely on the self-attention mechanism to capture global dependencies have dominated in natural language modelling and their use in other domains, e.g. speech processing, has shown great potential. The impressive results obtained on these domains leads computer vision researchers to apply transformers to visual data. However, the application of an architecture designed for sequential data is not straightforward for data represented as 2-D matrices. This chapter presents how Transformers were introduced in the domain of vision processing, challenging the historical Convolutional Neural Networks based approaches. After a brief reminder about historical methods in computer vision, namely convolution and self-attention, the chapter focuses on the modifications introduced in the Transformers architecture to deal with the peculiarities of visual data, using two different strategies. In a last part, recent work applying Transformer architecture in a multimodal context is also presented.

Keywords: Convolutional neural networks · Vision transformers · Multimodal transformer

1 Introduction

Transformers introduced by Vaswani et al. in 2017 [23] are learning models designed to handle sequential data using attention mechanisms. In particular, they allow computers to learn sequences automatically, without having been programmed specifically for this purpose. The Transformer is an instance of the sequence-to-sequence (seq2seq) learning models, taking a sequence as input, processing it, before returning another as output. If the Transformer uses an attention mechanism, it still inherited the encoder-decoder pattern system from the Recurrent Neural Networks (RNNs), the encoder being the input to the sequence and the decoder being the output. Each of these two blocks includes two layers of neural networks: the so-called self-attention layer which allows to keep the interdependence of data in a sequence, and the layer called Feed-forward Neural Network that leads the data to the output.

Transformers, originally designed for Natural Language Processing tasks: translation, question-answering, etc. have been successfully applied in the field of speech processing, particularly in speech synthesis [19], as presented in [9]. The impressive results obtained on other domains leads computer vision researchers

© Springer Nature Switzerland AG 2023
M. Chetouani et al. (Eds.): ACAI 2021, LNAI 13500, pp. 106–122, 2023.
https://doi.org/10.1007/978-3-031-24349-3_7

to apply transformers to visual data. However, the application of an architecture designed to be applied to sequential data (such as text or speech) is not straightforward for data represented as 2-D matrix and containing spatial dependencies. This difficulty becoming even greater for video data that add a temporal dimension.

This chapter aims at presenting the adaptation of the Transformers architecture, as it was developed in the Natural Language Processing domain, to visual or multi-modal data to solve vision or multimedia tasks. A particular focus is made on data representation for machine learning approaches, starting from the historical Convolutional Neural Networks (CNN) and self-attention mechanism, described in Sect. 2 to the Vision Transformers, proposed recently by Dosovitskiy et al. [8]. Finally, in the last Section, recent work applying Transformers in a multi-modal context is presented.

In summary, the learning objectives presented in this paper are the following:

- reminisce the historical approaches for computer vision, namely convolutions and self-attention;
- understand the adaptation of the Transformers architecture to deal with the visual data peculiarities, using two different strategies;
- grasp the functioning principles of recent work applying Transformers architecture to multimodal tasks and data.

2   From Convolutional Neural Networks to Transformers

Computer vision is concerned with the automatic extraction, analysis and understanding of useful information from a single image or a sequence of images. Computer vision tasks include object or event detection, object recognition, indexing, motion estimation, image restoration, etc. The most established algorithm among various deep learning models is Convolutional Neural Network (CNN), a class of artificial neural networks that has been a dominant method in computer vision tasks since the astonishing results reported in 2012 in [14].

2.1   Convolutional Neural Networks (CNN)

In the context of computer vision, a Convolutional Neural Network (CNN) is a Deep Learning algorithm that can take in an input image, identify salient regions in the image, through learnable weights and biases, and is able to differentiate one image from the others. A convolutional neural network architecture is composed of a stack of processing layers: the **convolutional layer** which processes the data of an input channel; the **pooling layer** which reduces the size of the intermediate image, performing some information compression; the correction layer; the **fully connected layer**, which is a perceptron-like layer. After several layers of convolution and max-pooling, the high level decision in the neural network is done through fully connected layers. Finally, the **loss Layer** specifies how the gap between the expected and the actual signal is penalized. It is usually

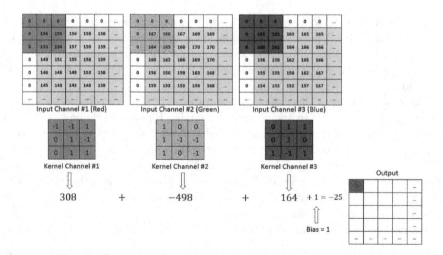

Fig. 1. Convolution of a 3 channel image with a $3 \times 3 \times 3$ kernel - Image from Rijul Vohra

the last layer in the network. For more details on the architecture and functioning of Convolutional Neural Network, see [7].

The goal of the convolutional layer is to provide a representation of the input image. Even if an image is just a matrix of pixel values, a simple flattening of the image as a vector would not be enough to represent complex images having pixel dependencies throughout. Therefore, to model the spatial and temporal dependencies in an image, convolutions were introduced to capture them through the application of relevant filters.

Figure 1 presents the process of applying a convolution filter to an image. At each step, a convolution takes a set of weights (a kernel, for 3D structures, or a filter, for 2-D arrays) and multiplies them with the input channels representing the image. Each filter multiplies the weights with different input values; the total inputs are summed, providing a unique value for each filter position. In the case of images with multiple channels (e.g. RGB), all the results are summed with the bias to give a value of the Convoluted Feature Output. To cover the entire image, the filter is applied from right to left and from top to bottom, giving the output matrix.

The advantage of convolutions is two-folds: they can be efficiently parallelized using GPUs and their operations impose two important spatial constraints that facilitate the learning of visual features. Indeed, the features extracted from a convolution layer are 1) not sensitive to the global position of a feature 2) locality sensitive as the operation only takes into account a local region of the image. However, the image representation obtained through convolution operations lack a global view of the image. If they are able to extract visual features, they are not able to model the dependencies between them.

Fig. 2. Show, attend and tell – examples of attending to the correct object - image extracted from [28]

2.2   Self-attention

To overcome these limitations, recent studies [2,3,25,28] have proposed to use self-attention layers in combination with or instead of convolutional layers. The main difference between convolutional and self-attention layers is that the computed value of a pixel depends on every other pixel of the image, instead of a K × K neighborhood grid.

Introduced by [1] for neural machine translation, attention shows the ability to learn to focus on important subparts of the input, as explained in [6]. This ability can also be used in computer vision where the objective of self-attention layers is to compute attention weights so each position in the image has information about all the other features in the same image. Self-attention layers can either replace or be combined with convolutions, as they are able to model dependencies between spatially distant features by attending to larger receptive fields than regular convolutions.

In [28], the attention mechanism is applied on images to generate captions. The image is first encoded by a convolutional neural network to extract features. To do so, the authors use a lower convolutional layer instead of a fully connected layer to allow the decoder to selectively focus on certain parts of an image by selecting a subset of all the feature vectors. Then a Long short-term memory (LSTM) decoder is used to generate a caption by producing one word at every time step based on a context vector, the previous hidden state and the previously generated words. Figure 2 presents examples of attending to the correct object where white, in the image, indicates the attended regions, and underline, in the text, indicates the corresponding word.

When combined with self-attention, convolution models can improve the results obtained on several vision tasks. For example, in [25], self-attention is used for video classification and object detection with performance that can compete or outperform with state-of-the-art approaches. Another milestone is [3], where the authors obtain improvements on image classification and achieve state-of-the-art results on video action recognition when using self-attention with convolution models. Finally, [2] augment convolutional operators with self-attention mechanism and show that attention augmentation leads to consistent improvements in image classification and object detection.

However, self-attention layers can have expensive computational costs for high resolution inputs, and can therefore be used only on small spatial dimensions. Some works have already presented ways to overcome this problem, as [24], which computes attention along the two spatial axes sequentially instead of dealing directly with the whole image or [18], which uses patches of feature maps instead of the whole spatial dimensions.

3   Transformers for Computer Vision

Instead of including self-attention within convolutional pipelines, other works have proposed to adapt the original encoder-decoder architecture presented for Transformers to Computer Vision tasks. In this section, works that have proposed to use the transformer architecture to deal with images are described with a focus on the way images are represented. As the original text Transformer takes as input a sequence of words to perform translation, classification, or other NLP tasks, two different strategies can be used to apply this architecture on image data. In the first one, the fewest possible modifications are made to the transformer while input are modified to add information about positions in the image. [8,21] and [4] are using this strategy. The second strategy consists in modifying the architecture, for example, by introducing convolutions to the vision transformer as proposed in [26] to fit images peculiarities.

3.1   Introduction of Positional Encodings

The first work that modifies the Transformer design to make it operate directly on images instead of words is the Vision transformers (ViT) proposed by Dosovitskiy et al. [8]. In this paper, the authors make the fewest possible modifications to the Transformer architecture and observe to which extend the model can learn about image structure on its own[1].

Figure 3 presents the Vision Transformers architecture that divides an image into a grid of square patches. Each patch is flattened into a single vector by concatenating the channels of all pixels in a patch and then linearly projecting it to the desired input dimension. To introduce information about the structure of the input elements, the authors add learnable position embeddings to each patch. The idea is to make the Vision Transformers learn relevant information about image structure from the training data and encode structural information in the position embeddings.

To gain some intuition into what the model learns, the authors propose two figures to visualize some of its internal workings. First, they present the position embeddings: the parameters learned by the model to encode the relative location

---

[1] https://github.com/google-research/vision_transformer.

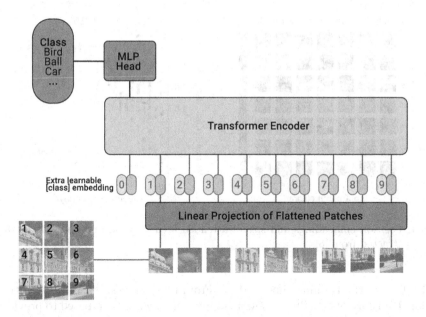

Fig. 3. Vision Transformers (ViT) architecture - image extracted from [8]

of patches. On the right part of Fig. 4, it can be seen that the vision transformer is able to reproduce the image structure as closer patches tend to have more similar position embeddings. Second, the authors also present the size of attended area by head and network depth in order to evaluate to which extend the network uses the ability to integrate information across the entire image, even in the lowest layers, thanks to self-attention. If for depths between 10 and 20 only large attention distances are visible, meaning that only global features are used, in the lowest layers, a large range in the mean attention distance, showing that the ability to integrate information globally, is indeed used by the model.

Table 1 reports the results obtained for variants of the ViT transformers, compared to previous state-of-the-art models, applied on popular image classification benchmarks. The first comparison model used is Big Transfer (BiT) which performs supervised transfer learning with large ResNets [13] and the second one is Noisy Student [27] which is a large EfficientNet trained using semi-supervised learning on ImageNet and JFT300M with the labels removed. From this table, we can see that the smaller ViT-L model, with a 16 × 16 image patch size, pre-trained on JFT-300M outperforms BiT-L, which is pre-trained on the same dataset, on all datasets. The larger model, ViT-H (with a 14 × 14 image patch size), further improves the performance, especially on ImageNet, CIFAR-100, and the VTAB suite, that are the more challenging datasets. The ViT-L model, with a 16 × 16 image patch size, pre-trained on the public ImageNet-21k dataset performs well on most tasks too. Finally, the last line of the Table reports the number of TPUv3-core-days taken to pre-train each of the models on TPUv3 hardware, that is, the number of TPU v3 cores (2 per chip) used for training

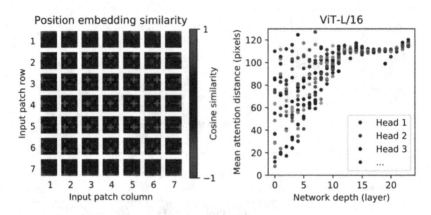

Fig. 4. Position embeddings and size of attended area by head and network depth - image extracted from [8]

multiplied by the training time in days. From these values, it can be seen that Vision Transformers results use fewer computing resources compared to previous state-of-the-art CNNs.

Table 1. Accuracy for Vision Transformers and state of the art approaches on 7 image classification benchmarks.

	ViT-H/14 JFT	ViT-L/16 JFT	ViT-L/16 I21k	BiT-L ResNet152 × 4	Noisy student EfficientNet-L2
ImageNet	88.55	87.76	85.30	87.54	88.5
ImageNet ReaL	90.72	90.54	88.62	90.54	90.55
CIFAR-10	99.50	99.42	99.15	99.37	
CIFAR-100	94.55	93.90	93.25	93.51	
Oxford-IIIT Pets	97.56	97.32	94.67	96.62	
Oxford Flowers-102	99.68	99.74	99.61	99.63	
VTAB (19 tasks)	77.63	76.28	72.72	76.29	
TPUv3-core-days	2.5k	0.68k	0.23k	9.9k	12.3k

If the Vision Transformers proposed in [8] reduces the need of computing resources compared to previous state-of-the-art CNNs, while presenting excellent results when trained with large labelled image dataset they do not generalize well when trained on insufficient amounts of data. Furthermore, the training of these models still involve extensive computing resources.

In order to overcome these problems, Touvron et al. [21] propose competitive convolution-free transformers trained on a single 8-GPU node in two to three days that is competitive with convolutional networks. Their Data-efficient Image Transformers (DeiT) has a similar number of parameters and uses Imagenet as the sole training set[2]. To do so, the authors proposed the knowledge distillation procedure specific for vision transformers. The idea of knowledge distillation is to train one neural network (the student) on an output of another network (the teacher). Such training improves the performance of the vision transformers. The authors have tested the distillation of a transformer student by a CNNs and a transformer teacher and surprisingly, image transformers learn more from CNNs than from another transformer.

In the distillation procedure a new *distillation token*—i.e. a trainable vector, appended to the patch tokens before the first layer—is included in order to interact with the class and patch tokens through the self-attention layers. Similarly to the class token, the objective of the distillation token is to reproduce the label predicted by the teacher, instead of the true label. Both the class and distillation tokens input to the transformers are learned by back-propagation. There are different types of distillation techniques, in [21], the authors use what is called hard-label distillation, so the loss penalizes the student when it mis-classifies real target and the target produced by the teacher.

To speed up the training of the system and improve its accuracy, [22] show that it is preferable to use a lower training resolution and fine-tune the network at the larger resolution. As the patch size stays the same when increasing the resolution of an input image, the number of input patches does change and, due to the architecture of transformer blocks and the class token, the model and classifier do not need to be modified to process more tokens. However, it is necessary to adapt the positional embeddings, because there are one for each patch. To do so, [8] and [21] interpolate the positional encoding when changing the resolution with a 2-D interpolation and a bicubic interpolation respectively.

Table 2 reports the accuracy obtained by DeiT models on ImageNet with no external training data, compared with two variants of ViT with 16 × 16 input patch size. It also presents the number of parameters and the throughput measured for images at resolution 224 × 224. This table first shows that DeiT models have a lower parameter count than ViT models, and a faster throughput, while having a better accuracy for images at resolution 384 × 384, when fine-tuned at a larger resolution. It also presents that the transformer-specific distillation increases the accuracy obtained for the three models DeiT-Ti, DeiT-S and DeiT-B.

3.2   Dynamic Positional Encodings

In the two previous systems, the absolute positional encodings were added to each token in the input sequence to take into account the order of the tokens. If these absolute positional encodings are effective, they also have a negative impact on the flexibility of the Transformers. For example, the encodings are often a vector of dimension equal to the length of the input sequence to the input sequence, which are jointly updated with the network weights during training, causing difficulty to handle the sequences longer than the ones in the training

---

[2] https://github.com/facebookresearch/deit.

Table 2. Accuracy and Throughput for Transformers model on ImageNet.

Model	Params	Image size	Throughput	Accuracy on ImageNet
ViT-B/16	86M	384^2	85.9	77.9
ViT-L/16	307M	384^2	27.3	76.5
DeiT-Ti	5M	224^2	2536.5	72.2
DeiT-S	22M	224^2	940.4	79.8
DeiT-B	86M	224^2	292.3	81.8
DeiT-B384	86M	384^2	85.9	83.1
DeiT-Ti dist	6M	224^2	2529.5	74.5
DeiT-S dist	22M	224^2	936.2	81.2
DeiT-B dist	87M	224^2	290.9	83.4

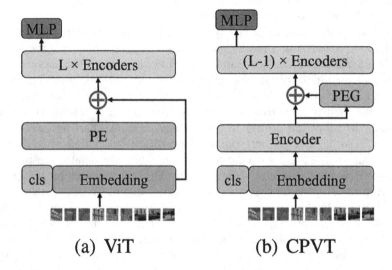

(a) ViT   (b) CPVT

Fig. 5. ViT vs. CPVT architecture - image extracted from [5]

data at test time. This limits the generalization of the Transformers. Moreover, by adding unique positional encodings to each token (or each image patch), these absolute positional encodings breaks the translation-invariance.

To overcome these limitations, Chu et al. propose the Conditional Positional Encoding Vision Transformers (CPVT) architecture, [5], that integrates positional encodings that are dynamically generated and conditioned on the local neighborhood of an input token[3]. Figure 5 presents the architecture of the Vision Transformers, proposed by [8], with explicit 1-D learnable positional encodings and the CPVT architecture proposed by [5] with conditional positional encoding

---

[3] https://github.com/Meituan-AutoML/CPVT.

from the proposed Position Encoding Generator (PEG) plugin. Except that the positional encodings are conditional, the authors exactly follow the Vision Transformers and the Data-efficient Image Transformers architectures to design their vision transformers. To condition the positional encodings on the local neighborhood of an input token, the authors first reshape the flattened input sequence used in the Vision Transformers [8] back in the 2-D image space. Then, a function is repeatedly applied to the local patch in the 2-D structure to produce the conditional positional encodings.

Table 3 presents the accuracy obtained by the Conditional Positional Encoding Vision Transformers (CPVT) [5] and the Data-efficient Image Transformers (DeiT) [21] on ImageNet for two image sizes with direct evaluation on higher resolutions without fine-tuning. From this Table, it can be seen that performance degrades when DeiT models are applied to 384 × 384 images while CPVT model with the proposed PEG can directly process the larger input images.

Table 3. Accuracy on ImageNet for 224 × 224 and 384 × 384 images, with direct evaluation on higher resolutions without fine-tuning.

Model	Params	Top-1@224	Top-1@384
DeiT-Ti	6M	72.2	71.2
DeiT-S	22M	79.9	78.1
DeiT-B	86M	81.8	79.7
CPVT-Ti	6M	72.4	73.2
CPVT-S	22M	79.9	80.4
CPVT-B	86M	81.9	82.3

To picture what the model learns, the authors compare the attention weights of three architectures, presented in Fig. 6. In the middle of the figure, the attention weights of DeiT with the original positional encodings, on the right, those of DeiT after the positional encodings are removed and on the left the weights of the CPVT model with PEG. In the middle of the figure, the attention weights are high on the diagonal but low for the rest of the image, suggesting that DeiT with the original positional encodings learns to attend the local neighbors of each patch. When the positional encodings are removed (on the left), all the patches produce similar attention weights meaning that they are not able to attend to the patches in their neighbourhood. Finally, like the original positional encodings, the model with PEG can also learn a similar attention pattern, which indicates that the proposed PEG can provide the position information as well.

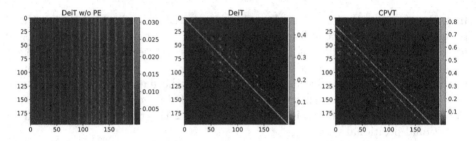

Fig. 6. Normalized attention scores from the second encoder block of DeiT, DeiT without position encoding (DeiT w/o PE), and CPVT on the same input sequence - image extracted from [5].

3.3   Convolution and Transformers

To apply the Transformers, designed for NLP, to vision tasks, the three previous architectures proposed minimal modifications. Despite the success of these models at large scale, their performances are still below similarly sized convolutional neural network (CNN) counterparts when trained on smaller amounts of data. This difference can be explained by the properties of convolutions. As explained in Sect. 2.1, convolutions are able to capture the local structure of an image, and also achieve some degree of shift, scale, and distortion invariance. To account for the properties of convolutions, Wu et al. proposed to introduce two convolution-based operations into the Vision Transformer architecture: Convolutional Token Embedding and Convolutional Projection.

The Convolution vision Transformer (CvT), [26], introduces convolutions to two core sections of the Vision Transformer architecture[4]. First, the authors create a hierarchical structure of Transformers by partitioning the Transformers in multiple stages. The beginning of each stage consists of a convolutional token embedding that performs an overlapping convolution operation with stride on a 2-D-reshaped token map, followed by layer normalization. Hence, the model proposed captures local information and progressively decreases the sequence length while increasing the dimension of token features across stages. This way the model achieves spatial downsampling while increasing the number of feature maps, as is performed in Convolutional Neural Networks. In a second step, the linear projection prior to every self-attention block in the Transformer module is replaced with a convolutional projection that allows the model to further capture local spatial context and reduce semantic ambiguity in the attention mechanism.

Table 4 reports the results of the CvT architecture, compared to the ones obtained by CNN and Vision Transformers on ImageNet. In this table, CvT-X stands for Convolutional vision Transformer with X Transformer Blocks in total. The authors also experiment with a wider model with a larger token dimension for each stage, namely CvT-W24 (W stands for Wide) to validate the scaling ability of the proposed architecture. On the upper part of the Table, it can be

---

[4] https://github.com/microsoft/CvT.

seen that the two convolution-based operations introduced in the Vision Transformer architecture yield improved performance when compared to CNN and to Vision Transformer for images with different resolutions. On the lower part of the table, when the models are pre-trained on ImageNet22k at resolution 224 × 224, and fine-tuned on ImageNet1k at resolution of 384 × 384 (or 480 × 480 for BiT), the accuracy of the CvT models are almost on par with the accuracy of Transformers and CNNs while having a much lower number of model parameters. Finally, when more data is involved, the wide model CvT-W24 pre-trained on ImageNet22k reaches 87.7% of accuracy surpassing the previous best Transformer Vit-L/16.

Table 4. Accuracy of CNN and Vision Transformers architectures on ImageNet. $Subscript_{22k}$ indicates that the model is pre-trained on ImageNet22k, and finetuned on ImageNet1k with the input size of 384 × 384 (except for BiT-M that is finetuned with input size of 480 × 480).

Method type	Network	Params	Image size	ImageNet top-1
Convolutional networks	ResNet-50 [11]	25	224^2	76.2
	ResNet-101 [11]	45M	224^2	77.4
	ResNet-152 [11]	60M	224^2	78.3
Transformers	ViT-B/16	86M	384^2	77.9
	ViT-L/16	307M	384^2	76.5
	DeiT-S	22M	224^2	79.8
	DeiT-B	86M	224^2	81.8
Convolutional transformers	CvT-13	20M	224^2	81.6
	CvT-21	32M	224^2	82.5
	CvT-13$\uparrow^{384}$	20M	384^2	83.0
	CvT-21$\uparrow^{384}$	32M	384^2	83.3
Convolutional Networks$_{22k}$	BiT$\uparrow^{480}$ [13]	928M	480^2	85.4
Transformers$_{22k}$	ViT-B/16$\uparrow^{384}$	86M	384^2	84.0
	ViT-L/16$\uparrow^{384}$	307M	384^2	85.2
	ViT-H/16$\uparrow^{384}$	632M	384^2	85.1
Convolutional transformers$_{22k}$	CvT-13$\uparrow^{384}$	20M	384^2	83.3
	CvT-21$\uparrow^{384}$	32M	384^2	84.9
	CvT-W24$\uparrow^{384}$	277M	384^2	87.7

4 Transformers for Multimedia Data

As the Transformers architecture has been diverted from its primary use in Natural Language Processing to be applied to other modalities (audio and image), very recent works have proposed to use the transformer architecture to solve multimodal challenges. For example, Sterpu et al. have proposed to adapt their tool, AV Align for Speech Recognition to the Transformer architecture [20]. In [16], Radford et al. present the Contrastive Language-Image Pre-training (CLIP) system that is able to learn image representations from scratch on a dataset of 400 million (image, text) pairs collected from the internet. Another example is the work of Gabeur [10] that uses video and text modalities to tackle the tasks of caption-to-video and video-to-caption retrieval (MMT). In the last section of this chapter, two multimodal systems using Transformers architectures are presented, CLIP and MMT.

The idea behind the Contrastive Language-Image Pre-training (CLIP) system proposed by Radford et al. [16] is to learn about images from free-text to recognize objects in a visual scene and solve a variety of visual tasks[5]. So instead of predicting the exact words of the text accompanying each image, the authors try to predict only which text as a whole is paired with which image. Concerning the training part of the system, given a batch of N (image, text) pairs, CLIP is trained to predict which of the $N \times N$ possible (image, text) pairings across a batch actually occurred. To do this, CLIP learns a multi-modal embedding space by jointly training an image encoder and text encoder to maximize the cosine similarity of the image and text embeddings of the N real pairs in the batch while minimizing the cosine similarity of the embeddings of the $N^2\text{-}N$ incorrect pairings. CLIP is trained from scratch without initializing the image encoder with ImageNet weights or the text encoder with pre-trained weights. They use only a linear projection to map from each encoder's representation to the multi-modal embedding space.

As CLIP is pre-trained to predict if an image and a text are paired together in its dataset, the authors reuse this capability to perform zero-shot classification of images. For each image dataset, they use the names of all the classes in the dataset as the set of potential text pairings and predict the most probable (image, text) pair according to CLIP. In a bit more details, they first compute the feature embedding of the image and the feature embedding of the set of possible texts with their respective encoders. The cosine similarity of these embeddings is then calculated and normalized into a probability distribution via a softmax operation.

The system was trained on 400M image-text pairs from the internet and evaluated on 27 image datasets that contains different kinds of images: satellite images, car models, medical images, city classification, etc. Figure 7 shows that CLIP is competitive with a fully supervised linear classifier fitted on ResNet-50 features as the CLIP classifier outperforms it on 16 datasets, including ImageNet. On the right of the figure, the number of labeled examples per class a linear classifier requires to match the performance of the zero-shot classifier is represented. Performance varies widely from still underperforming a one-shot classifier on two datasets to matching an estimated 184 labeled examples per class.

---

[5] https://github.com/openai/CLIP.

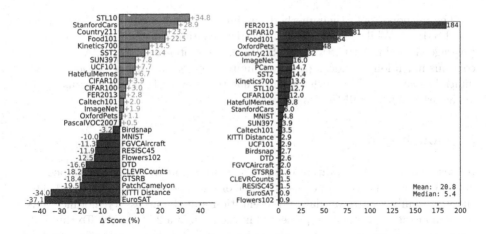

Fig. 7. CLIP performance on 27 image datasets - image extracted from [16]

The second example of multi-modal transformers is the "Multi-modal transformer for video retrieval"[6] (MMT) proposed in [10]. This system tries to solve two tasks. In the first task of caption-to-video retrieval, it is given a query in the form of a caption (e.g., "How to build a house") and its goal is to retrieve the videos best described by it (i.e., videos explaining how to build a house). The other task is video-to-caption retrieval where it has to find among a collection of captions the ones that best describe the query video. To solve these two tasks, the multi-modal transformers use the self-attention mechanism to collect cross-modal and temporal cues about events occurring in a video. The multi-modal transformer is integrated in a cross-modal framework, which takes into account both captions and videos, and estimates their similarity.

The video-level representation computed by the multi-modal transformer (MMT) consists of stacked self-attention layers and fully collected layers. The input is a set of embeddings, all of the same dimension, each of them representing the semantics of a feature, its modality, and the time in the video when the feature was extracted. In order to learn an effective representation from different modalities, the authors use video feature extractors called "experts". Each expert is a model trained for a particular task that is then used to extract features from video. A transformer encoder produces an embedding for each of its feature inputs, resulting in several embeddings for an expert. To obtain a unique embedding for each expert, an aggregated embedding is defined to collect the expert's information. To take into account the cross-modality information, the multi-modal transformer needs to identify which expert it is attending to. To do so, the authors learn N embeddings to distinguish between embeddings of different experts. Finally the temporal embeddings provide temporal information about the time in the video where each feature was extracted to the multi-modal transformer.

---

[6] https://github.com/gabeur/mmt

The authors apply their method on three datasets: MSRVTT, ActivityNet and LSMDC. While MSRVTT and LSMDC contain short video-caption pairs (average video duration of 13s for MSRVTT, one-sentence captions), ActivityNet contains much longer videos (several minutes) and each video is captioned with multiple sentences. The authors show that the proposed system obtains state-of-the-art results on all the three datasets.

5   Conclusion

In this chapter, the adaptation of the Transformers architecture, developed for natural language processing tasks, to visual or multimodal data is presented. The chapter mainly focuses on data representation and the necessary modifications to the management of data represented in the form of a 2-D matrix. To this end, some papers proposed to introduce positionnal embeddings, either absolute or dynamically generated, while others integrate convolutions in the Transformers architecture to capture local spatial context. Dealing with video data further complicates the problem as it requires to account for the temporal dimension. These recent applications of the Transformers architecture to these new domains have shown great potential, outperforming previous approaches when apply on purely visual data to reaching state-of-the-art results on multi-modal data.

In order to go further in understanding the issues related to the use of Transformers in computer vision, several additional readings are recommended. Concerning the specificities related to the representation of images, Dong Ping Tian proposes an extensive overview on image feature extraction and representation techniques in Computer Vision [15]. More details about CNNs architecture can be found in [12] to understand both the theory behind CNNs and to gain hands-on experience on the application of CNNs in computer vision. Finally, regarding the internal representation structure of Vision Transformers (ViT) and CNNs, Raghu et al. analyze the differences between the two architectures, how are Vision Transformers solving these tasks; are they acting like convolutional networks, or learning entirely different visual representations [17]?

References

1. Bahdanau, D., Cho, K., Bengio, Y.: Neural machine translation by jointly learning to align and translate. In: Proceedings of the International Conference on Learning Representations (2015)
2. Bello, I., Zoph, B., Vaswani, A., Shlens, J., Le, Q.V.: Attention augmented convolutional networks. In: Proceedings of the IEEE/CVF International Conference on Computer Vision, pp. 3286–3295 (2019)
3. Chen, Y., Kalantidis, Y., Li, J., Yan, S., Feng, J.: A^ 2-nets: double attention networks. Adv. Neural. Inf. Process. Syst. **31**, 352–361 (2018)
4. Chu, X., et al.: Conditional positional encodings for vision transformers. arXiv preprint arXiv:2102.10882 (2021)
5. Chu, X., Zhang, B., Tian, Z., Wei, X., Xia, H.: Do we really need explicit position encodings for vision transformers? arXiv e-prints, pages arXiv-2102 (2021)

6. Yvon, F.: Transformers in natural language processing. Advanced Course on Human-Centered AI (2022)

7. Crowley, J.: Convolutional neural networks. Advanced Course on Human-Centered AI (2022)

8. Dosovitskiy, A., et al.: An image is worth 16×16 words: transformers for image recognition at scale. In: International Conference on Learning Representations (2020)

9. Evrard, M.: Transformers in automatic speech recognition. Advanced Course on Human-Centered AI (2022)

10. Gabeur, V., Sun, C., Alahari, K., Schmid, C.: Multi-modal transformer for video retrieval. In: Vedaldi, A., Bischof, H., Brox, T., Frahm, J.-M. (eds.) ECCV 2020. LNCS, vol. 12349, pp. 214–229. Springer, Cham (2020). https://doi.org/10.1007/978-3-030-58548-8_13

11. He, K., Zhang, X., Ren, S., Sun, J.: Deep residual learning for image recognition. In: Proceedings of the IEEE Conference on Computer Vision and Pattern Recognition, pp. 770–778 (2016)

12. Khan, S., Rahmani, H., Shah, S.A.A., Bennamoun, M.: A guide to convolutional neural networks for computer vision. Synthesis Lect. Comput. Vis. 8(1), 1–207 (2018)

13. Kolesnikov, A., et al.: Big transfer (BiT): general visual representation learning. In: Vedaldi, A., Bischof, H., Brox, T., Frahm, J.-M. (eds.) ECCV 2020. LNCS, vol. 12350, pp. 491–507. Springer, Cham (2020). https://doi.org/10.1007/978-3-030-58558-7_29

14. Krizhevsky, A., Sutskever, I., Hinton, G.E.: ImageNet classification with deep convolutional neural networks. Adv. Neural Inf. Process. Syst. 25, 84–90 (2012)

15. Tian, D.P.: A review on image feature extraction and representation techniques. Int. J. Multimed. Ubiquit. Eng. 8(4), 385–396 (2013)

16. Radford, A., et al.: Learning transferable visual models from natural language supervision. Image 2, T2 (2021)

17. Raghu, M., Unterthiner, T., Kornblith, S., Zhang, C., Dosovitskiy, A.: Do vision transformers see like convolutional neural networks? In: Advances in Neural Information Processing Systems (2021)

18. Ramachandran, P., Parmar, N., Vaswani, A., Bello, I., Levskaya, A., Shlens, J.: Stand-alone self-attention in vision models. Adv. Neural Inf. Process. Syst. 32 (2019)

19. Ren, Y., et al.: FastSpeech: fast, robust and controllable text to speech. Adv. Neural Inf. Process. Syst. 32 (2019)

20. Sterpu, G., Saam, C., Harte, N.: Should we hard-code the recurrence concept or learn it instead? Exploring the transformer architecture for audio-visual speech recognition. In: Interspeech (2020)

21. Touvron, H., Cord, M., Douze, M., Massa, F., Sablayrolles, A., Jégou, H.: Training data-efficient image transformers & distillation through attention. In: International Conference on Machine Learning, pp. 10347–10357. PMLR (2021)

22. Touvron, H., Vedaldi, A., Douze, M., Jegou, H.: Fixing the train-test resolution discrepancy. Adv. Neural. Inf. Process. Syst. 32, 8252–8262 (2019)

23. Vaswani, A., et al.: Attention is all you need. In: Advances in Neural Information Processing Systems, pp. 5998–6008 (2017)

24. Wang, H., Zhu, Y., Green, B., Adam, H., Yuille, A., Chen, L.-C.: Axial-deeplab: stand-alone axial-attention for panoptic segmentation. In: Vedaldi, A., Bischof, H., Brox, T., Frahm, J.-M. (eds.) ECCV 2020. LNCS, vol. 12349, pp. 108–126. Springer, Cham (2020). https://doi.org/10.1007/978-3-030-58548-8_7

25. Wang, X., Girshick, R., Gupta, A., He, K.: Non-local neural networks. In: Proceedings of the IEEE Conference on Computer Vision and Pattern Recognition, pp. 7794–7803 (2018)
26. Wu, H., et al.: CvT: introducing convolutions to vision transformers. In: Proceedings of the IEEE/CVF International Conference on Computer Vision, pp. 22–31 (2021)
27. Xie, Q., Luong, M.-T., Hovy, E., Le, Q.V.: Self-training with noisy student improves ImageNet classification. In: Proceedings of the IEEE/CVF Conference on Computer Vision and Pattern Recognition, pp. 10687–10698 (2020)
28. Xu, K., et al.: Show, attend and tell: neural image caption generation with visual attention. In: International Conference on Machine Learning, pp. 2048–2057. PMLR (2015)

Transformers in Automatic Speech Recognition

Marc Evrard[(✉)][iD]

LISN Paris-Saclay, Gif-sur-Yvette, France
marc.evrard@lisn.upsaclay.fr
https://www.lisn.upsaclay.fr

Abstract. The Transformer, a model relying entirely on the attention mechanism, brought significant improvements in performance on several natural language processing tasks. This chapter presents its impact on the speech processing domain and, more specifically, on the automatic speech recognition task. A short history of the evolution of automatic speech recognition systems is also given. A selection of important works making use of transformers are presented, as well as pretraining self-supervised architectures.

Keywords: Transformers · Automatic Speech Recognition (ASR)

1 Introduction

Spoken communication is a fast, natural, and simple way of communicating information that we learn from an early age to make us all experts. It is thus an obvious way of communicating and interacting with a system. In order to transmit the information for further processing, the conversion to text is typically required. This is done through a process called *automatic speech recognition* (ASR). In this chapter, we will focus on the use of the Transformer architecture for ASR systems.

A speech signal contains much more information than its pure verbal aspects. It contains the speaker's voice characteristics. It varies according to the expressivity and psychological state of the speaker, among several other factors. Several variations may occur: the timbre, the vocal quality, the disfluencies, or the prosody (i.e., melody, intensity, rhythm, etc.). Hence, it is a complex mixture of variations. Naturally, we tend to adjust our articulation of each phoneme production according to its direct context, before or after. This phenomenon is called *coarticulation*. Moreover, coarticulation leads to the perception that the signal is continuous. There is thus no obvious segmentation at each phoneme or even word boundary. There is also the problem of rate variation, which induces temporal distortions. Speech information does not only depend on production but also transmission, perception, and understanding constraints, the context variability of acoustic conditions, the attention of the listener, their hearing abilities,

M. Chetouani et al. (Eds.): ACAI 2021, LNAI 13500, pp. 123–139, 2023.
https://doi.org/10.1007/978-3-031-24349-3_8

etc. Besides variation, another challenge arises from the linguistic point of view: homophonies, i.e., when different words are pronounced identically.

This chapter will be presented from a historical perspective. After this introduction, we will start in Sect. 2 with a summary of the history of ASR architectures, long before the advent of Transformers. In Sect. 3, we will describe some prominent solutions designed around Transformers. In Sect. 4, we will talk more generally about Transformers as representations of speech and introduce self-supervised learning in the context of ASR applications.

2   Historical Perspective

2.1   The Prehistory

The 60s: Rule-Based Approach (Dawn of AI). In 1960, Gunnar Fant, a Swedish researcher who specialized in speech synthesis, published the book *Acoustic theory of speech production* [12], which introduced the *source-filter model* of speech production. The source-filter model proposes to approximate speech production as a combination of a sound source, the vocal folds, and a linear filter, the vocal tract. Its simplicity and good approximation allowed the building of robust systems both in speech synthesis and speech recognition applications.

In 1966, Fumitada Itakura (Nagoya University) and Shuzo Saito (Nippon Telegraph and Telephone, NTT) proposed the Linear predictive coding (LPC) method to model speech for speech recognition [41]. LPC is based on the source-filter model approximation, with the assumption that voiced phonemes are produced by a buzzer at the end of a tube. Some other simple noises are included for voiceless consonants (e.g., sibilants and plosives). Despite its simplicity, this model offers a reasonable approximation of speech production in practice.

The 70s: Pattern Recognition (Isolated Words). In 1971, the Advanced Research Projects Agency (ARPA, now DARPA) funded a five-year program to demonstrate the capability of a large-vocabulary-connected speech understanding system. The program led to the birth of the Carnegie Mellon's *Harpy* speech-understanding system in 1976 [31]. It was able to recognize 1011 words through a graph search. It used finite-state machines to represent each word in terms of its phonemes and expanded the result into a network of possible phoneme sequences. Given an input, it performed a probabilistic search through the network, taking into account the acoustic matches between phonemes and segments of the acoustic signal [40].

In 1968, Vintsyuk, a Ukrainian researcher, invented the dynamic time warping (DTW) algorithm [45] to tackle speech recognition by taking into account the variation in speaking speed. The principle was to process speech signals into short frames and align them to those of a reference speech recording of a list of words. Then, using a distance metric, the closest word to the processed signal was selected as the transcription candidate. The success of this approach for the recognition of isolated words illustrates the success of engineering approaches.

2.2 Statistical-Based ASR

The 80s: Statistical Approaches (Continuous Speech). Since the late 70s, James and Janet Baker, a couple of researchers from Carnegie Mellon University (CMU), began using the hidden Markov model (HMM) for speech recognition. The main advantage of the HMM is that it is a doubly stochastic process allowing to take into account both the intrinsic variability of speech and the structure of the language in a unified probabilistic model. James and Janet Baker later founded Dragon systems, which would later develop the first consumer product for speech recognition.

During the same period, Frederick Jelinek and his colleagues at IBM independently discovered the use of HMMs for speech recognition. They built Tangora, a voice-activated typewriter that could handle a 20,000-word vocabulary. Even though HMMs were supposed to be too simplistic to account for the complexity of human languages, their performance on speech recognition tasks surpassed those of rule-based systems built by linguists. Jelinek famously said: *Anytime a linguist leaves the group, the recognition rate goes up.*

A crucial development for speech recognition during the same period is the use of the n-gram language model (LM) that estimates the conditional probability of a word given its previous sequence of n words. In 1987, Katz proposed the back-off model [24] that made the n-gram model practical for generative purposes, despite its sparsity issue. It allowed the smoothing of probabilities by progressively decreasing sequence length when a particular sequence was not present in the training corpus.

The 90s: Birth of Neural Architectures. In 1990, Dragon Systems released *Dragon Dictate*, the first consumer product for speech recognition. It was followed in 1997 by the initial release of the software package *Dragon NaturallySpeaking*, which still exists today and is now owned by Nuance Communications.

In 1992, Lawrence Rabiner and his team at AT&T Bell Laboratories developed the Voice Recognition Call Processing (VRCP), a service to route telephone calls without the intervention of human operators [37].

During the same decade, several critical neural architectures that will allow for speech representation were proposed.

In his diploma thesis at the Technical University of Munich, Sepp Hochreiter, under the supervision of Jürgen Schmidhuber, outlined the initial version of a solution to the vanishing gradient problem in recurrent neural networks (RNN): the Long short-term memory (LSTM) [18]. This architecture will later become the leading architecture used for sequence-to-sequence problems such as machine translation or speech recognition.

In 1995, Yann LeCun, in collaboration with Yoshua Bengio, both also at AT&T Bell Laboratories at that time, developed the Convolutional neural network (CNN) [25], initially in the context of optical character recognition. They also developed a version of the *gradient descent* algorithm for neural networks [26]: *gradient back-propagation*. It allowed breakthrough speed performance in neural networks training convergence.

The 2000s: International Evaluation Campaigns. Since the end of the 90s and through the 2000s, the DARPA and the National Institute of Standards and Technology (NIST) funded and started coordinating annual international assessment campaigns. These campaigns made several large corpora available, such as DARPA, which funded the famous collection of the Switchboard telephone speech corpus. These large corpora, along with the increased performance of computers and algorithms, participated in the steep rise of ASR systems.

2.3   Neural-Based ASR

The 2010s: Introduction of Deep Neural Networks. Neural networks were initially applied mainly to the LM component of ASR systems[1]. However, since 2010, there has been a steady increase in the use of Deep neural network (DNN) architectures for acoustic modeling [17] as well. The use of these architectures led to a significant improvement of speaker-independent ASR. Previously, systems used to require an adaptation training phase to be able to recognize new speakers' voices.

This period also saw the multiplication of free consumer applications, e.g., Apple Siri in 2011, Google Now in 2012, and Microsoft Cortana in 2014.

In 2017, Microsoft announced that the Human parity milestone was reached on the Switchboard conversational speech recognition corpus [48].

Early DNN-Based Architectures. The ASR task aims to find the most likely text sequence Y^* that produced the given audio features X. The acoustic and LMs specify the most likely sequence Y^* explicitly through:

$$Y^* = \underset{Y}{\mathrm{argmax}}\, P(X \mid Y)\, P(Y) \tag{1}$$

The different components required to perform ASR were initially specialized and relied on principles and techniques that were specific to their domain. The idea was to combine state-of-the-art architectures that improve all components of the ASR system when compared to the standard statistical approach (see Fig. 1). Here are examples of papers proposing neural architectures that could be combined as components depicted in Fig. 1:

1. *Learning a better representation of speech sound waves using restricted Boltzmann machines* [20]
2. *Deep neural networks for acoustic modeling in speech recognition* [17]
3. *Grapheme-to-phoneme conversion using Long Short-Term Memory recurrent neural networks* [39]
4. *Recurrent neural network-based language model* [32]

---

[1] For more information on neural networks applied to language modeling, see François Yvon, *Transformers in Natural Language Processing*, Advanced course on Human-Centered AI, Editors Mohamed Chetouani, Virginia Dignum, Paul Lukowicz, and Carles Sierra, Springer Lecture Notes in Artificial Intelligence (LNAI), 2022.

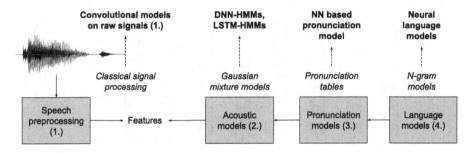

Fig. 1. Example of architecture including state-of-the-art neural-based components, compared to former statistical approach (inspired by Stanford cs224n 2017 class lecture 12).

Since each component is trained independently, according to different objective functions, errors within each component may amplify those in others. Although all components offer good performance for each task they were trained for, their combination may lead to a suboptimal solution.

2.4   End-to-End Approach

A solution to solve the problem of independent component-based ASR architecture would be to train a global end-to-end model, which encompasses all components with a unique objective function [14].

Connectionist Temporal Classification Loss. A challenge of end-to-end models is to find an objective function that can fit the possibly very different structures of the input and output sequences.

Connectionist temporal classification (CTC) [13] is a loss function for training recurrent neural networks in the context of sequence-to-sequence problems where timing may differ between the input and output sequences. It is typically used for tasks such as handwriting recognition, phone-based, or character-based speech recognition.

The principle is to find the best path through a matrix of softmax outputs at each frame targeting the whole dictionary (and a blank token). It can be solved efficiently through a dynamic programming algorithm.

Gradients can be calculated from the CTC scores and be back-propagated to update the neural network weights. As shown in Fig. 2, a softmax is first computed through the network for each feature frame. Figure 3 shows an example of a result of finding the best path through the matrix of softmax at each frame for the word *cat*.

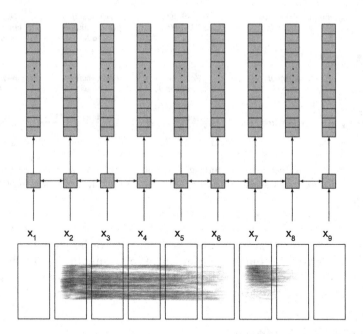

Fig. 2. CTC: A matrix of softmax, corresponding to the token vocabulary probability distribution at each frame (inspired by Stanford cs224n 2017 class lecture 12).

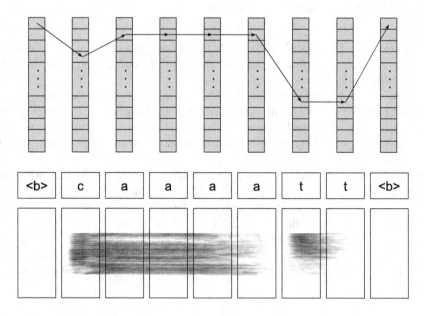

Fig. 3. CTC: Find the best path through the matrix of softmax for the word "cat" (inspired by Stanford cs224n 2017 class lecture 12).

3 Transformers for ASR

3.1 Attention for Speech

Attention in Neural Machine Translation. There is still an issue with end-to-end sequence-to-sentence models. As Raymond Mooney stated during the opening of his invited talk at the ACL-2014 Workshop on Semantic Parsing: *You can't cram the meaning of a whole %&!$# sentence into a single $&!#% vector!*.

The main aim of attention is thus to provide a solution to this sequence-to-sequence bottleneck problem[2]. The core idea of attention is that on each step of the decoder, a direct connection encoder is provided to focus on a particular part of the source sequence. Decoders allow looking directly at the source, bypassing this bottleneck. It thus significantly decreases the vanishing gradient problem by providing shortcuts to distant states.

Attention also allows for some interpretability since one can inspect what the decoder was focusing on through its soft alignment values. At last, this soft alignment allows learning a structure without the need for an explicit loss.

Attention in General. In lecture 7 of his cs224n class at Stanford, Christopher Manning proposes this intuitive general definition of attention:[3]

A technique to compute a weighted sum of vector values, depending on a vector query. The query attends to the values. For example, in the sequence-to-sequence and attention Model, the query vector serves as a hidden state decoder, and the values vector encodes the hidden states.

The attention-weighted sum could be thought of as a selective summary of the information contained in the values, with the query determining which values to highlight. It is a way to obtain a fixed-size representation of a set of representations (the values) depending on some other representation (the query) (see Footnote 2).

Attention in Speech: Listen, Attend and Spell. To the best of our knowledge, the paper "Listen, Attend and Spell" [5] is the first work to implement attention in speech processing. It consists of an ASR system based on a neural network architecture NN that learns to transcribe speech utterances to characters. Unlike traditional DNN-HMM-based models, it learns all components of a speech recognizer jointly.

It is based on two main parts: the *listener* and the *speller*. The listener consists of an RNN, which serves as an encoder. More precisely, it is based on a

---

[2] For more information on the use of attention for language modeling, see François Yvon, *Transformers in Natural Language Processing*, Advanced course on Human-Centered AI, Editors Mohamed Chetouani, Virginia Dignum, Paul Lukowicz, and Carles Sierra, Springer Lecture Notes in Artificial Intelligence (LNAI), 2022.

[3] http://web.stanford.edu/class/cs224n/slides/cs224n-2021-lecture07-nmt.pdf (Stanford cs224n Lecture 7, 2021).

pyramidal bidirectional LSTM (BLSTM) structure. It takes as input sequence the speech expressed as filterbank spectrum (FB) **x** and encodes it into the hidden layer **h**. The speller is an attention-based BLSTM decoder that generates the characters y from the hidden layer **h**.

The attention method is based on a probability distribution. For each output step, the speller LSTM produces a probability distribution over the next character, conditioned on all previous characters, through a *softmax layer*.

3.2   Attention in Speech

Transformers: Why Not Use only Attention? Recurrent sequence-to-sequence models using encoder-decoder architecture yield good performance in speech recognition, but their recurrence process limits the training parallelization, which makes them slow. A solution to improve speed would be to compute speech representation through self-attention instead of recurrent networks, such as LSTM or Gated recurrent unit (GRU). Transformers implement two types of attention: self-attention for representation and encoder-decoder attention [44].

3.3   Transformer-Based ASR Models

Speech-Transformer. An early adaptation of the Transformer architecture for a speech recognition system is the *Speech-Transformer* [9]. It presents minimal changes in the architecture when compared to the original Transformer model. As expressed in the title of the paper, it is thus a sequence-to-sequence model without recursion. It takes as input of the encoder the spectral representation of the speech and produces words as outputs of the decoder.

Two adaptations were necessary to accommodate for speech.

(1) The input embeddings were produced using a CNN layer. This approach notably facilitates the alignment of the speech frames given as input and the output sequence of words, which typically are of different lengths.

(2) The attention mechanism was modified to accommodate the characteristics of the spectral input features. A novel 2D-Attention mechanism is proposed to attend jointly for the time and the frequency axes. As shown in Fig. 4, it still resorts to multi-head attention as in the original model.

Three CNNs are first applied to the spectrograms to build the queries, keys, and values representations independently. Two types of attention are then performed to attend to both temporal and spectral dependencies. The outputs of the 2D-Attention module are finally concatenated and fed into the last CNN layer. The rest of the architecture is similar to the original Transformer model.

The system exhibits slightly lower performance than traditional state-of-the-art models, it seemed to be proposed rather as a proof of concept than as a new architecture with a strongly competitive contribution.

The authors report their evaluation on the Wall Street Journal (WSJ) speech recognition dataset: 10.92% word error rate (WER) for their best model (WSJ, eval92 [35]). The state-of-the-art character-based results without LM and using a conventional sequence-to-sequence model were given by the Very deep convolutional networks model [49] with 10.53%.

Moreover, the training time reported by the authors was of 1.2 days on a single GPU (NVIDIA Tesla K80), while a training time of 5 days on 10 GPUs was reported for the same corpus by Zhang and colleagues [49] (the GPU models were not reported), which seems an impressive improvement. Though, a system based on a combination of CNN and pyramidal BLSTM layers with attention, provided in the ESPnet toolkit and published the same year (2018) [46], reached a WER of 10.1% in just 5 h of training on the same corpus on a single GPU as well.

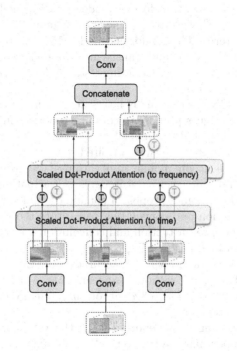

Fig. 4. 2D-Attention mechanism. Circled T's represent transposition operations (Fig. inspired by [9]).

CTC Loss and Transformers. To try to improve the Speech-Transformer model, Karita and colleagues [23] proposed to integrate the CTC loss into the speech transformer architecture.

According to the authors, CTC addresses two problems with transformer-based ASR architectures.

(1) *Slower convergence.* Recent advances in RNN-based ASR systems [19,46] allow for a faster increase in validation accuracy over wall clock time when compared to the Speech-Transformer implementation. If the latter tends to take less time per iteration, it needs many more epochs to converge.

(2) *The complex integration of the LM in joint beam search decoding.* They reported drastically different behaviors between the Speech-Transformer system and the LM component, which made them difficult to combine. CTC joint training and decoding applied to transformer-based ASR architecture made the convergence of the model faster since CTC allows for learning the alignment of speech features and transcription explicitly [13]. A performance increase in terms of WER was also reported: 10.2% on the WSJ without LM (and 4.5% using an LM).

Conformer. So far, we have seen that transformer-based models, as well as mixtures of CNN-RNN models, can be fast while offering state-of-the-art performance. Though, in principle, transformer models are designed to capture global information effectively. However, CNN layers are more capable of extracting fine-grained local patterns. The Conformer model [15] aims to find a parameter-efficient way of combining CNN and transformers to model both local and global dependencies of audio sequences. Conformer stands for *convolution-augmented transformer for speech recognition.*

One limitation of CNN is that many layers are required to capture the global context. Bello and colleagues propose to combine convolution and self-attention to learn both local and global features [4].

The Conformer architecture was inspired by an architecture targeting machine translation tasks on mobile applications [47], using a multi-branch architecture that splits and then concatenates self-attention and convolution branches. Gulati and colleagues propose a combination of self-attention to capture the global interaction and convolution to capture the relative-offset-based local correlations. These self-attention and convolution are sandwiched between a pair of feed-forward modules (see Fig. 5).

The authors report state-of-the-art accuracies on the LibriSpeech benchmark [34]: 2.1% WER (4.3% without using an LM). Moreover, they report a competitive performance of 2.7% (6.3% without using an LM) with a constrained model to 10M parameters.

Unfortunately, no results are reported using the WSJ corpus, although Lee and colleagues [27] report 9.9% WER on the WSJ eval92 test set with a modified version of the Conformer, on which they applied a CTC loss.

4 Transformers as Representations of Speech

In order to obtain state-of-the-art results, ASR models require large transcribed audio corpora. In natural language processing, the BERT model [8] and its clones[4] provide several extended context representations trained on large

---

[4] For more information on Transformers as representations in natural language processing, see François Yvon, *Transformers in Natural Language Processing*, Advanced course on Human-Centered AI, Editors Mohamed Chetouani, Virginia Dignum, Paul Lukowicz, and Carles Sierra, Springer Lecture Notes in Artificial Intelligence (LNAI), 2022.

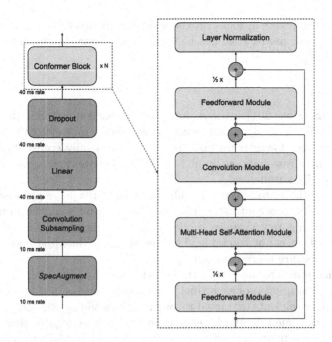

Fig. 5. Conformer encoder model architecture: two feed-forward layers with residual connections (Fig. inspired by [15]).

unlabeled data. These representations can then be used with or without resorting to fine-tuning to perform downstream tasks with usually substantial performance improvements.

The question is: can SSL be effectively applied to speech?

4.1 Self-attention in Speech

The textual representation is a discrete, symbolic form of information. The speech signal is continuous. It thus needs to be discretized to obtain a *spoken element dictionary* and a tractable representation problem. It could be argued that, since speech is sampled and quantized to be stored and processed within a computer, it is in practice discrete rather than continuous. Though, the large number of samples and possible values on, e.g., a 16 bits-scale at 16 kHz, makes the modeling of a given frame impractical.

Different options are proposed to discretize the speech features. Liu and colleagues [29] use a simple *reshape* approach as a downsampling technique. Dong and colleagues, on their Speech-Transformer [9], use CNN layers with a particular stride. On vq-wav2vec [2] and wav2vec 2.0 [3], a vector quantization approach was proposed.

In this section, we will focus on the wav2vec architecture and its evolution since it is the SSL model that has had the most impact in the field of speech processing so far.

4.2 Wav2vec

First Version. Since 2017, various works have tackled speech SSL [6,7,22] and, more recently, Wav2vec [3], which focused primarily on improving the supervised speech recognition downstream task. It consists of a fully convolutional architecture that takes raw audio as input to generate a contextual representation. It can thus be easily parallelized.

Similarly to the word2vec model [33]—in natural language processing applications, it resorts to a contrastive loss to predict future samples from a given context. Predicting raw samples would require the fine modeling of the data distribution, which is not tractable. The raw signal is thus first encoded into a downsampled feature representation.

The model resorts to two CNNs, the encoder and the aggregator. The encoder produces a representation of each time step, which consists in a frame of 80 log-Mel filterbank coefficients extracted through a 25 ms sliding window every 10 ms (100 Hz). At the same rate and for each time step, the aggregator then combines multiple time steps in an aggregated representation. At last, given an aggregated representation, the model is trained to discriminate a sampled representation positioned k steps ahead, from uniformly sampled distractors, by minimizing the contrastive loss.

A low-resource setup is simulated to illustrate the ASR improvement in terms of WER when using the pretrained wav2vec model. The wav2vec model is pretrained on WSJ (81 h) and LibriSpeech (960 h) datasets. The acoustic model performing the ASR task is based on the wav2letter++ [36] system. The baseline is given by using log-Mel filterbanks features. To simulate the low-resources setup, the training set is limited to 8 h out of the 81 h of the WSJ training set (si284). When wav2letter++ is trained on features extracted from the wav2vec pretrained model, the authors report a WER of 9.7%, compared to 15.2% for the baseline (36% increase) on the WSJ eval92 test set. It should be noted that wav2letter++ includes an LM, so the result should not be compared to the results of the models presented in previous sections.

Vector Quantization. The original wav2vec model was purely convolutional. The next version, named vq-wav2vec [2], aimed at taking advantage of SSL transformer-based architecture such as BERT. As explained in Sect. 4.1, speech needs to be discretized to obtain a tractable representation to create speech units that correspond to some sort of *spoken element dictionary*. Hence, vq-wav2vec includes an algorithm that can identify these speech units and learn them on the fly by quantizing the data.

First, as in the original wav2vec model, the 25 ms raw audio chunks are fed into a CNN layer, the encoder, which outputs a speech representation. This representation is then assigned to a fixed inventory of discrete representations that act as labels. These quantized representations are fed in another CNN layer, the aggregator, similarly to the original wav2vec model, to obtain the larger contextual units. Two techniques were investigated to choose the discrete variables: the Gumbel-Softmax approach [21] and the online k-means clustering [10,43].

The quantized representations are treated by the model as if they were word vectors, just like in natural language processing applications. The BERT model is then trained on the representations, and the process becomes identical to the one in a sequence-to-sequence model.

The WER results are reported using vq-wav2vec Gumbel-Softmax and BERT-base model on the WSJ eval92 test set, without resorting to an LM: 9.39%. Using the 4-gram character-based LM [16]: 3.62%. With the convolutional character-based LM (CharConvLM) [28]: 2.34%.

Wav2vec 2.0. The current iteration of the model is named Wav2vec 2.0 [3]. Instead of resorting to the BERT model after the quantization of the representation, Wav2vec 2.0 incorporates its own transformer network. Its architecture allows the model to jointly learn the inventory—using similar techniques as in the vq-wav2vec model—and the context representations through the transformer architecture. It looks at the entire sequence at every 25 ms raw audio frame encoded with the CNN layer.

This version of wav2vec is bidirectional. It still resorts to contrastive losses, but contrary to the vq-wav2vec model, it is not causal. Masked frames are obtained by randomly sampling starting frame positions and expanding the spans to 10 frames in total to obtain large enough chunks of audio (span lengths are 250 ms or larger since span overlaps may occur). The aim is to ensure that the prediction task is not too trivial. The redundancy of speech signals makes the prediction of small chunks too simple. At last, to prevent the collapse case when the model always predicts the same speech unit, a diversity penalty is introduced, using an entropy prior.

To fine-tune the model, a single linear projection is applied to the output of the model and trained using a CTC loss. As in the vq-wav2vec model, the decoder is the wav2letter model using the 4-gram LM, as well as the Transformer LM.

Unfortunately, no results have been reported on the WSJ in Wav2vec 2.0's paper; they instead used the LibriSpeech dev/test sets. The model reaches 1.8/3.3 WER on the clean/other test sets, using all available labeled data of LibriSpeech. In the low-resource condition, it achieves 4.8/8.2 WER with a limit of 10 min of labeled data and 53k hours of pretraining on unlabeled data (Fig. 6).

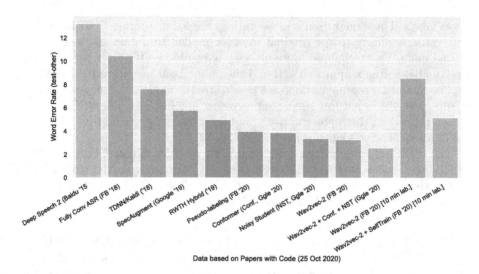

Fig. 6. LibriSpeech benchmark with performance in WER on the test-other dataset (Fig. inspired by [1])

5   Conclusion

After a brief overview of the historical evolution of ASR, a selection of recent transformer-based architectures was presented. Few modifications were necessary to apply the transformer architecture to speech signals. Mainly the segmentation and quantization of the signal, usually through the use of CNN layers and the application of a two-dimensional attention mechanism to attend to both the time and frequency domains.

After several iterations from the earlier implementations, significant improvements are observed for tasks involving a language model, as well as those without any language knowledge input.

Solutions based on self-supervised pretraining exhibit impressive results. However, few experiments have been published yet to reproduce these results on other datasets. One such attempt, LeBenchmark [11], trained their own SSL models for French and evaluated them for different speech tasks, including ASR. If they found that their learned SSL models were particularly beneficial for most low-resource tasks, they reported similar results for end-to-end ASR when compared to more classical approaches based on spectral inputs (Mel Filterbanks).

We are still at the beginning of the study of these architectures; more work is required to understand them better and improve their performances. It is also possible that the research trends are about to turn back to more classical neural networks. In the computer vision field, for instance, several recent works challenge transformer-based to more classical convolutional network approaches [30,38,42].

References

1. Auli, M.: Wav2vec: self-supervised learning of speech representations. Talk at MIT, CMU, U of Edinburgh, Spring 2021 (2021)
2. Baevski, A., Schneider, S., Auli, M.: VQ-wav2vec: self-supervised learning of discrete speech representations. In: International Conference on Learning Representations (2019)
3. Baevski, A., Zhou, Y., Mohamed, A., Auli, M.: Wav2vec 2.0: a framework for self-supervised learning of speech representations. In: Advances in Neural Information Processing Systems, vol. 33, pp. 12449–12460 (2020)
4. Bello, I., Zoph, B., Vaswani, A., Shlens, J., Le, Q.V.: Attention augmented convolutional networks. In: Proceedings of the IEEE/CVF International Conference on Computer Vision, pp. 3286–3295 (2019)
5. Chan, W., Jaitly, N., Le, Q., Vinyals, O.: Listen, attend and spell: a neural network for large vocabulary conversational speech recognition. In: 2016 IEEE International Conference on Acoustics, Speech and Signal Processing (ICASSP), pp. 4960–4964. IEEE (2016)
6. Chorowski, J., Weiss, R.J., Bengio, S., Van Den Oord, A.: Unsupervised speech representation learning using wavenet autoencoders. IEEE/ACM Trans. Audio Speech Lang. Process. 27(12), 2041–2053 (2019)
7. Chung, Y.A., Weng, W.H., Tong, S., Glass, J.: Unsupervised cross-modal alignment of speech and text embedding spaces. In: Advances in Neural Information Processing Systems, vol. 31 (2018)
8. Devlin, J., Chang, M.W., Lee, K., Toutanova, K.: BERT: pre-training of deep bidirectional transformers for language understanding. In: Proceedings of the 2019 Conference of the North American Chapter of the Association for Computational Linguistics: Human Language Technologies, (Long and Short Papers), vol. 1, pp. 4171–4186 (2019)
9. Dong, L., Xu, S., Xu, B.: Speech-transformer: a no-recurrence sequence-to-sequence model for speech recognition. In: 2018 IEEE International Conference on Acoustics, Speech and Signal Processing (ICASSP), pp. 5884–5888. IEEE (2018)
10. Eloff, R., et al.: Unsupervised acoustic unit discovery for speech synthesis using discrete latent-variable neural networks. In: INTERSPEECH (2019)
11. Evain, S., et al.: Lebenchmark: a reproducible framework for assessing self-supervised representation learning from speech. In: INTERSPEECH 2021: Conference of the International Speech Communication Association (2021)
12. Fant, G.: Acoustic Theory of Speech Production. Mouton & Co., The Hague (1960)
13. Graves, A., Fernández, S., Gomez, F., Schmidhuber, J.: Connectionist temporal classification: labelling unsegmented sequence data with recurrent neural networks. In: Proceedings of the 23rd International Conference on Machine Learning, pp. 369–376 (2006)
14. Graves, A., Jaitly, N.: Towards end-to-end speech recognition with recurrent neural networks. In: International Conference on Machine Learning, pp. 1764–1772. PMLR (2014)
15. Gulati, A., et al.: Conformer: convolution-augmented transformer for speech recognition. In: Proceedings of the Interspeech 2020, pp. 5036–5040 (2020)
16. Heafield, K., Pouzyrevsky, I., Clark, J.H., Koehn, P.: Scalable modified Kneser-Ney language model estimation. In: Proceedings of the 51st Annual Meeting of the Association for Computational Linguistics (Volume 2: Short Papers), pp. 690–696 (2013)

17. Hinton, G., et al.: Deep neural networks for acoustic modeling in speech recognition: the shared views of four research groups. IEEE Signal Process. Mag. **29**(6), 82–97 (2012)

18. Hochreiter, S., Schmidhuber, J.: Long short-term memory. Neural Comput. **9**(8), 1735–1780 (1997)

19. Hori, T., Watanabe, S., Zhang, Y., Chan, W.: Advances in joint CTC-attention based end-to-end speech recognition with a deep CNN encoder and RNN-LM. In: Proceedings of the Interspeech 2017, pp. 949–953 (2017)

20. Jaitly, N., Hinton, G.: Learning a better representation of speech soundwaves using restricted Boltzmann machines. In: 2011 IEEE International Conference on Acoustics, Speech and Signal Processing (ICASSP), pp. 5884–5887. IEEE (2011)

21. Jang, E., Gu, S., Poole, B.: Categorical reparameterization with gumbel-softmax. In: ICLR 2017 Conference (2016)

22. Kamper, H., Jansen, A., Goldwater, S.: A segmental framework for fully-unsupervised large-vocabulary speech recognition. Comput. Speech Lang. **46**, 154–174 (2017)

23. Karita, S., Soplin, N.E.Y., Watanabe, S., Delcroix, M., Ogawa, A., Nakatani, T.: Improving transformer-based end-to-end speech recognition with connectionist temporal classification and language model integration. In: Proceedings of the Interspeech 2019, pp. 1408–1412 (2019)

24. Katz, S.: Estimation of probabilities from sparse data for the language model component of a speech recognizer. IEEE Trans. Acoust. Speech Signal Process. **35**(3), 400–401 (1987)

25. LeCun, Y., Bengio, Y., et al.: Convolutional networks for images, speech, and time series. Handb. Brain Theory Neural Netw. **3361**(10), 1995 (1995)

26. LeCun, Y., Bottou, L., Bengio, Y., Haffner, P.: Gradient-based learning applied to document recognition. Proc. IEEE **86**(11), 2278–2324 (1998)

27. Lee, J., Watanabe, S.: Intermediate loss regularization for CTC-based speech recognition. In: 2021 IEEE International Conference on Acoustics, Speech and Signal Processing (ICASSP), ICASSP 2021, pp. 6224–6228. IEEE (2021)

28. Likhomanenko, T., Synnaeve, G., Collobert, R.: Who needs words? Lexicon-free speech recognition. In: Proceedings of the Interspeech 2019, pp. 3915–3919 (2019)

29. Liu, A.T., Yang, S., Chi, P.H., Hsu, P., Lee, H.: Mockingjay: unsupervised speech representation learning with deep bidirectional transformer encoders. In: 2020 IEEE International Conference on Acoustics, Speech and Signal Processing (ICASSP), ICASSP 2020, pp. 6419–6423. IEEE (2020)

30. Liu, Z., Mao, H., Wu, C.Y., Feichtenhofer, C., Darrell, T., Xie, S.: A convnet for the 2020s. In: Proceedings of the IEEE/CVF Conference on Computer Vision and Pattern Recognition, pp. 11976–11986 (2022)

31. Lowerre, B.T.: The Harpy Speech Recognition System. Carnegie Mellon University (1976)

32. Mikolov, T., Karafiát, M., Burget, L., Cernocky, J., Khudanpur, S.: Recurrent neural network based language model. In: Interspeech, vol. 2, pp. 1045–1048. Makuhari (2010)

33. Mikolov, T., Sutskever, I., Chen, K., Corrado, G.S., Dean, J.: Distributed representations of words and phrases and their compositionality. In: Advances in Neural Information Processing Systems, vol. 26 (2013)

34. Panayotov, V., Chen, G., Povey, D., Khudanpur, S.: Librispeech: an ASR corpus based on public domain audio books. In: 2015 IEEE International Conference on Acoustics, Speech and Signal Processing (ICASSP), pp. 5206–5210. IEEE (2015)

35. Paul, D.B., Baker, J.: The design for the wall street journal-based CSR corpus. In: Speech and Natural Language: Proceedings of a Workshop Held at Harriman, New York, 23–26 February 1992 (1992)
36. Pratap, V., et al.: Wav2letter++: a fast open-source speech recognition system. In: 2019 IEEE International Conference on Acoustics, Speech and Signal Processing (ICASSP), ICASSP 2019, pp. 6460–6464. IEEE (2019)
37. Rabiner, L.R.: Applications of speech recognition in the area of telecommunications. In: 1997 IEEE Workshop on Automatic Speech Recognition and Understanding Proceedings, pp. 501–510. IEEE (1997)
38. Raghu, M., Unterthiner, T., Kornblith, S., Zhang, C., Dosovitskiy, A.: Do vision transformers see like convolutional neural networks? In: Advances in Neural Information Processing Systems, vol. 34 (2021)
39. Rao, K., Peng, F., Sak, H., Beaufays, F.: Grapheme-to-phoneme conversion using long short-term memory recurrent neural networks. In: 2015 IEEE International Conference on Acoustics, Speech and Signal Processing (ICASSP), pp. 4225–4229. IEEE (2015)
40. Ringger, E.: A robust loose coupling for speech recognition and natural language understanding. Ph.D. thesis, The University of Rochester (1995)
41. Saito, S., Itakura, F.: The theoretical consideration of statistically optimum methods for speech spectral density. Electrical Communication Laboratory, NTT, Tokyo, Rep 3107 (1966)
42. Trockman, A., Kolter, J.Z.: Patches are all you need? arXiv preprint arXiv:2201.09792 (2022)
43. Van Den Oord, A., Vinyals, O., et al.: Neural discrete representation learning. In: Advances in Neural Information Processing Systems, vol. 30 (2017)
44. Vaswani, A., et al.: Attention is all you need. In: Proceedings of the 31st International Conference on Neural Information Processing Systems, pp. 6000–6010 (2017)
45. Vintsyuk, T.K.: Speech discrimination by dynamic programming. Cybernetics 4(1), 52–57 (1968). Russian Kibernetika 4(1):81–88 (1968)
46. Watanabe, S., et al.: ESPNet: end-to-end speech processing toolkit. In: Proceedings of the Interspeech 2018, pp. 2207–2211 (2018)
47. Wu, Z., Liu, Z., Lin, J., Lin, Y., Han, S.: Lite transformer with long-short range attention. In: International Conference on Learning Representations (2019)
48. Xiong, W., et al.: Achieving human parity in conversational speech recognition. IEEE/ACM Trans. Audio Speech Lang. Process. (2016). https://doi.org/10.1109/TASLP.2017.2756440
49. Zhang, Y., Chan, W., Jaitly, N.: Very deep convolutional networks for end-to-end speech recognition. In: 2017 IEEE International Conference on Acoustics, Speech and Signal Processing (ICASSP), pp. 4845–4849. IEEE (2017)

Interactive Robot Learning: An Overview

Mohamed Chetouani[(✉)] [ID]

Institute for Intelligent Systems and Robotics, CNRS, UMR7222,
Sorbonne University, Paris, France
mohamed.chetouani@sorbonne-universite.fr

Abstract. How do people teach robots tasks? Here, we focus on main methods and models enabling humans to teach embodied social agents such as social robots, using natural interaction. Humans guide the learning process of such agents by providing various teaching signals, which could take the form of feedback, demonstrations and instructions. This overview describes how human teaching strategies are incorporated within machine learning models. We detail the approaches by providing definitions, technical descriptions, examples and discussions on limitations. We also address natural human biases during teaching. We then present applications such as interactive task learning, robot behavior learning and socially assistive robotics. Finally, we discuss research opportunities and challenges of interactive robot learning.

Keywords: Robot learning · Interactive machine learning · Reinforcement learning · Learning from feedback · Learning from demonstrations · Learning from instructions · Human teaching strategies

1 Introduction

Robot learning deals with algorithms, methods and methodologies allowing a robot to master a new task such as navigation, manipulation and classification of objects. At the intersection of machine learning and robotics, robot learning addresses the challenge of task learning, which is defined by a goal (e.g. grasping an object). The aim is to identify a sequence of actions to achieve this goal. Multi-task learning, transfer learning or life-long learning are also considered for this purpose.

Several trends of robot learning take inspiration from human learning by studying developmental mechanisms [61]. In particular, several of such trends focus *social learning* since human learning often occurs in a social context. The computational approaches of social learning are formulated

This work has received funding from European Union's Horizon 2020 ICT-48 research and innovation actions under grant agreement No 952026 (HumanE-AI-Net) and from the European Union's Horizon 2020 research and innovation programme under grant agreement No 765955 (ANIMATAS).

M. Chetouani et al. (Eds.): ACAI 2021, LNAI 13500, pp. 140–172, 2023.
https://doi.org/10.1007/978-3-031-24349-3_9

as an interaction between a tutor/teacher/demonstrator and an artificial learner/student/observer. The aim of the teacher is to influence the behavior of the learning agent by providing various cues such as feedback, demonstrations or instructions. Interactive task learning [56] aims at translating such interactions into efficient and robust machine learning frameworks. Interactive task learning is usually considered to be an alternative to autonomous learning. The latter requires an evaluation function that defines the objective of the task. The robot autonomously learns the task by continuously evaluating its actions using this function. Interactive learning assumes that a human will be able to assist the robot in the evaluation by providing feedback, guidance and/or showing optimal actions. In this chapter, we describe the fundamental concepts of interactive robot learning with the aim of allowing students, engineers and researchers to get familiar with main definitions, principles, methodologies, applications and challenges.

The chapter is structured as follows. Section 2 presents learning objectives, notations, abbreviations and relevant readings. Section 3 provides a background on reinforcement learning and robot learning. Section 4 describes the types of human interventions in both traditional supervised machine learning and interactive machine learning. Section 5 discusses human teaching strategies in interactive robot learning. In Sects. 6 to 8, we provide definitions, describe learning methods and examples as well as limitations of each strategy: feedback (Sect. 6), demonstrations (Sect. 7) and instructions (Sect. 8). Section 9 gives deeper insights about modeling approaches to take into account natural human biases during teaching. Section 10 presents several applications of interactive robot learning: interactive task learning, learning robot behaviors from human demonstrations or instructions, and socially assistive robotics. Finally, in Sect. 11 sums up main observations and describes several opportunities and challenges of interactive robot learning.

2 Tutorial Scope and Resources

2.1 Learning Objectives

- Awareness of the human interventions in standard machine learning and interactive machine learning.
- Understand human teaching strategies
- Gain knowledge about learning from feedback, demonstrations and instructions.
- Explore ongoing works on how human teaching biases could be modeled.
- Discover applications of interactive robot learning.

2.2 Notations

- s, a: state and action, $s \in S$ and $a \in A$.
- a^*: optimal action.

- $H(s,a)$: Human Feedback at state s for robot action a.
- $D = \{(s_t, a_t^*), (s_{t+1}, a_{t+1}^*)....\}$: Human Demonstrations, a state-action sequence.
- $I(s)$: Human Instruction at state s, $Pr_t(a|i)$.
- $Pr(s'|s,a)$: the probability of going from state s to state s' after executing action a.
- $<S, A, T, R, \gamma>$: State & Action spaces, State-Transition probability function $(Pr(s'|s,a))$, Reward function, and the discount factor $([0,1])$.
- $r(s,a)$: reward at state s for action a.
- π: agent/robot policy.
- $V^\pi(s)$: state-value function.
- $Q^\pi(s,a)$: action-value function.

2.3 Acronyms

- AI: Artificial Intelligence
- HRI: Human Robot Interaction
- IML: Interactive Machine Learning
- IRL: Inverse Reinforcement Learning
- ITL: Interactive Task Learning
- LfD: Learning from Demonstrations
- MDP: Markov Decision Process
- ML: Machine Learning
- RL: Reinforcement Learning

2.4 Selected Relevant Readings

- Robot learning from human teachers, Chernova & Thomaz (2014) [21]
- Interactive task learning, Laird et al. (2017) [56]
- Recent advances in leveraging human guidance for sequential decision-making tasks, Zhang et al. (2021) [100]
- Reinforcement Learning With Human Advice: A Survey, Najar & Chetouani (2020) [67]
- Survey of Robot Learning from Demonstration, Argall et al. (2009) [6]
- Recent advances in robot learning from demonstration, Ravichandar et al. (2020) [80]
- A survey on interactive reinforcement learning: Design principles and open challenges, Cruz et al. (2020) [24]
- On studying human teaching behavior with robots: A review, Vollmer & Schillingmann (2018) [96]
- Cognitive science as a source of forward and inverse models of human decisions for robotics and control, Ho & Griffiths (2022) [40]
- Towards teachable autonomous agents, Sigaud et al. (2022) [85].

3 Background

3.1 Fundamentals of Reinforcement Learning

Reinforcement Learning (RL) is a branch of machine learning concerned with how an *autonomous agent* learns sequential decisions in an uncertain environment by maximizing a cumulative reward [87]. This category of problems is modeled as a Markov Decision Process (MDP), which is defined by a tuple $<S, A, T, R, \gamma>$ with S the state space, A the action space, $T : S \times A \rightarrow Pr(s'|s, a)$ state-transition probability function, where $Pr(s'|s, a)$ is the probability of going from state s to state s' after executing action a and $R : S \times A \rightarrow R$ the reward function, which represents the reward $r(s, a)$ that the agent gets for performing action a in state s. The reward function R defines the objective of the task. A discount factor γ ($[0, 1]$) controls of the trade-off between immediate reward and delayed reward. In the reinforcement learning framework, the dynamics of the autonomous agent is captured by the transition function T: at time t, the agent performs an action a_t from state s_t, it receives a reward r_t and transitions to state s_{t+1}.

Example: Figure 1 illustrates the concept of RL in robotics in which the state space describes the environment: position of boxes; action space the possible robot actions: arm motion. After each action, the robot receives a binary reward.

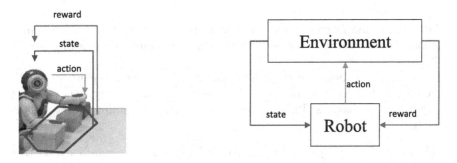

Fig. 1. RL learning framework used to model the environment (state space S), robot actions (action space A) and the task that should be achieved formulated by an MDP (Markov Decision Process). The robot receives a reward R after each action (adapted from [66])

The aim of RL is to find a policy $\pi : S \rightarrow A$ which maps from the state s to a distribution on the action A, this is the decision function. An agent endowed with a policy π will behave in a certain manner to achieve a task. The policy could be either deterministic or stochastic [87]. The optimal policy π^* maximizes agent's long-term rewards. Learning is performed with a trial-and-error strategy. The long-term view is defined by the *state-value function* $V^\pi(s)$, which specifies the expected gain for an agent to be in a particular state s with a policy π. Similarly, the *action-value function* $Q^\pi(s, a)$ defines the expected gain for policy π starting from state s taking action a.

Several algorithms of RL have been proposed (see [87] for an overview). A fundamental problem faced by some of the RL algorithms, is the *dilemma between the exploration and exploitation*. Exploration allows the autonomous agent to gather new information that may improve future reward and consequently the policy (eg., ϵ−greedy approach). The exploitation refers to making the best decision given the current model. Several modern RL algorithms have been proposed to tackle this critical dilemma of exploration and exploitation.

3.2   Robot Learning

RL and Robotics. In [52], the authors discuss the challenges, problems and opportunities of reinforcement learning in the context of robotics. In particular, the physical embodied nature of robots, the nature of tasks and the limited perception of the environment often result in problems that should be represented with high-dimensional continuous states and actions. In addition, these states are not always completely observable. Exploration of actions is costly, difficult to reproduce and sometimes unsafe. The specification of a "good" reward function is not always straightforward and requires a significant amount of domain knowledge.

Human Interventions in the Robot Learning Process. In the context of human-robot interaction, reinforcement learning could be employed for several purposes:

- *Interactive Task Learning.* The aim is to learn to perform tasks with a human involved in the learning process by evaluating and guiding the learning process [92].
- *Learning Communicative Behaviors.* The aim is to learn to generate multimodal robot behaviors such as legible motion (transparency) [16] or select appropriate behaviors during interaction in order to adapt to the human partner [64].

The focus of this chapter is Interactive Task Learning. We consider tasks that are performed by embodied agents in the physical world or in a simulation of it. Such agents could use their sensors and effectors to both perform the task and communicate with the human: manipulating an object, pointing to indicate an object. This chapter discusses the role of interaction in the agent/robot learning process.

Communication in the Robot Learning Process. Human interventions could enrich task learning in the form of teaching signals to guide the learning process such as gaze at objects or spoken language for feedback. Demonstration of a task is an interesting paradigm since it gathers action and communication about it at the same time. Similarly, robot communication using transparency and explainability mechanisms of robots could include both task and communicative goals directed actions. For example, generation of legible motions [28,98] facilitates human interpretation of the robot task.

The objective of a task could be to communicate. For example to address the symbol grounding problem [88], both physical and social symbol grounding, there is a need for agent to connect sensory and symbolic representations in order to be able to process them, reason about them, generate new concepts and communicate with humans in particular.

The distinction between task achievement and communication is not always easy and sometimes not relevant at all. However, being able to qualify the goal of learning is important for interactive and autonomous agents. For this purpose, interactive learning is conceptualized as a mutual exchange process using two main communication channels, the social channel and the task channel with valuable interpretations of several learning strategies from: observation, demonstration, instruction or feedback [85].

4   Interactive Machine Learning vs. Machine Learning

The purpose of this section is to introduce the main concepts of interactive machine learning. Reviewing all the mechanisms of interactive machine learning is beyond the scope of this chapter. However, understanding the impact of human interventions during the learning process is important for the content of this chapter. For this purpose and for a sake of clarity, we only discuss the human interventions on both the traditional and interactive machine learning processes.

4.1   Human Interventions in the Supervised Machine Learning Process

Human interventions are already present in the traditional machine learning process (Fig. 2). The obvious case is *human machine interaction*: the objective is to support end-users interaction. However, in most of the machine learning approaches, humans are present at different stages. They could provide data, annotations, design the algorithms, evaluate the model, design the interaction and interact with it (Fig. 2). These interventions are made by different profiles: users, domain expert, machine learning expert, human-machine expert and end-users and at different steps corresponding to different time scales in the process: data collection, annotation, data analysis, algorithm design, interaction design, model training and evaluation and final end-user model interaction. The impacts of such interventions are of different natures.

Example: Human emotion recognition systems require data and annotations to build robust and efficient systems. Data collection is a key phase and usual approaches rely either on acted or real-life scenarios. In addition, various methodologies have been proposed to annotate emotions with different representations (discrete vs. dimensional). Self-assessment (e.g., asking the data provider for annotation) or assessment from an external observer [1]. All these methodological and experimental choices impact the design, performance and robustness of the emotion recognition system.

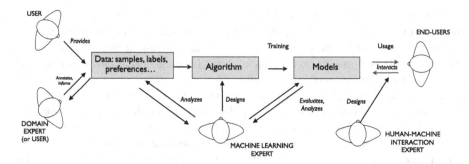

Fig. 2. Humans in the Machine Learning Process. Data Providers, Domain, Machine Learning and Human-Machine Interaction Experts as well as End-Users play a key role in the machine learning process.

4.2   Human Interventions in the Interactive Machine Learning Process

Interaction with humans is at the core of the Interactive Machine Learning (IML) process [4]: from the design to the usage (Fig. 3). There is a growing interest for IML for several applications: web recommendation, e-mail processing, chatbots or rehabilitation. *Interactive Machine Learning* is at the intersection of *Machine Learning* and *Human-Computer/Machine Interaction.*

Human interventions are of different nature. While in traditional ML (Fig. 2), it is usual to collect and process very large datasets with multiple users, interactive ML relies on the interaction with the end-user to collect data. The training, evaluation and usage phases are intrinsically linked, which requires specific approaches for the design of both algorithms and interactions.

Interestingly, interactive ML opens new ways of lifelong learning, adaptation and personalization of models, which could improve usage and trust. However, having humans at the center of the process also raises several ethical questions [56,84] that should be addressed including the definition of requirements to develop human-centric AI that minimizes negative unintended consequences on individuals and on the society as a whole [30,57].

Interactive Robot Learning approaches are grounded in Interactive ML [21]. The embodied nature of robots make the researchers to also take inspiration from human social learning [92] or even modeling its key mechanisms of child development as done in developmental robotics [61,85]. In the following sections, we will describe human's teaching strategies and how they are represented and modeled to fit interactive machine learning frameworks.

5   Overview of Human Strategies

In this section, we give an overview of the main strategies employed by humans to teach robots. We consider the situation in which a human provides teaching

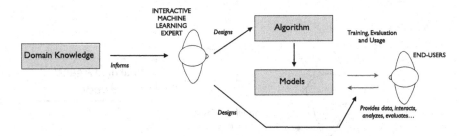

Fig. 3. Humans in the Interactive Machine Learning Process. End-users are both data providers and model evaluators. Designing the interaction is as important as designing the models. The Expert becomes an *Interactive Machine Learning Expert.*

signals to a learning agent (Fig. 4). Teaching signals could take different forms (e.g., demonstration, instruction) and are at the core of the human teaching strategy. Most of these strategies assume that humans are rational intentional agents, optimal with respect to their decisions, actions and behaviors. The concept of intention is used to characterize both the human's actions and mental states [13]. In case of interactive robot learning, this means that humans provide teaching signals with an intention, which is translated into a sequence of actions aiming at influencing the robot learning.

In Table 1, we describe the main teaching signals considered in human-robot interaction: *feedback, demonstration and instruction.* They are respectively used to communicate specific intentions: evaluating/correcting, showing and telling. Social and task channels are employed to communicate intentions (Fig. 4). Instructions, gaze or pointing are considered as being conveyed by the social channel. Manipulation of objects to demonstrate a task exploit the task channel. These channels could be combined and exploited by both the human and the robot during the learning process.

The learning agent needs to infer human's intention from the teaching signals. However, intentions are not explicit. Ambiguities could occur during communication. Humans could also intentionally deviate from optimality and apparently behave as non-rational agents (Sect. 9). The most common strategies are certainly to learn new tasks by providing feedback, demonstration or instructions (Table 1). In the following sections, we propose definitions, mathematical formulations and discuss interpretations and teaching/learning costs of such strategies.

6   Feedback

6.1   Representation

Human feedback $H(s, a)$ is considered as an observation about the reward $r(s, a)$. Binary and Real-valued quantities have been considered in interactive reinforcement learning.

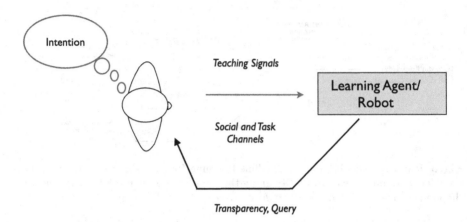

Fig. 4. Interactive Robot Learning Paradigm: The Human Teacher provides Teaching signals using Social and/or Task Channels. Teaching signals are performed with an intention. The Learning Agent/Robot infers the intention from the teaching signal and exploits them to learn a task. Learning agents could improve learning by increasing transparency and/or asking for additional information (e.g., labels, features).

Table 1. Description of main Human Teaching Strategies. Robot action is performed at time-step t. A teaching signal is the physical support of the strategy using social and/or task channels.

Teaching signals		Feedback	Demonstration	Instruction
Nature	Notation	$H(s,a)$	$D = \{(s_t, a_t^*), (s_{t+1}, a_{t+1}^*)....\}$	$I_\pi(s) = a_t^*$
	Value	Binary/Scalar	State-Action pairs	Probability of an action
Time-step	$t-1$		✓	✓
	t		✓	
	$t+1$	✓		
Human	Intention	Evaluating/Correcting	Showing	Telling
	Teaching cost	Low	High	Medium
Robot	Interpretation	State-Action evaluation Reward-/Value-like	Optimal actions Policy-like	Optimal action Policy-like
	Learning cost	High	Low	High

6.2 Definition

Human feedback H is produced at $t + 1$, after the evaluation of the robot's action (Table 1). Human feedback is provided with the intention of evaluating the robot's action (critique). Human Feedback is considered to communicate about the performance of a robot's action. Human feedback is usually termed as *evaluative feedback*: the human observes the states s_t and s_{t+1} and the last robot action a and then gives a reward signal. The value of the evaluative feedback depends on the last action performed by the robot.

Teaching with evaluative feedback is a low cost strategy (Table 1). The actions are performed by the robot using exploration algorithms. The human only delivers feedback on the observed actions. However, intervention at each time-step is not realistic and imposes a significant burden on the human teacher. This calls for new algorithms able to efficiently integrate human feedback during learning.

6.3   Learning from Evaluative Feedback

An intuitive way is to remove the reward function R from the reinforcement approach for task specification (Sect. 3). This results in an $MDP \backslash R$, an MDP without a reward function. The reward is then replaced by the human feedback. Understanding human's feedback strategy has been the focus of several works [42, 47, 68, 90]. They all highlight the importance of understanding human's intentions and the design of adequate algorithms for the exploitation of teaching signals. To efficiently learn from human feedback, there is a need to go beyond just considering the human feedback as a reward and eventually combining it with the reward of the environment.

The usual approach is to design models of human feedback that are able to capture specific properties of human strategies. This leads to various integration strategies of Human feedback H into RL systems. There is no clear agreement on the many ways of achieving this integration but the main approaches rely on shaping such as:

- Human feedback H as a reward r: *reward shaping*
- Human feedback H as a value V or Q: *value shaping*
- Human feedback H as a policy π: *policy shaping*

We detail the approaches that result from three different interpretations of human feedback. They all consider shaping as a method to influence the agent behavior towards a desired behavior [49, 68, 69].

6.4   Reward Shaping

Human feedback is interpreted as a reward (Table 1). When the agent interacts with its environment, modeled as a Markov Decision Process (MDP), it receives a reward $r(s, a)$ and an additional reward shaping reward $H(s, a)$:

$$r'(s, a) = r(s, a) + \beta * \hat{H}(s, a). \tag{1}$$

where β, a decaying weight factor, controls the contribution of human feedback $H(s, a)$ over the environment reward $r(s, a)$.

The reward $r(s, a)$ is first augmented by the human feedback $\hat{H}(s, a)$. Then, the augmented reward $r'(s, a)$ is used to shape the agent. This is usually considered as an indirect shaping approach [68, 77].

6.5   Value Shaping

Human feedback is interpreted as a human value function (Table 1). The human evaluates the action by providing a rating of the current agent's action with respect to some forecast of future behavior [23, 43, 48, 68, 100]. This rating is employed to augment the action-value function $Q(s, a)$. Shaping method have been considered in the literature [68]:

$$Q'(s, a) = Q(s, a) + \beta * \hat{H}(s, a), \tag{2}$$

where β is a decaying weight factor (see also Eq. 1).

Other approaches consider an estimation of the human value function as done in TAMER [49] (Sect. 6.7).

6.6   Policy Shaping

Human feedback is still interpreted as a value (Table 1) but employed to directly influence the agent's policy [68, 77, 100]. Two main methods have been considered so far [50]:

– Action biasing: The shaping is only performed during the decision-making step. The value function is not directly perturbed by the human feedback augmentation:

$$a^* = \arg\max[Q(s, a) + \beta * \hat{H}(s, a)], \tag{3}$$

– Control sharing: This method arbitrates between the MDP policy and human value function. The human policy derived from feedback is used for action selection given the probability β:

$$Pr\left[a = \arg\max\left(\hat{H}(s, a)\right)\right] = \min(\beta, 1) \tag{4}$$

Other approaches have been proposed in the literature such as combination of policies using multiplication of probability distributions [36, 69, 78]. COACH (Convergent Actor-Critic by Humans) algorithm [62] is motivated by the observation that human policy is influenced by learner's current policy. The authors argue that *the advantage function* [87] is a good model of human feedback. They use actor-critic algorithms to compute an unbiased estimate of the advantage function.

6.7   Example: The TAMER Architecture

The TAMER architecture (Training an Agent Manually via Evaluative Reinforcement) [49] assumes that the human has an internal function H that maps observed agent action in a feedback (negative, neutral or positive). The human has in mind a desired policy π_H and wants to communicate it to the agent through feedback. In other words, TAMER estimates human's intention (Table 1) from the observation of feedback. The internal function H is called the "Human

Reinforcement Function". TAMER approximates the human internal function by a regression model $\hat{H}^*$ trough minimizing a standard squared error loss between $H(s_t, a_t)$ and $\hat{H}(s_t, a_t)$. TAMER is formulated as an MPD without a reward ($MDP\backslash R$). The agent uses this function to perform action selection:

$$\pi(s) = \arg\max_a \hat{H}^*(s, a) \tag{5}$$

TAMER interprets Human feedback as a value. In [51], the authors address delays in human evaluation (human's feedback) through credit assignment, which includes creation of labels from delayed reward signals. TAMER has been successfully combined with Reinforcement learning (TAMER+RL) [50] and recently Deep Learning (Deep TAMER) in order to deal with high-dimensional state spaces [99].

6.8 Limitations

Understanding human feedback strategies is essential in the design and development of learning from evaluative feedback algorithms. Previous works have identified numerous issues such as:

- *Credit assignment problem*: humans provide feedback with a delay by considering actions happened in the past [24].
- *Policy dependent*: humans' feedback strategy is influenced by learner's current policy [62].
- *Positively biased feedback*: positive and negative feedback are not employed in the same way by humans [43,89]. Whether providing both positive and negative rewards is necessary is an open question [77].
- *Reward hacking*: this describes situations in which non anticipated actions are introduced by the agent in order to obtain a positive human feedback. Several works show that is difficult to anticipate failure behaviors aroused from reward functions [24,77].
- *Autonomous/self agent exploration vs social interaction*: relying only on human feedback is not efficient and imposes a significant burden on the human teacher. Current trends combine agent exploration and human feedback in order to improve robustness to sparse and/or erroneous teaching signals.

Current and future works of the domain are addressing such issues by both conducting human studies as well as developing new machine learning algorithms and human-machine interaction designs.

7 Demonstrations

7.1 Representation

Human demonstrations D are usually represented by a state-action sequence (Table 1): $\{(s_t, a_t^*).\}$. Where a_t^* is the optimal human action at time-step t given a state s_t.

7.2 Definition

A demonstration D is produced by the human demonstrator with the intention of *showing a state-action sequence to the robot* (Table 1). The paradigm assumes that the human expert shows the optimal actions a_t^* for each state. The state-action sequence is then reproduced by the robot.

The identification of a mapping between the human teacher and robot learner actions, which allows the transfer of information from one to the other, is called the *correspondence problem* [6]. Contrary to evaluative feedback, demonstrations could be provided before (time-step $t-1$) or simultaneously (time-step t) to robot actions (Table 1).

7.3 Methods

Teaching with a demonstration strategy imposes a significant burden on the human teacher. The assumption is that the human teacher is being able to perform the task in order to communicate optimal actions a_t^* through the task channel (see Fig. 4). The set of demonstrations are interpreted as a human policy of the task (π_h) (Table 1). For such reasons, *Interaction Design* plays an important role in learning from demonstrations (see Fig. 3). Three general methods are usually considered in the literature [80]: *kinesthetic, teleoperation and observation*.

Kinesthetic demonstration is an example of simultaneous teacher-learner interactions through demonstrations, in which the teacher directly manipulates the robot. This approach eliminates the correspondence problem and simplifies the machine learning process. Several industrial robots are now proposing this approach to facilitate task learning (Sect. 10). Kinesthetic demonstration facilitates the mapping and it facilitates the production of human demonstrations. However, the quality of demonstrations is known to be low as it depends on the dexterity and smoothness of the human demonstrator during the manipulation of the robot [80]. With teleoperation, the human demonstrator can provide demonstrations of robots with high degrees-of-freedom (HOF) as well as facilitating mapping. However, teleoperation requires the development of specific interfaces (including virtual/augmented reality) [80]. Observation of human demonstrations offers a natural interaction mode to the users. However, learning from demonstrations by observation of human actions using a camera or a motion capture is not sufficient to compute the mapping. Several challenges of machine perception are faced including motion tracking, occlusion or high degrees-of-freedom of human motion.

7.4 Learning from Demonstrations

Demonstration facilitates engagement of non-expert users in robot programming. They can teach new tasks by showing examples rather than programming them (see Sect. 10). Interest in learning from demonstrations is shown by the number of publications in recent years (see [80] for an overview), resulting also in various terminologies: *imitation learning, programming by demonstration, behavioral cloning and Learning from Demonstrations (LfD)*.

The challenge of learning from demonstrations in robotics has been addressed by methods and models of supervised, unsupervised and reinforcement learning. In [6], the authors argue that LfD could be seen as a subset of Supervised Learning. The robot is presented with human demonstrations (labeled training data) and learns an approximation to the function which produced the data. In the following, we discuss two different perspectives: (i) behavioral cloning (supervised learning) and sequential decision-making (reinforcement learning). Inverse Reinforcement Learning (IRL) is presented as an example in Sect. 7.7.

7.5   Behavioral Cloning

Behavioral cloning employs supervised learning methods to determine a robot policy that imitates the human expert policy. This is performed by minimizing the difference between the learned policy and expert demonstrations (state-action pairs) with respect to some metric (see Algorithm 1).

Algorithm 1. Behavioral Cloning

1: **procedure** BEHAVIORAL CLONING
2:      Collect a set of expert demonstrations $D = \{(s_t, a_t^*), (s_{t+1}, a_{t+1}^*)...\}$
3:      Select an agent policy representation π_θ
4:      Select a loss function L
5:      Optimize L using supervised learning: $L(a^*, \pi_\theta(s, a))$
6:      Return π_θ

A series of recommendations are made in [75] regarding nature of demonstrations (trajectory, action-state space), choice of Loss Functions (quadratic, l_1, log, hinge and Kullback-Leibler divergence) and supervised learning methods (regression, model-free and model-based).

7.6   Imitation Learning as a Sequential Decision-Making Problem

In [81], the authors argue that imitation learning could not be addressed as a standard supervised learning problem, where it is assumed the training and testing data are independent and identically distributed (i.i.d). They show that imitation learning is a *sequential decision-making problem*. For this reason, reinforcement learning techniques and interactive supervision techniques have been considered to address imitation learning.

7.7   Example: Inverse Reinforcement Learning

Inverse Reinforcement Learning (IRL) [70] is a popular approach in imitation learning. IRL aims to recover an unknown reward function given a set of demonstrations and then to find the optimal policy (conditioned by the learned reward function) using reinforcement learning (see Fig. 5).

IRL methods consider the set of expert's demonstrations as *observations of the optimal policy* π^*. Interpretation of demonstrations follows a *policy-like* vision (Table 1). From a set of demonstrations, the goal of IRL is to estimate the unknown reward function parameters of a policy $\hat{\pi}^*$ that imitates expert's policy π^*. The reward function is then analyzed to understand and/or to explain the expert's policy. Standard IRL algorithms consider the reward function as a linear combination (ψ^T) of features $f(s, a)$ of the environment:

$$r_\psi(s, a) = \psi^T f(s, a) \tag{6}$$

This approach assumes that the expert is acting accordingly in the environment. Modern approaches consider non-linear combinations using neural network based estimators of $r_\psi(s, a)$. IRL is an ill-posed problem since there are infinitely many reward functions consistent with the human expert's demonstrations.

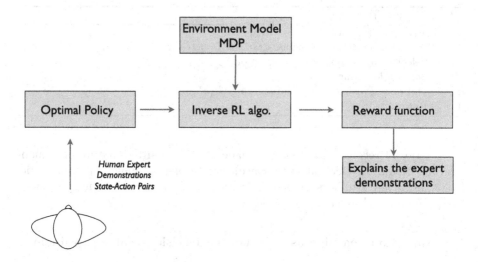

Fig. 5. Inverse Reinforcement Learning (IRL): Human expert provides demonstrations (state-action pairs). Demonstrations are interpreted as a policy. The goal of IRL is to compute the underlying reward function from the demonstrations.

7.8   Limitations

LfD methods assume that the demonstrations, state-action pairs (s_t, a_t^*), are the only teaching signals available to the learner (Table 1). After human demonstrations recording, the learner attempts to learn the task using these teaching signals. This approach has been formulated as an MDP without a reward function $(MDP\backslash R)$. As previously mentioned, demonstrations could be interpreted as a *human policy* π_h (Table 1). Similarly to learning from evaluative feedback, a current challenge of LfD is to *include other forms of rewards* in the learning, in particular those computed from environment and/or intrinsic motivations [85].

As discussed in [80], the *choice of learning methods* is compelling: (i) the optimal behavior cannot be scripted, (ii) the optimal behavior is not always easily defined in the form of a reward function, and (iii) the optimal behavior is only available through human teacher demonstrations. This leads to several challenges at the intersection of machine learning (e.g. learning methods), robotics (e.g. control of physical robots) and human-robot interaction (e.g., human factors, interaction design). In [75], a series of questions summarizes the current challenges of imitation learning:

- *Why and when should imitation learning be used?*
- *Who should demonstrate?*
- *How should we record data of the expert demonstrations?*
- *What should we imitate?*
- *How should we represent the policy?*
- *How should we learn the policy?*

Answering these questions is required for the design of imitation learning based systems (more details are available in [75]).

8 Instructions

8.1 Representation

Human instructions are usually represented as a probability distribution over actions: $Pr_t(a|i)$ and $a \in A$.

8.2 Definition

An instruction is produced by the human with the intention of communicating the action to be performed in a given task state (Table 1). This could be formulated as *telling*, which is a language based perspective of the interaction. Examples of instructions could be *turn left, pick up the object* or *go forward*.

Telling offers other opportunities to the teacher compared to *evaluating* (feedback) and *showing* (demonstration). A recent work of [86] studies how humans teach concepts using either demonstrations or language. The results suggest that language communicates more complex concepts by directly transmitting abstract rules (e.g., shapes and colors), while demonstrations transmit positive examples (e.g. manipulation of objects) and feedback evaluates actions. Inferring rules from demonstrations or feedback is supposed to be more complex.

Instructions are of different nature and are produced with different intentions grouped in the notion of *advice* [68]: guidance, critique, action advice. In [54], two different methods are compared: critique and action advice. In the critique based teaching method, the learning agent is trained using positive and negative verbal critiques, such as *good job*, and *don't do that*. As described in Sect. 6, such verbal critiques are binary feedback. In the action advice based teaching method, the learner is trained using action advice such as *move right* and *go left*. The authors show that action advice creates a better user experience compared to an agent that learns from binary critique in terms of frustration, perceived performance, transparency, immediacy, and perceived intelligence.

8.3   Learning from Instructions

Learning from instructions is formulated as *mapping instructions (often in natural language) to a sequence of executable actions* [12,60]. Mutual understanding (human/learning agent) of the meaning of instructions is usually assumed, which obviously facilitates the *instruction-to-action mapping*. The usual approach is to pre-define the mapping, which raises with several issues such as engineering and calibration phases [37,68], adaptation and flexibility [37,68], intermediate semantic representation [2,63,88], and reward inference from language [58].

We could distinguish between methods that focus on simple commands and the ones addressing sequence of instructions. The latter are employed to compose complex robot/agent behaviors with the interventions of a human teacher [27, 76,82]. In [27], the authors describe a Spoken Language Programming (SLP) approach that allows the user to guide the robot through an arbitrary, task relevant, motor sequence via spoken commands, and to store this sequence as a re-usable macro. Most of these approaches model the task through a graph [88].

Learning from instructions has been combined with learning from demonstrations [72,82] and evaluative feedback (critique) [54]. In [25], the authors combine reinforcement learning, inverse reinforcement learning and instruction based learning using policy shaping through action selection guidance. During training, an external teacher is able to formulate verbal instructions that will change a selected action to be performed in the environment. The results indicate that interaction helps to increase the learning speed, even with an impoverished Automatic Speech Recognition system.

8.4   Example: The TICS Architecture

The TICS architecture (Task-Instruction-Contingency-Shaping) [69] combines different information sources: a predefined reward function, human evaluative feedback and unlabeled instructions. Dealing with unlabeled instructions denotes that the meaning of the teaching signal is unknown to the robot. There is a lack of mutual understanding. TICS focuses on grounding the meaning of teaching signals (instructions).

TICS architecture enables a human teacher to shape a robot behavior by interactively providing it with unlabeled instructions. Grounding is performed during the task-learning process, and used simultaneously for guiding the latter (see Fig. 6).

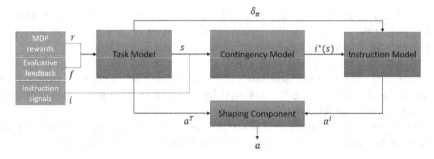

Fig. 6. The TICS architecture includes four main components: a Task Model learns the task, a Contingency Model associates task states with instruction signals, an Instruction Model interprets instructions, and a Shaping Component combines the outputs of the Task Model and the Instruction Model for decision-making (adapted from [69]).

Finally, TICS combines:

- standard RL with a predefined reward function (MDP rewards),
- learning from evaluative feedback based on policy shaping approach,
- learning from instructions, which are represented as a policy.

The Contingency Model plays a key role in grounding and it is defined for a given state as a probability distribution over detected teaching signals. In [69], a co-occurrence matrix is employed to estimate this probability distribution. TICS enables human teachers to employ unlabeled instructions as well as evaluative feedback during the interactive learning process. The robot is also learning from its own experience using the predefined reward function. The results show that in addition to the acceleration of learning, TICS offers more adaptability to the preferences of the teacher.

8.5 Limitations

Learning from instructions suffers from similar limitations as learning from evaluative feedback and demonstrations. Here, we report some specific limitations:

- *Speech recognition*: Instructions are usually provided through natural spoken language. Speech recognition is challenging in human-robot interaction contexts. Most of the approaches are impacted by the performance of speech recognition systems [25, 27, 76].
- *Instruction-to-action mapping*: Learning from instructions is mainly formulated as an instruction-to-action mapping. Going beyond engineering based approaches requires to address the Symbol Grounding problem [39], which facilitates the correspondence between natural language instructions and agent actions [2, 69]
- *Descriptions and Explanation*: Instructions explicitly communicate about robot/agent actions by either advise or critique. Language allows other forms

of teaching such as explanations [74,93] and descriptions [22,71]. Counterfactual explanations evaluate what would happen if an alternative action is performed. There is a less restrictive nature in a description.

- *Pragmatics*: Natural language conveys more than the literal interpretation of words [35]. There is an increasing interest in the introduction of pragmatics in interactive learning, often inspired by research in linguistics and cognitive science [18,34,38,41].
- *Emotions*: Spoken language is also employed to communicate emotions, which have to be taken into account for interpretation of instructions [53].

Most of these limitations call for methods able to handle uncertainty of spoken natural language in order to build efficient interactive robot/agent learning methods.

9   Modeling Human Teaching Strategies

Interactive robot learning is a joint activity allowing robots to learn a task by exploiting observable human behaviors (Fig. 3). Most of the methods assume the observation of *overt teaching signals* such as feedback, demonstrations and/or instructions. The *decoding phase*, i.e. interpretation of teaching signals (Table 1), is usually pre-specified by designers and engineers. This approach does not consider *covert communication* such as intentions, beliefs, goals, emotions or attitudes. Humans change their behavior in response to the actions of the robot they are interacting with. Several works have shown that people modify their tutoring behavior in robot-directed interaction [14,47,90,91,95]. When humans demonstrate a task to another human or agent, the demonstrations are directed not just towards the objects that are manipulated (*instrumental action*), but they are also accompanied by *ostensive communicative cues* such as eye gaze and/or modulations of the demonstrations in the space-time dimensions (*belief-directed action*). This modulation results in behaviors that might appear to be sub-optimal, such as pause, repetition and exaggeration, while they are the result of simultaneous instrumental and belief-directed actions, i.e. *performing the action and communicating about it*.

To address such limitations, several research directions have been proposed. For example, *computer vision and signal processing techniques* are largely employed in human-robot interaction for the analysis and modeling non-verbal cues (e.g. tone of the voice, gesture, facial expressions, gaze) in order to infer human's mental states, intentions, engagement, emotions and attitudes [5,94]. Another research direction focuses on *human-decision making* by studying forward models of human decision-making and inverse models of how humans think about others decision-making [40]. The approaches draw inspiration from research on how humans interpret observed behaviors as *goal-directed actions* and address the *challenge of communication in action* [40]: actor intends to not just perform the ordinary action, but also to convey something about it. In [40], a general mathematical framework of probabilistic inference and decision-making has been proposed to characterize the underlying beliefs, intentions and goals of communicative demonstrations. The framework is largely inspired by language in which literal interpretation and pragmatic inference of linguistic and paralinguistic content are performed. These approaches exploit models and methodologies of computational cognitive science and behavioral economics making them relevant for interactive machine learning. How humans make decisions reveal their beliefs, intentions and goals. In the following, we describe some examples of natural human teaching biases (Sect. 9.1) and a Bayesian approach of modeling human decisions (Sect. 9.2).

9.1 Natural Human Teaching Biases

Human teaching biases have been observed in several situations. In Sect. 6.8, we described several natural biases of human feedback strategies, which include delay in feedback delivery [24], influence of robot actions [62] and a tendency to generate more positive feedback than negative ones [89]. Natural deviations to optimal behaviors also occur during communicative demonstrations. In [42], the authors showed the differences in behavior when a human trainer is intentionally teaching (*showing*) versus merely *doing* the task. All these studies call for new methods that go beyond naive and literal interpretations of teaching signals (Table 1) such as *evaluating/correcting, showing and telling*.

Learning situations with children have inspired robotics researchers for the study of natural human biases during teaching others. We describe two dimensions of interest in human-robot interaction: (i) *modulation of non-verbal teacher behaviors in the space-time dimensions* (ii) *teacher training strategy*.

Non-verbal Teacher Behaviors Modulation. Human teaching situations are characterized by significant changes in various adult behaviors such as prosody (*motherese* [83]) or motion (*motionese*). In [95], the authors compared Adult-Child/Adult-Adult/Adult-Robot Interactions. They identified significant differences in hand movement velocity, motion pauses, range of motion, and eye gaze in an Adult-Child Interaction, opposed to an Adult-Adult Interaction. This decrease is even higher in the Adult-Robot Interaction.

There is a large body of research in cognitive science showing that humans are specifically efficient in the communication of generic knowledge to other individuals. This ability has been described in [26] as a communication system called the *'Natural Pedagogy'*. This work and others show that humans seem inherently sensitive to *ostensive communicative signals* such as eye gaze, gesture as well as tone of the voice. In particular, these works show that contingency of ostensive signals is a natural characteristic of social interaction in humans, which has inspired several studies of human teaching behavior [96].

Teacher Training Strategy. Interactive learning requires that human teachers organize the way they provide training examples to the robot. They select which examples to present and in which order to present them to the robot in the form of instructions, demonstrations and/or feedback. Organization of a training strategy is termed *curriculum learning* [8], which is a key element in human teaching. Several human curriculum learning strategies have been observed and often result in gradually increasing the level of task complexity, i.e. presentation of simple examples then more complex examples. AI and Machine learning techniques have been derived from this notion of curriculum learning with the idea that guiding training will significantly increase the learning speed of artificial agents. Several works are focusing on the question of how to effectively teach agents with the emergence of *computational machine teaching* as an inverse problem of machine learning [101].

Example: In [46], the authors conduct a study in which participants are asked to teach a robot the concept of "graspability", i.e. if an object can be grasped or not with one hand. To teach the binary task (graspable vs. not graspable), the participants are provided several cards with photos of common objects (e.g., food, furniture, and animals). They have to pick up the cards from the table and show them to the robot while teaching them the concept of "graspability". The authors observed three different human teaching strategies [46]: (1) the extreme strategy, which starts with objects with extreme ratings and gradually moves toward the decision boundary; (2) the linear strategy, which follows a prominent left-to-right or right-to-left sequence; and (3) the positive-only strategy, which involves only positively labeled examples. Building up on such observations, they propose a computational framework as a potential explanation for the teaching strategy that follows a curriculum learning principle.

In [91], observation of various human teaching strategies raised the following question: can we influence humans to teach optimally? The authors developed Teaching Guidance algorithms that allow robots to generate instructions for the human teacher in order to improve their input. They performed experiments to compare human teaching with and without teaching guidance and show that Teaching Guidance substantially improves the data provided by teachers. The experiments demonstrate that humans are not spontaneously as good as computational teachers.

9.2   A Noisily-Rational Decision Model

A more accurate model of human behavior would help in interpreting, anticipating and predicting behaviors, in particular when they are not optimal. A common approach is to formalize human intent via a reward function, and assume that the human will act rationally with regard to the reward function [45,55]. The Boltzmann noisily-rational decision model [59] is often employed for this purpose. This model assumes that people choose trajectories in proportion to their exponentiated reward.

The Boltzmann noisily-rational decision model quantifies the likelihood that a human will select any particular option $o \in O$ (e.g. any teaching signal or example). If each option o has an underlying reward $R(o)$, the Boltzmann model computes the desirability of an option as:

$$P(o) = \frac{e^{R(o)}}{\sum_{i \in O} e^{R(i)}} \tag{7}$$

Interactive robot learning usually considers a sequence of human states and actions, called a trajectory $\tau = (s_1, a_1, ..., s_T, a_T)$. Boltzmann noisily-rational decision model is usually approximated to estimate the probability the human will take a trajectory is proportional to exponentiated return times a "rationality coefficient" β ("inverse temperature"):

$$P(\tau) \approx \exp\left\{ \beta \sum_{t=1}^{T} \gamma^t R(s_t, a_t) \right\} \tag{8}$$

The rationality coefficient β captures how good an optimizer the human is. The following values are usually considered:

- $\beta = 0$ would yield the uniform distribution capturing a random human type;
- $\beta \to \infty$ would yield a perfectly rational human type.

The goal of a noisily-rational decision mode is to draw inference from the observation of human actions. In [45], the authors introduce a formalism exploiting such a framework to interpret different types of human behaviors called *the reward-rational choice*. Within this framework, the robot is able to interpret a large range of teaching signals such as demonstrations, reward/punishment and instructions. However, several works have demonstrated the limits of the Boltzmann based modeling approach (see for example [9]): needs to identify alternatives of an option (Eq. 7), suited for trajectories but not policies [55], and only one parameter β is employed to model rationality. In addition, the approach does not take into account human reactions to machine actions (i.e. continuous adaption of human partner to the robot). As described in [40], there is a need to build better *Human Models of Machines* to address such issues by exploiting recent research in cognitive science.

10 Applications

In this section, we illustrate how Interactive Robot Learning Algorithms have been applied to several domains such as *Interactive Task Learning*, *Behavior Generation/Composition*, and *Socially Assistive Robotics*. In all these applications, it is necessary to define the role of the human, the agent and their interactions during the learning and use phases.

10.1 Interactive Task Learning

Interactive Task Learning (ITL) [56] is one of the main areas of applications of methods and algorithms presented in this chapter. The aim of ITL is to develop agents able to learn a task through natural interaction with a human instructor.

Numerous applications have been considered and some of them transferred to industry.

A use-case, *object sorting task*, is presented in Fig. 7. The robot has to learn to sort two types of objects: *Plain* (left) and *Pattern* (right), with two different sizes and three colors. In [69], the TICS architecture (Sect. 8.4) has been employed to achieve this learning with a human teacher. The results show that the interactive learning perspective facilitates *programming* by including real-time interaction with humans, and improves flexibility and adaptability of communication.

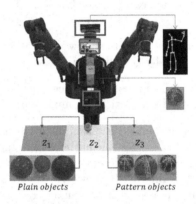

Fig. 7. Teaching object sorting (adapted from [66]).

10.2   Learning Robot Behaviors from Human Demonstrations

Figure 8 describes how Inverse Reinforcement Learning (IRL) is employed to learn robot behaviors: how a mobile robot approaches a moving human?. As described in Sect. 7.7, IRL starts with the recording of human demonstrations. In [79], demonstrations collection is performed off-line: humans were asked to teleoperate a mobile robot with the aim of approaching humans (Fig. 8a). Based on such demonstration, IRL is then used to learn a reward function that could replicate navigation behaviors. This work contributes to the challenge of generating legible robot motion [28] that should be addressed with a human-in-the-loop perspective [97].

10.3   Learning Robot Behaviors from Human Instructions

Spoken language based programming of robots has been described in Sect. 8.3. Humans simply describe actions and behaviors through natural language, which take the form of instructions. The ambition is to go beyond simple commands and enable end-users to create new personalized behaviors through natural interactions. In [76], a cognitive architecture has been developed for this purpose

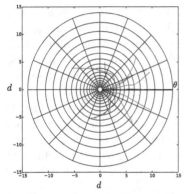

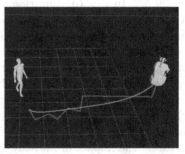

(a) Human demonstrations of the robot approaching the target person.

(b) Robot approaching solution using IRL. A smooth trajectory is generated using a Bézier curve.

Fig. 8. Learning how to approach humans using Inverse Reinforcement Learning (adapted from [79]).

(Fig. 9). This approach has been successfully transferred to industry and implemented in a Pepper robot with SoftBank Robotics. The cognitive architecture has been evaluated within the Pepper@Home program. The results demonstrate that end-users were able to create their own behaviors and share them with other end-users.

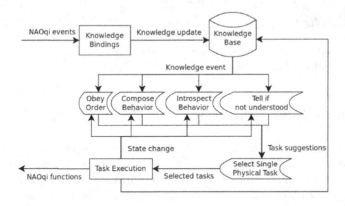

Fig. 9. Teaching new robot behaviors using natural language (adapted from [76]).

10.4   Socially Assistive Robotics

There is a substantial body of work in the design and development of socially assistive robotics where interactive robot learning plays an important role. The research works explore whether a robot could facilitate reciprocal social interaction in cases in which the robot was more predictable, attractive and simple [11,29,32]. In Fig. 10, imitation learning has been employed with children with Autism Spectrum Disorders. The children are asked to teach robots new postures, which is unusual in rehabilitation. Having the children teaching the robot has been shown to be relevant in rehabilitation and education (*protégé effect*) (see [33] for a use-case on dysgraphia). Contrary to the usual assumption of interactive robot learning, the challenge is to learn with children who do not fully master the task. The impact of the human teacher has been analyzed and exploited to capture *individual social signatures* [10] (Fig. 10). Using different imitation experiments (posture, facial expressions, avatar-robot), we were able to assess the impact of individual partners in the learning.

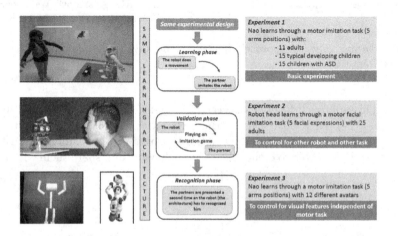

Fig. 10. Exploitation of Imitation Learning in Psychiatry, Developmental and Cognitive Sciences (adapted from [10]).

11   Conclusions, Challenges and Perspectives

In this chapter, we introduced the main concepts of Interactive Robot Learning, which were illustrated by several examples and applications. The chapter shows that the design of human interventions is as important as the design of algorithms in the efficiency of interactive robot learning. There is a substantial body of literature documenting interactive robot/machine learning methods and models (see also relevant readings in Sect. 2.4).

In the following, we report some relevant challenges of the domain shared by all human intervention strategies.

Autonomous - Interactive Learning. Collecting human teaching signals is expensive and a limited number of teaching signals could be collected. This issue refers to sample efficiency of algorithms and most of the interactive approaches are sample inefficient since they require a large number of human interventions. In addition, introducing human interventions in algorithms not designed for such purpose raises new issues not always expected (e.g., credit assignment, reward hacking, non-optimal human behaviors, implicit feedback or emotion). There has been several attempts aiming at combining rewards from multiple sources such as from the human and the environment.

This leads to challenges at the core of Human Centered AI, in particular how to build hybrid teams that are more efficient than each team member. In addition, following a Human Centered AI perspective, the aim is to augment the human and not to replace it. In [85], we discuss a range of reinforcement learning agents equipped with different skills that could handle such situations (including intrinsic motivations [77] and curriculum learning).

Evaluation and Replicability. Comparing, selecting and adapting models is essential in Interactive Robot Learning. Machine Learning and Robotics have set-up evaluation metrics that could be employed there. Similar to Human-Robot Interaction (HRI) methodology, there is a need to complement the evaluation by *human oriented metrics*, which could include questionnaires (see for example engagement evaluation in HRI [73]) as well as assessment of interaction load (e.g., number of interactions [69]).

Another important factor allowing to obtain consistent results is replicability (repeatability + reproducibility). Compared to standard machine learning, the data are collected during training through interaction with humans. In Interactive Robot Learning, data collection is about collecting data from both humans & robots. As mentioned in Sect. 7, recording of teaching signals is part of the interaction design and exploit various modalities: speech signals, gesture, robot motion... Consequently standardization of data collection is challenging. In addition, as mentioned in Sect. 6.8, reciprocal (human-robot) interdependence is observed during interactive robot learning scenarios, which impacts repeatability of experiments. This calls for new ways of collecting and sharing data for improving reproducibility of works.

Multiple and Multimodal Human Interventions. The most common strategies are certainly to learn new tasks by providing feedback, demonstration or instructions (Table 1). However, many other interventions have been considered in the literature such as human preference given in regards to pairwise agent behaviors [77,100], (joint) attention to states and/or actions during learning [31,100] and expressing hierarchy of a task [100].

Humans are per definition multimodal and should be enabled to produce multimodal teaching signals. Most of the current works consider only one modality such as facial expressions [10,15], gesture [69], social signals [65], or physiological signals [3].

Grounding multiple and multimodal teaching signals into actions is required to facilitate interpretation and learning. How to design interactions, interfaces, methods and models able to handle multimodal teaching signals is still an open question.

Mutual Understanding. The ability of agents to predict others and to be predicted by others is usually referred to as *mutual understanding*, which plays an important role in collaborative human-robot settings [44]. This could be achieved by transparency/explainability of robots [19,98] through the generation of verbal and non-verbal cues including gaze [7], legible motion [28], emotional expressions [16], queries/questions and dialog [17,20].

Being able to understand humans is also required and this will result in better *Computational Human Models of Machines.* In such direction, several recent contributions deal with *inferential social learning* to understand how humans think, plan, and act during interactive robot/agent learning [18,40,45,58,97]. This calls for new interdisciplinary research grounded in Cognitive Science, Machine Learning and Robotics [40,85].

References

1. Aigrain, J., Spodenkiewicz, M., Dubuisson, S., Detyniecki, M., Cohen, D., Chetouani, M.: Multimodal stress detection from multiple assessments. IEEE Trans. Affect. Comput. **9**(4), 491–506 (2018). https://doi.org/10.1109/TAFFC.2016.2631594

2. Akakzia, A., Colas, C., Oudeyer, P., Chetouani, M., Sigaud, O.: Grounding language to autonomously-acquired skills via goal generation. In: Ninth International Conference on Learning Representation, ICLR 2021, Vienna/Virtual, Austria (2021)

3. Akinola, I., et al.: Accelerated robot learning via human brain signals. In: 2020 IEEE International Conference on Robotics and Automation (ICRA), pp. 3799–3805 (2020). https://doi.org/10.1109/ICRA40945.2020.9196566

4. Amershi, S., Cakmak, M., Knox, W.B., Kulesza, T.: Power to the people: the role of humans in interactive machine learning. AI Mag. **35**(4), 105–120 (2014). https://doi.org/10.1609/aimag.v35i4.2513

5. Anzalone, S.M., Boucenna, S., Ivaldi, S., Chetouani, M.: Evaluating the engagement with social robots. Int. J. Soc. Robot. **7**(4), 465–478 (2015)

6. Argall, B.D., Chernova, S., Veloso, M., Browning, B.: A survey of robot learning from demonstration. Robot. Auton. Syst. **57**(5), 469–483 (2009). https://doi.org/10.1016/j.robot.2008.10.024

7. Belkaid, M., Kompatsiari, K., Tommaso, D.D., Zablith, I., Wykowska, A.: Mutual gaze with a robot affects human neural activity and delays decision-making processes. Sci. Robot. **6**(58), eabc5044 (2021). https://doi.org/10.1126/scirobotics.abc5044

8. Bengio, Y., Louradour, J., Collobert, R., Weston, J.: Curriculum learning. In: Proceedings of the 26th Annual International Conference on Machine Learning, ICML 2009, pp. 41–48. Association for Computing Machinery, New York (2009). https://doi.org/10.1145/1553374.1553380

9. Bobu, A., Scobee, D.R.R., Fisac, J.F., Sastry, S.S., Dragan, A.D.: Less is more: rethinking probabilistic models of human behavior. In: Proceedings of the 2020 ACM/IEEE International Conference on Human-Robot Interaction, HRI 2020, pp. 429–437. Association for Computing Machinery, New York (2020). https://doi.org/10.1145/3319502.3374811

10. Boucenna, S., Cohen, D., Meltzoff, A.N., Gaussier, P., Chetouani, M.: Robots learn to recognize individuals from imitative encounters with people and avatars. Scientific Reports (Nature Publishing Group) srep19908 (2016)
11. Boucenna, S., Anzalone, S., Tilmont, E., Cohen, D., Chetouani, M.: Learning of social signatures through imitation game between a robot and a human partner. IEEE Trans. Auton. Ment. Dev. **6**(3), 213–225 (2014). https://doi.org/10.1109/TAMD.2014.2319861
12. Branavan, S.R.K., Chen, H., Zettlemoyer, L.S., Barzilay, R.: Reinforcement learning for mapping instructions to actions. In: Proceedings of the Joint Conference of the 47th Annual Meeting of the ACL and the 4th International Joint Conference on Natural Language Processing of the AFNLP, ACL 2009, Stroudsburg, PA, USA, vol. 1, pp. 82–90. Association for Computational Linguistics (2009)
13. Bratman, M.E.: Intention and personal policies. Philos. Perspect. **3**, 443–469 (1989)
14. Breazeal, C., Thomaz, A.L.: Learning from human teachers with socially guided exploration. In: 2008 IEEE International Conference on Robotics and Automation, pp. 3539–3544 (2008). https://doi.org/10.1109/ROBOT.2008.4543752
15. Broekens, J.: Emotion and reinforcement: affective facial expressions facilitate robot learning. In: Huang, T.S., Nijholt, A., Pantic, M., Pentland, A. (eds.) Artifical Intelligence for Human Computing. LNCS (LNAI), vol. 4451, pp. 113–132. Springer, Heidelberg (2007). https://doi.org/10.1007/978-3-540-72348-6_6
16. Broekens, J., Chetouani, M.: Towards transparent robot learning through TDRL-based emotional expressions. IEEE Trans. Affect. Comput. **12**(2), 352–362 (2021). https://doi.org/10.1109/TAFFC.2019.2893348
17. Cakmak, M., Thomaz, A.L.: Designing robot learners that ask good questions. In: 2012 7th ACM/IEEE International Conference on Human-Robot Interaction (HRI), pp. 17–24 (2012). https://doi.org/10.1145/2157689.2157693
18. Caselles-Dupré, H., Sigaud, O., Chetouani, M.: Pragmatically learning from pedagogical demonstrations in multi-goal environments (2022). https://doi.org/10.48550/arxiv.2206.04546
19. Chakraborti, T., Kulkarni, A., Sreedharan, S., Smith, D.E., Kambhampati, S.: Explicability? legibility? predictability? transparency? privacy? security? the emerging landscape of interpretable agent behavior. In: Proceedings of the International Conference on Automated Planning and Scheduling, vol. 29, no. 1, pp. 86–96 (2018)
20. Chao, C., Cakmak, M., Thomaz, A.L.: Transparent active learning for robots. In: 2010 5th ACM/IEEE International Conference on Human-Robot Interaction (HRI), pp. 317–324 (2010). https://doi.org/10.1109/HRI.2010.5453178
21. Chernova, S., Thomaz, A.L.: Robot learning from human teachers. Synthesis Lect. Artif. Intelligence Mach. Learn. **8**(3), 1–121 (2014)
22. Colas, C., et al.: Language as a cognitive tool to imagine goals in curiosity-driven exploration. arXiv preprint arXiv:2002.09253 (2020)
23. Colombetti, M., Dorigo, M., Borghi, G.: Behavior analysis and training-a methodology for behavior engineering. IEEE Trans. Syst. Man Cybern. Part B (Cybern.) **26**(3), 365–380 (1996). https://doi.org/10.1109/3477.499789
24. Cruz, C.A., Igarashi, T.: A survey on interactive reinforcement learning: design principles and open challenges. In: Proceedings of the 2020 ACM Designing Interactive Systems Conference (2020)
25. Cruz, F., Twiefel, J., Magg, S., Weber, C., Wermter, S.: Interactive reinforcement learning through speech guidance in a domestic scenario. In: 2015 International

Joint Conference on Neural Networks (IJCNN), pp. 1–8 (2015). https://doi.org/10.1109/IJCNN.2015.7280477

26. Csibra, G., Gergely, G.: Natural pedagogy. Trends Cogn. Sci. **13**, 148–153 (2009)
27. Dominey, P., Mallet, A., Yoshida, E.: Real-time spoken-language programming for cooperative interaction with a humanoid apprentice. Int. J. Humanoid Robot. **6**, 147–171 (2009). https://doi.org/10.1142/S0219843609001711
28. Dragan, A.D., Lee, K.C., Srinivasa, S.S.: Legibility and predictability of robot motion. In: 2013 8th ACM/IEEE International Conference on Human-Robot Interaction (HRI), pp. 301–308. IEEE (2013). https://doi.org/10.1109/HRI.2013.6483603
29. Duquette, A., Michaud, F., Mercier, H.: Exploring the use of a mobile robot as an imitation agent with children with low-functioning autism. Auton. Robot. **24**(2), 147–157 (2008)
30. Floridi, L., et al.: AI4People—an ethical framework for a good AI society: opportunities, risks, principles, and recommendations. Mind. Mach. **28**(4), 689–707 (2018). https://doi.org/10.1007/s11023-018-9482-5
31. Fournier, P., Sigaud, O., Chetouani, M.: Combining artificial curiosity and tutor guidance for environment exploration. In: Workshop on Behavior Adaptation, Interaction and Learning for Assistive Robotics at IEEE RO-MAN 2017, Lisbon, Portugal (2017). https://hal.archives-ouvertes.fr/hal-01581363
32. Fujimoto, I., Matsumoto, T., De Silva, P.R.S., Kobayashi, M., Higashi, M.: Mimicking and evaluating human motion to improve the imitation skill of children with autism through a robot. Int. J. Soc. Robot. **3**(4), 349–357 (2011)
33. Gargot, T., et al.: "It is not the robot who learns, it is me" treating severe dysgraphia using child-robot interaction. Front. Psychiatry **12** (2021). https://doi.org/10.3389/fpsyt.2021.596055
34. Goodman, N.D., Frank, M.C.: Pragmatic language interpretation as probabilistic inference. Trends Cogn. Sci. **20**(11), 818–829 (2016). https://doi.org/10.1016/j.tics.2016.08.005
35. Grice, H.P.: Logic and conversation. In: Cole, P., Morgan, J.L. (eds.) Syntax and Semantics: Speech Acts, vol. 3, pp. 41–58. Academic Press, New York (1975)
36. Griffith, S., Subramanian, K., Scholz, J., Isbell, C.L., Thomaz, A.: Policy Shaping: integrating human feedback with reinforcement learning. In: Proceedings of the 26th International Conference on Neural Information Processing Systems, NIPS 2013, pp. 2625–2633. Curran Associates Inc. (2013)
37. Grizou, J., Iturrate, I., Montesano, L., Oudeyer, P.Y., Lopes, M.: Interactive learning from unlabeled instructions. In: Proceedings of the Thirtieth Conference on Uncertainty in Artificial Intelligence, UAI 2014, Arlington, Virginia, USA, pp. 290–299. AUAI Press (2014)
38. Gweon, H.: Inferential social learning: cognitive foundations of human social learning and teaching. Trends Cogn. Sci. (2021)
39. Harnad, S.: The symbol grounding problem. Physica D **42**, 335–346 (1990)
40. Ho, M., Griffiths, T.: Cognitive science as a source of forward and inverse models of human decisions for robotics and control. Ann. Rev. Control Robot. Auton. Syst. **5**, 33–53 (2022). https://doi.org/10.1146/annurev-control-042920-015547
41. Ho, M.K., Cushman, F., Littman, M.L., Austerweil, J.L.: Communication in action: planning and interpreting communicative demonstrations (2019)
42. Ho, M.K., Littman, M.L., Cushman, F., Austerweil, J.L.: Teaching with rewards and punishments: reinforcement or communication? In: Proceedings of the 37th Annual Meeting of the Cognitive Science Society (2015)

43. Ho, M.K., MacGlashan, J., Littman, M.L., Cushman, F.: Social is special: a normative framework for teaching with and learning from evaluative feedback. Cognition **167**, 91–106 (2017)
44. Jacq, A.D., Magnan, J., Ferreira, M.J., Dillenbourg, P., Paiva, A.: Sensitivity to perceived mutual understanding in human-robot collaborations. In: Proceedings of the 17th International Conference on Autonomous Agents and MultiAgent Systems, AAMAS 2018, Richland, SC, pp. 2233–2235. International Foundation for Autonomous Agents and Multiagent Systems (2018)
45. Jeon, H.J., Milli, S., Dragan, A.: Reward-rational (implicit) choice: a unifying formalism for reward learning. In: Proceedings of the 34th International Conference on Neural Information Processing Systems, NIPS 2020. Curran Associates Inc., Red Hook (2020)
46. Khan, F., Zhu, X., Mutlu, B.: How do humans teach: on curriculum learning and teaching dimension. In: Proceedings of the 24th International Conference on Neural Information Processing Systems, NIPS 2011, pp. 1449–1457. Curran Associates Inc., Red Hook (2011)
47. Knox, W.B., Stone, P.: Reinforcement learning from human reward: discounting in episodic tasks. In: 2012 IEEE RO-MAN: The 21st IEEE International Symposium on Robot and Human Interactive Communication, pp. 878–885 (2012). https://doi.org/10.1109/ROMAN.2012.6343862
48. Knox, W.B., Breazeal, C., Stone, P.: Learning from feedback on actions past and intended. In: In Proceedings of 7th ACM/IEEE International Conference on Human-Robot Interaction, Late-Breaking Reports Session (HRI 2012) (2012)
49. Knox, W.B., Stone, P.: Interactively shaping agents via human reinforcement: the TAMER framework. In: Proceedings of the Fifth International Conference on Knowledge Capture, K-CAP 2009, pp. 9–16. ACM, New York (2009). https://doi.org/10.1145/1597735.1597738
50. Knox, W.B., Stone, P.: Combining manual feedback with subsequent MDP reward signals for reinforcement learning. In: Proceedings of the 9th International Conference on Autonomous Agents and Multiagent Systems, AAMAS 2010, Richland, SC, vol. 1, pp. 5–12. International Foundation for Autonomous Agents and Multiagent Systems (2010)
51. Knox, W.B., Stone, P., Breazeal, C.: Training a robot via human feedback: a case study. In: Herrmann, G., Pearson, M.J., Lenz, A., Bremner, P., Spiers, A., Leonards, U. (eds.) ICSR 2013. LNCS (LNAI), vol. 8239, pp. 460–470. Springer, Cham (2013). https://doi.org/10.1007/978-3-319-02675-6_46
52. Kober, J., Bagnell, J.A., Peters, J.: Reinforcement learning in robotics: a survey. Int. J. Rob. Res. **32**(11), 1238–1274 (2013). https://doi.org/10.1177/0278364913495721
53. Krening, S., Harrison, B., Feigh, K.M., Isbell, C.L., Riedl, M., Thomaz, A.: Learning from explanations using sentiment and advice in RL. IEEE Trans. Cogn. Dev. Syst. **9**(1), 44–55 (2017). https://doi.org/10.1109/TCDS.2016.2628365
54. Krening, S., Feigh, K.M.: Interaction algorithm effect on human experience with reinforcement learning. J. Hum.-Robot Interact. **7**(2) (2018). https://doi.org/10.1145/3277904
55. Laidlaw, C., Dragan, A.D.: The Boltzmann policy distribution: accounting for systematic suboptimality in human models. arXiv abs/2204.10759 (2022)
56. Laird, J.E., et al.: Interactive task learning. IEEE Intell. Syst. **32**(4), 6–21 (2017). https://doi.org/10.1109/MIS.2017.3121552

57. Lepri, B., Oliver, N., Pentland, A.: Ethical machines: the human-centric use of artificial intelligence. iScience **24**(3), 102249 (2021). https://doi.org/10.1016/j. isci.2021.102249

58. Lin, J., Fried, D., Klein, D., Dragan, A.: Inferring rewards from language in context (2022). https://doi.org/10.48550/arxiv.2204.02515

59. Luce, R.D.: The choice axiom after twenty years. J. Math. Psychol. **15**, 215–233 (1977)

60. Luketina, J., et al.: A survey of reinforcement learning informed by natural language. In: Kraus, S. (ed.) Proceedings of the Twenty-Eighth International Joint Conference on Artificial Intelligence, IJCAI 2019, Macao, China, 10–16 August 2019, pp. 6309–6317. ijcai.org (2019). https://doi.org/10.24963/ijcai.2019/880

61. Lungarella, M., Metta, G., Pfeifer, R., Sandini, G.: Developmental robotics: a survey. Connect. Sci. **15**(4), 151–190 (2003). https://doi.org/10.1080/09540090310001655110

62. MacGlashan, J., et al.: Interactive learning from policy-dependent human feedback. In: Proceedings of the 34th International Conference on Machine Learning, vol. 70, pp. 2285–2294. JMLR. org (2017)

63. Matuszek, C., Herbst, E., Zettlemoyer, L., Fox, D.: Learning to parse natural language commands to a robot control system. In: Desai, J.P., Dudek, G., Khatib, O., Kumar, V. (eds.) Experimental Robotics. STAR, pp. 403–415. Springer, Heidelberg (2013). https://doi.org/10.1007/978-3-319-00065-7_28

64. Mitsunaga, N., Smith, C., Kanda, T., Ishiguro, H., Hagita, N.: Robot behavior adaptation for human-robot interaction based on policy gradient reinforcement learning. In: 2005 IEEE/RSJ International Conference on Intelligent Robots and Systems, pp. 218–225 (2005). https://doi.org/10.1109/IROS.2005.1545206

65. Moerland, T.M., Broekens, J., Jonker, C.M.: Emotion in reinforcement learning agents and robots: a survey. Mach. Learn. **107**(2), 443–480 (2017). https://doi.org/10.1007/s10994-017-5666-0

66. Najar, A.: Shaping robot behaviour with unlabeled human instructions. Ph.D. thesis, Paris 6 (2017)

67. Najar, A., Chetouani, M.: Reinforcement learning with human advice. a survey. arXiv preprint arXiv:2005.11016 (2020)

68. Najar, A., Chetouani, M.: Reinforcement learning with human advice: a survey. Front. Robot. AI (2021). https://doi.org/10.3389/frobt.2021.584075

69. Najar, A., Sigaud, O., Chetouani, M.: Interactively shaping robot behaviour with unlabeled human instructions. Auton. Agent. Multi-Agent Syst. **34**(2), 1–35 (2020). https://doi.org/10.1007/s10458-020-09459-6

70. Ng, A.Y., Russell, S.J.: Algorithms for inverse reinforcement learning. In: Proceedings of the Seventeenth International Conference on Machine Learning, ICML 2000, San Francisco, CA, USA, pp. 663–670. Morgan Kaufmann Publishers Inc. (2000)

71. Nguyen, K., Misra, D., Schapire, R.E., Dudak, M., Shafto, P.: Interactive learning from activity description. In: 2021 International Conference on Machine Learning (2021)

72. Nicolescu, M.N., Mataric, M.J.: Natural methods for robot task learning: instructive demonstrations, generalization and practice. In: Proceedings of the Second International Joint Conference on Autonomous Agents and Multiagent Systems, AAMAS 2003, pp. 241–248. ACM (2003). https://doi.org/10.1145/860575.860614

73. Oertel, C., et al.: Engagement in human-agent interaction: an overview. Front. Robot. AI **7**, 92 (2020). https://doi.org/10.3389/frobt.2020.00092

74. Olson, M.L., Khanna, R., Neal, L., Li, F., Wong, W.K.: Counterfactual state explanations for reinforcement learning agents via generative deep learning. Artif. Intell. **295**, 103455 (2021). https://doi.org/10.1016/j.artint.2021.103455

75. Osa, T., Pajarinen, J., Neumann, G., Bagnell, J.A., Abbeel, P., Peters, J.: An algorithmic perspective on imitation learning. Found. Trends Robot. **7**(1–2), 1–179 (2018). https://doi.org/10.1561/2300000053

76. Paléologue, V., Martin, J., Pandey, A.K., Chetouani, M.: Semantic-based interaction for teaching robot behavior compositions using spoken language. In: Ge, S.S., et al. (eds.) ICSR 2018. LNCS (LNAI), vol. 11357, pp. 421–430. Springer, Cham (2018). https://doi.org/10.1007/978-3-030-05204-1_41

77. Poole, B., Lee, M.: Towards intrinsic interactive reinforcement learning (2021). https://doi.org/10.48550/ARXIV.2112.01575

78. Pradyot, K.V.N., Manimaran, S.S., Ravindran, B., Natarajan, S.: Integrating human instructions and reinforcement learners: an SRL approach. In: Proceedings of the UAI Workshop on Statistical Relational AI (2012)

79. Ramírez, O.A.I., Khambhaita, H., Chatila, R., Chetouani, M., Alami, R.: Robots learning how and where to approach people. In: 2016 25th IEEE International Symposium on Robot and Human Interactive Communication (RO-MAN), pp. 347–353 (2016). https://doi.org/10.1109/ROMAN.2016.7745154

80. Ravichandar, H., Polydoros, A.S., Chernova, S., Billard, A.: Recent advances in robot learning from demonstration. Ann. Rev. Control Robot. Auton. Syst. **3**(1), 297–330 (2020). https://doi.org/10.1146/annurev-control-100819-063206

81. Ross, S., Bagnell, D.: Efficient reductions for imitation learning. In: Teh, Y.W., Titterington, M. (eds.) Proceedings of the Thirteenth International Conference on Artificial Intelligence and Statistics. Proceedings of Machine Learning Research, Chia Laguna Resort, Sardinia, Italy, vol. 9, pp. 661–668. PMLR (2010)

82. Rybski, P.E., Yoon, K., Stolarz, J., Veloso, M.M.: Interactive robot task training through dialog and demonstration. In: 2007 2nd ACM/IEEE International Conference on Human-Robot Interaction (HRI), pp. 49–56 (2007). https://doi.org/10.1145/1228716.1228724

83. Saint-Georges, C., et al.: Motherese in interaction: at the cross-road of emotion and cognition? (a systematic review). PLOS ONE **8**(10) (2013). https://doi.org/10.1371/journal.pone.0078103

84. Scheutz, M.: The case for explicit ethical agents. AI Mag. **38**(4), 57–64 (2017). https://doi.org/10.1609/aimag.v38i4.2746

85. Sigaud, O., Caselles-Dupré, H., Colas, C., Akakzia, A., Oudeyer, P., Chetouani, M.: Towards teachable autonomous agents. CoRR abs/2105.11977 (2021). arxiv.org/abs/2105.11977

86. Sumers, T.R., Ho, M.K., Griffiths, T.L.: Show or tell? Demonstration is more robust to changes in shared perception than explanation (2020). https://doi.org/10.48550/ARXIV.2012.09035. arxiv.org/abs/2012.09035

87. Sutton, R.S., Barto, A.G.: Reinforcement Learning: An Introduction. MIT Press, Cambridge (1998)

88. Tellex, S., et al.: Approaching the symbol grounding problem with probabilistic graphical models. AI Mag. **32**(4), 64–76 (2011). https://doi.org/10.1609/aimag.v32i4.2384

89. Thomaz, A.L., Breazeal, C.: Asymmetric interpretations of positive and negative human feedback for a social learning agent. In: The 16th IEEE International Symposium on Robot and Human Interactive Communication, RO-MAN 2007, pp. 720–725 (2007). https://doi.org/10.1109/ROMAN.2007.4415180

90. Thomaz, A.L., Breazeal, C.: Reinforcement learning with human teachers: evidence of feedback and guidance with implications for learning performance. In: Proceedings of the 21st National Conference on Artificial Intelligence, AAAI 2006, Boston, Massachusetts, vol. 1, pp. 1000–1005. AAAI Press (2006)

91. Thomaz, A.L., Breazeal, C.: Teachable robots: understanding human teaching behavior to build more effective robot learners. Artif. Intell. **172**(6), 716–737 (2008). https://doi.org/10.1016/j.artint.2007.09.009

92. Thomaz, A.L., Cakmak, M.: Learning about objects with human teachers. In: Proceedings of the 4th ACM/IEEE International Conference on Human Robot Interaction, HRI 2009, pp. 15–22. ACM, New York (2009). https://doi.org/10.1145/1514095.1514101

93. Tulli, S., Melo, F., Paiva, A., Chetouani, M.: Learning from explanations with maximum likelihood inverse reinforcement learning (2022). https://doi.org/10.21203/rs.3.rs-1439366/v1

94. Vinciarelli, A., et al.: Open challenges in modelling, analysis and synthesis of human behaviour in human–human and human–machine interactions. Cogn. Comput. **7**(4), 397–413 (2015). https://doi.org/10.1007/s12559-015-9326-z

95. Vollmer, A.L., et al.: People modify their tutoring behavior in robot-directed interaction for action learning. In: 2009 IEEE 8th International Conference on Development and Learning, pp. 1–6 (2009). https://doi.org/10.1109/DEVLRN.2009.5175516

96. Vollmer, A.-L., Schillingmann, L.: On studying human teaching behavior with robots: a review. Rev. Philos. Psychol. **9**(4), 863–903 (2017). https://doi.org/10.1007/s13164-017-0353-4

97. Wallkötter, S., Chetouani, M., Castellano, G.: SLOT-V: supervised learning of observer models for legible robot motion planning in manipulation. In: SLOT-V: Supervised Learning of Observer Models for Legible Robot Motion Planning in Manipulation (2022)

98. Wallkötter, S., Tulli, S., Castellano, G., Paiva, A., Chetouani, M.: Explainable embodied agents through social cues: a review. ACM Trans. Hum.-Robot Interact. **10**(3) (2021). https://doi.org/10.1145/3457188

99. Warnell, G., Waytowich, N., Lawhern, V., Stone, P.: Deep tamer: interactive agent shaping in high-dimensional state spaces. In: Proceedings of the AAAI Conference on Artificial Intelligence, vol. 32, no. 1 (2018). https://doi.org/10.1609/aaai.v32i1.11485

100. Zhang, R., Torabi, F., Warnell, G., Stone, P.: Recent advances in leveraging human guidance for sequential decision-making tasks. Auton. Agent. Multi-Agent Syst. **35**(2), 1–39 (2021). https://doi.org/10.1007/s10458-021-09514-w

101. Zhu, X.: Machine teaching: an inverse problem to machine learning and an approach toward optimal education. In: Proceedings of the AAAI Conference on Artificial Intelligence, vol. 29, no. 1 (2015). https://doi.org/10.1609/aaai.v29i1.9761

Explainable AI

Explainable for Trustworthy AI

Fosca Giannotti⬥, Francesca Naretto⬥, and Francesco Bodria⁽⊠⁾⬥

Scuola Normale Superiore, Pisa, Italy
{fosca.giannotti,francesca.naretto,francesco.bodria}@sns.it

Abstract. Black-box Artificial Intelligence (AI) systems for automated decision making are often based on over (big) human data, map a user's features into a class or a score without exposing why. This is problematic for the lack of transparency and possible biases inherited by the algorithms from human prejudices and collection artefacts hidden in the training data, leading to unfair or wrong decisions. The future of AI lies in enabling people to collaborate with machines to solve complex problems. This requires good communication, trust, clarity, and understanding, like any efficient collaboration. Explainable AI (XAI) addresses such challenges, and for years different AI communities have studied such topics, leading to different definitions, evaluation protocols, motivations, and results. This chapter provides a reasoned introduction to the work of Explainable AI to date and surveys the literature focusing on symbolic AI-related approaches. We motivate the needs of XAI in real-world and large-scale applications while presenting state-of-the-art techniques and best practices and discussing the many open challenges.

Keywords: Explainable AI · Trustworthy AI · Transparent by design

1 Introduction

Artificial Intelligence (AI) systems have witnessed increasing popularity during the past few years due to their excellent results. Unfortunately, for many years the primary goal of AI systems has been to solve a particular task in the best possible way, both in terms of time consumption and performance metrics. Due to these goals, the transparency of the model has been sacrificed for its performance. However, recent use cases have raised questions about such AI systems' fidelity and precision. In particular, one of these is the COMPAS: an AI system able to predict the risk of recidivism to support judges in such decisions. A few years ago, ProPublica[1] published an article in which they highlighted a racial bias in the COMPAS model employed by the judges in the USA to

---

[1] https://www.propublica.org/datastore/dataset/compas-recidivism-risk-score-data-and-analysis.

Supported by the European Community Horizon 2020 programme under the funding schemes: G.A. 871042 *SoBigData++* (sobigdata), G.A. 952026 *HumanE AI Net* (humane-ai), G.A. 825619 *AI4EU* (ai4eu), G.A. 834756 *XAI* (xai), and G.A. 952215 *TAILOR* (tailor).

© Springer Nature Switzerland AG 2023
M. Chetouani et al. (Eds.): ACAI 2021, LNAI 13500, pp. 175–195, 2023.
https://doi.org/10.1007/978-3-031-24349-3_10

predict recidivism. The problem with this algorithm was that it predicted a higher recidivism risk for black people since the dataset used for training contained a bias. This fact highlighted the need for an in-depth analysis for understanding the reasoning of the models. Here lies the eXplainable AI (XAI), whose goal is to make these systems more understandable to humans. Explainability is at the heart of Trustworthy AI and must be guaranteed for developing AI systems that empower and engage people across multiple scientific disciplines and industry sectors. Essentially, the explanation problem for a decision support system can be understood as "where" to place a boundary between what algorithmic details the decision-maker can safely ignore and what meaningful information the decision-maker should absolutely know to make an informed decision. Therefore, the explanation is intertwined with trustworthiness (what to ignore safely), comprehensibility (meaningfulness of the explanations), and accountability (humans keeping the ultimate responsibility for the decision).

In this chapter, we present the topics analyzed during our tutorial at the ACAI school, held in Berlin, October 2021. The purpose of the tutorial was to provide a reasoned introduction to the work of Explainable AI (XAI) to date and surveys the literature with a focus on machine learning and symbolic AI related approaches. Then, the challenges and current achievements of the ERC project "XAI: Science and technology for the eXplanation of AI decision making"[2] will also be presented. We will motivate the needs of XAI in a real-world and large-scale application while presenting state-of-the-art techniques and best practices, as well as discussing the many open challenges. In Sect. 2 it is described what Explainable AI means and the different areas of research, and the open points in the state-of-the-art. Several real-case scenarios were presented to the students, in which it is of utmost importance to understand the behaviour of the machine learning model: criminal justice, financial credit scoring and loan approval or health care applications. Section 2.2 introduces the various types of explanations currently proposed in the literature, the desired properties and the metrics for evaluating its goodness. In particular, we present the metrics for evaluating the goodness of an explanation, both from a quantitative point of view and a qualitative one. Then, Sect. 3 presents the available methods in the literature, by dividing them into the two primary approaches of XAI, namely *post-hoc explanation methods* (Sect. 3.1) and *Transparent by-design methods* (Sect. 3.5). Firstly, we analyze the tabular data, then the images and the text data. Lastly, Sect. 4 concludes the presentation by collecting ideas and opinions of the school's students.

2 Explainable AI

Artificial Intelligence (AI) is becoming an integral part of our lives in many sectors. It is used in various fields: suggesting what to buy on Amazon, recommending the songs on Spotify, to detect face mask violations in the recent pandemic. However, other fields are involved in this AI revolution, such as healthcare, banking, retail, and many more. However, many AI systems trained (ML)

---

[2] https://xai-project.eu/.

models are also called black-boxes: they perform well from a technical point of view, but they do not explain their predictions so that humans can understand the internal reasoning of the model. Predictive models' lack of transparency and accountability has had severe consequences, especially in high-stack scenarios. As mentioned in the Introduction, with the case of COMPAS, we discover unfair behaviour of the ML model used to determine recidivism. However, this is not the only case: there are several concerns about the novel ML-aided apps in health-care, such as those that help you lose weight. Many doctors stated that these apps do not work and are not based on the same doctors' knowledge[3]. Another alarming situation is presented in this article: an AI model incorrectly concluded that people with pneumonia were less likely to die if they had asthma. This error could have led doctors to deprive asthma patients of extra care. Lastly, there is also the simplest case, such as the one presented in LIME [41], in which an ML model is making mistakes in detecting wolves or husky dogs because it is only focusing on the background of the training data (snow for wolves and grassland for husky). There have been cases of people incorrectly denied loans, ML-based pollution models stating that highly polluted air was safe to breathe and gener-ally poor use of limited valuable resources in criminal justice, medicine, energy reliability, finance, and other domains. As we start using AI, we need to under-stand why the algorithm made certain decisions and why not others. The higher transparency we can get into the AI black-box, the easier it would be to believe and use it. This exact thought gave rise to the field of eXplainable AI (XAI).

As we start using AI more and more for decision making, there could be several reasons why we will look for an explanation of the decision:

- *To Build Trust*: If the systems are transparent, it is easier for people to trust them and use them.
- *To enable auditing*: This will help systems comply with government regula-tions.
- *To improve the model*: Looking at the explanations, Data Scientists will be able to fine-tune the models and draw better results.

However, this is just the tip of the iceberg: many researchers and companies provide XAI algorithms, and the list is increasing every day.

2.1 Types of Explanations

An XAI method can produce different types of explanations, and they are tied with the type of data to explain. Since the type of data we face is very different, the explanation returned are also different. There are three principal data types recognized in the literature: *tabular* data, *images* and *text*. For each of them, we can have different types of explanations, as illustrated in Table 1. We list the most common ones, and in the following sections, we present the specific definitions depending on the type of data considered:

---

[3] https://www.scientificamerican.com/article/artificial-intelligence-is-rushing-into-patient-care-and-could-raise-risks/.

Table 1. Types of different explanations

<table>
<tr><td>

Rule-Based (RB)
A set of premises that the record must satisfy in order to meet the rule's consequence.

$$r = Education \leq College \rightarrow \leq 50k$$

</td></tr>
<tr><td>

Feature Importance (FI)
A vector containing a value for each feature. Each value indicates the importance of the feature for the classification.

capitalgain	0.00
education-num	14.00
relationship	1.00
hoursperweek	3.00

</td></tr>
<tr><td>

Prototypes (PR)
The user is provided with a series of examples that characterize a class of the black-box

$p =$ $\rightarrow$ "cat"

</td></tr>
<tr><td>

Counterfactuals (CF)
A set of rules to change his prediction or a counter-example of the opposite class.

$q =$ [image] $\rightarrow$ "3" $c =$ [image] $\rightarrow$ "8"

</td></tr>
</table>

- **Feature Importance (FI)** methods assign a score for every input feature based on their importance to predict the output. The more the features will be responsible for predicting the output, the bigger their score will be.
- **Rule-Based (RB)** methods are methods that output a set of premises that the record must satisfy in order to meet the rule's consequence.
- **Prototypes (PR)** are a kind of explanation where the user is provided with a series of examples that characterize a class of the black-box.
- **Counterfactuals (CF)** are a type of explanation in which the user is given either a set of rules to change the prediction or a counter-example of the opposite class.

2.2   Desiderata of an Explanation

The study of XAI is still in its infancy, so there are many different concepts to deal with and many different opinions regarding the desiderata for an explanation. First of all, the literature agrees that there is no universal type of explanation that is good for everyone and for all purposes: in some contexts, a more high-level explanation is needed; in others, a more technical one, depending on who is receiving the explanation and why the explanation is required. This section proposes some of the most popular desiderata of an explanation, referring to the state-of-the-art literature.

The goodness of an explanation should be evaluated considering its validity and utility. In the literature, these desiderata are evaluated in terms of goodness, usefulness, and satisfaction of explanations. The state-of-the-art provides both qualitative and quantitative methodologies for evaluating explanations.

Regarding the *qualitative evaluation*, it values the actual usability of explanations from the point of view of the end-user, such as if they satisfy human curiosity and trust. A large body of research has identified that one of the critical variables that may influence decisions about automation use is a user's trust in the automation. Users tend to use AI that they trust while rejecting the one they do not. For appropriate use to occur, users' trust must match the true capabilities of the AI system. The appropriateness of trust can be evaluated in terms of its calibration [31], or "the correspondence between a person's trust in the automation and the automation's capabilities". Trust is often seen as a 'single-direction road,' i.e. something that needs to be increased. However, 'trust' in AI technologies needs to be reduced to boost transparency based models. In this context, an interesting work of Doshi-Velez [16] proposes a systematization of evaluation criteria into three categories:

1. **Functionally-grounded** metrics aim to evaluate the interpretability by exploiting some formal definitions that are used as proxies, and they do not require humans for validation.
2. **Application-grounded** evaluation methods require human experts able to validate the specific task and explanation under analysis [45,49].
3. **Human-grounded** metrics evaluate the explanations through humans who are not experts. The goal is to measure the overall understandability of the explanation in simplified tasks [26,29].

Regarding *quantitative evaluation*, in this case the evaluation focuses on the performance of the explainer and how close the explanation method f is to the black-box model b. There are two different *criteria*: (i) **Completeness w.r.t. the black-box model**, in which the metrics aim at evaluating how closely f approximates b; (ii) **Completeness w.r.t. to specific task**, in which the evaluation criteria are tailored for a particular task.

Regarding the first criterion, one of the metrics most used in this setting is the *fidelity* that aims to evaluate how good is f at mimicking the black-box decisions. There may be different specializations of fidelity, depending on the type of explanator under analysis [20]. For example, in methods where a surrogate

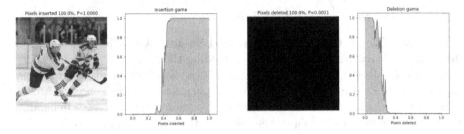

Fig. 1. Example of Insertion (on the left) and Deletion (on the right) metric computation performed on LIME and a hockey player image.

model g to mimic b, fidelity compares the prediction of b and g on the instances Z used to train g.

Another measure of completeness w.r.t. b is the *stability*, which aims at validating how stable the explanations are for similar records. Stability can be evaluated by exploiting the *Lipschitz constant* [2] as $L_x = \max \frac{\|e_x - e_{x'}\|}{\|x - x'\|}, \forall x' \in \mathcal{N}_x$ where x is the explained instance, e_x the explanation and $\mathcal{N}_x$ is a neighborhood of instances x' similar to x. Another kind of metric available is called *deletion* and *insertion* [38] (Fig. 1). The intuition behind deletion is that removing the "cause" will force the black-box to change its decision. Among the deletion methods, there is the *faithfulness* [2] which is tailored for FI explainers. The idea is that, by deleting a feature at the time, starting from the most important, the model's performance should decrease. The insertion metric, instead, takes a complementary approach. *Monotonicity* is an implementation of an insertion method: it evaluates the effect of b by incrementally adding each attribute in order of increasing importance. In this case, we expect that the black-box performance increases by adding more and more features, thereby resulting in monotonically increasing model performance. Finally, other standard metrics are considered to evaluate the performance of the explanation method, such as *accuracy*, *precision*, *recall* and *running time*.

3   XAI Methods

There are different ways of categorizing explanatory methods in the literature, but a common taxonomy has emerged in recent years. The first distinction is made according to the type of explanatory method that is considered, i.e. methods that can be explained by design or black-box explanation methods:

- ***Transparent by design methods*** are *Intrinsically* explainable methods that returns a decision, and the reasons for the decision are directly accessible because the model is transparent.
- ***Black-box explanation*** are *Post-Hoc* explanation methods that provides explanations for a black-box model that takes decisions.

The second differentiation distinguishes post-hoc explanation methods in global and local:

- **Global** explanation methods aim at explaining the overall logic of a black-box model. Therefore the explanation returned is a global, complete explanation valid for any instance;
- **Local** explainers aim at explaining the reasons for the decision of a black-box model for a specific instance.

The third distinction categorizes the methods into model-agnostic and model-specific:

- **Model-Agnostic** explanation methods can be used to interpret *any type* of black-box model;
- **Model-Specific** explanation methods can be used to interpret *only a specific type* of black-box model.

This section presents some of the available XAI methods in the state-of-the-art. We will first analyze the *post-hoc explanation* methods in Sect. 3.1. Then, we present the available *transparent* methods in Sect. 3.5

There are various industry companies where research is happening on XAI techniques. The leading cloud providers such as Google, Amazon, and Microsoft have products in the Automated (AutoML) domain. XAI efforts from significant industry leaders include:

- What-If: a tool from Google that provides a visual way to understand the prediction of a model by allowing the user to change the feature in real-time[4]
- A custom Framework made by H2O where the user can choose which explanation best fits for him[5]
- An Open Source Model Interpretability Library, which includes most state-of-the-art interpretability algorithms[6]
- Interpretability with Azure by Microsoft[7]

3.1   Post-hoc Explanations Methods

This section provides an overview of the methods presented in the tutorial. In particular, we present post-hoc explanation methods, i.e. methods to explain black-box models already created. We start presenting the post-hoc XAI algorithms tailored for tabular data (3.1), then for images (3.1), text (3.2) and time series (3.3). We conclude this section by presenting the methods employed during the hands-on session at the XAI Tutorial, in 3.4.

---

[4] https://cloud.google.com/explainable-ai/.
[5] https://www.h2o.ai/products-dai-mli/.
[6] https://captum.ai/.
[7] https://docs.microsoft.com/en-us/azure/machine-learning/how-to-machine-learning-interpretability.

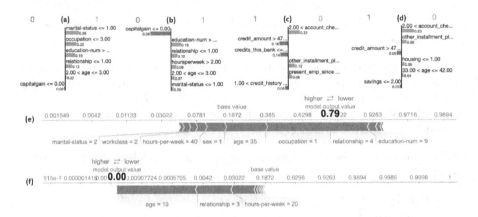

Fig. 2. *TOP*: Example of LIME application for different black-boxes. All the models correctly predicted the output class. *BOTTOM*: Force plot returned by SHAP explaining two records: the first one labeled as class 1 and the latter labeled as class 0. Only the features that contributed more (i.e. higher values) to the classification are reported.

Tabular Data

Feature Importance. For tabular data, feature importance is a kind of explanation that provides an importance value for each feature the model considers. The importance value represents how important the feature under analysis was for the prediction. There may be a global feature importance explanation. The importance considers how the overall model behaves, depending on the class under analysis or local feature importance. The importance is computed for only one particular record at a time. Formally, given a record x, an explainer $f(\cdot)$ models a feature importance explanation as a vector $e = \{e_1, e_2, \ldots, e_m\}$, in which the value $e_i \in e$ is the importance of the ith feature for the decision made by the black-box model $b(x)$. To understand each feature's contribution, the sign and the magnitude of each value e_i are considered. W.r.t. the sign, if $e_i < 0$, it means that feature contributes negatively for the outcome y; otherwise, if $e_i > 0$, the feature contributes positively. The magnitude, instead, represents how significant the contribution of the feature is to the final prediction y. In particular, the greater the value of $|e_i|$, the greater its contribution. In the context of feature importance explanations, there are some popular explanation methods, such as LIME [41], SHAP [34] and DALEX [5]. Many methods also provided an updated Python library, making them available for general use and improvements. In Fig. 2 is reported an example of explanation returned by LIME and SHAP.

Rules. Another interesting explanation method is the *rule*, also called decision rules, factual or logic rules. A rule aims at explaining the reasons that lead the model to the final prediction. It has the form $p \rightarrow y$, in which p is a premise composed of a Boolean condition on feature values, while y is the consequence of the rule. In particular, p is a conjunction of split conditions of the form

$x_i \in [v_i^{(l)}, v_i^{(u)}]$, where x_i is a feature and $v_i^{(l)}, v_i^{(u)}$ are lower and upper bound values in the domain of x_i extended with $\pm\infty$. Rules may provide both a global and a local explanation. Regarding global explanations, usually, a set of rules is defined to represent the decisions of a particular class. Instead, rules explain the conditions that lead a particular record to its prediction for the local explanations. In particular, an instance x *satisfies* r, or r *covers* x, if every Boolean conditions of p evaluate to true for x. One of the most important strong points about rules is that they are considered human-readable, thanks to their logical structure. Hence, they are preferred in contexts where a non-expert end-user is considered. Several methods have been proposed during the past few years regarding the available methods. Rule explanations are one of the oldest kinds of explanation, and the first algorithm, TREPAN [14] was published in 1996. Then there is also MSFT [13] and DecText [8]. To the best of our knowledge, two post-hoc local explanation methods provide rules and also have a Python library implementation: ANCHOR [42] and LORE [20].

Prototypes. Another popular form of explanation is the *prototype*. It is an object representing a set of similar records. It can be *(i)* a record from the training dataset close to the input data x; *(ii)* a centroid of a cluster to which the input x belongs. Alternatively, *(iii)* even a synthetic record, generating following some ad-hoc process. Prototypes serve as examples: the user understands the model's reasoning by looking at records similar to his/hers. Several definitions and requirements for the prototype explanations are available in the literature, depending on the different kinds of prototypes considered. Among the explanation methods available in this context, there are Prototype Selection [6], ProtoDash [21] and MMD-Critic [27].

Counterfactual. An interesting approach that has received much attention lately is the *counterfactual* explanation. Counterfactual focuses on the differences w.r.t. the record in input to obtain the opposite prediction w.r.t. $b(x) = y$. Moreover, they are often addressed as the prototypes' opposite. They describe a dependency on external facts that led to a particular decision made by the black-box model. Since it is quite a novel explanation approach, counterfactuals have several definitions. In this chapter, we consider the one presented in [48]. It is a general formalization of a counterfactual explanation. An explanation tells us that $b(x) = y$ was returned because variables of x has values $x_1, x_2, ..., x_n$. Instead, a counterfactual reasons about the opposite prediction: if x had values $x_1^1, x_2^1, ..., x_n^1$ and all the other variables has remained constant, $b(\overline{x}) = \neg y$ would have been returned, where $\overline{x}$ is the record x with the suggested changes. An ideal counterfactual should alter the values of the variables as little as possible to find the closest setting under which y is returned instead of $\neg y$. There are many desiderata of a counterfactual in this context, such as efficiency, robustness, diversity, actionability, and plausibility. There are several methods in the context of counterfactual explanations, even if the majority are only defined from a theoretical point of view and do not have code available. Regarding the methods available, the most popular are: C-CHVAE [37], FACE [40], CEM [15] and MAPLE [39].

Image Data

Saliency Maps. For image data, one of the most popular type of explanation is called *Saliency Maps* (Fig. 3). A Saliency Map (SM) is an image where a pixel's brightness represents how salient the pixel is. Formally, a SM is modelled as a matrix S, in which dimensions are the sizes of the image we want to explain, and the values s_{ij} are the saliency values of the pixels ij. The greater the value of s_{ij}, the bigger is the saliency of that pixel. To visualize SM, we can use a divergent colour map, for example, ranging from red to blue. A positive value (red) means that the pixel ij has contributed positively to the classification, while a negative one (blue) means that it has contributed negatively. There are two methods for creating SMs. The first one assigns to every pixel a saliency value. The second one segments the image into different pixel groups using a segmentation method, assigning a saliency value for each segmented group.

Fig. 3. Example of saliency maps, the red pixel highlight the pixel most important to the predicted class while blue pixel are most important for other classes. (Color figure online)

The majority of the methods presented in the literature are *pixel-based saliency maps*. The pioneering technique in this type of explanation is Layer-wise Relevance Propagation. Layer-wise Relevance Propagation (LRP) [3] a model-specific method which produce post-hoc local explanations for any type of data. LRP explains the classifier's decisions by decomposition. It redistributes the prediction y backwards using local redistribution rules until it assigns a relevance score R_i to each pixel value. This idea of "back-propagating" the relevance back to the input has become more popular over the years leading to a multitude of variations of LRP [30,32,35]. The other common technique for creating pixel-based saliency maps is using the black-box's gradients. This technique is widespread since most black-boxes in the image domain are differentiable Neural Networks. Integrated Gradient [46] utilizes the gradients of a black-box along with the sensitivity techniques like LRP. Formally, given b and x, let x' be the baseline input. The baseline x' is generally a black or a white image. INTGRAD constructs a path from x' to x and computes the gradients of points along the path. The points are taken by overlapping x on x' and gradually modifying the opacity of x. Integrated gradients are obtained by cumulating the gradients of these points. The most known method for creating *segmented based SMs* is LIME [41]. More in detail, LIME divides the input image into segments called *super-pixels*. Then it creates the neighbourhood by randomly substituting the super-pixels with a uniform, possibly neutral, colour. This neighbourhood is then fed into the black-box, and a sparse linear model is learned. However, LIME is an old approach, and several works have outperformed it. XRAI [25] is based on INTGRAD and inherits its properties, but it adds segmentation to the approach. The algorithm is divided into three steps: *segmentation, get attribution,* and *selecting regions.* The image segmentation is repeated several times with different segments to reduce the dependency on the image segmentation algorithm. For attribution, XRAI uses INTGRAD while, for select regions, it leverages the fact that, given two regions, the one that sums to the more positive value should be more important to the classifier. From this observation, XRAI starts with an empty mask and then selectively adds the regions that yield the maximum gain in the total attributions per area. Other methods for creating saliency maps involve the use of the gradients of the feature maps created in the last layer of a convolutional network [9,36,44] or masking several parts of the image [38].

Concept Attribution. Most ML models operate on low-level features like edges and lines in a picture that does not correspond to high-level concepts that humans can easily understand. In [1,52], they pointed out that feature-based explanations applied to state-of-the-art complex black-box models can yield nonsensible explanations. *Concept-based explainability* constructs the explanation based on human-defined concepts rather than representing the inputs based on features and internal model (activation) states. This idea of high-level features is more familiar to humans, that are more likely to accept it.

TCAV, Testing with Concept Activation Vectors [28] provides a quantitative explanation of how important is a concept for the prediction. Every concept is represented by a particular vector called *Concept Activation Vectors (CAVs)* created by interpreting an internal state of a neural network in terms of human-friendly concepts. TCAV uses directional derivatives to quantify the degree to which a user-defined concept is *vital* to a classification result. For example, TCAV can understand how sensitive a prediction of "zebra" is to the presence of "stripes". The problem with this algorithm is that the user defines the concepts, which is challenging and time-consuming. ACE, Automated Concept-based Explanation [17], is the evolution of TCAV, and it does not need any concept example. It automatically discover them. It takes training images and segments them using a segmentation method. These super-pixels are fed into the black-box model, as they were input images clustered in the activation space. Then we can obtain, like in TCAV, how much these clusters contributed to the prediction of a class.

Prototypes. Another possible explanation for images is to produce *prototypical images* that best represent a particular class. Human reasoning is often prototype-based, using representative examples as a basis for categorization and decision-making. Similarly, prototype explanation models use representative examples to explain and cluster data. For images, there is MMD-CRITIC [27] which selects prototypes by measuring the difference between the distribution of the instances and the instances in the whole dataset. Prototypes are the set of instances nearer to the data distribution, and the farthest are called criticisms. PROTOPNET [10] has a different approach: it figures out some prototypical parts of images (named prototypes) and then uses them to classify, making the classification process interpretable. A special architecture is needed to produce prototypes. The model identifies several parts on the test image that look like some training image prototypical parts. Then, it predicts based on a weighted combination of the similarity scores between parts of the image and the learned prototypes. The performance is comparable to the actual state of the art but with more interpretability.

Counterfactuals. As output, counterfactual methods for images produce images similar to the original one but with altered predictions. For this reason, they are usually called counter-exemplars. Some methods output only the pixel variation, others the whole altered image. Interpretable Counterfactual Explanations Guided by Prototypes [47], perturbs the input image to find the closest image to the original one but with a different classification by using an objective loss function $\mathcal{L} = cL_{pred} + \beta L_1 + L_2$ optimized using gradient descent. The first term, cL_{pred}, encourages the perturbed instance to predict another class then x while the others are regularisation terms. CEM, Contrastive Explanation Method [15], creates counterfactual explanations in terms of Pertinent Positives (PP) or Pertinent Negatives (PN). PP's or PN's are the pixels that lead to the same or a different class, w.r.t. the original instance. To create PP's and PN's, feature-wise perturbation is done by keeping the perturbations sparse and close to the original instance through an objective function that contains an elastic net $\beta L_1 + L_2$ regularizer. ABELE, Adversarial black-box Explainer generating Latent Exemplars) [18], is a local, model-agnostic explainer that produces explanations composed of: *(i)* a set of exemplar and counter-exemplar images, and *(ii)* a saliency map. The end-user can understand the classification by looking at images similar to those under analysis that received the same prediction or a different one. Moreover, by exploiting the SM, it is possible to understand the areas of the images that cannot be changed and varied without impacting the outcome. ABELE exploits an adversarial autoencoder (AAE) to generate the record's local neighbourhood to explain x. It builds the neighbourhood on a latent local decision tree, which mimics the behaviour of b. Finally, exemplars and counter-exemplars are selected, exploiting the rules extracted from the decision tree. The SM is obtained by a pixel-by-pixel difference between x and the exemplars.

3.2   Text Data

For text data, we can distinguish the following types of explanations: *Sentence Highlighting (SH)*, and *Attention-Based methods (AB)*.

Sentence Highlighting is a saliency map applied to text and consists of assigning to every word a score based on the importance that word had in the final prediction. Several methods can produce this type of explanation. LIME [41] can be applied to text with a modification to the perturbation of the original input. Given an input sentence x, LIME creates a neighbourhood of sentences by replacing multiple words with spaces. Another possible variation is to insert a similar word instead of removing them. INTGRAD [46] can also be exploited to explain text classifiers. Indeed, gradient-based methods are challenging to apply to NLP models because the vector representing every word is usually averaged into a single sentence vector. Since a mean operation gradient does not exist, the explainer cannot redistribute the signal to the original vectors. On the other hand, INTGRAD is immune to this problem because the saliency values are computed as a difference with a baseline value. INTGRAD computes the saliency value of a single word as a difference from the sentence without it.

Attention was proposed in [51] to improve the model performance. Through an attention layer, the authors managed to show which parts of the images contributed most to realizing the caption. Attention is a layer to put on top of the model that, for each word, ij of the sentence x generates a positive weight α_{ij}, i.e., the *attention* weight. This value can be interpreted as the probability that a word ij is in the right place to focus on producing the next word in the caption. Attention mechanisms allow models to look over all the information the original sentence holds and learn the context [4,50]. Therefore, it has caught the interest of XAI researchers, who started using these weights as an explanation. The explanation e of the instance x is composed of the attention values (α), one for each feature x_i. Attention is nowadays a delicate argument, and while it is clear that it augments the performance of models, it is less clear if it helps gain interpretability and the relationship with model outputs [24].

3.3   Time Series

Tabular data, images, and texts are the most popular data types used when developing a black-box model. Time series is a type of data representing any variable that varies over time. There are areas such as the medical field where temporal data is critical. The majority of the algorithms in this field are composed of very deep black-boxes, which means that eXplainable Artificial Intelligence is crucial for time series data. The most important difference with the other types of data relies on the explanation produced. Shapelet is the most characteristic explanation for time series data. They are time series subsequences that are maximally representative of a class. Saliency maps adopt a similar approach, and it consists of highlighting which part of the series has contributed the most to the classification. Finally, since also text can be interpreted as a time series, the attention methods explained before can also be applied to time series data.

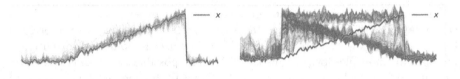

Fig. 4. Example of explanation for time series data given by LASTS [19]. On the left a representation of time series similar to the original one, while on the right are represented the counterfactual ones.

3.4 Post-hoc Explanations: Hands-on the Code

In the Tutorial at ACAI 2021, we show the majority of the methods present in this Section[8]. For the hand-on code on post-hoc explanations we started with a general view of tabular data using two very well known datasets in the literature `Adult`[9] and `German`[10]. We used LIME, LORE and SHAP to show different types of explanations for a Random Forest classifier trained on these two datasets. For images, we used the `MNIST` dataset[11] and showed different types of explanations using INTGRAD, LIME, RISE, LORE and ABELE. There was no time for text. However, in the Github, we provided an example of a LIME application.

3.5 Transparent by Design Methods

There has been a recent explosion of work on 'explainable ML', where a second (post-hoc) model is created to explain the first black-box model. This is because it is easy to create a black-box model with reasonable accuracy. In this setting, it only matters the quantity and the quality of the data. Often, companies and researchers throw all the data into the model, and something will come up. The prediction explanation only comes in second after a model with acceptable accuracy has been obtained. However, this is problematic since post-hoc explanations are often not reliable and often misleading. The problem with Post-Hoc explanations is that they must be wrong. They cannot have perfect fidelity with respect to the original model. If the explanation were completely faithful to what the original model computes, the explanation would equal the original model. One would not need the original model in the first place, only the explanation. This leads to the danger that any explanation method for a black-box model can accurately represent the original model in parts of the feature space. An inaccurate explanation model limits trust in the explanation and, by extension, trust in the black-box it is trying to explain. An explainable model that has a 90% agreement with the original model indeed explains the original model most of the time. However, an explanatory model that is correct 90% of the time is wrong 10% of the time. If a tenth of the explanations is incorrect, one

---

[8] Code available here https://github.com/rinziv/XAI_lib_HAI-net_Tutorial.
[9] https://archive.ics.uci.edu/ml/datasets/Adult.
[10] https://archive.ics.uci.edu/ml/datasets/statlog+(german+credit+data).
[11] http://yann.lecun.com/exdb/mnist/.

cannot trust the explanations, and thus one cannot trust the original black-box. If we cannot know whether our explanation is correct, we cannot trust either the explanation or the original model. Transparent by design methods come to solve this problem. Due to the intrinsic transparency nature, the decision process about predictions is known by construction. However, the accuracy of the prediction would suffer from this design. Usually, transparent by design models are weaker in terms of accuracy than black-box models. Also, they are usually difficult to build since they require considerable knowledge of the data used.

In most cases, it is a matter of a trade-off between accuracy and transparency, and the use depends on the case. In high-stack decision-making problems, like healthcare, it is usually preferable to use a transparent method since there is the need to justify the action. However, even in this case, if there is an algorithm that can save lives with a 10% improvement against the transparent model, why would you not use it? The following section will review the recent advances in transparent design methods concerning their data type.

3.6 Tabular Data

Decision Trees have been the primary type of interpretable algorithm by design models for quite a while. Due to their high interpretability, they are the go-to algorithm for real-world business applications. They can be explained as a series of questions of the type if-else statements that are very human-friendly. Also, the time required for the learning algorithm to make predictions is very low, and no missing value imputation is required since the algorithm can adapt accordingly. However, they are unstable, relatively inaccurate, and prone to overfitting. A small change in data can lead to a vastly different decision tree. This can be rectified by replacing a single decision tree with a random forest of decision trees. By doing this, we increase the complexity of the model and, therefore, lower its transparency. Tools like Xgboost [11], which relies on Boosting Tree, have implemented some Feature Relevance in years to explain their prediction, but they remain a black-box for all intents. A ruled-based classifier is a similar approach to Decision trees [22], always based on rule explanation. It provides an output set of rules, requiring no further explanations. Nevertheless, the comprehensibility of rule models is also not without caveats. For example, while individual rules may be well understood, the complete rule model may lose its explainability if there are too many rules. Interpretable Decision Sets (IDS) [29] is a rule learning algorithm that provides means for balancing the model size and also other facets of interpretability with prediction performance through user-set weights.

Furthermore, ruled-based methods are not the only methods to make transparent by design models. InterpretML[12] is a package from Microsoft which offers a new interpretability algorithm called Explainable Boosting Machine (EBM), which is based on Generalized Additive Models (GAMs). Generalized additive models were initially invented by Trevor Hastie and Robert Tibshirani in 1986 [23]. Although GAM does not receive sufficient popularity yet as a random

---

[12] https://interpret.ml/.

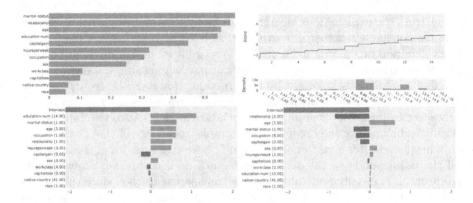

Fig. 5. Explanations given by EBM. *TOP*: Overall global explanation (left), example of a global explanation (right). *BOTTOM*: Local explanations: left, a record classified as 1; right a record classified as 0.

forest or gradient boosting in the data science community, it is undoubtedly a powerful yet simple technique. The idea of GAM is that the relationships between the individual predictors and the dependent variable follow smooth functions that can be linear or nonlinear. These relationships can be estimated simultaneously then added up. $y = f_1(x_1) + f_2(x_2) + \ldots$ This allows computing the exact contribution of each feature to the final prediction y. Although a GAM is easy to interpret, its accuracy is significantly less than more complex models that permit interactions. For this reason Lou et al. [33] also added interaction terms in the sum of the contributions and called it GA2M: $y = \sum f_i(x_i) + \sum f_{ij}(x_i, x_j)$ As a result, GA2M significantly increases the prediction accuracy but still preserves its nice interpretability. Although the pairwise interaction terms in GA2M increase accuracy, it is highly time-consuming and CPU-hungry. EBM solves the computational problem by learning each smooth function f() using bagging and gradient boosting techniques. The functions are modelled as straightforward decision trees, and the resulting adding function of the prediction is a stepwise function. This results in a better computational cost without losing accuracy or interpretability. An example for the `adult` dataset is shown in Fig. 5

3.7   Image Data

For years Deep Neural Networks have been predominant in the image domain world. Due to the data's complexity, transparent design methods suffer in performance more than when dealing with tabular data. New techniques are arising that promise to enhance the transparency of Deep Neural Networks, but we are far from creating a fully transparent by design method.

The most promising approach to transparency in the image domain is by using Concepts. As for Post-Hoc methods, high-level concepts could be used to design a transparent model for images. During training, each layer of a deep learning model encodes the features of the training images into a set of numerical values and stores them in its parameters. This is called the latent space of the AI model. The lower layers of a multilayered convolutional neural network will generally learn basic features such as corners and edges. The higher layers of the neural network will detect more complex features such as faces, objects, and entire scenes. Ideally, a neural network's latent space would represent concepts relevant to the classes of images it is meant to detect. Nevertheless, we do not know that, and deep learning models are prone to learning the most discriminative features, even if they are the wrong ones. Here comes the Concept Whitening approach [12]. The main logic behind "Concept Whitening" is the development of neural networks such that their Latent Space is aligned with the relevant concepts to what it has been trained. This will reduce the errors by neural networks, and their internal working can be explained much easier. However, the user still defines these concepts manually, which is challenging. There are several concepts for a single class image, and usually, in the image classification task, the classes are of the order of a thousand.

3.8   Text Data

For text data, the complexity of models is even higher than for images. Here the best model architecture is a even deeper Neural Network called Transformers. Transformers rely upon a mechanism called self-attention, which relates different positions of a single sequence to compute a representation of the sequence. There are no transparent by design methods capable of reproducing this type of architecture transparently.

3.9   Interpretable by Design Explanations: Hands-on the Code

In the Tutorial at ACAI 2021, we showed the majority of the methods present in this Section[13]. For the hand-on code on interpretable by design explanations, we show the explanations returned by EBM on the German dataset already used for post-hoc explanations.

4   Conclusion and Open Challenges

This chapter presented an overview of the tutorial conducted during the summer school ACAI 2021 in Berlin. We first presented what is Explainable AI, describing the different kinds of explanations available, such as feature importance, rules, prototypes and counterfactuals. Then, we proposed an overview of the desiderata of an explanation. We then moved to the presentation of post-hoc explanations and transparent by design methods. For these approaches, we presented the methods from a technical point of view, dividing the analysis into

---

[13] Code available here https://github.com/rinziv/XAI_lib_HAI-net_Tutorial/blob/main/EBM_example.ipynb.

the type of input data, such as tabular, images and text data. We also presented the hands-on code session that we conducted by exploiting a Python library developed by our research group. This is just a short description of this area of research. For the interested user, we suggest reading [7], an in-depth survey about these topics from our KDD Lab. Moreover, we did not consider other data types in this chapter, such as graphs or time series. Hence we suggest [43,53]. The topics covered in this tutorial proved to be very interesting for the participants, who raised an interesting debate on the challenges and open points in the literature. Most of the participants pointed out problems in the current XAI algorithms, such as slow execution and many assumptions to be made to obtain an explanation, like the number of synthetic neighbours to be generated, the type of surrogate and the granularity of the explanation. As an example, SHAP allows masks to speed up the computation, thus selecting fewer features to compute the SHAP values. However, this process requires setting a different granularity of the explanation that is not straightforward to select and may require expert knowledge of the kind of data. Moreover, one of the most interesting arguments pointed out regards the metrics: at the moment, we have several explanation algorithms, but few ways to compare them and validate at a theoretical and technical level the goodness of the obtained explanations. This is an alarming situation for many researchers since we may propose explanations that are not faithful to the black-box model we aim to explain. Lastly, most explanation algorithms are for tabular data and images, while text, time series and graphs are less considered.

References

1. Adebayo, J., Gilmer, J., Muelly, M., Goodfellow, I., Hardt, M., Kim, B.: Sanity checks for saliency maps. In: Advances in Neural Information Processing Systems, pp. 9505–9515 (2018)
2. Alvarez Melis, D., Jaakkola, T.: Towards robust interpretability with self-explaining neural networks. In: Advances in Neural Information Processing Systems, vol. 31, pp. 7775–7784 (2018)
3. Bach, S., Binder, A., Montavon, G., Klauschen, F., Müller, K.R., Samek, W.: On pixel-wise explanations for non-linear classifier decisions by layer-wise relevance propagation. PLoS One **10**(7), e0130140 (2015)
4. Bahdanau, D., Cho, K., Bengio, Y.: Neural machine translation by jointly learning to align and translate. arXiv preprint. arXiv:1409.0473 (2014)
5. Biecek, P., Burzykowski, T.: Explanatory model analysis, 2020 Data Science Series
6. Bien, J., Tibshirani, R.: Prototype selection for interpretable classification. Annals Appl. Stat. **5**(4), 2403–2424 (2011)
7. Bodria, F., Giannotti, F., Guidotti, R., Naretto, F., Pedreschi, D., Rinzivillo, S.: Benchmarking and survey of explanation methods for black box models (2021)
8. Boz, O.: Extracting decision trees from trained neural networks. In: ACM SIGKDD (2002)
9. Chattopadhay, A., Sarkar, A., Howlader, P., Balasubramanian, V.N.: Grad-cam++: Generalized gradient-based visual explanations for deep convolutional networks. In: 2018 IEEE Winter Conference on Applications of Computer Vision (WACV), pp. 839–847. IEEE (2018)

10. Chen, C., Li, O., Tao, D., Barnett, A., Rudin, C., Su, J.K.: This looks like that: deep learning for interpretable image recognition. In: Advances in Neural Information Processing Systems, pp. 8930–8941 (2019)

11. Chen, T., et al.: Xgboost: extreme gradient boosting. R package version 0.4-2 1(4), 1–4 (2015)

12. Chen, Z., Bei, Y., Rudin, C.: Concept whitening for interpretable image recognition. Nature Mach. Intell. 2(12), 772–782 (2020)

13. Chipman, H., George, E., McCulloh, R.: Making sense of a forest of trees. Comput. Sci. Stat. (1998)

14. Craven, M., Shavlik, J.W.: Extracting tree-structured representations of trained networks. In: NIPS, pp. 24–30 (1996)

15. Dhurandhar, A., et al.: Explanations based on the missing: towards contrastive explanations with pertinent negatives. In: Advances in Neural Information Processing Systems (2018)

16. Doshi-Velez, F., Kim, B.: Towards a rigorous science of interpretable machine learning. arXiv preprint. arXiv:1702.08608 (2017)

17. Ghorbani, A., Wexler, J., Zou, J.Y., Kim, B.: Towards automatic concept-based explanations. In: Advances in Neural Information Processing Systems, pp. 9277–9286 (2019)

18. Guidotti, R., Monreale, A., Matwin, S., Pedreschi, D.: Black box explanation by learning image exemplars in the latent feature space. In: Brefeld, U., Fromont, E., Hotho, A., Knobbe, A., Maathuis, M., Robardet, C. (eds.) ECML PKDD 2019. LNCS (LNAI), vol. 11906, pp. 189–205. Springer, Cham (2020). https://doi.org/10.1007/978-3-030-46150-8_12

19. Guidotti, R., Monreale, A., Spinnato, F., Pedreschi, D., Giannotti, F.: Explaining any time series classifier. In: 2020 IEEE 2nd International Conference on Cognitive Machine Intelligence (CogMI), pp. 167–176. IEEE (2020)

20. Guidotti, R., et al.: Factual and counterfactual explanations for black box decision making. IEEE Intell. Syst. 34(6), 14–23 (2019)

21. Gurumoorthy, K., et al.: Efficient data representation by selecting prototypes with importance weights. In: ICDM, pp. 260–269. IEEE (2019)

22. Hastie, T., Tibshirani, R., Friedman, J.H., Friedman, J.H.: The Elements of Statistical Learning: Data Mining, Inference, and Prediction, vol. 2. Springer, New York (2009)

23. Hastie, T.J., Tibshirani, R.J.: Generalized Additive Models. Routledge, Milton Park (2017)

24. Jain, S., Wallace, B.C.: Attention is not explanation. arXiv preprint arXiv:1902.10186 (2019)

25. Kapishnikov, A., Bolukbasi, T., Viégas, F., Terry, M.: Xrai: better attributions through regions. In: Proceedings of the IEEE International Conference on Computer Vision, pp. 4948–4957 (2019)

26. Kim, B., Chacha, C.M., Shah, J.A.: Inferring team task plans from human meetings: a generative modeling approach with logic-based prior. J. Artif. Intell. Res. 52, 361–398 (2015)

27. Kim, B., Khanna, R., Koyejo, O.: Examples are not enough, learn to criticize! criticism for interpretability. In: NIPS'16 (2016)

28. Kim, B., Wattenberg, M., Gilmer, J., Cai, C., Wexler, J., Viegas, F., et al.: Interpretability beyond feature attribution: quantitative testing with concept activation vectors (TCAV). In: International Conference on Machine Learning, pp. 2668–2677. PMLR (2018)

29. Lakkaraju, H., Bach, S.H., Leskovec, J.: Interpretable decision sets: a joint framework for description and prediction. In: Proceedings of the 22nd ACM SIGKDD International Conference on Knowledge Discovery and Data Mining, pp. 1675–1684 (2016)

30. Lapuschkin, S., Wäldchen, S., Binder, A., Montavon, G., Samek, W., Müller, K.R.: Unmasking clever Hans predictors and assessing what machines really learn. Nat. Commun. **10**(1), 1–8 (2019)

31. Lee, J.D., See, K.A.: Trust in automation: designing for appropriate reliance. Hum. Factors **46**(1), 50–80 (2004)

32. Li, H., Tian, Y., Mueller, K., Chen, X.: Beyond saliency: understanding convolutional neural networks from saliency prediction on layer-wise relevance propagation. Image Vis. Comput. **83**, 70–86 (2019)

33. Lou, Y., Caruana, R., Gehrke, J., Hooker, G.: Accurate intelligible models with pairwise interactions. In: Proceedings of the 19th ACM SIGKDD International Conference on Knowledge Discovery and Data Mining, pp. 623–631 (2013)

34. Lundberg, S.M., Lee, S.I.: A unified approach to interpreting model predictions. In: Proceedings of the 31st International Conference on Neural Information Processing Systems, pp. 4768–4777 (2017)

35. Montavon, G., Lapuschkin, S., Binder, A., Samek, W., Müller, K.R.: Explaining nonlinear classification decisions with deep taylor decomposition. Pattern Recogn. **65**, 211–222 (2017)

36. Muhammad, M.B., Yeasin, M.: Eigen-cam: Class activation map using principal components. In: 2020 International Joint Conference on Neural Networks (IJCNN), pp. 1–7. IEEE (2020)

37. Pawelczyk, M., Broelemann, K., Kasneci, G.: Learning model-agnostic counterfactual explanations for tabular data. In: Proceedings of The Web Conference 2020. WWW'20 (2020)

38. Petsiuk, V., Das, A., Saenko, K.: Rise: randomized input sampling for explanation of black-box models. arXiv preprint. arXiv:1806.07421 (2018)

39. Plumb, G., Molitor, D., Talwalkar, A.S.: Model agnostic supervised local explanations. In: Advances in Neural Information Processing Systems (2018)

40. Poyiadzi, R., Sokol, K., Santos-Rodriguez, R., De Bie, T., Flach, P.: Face: feasible and actionable counterfactual explanations. In: Proceedings of the AAAI/ACM Conference on AI, Ethics, and Society (2020)

41. Ribeiro, M.T., Singh, S., Guestrin, C.: " why should i trust you?" explaining the predictions of any classifier. In: Proceedings of the 22nd ACM SIGKDD International Conference on Knowledge Discovery and Data Mining, pp. 1135–1144 (2016)

42. Ribeiro, M.T., Singh, S., Guestrin, C.: Anchors: High-precision model-agnostic explanations. In: AAAI, vol. 18, pp. 1527–1535 (2018)

43. Rojat, T., Puget, R., Filliat, D., Ser, J.D., Gelin, R., Díaz-Rodríguez, N.: Explainable artificial intelligence (xai) on timeseries data: a survey (2021)

44. Selvaraju, R.R., Cogswell, M., Das, A., Vedantam, R., Parikh, D., Batra, D.: Gradcam: visual explanations from deep networks via gradient-based localization. In: Proceedings of the IEEE International Conference on Computer Vision, pp. 618–626 (2017)

45. Suissa-Peleg, A., et al.: Automatic neural reconstruction from petavoxel of electron microscopy data. Microsc. Microanal. **22**(S3), 536–537 (2016)

46. Sundararajan, M., Taly, A., Yan, Q.: Axiomatic attribution for deep networks. arXiv preprint. arXiv:1703.01365 (2017)

47. Van Looveren, A., Klaise, J.: Interpretable counterfactual explanations guided by prototypes. arXiv preprint. arXiv:1907.02584 (2019)

48. Wachter, S., Mittelstadt, B., Russell, C.: Counterfactual explanations without opening the black box: automated decisions and the GDPR. Harv. J. Law Tech. **31**, 841 (2017)

49. Williams, J.J., et al.: Axis: generating explanations at scale with learnersourcing and machine learning. In: Proceedings of the 3rd (2016) ACM Conference on Learning @ Scale. L@S'16 (2016)

50. Wu, Z., Ong, D.C.: Context-guided bert for targeted aspect-based sentiment analysis. arXiv preprint. arXiv:2010.07523 (2020)

51. Xu, K., et al.: Show, attend and tell: neural image caption generation with visual attention. In: International Conference on Machine Learning, pp. 2048–2057 (2015)

52. Yang, M., Kim, B.: Bim: towards quantitative evaluation of interpretability methods with ground truth. arXiv preprint. arXiv:1907.09701 (2019)

53. Yuan, H., Yu, H., Gui, S., Ji, S.: Explainability in graph neural networks: a taxonomic survey (2021)

Why and How Should We Explain AI?

Stefan Buijsman[(⊠)] [iD]

Department of Values, Technology and Innovation, Delft University of Technology,
Jaffalaan 5, Delft, The Netherlands
s.n.r.buijsman@tudelft.nl

Abstract. Why should we explain opaque algorithms? Here four papers
are discussed that argue that, in fact, we don't have to. Explainability,
according to them, isn't needed for trust in algorithms, nor is it needed for
other goals we might have. I give a critical overview of these arguments,
showing that there is still room to think that explainability is required for
responsible AI. With that in mind, the second part of the paper looks at
how we might achieve this end goal. I proceed not from technical tools in
explainability, but rather highlight accounts of explanation in philosophy
that might inform what those technical tools should ultimately deliver.
While there is disagreement here on what constitutes an explanation, the
three accounts surveyed offer a good overview of the current theoretical
landscape in philosophy and of what information might constitute an
explanation. As such, they can hopefully inspire improvements to the
technical explainability tools.

Keywords: Explainability · Trust · AI ethics

1 Introduction

Artificial intelligence, and in particular machine learning methods, is fast gaining
ground. Algorithms trained on large datasets and comprising numerous hidden
layers, with up to a trillion parameters, are becoming common. Such models
are difficult to explain to lay users with little understanding of the basis of
machine learning, but they are also hard to interpret for those who designed and
programmed them. The calculations that are carried out by the algorithm are
not assigned an easily understandable meaning, aside from there being far too
many of these calculations to actually follow. The outputs of algorithms are, as a
result, hard to predict and to explain. Why did the algorithm output that there
is a cat on this picture? We don't really know, certainly not without additional
help in the form of explainability tools.

Reducing this vast range of calculations to an explanation that is accessible
and helpful is a huge challenge, and one that is laid out in more technical detail in
chapter [8]. Instead, I focus on the question: is it a problem that machine learning
models are hard to interpret? This links closer to the tutorials on Ethics in AI,
such as the chapters [2,15,20]. For there is a philosophical question at the very

© Springer Nature Switzerland AG 2023
M. Chetouani et al. (Eds.): ACAI 2021, LNAI 13500, pp. 196–215, 2023.
https://doi.org/10.1007/978-3-031-24349-3_11

start of any attempt to make machine learning models more explainable: *why do we need explainability?* And, furthermore, if we decide that explainability is important, what is it exactly that the tools we aim to develop should provide? What information is needed to constitute an explanation? When is a machine learning model interpretable?

These are big questions, and require far more discussion to be fully answered than I can provide here. So, to narrow the scope I primarily look at the recent increase in arguments against the need for explainable machine learning methods. I discuss the philosophical angles taken here, using four recent publications on the topic. I leave aside most technical work on explainability methods, for the interested readers see chapter [8] or the literature overviews in [1,4,10]. Instead I focus on philosophical accounts of explanations in the second part, presenting three different accounts of what explanations are and thus what information we should aim to provide in our explainability methods. As such, this chapter should give a more conceptual overview of reasons we have for wanting to explain machine learning/AI algorithms and what that might entail.

1.1 Learning Objectives

At the end of this chapter readers will have:

- Awareness of the recent arguments against the need for explanations of machine learning algorithms
- Ability to discuss the merits of these arguments
- Knowledge of the main accounts of explanation in the philosophical literature

2 Why Should We Explain Algorithms?

With the growing use of machine learning algorithms, and the benefits they may deliver, there has also been an increase in discussions about the conditions in which we can use these algorithms. Do we require algorithms to be explainable or is it acceptable to use algorithms even when we can't say why they produce the outputs they do? I discuss four different (sets of) arguments that aim to establish that explainability is not necessary to trust, or acceptably use, an algorithm. They help set up a discussion of the aims of explainable AI (XAI) tools and cover the philosophical literature up to 2021. While this leaves out some discussions from computer science [18] in the same period, it gives a good overview of the arguments that circulate against a requirement of explainability. Do we need explanations for trust in AI? [7] What about other goals we might have for such tools? Are they such that all, or most, machine learning algorithms require XAI support? The four papers have been chosen to reflect these questions: from arguments against needing explainability for trust (2.1 – 2.3) to arguments considering the wider range of goals explainability might serve (2.4).

2.1   Robbins: The Impacts of AI and a Catch-22

Robbins [17] would certainly answer this last question with a resounding 'no'. He presents two arguments for this conclusion, but starts with the idea that any requirement on explainability wouldn't attach to the algorithm as such, but rather to the decisions that are made with/by the algorithm. For example, we don't require people to be generally explainable; it's fine if some actions (e.g. a sudden urge to dance by a child) are left unexplained. Likewise, I don't need to explain why I crave Chinese food for dinner, though I do need to offer an explanation were I to hit someone. It's the impact, presumably, of these different decisions on other people that makes all the difference. If the impacts are, or can be, high, then we require explanations. If they are low and nobody would be affected by my decisions, then I can make them however I like. So Robbins [17] argues, and so I'll assume here to trace out the argument.

For it is what happens in the different cases where it gets interesting. The low-risk situation, where an algorithm's outputs aren't really capable of leading to harms, are supposed to be ones where we don't need explanations. As with people, where decisions of little import to others can be made without needing a good reason for them, so algorithms too shouldn't have to be explainable. Robbins [17] uses the example of AlphaGo, the choices of which cannot be readily explained. The lack of any risks associated with AlphaGo's outputs means that nobody considered this problematic, though perhaps we would find it valuable additional information. The point is rather that the lack of potential harms means that there is no *requirement* of explainability. If the algorithm fulfills its function well enough, it should be acceptable to use it.

So far the argument is uncontroversial. Proponents of a requirement of explainability typically point to high-stakes cases such as algorithms making medical diagnoses, as it is in these situations that we would expect explanations from people. Here Robbins [17] discusses a 'Catch-22' argument to show that requiring machine learning algorithms to be explainable would make them redundant. The idea is that "in order for the explanation given by explainable AI to be useful we must have a human capable of knowing which considerations are acceptable and which are not. If we already know which considerations are acceptable, then there is no reason to use ML in the first place. We could simply hard-code the considerations into an algorithm - giving us an automated decision using pre-approved, transparent, reasoning." [17, p.510] Explanations can only be used to calibrate trust if we know what good reasons for a decision are, and Robbins claims that if we have that knowledge then we could just as well program a transparent, rules-based, algorithm.

It's this last claim that I consider problematic, as we often do seem to be capable of evaluating decisions even if we can't write down the exact steps needed for making or even evaluating the decision. The sheer amount of work by cognitive scientists to figure out how e.g. our visual processing functions, is a good example of this. We are very good at identifying objects and telling whether someone has correctly done so and on the correct basis, but formulating general rules that capture all this (e.g. defining when an object is a cat) turns out to be very difficult. We're bad at giving necessary and sufficient conditions, and at providing dictionary definitions even though we know perfectly well what our words mean and which objects are cats. The same holds for less conceptual tasks such as driving, where we can tell whether someone is a good driver, and whether decisions were made for appropriate reasons, but have a hard time giving a full functional description of how we drive. The very reason we started with machine learning was this observation that it is extremely difficult to formulate exact rules that capture our cognitive abilities. So the claim that the ability to evaluate explanations is sufficient to formulate transparent GOFAI (Good Old-Fashioned AI) algorithms seems blatantly false. As a result, the argument for the redundancy of explainable machine learning algorithms fails. For even if we can evaluate explanations (tell whether the algorithm looks at the right things to decide whether something is a cat), that doesn't imply that we could specify a rules-based algorithm instead. Explainability can still be a reasonable requirement on machine learning algorithms, at least in situations where the potential impact is serious enough.

2.2 London: A Lack of Explanations Elsewhere

If the reason that we get out of the Catch-22 in [17] is that we often can't provide the detailed descriptions needed for a transparent algorithm, then isn't that lack of transparency on our side a reason to question a requirement of explainability? Aren't we requiring something of algorithms that people wouldn't be able to supply, when we claim that they should be interpretable? This is the direction of critique in London [14], who claims that "The opacity, independence from an explicit domain model, and lack of causal insight associated with some powerful machine learning approaches are not radically different from routine aspects of medical decision-making." [14, p.17] The examples that London uses to make this point are important for the evaluation of the argument. For he points out that:

> [M]odern clinicians prescribed aspirin as an analgesic for nearly a century without understanding the mechanism through which it works. Lithium has been used as a mood stabilizer for half a century, yet why it works remains uncertain. Large parts of medical practice frequently reflect a mixture of empirical findings and inherited clinical culture. In these cases, even efficacious recommendations of experts can be atheoretic in this sense: they reflect experience of benefit without enough knowledge of the underlying causal system to explain how the benefits are brought about. [14, p.17]

In other words, we might not always be able to explain why a certain treatment is effective, even if it is the responsible decision to prescribe that treatment. London reinforces that point with an example of treatments that were chosen based on theoretical reasoning, which was later disproved (and showed that the chosen treatments in fact harmed patients). "In medicine, the overreliance on theories that explain why something might be the case has sometimes made it more difficult to validate the empirical claims derived from such theories, with disastrous effects." [14, p.18] It is the efficacy of the treatments, verified in randomized clinical trials (RCT) that offers the best basis for deciding which treatment to offer. And so, London argues by analogy, we should decide which algorithms to trust/use based on their efficacy and not based on whether we have a thorough understanding of them.

The question is whether this comparison to our (in)ability to explain why treatments work is a good one. For despite the fact that we may not know the underlying causal mechanisms, doctors are clearly able to explain why they choose to prescribe a certain treatment: it is, for example, the experience that it has worked for patients with similar symptoms, ideally backed up by RCTs. Similarly, they will have reasons available (that can be evaluated by other medical professionals) to support their diagnosis. It is therefore important to consider the role that machine learning algorithms are supposed to play. They are not a type of treatment about which decisions are made, but a tool to aid or replace decision making, much closer to the diagnostic tools such as MRI machines that are used and whose functioning we can explain in detail. In the case of decision making we can, and frequently do, receive explanations.

Now, this doesn't quite settle the matter, as we can also ask whether we trust our doctor and machinery (and consider a diagnosis and treatment decision a good one) based on an ability to explain a decision, or based on a track record of previous good decisions. Perhaps here there is a similar case to be made that what we value is their reliability, rather than their ability to give reasons for decisions. The point to make regarding London's argument, however, is that the lack of understanding of causal processes that explain the efficacy of treatments is largely besides the point. These treatments don't constitute decisions or diagnoses. There is no rational deliberation here, nor is there a question of what a decision was based on. Instead, the cases he highlights show that making decisions for the wrong reasons (theoretical ones rather than evaluated efficacy) can be damaging, and so that having these reasons can be an important part of figuring out how good a decision is. Perhaps, without meaning to, this gives us precisely a reason to prefer or require explainable AI so that there too (automated) decisions can be shown to be based on the relevant features, considered in an appropriate manner.

2.3 Durán and Jongsma: Reliabilism and Explainability

Still, I consider the question whether there is a requirement of explainability on machine learning algorithms to be far from settled. London's examples may not give as strong an argument against such a requirement as he hoped, there are more perspectives from which to proceed. A more principled one is that of reliabilism, a philosophical position in epistemology that (in a very simple, process reliabilism formulation) analyses our justification to believe a proposition to be true in terms of the reliability of the process that led to this belief [9]. If the process is reliable (enough), then the belief is justified. If it isn't reliable, then there is no justification. How much of this we are aware of, or the internal reasons we have, is of little matter: the only thing that counts is the (externally determined) reliability of the process.

It is with this account in mind, though with a somewhat more involved notion of reliability than standard in the epistemological literature, that Durán and Jongsma [6] argue against a requirement of explainability on machine learning algorithms. While their main point is that (computational) reliabilism can offer an account of when to trust machine learning algorithms, they also give an argument against explainability. "transparency is a methodology that does not offer sufficient reasons to believe that we can reliably trust black box algorithms. At best, transparency contributes to building trust in the algorithms and their outcomes, but it would be a mistake to consider it as a solution to overcome opacity altogether." [6, p.2] The underlying issue, as they see it, is one of infinite regress: our explainability tools will never succeed in making machine learning algorithms transparent, because of the need for transparency in the tools themselves. In their words:

> To see this, consider P again, the interpretable predictor that shows the inner workings of A, the black box algorithm. The partisan of transparency, S, claims that P consists of a sequence of procedures of which a given p_i entails A (or some of its outputs). But what reasons does S have to believe this? All that S holds is a very appealing visual output produced by P, like heatmaps or decision trees, and the - still unjustified - belief that such an output represents the inner workings of A. For all S knows, P is as opaque as A (eg, it can misleadingly create clusters which are biased, it can ignore relevant variables and functions that compromise the integrity of the results, etc). It follows that all we can say is that P induces on S the belief that S knows the output of A (ie, the idea that A is transparent), but at no point P is offering genuine reasons to believe that S has interpreted A. For this to happen, for S to be justified in believing that A is transparent, P must be sanctioned as transparent too. The problem has now been shifted to showing that P is transparent. [6, p.2]

There are two related concerns here that one might have about explainability tools. First, the tool itself might not be transparent, so e.g. the way in which a particular heatmap is output may not be explained. Why does the tool provide is with this explanation of the output rather than with another explanation? In other words, tool P may be a black box algorithm that in itself requires additional tools for its workings to be explained. Second, it might not be the tool itself that is opaque, but rather the fidelity of its explanations. We may know perfectly well how P generates explanations, but be unsure whether the explanations by P are indeed correct descriptions of why algorithm A reached that output. Linear approximations, for example, might be transparent in the first sense, but evaluating whether the explanations offered by them are a good representation of the reasons the machine learning model made its decisions is far more difficult. I think that Durán and Jongsma [6] aim to point to the second worry, about the fidelity of P, rather than the first, also since explainability tools often do not involve machine learning and so are generally not opaque in the first sense.

Would a regress occur here? Clearly it would if the first case was true: if all explainability tools are themselves black boxes, we wouldn't manage to get rid of black boxes by using XAI tools. That isn't the case, so they need a regress on determining the fidelity of these explainability tools. Is there some way to determine the fidelity of an explainability tool where we are sure that the answers are correct, or at least don't need yet another method to determine their correctness?

This will depend on the explainability methods we look at. Indeed, decision trees and linear approximations have this question of their fidelity to the model. And it is difficult to interpret heatmaps correctly, as there is a tendency to conceptualize the highlighted areas (e.g. a shovel) in terms of the concepts we typically use, whereas the algorithm might use the colour, shape, or some more complex combination of factors to make its decisions. While heatmaps highlight which areas are important for the algorithm's output, they do not explain *why* these areas are important. Yet the fidelity of these explainability tools is not directly in question: heatmaps, and feature importance methods in general, correctly represent part of the algorithm's behaviour. Similarly, counterfactual explanations correctly identify which minimal changes (under a chosen distance function, which is transparent – or can be transparent) lead to a change in output. Granted, these methods do not manage to make the algorithm transparent, but it is not their lack of fidelity that leads to this issue. I see, therefore, no reason to suspect a principled regress here on the question whether explainability tool P correctly describes the behaviour of algorithm A. Yes, we haven't found tools yet that manage to truly explain black-box algorithms (and probably this is why there are so many attempts to argue that algorithms can still be used even if they aren't explainable), but that alone is insufficient reason to think that it is impossible to achieve transparency.

Of course, Durán and Jongsma [6] offer a more constructive account of when people are justified to trust a machine learning algorithm, using reliabilism. It is not my intention to evaluate this account, on which explanations aren't needed for trustworthy algorithms, here (primarily for reasons of space). Rather, I aim to consider whether the arguments against a requirement of explainability hold up. Is it possible to hold that explainability is needed for trust? So far it seems that the answer is yes, as the arguments against such a requirement seem to fall short. It may still turn out that computational reliabilism, which they defend, is the correct account, but there is more room to argue for transparency than they suggest. In the case of an argument for explainability as a pre-requisite for trust, but also for an explainability requirement due to other reasons. It is this broader view that I explore in the next subsection, with the arguments of Krishnan [12] who goes through a range of possible ends to which explainability is a means.

2.4   Krishnan: Reasons to Explain

There are various reasons we might have to require, or strive for, explainability of machine learning algorithms. There is, as she terms it, the 'justification problem', closely related to questions about trust in algorithms. Explainability is often seen as a way to improve trust, and the above attacks on explainability have tended to focus on this aspect of the question (though Robbins actually focuses on control in his text). Her response here, as that of Durán and Jongsma, is to point to reliabilist accounts in epistemology. There are well-respected theories on which justification isn't linked to interpretability or some kind of awareness of reasons, and only links to reliability. So, putting forward a strong requirement of explainability motivated by trust is neglecting such alternatives, and might be wrong if reliabilist epistemologies are correct.

Trust/justification in general might then be in place without transparency. But a closely related reason to strive for explainability, or perhaps even require it in high stakes contexts, is often overlooked in these discussions. Yes, the algorithm might be trustworthy in general, because it gets it right often enough. But how about our trust in individual outputs? We might be justified to believe these, but surely we'd prefer to have a way to tell whether the algorithm makes good decisions in individual cases. For example, algorithms will perform worse in outlier cases, even when they are generally accurate. Understanding why the algorithm presents a certain output may help to gain a more fine-grained justification, and avoid mistakes that would arise if the algorithm is given blanket trust.

Krishnan would probably respond to this that there are other methods to detect such situations, such as outlier detection methods, which do not require the algorithm to be explainable. At least, that is the argument structure she uses for the other goals that explainability might serve. I can only agree here, such tools are available, and we have a fairly good idea of which conditions impact the reliability of our algorithms. But here, too, we can't make distinctions between outliers where the algorithm makes decisions in a way that seems reasonable, and ones where the algorithm makes decisions in an outlandish manner. For which outliers did the model generalize correctly, and for which will it make gross mistakes? Outlier detection won't be able to tell us. More insight into the processing of the algorithm might, however, provided that we have enough domain knowledge to evaluate its functioning. So there might actually be epistemic reasons to prefer explainability which cannot be readily replaced by accuracy measures. I'll leave this question aside though – I suspect that it's in part an empirical matter whether people actually are better at spotting mistakes if they understand why the algorithm gives a certain output – to move on to the other reasons one might have to demand explainability.

The second such reason that Krishnan discusses is that of fairness, or anti-discrimination in her terms. She naturally agrees that we should tackle this problem, but argues that explainability might not be a necessary ingredient to do so effectively. Fairness measures, possibly supported by synthetic datasets, might do most of the work here. Further investigations into biases of the training data can also help diagnose the source of discrimination by algorithms. Identifying and solving this issue, she argues, is something we can do largely by examining outcomes and training data. The algorithms needn't be transparent for that. I think that's a fair conclusion to draw, though as some of the participants in the workshop pointed out it doesn't mean that explainability methods will not help. Nor is there a guarantee that fairness measures, synthetic datasets, and so on will in practice spot all problems. Perhaps we can do this more effectively if algorithms are transparent than if they are not. For practical reasons, then, we still might prefer explainable algorithms over black boxes for this reason. Time will tell whether it is needed or not, but as she says "Interpretability is more plausibly construed as one tool among many which may prove useful against discrimination." [12, p.497]

The third reason that Krishnan puts forward is that one might want explainability to help weigh the output of the algorithm against other sources of information, or to solve disagreements. Generally speaking, it is the question of "how to synthesize the outputs of different sources into an overall decision and corresponding level of confidence in that decision" [12, p.497]. This is fairly close to the point made above, about the question whether we can trust individual decisions and the role that explainability may have to play there. Krishnan, however, focuses specifically on disagreements and balancing the output of an algorithm with other sources of evidence. It's a related case, but one that focuses primarily on disagreements. Her take on such disagreements is that here, too, we can do without detailed knowledge of why the algorithm reaches a certain output:

When human processes and ML processes track different indicators, they are independent sources whose coincidence should strengthen confidence in the accuracy of a shared conclusion, whereas tracking the same indicators (and especially using the same indicators in a different way) can strengthen confidence in the aptness of the way that human reasoners are processing a given data set, without providing fully independent evidence in favor of the accuracy of that conclusion. Both scrutiny of the content of training data sets and ways of testing classifiers to see what features they actually track are viable ways of extracting this information without scrutiny of the steps that the algorithm performs in arriving at categorizations. [12, p.498]

Having this knowledge of features will certainly help, though I worry that resolving disagreements will not be as straightforward as this. When the same indicators are used, but different conclusions are reached, we surely want to know which way of considering the indicators is better. When people are given the same case, but disagree, we ask them why they reach their respective conclusions, to evaluate which arguments make the most sense. Similarly in the case with the AI, we would want to know whether the disagreement implies that we should trust the algorithm less, or the human judgement. Is one of the two clearly mistaken, or are there good reasons to put forward for both sides, which leads to suspension of judgement in this case of disagreement? Having this information about indicators is useful, but it alone doesn't tell us which confidence levels need to be adjusted downwards in cases of disagreement. Other measures, such as whether the case is dissimilar to the training data of the algorithm, might help here but won't give as much clarity as when the reasons for the output can be evaluated.

Similar issues arise if the algorithm has considered the same indicators, but agrees with us. Should this raise our confidence in the aptness of people's reasoning? Surely this depends, for example on whether the algorithms output is biased (we wouldn't want to say that the person's biased reasoning is apt because it coincides with a similarly biased AI output) or based on spurious correlations. Granted, the question of bias was tackled earlier, but here too we see that whether we raise our confidence or not depends on the type of process that led to the AI output. Krishnan nicely points out that we might learn a lot about this proces without it being transparent, and without explainability tools. Can we really learn all that we need to handle disagreements and reconcile evidence from different sources though? If we look at disagreements with people, then they do seem to resort to answers to why-questions in order to settle disputes. We ask people for their reasons to hold something true or false. Merely resorting to which factors were considered does not seem a sufficient substitute for that, though we might get further than we originally thought should it prove too difficult to make black box algorithms interpretable.

Furthermore, there might be other reasons to require interpretability of (some) algorithms. Krishnan lists two at the end of her paper [12, §3.4]. First, using machine learning in scientific contexts, to generate causal explanations and make scientific discoveries. Second, interpretability might be needed for public trust in these systems, even if it isn't necessary to be justified in believing the outputs. Perhaps, she reasons, society simply won't accept opaque machine learning models in some contexts, partly due to experts who favour explainability requirements. I, and the attendants at the workshop, think we can readily add a number of other goals to which explainability might contribute. Contestability is one, and is part of the reason that counterfactual explanations were introduced [21]. Explanations might also help with accountability, control and model debugging, to name a few.

I should stress, however, that this does not mean that I have now given a positive argument to *require* explainability in certain contexts. All I have room to add here is that the arguments surveyed aim to show that a common practice among people – giving reasons for actions – can be replaced in the AI setting by input features and outcome measures. I'm skeptical that we'll be able to do everything with these substitutes that we can with reasons. Evaluations of the merits of individual decisions, for example, are harder to do even if we can get quite a lot out of knowing what features were used and how reliable the algorithm is. Likewise, figuring out what to do in disagreements between algorithms or between algorithms and people is harder without reasons. One may argue that what we can do without reasons is good enough, and that explainability methods would be a great addition but not a necessary one. An answer to such an argument should depend on more specific cases, with the stakes laid out and our tolerance for mistakes, alongside the capability to detect and handle such mistakes with and without explainability methods. In setting medical diagnoses, for example, we might point to the serious impacts of mistakes and thus the desire for accountability mechanisms and a way to improve after a mistake has been made. Explainability can be important as a result, although it is to be carefully weighed against potentially reduced accuracy. Credit scoring algorithms will present outcomes that are still very impactful, but less so than the life-and-death situations of some medical decisions. Consequently the balance may shift there. In addition, Krishnan and others show that explainability is not a silver bullet: factors such as reliability, bias detection and the interaction between humans and the system all matter for responsible use of AI. Explainability might help, but likely will not solve everything.

In fact, it might turn out that *current* explainability methods don't deliver understanding of AI outputs, and that we also don't want to accept the use of black box algorithms. The conclusion, then, would be that we should work on developing interpretable algorithms instead of black box algorithms. For an argument to that effect, I refer the reader to [18]. It's an interesting argument about what we should give most priority to in current development practices, but one I'll leave aside here. As in the workshop, I want to focus on explainability methods for black box algorithms, and the question of how we should explain algorithms, if we agree that there are good reasons to strive for such explanations. I turn to that in the next section.

3   What Constitutes an Explanation?

The question posed here, 'what constitutes an explanation?' is deliberately abstract. For it is not my goal to offer concrete guidelines on how existing explainability tools are to be improved. Instead, I want to offer some theoretical perspectives that may be unfamiliar to those working in the field of explainable AI, yet may prove fruitful. Philosophers, namely, have thought about the nature of explanation (primarily in the context of the natural sciences) for at least a century. They have tried to unravel the structure that explanations follow, and theorized what it is about those bits of information that provides us with insight. As we strive for similar insight into the workings of machine learning algorithms, it may be that these different views of what information makes up an explanation offer a goal on the horizon to work towards.

One place to start is that in philosophical discussions there is a fairly widespread agreements that whatever explanations are exactly, they are answers to *contrastive* why-questions. The idea is that when we ask for explanations, we typically do so by asking 'why?'. When scientists want an explanation for a phenomenon, they ask why it occurred. When we want an explanation for an action, we ask why that person did it. However, the idea is that these questions have a more specific focus than just the phenomenon or action; they seek an explanation for a specific aspect of it. As Peter Lipton puts it in his influential book on inference to the best explanation:

> We do not explain the eclipse tout court, but only why it lasted as long as
> it did, or why it was partial, or why it was not visible from a certain place.

Which aspect we ask about depends on our interests, and reduces the number of causal factors we need consider for any particular phenomenon, since there will be many causes of the eclipse that are not, for example, causes of its duration. More recently, it has been argued that the interest relativity of explanation can be accounted for with a contrastive analysis of the phenomenon to be explained. What gets explained is not simply 'Why this?', but 'Why this *rather than* that?' (Garfinkel1981:28–41; vanFraassen 1980:126–9). A contrastive phenomenon consists of a fact and a foil, and the same fact may have several different foils. We may not explain why the leaves turn yellow in November simpliciter, but only for example why they turn yellow in November rather than in January, or why they turn yellow in November rather than turn blue. [13, p.33]

That in itself doesn't tell us what the answers to contrastive why-questions look like, but it does point to something that might be missing from current explainability methods. Those do not offer a mechanisms for interest relativity, nor is there an option to consider explanations as operating with both a fact to be explained and a foil for which this explanation should operate. As a final example from Lipton to drive home the relevance of such contrasts: "When I asked my, then, 3-year old son why he threw his food on the floor, he told me that he was full. This may explain why he threw it on the floor rather than eating it, but I wanted to know why he threw it rather than leaving it on his plate." [13, p.33]

Granting that such contrasts are relevant, and that explanations might be construed as answers to contrastive why-questions, the natural follow-up question is: what do such answers look like? Here opinions differ among philosophers, and as a result I discuss three different accounts of what explanations are. I start with the kind of causal account that Lipton hints at, and has become more prominent since under the label of interventionism (and sometimes also manipulationism). Second, I discuss the unificationist framework of scientific explanation, and finally the mechanist framework of such explanations. I stick to brief overviews of these, and won't be arguing for any of the three frameworks over and above the other. Instead, I hope that this section can act as inspiration to further explore these rich discussions of explanations.

3.1   Causal/Interventionist

One possible answer to contrastive why-questions is to offer relevant causes. Why do leaves turn yellow in November rather than in January? Well, we can say something about the causal process that makes them turn yellow, and how this depends on the temperature drops that we already see in November. Not only is that a kind of answer we give routinely, it also matches nicely with the idea that explanations are asymmetrical: we can e.g. explain the length of a shadow based on the length of the object that casts the shadow. It would strike us as strange, however, to explain the length of an object by talking about how long the shadow it casts is, and what the position of the sun is at that time.

Causes can help account for this asymmetry, as it is the object that causes the shadow to be there, and not the other way around.

And so philosophers, such as Woodward [22] have tried to fill in the details of how causes might act as explanations. He starts out defining causation (or rather, a way to determine whether something is a cause, as the definition relies on a previous understanding of cause) on the basis of interventions. The idea is, basically, that X is a cause of Y iff an intervention on X that changes the value from x_1 to x_2 leads to a corresponding change in the value of Y, from y_1 to y_2. The important part here is how we understand interventions, where I is an intervention-variable on X with respect to Y if and only if:

I1. I causes X.

I2. I acts as a switch for all the other variables that cause X. That is, certain values of I are such that when I attains those values, X ceases to depend on the values of other variables that cause X and instead depends only on the value taken by I.

I3. Any directed path from I to Y goes through X. That is, I does not directly cause Y and is not a cause of any causes of Y that are distinct from X except, of course, for those causes of Y, if any, that are built into the I-X-Y connection itself; that is, except for (a) any causes of Y that are effects of X (i.e., variables that are causally between X and Y) and (b) any causes of Y that are between I and X and have no effect on Y independently of X.

I4. I is (statistically) independent of any variable Z that causes Y and that is on a directed path that does not go through X. [22, p.98]

Using this understanding of causes, it is possible to define minimal conditions on when a cause acts as an explanation E for explanandum M. The basic idea behind this definition is that causal explanations should give us information on the value that variable Y actually takes (e.g. the actual output of the algorithm) and inform us how this value changes should the value of X change. Which changes we're interested in depends on the contrast we focus on in our why-question. That then leads to the following more formal definition:

Suppose that M is an explanandum consisting in the statement that some variable Y takes the particular value y. Then an explanans E for M will consist of

(a) a generalization G relating changes in the value(s) of a variable X (where X may itself be a vector or n-tuple of variables X_i) and changes in Y, and

(b) a statement (of initial or boundary conditions) that the variable X takes the particular value x.

A necessary and sufficient condition for E to be (minimally) explanatory with respect to M is that (i) E and M be true or approximately so; (ii) according to G, Y takes the value y under an intervention in which X takes the value x; (iii) there is some intervention that changes the value of X from x to x' where $x \neq x'$, with G correctly describing the value y' that Y would assume under this intervention, where $y' \neq y$. [22, p.203]

While this definition really is rather minimal – a single counterfactual case will do – it showcases the underlying idea of causal explanations. The role of pointing to causes is so that you can determine what would happen if the situation (e.g. the inputs) had been different. Causes are simply those things that affect the outcome/output, and therefore the relevant factors to present. The goal of explanations, on this interventionist account, is thus to be able to tell how changes in the input result in changes to the output. Note that this is thus rather different from the explainability tools that are known as 'counterfactual', as those focus on presenting a single case in which the outcome is different. They do not give us a generalization that covers the actual case and a range of counterfactual cases.

If there's one thing to take away from this account of explanations, then it is the focus on the question: what happens if things are different? Good explanations should answer a wide range of such questions, on this account, and doing so with higher accuracy is naturally better. Furthermore, the range shouldn't be restricted to cases where the outcome is the same (as currently often happens for rule-based local explanations in XAI), but should cover how the outcome/output changes too. In a way this is quite similar to the other two accounts, as the unificationist for example focuses on deriving as many outcomes as possible with the same explanation, though the focus on causes is specific to the interventionist. With that, I leave causes aside, and move to the next account where derivations are the central element of explanations.

3.2   Unificationist

The basic idea behind this second account of explanation, unificationism (defended e.g. by Kitcher in [11]) is that the main role of explanations is to unify a range of different phenomena/observations. For example, Newton's laws of motion gave us a far better understanding of the physical world not because they point to causes, but because they presented us with formulas that showed how a range of different phenomena (e.g. different forces) all behave in the same way. They give a unified way to derive motions on Earth and in the heavens (stars, planets), something which was until that point unavailable. Gravity was derivable as simply another force, of which falling motions on Earth were but one example. It is such an ideal of unification, where a theory manages to give a single set of rules that bring together a wide range of phenomena, that Kitcher holds as the paradigmatic example of succesful explanations.

Yet, what does it mean to unify different phenomena (in the AI case that would be different outputs)? To make this more precise, Kitcher appeals to the notion of argument patterns that can be filled in different ways. The idea is that we start with sentences that have variables in them, that can take different values. Such sentences are schematic:

A schematic sentence is an expression obtained by replacing some, but not necessarily all, the nonlogical expressions occurring in a sentence with dummy letters. Thus, starting with the sentence "Organisms homozygous for the sickling allele develop sickle-cell anemia," we can generate a number of schematic sentences: for example, "Organisms homozygous for A develop P" and "For all x, if x is O and A then xis P" [11, p.432]

To turn a schematic sentence back into a 'normal' sentence, you need to add filling instructions, which specify what values the variables in the schematic sentence take. For example, A can be specified as taking the value 'allele' in the above schematic sentence. Once there are filling instructions for all variables in the schematic sentence, it is no longer schematic and simply a sentence. This functioning of schematic sentences allows for the construction of more abstract argument patterns, which form the basis of the unificationist account. With a little more setup, the basic idea is that we can go through the same procedure for arguments:

A schematic argument is a sequence of schematic sentences. A classification for a schematic argument is a set of statements describing the inferential characteristics of the schematic argument: it tells us which terms of the sequence are to be regarded as premises, which are inferred from which, what rules of inference are used, and so forth. Finally, a general argument pattern is a triple consisting of a schematic argument, a set of sets of filling instructions, one for each term of the schematic argument, and a classification for the schematic argument. [11, p.432]

If we can find a single argument pattern (like Newton's laws of motion) that allows for a very broad set of derivations, then we've succeeded in the goal of unifying phenomena. In Kitcher's words: "Science advances our understanding of nature by showing us how to derive descriptions of many phenomena, using the same pattern of derivation again and again, and in demonstrating this, it teaches us how to reduce the number of facts we have to accept as ultimate" [11, p.432]. Unificationists, then, care about the number of outcomes/outputs that can be correctly derived from the explanation (argument pattern) that is offered. There is no particular focus on cases where the outcome is different, as with the interventionist framework of explanation. Nor do the argument patterns have to involve causes. Of course, it might turn out that general argument patterns often appeal to causes, but the unificationist can be rather more flexible here in what can figure in an explanation.

As a result, the unificationist framework might be closer to the current explainability methods. Of course, local explanations using decision rules/trees don't manage to unify very many outcomes, and aren't always correct in their predictions of model behaviour. But the basic direction is one that a unificationist, looking for patterns from which different outcomes can be derived, might endorse. There are more ways to go, however, as one might look not just at unifying different outputs of the same algorithm, but strive for argument patterns that work across algorithms or for connecting the outputs of one algorithm with theories in that domain of application. At least in the case of healthcare, Durán has made an argument for precisely such a connection with scientific theories in the explanations of algorithms [5]. Drawing more of these connections may be a way to push explanations forward. Although it may also help to, instead of unifying with parts outside of the algorithm, look at the inner mechanism more. That, at least, is the idea behind the last account I discuss.

3.3 Mechanists

Finally, there is a third account that again looks at causes to some extent. It differs from interventionism, however, in that the real focus here is on models that capture the mechanisms of a system. Those models are what do the explaining, and it is the representation of mechanisms in virtue of which these models explain. These accounts have changed somewhat compared to when it was first presented by Salmon [19], as they now look at constitutive explanations rather than etiological ones:

> Etiological explanations reveal the antecedent events that cause the explanandum phenomenon. Constitutive explanations, in contrast, reveal the organized activities of and interactions among parts that underlie, or constitute, the explanandum phenomenon. More specifically, they describe features of the mechanism for a phenomenon, where the mechanism includes the set of all and only the entities, activities and organizational features relevant to that phenomenon. [3, p.297]

This is a view of explanation that seems to work quite naturally in, for example, biology where if we want to understand the human body we're interested in a model that captures the functioning of the different parts and their causal role in the whole. The difficulty in applying this conception to AI is that machine learning models are far too complex for a complete model of their workings (which we have, after all) to offer much insight. And it's not just machine learning where this is the case, as we can wonder for the human body too how detailed these mechanistic models should be. Do they have to include absolutely everything that is relevant? Are more details automatically better? The point of [3] is to argue that this isn't the case, and that only those factors that are causally relevant matter. This is reflected in why they think that mechanistic models explain:

> A constitutive mechanistic model has explanatory force for phenomenon P versus P' if and only if (a) at least some of its variables refer to internal details relevant to P versus P', and (b) the dependencies posited among the variables refer causal dependencies among those variables (and between them and the inputs and outputs definitive of the phenomenon) relevant to P versus P'. [3, p.401]

Note again the focus on a contrast between P, which we want to explain, and P' from which it needs to be distinguished. Such contrasts can limit which parts of the mechanism are relevant. Furthermore, not every detail matters: only those that are causally relevant do. The question is where this leaves us with machine learning models, as here every parameter might have some causal relevance for the output of the algorithm. Can we really restrict the model to a manageable set of factors, then, in the case of machine learning algorithms? Perhaps not if we look at explanations of the internal mechanism for the algorithm itself, but if we take a slightly broader view of the system at play there is room for applying the account to AI. The training set, hyperparameters, number of layers, etc. all influence the outcomes, namely. They are causally relevant, and there aren't so overwhelmingly many of them that a complete mechanistic model would fail to generate real insights. An option, then, to apply the mechanistic account to AI is to take the factors not on the level of individual parameters (of which there are millions to trillions), but on a slightly more abstract level. It still makes sense to speak of a mechanistic model, and all the different factors are causally relevant for the outcome. So, an explanation in this sense looks at that interplay of factors, and as such offers a somewhat different way of considering causation in the explanation of AI outputs.

3.4 Bringing Theory into Practice

The types of explanations found in the philosophical literature are far from what current XAI tools provide. So, what can developers of (X)AI tools do about this discrepancy? First of all, as can be seen explicitly in most accounts, explanations are ideally presented in a contrastive format. That is, they answer questions of the form 'why P rather than Q?' instead of plainly 'why P?'. As pointed out elsewhere [16] this is a common feature of how humans explain, yet is not found in current XAI tools. Incorporating contrasts, and using these to direct the explanation, can be a first step towards XAI that more squarely fits the philosophical definitions of explanation.

Second, while current XAI tools might not conform to the definitions of explanation, that does not entail that they can serve none of the goals of explainability. Feature importance maps and counterfactuals can hint that the model looks at features that we think are irrelevant, even if they generally do not enlighten us as to why the model looks at those features. Similarly, bias detection can be aided by current XAI tools if part of the features the model uses are protected. In practice, therefore, XAI tools can still be useful even if they do not provide explanations proper.

Finally, I hope that the definitions provided here can help in the development of new explainability tools that do get closer to explanations as conceptualized in philosophy. A focus on generalizations that include counterfactuals (a combination that is rare in current XAI methods) is suggested by both causal and mechanistic accounts of explanation. In addition, Tools or explanations that consider what happens if training data or hyperparameters are changed, that to my knowledge do not yet exist, are also suggested by these accounts and might help us understand how we can improve AI systems. Most of all, the challenge is to design tools that can highlight the patterns used by AI models, as the unificationist account also points out. That is easier said than done, given both the non-linearity of machine learning models and their complexity. Still, clear definitions of explanation have been lacking in the literature on XAI and here philosophy can be helpful.

4   Conclusion

I have given a brief overview here of the reasons put forward against a requirement of explainability, and of accounts that might help us fill in what this end goal of explainability might mean. I've argued that providing such explanations doesn't make opaque machine learning methods redundant, as we typically can evaluate reasons without being able to replicate our thinking in decision rules. It also doesn't have to be unfair to ask for explanations in this case, as the examples pushed by London aren't of decision making processes, but rather focus on the treatments about which we decide. That brought us to reliabilism, and the question of whether there isn't some kind of regress in asking for explainability. While I think that such a regress is unlikely, there is a question of whether explainability is truly a requirement for trust/justification. Perhaps reliabilism offers an account on which we can do without explainability, and perhaps we can do more with input/output measures than we thought – as Krishnan points out. Still, there seem to remain good reasons to develop explainability methods, even if we don't end up requiring algorithms to be transparent.

Because of those reasons I went on a brief tour through accounts of explanation in the philosophical literature. For if we aim to make machine learning explainable, it might help to have a better sense of what explanations would ideally look like. Views differ here, but there is a surprising amount of agreement about the contrastive nature of explanations. One that, surprisingly, we do not yet see in technical explainability tools. Proceeding from there we see a range of options: interventionists who focus on causal dependencies and the ability to say what the output would be if the input were different. Unificationists who look at argument patterns that are as general as possible, allowing us to derive a wide range of outcomes. And finally mechanistic accounts, who focus on models that describe the inner workings of a system with as many causally relevant details as possible. Hopefully these can inspire improvements to explainability methods.

5   Suggested Readings

- Rudin, Stop explaining black box machine learning models for high stakes decisions and use interpretable models instead [18]
- Miller, Explanation in artificial intelligence: Insights from the social sciences [16]

- Woodward, Making things happen: A theory of causal explanation [22]
- Kitcher, Explanatory unification and the causal structure of the world [11]
- Craver and Kaplan, Are more details better? On the norms of completeness for mechanistic explanations [3]

References

1. Adadi, A., Berrada, M.: Peeking inside the black-box: a survey on explainable artificial intelligence (XAI). IEEE Access **6**, 52138–52160 (2018)
2. Boella, G., Mori, M.: An introduction to ethics and AI. In: Chetouani, M., et al. (eds.) ACAI 2021. LNCS, vol. 13500, pp. 245–260. Springer, Cham (2022)
3. Craver, C.F., Kaplan, D.M.: Are more details better? on the norms of completeness for mechanistic explanations. Br. J. Philos. Sci. **71**(1), 287–319 (2020)
4. Das, A., Rad, P.: Opportunities and challenges in explainable artificial intelligence (XAI): a survey. arXiv preprint. arXiv:2006.11371 (2020)
5. Durán, J.M.: Dissecting scientific explanation in AI (sXAI): a case for medicine and healthcare. Artif. Intell. **297**, 103498 (2021)
6. Durán, J.M., Jongsma, K.R.: Who is afraid of black box algorithms? on the epistemological and ethical basis of trust in medical AI. J. Med. Ethics **47**(5), 329–335 (2021)
7. Ferrario, A., Loi, M.: How explainability contributes to trust in AI. SSRN 4020557 (2022)
8. Giannotti, F., Naretto, F., Bodria, F.: Explainable machine learning for trustworthy AI. In: Chetouani, M., et al. (eds.) ACAI 2021. LNCS, vol. 13500, pp. 175–195. Springer, Cham (2022)
9. Goldman, A.: What is justified belief? In: Pappas, G.S. (ed.) Justification and Knowledge, pp. 1–23. Springer, Dordrecht (1979)
10. Guidotti, R., Monreale, A., Ruggieri, S., Turini, F., Giannotti, F., Pedreschi, D.: A survey of methods for explaining black box models. ACM Computi. Surv. (CSUR) **51**(5), 1–42 (2018)
11. Kitcher, P.: Explanatory unification and the causal structure of the world (1989)
12. Krishnan, M.: Against interpretability: a critical examination of the interpretability problem in machine learning. Philos. Technol. **33**(3), 487–502 (2020). https://doi.org/10.1007/s13347-019-00372-9
13. Lipton, P.: Inference to the Best Explanation. Routledge, Milton Park (2003)
14. London, A.J.: Artificial intelligence and black-box medical decisions: accuracy versus explainability. Hastings Cent. Rep. **49**(1), 15–21 (2019)
15. Methnani, L., Brännström, M., Theodorou, A.: Operationalising AI ethics: conducting socio-technical assessment. In: Chetouani, M., et al. (eds.) ACAI 2021. LNCS, vol. 13500, pp. 304–321. Springer, Cham (2022)
16. Miller, T.: Explanation in artificial intelligence: insights from the social sciences. Artif. Intell. **267**, 1–38 (2019)
17. Robbins, S.: A misdirected principle with a catch: explicability for AI. Mind. Mach. **29**(4), 495–514 (2019). https://doi.org/10.1007/s11023-019-09509-3
18. Rudin, C.: Stop explaining black box machine learning models for high stakes decisions and use interpretable models instead. Nat. Mach. Intell. **1**(5), 206–215 (2019)
19. Salmon, W.C.: Scientific explanation: three basic conceptions. In: PSA: Proceedings of the Biennial Meeting of the Philosophy of Science Association, pp. 293–305. no. 2. Philosophy of Science Association (1984)

20. Slavkovik, M.: Mythical ethical principles for AI and how to attain them. In: Chetouani, M., et al. (eds.) ACAI 2021. LNCS, vol. 13500, pp. 275–303. Springer, Cham (2022)
21. Wachter, S., Mittelstadt, B., Russell, C.: Counterfactual explanations without opening the black box: automated decisions and the GDPR. Harv. J. Law Tech. **31**, 841 (2017)
22. Woodward, J.: Making Things Happen: A Theory of Causal Explanation. Oxford University Press, Oxford (2005)

Artificial Visual Intelligence

Perceptual Commonsense for Human-Centred Cognitive Technologies

Mehul Bhatt[1,3(✉)] and Jakob Suchan[2]

[1] Örebro University, Örebro, Sweden
mehul.bhatt@oru.se
[2] German Aerospace Center (DLR), Oldenburg, Germany
jakob.suchan@dlr.de
[3] CoDesign Lab EU/Cognition. AI. Interaction. Design., Stockholm, Sweden
https://codesign-lab.org

Abstract. We address computational cognitive vision and perception at the interface of language, logic, cognition, and artificial intelligence. The chapter presents general methods for the processing and semantic interpretation of dynamic visuospatial imagery with a particular emphasis on the ability to abstract, learn, and reason with cognitively rooted structured characterisations of commonsense knowledge pertaining to space and motion. The presented work constitutes a systematic model and methodology integrating diverse, multi-faceted AI methods pertaining Knowledge Representation and Reasoning, Computer Vision, and Machine Learning towards realising practical, human-centred artificial visual intelligence.

Keywords: Cognitive vision · Knowledge representation and reasoning · Commonsense reasoning · Deep semantics · Declarative spatial reasoning · Computer vision · Computational models of narrative · Human-centred computing and design · Spatial cognition and AI · Visual perception · Multimodal interaction · Autonomous driving · HRI · Media · Visual art

Chapter Objectives. We present a conceptual overview of computational cognitive vision together with practical demonstrations as follows:

- human-centred, explainable model of computational visuospatial intelligence primarily at the interface of symbolic and neural techniques is presented; a systematic integration of techniques in AI and Vision is emphasised;
- we introduce deep semantics, entailing systematically formalised declarative (neurosymbolic) reasoning and learning with aspects pertaining to space, space-time, motion, actions & events, and spatio-linguistic conceptual knowledge;

M. Chetouani et al. (Eds.): ACAI 2021, LNAI 13500, pp. 216–242, 2023.
https://doi.org/10.1007/978-3-031-24349-3_12

- ▶ we present general foundational commonsense abstractions of space, time, and motion needed for representation mediated reasoning and learning with dynamic visuospatial stimuli in human-centred cognitive technologies;
- ▶ applied case-studies of socio-technological significance in domains such as autonomous driving, cognitive robotics, media studies are demonstrated; and
- ▶ we make a case for an interdisciplinary method for realising computational visual intelligence, and also indicate avenues for further research.

1   Introduction

We characterise *artificial visual intelligence* as:

> the computational capability to semantically process, interpret, and explain diverse forms of visual stimuli (typically) emanating from sensing embodied multimodal interaction of/amongst humans and other artefacts in diverse naturalistic situations of everyday life and profession.

Through semantic processing, interpretation, and explanation, alluded here are a wide-spectrum of high-level human-centred *sensemaking* capabilities. These capabilities encompass functions such as visuospatial conception formation, commonsense/qualitative generalisation, hypothetical reasoning, analogical inference, argumentation, event based episodic maintenance & retrieval for perceptual narrativisation, counterfactual reasoning and explanation etc. In essence, in scope are all high-level commonsense visuospatial sensemaking capabilities –be it mundane, analytical, or creative in nature– that humans acquire developmentally or through specialised training, and are routinely adept at performing seamlessly in their everyday life and work.

(Artificial) Visual Intelligence: A Multi-faceted Approach

We posit that building general artificial visual intelligence systems –in the manner characterised herein– requires the integration of diverse, multi-faceted methods from multiple sub-fields in Artificial Intelligence, Cognitive Science, and Visual Perception. Furthermore, the incorporation and realisation of human-centred considerations in the design and engineering of computational visual intelligence particularly requires interdisciplinary input from behavioural research areas concerning cognitive human factors relevant to:

1. the structure and function of natural vision and visual perception (e.g., (in)attention, search, change blindness, event perception) from the viewpoint of cognitive neuroscience and psychology; and
2. embodied multimodal interaction under *ecologically valid* (application-centred) naturalistic conditions inherent to particular everyday social and professional contexts.

In essence, building human-centred visual intelligence systems will require a systematic study and exploration of synergies between both the artificial and human aspects of visual intelligence. Given the objectives and scope of this chapter, of primary focus here are Knowledge Representation and Reasoning, Declarative Spatial Reasoning, Computer Vision, Machine Learning, and (from an applied viewpoint) Visual Perception.

Cognitive Vision and Perception

In the backdrop of the aforestated functional perspective on artificial visual intelligence, the central focus of this chapter is to present recent developments in that regard in the backdrop of our research in (computational) cognitive vision and perception. These developments have been driven by bringing together a novel combination of methodologies from Artificial Intelligence, Vision and Machine Learning, Cognitive Science and Psychology, Visual Perception, and Spatial Cognition and Computation towards realising and demonstrating a much-needed functional model of human-centred computational or artificial visual intelligence.

From a methodological viewpoint, our research (in cognitive vision and perception) explicitly addresses visual, visuospatial and visuo-locomotive perception and interaction from the viewpoints of (spatial) language, (spatial logics), and (spatial) cognition (e.g., [9]). To reiterate, the principal technical focus is on a systematic integration of methods in knowledge representation & reasoning and commonsense spatial reasoning with visual computing techniques in computer vision. This systematic integration –bridging "AI and Vision"– is pursued from the viewpoint of applied functional (perceptual sensemaking) challenges such as:

1. Commonsense scene understanding
2. Explainable visual interpretation
3. Semantic question-answering
4. Concept learning & analogical inference
5. Visuospatial (concept) representation learning
6. Image-schematic generalisation
7. Multimodal event perception

In this backdrop, the central aim of this chapter is two-fold:

– to highlight research in cognitive vision and perception as a model for artificial visual intelligence, thereby also providing a roadmap for the development of human-centred visuospatial sensemaking solutions.
– to conceptually illustrate systematically formalised, general methods based on an integration of (relational) AI and (deep learning based) computer vision, and showcase their applications in multidisciplinary areas of socio-technological impact.

Secondarily, we also present concrete working examples pertaining diverse application domains such that functional capabilities of general methods for cognitive vision and perception are operationally visible (at least to some extent).

The rest of the chapter is structured as follows:

Table 1. Visuospatial commonsense reasoning and learning (select examples; Sect. 4)

Examples	Scope	Page
Ex. 1	Semantic Q/A with Video and Eye-Tracking	Pg. 226
Ex. 2	Declarative Grounding of Embodied Interactions	Pg. 228
Ex. 3	Joint Abduction of Scene Dynamics and Object Motion	Pg. 230
Ex. 4	Declarative Explainability – Case of Human-Centred Symmetry	Pg. 233
Ex. 5	Learning Relational Space-Time Structure	Pg. 235

► **Section** 2 motivates with key applications that presently inspire the development of computational cognitive vision; we aim to indicate key technical considerations that are identifiable in view of application needs.

► **Section** 3 introduces the crucial notion of deep semantics, essentially characterising the domain-neutral or foundational crux of commonsense reasoning and learning about space and motion.

► **Section** 4 builds on Sects. 2–3 by providing a practical or operational view of visuospatial commonsense reasoning and learning through five complementary examples (Table 1); here, Examples 1–5 illustrate capabilities for visuospatial question-answering, abductive inference, and relational learning. We reflect upon the overall line of this research in Sect. 5, also pointing out select open as well as long-range challenges.

Appendices A–B provide supplementary information intended to guide readers seeking go deeper into the presented material.

2   Application: Human-Centred Cognitive Technologies

From an applied viewpoint, foundational computational capabilities pertaining to deep (visuospatial) semantics (are intended to) translate to:

> (human-centred) techniques and methods for modelling, interpreting and anticipating human-behaviour (e.g., from data pertaining to physical interactions) encompassing (interactive, real-time, or even offline) derivation of knowledge, desires, preferences, attitude, and sentiments in a variety of joint man-machine cognitive systems.

Cognitive vision research, and particularly the articulation of deep (visuospatial) semantics (Sect. 3) and the design of corresponding computational models, is inspired –if not fully driven– by real-world application demands encountered in a range of human-centred cognitive technologies involving the offline and online/realtime interpretation of embodied multimodal interaction. Naturally, application potentials are aplenty and perhaps non-exhaustive; case-studies that we focus on –at least in so far as this chapter is concerned– include autonomous driving, commonsense cognitive robotics, (eye-tracking driven) visual media reception, computational aesthetics, and behavioural research in embodied visual and

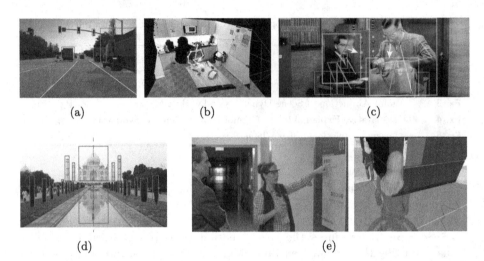

(a)   (b)   (c)

(d)   (e)

Fig. 1. Application scenarios: autonomous systems, minds and media studies, behavioural research in multimodality interaction.

visuo-locomotive interaction (both in real as well as virtual environments) vis-a-vis their relevance for the design of products/experiences (e.g., for architecture design) (Fig. 1):

▶ **Autonomous Systems/Self-Driving Vehicles. Cognitive Robotics.** Here, opportunities range from active visual sensemaking (e.g., through grounded visual abduction and mental simulation) to post-hoc analysis of quantitative archives, natural human-machine interaction, and standardisation from the viewpoint of licensing and validation [44,45]. Within cognitive robotics in particular, the role of semantically grounded low-level motion control, and significance of representation in semantic behavioural policy learning, dialog based social interaction is also crucial.

▶ **Minds and Media Studies/Visuoauditory Media. Visual Perception. Computational Aesthetics.** Cognitive media studies—encompassing film, news, animation, virtual reality etc.—has emerged as an area of research at the interface of disciplines as diverse as AI, psychology, neuroscience, film theory, aesthetics, and cognitive science. Here, opportunities for computational cognitive vision range from technological capabilities aimed at investigating attention & recipient effects vis-a-vis visuoauditory media, e.g., encompassing high-level analysis of subject's visual fixation patterns and correlating this explainable semantic analysis of the digital media under consideration. Computational cognitive vision can been seen as a general AI-based assistive technology platform for cognitive media studies in particular, and the computational explainable interpretation, analysis, archiving (etc.) of visuoauditory art in general.

▶ **Behavioural Research in Embodied Multimodal Interaction.** Here, we allude to behavioural multimodality research in cognitive science and psychology aimed at the study of embodied multimodal interaction of humans under real world, naturalistic conditions, i.e., "in-the-wild". The multimodality that is alluded to here stems from an inherent synergistic value in the integrated processing and interpretation of a range of data sources such as vision, gesture, speech, language, visual attention, facial expressions, tactile interactions, olfaction [6].

Irrespective of a specific application domain, the general underlying impetus and functional requirement is to cognitively assist and empower in planning, decision-making, design situations requiring an interplay of commonsense, creative, and specialist (visuospatial) intelligence.

3 Deep Semantics: On Neurosymbolic Explainability

Computational visual intelligence requires a systematically developed general and modular integration of high-level techniques concerned with "commonsense and semantics" with low-level methods –neural or otherwise– capable of computing primitive features of interest in visual data. In view of this notion of neurosymbolism, we demonstrate the significance of semantically-driven methods rooted in knowledge representation and reasoning (KR) in addressing research questions pertaining to explainability and human-centred AI particularly from the viewpoint of (perceptual) sensemaking of dynamic visual imagery (Sect. 3.1). For demonstration purposes, this is done in the backdrop of diverse application areas where embodied multimodal interaction in naturalistic everyday settings is of the essence (Sect. 2).

3.1   What is Deep Semantics?

The development of domain-independent computational models of perceptual sensemaking—e.g., encompassing visuospatial Q/A, learning, abduction—with multimodal human behavioural stimuli such as RGB(D), video, audio, eye-tracking requires the representational and inferential mediation of commonsense and spatio-linguistically rooted abstractions of space, motion, actions, events and interaction.

We characterise deep (visuospatial) semantics as:

▸ the existence of declarative models –e.g., pertaining to space, space-time, motion, actions & events, spatio-linguistic conceptual knowledge– and corresponding formalisation supporting (domain-neutral) commonsense cognitive reasoning capabilities –such as visuospatial question-answering and learning, non-monotonic visuospatial abduction– with quantitatively sensed dynamic visual imagery. Here, it is of the essence that an expressive ontology consisting of, for instance, space, time, space-time motion primitives as first-class objects is accessible within the (declarative) programming paradigm under consideration

Deep semantics therefore emphasises generality, modularity, and elaboration tolerance in the processing and semantic interpretation of dynamic visuospatial imagery with an emphasis, in so far as the present chapter is concerned, on the ability to **abstract, learn, and reason** with cognitively rooted structured characterisations of commonsense knowledge about **space and motion.** Formal semantics and computational models of deep semantics manifest themselves in declarative AI settings such as Constraint Logic Programming (CLP) [26], Inductive Logic Programming (ILP) [30], and Answer Set Programming (ASP) [12]. Naturally, a practical illustration of the integrated "AI and Vision" method requires a tight but modular integration of the (declarative) commonsense spatio-temporal abstraction and reasoning (Sect. 3.2) with robust low-level visual computing foundations (primarily) driven by state of the art visual computing techniques (e.g., for visual feature detection, tracking, Appendix B).

At a higher level of abstraction, deep semantics entails inherent support for tackling a range of challenges concerning *epistemological* and *phenomenological* aspects relevant to a wide range of *dynamic spatial systems* [4,5,8]:

- **interpolation and projection** of missing information, e.g., what could be hypothesised about missing information (e.g., moments of occlusion); how can this hypothesis support planning an immediate next step?
- object **identity maintenance** at a semantic level, e.g., in the presence of occlusions, missing and noisy quantitative data, error in detection and tracking
- ability to make **default assumptions**, e.g., pertaining to persistence objects and/or object attributes
- maintaining **consistent beliefs** respecting (domain-neutral) commonsense criteria, e.g., related to compositionality & indirect effects, space-time continuity, positional changes resulting from motion
- inferring/computing **counterfactuals**, in a manner akin to human cognitive ability to perform mental simulation for purposes of introspection, performing "what-if" reasoning tasks etc.

Addressing such challenges—be it realtime or post-hoc—in view of human-centred AI concerns pertaining to representations rooted to natural language, explainability, ethics and regulation requires a systematic (neurosymbolic) integration of **Semantics and Vision**, i.e., robust commonsense representation & inference about *spacetime dynamics* (Sect. 3.2) on the one hand, and powerful low-level visual computing capabilities, e.g., pertaining to object detection and tracking on the other (Appendix B). Furthermore, of at least equal importance are the *modularity* and *elaboration tolerance* of the framework, enabling seamless integration and experimentation with advances in fast evolving computer vision methods, as well as experimenting with different forms of formal methods

Table 2. Commonsense abstractions of space and motion

SPACE-TIME DOMAIN	Spatial, Time, Motion Relations ($\mathcal{R}$)	Entities ($\mathcal{E}$)
Mereotopology	disconnected (dc), external contact (ec), partial overlap (po), tangential proper part (tpp), non-tangential proper part (ntpp), proper part (pp), part of (p), discrete (dr), overlap (o), contact (c)	arbitrary rectangles, circles, polygons, cuboids, spheres
Incidence	interior, on boundary, exterior, discrete, intersects	2D point with rectangles, circles, polygons; 3D point with cuboids, spheres
Orientation	left, right, collinear, front, back, on, facing towards, facing away, same direction, opposite direction	2D point, circle, polygon with 2D line
Distance, Size	adjacent, near, far, smaller, equi-sized, larger	rectangles, circles, polygons, cuboids, spheres
Motion	moving: towards, away, parallel; growing / shrinking: vertically, horizontally; splitting / merging; rotation: left, right, up, down, clockwise, couter-clockwise	rectangles, circles, polygons, cuboids, spheres
Time	before, after, meets, overlaps, starts, during, finishes, equals	time-points, time intervals

for *reasoning about space, actions, and change* [4, 8] that could either be embedded directly within specialised commonsense reasoning frameworks, or possibly be utilised independently as part of other general declarative frameworks for knowledge representation and reasoning.

3.2   Commonsense, Space, Change

Commonsense spatio-temporal relations and patterns (e.g., *left, touching, part of, during, collision*; Table 2) offer a human-centered and cognitively adequate formalism for semantic grounding and automated reasoning for everyday (embodied) multimodal interactions [9, 29]. Qualitative, multi-domain[1] representations of spatial, temporal, and spatio-temporal relations and motion patterns (e.g., Figs. 2–3), and their mutual transitions can provide a mapping between high-level semantic models of actions and events on one hand, and low-level/quantitative trajectory data emanating from visual computing algorithms (Appendix B) on the other. For instance, by spatio-linguistically grounding complex trajectory data –e.g., pertaining to on-road moving objects– to a formal framework of space and motion, generalized (activity-based) commonsense reasoning about dynamic scenes, spatial relations, and motion trajectories denoting single and multi-object path & motion predicates can be supported. For

---

[1] Multi-domain refers to more than one aspect of space, e.g., topology, orientation, direction, distance, shape; this requires a mixed domain ontology involving points, line-segments, polygons, and regions of space, time, and space-time [21, 35, 48].

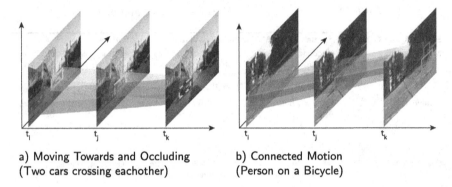

a) Moving Towards and Occluding   b) Connected Motion
(Two cars crossing eachother)   (Person on a Bicycle)

Fig. 2. Space-time histories in context: motion tracks under conditions of occlusion and partial overlap

instance, such predicates can be abstracted within a region-based 'space-time' framework [35] (Fig. 2–3), object interactions [15,16], or even spatio-temporal narrative knowledge. An adequate commonsense spatio-temporal representation can, therefore, connect with low-level quantitative data, and also help to ground symbolic descriptions of actions and objects to be queried, reasoned about, or even manipulated in the real world.

4   Visuospatial Commonsense: On Neurosymbolic Reasoning and Learning

Cognitive vision research is driven by (but not limited to) applications where, for instance, the processing and semantic interpretation of (potentially large volumes of) highly dynamic visuo-spatial imagery is central: autonomous systems, human-machine interaction in cognitive robotics, visuoauditory media technology, and psychology & behavioural research domains where data-centred analytical methods are gaining momentum. For this chapter, we position mutually related/complementary works that are representative of the crux of *deep semantics* (Fig. 4):

- human-centred representation & relational explainability,
- declarative reasoning enabled by systematic formalisation, and
- domain-independence vis-a-vis commonsense spatio-linguistic abstractions supported for modelling space, events, actions, motion, and (inter)action.

What follows is a practical or operational view of visuospatial commonsense reasoning and learning through a series of complementary illustrations in Examples 1–5 showcasing capabilities for visuospatial question-answering, abductive inference, and relational learning:[2]

---

[2] Select publications relevant to these chosen examples include: visuospatial questions-answering [37,39–41], visuospatial abduction [43,45,47,49], and integration of learning and reasoning [42,46].

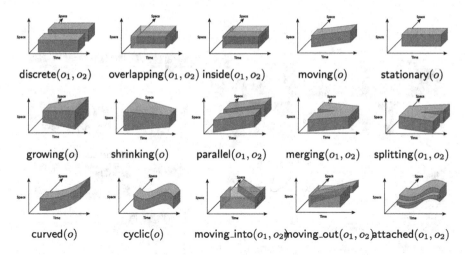

Fig. 3. Commonsense spatial reasoning with spatio-temporal entities. Illustrated are: space-time histories for spatio-temporal patterns and events

I. Visuospatial Question-Answering

Focus is on a computational framework for semantic-question answering with video and eye-tracking data founded in constraint logic programming is developed; we also demonstrate an application in cognitive film & media studies, where human perception of films vis-a-via cinematographic devices [39] is of interest.

▶ **Example** 1   applies deep semantics for query answering and semantic sense-making of spectators eye-tracking behaviour vis-a-vis the moving image.

▶ **Example** 2   presents declarative space and motion for embodied grounding of everyday activities in a cognitive robotics setting.

II. Visuospatial Abduction

Focus is on a hybrid architecture for systematically computing robust visual explanation(s) encompassing hypothesis formation, belief revision, and default reasoning with video data (for active vision for autonomous driving, as well as for offline processing). The architecture supports visual abduction with *space-time histories* as native entities, and founded in (functional) answer set programming based spatial reasoning [47, 48].

▶ **Example** 3   showcases visual abduction for jointly abducing object tracks together with high-level explanations in the context of autonomous driving.

III. Relational Visuospatial Learning

Focus is on a general framework and pipeline for: relational spatio-temporal (inductive) learning with an elaborate ontology supporting a range of space-time features; and generating semantic, (declaratively) explainable interpreta-

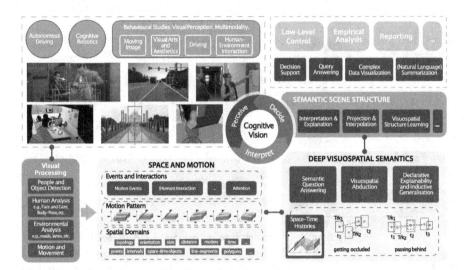

Fig. 4. Cognitive vision and perception: deep semantics for space, action and motion – integrated vision and AI foundations for human behavioural research in embodied multimodal interaction; E.g., *"multimodal visuoauditory computing in context for the case of media studies, and everyday activity analysis from the viewpoint of cognitive robotics"*.

tion models in a neurosymbolic pipeline (demonstrated for the case of analysing visuospatial symmetry in (visual) art);

▶ **Example** 4   presents declarative explainability in the context of a multi-level characterisation of (reflectional) symmetry.

▶ **Example** 5   uses inductive logic programming (ILP) for learning rules about symmetrical spatial structure.

Other works closely related to the development and application of the deep semantics methodology address relational inductive-abductive inference with video [19], and modelling and interpretation of embodied multimodal interaction in cognitive robotics [37, 41].

Example 1. Semantic Q/A with Video and Eye-Tracking

Semantic interpretation and question-answering is applied in the context of empirical research concerned with the human reception of films, where visual question-answering is demonstrated in support of visual perception research in *Cognitive Film Studies.*

To facilitate this analysis, relational characterisations of visual perception are developed and declaratively grounded with respect to primitive spatio-temporal entities and motion patterns, pertaining to the structure of the scene and the dynamics of spectators gaze, i.e., obtained from a computational pipeline for visual processing and gaze analysis. In particular we extract geometric entities representing the following scene elements and perceptual artefacts:

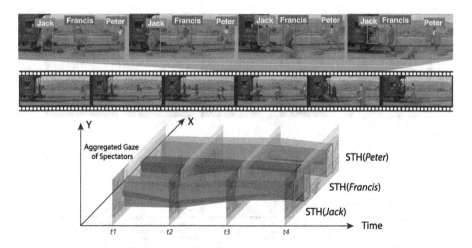

Fig. 5. Semantic scene structure and attention: people movement and fixation clusters.

- *Structural elements of the scene*, e.g., object/character identity and placement, shots and shot types, categories of camera movement.
- *Perceptual artefacts*, e.g., visual fixation, saccadic movements, gaze patterns, pertaining to the *perception and reception* of the moving image.

Scene dynamics are represented using space-time histories of people tracks and spectators eye-tracking data aggregated to Areas of Attention (AOA).

For the sample movie scene depicted in Fig. 5 one could, for instance, formulate a query to determine **what happened** when the AOA following *Jack* and *Francis* merged?

Here we query the corresponding space-time histories of characters Jack and Francis, and the aggregated AOAs, using the *sth* predicate. The predicates *occurs_in* and *occurs_at* are used to query the motion pattern of the *sths*, i.e., the AOAs following the characters and the merging of the AOAs. Further we use the *occurs_in* predicate to query the motion pattern that occurs in the time interval when the AOAs are merging.

```
?- Int = interval(_, _), TP = timepoint(_),
   sth(jack, STH_jack), sth(francis, STH_francis),
   sth(attention(AOA_1), STH_AOA_1), sth(attention(AOA_2), STH_AOA_2),
   occurs_in(attn_following(STH_AOA_1, STH_jack), _),
   occurs_in(attn_following(STH_AOA_2, STH_francis), _),
   occurs_at(merge([STH_AOA_1, STH_AOA_2], _), TP),
   occurs_in(Obs, Int), time(TP, Int, during).
```

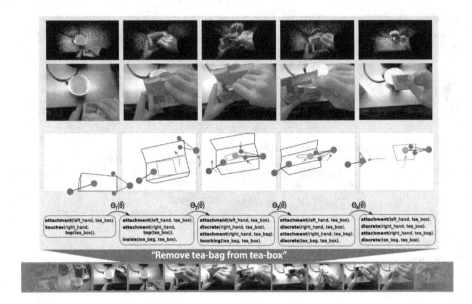

Fig. 6. Relational grounding of everyday activity: "making a cup of tea" (egocentric view from a head-mounted RGB-D capture device)

As a result we get that *Francis* is approaching *Jack* when the respective AOA merge.

```
Obs = approaching(francis, jack),
Int = interval(25, 30),
TP = 28;
...
```

Such question answering provides a basis for analysing the correlation between scene structure and eye-movements, and serve as an intermediate semantic abstraction layer for summarising and externalising the dynamics of visual attention vis-a-vis the moving image.

Example 2. Declarative Grounding of Embodied Interactions

Embodied grounding refers to the ability to link high-level conceptual knowledge, e.g., pertaining to vision, touch, and bodily motion, to (spatio-temporal) experiences in everyday life [20]. In this context qualitative space and motion provide an intermediate (image schematic) abstraction layer for representing and reasoning about everyday activities.

For instance, consider Fig. 6 consisting of a sample human activity—"*making a cup of tea*"—as captured from an egocentric viewpoint with a head-mounted RGB-D capture device. From a commonsense viewpoint, this activity may be represented as a sequence of dynamic visuospatial interactions, such as the following:

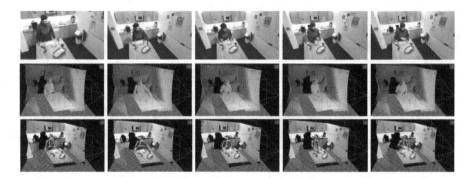

Fig. 7. RGB-D data of human activities with corresponding skeleton data

opening the tea-box, removing a tea-bag from the box and putting the tea-bag inside a tea-cup filled with water while holding the tea-cup.

Such interactions correspond to high-level spatial and temporal relationships between the agent and other involved objects, constituting an embodied grounding, e.g., involving conceptual representations of contact and containment that hold across specific time-intervals. In this context, manipulation and control actions $(\Theta_1(\vec{\theta}), ...\Theta_n(\vec{\theta}))$ cause state transitions in the world, modelled as changes in the spatio-temporal relations amongst involved domain entities. Similarly the activity of making a sandwich (depicted in Fig. 7) may be characterised with respect to the interactions between a human and its environment as follows:

Person1 *reaches* for the bread, *picks up* a slice of bread, and *moves* the hand together with the bread *back* to the chopping board.

The scene is captured using an RGB-D sensor providing 3D positions of skeleton joints and tabletop objects for each time-point.

```
at(joint(id(0), person(id(1))),
   tracking_status(2), pos_3d(point(0.230083,-0.0138919,2.05633)), time_point(2168577589)).
at(joint(id(1), person(id(1))),
   tracking_status(2), pos_3d(point(0.228348,0.275798,1.98048)), time_point(2168577589)).
...
at(object(id(0)), type(bread),
  pos_3d(point(0.223528,0.500194,1.92038)), time_point(2168577589)).
...
```

Using declarative characterisations of these interactions defined based on spatio-temporal relations this data can be used to query the sequence of interactions identified in the example sequence and their respective grounding with respect to the spatio-temporal dynamics constituting the interaction, i.e., the following query searches for an interactions and its grounding based on the above sensor data:

```
?- grounded_interaction(occurs_in(Interaction, Interval), Grounding).
```

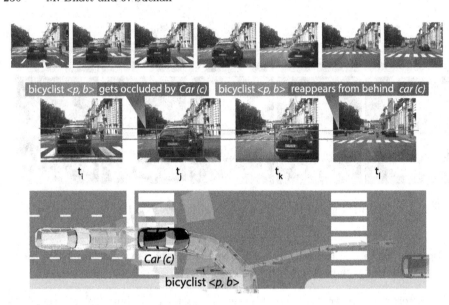

Fig. 8. Out of sight but not out of mind: the case of hidden entities: e.g., an occluded cyclist.

These groundings describe the spatio-temporal dynamics underlying the interactions. In particular, the interaction *reach_for(person(id(1)), object(bread))* occurring between time-point $t1$ and $t3$ is composed of the spatio-temporal pattern of *approaching*, stating that the right hand of person 1 is approaching the bread during time-interval $t1$ to $t2$, and the pattern *touching*, stating that the right hand of person 1 is touching the bread during time-interval $t2$ to $t3$. Similarly the interaction *pick_up(person(id(1)), object(bread))* is composed of *grasping, attachment* and *upwards movement*, with the difference, that grasping itself is an interaction, that can be further grounded in movement dynamics.

```
Interaction = reach_for(person(id(1)), object(bread)),
Interval = interval(t1, t3),
Grounding = [
  holds_in(approaching(body_part(right_hand, person(id(1))), object(bread)), interval(t1,t2)),
  holds_in(touching(body_part(right_hand, person(id(1))), object(bread)), interval(t2,t3)];

Interaction = pick_up(person(id(1)), object(bread)),
Interval = interval(t4, t6),
Grounding = [
  occurs_at(grasp(body_part(right_hand, person(id(1))), object(bread)), timepoint(t4),
  holds_in(attached(body_part(right_hand, person(id(1))), object(bread)), interval(t5,t8)),
  holds_in(move_up(body_part(right_hand, person(id(1)))), interval(t5,t6))];
  ...
```

Example 3. Joint Abduction of Scene Dynamics and Object Motion

Consider the situation depicted in Fig. 8, where a cyclist riding on the road gets occluded by a car turning right. This situation may be described in natural language as follows:

Car (c) is in-front, and indicating to turn-right; during this time, person (p) is on a bicycle (b) and positioned front-right of c and moving-forward. Car c turns-right, during which the bicyclist $< p, b >$ is not visible. Subsequently, bicyclist $< p, b >$ reappears.

Visual abduction aims at explaining the perceived spatio-temporal changes in terms of high-level object dynamics, i.e., finding a set of events that explain the sudden disappearance of the cyclist together with the corresponding motion tracks. For the example situation we can hypothesise that the cyclist got occluded by the car in-front, based on the relational spatio-temporal structure of the scene.

To support this, we implement a general and online capable visual abduction method driven by ASP, that facilitates joint abduction and motion tracking. For generating the motion tracks, we define actions that control how observations are assigned to tracks, i.e., for the purpose of this example we only consider the case that an observation is assigned to a track, and the case where no observation can be assigned to the track and the track is halted.

Here we define two choice rules stating that for each track Trk there is either a detection Det that gets assigned to the track, or the track gets halted if there is no detection to assign to the track.

```
1{
    assign(Trk, Det): det(Det, _, _);
    halt(Trk);
    ...
}1 :- trk(Trk, _).
1{
    assign(Trk, Det): trk(Trk, _);
    ...
}1 :- det(Det, _, _).
```

Further, we define a set of choice rules explaining these assignments, i.e., for this example we define the event *hides_behind* stating that a track Trk can get halted if the track hides behind another track $Trk2$. The corresponding choice rule states that a track can only get halted when there is an event explaining this, i.e. in this case the event *hides_behind*.

```
1{
    occurs_at(hides_behind(Trk, Trk2), curr_time): trk(Trk2,_);
    ...
}1 :- halt(Trk).
```

Events and corresponding event dynamics may be defined in standard KR based languages for reasoning about action and change. For instance, here the event *hides_behind* is defined using event calculus [27] by stating the conditions under which the event may occur (by defining the *poss* predicate for the event). In this case we define that a track $Trk1$ may hide behind another track $Trk2$ if the two tracks are overlapping and are not *not_visible*, i.e., both tracks need to be at least partially visible.

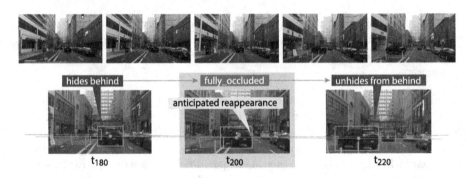

Fig. 9. Abducing occlusion to anticipate reappearance

```
poss(hides_behind(Trk1, Trk2)) :-
    trk(Trk1, _), trk(Trk2, _),
    position(overlapping, Trk1, Trk2),
    not holds_at(visibility(Trk1), not_visible, curr_time),
    not holds_at(visibility(Trk2), not_visible, curr_time).
```

Based on these rules we can jointly abduce scene dynamics and object motion, resulting in associations of detections to motion tracks and corresponding event sequences explaining these associations.

Lets now look at the situation depicted in Fig. 9 where a car gets occluded by another car turning left and reappears *in front of* the autonomous vehicle. Here we can hypothesize that the car got *occluded* and anticipate its reappearance based on the perceived scene dynamics. Towards this, each track is given by the predicted bounding box, the state in which the track currently is, and the type of the tracked object:

```
trk(trk_3, car). trk_state(trk_3, active).
...
trk(trk_41, car). trk_state(trk_41, active).
...

box2d(trk_3, 660, 460, 134, 102).
...
box2d(trk_41, 631, 471, 40, 47).
...
```

Based on this problem specification the event $hides\_behind(trk\_41, trk\_3)$ is abduced, as there is no detection that could be associated with trk_41 and trk_3 is partially overlapping with trk_41:

```
... occurs_at(hides_behind(trk_41,trk_3),179) ...
```

The abduced explanation together with the object dynamics may then be used to anticipate the reappearance of the car. Towards this we define a rule for anticipating the event $unhides\_from\_behind(Trk1, Trk2)$ stating that a *hidden* object may *unhide* from behind the object it is hidden by and anticipate the time point t based on the object *movement* as follows:

```
anticipate(unhides_from_behind(Trk1, Trk2), T) :-
    time(T), curr_time < T,
    holds_at(hidden_by(Trk1, Trk2), curr_time),
    topology(proper_part, Trk1, Trk2),
    movement(moves_out_of, Trk1, Trk2, T).
```

We can then interpolate the objects movement to predict when the object may *reappear*, i.e., for the occluded car in our example we get the following prediction:

```
anticipate(unhides_from_behind(trk_41, trk_2), 202)
```

Such predictions may then be used in decision-making to reason about appropriate control actions, i.e., in this case slowing down to give space to the car in front.

Example 4. Declarative Explainability – Case of Human-Centred Symmetry

Subjective perception of symmetrical image structure serves as a testbed for developing explainability driven visuospatial characterisations where high-level semantic concepts are directly grounded within low-level (neural) visual features, e.g. extracted from deep neural networks. In this context, and as one example, we develop a multi-level characterisation for analysing (reflectional) symmetry, encompassing three layers (L1–L3, as defined in [46] and illustrated in Fig. 10):

L1. *Symmetrical (spatial) composition*:   Spatial arrangement of objects in the scene with respect to a structural representation of position, size, orientation, etc.;

L2. *Perceptual similarity*:   Perceptual similarity of features in symmetrical image patches, based on the low-level feature based appearance of objects, e.g., color, shape, patterns, etc.;

L3. *Semantic similarity*:   Similarity of semantic categories of the objects in symmetrical image patches, e.g., people, object types, and properties of these objects, such as peoples gazing direction, foreground/background etc.

This characterisation may serve as the foundation for analysing and interpreting symmetrical structures in visual imagery; in particular it can be used to identify the elements of the image supporting the symmetrical structure, and those not in line with the symmetry, e.g., elements breaking the symmetry.

For instance, consider the image depicted in Fig. 11, here the symmetry model can be used to query symmetrical (and non-symmetrical) elements of the image using the following rules, stating that an element is considered symmetrical, if it is symmetric in it self or if it is part of a pair of symmetrical elements.

```
symmetrical_element(E) :- symmetrical(E).
symmetrical_element(E) :- symmetrical(E, _); symmetrical(_, E).
```

Aggregating results for the symmetrical_element(E) predicate for the example image results in a list of all symmetrical image elements:

```
SYMETRICAL = [0, 2, 8, 10, 11, 12, 14, 15, 17|...]
```

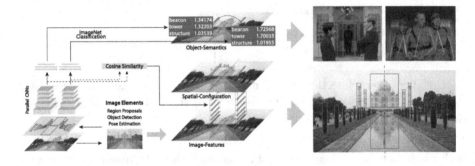

Fig. 10. A computational model of multi-level semantic symmetry.

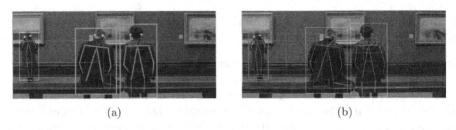

(a)   (b)

Fig. 11. Analysing symmetry: (a) symmetrical, and (b) non-symmetrical elements of an image.

Similarly we can query for non symmetrical elements of the image using the following rule, stating that every element that is not part of a symmetrical structure is considered non symmetrical.

```
non_symmetrical_element(E) :- image_element(E), not(symetrical_element(E)).
```

```
NON_SYMETRICAL = [1, 3, 4, 5, 6, 7, 9, 13, 16|...].
```

Further, the model supports querying of divergence of a image elements from the optimal symmetrical configuration and perceptual and semantic similarity of pairs of image elements as follows:

The predicate *divergence* is used to obtain reassures on how much an image element or a pair of image elements differ from a fully symmetrical configuration in terms of *size*, *aspectratio*, and *position*.

```
?- divergence(symmetrical(id(E1), id(E2)), Div_Size, Div_Aspect_Ratio, Div_Pos).
```

```
...
E1 = 170, E2 = 200,
Div_Size = div_size(9.0, 18.0),
Div_Aspect_Ratio = div_aspect_ratio(0.0595206914614983),
Div_Pos = div_pos(3.905124837953327);
...
```

Fig. 12. Symmetrical spatial configuration: examples for object level symmetry.

The predicate *similarity* is used to query how similar two image elements are in terms of *perceptual symmetry*, i.e., based on visual features, and *semantic similarity*, i.e., based on object categories.

```
?- similarity(pair(id(E1), id(E2)), Percept_Sim, Semantic_Sim).
...
E1 = 170, E2 = 200,
Percept_Sim = 0.70728711298,
Semantic_Sim = 0.6666666666666666;
...
```

These measures provide the basis for the semantic analysis of symmetry structures in the image and can for instance be used to create statistics on the symmetrical features of an image, e.g., to train a classifier based on the semantic characterisations of symmetry. Additionally, the relational spatio-temporal characterisations may be used in the context of inductive learning to learn spatio-temporal structures defining symmetry, as described in Sect. 5.

Example 5. Learning Relational Space-Time Structure

Symmetrical spatial structure, both in space and time, may be inductively learned by finding spatio-temporal relations holding between basic spatial entities representing the image elements. For simplicity, consider the task of learning when a spatial structure is considered to be symmetrical (e.g., as depicted in Fig. 12) vis-a-via relative placement/arrangement of the objects in the scene. To solve this and a similar class of visuospatial learning problems, we build on foundations in inductive logic programming [30] with the aim to learn the general relational structure of a domain through inductive generalisation based on available positive and negative examples; practically, the method is realised using the ILP system Aleph [38]. Within Aleph, the predicate *modeh* is used to specify the head of the rule that is to be learned, and the predicate *modeb* is used to specify the predicates that can be used in the body of the rule. We use *symmetric*($+img$) as the head (i.e., *modeh*) and further specify the predicates to be used in the body of the learned rule (i.e., *modeb*) constituting the basic *spatial entities* and the spatial relations (e.g., *topology, orientation, distance,* and *size*) among the involved spatial entities:

```
:- modeh(1,symmetric(+img)).                    :- modeb(*,entity(#ent,-obj,+img)).
:- modeb(*,topology(rcc8(#rel),+obj,+obj)).  :- modeb(*,distance(#rel,+obj,+obj)).
:- modeb(*,orientation(#rel,+obj,+obj)).      :- modeb(*,size(#rel,+obj,+obj)).
```

Rules about symmetrical spatial configuration are then learned based on positive and negative examples directly obtained from the images. For instance, when trained on examples where the object level symmetry is determined by two people being equally far away from the symmetry axis, the system learns the following spatial structure:

```
sym(A) :-
    entity(center(person(0)),B,A), entity(center(person(1)),C,A),
    entity(symmetry_object(center_axis),D,A), distance(equidistant,D,C,B).
```

In this way, inductive generalisation may be used to learn structural regularities in the underlying visuospatial imagery and provide the means to learn commonsense rules about the domain of interest.

5   Reflection and Outlook

The research reported in this chapter is being pursued as part of what we articulate as "Cognitive Vision and Perception", where one of the key technical goal is to develop general methods for the processing and semantic interpretation of dynamic visuospatial imagery with a particular emphasis on the ability to abstract, learn, and reason with cognitively rooted structured characterisations of commonsense knowledge pertaining to space and motion[3]. The vision that drives this line of work is:

> to shape the nature and character of (machine-based) artificial visual intelligence with respect to human-centred cognitive considerations, and actively create an exemplar for developing , applying, and disseminating such methods in socio-technologically relevant application areas where embodied (multimodal) human-system interaction is of the essence.

In the conceptual overview and practical illustrations of this chapter, we have centralised select basic research and developmental challenges categorically focussing on:[4]

> explainable interpretation –by integrated reasoning and learning– of human-scale motion and multimodal interaction from the viewpoint of integrating neural and symbolic methods, and vis-a-vis the impact of explainable neurosymbolism on the design and development of AI technologies concerned with human-in-the-loop decision-making, planning, and analysis.

The reported development of formally characterised, modular, and general visuospatial sensemaking methodologies opens up several immediate technical possibilities as well as long-range challenges for investigation.

---

[3] A summary is available in [10].
[4] Select readings are indicated in Appendix A.

Immediate Technical Extensions

Immediate possibilities for technical developments/extensions to the presented model of deep visuospatial semantics worth alluding to include development of specialised (but domain independent) visuospatial commonsense capabilities, and the development of datasets and benchmarks that centralise human-centred performance benchmarks:

- Specialised commonsense theories about multi-sensory integration, and multi-agent (spatio-temporal) belief merging would constitute a foundational extension to the existing capabilities for reasoning about space and motion.
- Multimodal stimuli datasets together with fine-grained, expert-guided, event-based annotations would be needed for community driven benchmarking of high-level visuospatial commonsense; here, the emphasis should on the nuances of high-level visual sensemaking and explainability capabilities of humans, and not on low-level performance metrics (alone) as is typical in computer vision research.

Long-Range Questions

Concerning behavioural research themes in visual perception and spatial cognition that have not been directly addressed in the chapter, the overarching motivations and the interdisciplinarity that Cognitive Vision and Perception research addresses are multi-faceted:

(a) how can a vision for the development of next generation of AI methods for visual cognition be driven by and intricately interwoven with empirically established human-centred characteristics;

(b) how can the cognitive & developmental psychology and cognitive neuro-science based views of human visual intelligence –even if in highly focussed interactional contexts– influence in systematically articulating the essential crux –e.g., design challenges, functional capabilities– of human-centred artificial visual intelligence;

(c) what can human-centred artificial visual intelligence do for fundamentally impacting the social and life sciences, e.g., through the power of semantically driven explainable sensemaking of large-scale, experimental multimodal human behavioural data.

These long-range research challenges call for continuing bottom-up interdisciplinarity for the study of human visual perception in naturalistic settings on the one hand, and the development of computational models of distinct visual sensemaking capabilities of humans –both in seemingly mundane tasks or even in specialist work related contexts– on the other. Such interdisciplinary studies –e.g., at the confluence of Cognition, AI, Interaction, and Design Science– are needed to better appreciate the complexity and spectrum of varied human-centred challenges for the design and (usable) implementation of artificial visual intelligence solutions in diverse human-system interaction contexts.

Appendices

A   Select Further Readings

Select readings pertaining to cognitive vision and perception are as follows:

▶ **Visuospatial Question-Answering**   [40] [39] [41] [37]
▶ **Visuospatial Abduction**   [43, 45] [47] [49]
▶ **Relational Visuospatial Learning**   [42] [46] [19]

Select readings pertaining to foundational aspects of commonsense spatial reasoning (within a KR setting) are as follows:

▶ **Theory (Space, Action, Change)**   [4,5,8,9]
▶ **Declarative Spatial Reasoning (CLP, ASP, ILP)** [7,35,42,48]

B   Visual Computing Foundations

A robust low-level visual computing foundation driven by the state of the art in computer vision techniques (e.g., for visual feature detection, tracking) is necessary towards realising explainable visual intelligence in the manner described in this chapter. The examples of this chapter (in Sect. 4), for instance, require extracting and analysing scene elements (i.e., people, body-structure, and objects in the scene) and motion (i.e., object motion and scene motion), encompassing methods for:

- **Image Classification** and **Feature Learning** – based on Big Data, (e.g., ImageNet [17,34]), using neural network architectures such as AlexNets [28], VGG [36], or ResNet [23].
- **Detection**, i.e., of *people and objects* [11,31–33], and *faces* [18,24].
- **Pose Estimation**, i.e., of body pose [13] (including fine grained hand pose), face and gaze analysis [1].
- **Segmentation**, i.e., semantic segmentation [14] and instance segmentation [22].
- **Motion Analysis**, i.e., optical flow based motion estimation [25] and movement tracking [2,3].

References

1. Baltrusaitis, T., Zadeh, A., Lim, Y.C., Morency, L.: OpenFace 2.0: facial behavior analysis toolkit. In: 2018 13th IEEE International Conference on Automatic Face Gesture Recognition (FG 2018), pp. 59–66, May 2018. https://doi.org/10.1109/FG.2018.00019
2. Bergmann, P., Meinhardt, T., Leal-Taixé, L.: Tracking without bells and whistles. In: The IEEE International Conference on Computer Vision (ICCV), October 2019
3. Bewley, A., Ge, Z., Ott, L., Ramos, F., Upcroft, B.: Simple online and realtime tracking. In: 2016 IEEE International Conference on Image Processing (ICIP), pp. 3464–3468 (2016). https://doi.org/10.1109/ICIP.2016.7533003

4. Bhatt, M.: Reasoning about space, actions and change: a paradigm for applications of spatial reasoning. In: Qualitative Spatial Representation and Reasoning: Trends and Future Directions. IGI Global, USA (2012)
5. Bhatt, M., Guesgen, H.W., Wölfl, S., Hazarika, S.M.: Qualitative spatial and temporal reasoning: emerging applications, trends, and directions. Spatial Cogn. Comput. **11**(1), 1–14 (2011). https://doi.org/10.1080/13875868.2010.548568
6. Bhatt, M., Kersting, K.: Semantic interpretation of multi-modal human-behaviour data - making sense of events, activities, processes. KI/Artif. Intell. **31**(4), 317–320 (2017)
7. Bhatt, M., Lee, J.H., Schultz, C.: CLP(QS): a declarative spatial reasoning framework. In: Egenhofer, M., Giudice, N., Moratz, R., Worboys, M. (eds.) COSIT 2011. LNCS, vol. 6899, pp. 210–230. Springer, Heidelberg (2011). https://doi.org/10.1007/978-3-642-23196-4_12
8. Bhatt, M., Loke, S.W.: Modelling dynamic spatial systems in the situation calculus. Spatial Cogn. Comput. **8**(1–2), 86–130 (2008). https://doi.org/10.1080/13875860801926884
9. Bhatt, M., Schultz, C., Freksa, C.: The 'space' in spatial assistance systems: conception, formalisation and computation. In: Tenbrink, T., Wiener, J., Claramunt, C. (eds.) Representing Space in Cognition: Interrelations of Behavior, Language, and Formal Models. Series: Explorations in Language and Space. Oxford University Press (2013). ISBN 978-0-19-967991-1
10. Bhatt, M., Suchan, J.: Cognitive vision and perception. In: Giacomo, G.D., Catalá, A., Dilkina, B., Milano, M., Barro, S., Bugarín, A., Lang, J. (eds.) 24th European Conference on Artificial Intelligence, ECAI 2020, Santiago de Compostela, Spain, 29 August–8 September 2020 - Including 10th Conference on Prestigious Applications of Artificial Intelligence (PAIS 2020). Frontiers in Artificial Intelligence and Applications, vol. 325, pp. 2881–2882. IOS Press (2020). https://doi.org/10.3233/FAIA200434
11. Bochkovskiy, A., Wang, C., Liao, H.M.: YOLOv4: optimal speed and accuracy of object detection. CoRR abs/2004.10934 (2020). https://arxiv.org/abs/2004.10934
12. Brewka, G., Eiter, T., Truszczyński, M.: Answer set programming at a glance. Commun. ACM **54**(12), 92–103 (2011). https://doi.org/10.1145/2043174.2043195
13. Cao, Z., Hidalgo Martinez, G., Simon, T., Wei, S., Sheikh, Y.A.: OpenPose: realtime multi-person 2D pose estimation using part affinity fields. IEEE Trans. Pattern Anal. Mach. Intell. **43**, 172–186 (2019)
14. Chen, L.C., Zhu, Y., Papandreou, G., Schroff, F., Adam, H.: Encoder-decoder with atrous separable convolution for semantic image segmentation. arXiv:1802.02611 (2018)
15. Davis, E.: Pouring liquids: a study in commonsense physical reasoning. Artif. Intell. **172**(12–13), 1540–1578 (2008)
16. Davis, E.: How does a box work? A study in the qualitative dynamics of solid objects. Artif. Intell. **175**(1), 299–345 (2011)
17. Deng, J., Dong, W., Socher, R., Li, L.J., Li, K., Fei-Fei, L.: ImageNet: a large-scale hierarchical image database. In: CVPR 2009 (2009)
18. Deng, J., Guo, J., Ververas, E., Kotsia, I., Zafeiriou, S.: RetinaFace: single-shot multi-level face localisation in the wild. In: CVPR (2020)
19. Dubba, K.S.R., Cohn, A.G., Hogg, D.C., Bhatt, M., Dylla, F.: Learning relational event models from video. J. Artif. Intell. Res. (JAIR) **53**, 41–90 (2015). https://doi.org/10.1613/jair.4395. http://dx.doi.org/10.1613/jair.4395
20. Hampe, B., Grady, J.E.: From Perception to Meaning. De Gruyter Mouton, Berlin (2008). https://www.degruyter.com/view/title/17429

21. Hazarika, S.M.: Qualitative spatial change : space-time histories and continuity. Ph.D. thesis, The University of Leeds, School of Computing (2005). Supervisor - Anthony Cohn

22. He, K., Gkioxari, G., Dollar, P., Girshick, R.: Mask R-CNN. IEEE Trans. Pattern Anal. Mach. Intell. **42**(02), 386–397 (2020). https://doi.org/10.1109/TPAMI.2018.2844175

23. He, K., Zhang, X., Ren, S., Sun, J.: Deep residual learning for image recognition. In: 2016 IEEE Conference on Computer Vision and Pattern Recognition, CVPR 2016, Las Vegas, NV, USA, 27–30 June 2016, pp. 770–778. IEEE Computer Society (2016). https://doi.org/10.1109/CVPR.2016.90

24. Hu, P., Ramanan, D.: Finding tiny faces. In: The IEEE Conference on Computer Vision and Pattern Recognition (CVPR), July 2017

25. Ilg, E., Mayer, N., Saikia, T., Keuper, M., Dosovitskiy, A., Brox, T.: FlowNet 2.0: evolution of optical flow estimation with deep networks. In: IEEE Conference on Computer Vision and Pattern Recognition (CVPR) (2017). http://lmb.informatik.uni-freiburg.de/Publications/2017/IMSKDB17

26. Jaffar, J., Maher, M.J.: Constraint logic programming: a survey. J. Logic Program. **19**, 503–581 (1994)

27. Kowalski, R., Sergot, M.: A logic-based calculus of events. In: Schmidt, J.W., Thanos, C. (eds.) Foundations of Knowledge Base Management, pp. 23–51. Springer, Heidelberg (1989). https://doi.org/10.1007/978-3-642-83397-7_2

28. Krizhevsky, A., Sutskever, I., Hinton, G.E.: ImageNet classification with deep convolutional neural networks. In: Bartlett, P.L., Pereira, F.C.N., Burges, C.J.C., Bottou, L., Weinberger, K.Q. (eds.) Advances in Neural Information Processing Systems 25: 26th Annual Conference on Neural Information Processing Systems 2012. Proceedings of a Meeting Held at Lake Tahoe, Nevada, United States, 3–6 December 2012, pp. 1106–1114 (2012). https://proceedings.neurips.cc/paper/2012/hash/c399862d3b9d6b76c8436e924a68c45b-Abstract.html

29. Mani, I., Pustejovsky, J.: Interpreting Motion - Grounded Representations for Spatial Language, Explorations in Language and Space, vol. 5. Oxford University Press, Oxford (2012)

30. Muggleton, S., Raedt, L.D.: Inductive logic programming: theory and methods. J. Log. Program. **19**(20), 629–679 (1994)

31. Redmon, J., Divvala, S.K., Girshick, R.B., Farhadi, A.: You only look once: unified, real-time object detection. In: 2016 IEEE Conference on Computer Vision and Pattern Recognition, CVPR 2016, Las Vegas, NV, USA, 27–30 June 2016, pp. 779–788. IEEE Computer Society (2016). https://doi.org/10.1109/CVPR.2016.91

32. Redmon, J., Farhadi, A.: YOLOv3: an incremental improvement. CoRR abs/1804.02767 (2018). http://arxiv.org/abs/1804.02767

33. Ren, S., He, K., Girshick, R.B., Sun, J.: Faster R-CNN: towards real-time object detection with region proposal networks. IEEE Trans. Pattern Anal. Mach. Intell. **39**(6), 1137–1149 (2017). https://doi.org/10.1109/TPAMI.2016.2577031

34. Russakovsky, O., et al.: ImageNet large scale visual recognition challenge. Int. J. Comput. Vis. **115**(3), 211–252 (2015). https://doi.org/10.1007/s11263-015-0816-y

35. Schultz, C., Bhatt, M., Suchan, J., Wałęga, P.A.: Answer set programming modulo 'space-time'. In: Benzmüller, C., Ricca, F., Parent, X., Roman, D. (eds.) RuleML+RR 2018. LNCS, vol. 11092, pp. 318–326. Springer, Cham (2018). https://doi.org/10.1007/978-3-319-99906-7_24

36. Simonyan, K., Zisserman, A.: Very deep convolutional networks for large-scale image recognition. In: International Conference on Learning Representations (2015)

37. Spranger, M., Suchan, J., Bhatt, M.: Robust natural language processing - combining reasoning, cognitive semantics and construction grammar for spatial language. In: 25th International Joint Conference on Artificial Intelligence, IJCAI 2016. AAAI Press, July 2016

38. Srinivasan, A.: The Aleph Manual (2001). http://web.comlab.ox.ac.uk/oucl/research/areas/machlearn/Aleph/

39. Suchan, J., Bhatt, M.: The geometry of a scene: on deep semantics for visual perception driven cognitive film, studies. In: 2016 IEEE Winter Conference on Applications of Computer Vision, WACV 2016, Lake Placid, NY, USA, 7–10, March 2016, pp. 1–9. IEEE Computer Society (2016). https://doi.org/10.1109/WACV.2016.7477712

40. Suchan, J., Bhatt, M.: Semantic question-answering with video and eye-tracking data: AI foundations for human visual perception driven cognitive film studies. In: Kambhampati, S. (ed.) Proceedings of the Twenty-Fifth International Joint Conference on Artificial Intelligence, IJCAI 2016, New York, NY, USA, 9–15 July 2016, pp. 2633–2639. IJCAI/AAAI Press (2016). http://www.ijcai.org/Abstract/16/374

41. Suchan, J., Bhatt, M.: Deep semantic abstractions of everyday human activities: on commonsense representations of human interactions. In: ROBOT 2017: Third Iberian Robotics Conference, Advances in Intelligent Systems and Computing 693 (2017)

42. Suchan, J., Bhatt, M., Schultz, C.P.L.: Deeply semantic inductive spatio-temporal learning. In: Cussens, J., Russo, A. (eds.) Proceedings of the 26th International Conference on Inductive Logic Programming (Short Papers), London, UK, vol. 1865, pp. 73–80. CEUR-WS.org (2016)

43. Suchan, J., Bhatt, M., Varadarajan, S.: Out of sight but not out of mind: an answer set programming based online abduction framework for visual sensemaking in autonomous driving. In: Kraus, S. (ed.) Proceedings of the Twenty-Eighth International Joint Conference on Artificial Intelligence, IJCAI 2019, Macao, China, 10–16 August 2019, pp. 1879–1885. ijcai.org (2019). https://doi.org/10.24963/ijcai.2019/260

44. Suchan, J., Bhatt, M., Varadarajan, S.: Driven by commonsense. In: Giacomo, G.D., et al. (eds.) ECAI 2020–24th European Conference on Artificial Intelligence, Santiago de Compostela, Spain, 29 August–8 September 2020 - Including 10th Conference on Prestigious Applications of Artificial Intelligence (PAIS 2020). Frontiers in Artificial Intelligence and Applications, vol. 325, pp. 2939–2940. IOS Press (2020). https://doi.org/10.3233/FAIA200463

45. Suchan, J., Bhatt, M., Varadarajan, S.: Commonsense visual sensemaking for autonomous driving - on generalised neurosymbolic online abduction integrating vision and semantics. Artif. Intell. **299**, 103522 (2021). https://doi.org/10.1016/j.artint.2021.103522

46. Suchan, J., Bhatt, M., Vardarajan, S., Amirshahi, S.A., Yu, S.: Semantic analysis of (reflectional) visual symmetry: a human-centred computational model for declarative explainability. Adv. Cogn. Syst. **6**, 65–84 (2018). http://www.cogsys.org/journal

47. Suchan, J., Bhatt, M., Walega, P.A., Schultz, C.P.L.: Visual explanation by high-level abduction: on answer-set programming driven reasoning about moving objects. In: 32nd AAAI Conference on Artificial Intelligence (AAAI-2018), USA, pp. 1965–1972. AAAI Press (2018)

48. Wałęga, P.A., Bhatt, M., Schultz, C.: ASPMT(QS): non-monotonic spatial reasoning with answer set programming modulo theories. In: Calimeri, F., Ianni, G., Truszczynski, M. (eds.) LPNMR 2015. LNCS (LNAI), vol. 9345, pp. 488–501. Springer, Cham (2015). https://doi.org/10.1007/978-3-319-23264-5_41

49. Walega, P.A., Schultz, C.P.L., Bhatt, M.: Non-monotonic spatial reasoning with answer set programming modulo theories. Theory Pract. Log. Program. **17**(2), 205–225 (2017). https://doi.org/10.1017/S1471068416000193

Ethics, Law and Society AI

An Introduction to Ethics and AI

Guido Boella[1]([✉]) and Maurizio Mori[2]

[1] University of Torino, Turin, Italy
guido.boella@unito.it
[2] Italian Society for the Ethics of Artificial Intelligence, Turin, Italy
maurizio.mori@unito.it
http://www.sipeia.it

Abstract. In this paper we discuss the relationship between Ethics and AI. First, we present a non-exhaustive panorama of ethical issues raised by AI, with a focus on the fact that not all problems can be solved by technological advancements. Second, we introduce what is Ethics and how AI may need changing it. Finally, we will consider how AI can impact current ethical theories.

Keywords: Ethics · Ethics of artificial intelligence · Bias · Explainability · Surveillance capitalism · Biomedical ethics

1 Introduction

This tutorial has as learning objectives:

– Having a glimpse about what is Ethics.
– Understanding that Ethics evolves over time, also as a result of the emergence of new technologies.
– Acquiring the width of the impact of AI on Ethics.

The following readings are suggested to deepen the arguments of this paper:

– Kate Crawford, Atlas of AI: Power, Politics, and the Planetary Costs of Artificial Intelligence. Yale University Press, 2021.
– Mark Coeckelbergh, AI Ethics. MIT Press, 2021.
– Shoshana Zuboff, The Age of Surveillance Capitalism: The Fight for a Human Future at the New Frontier of Power. Public Affairs, 2019.
– Anthony Elliott, The Culture of AI Everyday Life and the Digital Revolution. Routledge, 2019.
– David Weinberger, Everyday Chaos. Harvard Business Review Press, 2019.

M. Chetouani et al. (Eds.): ACAI 2021, LNAI 13500, pp. 245–260, 2023.
https://doi.org/10.1007/978-3-031-24349-3_13

2   Ethics of AI (by Guido Boella)

In this section, we discuss some ethical aspects of AI. We are talking here about Ethics of AI, which addresses the ethical issues raised by AI, while in the next chapters we discuss about Ethics AND AI: how AI will affect Ethics itself. We will not consider instead another large field connecting the two topics, i.e., "machine ethics": how to develop machines that are able (or could be able) to make ethical reasoning when making decisions, such as an autonomous car that by explicitly considering ethical principles has to decide whether to endanger the safety of the occupants or the one of a pedestrian unexpectedly crossing the road in front of the car.

First of all, we should ask ourselves if there is an ethical problem with AI. Does AI create risks? If yes, which are those risks, and how and why do they emerge? how can they be addressed? Are these risks different from those created by other technologies, such as biotechnology or nanotechnology? Do they need different solutions?

We must also be aware that these are not simple problems and cannot be solved easily. As Algorithm Watch, an activist organization on Ethics and ICT, observes, there are more than 160 guidelines[1] on Ethics and AI, but they are "paper tigers"[2]: ineffective. This happens as they are not enough specific, they cannot be implemented in practice, and there are rarely enforcements mechanisms. Moreover, they are mostly from EU and US. They put together principles, such as the four principles of Bio-medical Ethics, and, sometimes, they end up being tools to make "Ethics washing" for companies, and even researchers: *"the question arises whether guidelines that can neither be applied nor enforced are not more harmful than having no ethical guidelines at all"*.

In the following, we will provide a panorama of the open ethical issues, briefly addressing a variety of them.

2.1   The Bias Problem

Bias in Computer Science is nowadays a main problem of Machine Learning (ML) algorithms: you want to learn from the data something that is not in the data. As Ruha Benjamin[3] recently said, *"feeding AI system on the word's beauty, ugliness and cruelty but expecting it to reflect only the beauty is a fantasy"*. We pretend to get only what we deem right and fair from the results of algorithms, even if we train them using the existing huge datasets representing not the ideal, but the actual world with all its unfairness and horrors. There are several consequences caused by a biased ML system:

– Quality of results: obviously results are not as we pretend them to be according to our ideal world.
– Negative effects on people: e.g., automated hiring systems; you could not be hired because you are a woman or from a minority, and, thus, you are discriminated.

---

[1] https://inventory.algorithmwatch.org/.

[2] https://algorithmwatch.org/en/ai-ethics-guidelines-inventory-upgrade-2020/.

[3] Ruha Benjamin. 2019. Race After Technology: Abolitionist Tools for the New Jim Code. Polity Press, Cambridge, UK.

– Psychological effects on users: besides the damage of being discriminated, you are harmed by feeling discriminated by the algorithms. Moreover, a biased AI may not only make discriminatory decisions, but it could also produce discriminatory content or hate speech on the Web against you on social networks: you end up being more discriminated, not only by people but also by machines.
– Proselytism of users convinced by what is produced by biased AI systems, e.g., hate speech posts on a social network. Or mislead by the autocomplete feature of a search engine, suggesting, e.g., "black shirt" (in the sense of fascist uniform) when typing "shirt" in the search bar, as recently happened to one of the authors.
– Feedback loops reinforcing the bias in the data due to further bias generated by biased AI systems and added to the learning corpus. This phenomenon has been widely discussed by Cathy O'Neil in her famous book *"Weapons of math destruction"*: for example, if a "predpol" AI system sends more police patrols in a high-density crime district populated by minorities, more crimes will be found and added to the dataset fed to the AI, making the district even more risky next time in the judgement of the AI system: more and more police patrols will be send there and the minorities living there more and more discriminated.

Related to the bias problem a widely debated news appeared beginning of this year: two major scientists at Google, part of the ethical team, have been fired. The public debate focused on the fact that two women (one immigrated in the US) have been fired, and did not highlight enough why they were fired. The reason is that in their paper *"On the Dangers of Stochastic Parrots. Can Language Models be too Big?"* they made very strong criticisms against the use of AI their employer does. There is a section in the pape dedicated to the *"Unfathomable training data"* - where the uncommon word "unfathomable" means "incapable of being fully explored or understood". There, concerning machine learning based on huge datasets of text from the web – a technology at the base of many of the most known services by Google - they highlight these problems:

– Encoded biases: for example, because English text on the web has been produced in a big percentage by white Anglo-Saxon males.
– Curation, documentation, accountability: there is not enough budget to curate, document and to analyze the collected dataset to identify biases.
– The size of training datasets does not guarantee diversity: data are taken from mainstream discussions on social media, while minority issues are often discussed on niche blogs not covered by the web spiders harvesting data.
– Data are static, the society changes: AI is trained on the past (data) and reflects the past reality (as represented in the data). E.g., movements like #MeToo or #BlackLivesMatter are new, and they are not reflected enough in the datasets. The state of the art of innovation seems to be conservative by design.

Moreover, the researchers say that "Any product development that involves operationalizing definitions around such shifting topics into algorithms is necessarily political (whether or not developers choose the path of maintaining the status quo ante)".

But there is more. They say that Google is morally bankrupt because their natural language processing engines are cheating and misleading users. Such systems are just manipulating strings of text and thanks to being able to deal with huge amounts of data they seem to users to be able to give meaningful replies. But the two authors notice that these systems are just exploiting our inner automatic tendency, as humans, to attribute intentions and beliefs to people talking with us, while there are no such mental states inside these machines: they are just manipulating text. Hence, the phrase in the title of the paper "Stochastic parrots". This is a very strong point of view. They also say that main AI players (like Google) are even deviating and corrupting public research on natural language processing as most researchers are trying to follow this approach, to test, improve and evaluate their systems, but going in a wrong research direction. And spending a lot of money for running deep learning algorithms (another topic in the paper is the energetic cost of machine learning systems). Amazingly, we are back in the '60s when the MIT AI Lab scientist Joseph Weizenbaum coded the ELIZA provocation, a sort of chatbot applying a simple pattern matching on the sentences of the users and producing a conversation that gives the impression to be at a Rogerian psychotherapist session. We should be aware that the same problem will be found in humanoid robotics: we are just misled by the facial expressions of emotions of robots, deluding us that they have some mental states. Emotion expression could be helpful, e.g., for therapeutic robots for elderly or autistic people, but in the general case this raises the question about the meaning of affection of humans towards machines that mislead them.[4]

But the main message we want to convey concerning bias is that bias is not a technical problem. We cannot solve the problem of bias by improving algorithms. The term bias has different meanings in different disciplines and contexts:[5]

- In law, bias refers to a preconceived notion or opinion, a judgment based on prejudices, as opposed to a decision from the impartial evaluation of the facts of a case.
- In psychology, Amos Tversky and Daniel Kahneman study "cognitive biases", or the ways in which human judgments deviate systematically from probabilistic expectations.
- Implicit biases emphasize the ways that unconscious attitudes and stereotypes "produce behaviors that diverge from a person's avowed or endorsed beliefs or principles".
- A systematic classification error that the system exhibits when presented with new examples.

Bias is not simply a type of technical error: it concerns human beliefs, stereotypes, or forms of discrimination. Liming discussion to the statistical meaning of the term makes us forget that the term has to do with equality and justice. Who is in charge of deciding what are the equality and justice principles that should correct the bias of an AI system? As suggested by Gebru and Mitchell above, this is a political question and not a technical one.

---

[4] A reading suggestion on this topic is the Nobel prize winner Kazuo Ishiguro's new novel: Clara and the Sun.

[5] Kate Crawford: Atlas of AI: Power, Politics, and the Planetary Costs of Artificial Intelligence, Yale University Press 2021.

Moreover, Kate Crawford argues that we cannot save ourselves from the bias problem by improving algorithms, because the AI systems we are talking about essentially make classification. Classification is an act of power: classifications are created to justify the order, the status quo of who is in power. The people who classify can decide which differences make a difference. They are political interventions hidden to us and become taken for granted, but still they play an active role and shape the social and material world. To contrast them we must actively resist.

Connected to this, Kate Crawford reminds us that AI in image recognition is going to create a so-called "digital epidermalization". The only data the machine can have, our images, do not contain all the information machines tend to take out of images: gender, cultural and political views. These categories are not biological traits that emerge from our face images, but are politically, culturally, and socially constructed relational concepts. Leaving image recognition AI systems taking information from us is alienating our right to define our true identity: they do not consider what are our subjective claims.

Furthermore, real datasets are used beyond their original purpose. For example, take one of the biggest: ImageNet. The underlying labelling of images was imported from WordNet, a database of word classifications first developed at Princeton for different purposes. Its nine top-level categories show plant, geological formation, natural objects, sport, artifact, fungus, person, animal and miscellaneous. If we go into detail and take, e.g., "human body", we see it is distinguished in male body, person, juvenile body, adult body, female body. It is a binary classification. Despite this, ImageNet is the most used dataset for training image recognition systems.

ImageNet is an open-source dataset and we can examine it; but what are Facebook and other companies doing? They use proprietary systems and don't allow us to probe or audit how images are classified: we cannot know which order they impose on us.

The world is full of meanings, irresolvable questions and contradictions. When you make a dataset, you make choices and simplifications. Kate Crawford reminds us that we have to know who makes choices and on what bases. We risk perpetuating asymmetries of power because AI developers– AI is produced mostly by big companies – are imposing and perpetuating classifications for their own business purposes.

A problem related to image recognition is emotion recognition. There is a huge problem on how this technology is applied. Consider the risks in China where the government wants to promote positive energy by monitoring people's expression of happiness, banning anger and sadness. But there are also technical problems as most of the systems on emotion recognition are based on the work of Paul Ekman[6], for its convenience in terms of formalization, but his theory is not anymore recognized in the psychology community as entirely correct and scientifically grounded.

A suggestion to deepen these issues is the movie Coded Bias. At its beginning, the MIT media lab afro-american researcher Joy Boulamwini recognizes that the image recognition system she is using is not working well on her face. It starts working only when she puts by chance a white mask on her face. Ironically the movie is distributed by Netflix that is one of the biggest developers of recommendation systems based on AI, clustering people in dozens of buckets and proposing to them different trailers.

---

[6] Paul Ekman. "Facial Expression and Emotion". American Psychologist. 48 (4): 384–92, 1993.

Another suggested reading is "Automating Inequality" from Virginia Eubanks that examines case studies on the effect of using AI in social assistance settings.

2.2 Explainability

Another widely discussed issue in the Ethics of AI is the *explainability* of the decisions of ML systems. A large part of the machine learning community is trying to create systems that are not entirely black boxes, but that are able to justify the classifications they make. This concept is so widespread in the community that it even ended up in the General Data Protection Regulation of EU (GDPR) of 2016. In recital 71, it is said that people have the right to obtain an explanation of the decision reached after assessment made by AI and to challenge the decision. Also consider the latter right: we are not allowed to discuss and negotiate the decision with the AI system that made it as we can do with human decision makers.

An anecdote on the obscurity of the reasoning happening within deep learning algorithm comes from the AlphaGo system defeating the (human) world champions: some of them said that it looked like playing against an alien.

Before rushing to say that achieving explainability of ML decisions would save AI, we have to understand what an explanation is. Do we really know? Can humans give explanations? Different disciplines have different points of view on the matter:

- Law is often advocated as an example, since judges motivate their judgements. However, Amedeo Santosuosso[7] reminds us that in law, motivations of judgements are just a recent social construct. In some legal systems, writing the motivations can be even delegated to assistants.
- The psychological point of view on explanations: as the economist Michael Polanyi discovered, explicit knowledge (the part that can be expressed linguistically and can be represented in a logical way) is only a part of our knowledge. There is another bigger part of knowledge which is the "*tacit knowledge*", concerning how to do things, for example how to ride a bicycle or how to be able to speak or even to reason. This knowledge is not accessible to our conscience and not expressible linguistically (and you cannot learn it from reading a book).

Then there are technical problems. How to explore the dependencies among tens of trillions of nodes constituting a deep neural network to reconstruct its reasonings?

Furthermore, do you trust machine or people giving explanations? Can we ask machines to do something that we are not able to do ourselves? How can we know if an HR AI system is actually not hiring someone for a racial reason while it explains its decision in another way?

Finally, as discussed in Everyday Chaos by David Weinberger[8], deep neural network systems could be literally unexplainable since, given their computational power, they are able to reason without resorting to the traditional conceptual models made by

---

[7] Amedeo Santosuosso. *Intelligenza artificiale e diritto. Perché le tecnologie di IA sono una grande opportunità per il diritto.* Mondadori, 2021.

[8] David Weinberger. Everyday Chaos. Harvard Business Review Press, 2019.

humans to decide and at the same time explain their decisions. These models are always simplifications of a complex reality due to our cognitive limitations.

2.3 Control and Accountability of Autonomous Systems

Self driving cars and autonomous drones pose many ethical problems. We can focus here on a couple of examples only. Philosophers devised the so-called trolley problem: an evil terrorist has tied 5 people on the track of a runaway trolley and one person on another track following a railway exchange, and you got in the horrible position of deciding whether to let the trolley go straight on its route and kill 5 people or to turn the switch and make the trolley kill just one. However, let to their devices, engineers have found their own solutions to this dilemma. Consider the report of the US National Transportation Safety Board about the famous accident in Arizona where an Uber self-driving car killed a poor woman who was crossing a large street while pushing her bicycle. The autonomous vehicle was able to recognize the obstacle of the pedestrian, but emergency breakers were not enabled when the car is on computer drive in order not to shake passengers.

Concerning autonomy, there is the huge debate about eventual deadly autonomous weapons like military drones. However, already now, when the drones are remotely piloted by humans AI creates ethical problems. The information pilots get on their monitors for taking their decisions is probably the result of AI algorithms (recognizing possible targets from camera imagines, tracking them, surveilling them on the social networks, etc.): the ethical problems of the role of AI in deciding to kill are already here.

2.4 Power and the Rhetoric Behind AI

In this paper we are not discussing only about technical issues, but also about power relationships and the struggle to maintain them. A big share of research on AI is nowadays made by companies. In "Atlas of AI" Kate Crawford (See footnote 5) warns us that AI is, first of all, connected to power. You can look at how power is distributed in our current world by looking at all the articulations of AI. She claims AI is not artificial, as it is embodied, it is material, it requires natural resources, human work and so on. It is not autonomous as it depends on datasets and people tagging them. It is capital intensive: deep learning computations cost hundred thousand dollars. She reminds us that when we talk about AI, we don't talk about a technology, but about the massive industrial formation that includes politics, labor, culture, and capital. When we talk about the Ethical aspects of AI we have to consider also these dimensions: we have to consider both the effect of AI tools on the society and of the corporations that are changing the economy using AI.

To gain and maintain their power positions, rhetoric is often used by the big AI players. This rhetoric is often mixed with *technochauvinism* and *inevitabilism*: the evolution of technology is considered to be always positive and not stoppable, since it is presented not as the result of the choice of someone, but a sort of natural evolutionary force. To bring an example, Larry Page, cofounder of Google, asked "What is Google" by a journalist replied: "if we did have a category it would be personal information. The places you have seen. Communication... sensors are really cheap... storage is cheap.

Cameras are cheap. People will generate enormous amounts of data… everything you have ever heard or seen or experienced will become searchable. Your whole life will be searchable". In this interview Page was manipulating us by providing something that is in the pure advantage of Google as something that is useful for everyone and presents it as something inevitable. Storage is cheap, then it is searchable. It is not like that. It is searchable because someone wants it to be searchable.

2.5 AI and Economics

Concerning the interplay between AI and economics we have space here only for listing some issues. The first one is the future of work. Since the beginning of past century newspapers had been warning us that machines would have made all us unemployed. One century after we are still here at work. Some show optimism: the Economist titled recently: "Robots threaten jobs less than fearmongers claim"[9]. But the Harvard Business School scholar Shoshana Zuboff in her "The age of surveillance capitalism"[10] argues that the usual argument that a new technology produces new kinds of work while destroying old ones may not be true anymore, since the very structure of our capitalist world is changing. In 1908 when the T-model car was produced by Henry Ford we were in a world where the employees of Ford after some years could afford buying that car. In the current economic world, we are not the customers of the enterprises that extract value from us. The positive feedback loop between production, income, consume of goods of the past century that produced new jobs is not anymore here. The customers of big ICT players are brands buying advertising space, while we are the unemployed source of data of the extraction capitalism. The future of work is not only a quantitative issue but also a qualitative one. Already Karl Marx saw automation technology as an unprecedented challenge for the individual and society. The workman "becomes an appendage of the machine, and it is only the most simple, most monotonous, and most easily acquired knack, that is required of him". AI is also becoming a means of control on the worker, as the extreme condition of work in Amazon warehouses show.

Another issue is to consider the effect of industrial revolutions on the functioning of the society itself. The French sociologist Emile Durkheim[11], examining the social transformation already gathering around him, observed that the specialization of work created by the division of labour was going outside the factories and gaining influence in politics, administration, the judiciary science and the arts. He sees specialization as something positive as it created interdependency and reciprocity among people by increasing respect and mutual trust, thus reinforcing the fabric of society. Whatever the effect of AI on work we must be aware that it could diminish the dependency among people thus affecting the moral force keeping society together. The industrial revolution from this point of view had positive effects but at the same time increased inequality, a great danger that leads to make conflicts to reclaim power and justice within society impossible. It seems that one of the risks of AI is a further increase in inequality.

---

[9] https://www.economist.com/special-report/2021/04/08/robots-threaten-jobs-less-than-fearmongers-claim.

[10] Zuboff, Shoshana. The age of surveillance capitalism: the fight for a human future at the new frontier of power. First edition, Public Affairs, 2019.

[11] Emile Durkheim, The Division of Labor in Society, 1893.

Finally, Shoshana Zuboff argues that there has been in the last 20 years a new appropriation of our data that are not used to improve services such as search engines, but are extracted and refined to sell predictions about our behavior to advertisers. This expropriation process can be seen as a further step in the development of commodity fictions, to use the term of the economist Karl Polanyi. Karl Marx had described the taking of lands and natural resources as the original "big bang" that ignited modern capital formation, calling it "primitive accumulation". For Polanyi this was only one step of the process. The first step was that human life could be subordinated to market dynamics and reborn as "labor" to be bought and sold. The second was that nature could be translated into the market and reborn as "land" or "real estate". The third was that exchange could be reborn as "money". The philosopher Hannah Arendt predicted that capitalism is made of such recurring phases in a repetitive cycle. Marx's original sin of simple robbery had eventually to be repeated or otherwise the motor of capital accumulation suddenly die down. Now we are attending another cycle of appropriation subordinating not only the natural world but also the social one to the market dimension.

3   How AI is Influencing Morality and Ethics (by Maurizio Mori)

I try to combine the little I know on AI and its impact on ethics. AI is a very complicated field which grew up in the last few decades and it now got a sense of maturity. AI is going to influence deeply out lifestyle and existence. On the one hand, for instance, robots are used for surgery and sometimes are even better than humans. This may be a problem. On the other hand, AI is influencing morality and ethics, this is the main topic of my talk. I try to clarify and to give ideas of what ethics and morality is. From my point of view, ethics and morality are synonymous. My talk is partly philosophical and partly empirical and sociological.

What is morality? My perspective is the one of an analytic philosopher. In philosophy there is a big distinction between the continental and analytical perspective. Every word must be examined and justified.

My talk is philosophical, and by philosophy here I mean analysis of concepts. I don't think that philosophy has a proper object but I think that philosophy is the analysis of any other field so we can have philosophy of AI, philosophy of morality.

What is a morality? Ethics or morality is a peculiar social institution. An institution is a social construct. An example of institution is law. Law is a solid institution as there are places in which this institution is exercised. It exists in time and space. There are other institutions that are not as solid as law. For instance, there are semi-solid institutions like politics. Politics is in part solid like law (there are parliaments, parties, political acts, etc.) but it is also fluid: when you talk to a friend in a bar, your talk could be a political act. Elections are a solid part of politics, but when you suggest to your neighbor to vote someone this is a very fluid. Having distinguished two different sorts of institutions, I can introduce another great institution: language. This is a prototype of fluid institution. The meaning of words and the structure of language is not invented by me or by anyone of us, but it is given. Yet certainly it is not solid (there is no such a thing as the "house of language"). Language is spread among people. Language does not depend on anyone and yet it exists. Morality is a kind of institution like language. It is spread in society and it is similar to language. No one owns morality. Morality is like a wind: you can feel but you cannot capture. It has an influence on you, but it is difficult to grasp as it is pervasive and has no definite point. The analogy between language and morality is classical and appears to be adequate so far, i.e., up to our time or a few decades ago.

In the last few years new problems have arisen connected with the new technologies. In the past, language grew up from the people and there was no way to control language. Some institutions could influence language more than normal native speakers. But now we have television or mass media that can influence language in a more profound way than it was possible in the past. So, in the essence, as a very recent phenomenon, we could say that we have a sort of "house of language". In a similar way we can say that advertisements are the products of a new "house of morality": ethics is not depending any longer on the individuals' contributions but can be deeply influenced by a new ad. We have to study the morality of this new situation, which is affected by the instruments that we have: television, social media, etc. These new problems are connected to AI, which appears to be one of the most powerful instruments that could facilitate a structural control of language as well as of morality. Up to now morality used to be spread among people as one's own mother tongue was: as no one could control the language so no one could control morality. Everyone could use and participate to the moral game like everyone could contribute to the language game without controlling it. Language is something more powerful than any of us. We don't invent the meaning of terms, but we can modify a little their meaning and use them in an extended or analogical sense, we can create new words and sometimes even new syntactical forms, contributing to the language. Our contributions to the language may be successful or not: nobody knows it in advance. Something similar occurs with moral values.

Morality is a special institution, and its peculiarity depends on its content and on the way it is uphold as well as on the ground it is based on. Content: there are moral duties which are at the core of any ethics, like the prohibition of killing or of stealing, etc. Of course, there are different interpretations of what it means "to kill" or "to steal", as well as about the subject not to-be killed and the object not-to-be stolen. There are other duties at the margin, that are discretional, in the sense that we can choose either a solution or the other and there is a margin of freedom in the choice. An example is clothing: one has to be dressed, and there are strict rules concerning the kind of clothing, but it is permitted to choose among different styles (of course even this example would require qualifications, but I hope it that is different from the former). In any case moral values and norms are followed spontaneously and for intimate conviction, because they are reckoned to be just. Instead, legal norms are followed in order to avoid penalty.

Which is the ground of morality? There are two different great basic answers to the question: on the one hand there is the idea that morality is a social institution which is given and founded in God and it is depended on religion. This is a very crucial point as we know that for many people morality is a special institution because it is not human. The most influential moral code are the Ten commandments. As you all know they have been given by God himself to Moses on the Mount Sinai. Is morality simply human or does it depend on religion?

Many people still think that either morality is connected to God, or it would collapse and vanish. This is not true, but it is true that the fact that morality is dependent on God (or not) has practical effects. At least for two aspects. First of all, if it is dependent on God, then morality will have absolute norms and prohibitions. Absolute means not dependent on conditions. This means that it is always valid and eternal, with no exception. Religion cannot be modified, cannot change. This is the first important consequence coming from the belief that morality is dependent on God. The shadow of such an absoluteness is flawing in morality. An example of this is the prohibition of divorce or of abortion, that was never allowed. Of course, in practice then such prohibitions are interpreted, because it is difficult to state what exactly God said. This is a difficult topic into which I do not want to enter. I can only say that we have different perspectives in Christianity as well as in other religions, and that even within a religion some moral precepts evolve. For instance, loan at interest (usury) was forbidden by the Roman Catholic church up to mid-XVIII century, and then permitted: something similar occurs in our days with divorce, which was absolutely prohibited up to the *Amoris Laetitia* (2016) and now it appears to be "in practice" permitted (at least in some cases).

The second point is formal, and it is about the reasons we have to comply with what morality requires. If morality is dependent on God, one should follow morality because God commanded, and the agent has to obey: obedience is what justifies moral compliance. I think that this is a poor and inadequate reason, because what is morally good or bad is dependent on rational justification and reason. This is the hallmark or the seal of morality as a human institution.

For this reason, my view is that morality is secular. Morality is a social institution that we follow because it has norms that are rationally justified. The goal of morality is to allow people to get an adequate level of social coordination that is required to reach personal self-realization. When the circumstances change, social coordination may modify as well and therefore some norms require to be qualified and changed. To have a rough idea, think of dressing: in winter, when it is cold, we wear heavy coats and hats in order to be warm, but in summer, when it is hot, we dismiss them and we wear linen. In our time the historical circumstances changed radically, and in fact we have different moralities because people try to adequate norms and values to the new conditions.

At this point one may legitimately ask how is it possible to talk about different moralities. How can they coexist? Shouldn't we say that there is just one universal morality? These are important questions that require an articulate answer with some premises. In abstract morality is universal and one, but this model has to be applied in our historical circumstances where the universal precepts have to be contextualized and the acquire some differences. As a matter of fact, we see that we have different moralities. Sometimes they can coexist peacefully, and sometimes they clash. In recent times things changed so quickly that people could hardly cope with such transformations and the result is that we speak of "culture wars", "cancel culture" etc., which is a different way to say that different ethics are in conflicts.

We can try to explain why there are ethical wars. One powerful reason is that in a few decades western societies had a rapid process of secularization as disenchantment of the world. As I said, up to half a century ago it was "normal" and taken for granted that morality was dependent on God. God sees everything in your heart and can see your intentions and actions. Therefore, if you copy an idea, you steal something and this is wrong because God does not want it. The God-eye perspective of ethics was dominant and undisputed.

Now this is still true for a fraction of people and they are scared that the world will be horrible if God won't continue to be the ruler. In this sense we have a clash of values. Do not forget that morality is rooted in the emotional part, and that emotion has a big role in ethics. Ideas move quickly and are light, but emotions are heavy and slow, and it takes time before they change. In this sense, we have a lot of people who are simply terrified at the idea that God is not prominent in morality, and they still adhere to traditional precepts and are proud to live according to the old customs. This is one of the main sources of the current moral war.

But the question is not only theoretical and abstract. It has quite practical effects that fuel the ethics war. Consider the issue of assisted reproduction. Should we limit the number of humans? Or should we get to infinite numbers? How many people are to enter in the world? Who and how should decide? These are only some of the questions that we can raise in the field and that morality has to face. In general, the approach is that if the moral norms are God-given, then we should leave the choice to the natural lottery. If the moral norms depend on human responsibility, then humans have to decide and articulate some criteria to the point. In our age we are encountering a big problem: are we allowed to control human reproduction? In the future reproduction will be totally assisted? How can different moralities coexist on the issue?

However, AI will fuel extra controversy, because there is a sense in which AI will substitute God's eye. Think. In the past, God could see all your actions. Now all our actions will be recorded by computers. For instance, I don't remember what I did in August 1st 1980 or 2 years ago. But I have a daughter who lives in London and she tells me that when she get the tube she pays with her mobile. Through her payments in the past, she is able to tell what she did in the past in a specific day. People have a full recording of everything. This will change our moral rules concerning privacy and our past life, and even our identity.

The possibility of recording everything and to keep any sort of data is going to modify our sense of history: let me explain. For thousands of years humans lived without scripture and recording the facts. That was pre-history. Then 5 thousand years ago humans invented writing in order to record what is happening. In this sense, we all have birth certificate, pictures of graduations, of weddings etc. This is history: History is a time in which we have some written documents recording of some events. "Pre-history", a time in which there were no written recording, while history is characterized by the recording of the most important events: actions, treatises, etc. Now the situation is quickly changing. Let's take an example: As an Italian, I went to Venice. Tourists used to take few pictures of Venice in the past. Now, tourists in Venice record everything. This is a dramatic change. We are entering what I propose to call "post-history". This empowerment will change deeply the historical condition and for this reason our morality will be modified. This is the main point of my thesis. In post-history we have recordings of everything. An important aspect is that all this information can be examined and analyzed. They can be used for good purposes, like to detect in advance medical problems. But even for bad purposes. This will deeply change our lives. We are entering in post-history in which everything is recorded, duplicated, and it will be hard to get what is relevant. For this reason, Big Data, data mining are aspects of the future.

We are in a stage in which we start something new because history will cease to exist. Of course, this is a remark concerning our description or representation of the matter. In reality, the flow of human events will continue as always. But our way of looking at the matter has to change. In a sense, my proposal is about technical language used to represent reality. Let me explain: we still have what we can call "the flow of human events", i.e., occurrence of things. In a sense, they represent the background of everything. The flow of human events started long ago and will continue up to the extinction of the human species. Of course, human events will continue but will include technological events. And this is a real problem because in essence technology enhances humans. We are already enhanced humans. We are no longer mere humans. We are supermen/wonder-women!

This is a problem for ethics because not to be enhanced is normal or is a lack of something? Everyone has a mobile. If someone has no mobile is like having something less than the others? Is it a kind of deficiency or defect?

Let's take another example. Nowadays everything is recorded and even the lecture this paper derives from is now recorded and can be shown in the future, 20 years from now. While there is no recording of Kant's lectures or of Verdi playing la Traviata. It is not the case to continue, but it is clear that this is a new feature of our new world: what will be the effect that my lecture will remain in the future? This is a permanent change in our conditions and therefore it will influence morality. This is a great problem. Algorithms will change our real life because life will be strongly conditioned by technology, peculiarly AI. This new technology will be pervasive, and it will induce a moral change. It is too early to predict the lines of the change, but it will occur.

This aspect raises new problems concerning the current behavior that people for example on Youtube. Algorithms decide when people can present their content or not, and maybe in the future even the content is conditioned. This could be interpreted as one sign among others of a sort of Machine-God, i.e., something trying to substitute the God-eye perspective. I think that such a hypothesis can be a risk as well as an opportunity! Think for instance what is going to happen in education. Now gathering together students in a class is done by chance. In the future, machines could choose how to match people in a class. Maybe weddings will be decided by algorithms. These are problems. For instance, in Sweden years ago there was a school very efficient in assisted reproduction that tried to select embryos. That was something seen under the microscope. Now all these processes of selection are processed by robots. What is better? Will we decide future life through robots? Which are the rational criteria to select someone rather than someone else?

Since we are open to enlarge our horizon to new perspectives, some few words can be said concerning another controversial issue, i.e., whether it is possible or even desirable that some Artificial Intelligence constructs will become "moral agent" or autonomous centers of action. This would mean that some AI artifacts will be able not only to calculate things, but also to feel them. I think this is a hypothesis that we should take seriously. We have already testified an enlargement of morality to non-humans (any sentient beings). If computers will become sentient as well as responsible of their actions, I think that we have to enlarge morality to include them. We have to be ready to modify our categories and enlarge them.

What is morality? Morality grants an adequate level of self-realization of every being capable of realizing themselves. Even non-human animals are able to get a kind of self-realization. So, they can be included in the moral game. If a robot will be able to consider a kind of self-realization, then even robots could be moral actors. This will depend on the future. But this is my view. This will be like an atomic bomb in morality. This will be a problem in the religious conception of morality. One should assume that God had the idea that humans can create computer. What will happen if computers could be able to replicate itself? (Should we use he or she?) These are fascinating issues.

More precisely, let's think what will happen if we had to program a new self-responsible robot. An issue will emerge immediately: moral bias. Moral bias is something that is not rational because it does not comply with equality and brings about a sort of discrimination. A bias is something unjust in the sense that it does not respect equality. But equality is not easy to understand in this way. To be equal is not to be identical (to have all similar properties). "Equal" in a moral sense means to be similar in some respect and not in others, but to deserve equal treatment because both have dignity. For instance, I am equal to Peter even though we have different faces. We are equal in dignity. We are not equal in other respects. To find out the similarities that create "equality" is a real problem. But we have to find it out, because bias is something unequal. In the next section, we will discuss if bias in machine learning has to do with rationality and how bias in morality is connected to the one in computer science.

4 AI and Ethics (by Guido Boella)

If AI impacts on what is Ethics, it will be not the first time that technology brings changes in Ethics. In the '70s there has been a revolution within Ethics as a consequence of the advances on bio-technology. We now think of AI as a tool, as other technologies. The historian Yuval Noah Harari[12] reminds us that the success of Sapiens with respect to the other human species is not due to the invention of tools. The real explosion of Sapiens happened with the cognitive revolution 70,000 years ago, a change that allowed us to talk not only about the reality, but also about fictional entities such as myths and gods. 6,000 years ago, in the middle east, artificial fictions such as temples, gods and then laws, allowed the Sumer to coordinate their society. Temples were employing people, owning lands, collecting taxes, etc., like they were real persons. Harari notices that these fictions are not so far from the modern concept of corporations, legal entities who own properties and employ people: they have a legal personhood (now detached from religion). Thanks to the possibility of coordinating people using such fictions, in a couple of millennia empires of over one million people became possible.

The American philosopher John Searle explains that we can coordinate in such a way our society thanks to the fact that we all share norms and costumes that create a socially constructed reality in which we are embedded in a seamless way: money, citizenship, laws are all fictional entities that work as long as we all agree upon them.

---

[12] Yuval Noah Harari, Sapiens, a brief history of humankind. Random House, 2014.

Technologies up to now had impact on our lives and only indirectly affected the socially constructed reality. Probably AI will have an impact on this dimension. So, the greatest impact of AI may not be autonomous weapons but how it will change these structures surrounding all of us. Consider, as an example, the notion of "Public sphere" by the German philosopher Jürgen Habermas, the realm of social life where public opinion is formed by public discussion: the social sites or arenas where meanings are articulated, distributed, and negotiated, as well as the collective body constituted by, and in this process, "the public". These mechanisms are increasingly substituted by personalization algorithms of social networks, deciding which different content to provide to each of us. How this change in the functioning of "Public sphere" will change our socially constructed reality?

Such deep changes will possibly need a change in Ethics itself. Up to now, many scholars, such as Floridi and Cowls, proposed to adopt for AI the same principles developed by Bio-medical Ethics: beneficence, non-maleficence, autonomy and justice. Take for example the beneficence principle: *"Beneficence: promoting well-being, preserving dignity, and sustaining the planet"*[13]. At some point some AI system will be used to provide information and judgements for the decision maker that must ethically evaluate another AI system according to this principle. So, we will use AI to evaluate AI itself from the ethical point of view. We have here a circular argument in applying current ethical principles to AI, invalidating the use of these principles. So, it is not possible to simply import them from the field of Bio-medical Ethics in the AI field without further considerations.

Moreover, we should not take for granted that a list of principles is the right approach to AI Ethics. As we noticed in Sect. 2, the generality of AI ethical guidelines makes them ineffective paper tigers. But also, as the authors of the Principles of Biomedical Ethics, Beauchamp and Childress[14], write:

Principlism, then, is not a mere list and analysis of four abstract principles. It is a theory about how principles link to and guide practice. We will be showing how these principles are connected to an array of transactions, practices, understandings, and forms of respect in health care settings, research institutions...

Beauchamp and Childress ground the principles in the common morality: "norms about right and wrong human conduct that are so widely shared that they form a stable social compact". The identification of very broad principles is only part of the contribution of Beauchamp and Childress: the other part is to use specification, balancing and (deductive) application to create a bridge between the moral situation and the relevant principles. In the Ethics of AI field, we are still lacking the *array of transactions, practices, understandings, and forms of respect*, that make concrete these principles. Hence, importing principles, as many authors do, is not the right way to proceed. We should learn from the history of Bio-medical Ethics in creating a new Ethics of AI tailored to the new risks created by technology.

---

[13] Luciano Floridi and Josh Cowls, A Unified Framework of Five Principles for AI in Society, Harvard Data Science Review, 1.1, 2019.

[14] Beauchamp, Tom L., and James F. Childress. Principles of Biomedical Ethics (5th ed.). New York: Oxford University Press, 1979.

5 Conclusion

As Ivana Bartoletti[15] says, *"if AI is both power and oppression, we should claim the first, and resist the second"*. We cannot just hope to rely on technical solutions and on existing ethical frameworks. Besides the work of researchers, we need the action of legislators, public opinion and the many activists and advocacy groups emerged in the last years, such as Electronic Frontier Foundation, Algorithm Watch, Algorithmic Justice League, and many others, among which the Italian Association for the Ethics of AI, SIpEIA that the authors recently co-founded.

---

[15] Ivana Bartoletti, An Artificial Revolution: On Power, Politics and AI. Indigo Press, 2020.

Law for Computer Scientists

Mireille Hildebrandt[1,2(✉)] and Arno De Bois[1]

[1] Vrije Universiteit Brussel, Pleinlaan 2, Brussel, Belgium
mireille.hildebrandt@vub.be
[2] Radboud University, Toernooiveld 212, Nijmegen, The Netherlands

Abstract. In this tutorial, we provide insights on what law does, how it operates and why it matters. We will more specifically dive into what law has to do with computer science or AI. In the second part we will zoom in on a set of texts that are highly relevant for computer science and AI. A first aspect we discuss the content of legal norms that apply to the processing of personal data, followed by a brief analysis of the proposed AI Act.

Keywords: Law · Data protection · GDPR · AI Act · Rule of law · Fundamental rights · AI · Personal data

1 Introduction

1.1 Learning Objectives

- Provide a better understanding of the inner workings of the law.
- Identify nonsensical headlines about the law as such (similar to tech headlines)
- Offer a taste of EU legislation that co-defines the global marketplace for AI systems (Brussels Effect: EU exporting rules and standards)
- Enable reasoning about the content of the law (the interpretation of legal conditions when deciding on legal effect)

1.2 Law and Computing Architectures

When we ask a room of computer scientists what law is, we often receive answers about constraints and about rules. This is, however, not what law is about [1].

In the end, law is about power relationships. The question should be asked whether the development of computing architectures is not also about power relationships. Indeed, many design decisions frame the choices we get to make. The difference with law, is that law is enacted by a democratic legislature by way of written legal norms, for everyone to read and to contest, whereas computing systems are often created behind closed doors and the relevant code is not accessible for those it affects. Another difference between law and computing systems, is that the latter's 'impact' is not limited to one jurisdiction.

Spelling out some of the differences between legal norms and computational rules, does not yet tell us what law is, what it does and how it does this. These questions are discussed in the next sections.

M. Chetouani et al. (Eds.): ACAI 2021, LNAI 13500, pp. 261–274, 2023.
https://doi.org/10.1007/978-3-031-24349-3_14

2 How Law Works

2.1 What Law is (Not)

Law is too often portrayed as the things it is not. For example, it is often described as a bag of rules. But law is different from a bag of rules, because there is a hierarchy between those rules, which is important in case those rules conflict. It is a complex system of rules and decisions.

Law is also not a set of orders, backed by threats, as is often claimed. Orders imply an external perspective, whereas a viable and legitimate legal system requires that norms have an internal aspect. Also, the law contains many types of rules. As such, there are prescriptions (telling what one should do), prohibitions (telling what one is not allowed to do) and permissions (telling what one is allowed but not prescribed). Other rules explain when someone may be punished (criminal law) or when compensation has to be paid (private & administrative law).

An important concept in understanding what law is and how it works, is the 'rule of law' [2]. The rule of law is about checks and balances and countervailing powers. It first of all means that the person enacting the rule is itself subject to the rule (nobody is above the law), based on the fundamental legal principle that the law is applied equally to equal cases. Rule of law also means that the institution that enacts the rule does not get to decide on how to interpret and apply that rule, which Montesquieu referred to as *iudex lex loquens* (the court is the mouth of the law). This was Montesquieu's opposition to *rex lex loquens*, where it was the king who decides the meaning of a rule. Iudex lex loquens means that even though the judge speaks the law in the name of the king, that king could no longer overrule the judge (who could not be fired by the king and thus became part of an independent judiciary, thus preventing the arbitrary rule of an absolute king) [3]. The rule of law thus ensures the contestability of the application and interpretation of enacted law. When we refer to the notion of Legal Protection by Design (LPbD) we refer to the idea of building contestability into computing architectures.

2.2 What Law Does (Not)

Law does things with words. It creates 'institutional facts' by way of written (e.g. deed) and spoken (e.g. contract) legal speech acts. It attributes 'legal effect' to events, actions, states of affair when the conditions of the relevant legal norm are satisfied. A legal effect is not caused or logically derived; it is attributed by the rules of positive law. Positive law is the law that is in force in a specific jurisdiction.

For example, killing somebody may have the effect of punishability, not of punishment. The latter depends on a court imposing punishment after a criminal offence has been charged and a number of procedural rules have been met, notably that the fact has been proven and found not to be justified (as in the case of self-defence) and found not to be excused (as in the case of force majeure). As another example, agreeing on the sale of a computer creates a legal obligation for the seller to provide property, and another legal obligation for the buyer to pay a price, but it does not have the legal effect of a transfer of property, which depends on another type of legal rule that is based on property law instead of the law of obligations. Though this may seem cumbersome, it makes a lot of sense, because property rules concern the relationship between a person and everyone else, whereas the law of obligations concerns relationships between two or more parties. Property can be enforced against everybody (so everybody needs to know about it), a contract can only be enforced against the party with which one concluded the contract (no need for recording every contract in a public registry).

2.3 Legal Norms

Legal norms are rules with binding force within a specific jurisdiction. This binding force is derived from the sources of law, which are respectively: international treaties, supranational legislation, statutory law, case law, fundamental principles of law and customary law. The lawmaker has to develop legal norms at the right level of abstraction, such that they are neither over- nor underinclusive. A relevant illustration of this is the definition of AI systems under the proposed Artificial Intelligence Act (AI Act) of the European Union, defining the object of regulation as 'AI systems' (not 'AI' in general). The AI Act does this in a pragmatic manner that is focused on protection against adverse impact on safety, health and fundamental rights.

Next to legislation, case law is a crucial source of law that allows courts to decide the 'ratio decidendi', that is the reasoning that justifies the decision of the court and – due to the principle of equality – requires that the legal effect will be decided similarly in subsequent cases that are similar in a relevant way.

Rules in law are different from logic (IFTTT) or causation (IFTT). Rules in law concern obligations and powers, they create a complex system of legitimate expectations – upheld by the state. Not all obligations are, however, legal obligations. We should distinguish them from deolontogical (moral) or social (prevalent common sense) norms. The difference between legal and other norms is their performative effect: legal norms create legal effect.

Under the rule of law, legal norms must be legitimate, lawful and instrumental. Legitimacy concerns justice. Lawfulness concerns legal certainty. Instrumentality concerns the fact that law serves goals decided by the government. In a constitutional democracy that is built on the rule of law, the government decides the goals based on democratic participation. Key to the combination of the rule of law and democratic rule is that governments must treat each and every citizen with equal respect and concern: this explains 'one person one vote', but it also explains that even a democratic majority must rule such that each and every person is respected. That is why democracy does not stand for tyranny of the majority.

2.4 Legal Rights

Legal rights are relational. They play out between legal subjects. As we have seen above, some rights are *erga omnes*, meaning they can be exercised against everyone (e.g. property). Other rights are *ad personam*, meaning they can only be exercised against specific parties (e.g. contract). Some rights have a correlating duty (e.g. right to obtain payment comes with an obligation to pay for the other party). Other rights have a correlating restriction (e.g. right to privacy).

Rights, which have effect between private parties, should also be distinguished from competences of public authorities based on public law, such as the competence to enact binding rules (constitution) or make decisions about individuals (administrative law).

2.5 Legal Reasoning

Legal reasoning results in the articulation of a syllogism: the application of major to a minor leads to a conclusion [4]. The major is the legal norm, the minor concerns the facts of the case, the conclusion concerns the attribution of legal effect. If certain legal conditions (articulated in a legal norm) apply (depending on the facts of the case), then the legal effect (articulated in the legal norm) is attributed. Note that the syllogism is not the method to achieve a conclusion. The syllogism itself is the end-result that justifies the attribution of legal effect. Legal reasoning is not just about finding the right answer, but about the right justification of a legal decision. The available legal norms thus constrain the decision space of the court, in order to rule out arbitrary decisions. As such, legal reasoning is not defined by logic, though it involves logic. The decision requires qualifying facts as relevant in light of a certain set of legal norms, while simultaneously interpreting a set of legal norms in light of the facts.

3 Data Protection

3.1 GDPR

This section elaborates on the General Data Protection Regulation (GDPR) [5], a highly relevant piece of legislation for the processing of personal data in the context of data-driven AI systems. We will mostly quote the precise wording of the text of the GDPR, because it is this text that has binding force, paraphrasing has no legal effort.

3.2 Objectives

According to art. 1, the GDPR has two objectives: (1) 'the protection of fundamental rights of natural persons' (i.e. not legal persons, such as corporations) 'with regard to the processing of personal data' and (2) 'the free movement of personal data' within the internal market of the EU. By harmonizing the legal norms that apply to the processing of personal data amongst the member states of the EU, the GDPR prevents obstacles within the internal market (the same rules apply everywhere) and simultaneously sets a threshold of legal protection. Note that the GDPR targets protection of fundamental rights and mentions specifically the right to data protection, without however mentioning privacy. It is a misunderstanding that the GDPR is focused on privacy. A whole range of other fundamental rights are at stake, notably non-discrimination and freedom of expression, right to a fair trial and the presumption of innocence.

3.3 The Object of Regulation

The GDPR regulates the processing of personal data. Personal data is understood as 'any information' (whether audio, written, video or under any other conceivable form) 'relating to an identified or identifiable individual (the 'data subject')'. Identifiability can be either direct or indirect. The latter significantly broadens the scope of the GDPR, because this means that even without an identified data subject, data that can be linked to an identifier constitutes personal data.

Processing under the GDPR is much broader than what is understood as the 'processing' stage in computer science. It is defined as 'any operation or set of operations performed on personal data, whether or not by automated means'. Any operation means any operation, including for example the collection, consultation, storage or destruction of data. The GDPR, much like the proposed AI act, thus starts with a broad scope, to offer broad protection.

3.4 Addressees: Controller and Processor

Accountability and liability for the processing of personal data is attributed to what the GDPR calls the data controller. This is not necessarily the entity carrying out the processing. The controller is the party that (co-)determines the purposes and means of the processing of personal data. Note that an entity without any technical expertise can nevertheless be a controller if it determines the purpose (while e.g. outsourcing the means).

The GDPR also defines the role of the so-called data processor, which is the party processing personal data 'on behalf of the controller'. This implies that as soon as a processor processes personal data for an own purpose, they become a controller with regard to that processing.

3.5 Principles

The GDPR in article 5 sets out the principles applicable to the processing. The use of the term 'principles' does not imply we are dealing with niceties or with ethical guidelines. The principles are rules that have to be followed. Article 5 prescribes that personal data shall be:

1. *processed lawfully, fairly and in a transparent manner in relation to the data subject ('lawfulness, fairness and transparency');*
   Lawfulness and fairness refer to the need to secure a legal basis (we will return to this when discussing art. 6) and the need to ensure the quality of the processing in light of potential infringements of fundamental rights.
2. *collected for specified, explicit and legitimate purposes and not further processed in a manner that is incompatible with those purposes; further processing for archiving purposes in the public interest, scientific or historical research purposes or statistical purposes shall [...] not be considered to be incompatible with the initial purposes ('purpose limitation');*

This is about honouring the legitimate expectations of data subjects. The purpose should be explicit and clearly defined, meaning that a purpose abstractly defined as 'collection of data for the creation of a dataset' will not be sufficient.

Note that under specific circumstances (for example in the context of scientific research) the GDPR allows for some flexibility when specifying the purpose, requiring that a more concrete finality crystallises in the course of the research.

3. *adequate, relevant and limited to what is necessary in relation to the purposes for which they are processed ('data minimisation');*

This principle stipulates that the controller must consider various alternatives before engaging in the processing of personal data. Data hoarding is not allowed. Under the previous legislation the threshold was less stringent, requiring appropriateness instead of necessity.

To the extent that it is difficult to establish what data will be necessary, the concrete purpose of processing may be to determine what data is needed. This may be especially relevant in a research context. Even in that case, however, the necessity cannot be taken for granted. For example, when patient treatment data is reused for scientific research, it may be the case that such data is incorrect and incomplete, because doctors may routinely change the diagnosis to ensure that the treatment is ensured. This raises questions about whether such data can possibly be necessary, noting it will easily result in incorrect output.

4. *accurate and, where necessary, kept up to date; every reasonable step must be taken to ensure that personal data that are inaccurate, having regard to the purposes for which they are processed, are erased or rectified without delay ('accuracy');*

This principle is very relevant for machine learning, where for example much behavioural data is highly likely to be irrelevant, as human behaviour is forever in flux (notably anticipating being targeted based on behavioural targeting, known as the so-called Goodhart effect in economics).

5. *kept in a form which permits identification of data subjects for no longer than is necessary for the purposes for which the personal data are processed; personal data may be stored for longer periods insofar as the personal data will be processed solely for archiving purposes in the public interest, scientific or historical research purposes or statistical purposes [...] subject to implementation of the appropriate technical and organisational measures [...] in order to safeguard the rights and freedoms of the data subject ('storage limitation');*

Note that in the context of scientific research, data will often have to be stored for a long time in order to allow for e.g. reproducibility testing. This is considered a valid reason for storage (noting that storage is defined as processing of personal data).

As to deletion and so-called subject access requests (SARs, based on GDPR transparency requirements), some companies are selling software systems under the heading of GDPR compliance tools. These tools are capable of detecting personal data in both structured and unstructured datasets, in order to delete or access them. These are obviously very invasive tools with a high potential for misuse. This demonstrates that compliance tools should not take singular legal rules out of context, as such an invasive tool easily presents likely high risks for fundamental rights and freedoms of natural persons (something data controllers need to check for, avoid if possible or mitigate, based on art. 35 GDPR).

6. *processed in a manner that ensures appropriate security of the personal data, including protection against unauthorised or unlawful processing and against accidental loss, destruction or damage, using appropriate technical or organisational measures ('integrity and confidentiality').*

This concerns robust security requirements, that result in liability in case of a data breach (see art. 33 GDPR), more details about appropriate technical and organizational measures can be found in art. 32 GDPR).

3.6 Legal Basis

In order for any processing to be lawful, the processing must be based on one of six legal grounds. Though those not familiar with the GDPR often think that processing is only allowed based on consent, this is not at all the case. Actually, consent is a weak legal ground, for instance because it can be withdrawn any time.

1. *the data subject has given consent to the processing of his or her personal data for one or more specific purposes;*
   Consent can only be provided for an explicit, specific and legitimate purpose. This links consent to purpose limitation, but also to necessity (as we have seen above). Even in the case of consent, the processing is only allowed when it is necessary for the purpose as explicitly specified and only if that purpose is legitimate.
   Also note that consent may also be required under the E-Privacy Directive, which regulates confidentiality in the case of telecommunication. In the latter case the consent requirement does not depend on whether or not data is personal data.

2. *processing is necessary for the performance of a contract to which the data subject is party or in order to take steps at the request of the data subject prior to entering into a contract;*
   Contract should not be confused with consent. Note that as soon as the contract has been performed, the legal basis may be exhausted.

3. *processing is necessary for compliance with a legal obligation to which the controller is subject;*
   Examples of such legal obligations are tax law and the GDPR itself (e.g. to comply with transparency requirements).

4. *processing is necessary in order to protect the vital interests of the data subject or of another natural person;*
   This means that you will for example not need to ask for consent to process data on the blood type of someone who is bleeding to death.

5. *processing is necessary for the performance of a task carried out in the public interest or in the exercise of official authority vested in the controller;*
   This normally concerns tasks carried out by public administration, but it can be argued that scientific research is processing in the public interest. The GDPR spells out that private companies can also do scientific research, provided that they adhere to the relevant methodological standards, which implies that research behind closed

doors (due to intellectual property rights or trade secrets) may not count as research in the public interest.

6. *processing is necessary for the purposes of the legitimate interests pursued by the controller or by a third party, except where such interests are overridden by the interests or fundamental rights and freedoms of the data subject which require protection of personal data, in particular where the data subject is a child.*

The legitimate interest is one of the most contentious grounds for the processing of personal data. Important is that the legitimate interest rhymes with a right to object from the data subject, which has to be explicitly communicated to the data subject, separately from any other information. In case of objection the processing can only continue if the controller demonstrates compelling legitimate grounds for the processing that override the interests, rights and freedoms of the data subject or for the establishment, exercise or defense of legal claims. In case of processing for direct marketing purposes, the objection by the subject is final and must be complied with.

3.7 Data Protection Impact Assessment

Whenever intended processing, according to an initial assessment, is 'likely to result in a high risk for fundamental rights and freedoms of natural persons' (note that this is much broader than a risk to 'privacy', and includes all rights, such as for example the right to non-discrimination or the right to a fair trial), the controller has to perform a Data Processing Impact Assessment (DPIA). As a likely high risk are considered in any case:

1. *systematic and extensive evaluation of personal aspects relating to natural persons which is based on automated processing, including profiling, and on which decisions are based that produce legal effects concerning the natural person or similarly significantly affect the natural person;*

For example, automated decisions on insurance premiums or eligibility, based on a web application or similar decision of student grants.

2. *processing on a large scale of special categories of data referred to in Article 9(1), or of personal data relating to criminal convictions and offences referred to in Article 10; or*

This concerns the processing of sensitive data, such as health data, data on ethnicity, political views, sexual preferences, etc.

3. *a systematic monitoring of a publicly accessible area on a large scale.*

For example in a shopping mall, or football stadion.
A data protection impact assessment contains at least:

1. *a systematic description of the envisaged processing operations and the purposes of the processing, including, where applicable, the legitimate interest pursued by the controller;*
2. *an assessment of the necessity and proportionality of the processing operations in relation to the purposes;*
3. *an assessment of the risks to the rights and freedoms of data subjects referred to in paragraph 1; and*
4. *the measures envisaged to address the risks, including safeguards, security measures and mechanisms to ensure the protection of personal data and to demonstrate compliance with this Regulation taking into account the rights and legitimate interests of data subjects and other persons concerned.*

The measures mentioned in the last point should aim to prevent, or at least to mitigate the potential impact of the processing on the fundamental rights and freedoms of the data subjects. The processing will also need to be followed-up. The controller must verify whether the described measures are effectively deployed in practice.

In a sense, the DPIA is similar to the impact assessment under the AI Act, the so-called conformity assessment that includes a dedicated assessment of risk to fundamental rights, brought about by high risk AI systems, both when used for their intended purpose and when used for reasonably foreseeable other purposes. On top of that, the AIA requires that providers of high risk AI systems make sure that claims on functionality are accurate, which only regards usage for their intended purpose. Note that the AI Act's impact assessment is not restricted the processing of personal data and not only concerns fundamental rights infringements, but also safety and health risks (think of robotics, Internet of Things).

3.8 Data Protection by Design and by Default

Article 25 prescribes data protection by design and by default [6]. The first paragraph describes data protection by design:

Taking into account the state of the art, the cost of implementation and the nature, scope, context and purposes of processing as well as the risks of varying likelihood and severity for rights and freedoms of natural persons posed by the processing, the controller shall, both at the time of the determination of the means for processing and at the time of the processing itself, implement appropriate technical and organisational measures, such as pseudonymization,

An example of technical and organizational measures would be Chinese walls that keep data separate from the relevant identifier (pseudonymization). Keep in mind that pseudonymised data, as defined by the GDPR, are personal data and not considered anonymised (as they can reasonably likely be linked with the identifiers).

Such technical and organization measures should be

(...) designed to implement data-protection principles, such as data minimisation, in an effective manner and to integrate the necessary safeguards into the processing

in order to meet the requirements of this Regulation and protect the rights of data subjects.

The next paragraph addresses data protection by default:

The controller shall implement appropriate technical and organisational measures for ensuring that, by default, only personal data which are necessary for each specific purpose of the processing are processed.

This highlights again that it is the purpose that determines what is necessary data, in terms of type, but also in terms of volume and precision:

That obligation applies to the amount of personal data collected, the extent of their processing, the period of their storage and their accessibility.

Polymorphous encryption could be such a technique addressing the accessibility:

In particular, such measures shall ensure that by default personal data are not made accessible without the individual's intervention to an indefinite number of natural persons.

4   Artificial Intelligence Act

4.1   The Proposal

As opposed to the GDPR, the AI Act is not yet a binding legal text but currently a proposal by the European Commission. It is thus still subject to change, due to negotiation between the Council and the Parliament of the EU; we expect the final version to come into force within the coming two or three years. The AI Act is part of administrative law, which is focused on the public interest and enforced by oversight bodies competent to conduct investigations and to impose administrative fines. Most of the responsibilities are attributed to the providers of high-risk AI systems. The Act does not settle private law liability issues (an update of the liability framework is expected in 2022). Neither does the AI Act attribute new individual rights to natural persons. The GDPR does impose private law liability and, as indicated above, it does provide specified individual rights to natural persons.

4.2   Defining AI Systems

As mentioned before, the AI Act is not concerned with the metaphysical discussion on what is or what isn't considered 'Artificial Intelligence'. The text adopts a pragmatic approach, listing out in its annex what falls within the scope of the regulation.

The scope as laid out is remarkably broad, just like is the case with the GDPR, offering by default a broad protection. The 'Annex I' lists out three types of approaches that must apply for software to qualify as an 'AI system':

(a) *Machine learning approaches, including supervised, unsupervised and reinforcement learning, using a wide variety of methods including deep learnin;*

(b) *Logic- and knowledge-based approaches, including knowledge representation, inductive (logic) programming, knowledge bases, inference and deductive engines, (symbolic) reasoning and expert system;*

This category in particular highlights the broad scope of the regulation, where it could be argued that for example an excel sheet when used for taking certain decisions (e.g. on social benefits), may be qualified as an AI system, provided the other elements of the definition apply (see below). In one of the draft versions of the Council (that co-determines the final version of the Regulation), an attempt was made to exclude what is called 'traditional software' from the application of the AI Act. However, (b) is left without changes, so in the end it would still be up to the Court of Justice of the European Union to decide what kind of systems falls within the scope of the Act.

(c) *Statistical approaches, Bayesian estimation, search and optimization methods.*

For a software system to fall within the scope of the Act, it does not suffice to establish that it deploys one of the above approaches. Art. 3(1) stipulates:

'artificial intelligence system' (AI system) means software that is developed with one or more of the techniques and approaches listed in Annex I and can, for a given set of human-defined objectives, generate outputs such as content, predictions, recommendations, or decisions influencing the environments they interact with;

This implies three legal conditions for the legal effect of 'qualifying as an AI system' to apply: (1) the system consists of software, whether or not embedded, (2) its objectives have been defined by human beings and (3) it generates specific kinds of output that influence the environments they interact with. The latter clarifies the focus on impact, the second point highlights that providers are held accountable for the way the system targets the intended purpose (and its reasonably foreseeable misuse). The more general the objectives of an AI system, the larger the scope of the impact assessment, as its reasonably foreseeable misuse will also expand.

4.3 Architecture of the Act

The Act is applicable to 'AI systems' as broadly defined, and more specifically to (1) prohibited 'AI practices', which are more narrowly defined, (2) high risk systems (see below) and (3) four additional types of systems that involve dedicated transparency requirements.

The main addressees of the act are the providers (and distributors and importers): whoever is making the system available on the market or putting it into service (under their own name or brand). This is the triggering event for the applicability of the Act. Note that making available on the market only qualifies as such if done 'in the course of a commercial activity', meaning that posting code on github or publishing prototypes outside a commercial context does not make developers or computer scientists liable as providers.

Other addressees of the act are the so-called users. They are not to be confused with end-users. The user is the party putting into service an AI system, deploying it under their own authority. Users would for example be governments, web shops, etc.

4.4   Qualification of AI Systems

The AI Act regulates mostly what are considered 'high risk' systems. Depending on how they are used, such systems may also fall within the scope of one of the prohibited practices, which are however very narrowly defined. High risk systems are summed up in Annexes II (mostly safety and health risks) and III (mostly fundamental rights risks). The European Commission can update the listing if new systems with similar risks emerge.

When an AI system qualifies as a high risk system, a set of requirements is triggered (Title III, chapters 2 and 3). These requirements form the core of the Act. They entail risk management, quality management, data and data governance requirements, human oversight, technical documentation, record keeping, transparency for users (note that this not about end-users), accuracy, robustness and cybersecurity requirements. The violation of these requirements can lead to fines up to 30 million euros, or 6% of the global turnover.

Risk Management. In case of high risk AI systems, a Risk Management System (RMS) must be set up for iterant, continuous impact assessment during the entire life cycle of the system. This includes the identification of known and foreseeable risks concerning use for both the intended purpose as well as reasonably foreseeable misuse (defined as use for other purposes). The risk management includes testing against predefined metrics and post-market monitoring (including some requirements regarding automated logging). The RMS also includes suitable measures for the prevention and mitigation of risks, taking into account post-market interactions with other systems. Finally, providers must provide clear instructions to users (again not to be confused with end-users).

Data Governance. The Act prescribes that training, validation and test data are subject to a series of governance and management practices that concern relevant design choices, data preparation, formulation of relevant assumptions and notably a prior assessment of the 'availability, quantity and suitability of data sets that are needed'. Potential bias, gaps and shortcomings must be addressed. This kind of assessment is core to the methodological integrity of data-driven AI systems; as such they should be welcomed by the AI community, since today many applications are experimental *crapware* built with low-hanging fruit. We may therefor expect higher quality next to the risk reduction that is core to the Act.

Human Oversight. This is not to be confused with the right to an explanation and the right not to be subject to automated decisions of the GDPR. The AI Act stipulates that the development of high risk AI systems is such that meaningful human oversight at the site of the user is built into the system or guaranteed by way of instructions to the user. It should allow the prevention or mitigation of risks to health, safety and fundamental rights, both when used for the intended purposes and in case of reasonably foreseeable other purposes. Those tasked with human oversight must enable understanding of both the capacities and the limitations of the system, resisting automation bias, proper interpretation of the behaviour and decisions of the system, and it must enable those tasked with human oversight to disregard, override or even interrupt or stop the system if needed.

Accuracy. High risk AI systems should be designed in a way that ensures persistent performance based on relevant accuracy metrics, resilience against errors, faults and inconsistencies. The design should also ensure robustness through for example redundancy solutions. It should prevent feedback loops (e.g. reinforcing bias, but also echo-chambers) and it should provide resilience against manipulation (e.g. against data poisoning and adversarial examples).

Quality Management Systems. This concerns a documented series of integrated technical and organizational measures to be taken by the provider to ensure compliance with the Act.

4.5   Final Note on Actionable Protection in the AI Act

To ensure the practical and effective protection the Act aims to offer, we would argue that it should include the following individual and collective rights:

A.   The right not to be subject to prohibited AI practices
B.   The right to object to decisions made by high-risk AI systems
C.   The right to file an injunction in a court of law, and to mandate that right to an NGO in case one is subjected to prohibited AI practices or to decisions made by high risk AI systems
D.   The right of dedicated NGO's to file an injunction in their own name with respect to the rights under A and B.

We assume that the upcoming liability framework will provide some forms of strict liability. This will most probably take the form of an update of e.g. the product liability directive [7], making sure that the relevant EU legislation applies to AI systems.

Recommendations for Further Readings (See Also the References)
Hildebrandt, M.: Law for Computer Scientists and Other Folk. Oxford University Press, Oxford (2020), available in Open Access at OUP: https://academic.oup.com/book/33735.
GDPR: Regulation (EU) 2016/679 of the European Parliament and of the Council of 27 April 2016 on the protection of natural persons with regard to the processing of personal data and on the free movement of such data, and repealing Directive 95/46/EC (General Data Protection Regulation), https://eur-lex.europa.eu/eli/reg/2016/679/oj.
AI Act (proposal): Proposal for a Regulation of the European Parliament and of the Council laying down harmonised rules on artificial intelligence (Artificial Intelligence Act), COM/2021/206 final, https://eur-lex.europa.eu/legal-content/EN/TXT/?uri=CELEX%3A52021PC0206.

References

1. Hildebrandt, M.: Law for Computer Scientists and Other Folk. Oxford University Press, Oxford (2020). https://doi.org/10.1093/oso/9780198860877.001.0001
2. Hildebrandt, M.: Law, democracy, and the rule of law. In: Law for Computer Scientists and Other Folk. Oxford University Press, Oxford (2020). https://doi.org/10.1093/oso/9780198860877.003.0002
3. Schoenfeld, K.M.: Rex, lex et judex: montesquieu and la bouche de la loi revisted. Eur. Const. Law Rev. **4**, 274–301 (2008)
4. Hildebrandt, M.: 2.1.3 Legal reasoning. In: Law for Computer Scientists and Other Folk, pp. 28–30. Oxford University Press, Oxford (2020). https://doi.org/10.1093/oso/9780198860877.003.0002
5. Hildebrandt, M.: Privacy and data protection. In: Law for Computer Scientists and Other Folk. Oxford University Press, Oxford (2020). https://doi.org/10.1093/oso/9780198860877.003.0005
6. Hildebrandt, M., Tielemans, L.: Data protection by design and technology neutral law. Comput. Law Secur. Rev. **29**, 509–521 (2013). https://doi.org/10.1016/j.clsr.2013.07.004
7. Product Liability Directive (85/374/EEC), see 'Civil liability – adapting liability rules to the digital age and artificial intelligence'. https://ec.europa.eu/info/law/better-regulation/have-your-say/initiatives/12979-Civil-liability-adapting-liability-rules-to-the-digital-age-and-artificial-intelligence_en

Mythical Ethical Principles for AI
and How to Attain Them

Marija Slavkovik[⊠]

University of Bergen, Bergen, Norway
marija.slavkovik@uib.no

Abstract. To have ethical AI two questions need to be answered: i) what is the ethical impact that an AI system can have, and, ii) what does it mean for an AI system to behave ethically. The lack of answers to both of these questions hinder the identification of what are the values or principles that we want upheld by AI and for AI. Identifying these principles is not enough, we also want to define them so that they can be operational, or at least understand what operational means here. There is a gap between moral philosophy and ethically behaving AI. The tutorial contributes towards closing this gap, by motivating researchers to interpret an abstract principle from moral philosophy into an algorithmic property that can be formally specified and measured or computationally implemented. The tutorial uses recent articles in AI ethics that attempt to define and identify pertinent ethical principles, as well as ethically motivated desirable algorithmic properties.

1   About This Tutorial

This tutorial is primarily intended for students of computer science and artificial intelligence (AI) who are interested in how to establish what ethical impact the research and products they develop have on individuals and society. The tutorial is also aimed for graduate students interested in doing research in AI ethics.

Intended Learning Outcomes

- Knowledge
    - Familiarity with ethical principles of interest to AI problems.
    - Familiarity with the definitions and main areas problems studied in: Accountability, Transparency, Explainability, Interpretability, Fairness, and Privacy.
- Skills
    - Ability to discern between ethically motivated computation properties of an AI system and the extent to which an AI system satisfies an ethical principle
    - Ability to appraise the ethical aspects of AI problems.
    - Familiarity with the some of the core literature in the computer science aspects of the AI Ethics research field

© Springer Nature Switzerland AG 2023
M. Chetouani et al. (Eds.): ACAI 2021, LNAI 13500, pp. 275–303, 2023.
https://doi.org/10.1007/978-3-031-24349-3_15

2   Introduction

Artificial intelligence ethics is a sub-field of artificial intelligence (AI). The subfield emerged in response to how computation and artificial intelligence are researched, developed, deployed, and used today in different societies. It is concerned with ensuring a non-negative ethical impact on people and societies while researching, developing, deploying and using artificial intelligence. The focus on the ethical impact of AI is motivated by the way AI and computation are used today changed, in contrast to how they were used up to one decade ago.

Both computation in general and artificial intelligence specifically, since their inception, have been used to automate tasks that require intelligence [16]. It is difficult to precisely discern between AI and 'just' computation. Today, tasks that require intelligence are automated in separation. For example, one algorithm is used for learning, another for scheduling tasks. This is not the aspect of computation that has changed a lot – what has changed is who develops and uses computation and artificial intelligence today.

Due to the development of computation technology and the wast connectivity enabled by the Internet, computation is now available to all, for all kinds of purposes. This is a positive development, but one that disables past methods of controlling for ethical impact of computation. For example, bias in the information that a decision making computer program uses could be controlled, against trade offs, by adequate training of knowledge engineers[1] and users [69]. This was possible in the past because it was known who the knowledge engineers and users were. Furthermore, if anything, ethical concerns regarding computation are exasperated because computation is used to supplement or replace humans in tasks where ethical considerations are necessary. Examples include medical decisions and digital first government services.

Ethics or moral philosophy is a sub-field of philosophy concerned with the development of concepts of right and wrong behavior. Although artificial intelligence is sometimes defined as "the field that studies the synthesis and analysis of computational agents that act intelligently." [63], computer programs do not, as of today, have agency in the standard philosophical sense [3]. Therefore it is perhaps wrong to consider the moral[2] behaviour of artificial intelligence. Instead we can consider the extent to which the research, development, deployment and use of artificial intelligence aligns with the moral values that a person, or a society, want to uphold.

Ethical values can also be defined in relation to ethical principles. Ethical principles are part of a normative theory that justifies or defends moral rules and/or moral decisions and reflect objective positions of right and wrong or what "ought" to be [38]. Most common ethical principles that are considered in moral philosophy are: beneficence, non-maleficence, fidelity, autonomy, freedom, and justice.

---

[1] Knowledge engineers are experts who identify information and represented into data that can be used by computers.

[2] Moral and ethical are used as synonyms throughout this text.

In AI ethics however, one does not measure to which extent does an algorithm's behaviour or impact of use align with moral principles. This is not surprising. On one hand, it is fairly clear that satisfying a moral principle is not a yes-or-no thing. For example we recognise that one behaviour brings about more beneficence to the world than another, while both bringing beneficence. On the other hand, the quantification of the level of compliance with a moral principle is very hard. Instead, in AI ethics one defines properties of algorithms that can be ascertained. These include: algorithmic accountability, fairness, transparency, explainability, interpretability and privacy. One also considers the properties of people who play a significant role in the ethical impact of AI. These properties include responsibility and trustworthiness.

Despite a direct measurement of satisfaction of a moral principle being out of reach, it is important to keep moral principles connected with the properties of algorithms. This means, keeping track of which algorithmic property advances or hinders which principles. Without this connection, we risk considering algorithmic properties that are easy to satisfy but do not in fact promote ethical values, or properties defined because they sound or appear ethical, while in fact not promoting ethical values. Both of these such practices effectively amounts to ethics washing [39, 78]. What is particularly challenging to accomplish are well defined ethical algorithmic properties. For example, number of iterations of a loop, or an amount of memory an algorithm uses are well defined algorithmic properties. Accountability, transparency and fairness in particular are not well defined, neither as algorithmic properties nor as ethical principles.

[40] identify five core principles for ethical AI: beneficence, non-maleficence, autonomy, justice and explicability. The first four occur in bioethics, while the fifth they define as a moral principle that explicitly applies to AI. We here will consider these five principles and how they are impacted by the six algorithmic properties commonly considered desirable in AI ethics: algorithmic accountability, fairness, transparency, explainability, interpretability and privacy.

3   Ethical Principles

We begin by defining and discussing the five moral principles that [40] identify the most relevant to AI. It is important to note that these principles, with the exception of the one that [40] themselves define, have long be discussed in moral philosophy. As such, there exists not one simple, exact, and uniformly adopted definition of beneficence, non-maleficence, autonomy, or justice.

Moral principles are the "product" or "tool" of normative ethics. Normative ethics is a branch of moral philosophy that is concerned with prescribing ways in which moral behaviour or state can be achieved [38]. While numerous moral principles have been proposed in normative ethics, some, like beneficence, non-maleficence, autonomy and justice, have been included in short-lists more frequently than others.

Each of the moral principles that are of concern to AI, and to which an AI system should be aligned, require a thorough consideration. To a large extent the principles can be made more specific in the context of AI, in general, and particular methods and applications of an AI system, in particular. This is done, for example, for the principle of justice [12], but not to the same extent with the others.

Beneficence. The idea that our actions and behaviour should benefit not only ourselves but also others, perhaps even at a cost to ourselves, is the essence of morality. In ethical theories the concept of beneficence effectively includes "all norms, dispositions, and actions with the goal of benefiting or promoting the good of other persons." [14].

Aligning the research, development, deployment, and use of AI with the moral principle of beneficence, clearly can be interpreted in many different ways. AI systems always are developed to further the interest of someone. Is that sufficient to declare that system aligned with the principle of beneficence? Numerous, so called "AI for good" initiatives[3][4][5][6] seek precisely the alignment with beneficence.

In the simplest and most broad sense, alignment with beneficence entails the obligation to engage in AI work that benefits humanity as a whole or to put it another way "to improve people's lives". In a more precise interpretation, the evaluation of the alignment of an AI system with beneficence necessarily involves the stakeholders affected by, or involved in, that AI system's development and operation. This, in turn is also not a trivial task [13].

It is perhaps most essential that the benefits of an AI systems are made explicit particularly when considering the possible harms that system can, or does incur.

Non-maleficence. Another core concept of morality is the principle of non-maleficence, or avoiding to incur harm. Non-maleficence is a cornerstone of medical bioethics, being enshrined by the *The Hippocratic Oath's* maxim of "first do no harm". In many ways, when we think about ethical AI we consider the same aim of an AI that does not do harm. This is perhaps also motivated by the first Asimov law of robotics "A robot may not injure a human being or, through inaction, allow a human being to come to harm. Second Law" [3].

In moral philosophy the principle of non-maleficence is one of the *prima facie* duties championed by [80]. He makes an effort to clearly distinguish that beneficence and non-maleficence are two separate duties, and puts non-maleficence as a duty that should be followed before all others [70]. The concept of harm is what introduces ambiguity when estimating to which extent has the principle of non-maleficence been uphold. To cause death is clearly to cause harm, but is a one-off verbal insult a harm? The line is virtually impossible to draw and it is very context dependent. A further point of "built-in imprecision" is brought by the realisation that harm can also be subjective: what is perceived as harm by one person is not perceived as harm by another.

---

[3] https://aiforgood.itu.int/.

[4] https://ai4good.org/.

[5] https://www.microsoft.com/en-us/ai/ai-for-good.

[6] https://ai.google/social-good/.

The deliberate development of AI systems that cause harm or break laws is the concern of responsible and legal AI [37]. AI ethics is concerned with unintentional harm. When considering autonomous vehicles, assisting devices, and robots it is clear to see that those can cause bodily harm. Psychological harms and other non-bodily harms, in contrast, are much more difficult to establish or even agree upon. As with beneficence, to evaluate what is the potential of an AI system to cause harm entails identifying the stakeholders affected by the AI system in question.

It is perhaps important to emphasise that both beneficence and non-maleficence extend not only to people but to animal welfare and overall sustainability. Sustainability is described as "development that meets the needs of the present without compromising the ability of future generations to meet their own needs." [20]. AI systems can have both a direct and indirect impact on sustainability [75].

Justice. The moral principle of justice embodies the duty to be concerned with how people are treated in the interest of treating individuals and groups justly [53]. Rawls [64] attempts to conceptualise justice by developing two principles: the principle of liberty and the principle of equality. The principle of liberty advances the idea that everyone has an equal right to basic liberties. The laws and liberties that Rawls lists as basic are not necessarily what one wants to always consider as such [50], but most constitutions do define what is considered to be basic human rights, mostly following the UN[7]. The principle of equality is then given in two sub-principles, one requiring fair equality of opportunity and the other permitting only those inequalities that are incurred to benefit the worst-of individuals in society.

Basl et al. [12] give a thorough consideration of the moral principle of justice, in its many values and forms, when applied to AI directly:

"The foundational value that underlies justice is the equal worth and political standing of people. The domain of justice concerns how to organize social, political, economic, and other systems and structures in accordance with these values. A law, institution, process, or algorithm is unjust when it fails to embody these values. So, the most general principle of justice is that all people should be equally respected and valued in social, economic, and political systems and processes". [12]

Basl et al. [12] also are careful to distinguish between fairness and justice, although recognising that the two terms are used interchangeably in AI ethics:

"In institutional contexts, 'fairness' is often used to refer to treatment in a particular context, whereas 'justice' refers to the institutional features that structure the context – a process (e.g., lending or criminal justice) can be unfair because the system is unjust (e.g., organized in a way that advantages some groups and disadvantages others)." [12]

---

[7] https://www.un.org/en/global-issues/human-rights.

Basl et al. [12] argue that set of more specific justice-oriented principles is needed, and gives the examples in Table 1[8].

Table 1. Justice oriented principles

Procedural	Distributive	Recognition
Non-discrimination A system or decision-making process should not be biased against certain groups	*Equality of Access* Everyone should be provided the same/similar access to benefits and services	*Same Treatment* Everyone should be treated the same regardless of the groups to which they belong
Equality of Opportunity Everyone should have equal/similar chanced of success (e.g. educational, social, or economic)	*Benefit Sharing* Everyone who contributes to a collective endeavor should share in its benefits	*Representational Accuracy* People or groups of people should not be mischaracterized
Equality of Participation People should be similarly empowered in social and political decision-making contexts and processes	*Decent Outcome* Everyone should have good enough (or minimally decent) social and economic outcomes	*Inclusion* People or groups of people (and their interests) should not be marginalized or excluded
Just Deserts People's social and economic outcomes should reflect their efforts and contributions	*Prioritizing Worst-Off* Practices and policies should prioritize those who are most vulnerable, dependent, or in need	*Reparative Justice* Past wrongful harms should be made up for and addressed so as not to create further harms or future disadvantages

It is clear from the example specifications of the justice principle in Table 1 that the ethical principles do overlap and it is often not possible to talk about one without talking about another. Equality of participation, for example, considers the empowerment of people in decision-making contexts. The idea that a person should have the power to make their own decisions is related to the principle we consider next, that of autonomy.

Autonomy. Floridi et al. [40] express a concern that "artificial autonomy may undermine the flourishing of human autonomy". The concept of autonomy is applied to both humans and machines and it both cases it means "self governance", however the expression of that self governance is necessarily defined by the abilities of the machine in question. Before we discuss the moral principle of autonomy, let us briefly outline autonomy of systems.

---

[8] Verbatim https://www.atlanticcouncil.org/in-depth-research-reports/report/specify ing-normative-content/#table-3.

When applied to machines (software and devices alike) the term autonomous refers to their capacity for independent operation without direct supervision or control by a human operator. Typically, with respect to their ability for independent operation, machines are divided into four categories: controlled, supervised, automatic and autonomous. Controlled machines have no ability of independent operation. Supervised machines can do some tasks independently but require regular intervention. For example, a washing machine, or a calculator need input from people and people to process the outcomes of their respective operations. Automatic machines can operate fully without supervision or intervention if placed in a specific working environment in which all interactions with the machine are fully predicted. Autonomous machines can operate in some unpredictable context, react to the environment, and learn from it to improve their executions of tasks. With the autonomous machines a separate hierarchy exists as to how much abilities of autonomy the machine has [60]. The lines are not easy to draw, but it is well understood that the machine autonomy is far bellow the capabilities for self governance of humans and complex animals.

Autonomy as a moral principle expresses protection for the ability of one to be their own person and "live one's life according to reasons and motives that are taken as one's own and not the product of manipulative or distorting external forces, to be in this way independent." [30]. Autonomy closely relates to the moral principle of freedom and we need to contrast them to better understand them both. Freedom concerns the ability of one individual to act without external or internal constraints and with sufficient resources and power to make one's desires effective [30]. The moral principle of freedom is to strive to ensure those abilities. Autonomy, in contrast, concerns the independence and authenticity of the desires that motivate the individual's actions.

The concern that artificial autonomy may undermine the autonomy of people and not their freedoms comes from numerous observations that we are influenced by technology, AI supported or otherwise [21,22]. AI systems can't, as of present, constrain us directly, which is perhaps why the freedom moral principle takes a backseat. We directly communicate with computer programs, not only acquiring information from them, but also supplying them with information. On one hand, the interfaces through which this interaction is executed can be deliberately designed to change our choices [58]. On the other hand, our behaviour and personality traits can be modeled with machine learning methods [46], leading to opportunities for taking advantage of people's vulnerabilities.

The principle of autonomy is perhaps least directly visible in AI ethics compared to those of justice and non-maleficence. However, issues of unethical impact that do violate this principle are called under many different names and are frequently brought forward in context of discussing the AI-boosted-power of social media[9].

Explicability is the moral principle that is particular for AI systems in contrast to the other four that are used in guiding human moral behaviour as well. Floridi et al. [40] define explicability, as "incorporating both the epistemological sense

---

[9] https://medium.com/@francois.chollet/what-worries-me-about-ai-ed9df072b704.

of intelligibility (as an answer to the question 'how does it work?') and in the ethical sense of accountability (as an answer to the question: 'who is responsible for the way it works?')."

We (people) share the same means by which we perceive the world – our bodies. Despite variations in bodies and environments, we each understand on a deep intuitive level what it means to be human. This shared experience brings about an understanding of the motivations and constraints that might govern one towards particular choices, abilities and acts. Furthermore, we have trained our entire lives how to be in a society of people. We use all these experiences to find out information that is meaningful to us. We also use these experiences to build systems of accountability that identify those that in a given situation can change a decision on one hand, and incentivize decisions-makers towards a particular behaviour, on the other hand.

We do not necessarily understand how a machine works. This is true today for virtually all complex machinery, including that which does not use artificial intelligence, like for example a microwave oven. AI, however, is used in automated decision-making and decision-aiding processes. The nature of this application drives the importance of how the decision-making system works. To use a microwave, as long as it has been certified as safe, you do not need to understand how it work. You only need to remember one rule: not to use metal in it. Understanding how a decision is reached and for which reasons directly impacts our abilities and available options in the larger context. If I know why I have been refused an opportunity, I can work on those reasons that have caused the refusal and ensure acceptance the next time.

The principle of explicability seeks to also ensure that a person affected by a decision or action made by an AI system, is somewhat empowered to influence that decision or action by ensuring that they can identify a human who is responsible for the way that AI system works.

Article 22 of the EU GDPR [61] can be seen as working towards protecting this principle of explicability, but does not directly refer to it as such:

> "The data subject shall have the right not to be subject to a decision based solely on automated processing, including profiling, which produces legal effects concerning him or her or similarly significantly affects him or her."

Accountability occurs not only as an ethical principle in AI but also directly as a property of an algorithm. Next we will discuss this and other algorithmic "properties" considered in AI ethics, what they mean and how each can advance the ethical principles we just outlined.

4   Algorithmic Accountability

First we will give a very brief overview of what algorithmic accountability is. Specifically, we discuss which properties an algorithm has when it is accountable. Next we will discuss how accomplishing algorithmic accountability aligns the behaviour of an AI system with the relevant ethical principles.

4.1 What is It?

Accountability can be defined as [19, p.447]:

> "a relationship between an actor and a forum, in which the actor has an obligation to explain and to justify his or her conduct, the forum can pose questions and pass judgement, and the actor may face consequences."

To develop a systematic review of what work is done under algorithmic accountability, Wieringa [81] collected 242 English articles published from the period starting with 2008 up to and including 2018. She observes that:

> "What is denoted with algorithmic accountability is this kind of accountability relationship where the topic of explanation and/or justification is an algorithmic system."

Both the actor and the forum in these definitions are concepts that can take on multiple meanings, also simultaneously. An actor is a person, or an organisation that has participated or conducted fully the development and deployment of the algorithmic system. The forum is the audience that "receives the account", but this concept of forum is more complex.

Bovens [19] considers five types of fora: political, legal, administrative (e.g. auditors inspecting a system), professional (e.g. insight by peers), and social (e.g. civil society). A parallel can be drawn between the concept of forum in the accountability relationship and the concept of stakeholder [13,27].

One notable difference is that the concept of stakeholder more clearly recognises the impact an algorithm's operation can have on a user, whereas in the forum concept individual users are ensconced in "civil society". On the other hand, a forum allows us to clearly distinguish that the legal accountability relationship, where the account justifies the alignment of the algorithm's operations with laws and regulations, has different requirements than the social accountability relationship.

Many aspects of the algorithmic accountability relationship are accomplished by accomplishing some of the other properties of algorithms (AI or otherwise) which we will discuss in the sections that follow. Algorithmic accountability can be challenging to consider as a property of algorithms, among else, because of two points of confusion. The first point is confusing the concept of accountability with that of *liability* and *auditability*. The second point is the assumption that algorithmic accountability is a property of AI algorithms only, at the exclusion of simple algorithms or devices. We clarify these points in turn.

To establish liability for an algorithm means to establish who is legally at fault for the violations of existing laws and regulations that algorithm commits. For example, if an unmanned vehicle causes physical damage to a building, the establishing of liability means to establish who is legally responsible for the damage. The concept of responsibility generalises the concepts of liability from strictly legal violations to violations of other, including moral, norms. Both liability and responsibility seek to identify an actor to punish. Punishment in law and society plays an important role in establishing incentives that deter the offending actor and other actors from repeating the violation. The concern about establishing algorithmic liability is not that of maintaining a relationship, but rather cancelling an affordance. An affordance is what the environment offers the individual. In this case the concern is that no liability is afforded to the actors due to the lack of legal and societal frameworks that identify clearly who is at fault together with a complex system in which it is not clear with whom the agency that guides the offending behaviour lies.

Auditability is the property of an operation (an algorithm, an organisation) to be inspected towards establishing compliance with given norms, laws, and guidelines. Numerous properties of algorithms make them uneasy to inspect by a third party. Algorithms can be developed in one country, executed from cloud servers in a second country and impact the lives of people in a third country. Proprietary rights to software, as well as security concerns, limit access to algorithms yet in an other way. However, the concern about establishing algorithmic auditability also is a concern of cancelling an affordance not one of maintaining a relationship. The same context that creates the lack of algorithmic liability affordance also creates the lack of auditability affordance. Unlike liability, auditability also comes with engineering challenges. For example, the question of how should one test or benchmark for the ethical impact of an AI algorithm is challenging in its own right.

To understand the algorithmic accountability relationship, consider the following example of a service and how it changes with the use of an AI algorithm. We will consider the reimbursement of expenses within an organisation. This service has two actors. One actor is the service user, which typically is an employee of the organisation. The second actor is the service provider, which typically is an economy department comprising of several employees. The user submits a claim supported by receipts. A member of the provider department evaluates whether the claim matches the supplied receipts, as well as the rights of the employee, and decides to approve the claim, reject it, or return it to the user.

No-automation Scenario. Assume that the claim is supported with a receipt that is handwritten and unclear. The person who is evaluating the claim would get in touch with the user (enacting the option to return the claim to the user), explain the situation and propose options: such as, for example, a bank statement that shows the same expense as the unclear receipt.

Automation Scenario. Object character recognition (OCR) is a technology (software and hardware device) that extracts a character of written or printed text from an image. OCR can, and is, used by organisations to automatically check whether the figure and text of a receipt matches those in a claim, thus establishing that a claim is supported by the adequate receipts. What happens when OCR is used to automate part of the role of the economy department? In the same situation of the unclear handwritten receipt, the OCR system will notify the claimant, the user, that one count of the claim does not have a receipt to support it. The OCR will not generate an explanation of why.

While in the no-automation scenario it was the task of the service provider to resolve the return of the claim, in the automation scenario it is the responsibility of the user to rectify the situation. The question is: is the user sufficiently empowered to do so? The same affordances do not exist for the user between the two scenarios. In the automation scenario the user needs to be given the information of which specific receipt is not recognised and also how to address the fail. An OCR system would need to be extended with additional features to give explanations. But even with that extension, the user would need to get in touch with the economy department to discuss possible substitutions for the receipt. To do so, the user needs to be provided with a contact person. Failure to adequately empower the user is a failure in the algorithmic accountability relationship.

To summarise and simplify, algorithmic accountability is a balance of powers: that of the actors who develop, implement, deploy and maintain an algorithm, with that of the forum that is concerned with managing the impact of the algorithm's operation. For that balance of powers to occur first the forum needs to be adequately empowered to demand it. Assuming the empowered forum, in the practical sense, the property of algorithmic accountability is established when it is clear for that algorithm:

- Which are the individual(s) that have the power to change the operation parameters of the algorithm resulting in a change of behaviour;
- Who are the individuals that can answer questions about the way the algorithm works;
- How can these individual(s) be reached by the forum;
- How can the forum ascertain that the required changes have been received, evaluated and implemented (or justifiably rejected) by the algorithm actor(s).

All of these activities, ensuring the right people are identified, do not read as properties of algorithms but properties of a society. However, ensuring that the interface between the algorithm and society contains necessary and usable communication information is a property of the algorithm. Further, building the algorithms in such a way that adequate changes to them are dynamically possible, is also a feature of the algorithm.

Failure to establish a contact with a specific person that can handle algorithmic issues is the easiest way to disrupt the algorithmic accountability relationship. This failure does not require that the algorithm is capable of any level of autonomy or intelligence. A simple web form that does not clarify where the entered data goes, how it is used, or who can modify it after it has been sent, already fails algorithmic accountability. Partial automation changes power relationships and this directly causes the algorithmic accountability relationship to also be disrupted. What does the balanced algorithmic accountability relationship contribute to the ethical impact of the algorithm?

4.2   Alignment with Ethical Principles

Algorithmic accountability as a property serves the purpose of balancing out the efficiency of the algorithm with the impact it has over individuals and society. Algorithmic accountability is thus the foundation of having a control over the ethical impact of an algorithm.

Beneficence & Non-maleficence. Computation is always used because it benefits someone. The concern with algorithms and AI is that they tip the power balance against the interests of society or vulnerable individuals in it. The power between actors in a relationships is balanced when neither of the actors can make the other act against their interests or will.

Algorithmic accountability as a property, when present, can demonstrate that computation is used to improve lives. When algorithms are used in such a way that they do not change or erode the balance of power between the agents in society, a service provider and service receiver, then the algorithms are aligned with the non-maleficence ethical principle.

Justice. Computation only takes into consideration inputs that are declared to the algorithm. A person, in contrast, can decide to pay attention to more information or less information when performing a task. This can be a feature, when handling unexpected situations, or it can be a hindrance, when needing to withhold personal and implicit bias in decision-making. Any algorithm that contributes to making decisions about people can increase the injustice in the world. Injustice is particularly directly incurred by:

- an algorithm whose behaviour you cannot impact, even when it has made a mistake;
- an algorithm which makes or aids decisions that impact your life without revealing the information and rules on which those decisions are based.

The disruption of power in society that algorithms can introduce, can heavily impact the state of justice. The forum, in an accountability relationship, has as a primary role to ensure that justice is observed. A well balanced accountability relationship, with a clear accountability properties for the algorithms, supports the ethical principle of justice.

Autonomy. The principle of autonomy is directly violated by:

- an algorithm that pre-selects options that are presented to a user without revealing which criteria are used to make the sub-selection or even that a sub-selection is being made;
- an algorithm which removes communication channels between a user and service provider;
- computation which has a direct and measurable impact on a person's life but of which the person in not aware is happening.

Autonomy is about having the power to choose for one self. This power is stripped directly when some available options of interest are hidden or removed. Consider a web based content platform where content is pre-selected for you based on your previous engagement. This pre-selection can save you a lot of time and increase your satisfaction, but at the same time it can also push you towards options that you would not choose were you to choose for yourself[10].

An adequately empowered forum can enforce a user's ability to access information about the decisions that an algorithm makes for them, and alter or

---

[10] https://www.wsj.com/articles/tiktok-algorithm-video-investigation-11626877477.

impact that algorithm. However, it is not sufficient that information is made available, but that it is made available in a meaningful way that does not additionally increase the cognitive burden on the user. The use of dark patterns, user interface design elements that manipulate the user towards making particular choices, can have a drastic impact on eroding the principle of autonomy. Even when a forum mandates that particular options and information is made available to users so that they can make an informed and autonomous choice, dark patterns can be used to erode autonomy [72].

Explicability. Accountability is an explicit part of the new ethical principle of explicability. Accountability enables explicability. On one hand it is the forum that demands the creation of an account on which are the operation domain, impact, effect etc. of an algorithm. On the other hand the accountability relationship enforces, not only the account, but also the possibility for a channel of communication that guarantees that additional information about the operation of the algorithm is made available when needed.

5   Transparency, Explainability, Interpretability

Transparency, explainability and interpretability are all properties of algorithms that are related to the creation and availability of the account in the algorithmic accountability relationship. There is not a great precision and rigour in the use of these terms in the literature. We cannot hope to establish a clear distinction once and for all in this tutorial, but he can offer the definitions of those who have attempted this task.

5.1   Transparency

When discussing the transparency of algorithms, one often contrasts algorithms that are *a black box* and those that are a *glass box*. In engineering and computing, a black box is a "fiction representing a set of concrete systems into which stimuli S impinge and out of which reactions R emerge. The constitution and structure of the box are altogether irrelevant to the approach under consideration, which is purely external or phenomenological." [23]. In other words, a black box is a system that is viewed only in terms of its inputs and outputs without knowledge of its internal workings. A glass box in contrast is a system whose inner workings are completely accessible. The existence of black box systems is not in its self unethical or problematic [26]. What is of concern is when a system participates as a black box in the accountability relationship.

   In the context of AI ethics, transparency is a property of algorithms that are subject to algorithmic accountability. Namely transparency is the property of availability of information about an algorithm allowing the forum to monitor the workings or performance of the algorithm [32,52]. In this context it becomes more clear that whether an algorithm will be "transparent" or not depends not only on access but also on *who* it is that is doing the accessing. This in consequence means that making an algorithm transparent does not necessarily make its behaviour and impact ethical [36]. Let us consider an illustrative example.

Consider for example a calculator. We input two numbers separated by the '+' sign and obtain their sum on output. We do not have access to the inner-workings of the calculator, thus this is a "black box". The assembly code for the calculation operations, as well as full schematics of the electronic circuits used, would make this calculator a "glass box". We do not need the calculator to be a "glass box" because we can verify the correctness of calculation impartially without an understanding of its inner working. We can also verify that the device is not connected to the internet and it does not communicate or manipulate any information other than the input numbers. The glass box information is only meaningful to those wishing to recreate the calculator or use it in a different manner.

The amount and type of information which make an algorithm transparent for a forum will depend on the algorithm and the forum. Both [32] and [82] observe that transparency is not a dichotomous property but one that comes in degrees and depends on the intentions, needs and composition of the forum. For example, a programmer may be able to identify a while-loop and consider it a transparent implementation of a function that identifies the length of sentence, but a user with different skills would not be able to "see" the same thing. Winfield et al. [82] give a definition of transparency, obtained after a comprehensive literature review on the topic:

> "the transfer of information from an autonomous system or its designers to a stakeholder, which is honest, contains information relevant to the causes of some action, decision or behavior and is presented at a level of abstraction and in a form meaningful to the stakeholder."

The standard that Winfield et al. [82] developed, IEEE P7001 recognises five distinct groups of stakeholders split into two groups: non-expert end users (and wider society), experts including safety certification engineers or agencies, accident investigators, and lawyers or expert witnesses. For each of these stakeholders levels 0 to 5 of increasing measurable transparency properties are identified. Each of the levels defines how much and which kind of information should be made available to the stakeholder. If we then try to define a fully transparent algorithm, it would be that algorithm for which the forum has the information it needs in the algorithmic accountability relationship.

The availability of information on the algorithm is not only a question of willingness to divulge that information (by the actors that have created and deployed it). The inner workings of an algorithm can be inaccessible because of many reasons. One reason is the level of complexity involved. The number of lines of code, interactions of different algorithm and systems and the way an algorithm adjusts to different users can have a net emergent behaviour that would not be easy to trace to a specific line of code. In the words of Lazer [48]:

> "You might imagine that they could just go into the next building and look directly at the code. However, looking at the algorithms will not yield much insight, because the interplay of social algorithms and behaviors yields patterns that are fundamentally emergent."

Another reason for a lack of transparency, and this is particularly of interest in AI, is due to the way a task is computed by the algorithm, namely, by not following the operations that a person takes when solving the same task. Neural networks are considered non-transparent because of this reason. To extract or create the information that is required to understand the workings of the complex computation process, additional steps need to be taken: *explainability* and *interpretability.*

The [42] considers transparency to be one of the seven requirements for accomplishing a trustworthy AI system[11]. Here transparency is defined as a combination of three elements: traceability, explainability, and communication. Traceability is the ability to maintain a complete account of the provenance of data, processes, and artefacts involved in the production of an AI decisions/action [57]. The [42] defines communications in the following way [pg.18]: " AI systems should not represent themselves as humans to users; humans have the right to be informed that they are interacting with an AI system. This entails that AI systems must be identifiable as such. In addition, the option to decide against this interaction in favour of human interaction should be provided where needed to ensure compliance with fundamental rights. Beyond this, the AI system's capabilities and limitations should be communicated to AI practitioners or end-users in a manner appropriate to the use case at hand. This could encompass communication of the AI system's level of accuracy, as well as its limitations. "

Explainability and interpretability, which is partly included in communication, are two separate fields in AI ethics, both concerned specifically with identifying, creating and making available information on the operation of an algorithm.

5.2 Explainability and Interpretability

Explainable AI (XAI) as a field in AI is concerned with the problem of generating the account in the algorithmic accountability relationship. Typically XAI is associated with AI involved in making and aiding decisions. Specifically, XAI is concerned with the problem of identifying the justifications for algorithmic generated decisions.

The inception of the term XAI was a DARPA[12] program started in 2017. The field, however pre-dates this program, with works such as [65] doing XAI without naming it as such. DAPRA explained the aims as follow:

"The Explainable AI (XAI) program aims to create a suite of machine learning techniques that:

---

[11] The seven key requirements for Trustworthy AI per the [42] are: (1) human agency and oversight, (2) technical robustness and safety, (3) privacy and data governance, (4) transparency, (5) diversity, non-discrimination and fairness, (6) environmental and societal well-being and (7) accountability.

[12] "The Defense Advanced Research Projects Agency (DARPA) is an agency of the United States Department of Defense responsible for the development of emerging technologies for use by the military." https://en.wikipedia.org/wiki/DARPA.

- Produce more explainable models, while maintaining a high level of learning performance (prediction accuracy); and
- Enable human users to understand, appropriately trust, and effectively manage the emerging generation of artificially intelligent partners" [74].

The field has since grown outside of the DARPA initiative and has expanded its field of interest beyond machine learning to other AI methods as well [41].

As an engineering problem, XAI is concerned with the issue of automatically generating a justification of why a specific output of an algorithm has been given instead of another, which specific data the algorithm has used, and/or its trace (history of past decisions and conditions under which they had been taken). The terms explanation and interpretation are sometimes used interchangeably in the literature. To explain typically refers to the process of tracing back the output's origin in the code, whereas to interpret means to assign corresponding meaning to a particular code segment or action. In contrast to the problem of generating explanations, interpretability is concerned with ensuring a sufficiently high degree of an understanding of that explanation by a specific stakeholder (or forum) [54,56]. Counter-intuitively thus, the product of explanability is information, whereas the product of interpretability are explanations.

Explainability, beyond the engineering challenges, seeks understanding of what it means to explain or interpret an algorithm, typically using methods from humanities and social sciences [55]. Understanding how to construct explanations [5] is primarily studied in computer science and artificial intelligence, but it is also an interdisciplinary problem.

In XAI we distinguish between the following approaches to generating explanation relevant information [5,17]:

- *Static vs interactive.* A static explanation is one-turn feedback that cannot respond to feedback from the user, while an interactive explanation is an explanation that is given in an interactive process with the user.
- *Local vs global.* When a specific decision is explained, we speak of a local explanation. For example, the answer to "why did my loan not get approved" is a local explanation. In contrast, if we want to know how a model classifies examples in general, we refer to global explanations. For example, the answer to "what are the properties of people whose loans were approved" requires a global explanation.
- *Direct vs post-hoc.* A direct explanation is a direct insight into an algorithm that is intrinsically transparent. A post-hoc explanation is the process of using other indirect means to interpret the operations of the algorithm which is not by nature transparent.
- *Model-agnostic vs. model-specific.* A model specific approach is one that is tailored and only works for a particular type of an algorithm (particularly in machine learning). In contract a model-agnostic approach does not depend on the inner workings of a specific algorithm, but can generate explanations for any algorithm that satisfies particular properties of input and output.

- *Surrogate and visualization.* These are not types of explanations but rather types of auxiliary algorithms that are built to interpret an algorithm that is too complex to be directly explained. A surrogate algorithm is a directly interpretive algorithm that approximates the original algorithm. A visualisation algorithm is one that visualizes parts of the original algorithm.

As to how the decision is being justified, we distinguish between [31]:

- *Attributive explanations* aim to answer the question: for what reasons, because of which problem attributes, has a particular decision been made. Examples of approaches for producing attributive explanations include logical inferences that support the decision and feature importance association with decisions.
- *Contrastive explanations* aim to answer the questions: why this decision or not another. For example, what was the decisive difference between the case that was decided as A and the case that was decided as B.
- *Counterfactual explanations* aim to answer the question of how a given difference in the case impacts a difference in the decision. Stepin et al. [73] offer a survey of methods for generating contrastive and counterfactual explanations.
- *Actionable explanations* aim to answer the question of what change in the case would lead to a desired decisions. For example, given the features of a person's loan application who has been rejected, an actionable explanation provides the information of which features need to be changed, least drastically or minimal number of features, to bring about the desired decision.

Numerous algorithms have been proposed that generate explanations particularly from deep neural networks and numerous surveys detail them, such as for example [4,11,24,33,43,77]. It has to be emphasised that explainable and interpretable AI as fields are not very precise, nor do they offer a taxonomy of terms and concepts so the algorithms will not always we situated within a taxonomy of approaches and types of applications.

None of the explanation generating algorithms that have been proposed "solves" the XAI problem. Each algorithm has strengths in addressing certain problems and weaknesses in others. Unlike a human explaining and interpreting "why I did that", no one algorithmic approach offers all the explanation types listed above. For example, one of the most well known algorithms is the LIME algorithm [65]. LIME stands for Local Interpretable Model-agnostic Explanations. This algorithm creates surrogates to generate attributive explanations of decisions reached by machine learning classification. Thus, while LIME can offer some information on which of your features had your loan application denied (being local), it cannot offer information on which feaures do the denied applicans have in common.

5.3 Information Availability and Ethical Principles

It is hard to measure the performance of algorithms in terms of how transparent, explainable or interpretable they are because transparency, explainability and interpretability are not simple to quantify. Furthermore, transparency, explainability and interpretability are subjective measures - it is the forum who needs to express satisfaction with the level of information it receives. The field of transparency has been focused on developing goals to direct algorithm developers towards algorithms that would be considered transparent by some forums in certain situations. Transparency answers the question: which information is the forum likely to need. Explainability and interpretability algorithms answer the challenge of how to extract the information that transparency has identified.

How does progress in transparency, explainability and interpretability advance the ethical principles of interest in AI? To answer this question, one needs to answer how being informed impacts the state of ethics in a society. This is clearly not a simple question to answer and goes beyond the scope of this tutorial. We sketch out some discussion points.

Explicability is directly advanced by transparency which in turn is enabled by efforts in explainability and interpretability of algorithms. An algorithm that is adequately transparent to a particular stakeholder advances the understanding of that stakeholder regarding how decisions are made, for which reasons, and how those decisions can be changed.

Autonomy is furthered particularly by providing counterfactual and actionable explanations. This information empowers people to efficiently find ways to address aspects of their life towards accomplishing their goals in ways that works for them. The same information also can elucidate when autonomy is violated, by showing which algorithmic decisions a user has no power to affect.

Beneficence, Non-maleficence, Justice. Asymmetry of information can cause harm by creating conditions in which the more informed party can take advantage of the less informed party. In the algorithmic accountability relationship, the account is generated to remove the informational asymmetry that exists, ensuring protection of the rights of the society and individuals that the forum represents. The availability of adequately selected and represented information promotes beneficence by enabling errors to be caught and promotes justice by elucidating what is the information used to make decisions.

6   Fairness

Algorithmic fairness is concerned with defining, evaluating and improving the fairness in decision making by AI algorithms. Clearly this necessarily involves defining what a fair algorithm is, in the first place. The field was recently motivated by the use of machine learning in the context of decision-making [62], however concerns for fairness extend to all algorithms and devices that are part of systems that ethically impact individuals and society. For example, a route finder that diverts traffic through a residential street in which there is less cars parked can increase unfairness by making that street no longer available for children to play in. An automated soap dispenser calibrated to respond only to white skinned hands, neither does decision-making nor uses machine learning, yet has a negative impact in a multi-cultural society.

Algorithmic fairness sounds as closest to being the ethical principle of justice expressed as a property of an algorithm. In reality an algorithm can easily be algorithmically fair and violate the ethical principle of justice at the same time. Kearns and Roth [45] in Chap. 2 give an example of how fairness definitions can be satisfied while still having unfair algorithmic decisions.

6.1   Algorithmic Fairness, Bias and Discrimination Definitions

Algorithmic fairness as of today is defined using a collection of statistic based measures for algorithms that make decisions [9,66]. The field of algorithmic fairness includes the study of fairness definitions and also methods for removing algorithmic bias from the decisions and algorithmic process. Tool-kits, like Aequitas [67] and AI(F)airness 360 (AIF360) [15], have become available to facilitate bias mitigation in machine learning specifically. Both tool-kites are open-source aim to serve not only software developers, but also researchers and students to better understand unfairness and how it is introduced. Aequitas was developed by the University of Chicago and offers an estimate of algorithmic fairness across several measures. Fairness 360 (AIF360) was developed by IBM and in offers pre-processing, in-processing and post-processing mitigation mechanisms for some machine learning methods. Other developed tool-kits include FairML [2] and Silva [83].

The concept of algorithmic bias, build on the concept of statistical bias, describes the situation where there is a discrepancy between the expected decisions that should be assigned and the decisions assigned by the algorithm. For example, if two groups of students are expected to be assigned the same grades, because they have similar performances in the course, a decision-making algorithm that awards high grades to one group and low to the other is considered to be biased.

The bias of an algorithm can be caused by using input that has some kind of skew in the data, or by having it built in its operation and use. These two causes are not clearly separated and often build into each-other. Algorithmic bias typically refers to the second type of cause: "Algorithmic bias is added by the algorithm itself and not present in the input data." [8]. Real world examples of the occurrences of data bias are listed in, for example [45,51].

The input-introduced bias is referred to as data bias. In machine learning, data bias refers to the existence of a skew in the training data. Data bias is particularly of concern in machine learning because data sets are not always purposefully build for training a particular prediction model for a particular task. Rather, data is collected and traded without a particular application lined up. This means that there is no possibility to model the data for the purpose, but also that data collected from some people, when applied to draw inferences about others can produce spurious and dangerous results, particularly in sensitive contexts such as medicine [25]. Mehrabi et al. [51] identify twenty three different types of bias in the literature, which of course can overlap.

Algorithmic discrimination describes algorithmic bias that occurs because a feature that should not have impact on a decisions, is somehow used by the algorithm and contributes to that decision. Typically these are by law *protected features* that are of interest such as for example, race, sexual orientation etc. A protected feature defines a protected group of people, or class. In the legal domain there are two main definitions of discrimination: disparate treatment and disparate impact [10,62]. Disparate treatment happens when an individual is intentionally treated differently than others based on their membership to a protected class. Disparate impact happens when members of a protected class are more frequently negatively affected by some phenomena than their counterparts outside of the protected class.

In algorithmic fairness studies we distinguish between *group fairness* and *individual fairness*. Group fairness takes the approach of identifying protected groups and requiring that (approximate) parity of some statistical measure across all of these groups is maintained [29]. Individual fairness is focused on individuals rather than groups requiring that "similar individuals should be treated similarly". Similarity is a task-specific metric determined on a case by case basis [34]. Individual fairness requires that there exists a commonly agreed measure of similarity among individuals.

Algorithmic fairness can be evaluated using measures of fairness. Algorithmic fairness in supervised machine learning is mainly concerned with ensuring equity in resource distribution. Specifically, if there exists a *desirable label*, such as for example "yes" for a loan approval or "unlikely to reoffend" in a parole evaluation, the concern is that the algorithm does not discriminate in its classification. Of course, data bias too can be a source of discrimination.

Pessach et al. [62] identify seventeen different measures of algorithmic fairness in the machine learning literature. Verma et al. [76] consider twenty, most prominent in their view, and attempt to explain the rationale behind them offering an intuitive analysis of why in some cases an algorithm can be considered fair according to some definitions and unfair according to others.

Quantifying fairness in machine learning is challenging to achieve for a variety of reasons [47]. Regardless the problem, there sometimes does not exists a solution which is universally fair, equitable and just. The additional requirement of fairness can come at a cost of efficiency - an algorithm can only be made more fair if it is made less correct. It has been shown that certain fairness types cannot be simultaneously achieved in machine learning [28]. In such situations, a trade-off would be necessary, meaning that we need to have a ways to resolve such conflicts fairly.

6.2   Fairness and Ethical Principles

The ethical principle that intuitively should be most aligned with algorithmic fairness is **justice**. An unfair algorithm has a direct impact on justice and equity. When there is bias in the decisions made by the algorithm, by definition there is a violation of the principle of justice. However satisfying a fairness property does not on its own guarantee an alignment with the justice ethical principle. For one, one may be forced to choose which fairness property to satisfy, or to sacrifice fairness in the interest of accuracy [44]. Chouldechova and Roth [29] argue that "statistical definitions of fairness do not on their own give meaningful guarantees to individuals or structured subgroups of the protected demographic groups. Instead they give guarantees to 'average' members of the protected groups." Justice for individuals is poorly reflected in group fairness definitions.

Algorithmic fairness contributes towards promoting the principle of **non-maleficence**. Bias in algorithms has been identified to cause *representational harms* and *allocation harms*.[13]. Representation harms can be caused by the way in which "individuals are represented differently in a feature space even before training a model" [1]. Allocation harm can occur when an individual is unjustly denied a desirable decision by an algorithm.

Representation harms are more difficult to assess than allocation harms. A representation harm occurs when data used to for decision making supports or exalts a past or existing undesirable phenomena in society. For example, in natural language processing, an algorithm can learn to associate certain professions with gender propagating sexism [18]. A search algorithm causes representational harm when returns a particular stereotypical image upon a search request. For example, searching for "gamer" return images of dark rooms and young men in front of a monitor, thus propagating the idea that a gamer is a socially undesirable activity and one that does not involve women or older people. A public perception such as this can directly harm both the gaming industry and individual image.

It is not clear when, how and who should decide to correct representation in data because this process can cause new representation harms while removing old ones. Representation harm can also cause allocation harm. For example, an algorithm that works off of historical data to predict who will make a good employee, can identify that being male is a strong indicator of good work performance because in the past all employees have been male. Thus a female candidate will be rejected because of her gender, causing allocation harm and the sexism will be propagated, causing representational harm. An algorithm that causes representational harm can also negatively impact persons and society **autonomy**.

Both the algorithmic bias and algorithmic fairness measures evaluate a particular given machine learning problem. However, local decisions, particularly when repeated over time, can lead to emerging global effects. Namely, by allowing a particular bias to go undetected or by invisibly, but consistently, preferring one type of behaviour and properties over another we may change our society. This can cause *emergent harm*. The risk of emerging effects from automated decision making are difficult to localise, measure and mitigate. More work in algorithmic fairness is needed to prevent this type of harm.

However, despite the shortcomings of the algorithmic fairness research, this field can also actively contribute to promoting **beneficence**. Discrimination and stereotypes can remain hidden in large volumes of text or wast amounts of data. Algorithmic fairness and bias measures can illuminate these historical

---

[13] K. Crawford. The trouble with bias. https://www.youtube.com/watch?v=fMym_BKWQzk, December 2017.

and entrenched injustices and bring attention to them. Even if it is not the job of an algorithm to correct for the wrong that exists in society, it can facilitate its removal.

7 Privacy

Privacy is often invoked when discussing AI ethics, however from an engineering and computer science aspect this field is, when compared to fairness for example, considerably under-explored outside of the scope of cybersecurity. It is very difficult to establish privacy as a property of an algorithm and quantify it when there is a very poor understanding in computer science what this concept means. Aligning privacy with the ethical principles of interest for AI also requires this understanding.

7.1 Definitions and Concerns

Matzner and Ochs [49] give a detailed account on the concept of privacy across disciplines and history. Privacy is a person's right rather than a moral principle or a norm. Originally privacy has been considered the right to be left alone [79]. The right has been developed to specify that privacy is about having the right to a space (both physical and metaphorical) where one can act or exist without undesired public scrutiny because under involuntary public scrutiny one cannot act freely and in the absence of others, infringements are likewise likely to also be absent [49].

One can distinguish between different types of privacy in the sense of absence of unwanted scrutiny in action or behaviour. Thus we can talk about bodily and psychological privacy as a right to not expose one's body or thoughts, intellectual privacy as the right to be able to make up ones mind or ideas without interference, communications privacy as the right to have conversations that are limited to the participants, associations privacy as the privacy to have relationships that are not scrutinized by people outside of them, behaviour privacy, informational privacy, decision privacy etc.

Only in understanding that privacy is the right to certain activities without an audience, we understand why privacy is often brought out as a concern in the digital age. As Matzner and Ochs [49] summarize, information before digitalization was characterized by clear ownership and access control: "Information was only accessible by third parties if actively passed along, or when third parties were granted physical access." Passing on written information included non-negligible effort, but also so did broadcast of information through television and radio. Passing on information without the knowledge of the person who owns it was extremely difficult. Digital technology facilitates digital data which is easy and cheap to story. Beyond mere holding information, data is very easy to create and a lot of the activities that have been private are no longer so because they leave digital traces, a process that is virtually inescapable [6]. In addition digital data can be very efficiently searched. The AI algorithms are increasingly more powerful in finding patterns in big data that could not be found by people.

There are at least two types of privacy concerns when working with data, both of which require different algorithmic considerations. One is the **access to and ownership control of specific data**. Specific data is any information that is specific, if not unique to one person and identifies that person such as their social security number or even their address of residence.

A big concern when it comes to specific data is anonymization. Here one is concerned that information about a specific individual can be identified in a collection of data that should not contain identifying information. The main algorithmic approach to handling this concern is k-anonymity [68] and differential privacy [35]. Both are collections of methods that measure how identifiable an individual is in a collection of data sets and offer methods for collecting, removing, or introducing noise in data to recover anonymity.

Another concern of specific data is that of its "fluidity". Specific data, as all data, is easy to share and can be shared without the knowledge of the person described by it. As Matzner and Ochs [49] summarized: "Information which may be voluntarily disclosed in one context and with a particular audience in mind, is now easily transported to other contexts where this might entail harm". For example data about ones sexual preferences would be completely in place to share in a dating app but not perhaps in a job search app. However, a person who has disclosed information to one application, has very little power to prevent it from being shared or sold to another. The main approach to counteract the problems of "fluidity" is the legal approach with regulation, such as the [61], being adopted to protect the right of individuals to control for what their specific information is used. However, legal solutions, not supported with technical means to allow direct control to users over their data, might not be sufficient [59].

A second privacy concern when working with data is the **access to and ownership control of applicable data patterns**. For example, a data pattern can identify a group of people that all have the same personality trait or mental health issue [46]. An individual's data belonging to a data pattern to which individuals of group X belong to, identifies a correlation with people from group X, rather than identifying that person as being a member of group X.

At first glance, compared to the dangers of sharing specific information, belonging to a group pattern may seem inconsequential. However, being identified with a data pattern of group X can lead to being given only the affordances of the group X members regardless of whether or not one belongs to group X. For example, you can be identified to have the similar browser history of people who are female and suffer from depression. Societal prejudice does not require proof and being suspected of a characteristic can be enough to be denied opportunities also in real life not only online.

It is particularly machine learning that allows for patterns to be found in big data. The numerous issues of being associated with different data patterns, as well as the difficulties in addressing this issue with technological and legal actions, are discussed in [71].

7.2 Privacy and Ethics

Privacy is perhaps the least quantifiable property of algorithms and it can be seen as wrong to consider it an algorithmic property. Even the very measurable K-anonymity [68] and differential privacy [35] evaluate data sets rather than algorithms. Privacy as a right is perhaps easiest to align with the ethical principles of interest. The two ethical principles that are perhaps most advanced when affording privacy are: **autonomy** and **non-maleficence**.

Protecting the right to make certain decisions or perform certain tasks without an undesirable audience and scrutiny directly protects autonomy. Privacy is even seen as a precondition for democratic institutions [49]: if a person is not allowed to make a decision in private, then that decision may not be autonomously made thus making collective decisions not democratic.

Protecting the anonymity of specific information outside of given contexts and the use of pattern affiliation in some contexts directly avoids doing harm to the individuals whose anonymity is protected. Harms from violations of privacy are not easy to measure or identify: we do change our behaviour when we are observed and it is not easy to determine whether that change benefits us and society or not until it has happened. It is also difficult to establish what we would have been like in the absence of a technology or computation after those changes have become fully integrated in society.

Protecting pattern affiliation anonymity also promotes the ethical principle of **justice**. AI is heralded as the ultimate "crystal ball" for use in predicting future behaviour and addressing issues before they arise. The ethical issues arise not from predicting the behaviour of people, but using those predictions to judge them and make decisions about them. Imagine a country T, 99% of whose population are compulsive thieves. We would find it unjust to detain a person carrying a passport from T at the border and put them in jail to prevent the thievery they are likely to commit. If a student is predicted to get a fail grade in a subject, it is unjust to treat that student as if they have already failed. Psychology recognises that people do live up or down to what is expected from them [7]. If we allow people to be judged by the estimates of their abilities, we risk limiting their liberty to choose to surpass them. We may be creatures of habit, but we are nonetheless fully autonomous agents.

Lastly we should mention that privacy is an ambivalent right. The protection of the right to privacy of one person can come at the expense of the rights of another. Protecting the right of privacy can cause the hindrance of ethical rather than their promotion.

In summary privacy as a property of algorithms and input to algorithms is a complex technical challenge, but one that needs to be addressed given how much direct impact the right of privacy has in advancing the ethical values we are interested in protecting.

8   Summary

This tutorial and lecture notes aim to highlights the distinction between: i) computation properties of algorithms and data; ii) ethical values promoted or suppressed by the existence and use of an algorithm. In AI ethics, the distinction between these two aspects of algorithms are too often blurred.

To improve the computer science student's understanding of ethical principles of interest to AI Ethics we give an overview of the five principles that Floridi et al. [40] identify as key. Clearly, theirs is only one opinion on what matters to AI from ethical principles and this list of key principles needs to be continuously re-assessed.

Computational algorithmic properties denote collection of approaches rather than well defined parameters that can be measured. We give an integral overview of the main groups of approaches, also discussing how they relate with each other.

By making the distinctions between ethical principles and algorithmic properties clear, we hope to contribute towards a better alignment between the two in research and the practice of AI Ethics.

9   Recommended Further Reading

Numerous references have been used throughout the tutorial and these all can be used to further ones knowledge in the topics touched upon in this tutorial. The following are particularly recommended.

Floridi et al. [40] give an analysis of existing AI ethics guidelines and refine those into the five proposed ethical principles we discussed here.

Wieringa [81] gives a thoughtful systematic review on the somewhat elusive topic of algorithmic accountability. It is a unique work on this topic.

Winfield et al. [82] give a very exhaustive overview of the topic of transparency that also goes into relating transparency with the topics of explainability and interpretability.

Chouldechova and Roth [29] give a very susinct overview of the state of the art and on-going challenges in the field of machine learnig fairness. An excellent chapter on bias and fairness in machine learning, particularly for people new to AI, is Rodolfa et al. [66]. The book as a whole deserves a read.

Matzner and Ochs [49] give a unique account on what is privacy and how digitalisation affects it.

Lastly, Parasuraman et al. [60] is a good starting point to better understand machine autonomy in relation to human autonomy.

References

1. Abbasi, M., Friedler, S.A., Scheidegger, C., Venkatasubramanian, S.: Fairness in representation: quantifying stereotyping as a representational harm. In: Proceedings of the 2019 SIAM International Conference on Data Mining (SDM), pp. 801–809. SIAM (2019)

2. Adebayo, J.: FairML : ToolBox for diagnosing bias in predictive modeling. Master's thesis, Massachusetts Institute of Technology, USA (2016)
3. Anderson, S.L.: Asimov's three laws of robotics and machine metaethics. AI Soc. **22**(4), 477–493 (2008)
4. Anjomshoae, S., Najjar, A., Calvaresi, D., Främling, K.: Explainable agents and robots: results from a systematic literature review. In: 18th International Conference on Autonomous Agents and Multiagent Systems (AAMAS 2019), Montreal, Canada, 13–17 May 2019, pp. 1078–1088. International Foundation for Autonomous Agents and Multiagent Systems (2019)
5. Arya, V., et al.: One explanation does not fit all: a toolkit and taxonomy of AI explainability techniques (2019)
6. Auxier, B., Rainie, L., Anderson, M., Perrin, A., Kumar, M., Turner, E.: Americans and privacy: concerned, confused and feeling lack of control over their personal information. Technical report, Pew Research Center (2019)
7. Babad, E.Y., Inbar, J., Rosenthal, R.: Pygmalion, galatea, and the golem: investigations of biased and unbiased teachers. J. Educ. Psychol. **74**(4), 459 (1982)
8. Baeza-Yates, R.: Bias on the web. Commun. ACM **61**(6), 54–61 (2018)
9. Barocas, S., Hardt, M., Narayanan, A.: Fairness and Machine Learning. fairmlbook.org (2019). http://www.fairmlbook.org
10. Barocas, S., Selbst, A.D.: Big data's disparate impact. Calif. Law Rev. **104**(3), 671–732 (2016)
11. Arrieta, A.B., et al.: Explainable artificial intelligence (XAI): concepts, taxonomies, opportunities and challenges toward responsible AI. Inf. Fusion **58**, 82–115 (2020)
12. Basl, J., Sandler, R., Tiell, S.: Getting from commitment to content in AI and data ethics: justice and explainability. Technical report, Atlantic Council Geothec Centre (2021). https://eur-lex.europa.eu/legal-content/EN/TXT/?uri=CELEX%3A52021PC0206
13. Baum, S.D.: Social choice ethics in artificial intelligence. AI Soc. **35**(1), 165–176 (2020)
14. Beauchamp, T.: The principle of beneficence in applied ethics. In: Zalta, E.N. (ed.), The Stanford Encyclopedia of Philosophy. Metaphysics Research Lab, Stanford University, Spring 2019 edition (2019)
15. Bellamy, R.K.E., et al.: AI fairness 360: an extensible toolkit for detecting, understanding, and mitigating unwanted algorithmic bias. CoRR, abs/1810.01943 (2018)
16. Bellman, R.E.: An Introduction to Artificial Intelligence: Can Computers Think? Boyd & Fraser Publishing Company, Boston (1978)
17. Biecek, P., Burzykowski, T.: Explanatory Model Analysis: Explore, Explain, and Examine Predictive Models. CRC Press, Boca Raton (2021)
18. Bolukbasi, T., Chang, K.W., Zou, J.Y., Saligrama, V., Kalai, A.T.: Man is to computer programmer as woman is to homemaker? Debiasing word embeddings. In: Proceedings of the 30th International Conference on Neural Information Processing Systems, NIPS 2016, pp. 4356–4364, Red Hook, NY, USA. Curran Associates Inc. (2016)
19. Bovens, M.: Analysing and assessing accountability: a conceptual framework. Eur. Law J. **13**(4), 447–468 (2007)
20. Brundtland Report. Report of the world commission on environment and development: Our common future. Technical report, United Nations (1987). https://sustainabledevelopment.un.org/content/documents/5987our-common-future.pdf
21. Bucher, T.: Want to be on the top? Algorithmic power and the threat of invisibility on Facebook. New Media Soc. **14**(7), 1164–1180 (2012)

22. Bucher, T.: IF...THEN: Algorithmic Power and Politics. Oxford University Press, New York (2018)
23. Bunge, M.: A general black box theory. Philos. Sci. **30**(4), 346–358 (1963)
24. Burkart, N., Huber, M.F.: A survey on the explainability of supervised machine learning. J. Artif. Int. Res. **70**, 245–317 (2021)
25. Cahan, E.M., Hernandez-Boussard, T., Thadaney-Israni, S., Rubin, D.L.: Putting the data before the algorithm in big data addressing personalized healthcare. NPJ Digit. Med. **2**(1), 78 (2019)
26. Castelvecchi, D.: Can we open the black box of AI? Nature **538**, 20–23 (2016). News feature
27. Charisi, V., et al.: Winfield, and Roman Yampolskiy. Towards moral autonomous systems. CoRR, abs/1703.04741 (2017)
28. Chouldechova, A.: Fair prediction with disparate impact: a study of bias in recidivism prediction instruments. Big Data **5**(2), 153–163 (2017)
29. Chouldechova, A., Roth, A.: A snapshot of the frontiers of fairness in machine learning. Commun. ACM **63**(5), 82–89 (2020)
30. Christman, J.: Autonomy in moral and political philosophy. In: Zalta, E.N. (ed.), The Stanford Encyclopedia of Philosophy. Metaphysics Research Lab, Stanford University, Fall 2020 edition (2020)
31. Cyras, K., et al.: Machine reasoning explainability (2020)
32. Diakopoulos, N.: Transparency. In: Dubber, M.D. Pasquale, F., Das, S. (ed.), The Oxford Handbook of Ethics of AI. Oxford University Press (2020)
33. Došilović, F.K., Brčić, M., Hlupić, N.: Explainable artificial intelligence: a survey. In: 2018 41st International Convention on Information and Communication Technology, Electronics and Microelectronics (MIPRO), pp. 0210–0215 (2018)
34. Dwork, C., Hardt, M., Pitassi, T., Reingold, O., Zemel, R.: Fairness through awareness. CoRR, abs/1104.3913 (2011)
35. Dwork, C., McSherry, F., Nissim, K., Smith, A.: Calibrating noise to sensitivity in private data analysis. J. Priv. Confidentiality **7**(3), 17–51 (2017)
36. Etzioni, A.: Is transparency the best disinfectant? J. Political Philos. **18**(4), 389–404 (2010)
37. European Commission. Proposal for a regulation of the european parliament and of the council laying down harmonised rules on artificial intelligence (artificial intelligence act) and amending certain union legislative acts com/2021/206 finalthat. Technical report (2021). https://eur-lex.europa.eu/legal-content/EN/TXT/?uri=CELEX%3A52021PC0206
38. Fieser, J.: Ethics. In: Boylan, M. (ed.), Internet Encyclopedia of Philosophy. ISSN 2161-0002 (2021)
39. Floridi, L.: Translating principles into practices of digital ethics: five risks of being unethical. Philos. Technol. **32**(2), 185–193 (2019)
40. Floridi, L., Cowls, J.: A unified framework of five principles for AI in society. Harv. Data Sci. Rev. **1**(1), 7 (2019). https://hdsr.mitpress.mit.edu/pub/l0jsh9d1
41. Gunning, D., Aha, D.: Darpa's explainable artificial intelligence (XAI) program. AI Mag. **40**(2), 44–58 (2019)
42. High-Level Expert Group on Artificial Intelligence. Ethics guidelines for trustworthy AI. Technical report, The Euruopean Comission (2019). https://ec.europa.eu/futurium/en/ai-alliance-consultation.1.html
43. Islam, S.R., Eberle, W., Ghafoor, S.K., Ahmed, M.: Explainable artificial intelligence approaches: a survey (2021)

44. Kearns, M., Neel, S., Roth, A., Wu, Z.S.: Preventing fairness gerrymandering: auditing and learning for subgroup fairness. In: Dy, J., Krause, A. (eds.), Proceedings of the 35th International Conference on Machine Learning, volume 80 of Proceedings of Machine Learning Research, pp. 2564–2572. PMLR, 10–15 July 2018

45. Kearns, M., Roth, A.: The Ethical Algorithm: The Science of Socially Aware Algorithm Design. Oxford University Press, Oxford (2019)

46. Kosinski, M., Stillwell, D., Graepel, T.: Private traits and attributes are predictable from digital records of human behavior. Proc. Natl. Acad. Sci. U. S. A. **110**(15), 5802–5 (2013)

47. Kusner, M.J., Loftus, J.R.: The long road to fairer algorithms. Nature 34–36 (2020)

48. Lazer, D.: The rise of the social algorithm. Science **348**(6239), 1090–1091 (2015)

49. Matzner, T., Ochs, C.: Privacy. Internet Policy Rev. **8**(4) (2019)

50. McLeod, S.K., Tanyi, A.: The basic liberties: an essay on analytical specification. Eur. J. Political Theory 14748851211041702 (2021)

51. Mehrabi, N., Morstatter, F., Saxena, N., Lerman, K., Galstyan, A.: A survey on bias and fairness in machine learning (2019)

52. Meijer, A.: Transparency. In: Bovens, M., Goodin, R.E., Schillemans, T. (eds.), The Oxford Handbook of Public Accountability. Oxford Handbooks Online (2014)

53. Miller, D.: Justice. In: Zalta, E.N. (ed.), The Stanford Encyclopedia of Philosophy. Metaphysics Research Lab, Stanford University, Fall 2021 edition (2021)

54. Miller, T.: Explanation in artificial intelligence: insights from the social sciences. Artif. Intell. **267**, 1–38 (2019)

55. Miller, T.: "But why?" Understanding explainable artificial intelligence. XRDS **25**(3), 20–25 (2019)

56. Molnar, C.: Interpretable machine learning. Lulu.com (2020)

57. Mora-Cantallops, M., Sánchez-Alonso, S., García-Barriocanal, E., Sicilia, M.-A.: Traceability for trustworthy AI: a review of models and tools. Big Data Cogn. Comput. **5**(2) (2021)

58. Narayanan, A., Mathur, A., Chetty, M., Kshirsagar, M.: Dark patterns: past, present, and future. Queue **18**(2), 67–92 (2020)

59. Nouwens, M., Liccardi, I., Veale, M., Karger, D., Kagal, L.: Dark patterns after the GDPR: scraping consent pop-ups and demonstrating their influence. CoRR, abs/2001.02479 (2020)

60. Parasuraman, R., Sheridan, T.B., Wickens, C.D.: A model for types and levels of human interaction with automation. IEEE Trans. Syst. Man Cybern. Part A Syst. Humans **30**(3), 286–297 (2000)

61. European Parlament and Council. Regulation (eu) 2016/679 of the european parliament and of the council of 27 April 2016 on the protection of natural persons with regard to the processing of personal data and on the free movement of such data, and repealing directive 95/46/ec (general data protection regulation) (2016)

62. Pessach, D., Shmueli, E.: Algorithmic fairness (2020)

63. Poole, D., Mackworth, A.: Artificial Intelligence: Foundations of Computational Agents, 2nd edn. Cambridge University Press, Cambridge, UK (2017)

64. Rawls, J.: Justice as fairness: political not metaphysical. Philos. Public Affairs **14**, 223–251 (1985)

65. Ribeiro, M.T., Singh, S., Guestrin, C.: Why should i trust you?: Explaining the predictions of any classifier. In: Proceedings of the 22nd ACM SIGKDD International Conference on Knowledge Discovery and Data Mining, KDD 2016, pp. 1135–1144, New York, NY, USA. Association for Computing Machinery (2016)

66. Rodolfa, K.T., Saleiro, P., Ghani, R.: Bias and fairness. In: Big Data and Social Science, pp. 281–312. Chapman and Hall/CRC, Boca Raton (2020)
67. Saleiro, P., et al.: Aequitas: a bias and fairness audit toolkit. CoRR, abs/1811.05577 (2018)
68. Samarati, P., Sweeney, L.: Protecting privacy when disclosing information: k-anonymity and its enforcement through generalization and suppression. Technical report, SRI International (1998). https://dataprivacylab.org/dataprivacy/projects/kanonymity/paper3.pdf
69. Shore, B.: Bias in the development and use of an expert system: implications for life cycle costs. Ind. Manag. Data Syst. **96**(4), 18–26 (1996). 2021/12/12
70. Skelton, A.: William David Ross. In: Zalta, E.N. (ed.), The Stanford Encyclopedia of Philosophy. Metaphysics Research Lab, Stanford University, Summer 2012 edition (2012)
71. Slavkovik, M., Stachl, C., Pitman, C., Askonas, J.: Digital voodoo dolls. In: Fourcade, M., Kuipers, B., Lazar, S., Mulligan, D.K. (eds.), AIES 2021: AAAI/ACM Conference on AI, Ethics, and Society, Virtual Event, USA, 19–21 May 2021, pp. 967–977. ACM (2021)
72. Htut Soe, T., Nordberg, O.E., Guribye, F., Slavkovik, M.: Circumvention by design - dark patterns in cookie consents for online news outlets. In: Proceedings of the 11th Nordic Conference on Human-Computer Interaction, 25–29 October 2020, Tallinn, Estonia. ACM (2020). https://arxiv.org/abs/2006.13985
73. Stepin, I., Alonso, J.M., Catala, A., Pereira-Fariña, M.: A survey of contrastive and counterfactual explanation generation methods for explainable artificial intelligence. IEEE Access **9**, 11974–12001 (2021)
74. Turek, M.: Explainable artificial intelligence (XAI) (2017). https://www.darpa.mil/program/explainable-artificial-intelligence. Accessed 10 June 2020
75. van Wynsberghe, A.: Sustainable AI: AI for sustainability and the sustainability of AI. AI Ethics **1**(3), 213–218 (2021)
76. Verma, S., Rubin, J.: Fairness definitions explained. In: Proceedings of the International Workshop on Software Fairness, FairWare 2018, pp. 1–7, New York, NY, USA, 2018. Association for Computing Machinery (2018)
77. Vilone, G., Longo, L.: Explainable artificial intelligence: a systematic review (2020)
78. Wagner, B.: Ethics As An Escape From Regulation. From Ethics-Washing To Ethics-Shopping?, pp. 84–89. Amsterdam University Press, Amsterdam (2019)
79. Warren, S.D., Brandeis, L.D.: The right to privacy. Harv. Law Rev. **4**(5), 193–220 (1890)
80. Ross, W.D.: The Right and the Good. Oxford University Press, Oxford (2007). Reprint edited by Philip Stratton-Lake. https://spot.colorado.edu/~heathwoo/readings/ross.pdf
81. Wieringa, M.: What to account for when accounting for algorithms: a systematic literature review on algorithmic accountability. In: Proceedings of the 2020 Conference on Fairness, Accountability, and Transparency, FAT* 2020, pp. 1–18, New York, NY, USA. Association for Computing Machinery (2020)
82. Winfield, A.F., et al.: IEEE P7001: a proposed standard on transparency. Front. Robot. AI **8**, 225 (2021)
83. Yan, J.N., Gu, Z., Lin, H., Rzeszotarski, J.M.: Silva: Interactively assessing machine learning fairness using causality. In: Proceedings of the 2020 CHI Conference on Human Factors in Computing Systems, CHI 2020, pp. 1–13, New York, NY, USA. Association for Computing Machinery (2020)

Operationalising AI Ethics: Conducting Socio-technical Assessment

Leila Methnani$^{(\boxtimes)}$ (iD), Mattias Brännström (iD), and Andreas Theodorou$^{(\boxtimes)}$ (iD)

Department of Computing Science, Umeå University, Umeå, Sweden
{leila.methnani,mattias.brannstrom,andreas.theodorou}@umu.se

Abstract. Several high profile incidents that involve Artificial Intelligence (AI) have captured public attention and increased demand for regulation. Low public trust and attitudes towards AI reinforce the need for concrete policy around its development and use. However, current guidelines and standards rolled out by institutions globally are considered by many as high-level and open to interpretation, making them difficult to put into practice. This paper presents ongoing research in the field of Responsible AI and explores numerous methods of operationalising AI ethics. If AI is to be effectively regulated, it must not be considered as a technology alone—AI is embedded in the fabric of our societies and should thus be treated as a socio-technical system, requiring multi-stakeholder involvement and employment of continuous value-based methods of assessment. When putting guidelines and standards into practice, context is of critical importance. The methods and frameworks presented in this paper emphasise this need and pave the way towards operational AI ethics.

Keywords: AI ethics · Responsible AI · Socio-technical assessment

1 Introduction

The use of Artificial Intelligence (AI) is increasing ubiquity in our societies and implies that it is reaching and impacting people in all corners of their daily lives. We can turn to several incidents that involve the deployment of AI technology in our societies that have resulted in harm to end users, e.g. minority groups who continue to face obstacles in the job market as a result of the bias perpetuated by AI-powered hiring algorithms [38], as well as involuntary bystanders, e.g. pedestrian deaths as a consequence of failed vision systems in automated vehicles [56]. Headlines like "Microsoft's AI chatbot gets a crash course in racism from Twitter" [26] or "Alexa, Can I Trust You?" [10] strike fear into their readers. These reported incidents lead to lack of trust, which in turn results in the formulation of a technological imaginary that influences the spread and acceptance of the technology [41].

Narratives promoting fear and mistrust reinforce the need for concrete policies around AI; effective governance, which puts socio-ethical values at the centre of any policy, is required to foster trust [55]. Yet, as regulatory bodies are trying

© Springer Nature Switzerland AG 2023
M. Chetouani et al. (Eds.): ACAI 2021, LNAI 13500, pp. 304–321, 2023.
https://doi.org/10.1007/978-3-031-24349-3_16

to push for governance—including the Commission's own "AI Act" [18]—there is a constant debate on what AI actually is [44]. There is not even a consensus on what constitutes 'true' AI or 'dumb' software. Drawn-out arguments on what constitutes AI and what does not only incentivises complexity or lack of governance and enables organisations to escape oversight [6]. While there is often a mysticism that is associated with it, AI is no 'magic abstraction' [7]. It is a technology researched, developed, and used by us for our own benefit. AI systems require code written by us, data produced by us, and machines designed by us. An AI system is more than a technology alone; due to its embedding and influence within societies, it needs to be understood as a socio-technical ecosystem [16]. Establishing and maintaining human control over AI is *always* a socio-technical problem. Technical solutions, in turn, can help keep track of compliance with socio-ethical solutions.

A universal definition of AI is not even required for operationalising AI ethics, but a common understanding of terms used in any policy amongst key stakeholders certainly is. Yet, an abstraction gap exists between the high-level requirements offered by numerous ethics guidelines rolled out by institutions globally, and the contexts for which they are to be applied [44]. The context is of critical importance; consideration of the stakeholders, projects, and societies that the system will be deployed into must be made throughout the design and development process. Furthermore, how socio-ethical legal values are interpreted must be clear and must be documented for reference. The process of operationalising AI ethics is necessarily elaborate and continuous. As Dignum [15] describes, it involves:

1. Ethics *in* Design; where development is influenced by socio-ethical issues.
2. Ethics *by* Design; where integration of ethical abilities as part of the behaviour of artificial intelligent systems occurs.
3. Ethics *for* Design; where codes of conduct, standards, and certification processes that ensure the integrity of developers and users are produced [15].

Responsible AI is not an afterthought; it should not be presented or promoted as a checklist: ticked once and henceforth forgotten [44]. Issues of bias, discrimination, and safety require overarching commitments and structured arrangements from institutions. Trust in AI should be derived from the trust in the entire socio-technical system that surrounds it. While there are various understandings of what constitutes AI, this paper aims to demonstrate to the reader that progress towards adequate AI governance through socio-technical assessment is achievable despite this, and paves the way towards the responsible use of AI. This will be presented through the lens of an ACAI 2021 tutorial, which shares the same title as this paper and was led by the authors. The Expected Learning Outcomes (ELOs) of the tutorial were:

1. Understand core concepts and misconceptions related to Responsible AI (RAI).
2. Gain knowledge about ongoing policy initiatives around AI.
3. Develop a practical grasp of why and how RAI is applied.
4. Explore ongoing research in the area of RAI.

This paper follows the same flow as the tutorial: first, to achieve ELO 1, a review of relevant background covering important terms and their definitions is presented in Sect. 2.1, along with some issues of misaligned conceptions. Then, to fulfill ELO 2, ideas of how to put ethics into practice are presented in Sect. 2.2 and Sect. 2.4. ELO 3 is targeted next, and illustrates these issues through the introduction and discussion of the role-playing serious game of *Protostrategos* in Sect. 3. Finally, to address ELO 4, we present additional tools for conducting continuous socio-technical assessment in Sect. 4; namely, the Responsible Artificial INtelligence (RAIN) framework, and other methods that take similar value-based approaches to operationalising AI ethics.

2   Background

2.1   What Is Responsible AI?

Before discussing what is meant by the term *responsible AI*, let us first consider what is meant by *AI*. John McCarthy—who was part of the Dartmouth Conference where the term was coined in the 1950s—described Artificial Intelligence as "the science and engineering of making intelligent machines". Here, intelligence is defined as "the computational part of the ability to achieve goals in the world" [33]. Per McCarthy's definition, a human, an advance robot such as R2D2[1], and even a thermostat all possess some level of intelligence: they can all be considered goal-seeking. This practical definition implies that *intelligence* is judged by behaviour [13]. It is the ability to perform the appropriate action at the appropriate time.

McCarthy highlights, however, that the relationship between the observer and the system also plays a role. In particular, the level of intelligence of a system is a function of how it is perceived, understood, or controlled by the observer. For instance, Weizenbaum's ELIZA programme—an early chatbot that simulated conversation through pattern matching—was still perceived as human-like and intelligent even after it was disclosed to users that they were interacting with a computer programme. This was simply a result of their perception and interpretation of the responses that ELIZA had offered. The users were said to "contribute much to clothe ELIZA's responses in vestments of plausibility." [51]. These illusions are misrepresentations of the systems they are interacting with, and can lead to mistrust, misuse, and/or disuse [45]. This extends to a misrepresentation of physical agents, onto which we often assign anthropomorphic attributes, including gender-based stereotypes [19,39].

These misrepresentations are often sculpted by the depiction of AI in popular media and science fiction, as social representation theory would suggest [25]. Most media are both responsible for and reinforced by the problematic term 'an AI', which is also worryingly used by scholars transitioning into the field. AI is never an entity that is entirely separate from the human [14]. Presenting the term in this way promotes the dystopian notion of 'superintelligence', i.e.

---

[1] A fictional robot from the popular Star Wars franchise.

that an AI system will become 'smart enough' to overthrow humanity, and runs the risk of misleading the public into thinking it cannot be effectively regulated or controlled, and that there is even an 'ultimate' algorithm to be discovered, further fuelling the 'AI Race' narrative [46].

Such a race would be difficult to win with an evolving definition of AI. McCarthy observed and described this phenomenon by simply stating: "as soon as it works, no one calls it AI any more" [35]. The association of mysticism and expectations with the 'briefcase word' *intelligence* results in us only classifying opaque complex techniques as 'intelligent'. Otherwise, like a magician whose tricks have been revealed, an AI system that is simple enough to be understood appears uninteresting, if not, unintelligent [58].

AI is always a product made by humans; an artefact designed by us and deployed in our societies to serve a purpose. Humans, the designers of these AI systems, are the moral agents; we cannot—and, arguably, should not—assign this type of agency to the machine [5,43]. It is through this lens that we discuss AI Ethics. While the term *AI Ethics*, like AI, has become an umbrella term for many things–including existential crisis, robot rights, governance, and others— we do not consider AI Ethics a new philosophical discipline. To clarify, we do not deny that AI provides opportunities to discuss and test existing frameworks. Instead, within the scope of this paper and its associated workshop, we consider the field to focus on application and observation of existing ethical frameworks within the *socio-technical* system that the AI system is a part of.

This implementation and assessment of ethical frameworks in AI requires ethics *in*, *by*, and *for* design [15]. Ethics in design says that development is influenced by socio-ethical legal issues. These are all specifications and values that should be protected. Ethics by design advises the integration of ethical abilities as part of behaviour of AI systems. Ethics for design promotes the code of conducts, standards, and certification processes that ensure the integrity of developers and users. Even without consensus on the definitions, interpretations can be assessed as to whether they comply with social norms and with the law. Ultimately, it is about the process, about the discourse and about maintaining control.

It is worth noting that ethics does not equate to law, nor does each equate to social norms [23]. While the latter two carry consequences when violated, ethics imposes no sanctions; and while norms often carry social repercussions, they do not result in legal liability. However, social accountability may lead to boycotting and other indirect measures against someone's actions if they are deemed as unethical or to be violating social norms [3].

Responsible AI is about understanding and making explicit the tension between the law, ethics, and social norms while also ensuring that our socio-technical systems adhere to concrete requirements firmly established in those three sources. As a Russian proverb suggests, "trust, but verify". In responsible AI, any compliance to socio-ethical legal values is audited and verified. Most importantly, responsible AI is about how the different actors who interact, affect, and are affected by the AI system acknowledge their responsibility and, if needed, accountability to any given outcome [16].

2.2 AI Governance

Building trust around AI systems is a necessity if the use of AI is to prosper within societies. Developers, investors, users, and bystanders should be able to trust that these systems perform as expected. Furthermore, the implications of the technology, from development to deployment and beyond, falls within socio-ethical legal specifications and values that should be protected. As a step in this direction, legislative bodies such as the European Commission have drafted and published strategies, policies and guidelines around AI and its trustworthy development [12]. This global movement to govern AI systems stems from the understanding that AI systems do not operate in isolation—they are embedded in the societies within which they are developed and deployed, forming *socio-technical systems* where the society, technology and organisation influence one another [47].

To best understand the current landscape of ethical governance, one needs to first comprehend the thread connecting ethical guidelines to regulation [55]. Ethical guidelines are what we refer to as *soft governance*; i.e. non-binding rules that are nonetheless provide some benefit to those following them. Guidelines, such as codes of conduct, provide means for organisations to demonstrate their due diligence and train personnel for their responsibilities. *Standards*, another type of soft governance, offer specifications or methodological guidelines that have been collectively agreed upon by a group of experts [42,55]. Following standards also enables organisations to demonstrate due diligence, provide features to their products, or better market their product or services. For example, specification standards, e.g. IEEE 802.11 (WiFi) [21], allow cross-compatibility between products. Another example are safety specifications standards, e.g. ISO 13482:2014 for robots [28], which explicitly dictate safety related performance requirements and help organisations to demonstrate the robustness of their solutions. *Hard governance* is a legally enforceable policy, i.e. legislation.

At the time of the tutorial, there was no legislation specifically for AI, only ongoing discussions related to the upcoming "AI Act" by the European Commission [22]. On the other hand, there has been a growing number of standardisation efforts related to AI [11,53], e.g. the "IEEE Standard for Transparency of Autonomous Systems" [27,54]. Still, the majority of existing policies related to AI are ethical guidelines and high-level investment strategies by intergovernmental and governmental institutions—over 700 of such policies are tracked by the OECD AI Observatory [37].

In a study conducted to compare and contrast various ethics guidelines and principles published across the globe [29], a convergence around 5 principles was identified: *transparency, justice and fairness, non-maleficence, responsibility,* and *privacy.* Moreover, significant divergence was identified with regards to how these principles are interpreted, what relevant issues, domains or actors are involved, and how they should be operationalised [44]. Indeed, values are not static; they are interpreted differently across communities, cultures, and contexts. It is not uncommon to observe different social circles endorsing the same values while coupling them with different behaviours [31]. Consider, for instance, the value of *fairness*: it can be perceived through the lens of equal opportunity (i.e. equity) or through the lens of equal outcome (i.e. equality).

While no universal morality exists, it is not needed in order to make good progress in the domain of AI ethics or in order to operationalise the principles therein and to govern effectively [1]. What is more important is the development of concrete methodologies for organisations to explicitly define and state their values transparently for both their internal and external users. These interpretations can subsequently be assessed as to whether they comply with social norms and with the law. Ultimately, it is about the process, about the discourse and about maintaining control.

2.3   Transparency and Control

In order to validate system compliance with a set relevant values, a sensible implementation of *transparency* is required. Properties like explainability are often linked—or even complimentary—to transparent systems. To be considered transparent, a system should expose its decision-making mechanism on-demand. A transparent system should present accurate interpretations of its goals, processes towards achieving goals, sensory inputs, and any unexpected behaviour [45].

Certainly, such information offered by the system supports the principle of human agency and oversight, the first of 7 requirements in the Ethics Guideline for Trustworthy AI [24]. Human-in-the-loop is one mechanism used to promote human oversight. It requires a human's involvement at every step of the system's decision cycle. Human-on-the-loop, on the other hand, allows autonomous decision actions by the system, but requires a human to consistently monitor such that manual intervention can be made at any step in the decision cycle. Human-out-of-the-loop requires no human involvement, and the system is expected to evaluate and execute decisions with full autonomy.

While these oversight mechanisms offer some level of human control, they are insufficient for what is known as *meaningful human control*. In the discourse around autonomous weapons and the ethical implications of their development, the principle of meaningful human control is presented [34]. It is argued that humans, not any computer or algorithm, must maintain control—and thus moral responsibility—of any such decision making process. For human control to be considered *meaningful*, the requirement of *tracking* and *tracing* must be fulfilled. The tracking condition requires that the decision-making system can demonstrate and respond to the human moral reasons relevant to the circumstance. The tracing condition requires that the system's actions and states can be traced back to at least one human's coherent moral understanding. That is, there is at least one identifiable human along the chain of responsibility, from the design, to programming, to operation, and finally system deployment, who is in the position of understanding the system's capabilities, the potential impacts, and legitimate moral responses to the system's role within the context within which it is deployed.

Both tracking and tracing offer transparency into the decision making process. For systems with variable autonomy (VA), where autonomy can be adjusted between fully manual to fully autonomous, this kind of transparency is not a perk but rather a *requirement* for effective transfer of control. VA systems, by design, promote meaningful human control [34]. For effective and responsible VA systems, roles and responsibilities must first be explicitly defined: who is responsible for transferring control? Of what? To whom? And when? VA both requires and ensures accountability, responsibility, and transparency. Overall, VA improves the performance of human-machine teaming.

For human users, interaction with complex intelligent artefacts involves the construction of mental models in attempts to understand and predict their behaviour. For instance, equipping a reactive planning robot with transparency into their action selection mechanism has been shown to aid users in their formulation of more accurate mental models and thus their understanding of the robot's behaviour [59].

In another study conducted using virtual reality (VR) to simulate a version of the trolley problem called "Slam the Brakes", perceptions of moral decisions in automated vehicles (AVs) was measured [52]. Participants were categorised into three groups each corresponding to different conditions. In the first, participants were informed that they will be driven in an AV and given no post-crash explanation. The second condition involved a transparent AV; the participants were given a post-crash explanation from the perspective of the vehicle as the decision-maker. That is, explanations were formulated as "the self-driving car made the decision on the basis that ... ". In the final condition, participants are told that they will be driven in a vehicle controlled by a human. However, there was no "real human" driver at all—the vehicle was automated in all conditions but this remained undisclosed to participants until the end of the study.

Interestingly, the key findings of this VR study showed that participants put the *least* blame on the 'human' driver, which was qualified as the least machine-like, medium blame to the opaque AV, which was qualified as "medium" machine-like, and the *most* blame on the transparent AV, qualified as the most machine-like. The increased attribution of moral responsibility is hypothesised to be due to realisation that the action was determined based on social values. What is suggested in the literature is that utilitarian action is more permissible— expected even—when a robot is to take a decision [32].

One outcome of transparency is that it offers an opportunity for the users to formulate a more accurate mental model of the AI artefact. Misunderstandings may lead to anxiety, mistrust, fear, misuse, and disuse. It can also lead to user self-doubt, questioning their own actions and competency with operating the system as opposed to the system being flawed itself. With sufficient transparency into the decision making mechanisms of the system, users can calibrate their trust in it, and as a result make better decisions about how to operate it—or whether they would like to operate it at all.

2.4   The End Game: Accountability

While it is key, transparency is not the end goal; it is merely a tool to guide control over the system. Instead, striving for responsibility and accountability is the desired destination [8].

When we refer to *responsibility* we are concerned with the role of the humans in the decision cycle of an AI system. Moreover, responsibility concerns itself with the system's ability to trace back to the human(s) who can be held responsible and to account for any decision, error, or unexpected result; i.e. there exists a *chain of responsibility* for any AI system [16].

Accountability is not only about punishment; it is about being answerable to actions, whether that is good or bad. When it concerns system issues, however, they must be addressed and action must be taken; the "threat" of legal liability does indeed motivate organisations (and individuals) to demonstrate due diligence. The Protostrategos case study, discussed next, demonstrates the need to thoroughly consider policies, decisions, and systems *together* in order to exercise due diligence.

3   Protostrategos

Protostrategos is a student-led Problem-Based Learning (PBL) activity. PBL is a type of learning that encourages the critical analysis of real-world problems by using student-led activities such as group discussions [57]. The use of problem-based learning in STEM courses not only enhances the students' knowledge, but it also increases their motivation for continuing education and long-term learning [30].

PBL activities do not focus on solutions themselves, but on the process of coming up with them. In the case of Protostrategos, we use a purpose-made case study of a fictional company called *Protostrategos*. The case study itself us based on Princeton's "Hiring by Machine" that explores the potential social, ethical, and legal implications of deploying AI systems into the real world [50]. The Protostrategos case is not just a localisation of Princeton's use case; it adds various game mechanics to ensure that students are active learners. Most specifically, Protostrategos can be seen as a serious game, i.e. a game developed for educational purposes [36].

The use of a serious game makes the activity enjoyable while also empowering the students to achieve their learning outcomes. Participants must thoroughly analyse and discuss the presented fictional scenario from various stakeholder viewpoints as they undertake a role (e.g. CTO, system developer, and others) throughout the exercise. In our tutorial, the role-playing mechanics of Protostrategos enable students to understand the contextualised nature of ethical socio-legal values as they represent different perspectives during the discussions. Furthermore, by adopting different stakeholder roles and considering their respective values, participants are encouraged to explore the complexities of—and most importantly the *need* for—AI assessment. In addition, various 'self-reflection' and 'discussion' points are distributed throughout the exercise; serving as check-points between the key tasks and offering opportunities for explicit knowledge transfer.

3.1 Scenario Overview

The scene is set in Sweden, where a group of army veterans aim to extend their civic duty and establish a non-profit technology company called *Protostrategos*. This company specialises in providing software products for Non-Governmental Organisations (NGOs) across the EU.

Protostrategos has a very homogeneous pool of employees: ex-military personnel. However, as it begins to attract more business, military experience is no longer a pre-requisite for working there. To aid them in their search for new talent, the developers at Protostrategos built an automated hiring system named THEMIS. The system passed internal testing for its candidacy to become a fully-fledged product offered by the company. In light of ongoing narratives related to AI system failures and to preserve their image as a trustworthy company, Protostrategos have decided to extend this process with an added 'ethics check' stage. A dedicated task force was assembled to investigate the system behaviour and draft a policy to guide the development and deployment for clients.

Participants are invited to select a role to play on this task force, and assume their position throughout discussion. The roles assigned in this exercise include both internal and external stakeholders. The Chief Technical Officer (CTO) is one example of an internal stakeholder role. The CTO is one of the most senior individuals in the company with both managerial and technical expertise. This role must align the company's technology resources with the organisation's short and long-term goals and may be held criminally responsible for actions taken by the company. The Citizen activist(s) advocating for underrepresented groups is an example of an external stakeholder. This role cares for the requirements directly related to the rights of underrepresented and marginalised groups. The activist does not use or otherwise benefit from the system, but represents a group of people that may be positively or negatively impacted by the system.

As a first task, the internal and external stakeholders must familiarise themselves with the "Ethics Guidelines for Trustworthy AI," which serves as a springboard into the discussion. Together, the stakeholders must consider which of the 7 requirements are relevant to the case and rank them in order of importance. This should be complimented with an explanation for the presented structure as well as the common vocabulary this ranking relies on. The vocabulary forms the foundation upon which the agreed structure can be built.

Next, the task force is to perform a preliminary assessment of the system with the help of either the "Assessment List for Trustworthy AI" released by the Commission's High-level Expert Group in AI [24] or the "Abbreviated Assessment List" released by AI4EU [17]. Each has its strengths and weaknesses. The European Commission presents a thorough list of more than one hundred questions, but includes a binary assessment that may be perceived as offering too little value. The abbreviated list offers a perhaps more useful assessment measure of 'maturity levels' to demonstrate varying compliance levels to the values in focus, but may still be perceived as too short to cover all risks. Regardless of the assessment checklist the group selects, the potential for adverse effects will remain, and the development of this fictional scenario is intended to demonstrate exactly this.

The scenario unfolds to reveal a concerning incident: one female applicant, Helena, was quickly rejected after applying for a well-suited position at Protostrategos. Upon her request for feedback, human resources manually reviewed her application and could not find any clear or reasonable explanation for the automated rejection. Upon face value, this application should have made it through to the next stage of the hiring process.

A call for further investigation was made over concerns that the system discriminated against Helena due to her physical disability. Helena was a wheelchair user, as were many veterans employed by the company. In fact, the developers designed the system with the intention of avoiding discrimination against protected groups; the team ensured any text relating to disabilities was excluded from the machine learning algorithm's input. The internal review revealed that it was Helena's lack of sports interest that resulted in her early rejection. As it turned out, THEMIS had learned to associate a history of sports with a 'good fit' for the company. Since Helena did not explicitly express the same interest in sports that the veterans at Protostrategos had expressed, she was subjected to a rejection by the automated system.

3.2 Students' Reflections

Helena's scenario demonstrates how emerging behaviours of an AI system can be difficult to predict. Is THEMIS discriminating against people with physical disabilities? Some participants brought forward arguments against this claim, emphasising that the system is not capable of discriminating; it is not sentient (nor intelligent, by some points of view). Here, the understanding of the term 'discriminatory' is in the deliberate act of unjustly distinguishing between groups of people and not in the technical sense of learning a decision boundary between classes in a machine learning model. The system has no interest in discriminating in this sense; it has simply learned a strong correlation based upon the data that it was fed during training. From this perspective, the discrimination is dealt by the employees of Protostrategos, for they have designed the system in a way that puts certain groups at a disadvantage.

Another argument that was brought forward is in support of Protostrategos' desire to preserve the status quo when it comes to company culture—they have remained transparent about seeking a certain demographic of employees for homogeneity. Does the company have any moral obligation or duty to build a more diverse workforce? Anti-discrimination laws in Europe require organisations to provide equal opportunities by not considering specific protected characteristics as a disadvantage. In Sweden, physical disabilities is one such characteristic protected by law. Indeed, if there was direct consideration of Helena's disability status in the system's decision-making process, Protostrategos would have violated Swedish law. THEMIS, however, used 'redundant encodings' in the training data that inferred such attributes. This is a typical example of how simply 'removing' a feature that is fed into a model is an insufficient way of avoiding discrimination. The model may very well learn to discriminate through proxy variables.

This stance argues that the model merely extends the human biases that already exist at Protostrategos. One might question whether the outcome would have differed at all if the process were not automated. It is certainly plausible that a hiring officer could relate to select applicants and feel compelled to favour their resumes over others. Human minds are black boxes too; one cannot simply peer into the mind of a Protostrategos employee and trace every step of the decision making process. Still, disinterest in sports is not a protected characteristic under Swedish law, and this is the stance that the company lawyers are ready to defend. Recall that ethics does not equate to law; while Protostrategos may be within legal compliance, this does not guarantee ethical compliance, nor would the reverse be true.

Participants were encouraged to consider further how one might address hidden biases using both technical (e.g. sanitising data) and socio-legal solutions. The task force is granted even more control in light of this controversy. As a group, they are to discuss what should be done about future developments. Should system deployment be rolled back? Should the system remain online but be used only for internal hires? Should it rather be sold to an external customer? To conclude the exercise, participants were asked to consider whether the ranking of their requirements and their interpretations of the various terms have shifted after learning about Helena's incident. After all, these definitions and interpretations are flexible and are likely to change in light of new information. This is as it should be. Moreover, the assessment conducted prior to the incident provides no guarantee of 'catching' every issue that might occur when the system is deployed into society. While it has performed well on an internal training data set, this set does not necessarily reflect the real world and cannot capture all its complexities. Countermeasures must be in place to account for incidents like this. From each stakeholder's point of view, the group was further prompted to discuss how trust in THEMIS can be rebuilt. Again, this requires discussion, agreement, and subsequent *action* as a continuous and iterative process.

The emphasis that was made throughout this exercise is the need for structured discourse and contextualising the problem at hand. The relevant stakeholders as well as the details of the application domain will influence which values are of prioritised and discussed. The definitions are of particular importance; they offer a foundation upon which more concrete design requirements can be constructed. In this exercise, the HLEG's 7 requirements for Trustworthy AI were suggested as a starting point, but any relevant and clearly defined principle or value can be brought to the discussion. Furthermore, the Commission's assessment list or AI4EU abbreviated assessment list were offered as tools to help guide the task force towards an agreed solution.

However, such checklists are often not enough to operationalise AI ethics. There is a glaring gap between the high-level values presented across various guidelines and the concrete contexts to which they might apply. This makes it particularly difficult to select a level of abstraction. For some it is too specific for others too vague, too generalised and may encompass any software, not just AI. Responsible AI Norms (RAIN) framework and tool, which is discussed next, presents a value-driven solution to fill this gap through socio-technical assessment.

4 Socio-ethical Values in Design and Development

RAIN is a structured framework established to enable organisations to move from high-level abstract values towards requirements that can be operationalised [9]. RAIN is more than just a methodology. Beyond this, it offers a concrete multi-stakeholder assessment framework, together with relevant tools to enable the audit and compliance validation of existing and upcoming AI systems. Both the methodology and assessment frameworks are being field tested by industrial partners and key stakeholders in the Nordic countries.

RAIN derives its theoretical basis from Value-Sensitive Design (VSD) [20], a methodology applied to the design of technical systems with an emphasis on value integration. VSD is an iterative process that begins with the articulation of high-level values and stakeholder perspectives, which are then intersected with technological contexts. To map values onto more tangible design requirements, a hierarchy of values can be constructed, where an intermediate layer of sub-norms are embedded and hold the structure together with the *specification* and *for the sake of* relation [40]. VSD also supports the identification of value conflicts. As a continuous process, it aims to be thorough and manual to foster fruitful discussion.

4.1 The Glass-Box Approach

An analysis that derives from VSD is employed in the glass-box approach [1], a versatile governance solution for ensuring an opaque system adheres to socio-ethical legal values. While opacity via the 'black box' can sometimes be unavoidable for technical, economic, or social reasons [2], adequate governance remains a necessity. This two-stage approach places a 'glass box' around the black box by mapping moral values onto explicit and verifiable norms that constrain and direct inputs and outputs of the systems. Adhering to the value in a specified context corresponds to these inputs and outputs remaining within the boundaries of the glass box. The interpretation stage is a structured process that translates abstract values into explicit norms and system design requirements. The observation stage involves observing the outputs produced by various inputs and approximating compliance with the list of requirements produced in the interpretation stage. These two stages are tethered in that they inform each other's values and result in system tuning. Overall, a link is established between testable requirements and high-level values. Still, this approach is intentionally manual in the interpretation step to reap the benefits of thorough discussion.

4.2 Interrogating the Black Box

Another approach is to interrogate the black box [49]. This process involves information seeking dialogues with a system to promote transparency. The auditing system—the 'investigator'—asks the AI system—the 'suspect'—a series of questions. Using argumentation semantics, the auditor can validate the consistency in these queries. Recall that we are not only concerned with auditing the intelligent system itself, but rather the larger socio-technical system as a whole. The glass-box approach and interrogating the black box do exactly this; these continuous processes validate a system's adherence to norms.

4.3 RAIN

RAIN, as a continuous and broad assessment tool, takes into consideration the wider socio-technical process that shapes the development, deployment and use of the system as a whole. It employs a reusable hierarchy of values that can be applied across organisations, where one might find different high-level values, different technical contexts, and a different suite of stakeholders. This hierarchy is derived from existing regulatory frameworks, standards, and policies by breaking them down by context features (Fig. 1). As a software, RAIN visualises, manages and tracks ethical and legal requirements for the development of responsible AI software with regards to this constructed hierarchy.

To integrate, monitor and evaluate AI software from an ethical and policy-compliance perspective, RAIN uses three operational layers. The setup layer involves the identification of the socio-technical context, which includes roles and responsibilities of the organisation, intention and function of the software, and known use-case risks. Using this information, the RAIN hierarchy finds the intersections between values, stakeholder perspectives, and identified context features. These intersections, RAI Norms, put focus on specific challenges and risks a given context feature presents given the policy values and stakeholder perspectives. The assessment layer assesses how well these risks are handled and produces scores on each RAI Norm on multiple levels of maturity ranging from 1 to 5. The assessment requirements also act as a guide for particular design features which can help resolve identified problems. The final results layer combine these partial maturity rating results on to any high-level value or stakeholder. Results can also be directly mapped back to the parts of external policies from which the hierarchy was derived, allowing RAIN to serve as a context-aware interface to more abstract policies or assessments.

The RAIN tool is intended to support companies like Protostrategos in their due diligence around AI projects. The focus is on contextualising values and translating them into tangible design requirements, guided by assessment scores.

Fig. 1. Example value breakdown in the Protostrategos case by interpreting fairness from the perspective of the job applicant, and further decompose it into requirements

5   Conclusion

While Protostrategos presents a fictional case, it is inspired by many real-world examples of similar incidents. These examples illuminate the influence AI systems can have on our society. AI systems are always a socio-technical system that reach people in all corners of their lives. This is why we need AI ethics.

Various understandings of what the term 'AI' means can result in misconceptions about what it means to practice AI ethics. It is therefore imperative to agree that we cannot assign any moral agency to an AI system. Rather, it is the human designers, developers and users who are the moral agents and who are to operationalise ethics. Ensuring system compliance to various ethical principles is a challenge when system limitations are not always clear, neither to the users nor the developers. In response to increasing public demand for trustworthy AI, various guidelines and standards have been produced to help inform the development AI systems, within which the principle of transparency plays a pivotal role. Transparency is the vector towards accountability and responsibility, where the human's role is of focus in the assessment of system behaviour.

Certainly, ethics is not an afterthought and ethical compliance should be assessed. Assessment, however, should not be reduced down to a checklist based on high-level guidelines that are completed once and then forgotten. When putting guidelines and standards into practice, context is of critical importance. Throughout the design and development process, the stakeholders, projects, and societies that the system will be deployed into must be carefully considered. How any socio-ethical legal value is interpreted must be clear and must be documented for reference. The methods and frameworks presented in this paper emphasise this need and pave the way towards operational AI ethics—a lengthy and often complex process about ethics *in*, *by*, and *for* design.

6   Further Reading

For further reading on Responsible AI, we recommend the book entitled "Responsible Artificial Intelligence: How to Develop and Use AI in a Responsible Way" by Dignum [16].

The following are recommended articles around putting governance into practice:

- IEEE P7001: A Proposed Standard on Transparency [54]
- Governance by Glass-Box [1]
- Translating Values into Design Requirements [40]
- Contestable Black Boxes [48]

Relevant readings also include the following whitepapers or analyses of the global governance landscape:

- Let Me Take Over: Variable Autonomy for Meaningful Human Control [34]
- Reflections on the EU's AI Act and How We Could Make It Even Better [22]
- Standards for AI Governance: International Standards to Enable Global Coordination in AI Research & Development [11]
- Ethical Governance is Essential to Building Trust in Robotics [55]
- Standardizing Ethical Design for Artificial Intelligence and Autonomous Systems [4]

In addition, the reader is advised to review the references for this article.

References

1. Aler Tubella, A., Theodorou, A., Dignum, F., Dignum, V.: Governance by glass-box: implementing transparent moral bounds for AI behaviour. In: Proceedings of the Twenty-Eighth International Joint Conference on Artificial Intelligence, IJCAI-2019, pp. 5787–5793. International Joint Conferences on Artificial Intelligence Organization, California, August 2019. https://doi.org/10.24963/ijcai.2019/802. http://arxiv.org/abs/1905.04994
2. Ananny, M., Crawford, K.: Seeing without knowing: limitations of the transparency ideal and its application to algorithmic accountability. New Media Soc. **20**(3), 973–989 (2018)
3. Bovens, M.: Analysing and assessing accountability: a conceptual framework. Eur. Law J. **13**(4), 447–468 (2007). https://doi.org/10.1111/j.1468-0386.2007.00378.x. https://onlinelibrary.wiley.com/doi/abs/10.1111/j.1468-0386.2007.00378.x. _eprint: https://onlinelibrary.wiley.com/doi/pdf/10.1111/j.1468-0386.2007.00378.x
4. Bryson, J., Winfield, A.: Standardizing ethical design for artificial intelligence and autonomous systems. Computer **50**(5), 116–119 (2017)
5. Bryson, J.J.: Patiency is not a virtue: the design of intelligent systems and systems of ethics. Ethics Inf. Technol. **20**(1), 15–26 (2018). https://doi.org/10.1007/s10676-018-9448-6. http://link.springer.com/10.1007/s10676-018-9448-6. ISBN 9781908187215
6. Bryson, J.J.: Europe is in danger of using the wrong definition of AI. Wired (2022). https://www.wired.com/story/artificial-intelligence-regulation-european-union/. Section: tags
7. Bryson, J.J., Diamantis, M.E., Grant, T.D.: Of, for, and by the people: the legal lacuna of synthetic persons. Artif. Intell. Law **25**(3), 273–291 (2017). https://doi.org/10.1007/s10506-017-9214-9

8. Bryson, J.J., Theodorou, A.: How society can maintain human-centric artificial intelligence. In: Toivonen, M., Saari, E. (eds.) Human-Centered Digitalization and Services. TSS, vol. 19, pp. 305–323. Springer, Singapore (2019). https://doi.org/10.1007/978-981-13-7725-9_16

9. Brännström, M., Theodorou, A., Dignum, V.: Let it rain for social good. In: Proceedings of the IJCAI-ECAI-22 Workshop on Artificial Intelligence Safety (AISafety 2022). CEUR-WS (2022)

10. Chung, H., Iorga, M., Voas, J., Lee, S.: Alexa, can I trust you? Computer **50**(9), 100–104 (2017)

11. Cihon, P.: Standards for AI governance: international standards to enable global coordination in AI research & development. University of Oxford, Future of Humanity Institute (2019)

12. European Commission: Communication from the commission to the European parliament, the council, the European economic and social committee and the committee of the regions youth opportunities initiative. Official Journal of the European Union (2011)

13. Dennett, D.C.: The age of post-intelligent design. In: The Age of Artificial Intelligence: An Exploration, p. 27 (2020)

14. Dignum, V.: Responsible autonomy. In: IJCAI International Joint Conference on Artificial Intelligence, pp. 4698–4704 (2017). https://doi.org/10.24963/ijcai.2017/655. ISSN 10450823

15. Dignum, V.: Ethics in artificial intelligence: introduction to the special issue. Ethics Inf. Technol. **20**, 1–3 (2018)

16. Dignum, V.: Responsible Artificial Intelligence: How to Develop and Use AI in a Responsible Way. Artificial Intelligence: Foundations, Theory, and Algorithms, Springer, Cham (2019). https://doi.org/10.1007/978-3-030-30371-6

17. Dignum, V., Nieves, J.C., Theodorou, A., Tubella, A.: An abbreviated assessment list to support the responsible development and use of AI. Department of Computing Sciences, Umeå University, Technical report (2021)

18. European Commission: Proposal for a regulation of the European parliament and of the council laying down harmonised rules on artificial intelligence (artificial intelligence act) and amending certain union legislative acts. Report, European Commission, Brussels (2021). https://eur-lex.europa.eu/legal-content/EN/TXT/HTML/?uri=CELEX:52021PC0206&from=EN

19. Fong, T., Nourbakhsh, I., Dautenhahn, K.: A survey of socially interactive robots. Robot. Auton. Syst. **42**(3–4), 143–166 (2003)

20. Friedman, B., Kahn, P.H., Borning, A., Huldtgren, A.: Value sensitive design and information systems. In: Doorn, N., Schuurbiers, D., van de Poel, I., Gorman, M.E. (eds.) Early Engagement and New Technologies: Opening Up the Laboratory. PET, vol. 16, pp. 55–95. Springer, Dordrecht (2013). https://doi.org/10.1007/978-94-007-7844-3_4

21. W.W.L.W. Group: IEEE standard for information technology-telecommunications and information exchange between systems local and metropolitan area networks-specific requirements - Part 11: Wireless LAN Medium Access Control (MAC) and Physical Layer (PHY) Specifications. Standard, The Institute of Electrical and Electronics Engineers (2016)

22. Haataja, M., Bryson, J.J.: Reflections on the EU's AI act and how we could make it even better. CPI TechREG Chronicle (2022)

23. Hildebrandt, M.: Closure: on ethics, code and law. In: Law for Computer Scientists, chap. 11 (2019)

24. High-Level Expert Group on Artificial Intelligence: Ethics guidelines for trustworthy AI (2019)
25. Höijer, B.: Social representations theory. Nordicom Rev. **32**(2), 3–16 (2017). https://doi.org/10.1515/nor-2017-0109
26. Hunt, E.: Tay, Microsoft's AI chatbot, gets a crash course in racism from twitter. The Guardian, March 2016. https://www.theguardian.com/technology/2016/mar/24/tay-microsofts-ai-chatbot-gets-a-crash-course-in-racism-from-twitter
27. IEEE Standards Association: IEEE 7001-2021 Standard for Transparency of Autonomous Systems. Technical report, IEEE Standards Association (2021). https://standards.ieee.org/ieee/7001/6929/
28. Robots and robotic devices - safety requirements for personal care robots. Standard, International Organization for Standardization, Geneva, CH (2014)
29. Jobin, A., Ienca, M., Vayena, E.: The global landscape of AI ethics guidelines. Nat. Mach. Intell. **1**(9), 389–399 (2019)
30. Lou, S.J., Shih, R.C., Ray Diez, C., Tseng, K.H.: The impact of problem-based learning strategies on STEM knowledge integration and attitudes: an exploratory study among female Taiwanese senior high school students. Int. J. Technol. Des. Educ. **21**(2), 195–215 (2011). https://doi.org/10.1007/s10798-010-9114-8
31. Maio, G.R.: Mental representations of social values. In: Advances in Experimental Social Psychology, vol. 42, pp. 1–43. Elsevier (2010)
32. Malle, B.F., Scheutz, M., Arnold, T., Voiklis, J., Cusimano, C.: Sacrifice one for the good of many? People apply different moral norms to human and robot agents. In: 2015 10th ACM/IEEE International Conference on Human-Robot Interaction (HRI), pp. 117–124. IEEE (2015)
33. McCarthy, J.: What is artificial intelligence? (2007). http://www-formal.stanford.edu/jmc/whatisai/whatisai.html
34. Methnani, L., Aler Tubella, A., Dignum, V., Theodorou, A.: Let me take over: variable autonomy for meaningful human control. Front. Artif. Intell. **4**, 133 (2021). https://doi.org/10.3389/frai.2021.737072. https://www.frontiersin.org/article/10.3389/frai.2021.737072
35. Meyer, B.: John McCarthy. https://cacm.acm.org/blogs/blog-cacm/138907-john-mccarthy/fulltext
36. Moradi, M., Noor, N.F.B.M.: The impact of problem-based serious games on learning motivation. IEEE Access **10**, 8339–8349 (2022). https://doi.org/10.1109/ACCESS.2022.3140434
37. OECD: National AI policies & strategies (2021). https://www.oecd.ai/countries-and-initiatives/
38. O'Neil, C.: Weapons of Math Destruction: How Big Data Increases Inequality and Threatens Democracy. Crown Publishing Group, USA (2016)
39. Otterbacher, J., Talias, M.: S/he's too warm/agentic!: the influence of gender on uncanny reactions to robots. In: Proceedings of the 2017 ACM/IEEE International Conference on Human-Robot Interaction, HRI 2017, New York, NY, USA, pp. 214–223. ACM (2017). https://doi.org/10.1145/2909824.3020220. http://doi.acm.org/10.1145/2909824.3020220
40. Poel, I.: Translating values into design requirements. In: Michelfelder, D.P., McCarthy, N., Goldberg, D.E. (eds.) Philosophy and Engineering: Reflections on Practice, Principles and Process. Philosophy of Engineering and Technology, vol. 15, pp. 253–266. Springer, Dordrecht (2013). https://doi.org/10.1007/978-94-007-7762-0_20
41. Sartori, L., Theodorou, A.: A sociotechnical perspective for the future of AI: narratives, inequalities, and human control. Ethics Inf. Technol. **24**, 1–11 (2022)

42. Schiff, D., Ayesh, A., Musikanski, L., Havens, J.C.: IEEE 7010: a new standard for assessing the well-being implications of artificial intelligence. In: 2020 IEEE International Conference on Systems, Man, and Cybernetics (SMC), pp. 2746–2753. IEEE (2020)
43. Theodorou, A.: Why artificial intelligence is a matter of design. In: Artificial Intelligence, pp. 105–131. Brill Mentis (2020)
44. Theodorou, A., Dignum, V.: Towards ethical and socio-legal governance in AI. Nat. Mach. Intell. 2(1), 10–12 (2020)
45. Theodorou, A., Wortham, R.H., Bryson, J.J.: Designing and implementing transparency for real time inspection of autonomous robots. Connect. Sci. 29(3), 230–241 (2017)
46. Tizhoosh, H.: The ethics room - can AI agents be ethical? (Ethics of artificial intelligence in medical imaging)
47. Trist, E.L.: The Evolution of Socio-Technical Systems, vol. 2. Ontario Quality of Working Life Centre Toronto (1981)
48. Aler Tubella, A., Theodorou, A., Dignum, V., Michael, L.: Contestable black boxes. In: Gutiérrez-Basulto, V., Kliegr, T., Soylu, A., Giese, M., Roman, D. (eds.) RuleML+RR 2020. LNCS, vol. 12173, pp. 159–167. Springer, Cham (2020). https://doi.org/10.1007/978-3-030-57977-7_12
49. Tubella, A.A., Theodorou, A., Nieves, J.C.: Interrogating the black box: transparency through information-seeking dialogues. arXiv preprint arXiv:2102.04714 (2021)
50. University Center for Human Values and Center for Information Technology Policy at Princeton: AI ethics case - hiring by machine (2017/18). https://aiethics.princeton.edu/wp-content/uploads/sites/587/2018/12/Princeton-AI-Ethics-Case-Study-5.pdf. Accessed 21 July 2022
51. Weizenbaum, J.: Eliza-a computer program for the study of natural language communication between man and machine. Commun. ACM 9(1), 36–45 (1966). https://doi.org/10.1145/365153.365168
52. Wilson, H., Theodorou, A., Bryson, J.: Slam the brakes: perceptions of moral decisions in driving dilemmas. In: AISafety@ IJCAI (2019)
53. Winfield, A.: Ethical standards in robotics and AI. Nat. Electron. 2(2), 46–48 (2019)
54. Winfield, A.F.T., et al.: IEEE p7001: a proposed standard on transparency. Front. Robot. AI 8, 225 (2021). https://doi.org/10.3389/frobt.2021.665729. https://www.frontiersin.org/article/10.3389/frobt.2021.665729
55. Winfield, A.F., Jirotka, M.: Ethical governance is essential to building trust in robotics and artificial intelligence systems. Philos. Trans. R. Soc. A Math. Phys. Eng. Sci. 376(2133), 20180085 (2018)
56. Wong, J.C., Levin, S.: Self-driving Uber kills Arizona woman in first fatal crash involving pedestrian. The Guardian, March 2018. https://www.theguardian.com/technology/2018/mar/19/uber-self-driving-car-kills-woman-arizona-tempe
57. Wood, D.F.: Problem based learning. BMJ 326(7384), 328–330 (2003). https://doi.org/10.1136/bmj.326.7384.328. https://www.bmj.com/lookup/doi/10.1136/bmj.326.7384.328
58. Wortham, R.H., Theodorou, A.: Robot transparency, trust and utility. Connect. Sci. 29(3), 242–248 (2017). https://doi.org/10.1080/09540091.2017.1313816
59. Wortham, R.H., Theodorou, A., Bryson, J.J.: What does the robot think? Transparency as a fundamental design requirement for intelligent systems. In: Ethics for Artificial Intelligence Workshop, IJCAI-2016 (2016)

Writing Science Fiction as an Inspiration for AI Research and Ethics Dissemination

Carme Torras[1]([✉])[iD] and Luís Gustavo Ludescher[2][iD]

[1] Institut de Robòtica i Informàtica Industrial, CSIC-UPC,
Llorens i Artigas 4-6, 08028 Barcelona, Spain
torras@iri.upc.edu
http://www.iri.upc.edu/people/torras
[2] Department of Computing Science, Umeå University, MIT-huset,
901 87 Umeå, Sweden
luisl@cs.umu.se
https://www.umu.se/en/staff/luis-ludescher/

Abstract. In this chapter we look at science fiction from a perspective that goes beyond pure entertainment. Such literary gender can play an important role in bringing science closer to society by helping to popularize scientific knowledge and discoveries while engaging the public in debates which, in turn, can help direct scientific development towards building a better future for all. Written based on a tutorial given by the first author at ACAI 2021, this chapter addresses, in its first part, how science and science fiction can inspire each other and, in its second part, how science fiction can be used as an educational tool in teaching ethics of AI and robotics. Each of the two parts is supplemented with sections containing the questions asked by the audience during the tutorial as well as the provided answers.

Keywords: Science fiction · Ethics · Artificial intelligence · Robotics · Education · Science and technology · Techno-ethics

1 Learning Objectives

– Familiarize the audience with cases of mutual inspiration between science and fiction, as well as initiatives to promote joint work in multidisciplinary teams.
– Increase awareness of new ethics issues raised by digital technologies, in particular Artificial Intelligence and Robotics.
– Learn about ways in which techno-ethics has been incorporated in engineering and computer science university degrees.
– Get to know recent science fiction literary works that have been used (or can be used) to teach techno-ethics and trigger debate.

The first author is supported by the European Research Council (ERC) within the European Union Horizon 2020 Programme under grant agreement ERC-2016-ADG-741930 (CLOTHILDE: CLOTH manIpulation Learning from DEmonstrations).

M. Chetouani et al. (Eds.): ACAI 2021, LNAI 13500, pp. 322–344, 2023.
https://doi.org/10.1007/978-3-031-24349-3_17

– Providing the attendants with a hands-on experience of the teacher's guide and presentation accompanying the novel *The Vestigial Heart*, so as to enable them to teach a course, some sessions or just trigger debate on "Ethics in AI and Robotics" using these free-of-charge ancillary materials [1].

2 Science and Fiction: Mutual Inspiration

The mutual inspiration between science and fiction is now more apparent than ever, perhaps due to the acceleration of scientific progress in recent decades and the emergence of digital technologies, which seem to have installed us in a fantasy future. Although only a few of us, as William Gibson, the father of Cyberpunk, said in an interview: "The future is here, but it is unevenly distributed." Fiction can also be inspiring in this regard, both by promoting the critical thinking needed to avoid dystopian risks and by guiding scientific research with an ethical perspective that leads us to a more equitable and sustainable future.

Just take a look at today's series, movies and narrative to see the growing presence of science fiction, and how recent scientific discoveries and technological innovations are the seed of most plots. There is no doubt that science is now a great source of inspiration for fiction. Every time science makes a discovery that revolutionizes our view of things, science fiction takes the idea and expresses it to the last detail. The splendid *Black Mirror* series is a good example of this: each chapter takes a digital technology, such as virtual reality, brain implants, social media, learning avatars or online games, and develops it often to the most dramatic extreme. The series is a true masterpiece, with a great ability to raise awareness and generate excellent debate.

And vice versa, there are many examples of science fiction inspiring science, from Jules Verne's "Twenty Thousand Leagues Under the Sea" to "Star Trek" with gadgets like the communicator, the forerunner of the mobile phone, not to mention robots of all kinds that have filled the imagination of past generations and have now become a reality even in the most complex cases such as robots with humanoid physiognomy. The list goes on and on, but perhaps it is worth noting how much space exploration owes to dreamers who imagined what might be on the neighboring planets.

The more we discover about our universe, the more fiction we write; the more fiction we write, the more inspiration there is for scientists. This is the fruitful feedback loop that we would like everyone to share, as adding the ethical ingredient would lead research, technology deployment and innovation to a deeper knowledge not only of what surrounds us, but also of our place in this uncertain future, in which we would like to make utopias possible such as 'evenly distributing' technological resources as suggested by Gibson.

3 Fostering the Confluence of Technoscientists and Writers/Artists

Many initiatives to put in contact SF writers and filmmakers with scientists and technology developers have emerged in recent years to foster the aforementioned feedback loop between science and fiction. Besides joint workshops, interdisciplinary research projects, exhibitions and performances, even top scientific journals have edited special issues devoted to SF inspiration.

A pioneer was the prestigious journal Nature, which to commemorate the fiftieth anniversary of the hypothesis of Hugh Everett III about parallel universes, published a volume entitled Many Worlds [2] containing articles from both researchers in quantum mechanics and SF writers. Its introduction states very clearly what role SF can play in anticipating the benefits and risks of scientific development: "Serious science fiction takes science seriously. [...] Science fiction does not tell us what the future will bring, but at its best it helps us understand what the future will feel like, and how we might feel when one way of looking at the world is overtaken by another."

Among other similar initiatives, MIT Technology Review publishes annually a volume entitled *Twelve Tomorrows* consisting of science fiction stories about different technologies, and Intel promoted *The Tomorrow Project* compiling four short stories about their products projected into the future. Even MIT Press is recently publishing science fiction stories to teach economics, artificial intelligence, robotics and roboethics.

We can thus conclude that science is also beginning to take science fiction seriously.

Let us mention another bridge that has been established between science, technology and science fiction. Neal Stephenson, a renowned science fiction writer, gave a talk entitled "Innovation starvation" [3], where he claimed that scientists had lost imagination after the big challenges of the microprocessor and the space exploration missions, and that they desperately needed imagination from science fiction writers. He said so in front of the Chair of Arizona State University, who took the challenge and created the Center for Science and the Imagination [4], which hosts interdisciplinary teams of artists and scientists to tackle very bold ideas, projects that may not seem feasible today, but they give them a try.

4   New Ethics Issues Raised by Artificial Intelligence

Working on assistive robotics [5], which entails a lot of AI-based human-robot interaction, has made us reflect about ethics and the social implications of the work we do. Many of the issues to be addressed concern programs that learn. As a simple example, some years ago Microsoft placed the Tay chatbot in Twitter to have regular conversations with people and, after only 16 h, it had to be removed because it had turned nasty, racist, sexist and it insulted everyone. This tells us that our interactions in the Internet can be learned by this type of programs that learn, and we should be very careful, so the responsibility is no longer only at the programmer side, it is also at the users side.

You may also have heard that this type of learning programs are prone to biases. Nowadays deep learning is trained with big data, which may have the biases inherent to historical records. There is a famous case of the judicial system in the United States that used a program to determine the probability of recidivism of prisoners and, since it was trained with historical data, it predicted that Afro Americans would recidive more than white people. This is what statistically happened in the past. Biases are in the data, in the history, in our prejudices, not in the learning algorithms themselves. Therefore, it is very important to clean up big data before training the algorithms.

Many of these issues are new, emerging now due to the spreading of AI applications. Another one is related to webs that offer to remove all our interventions in Internet, such as the web called Suicide Machine [6]. You know this cannot be entirely done: some posts can be at least hidden in platforms like Facebook or Twitter, but all the things that were downloaded by particular users to their computers cannot be removed, thus we should be very careful of what we put in these social networks and webs. And there is also the opposite: webs that offer virtual immortality. How? By compiling all our interventions in the net; for instance, all the likes we place, the things we buy, the movies, the photographs, who we interact with, our opinions, etc. are there and configure an avatar of us. They offer this avatar, first when you are alive just to answer mail for you, but for people that die, they offer it also to their families, saying that they can continue interacting with the dead relative. This is also plotted in an episode of the series we were mentioning at the beginning, *Black Mirror*. But it happens also in reality, there are many, up to four at least, webs that offer this virtual immortality [7–10]. Things are changing quickly and we must be aware of all this.

Some other issues raised by AI and social robotics were shared with other technologies in the past. For instance, the incidence on the job market is not new, since in the industrial revolution some tasks or jobs were automated and this had implications for people. Likewise, legal liability, privacy and social divides are not new issues. What is new about AI and all these new digital technologies? That these programs enter domains that were thought to be just human, like communication, feelings and relationships, and decision making. Some of these programs, for instance in the medical area, may make decisions for us and this should be regulated. Moreover, they may intervene in our feelings and relationships; we get attached to these devices that help us so much and may even have a human or quasi-human appearance. Implants and human enhancement through technology raise also many questions, and people are debating a lot about bioconservatism, transhumans and posthumans.

In sum, the field of techno-ethics appeared already some years ago because the AI community and the robotics community are really very worried about all these issues, not to mention military applications. Techno-ethics is a subfield of applied ethics studying both the positive and negative implications of robotics and AI for individuals and society. And it has two branches: one is human ethics applied to robotics and AI, where the history of philosophical thinking about ethics can be applied and some conclusions be drawn for these new issues that are appearing. And a second, new branch is that some codes of ethics are being embedded in the robots and programs themselves, what is termed machine ethics. There are many research groups working on values to be introduced in the programs so that there are some red lines that these programs cannot cross.

Let us talk just a bit about organisms, institutions and professional societies that are putting in place regulations and standards for these new issues that are appearing. For instance, the European Parliament launched the "Civil law rules on robotics"[1] four years ago already, which are very general principles derived from human rights. All regulations we will mention are available on the Internet. Specifically for AI, the high-level expert group on AI issued a draft on "Ethics guidelines for trustworthy AI"[2]. It is very informative, much more detailed than the aforementioned rules for robotics, and very handy for people working in this area of artificial intelligence.

There are also several networks and AI projects that have also issued some ethics guidelines. The Standards Association within the IEEE, the Institute of Electrical and Electronics Engineers, has released the document "Ethically Aligned Design"[3] that covers 12 areas in which robots and intelligent systems are being applied, for instance at schools, in the workplaces, the military also, etc. This is a well developed and very informative document, whose reading for specific issues we recommend very much.

5   Introducing Techno-Ethics in the Curricula

Complementary to regulation is ethics education at all levels, from primary school, to high-school, university and the general citizenship. Here we will focus on introducing techno-ethics in the curricula of technological degrees, and especially teaching it through science fiction narrative. Since several years ago, one of the 18 knowledge areas in the IEEE ACM Computer Science curriculum[4] is "social issues and professional practice", that includes courses on professional ethics, technology and society, and the like.

Barbara Grosz, a professor in computer science at Harvard University, says that "by making ethical reasoning a central element in the curriculum, students can learn to think not only about what technology they could create, but also whether they should create that technology" [11], thus making students aware of the implications of creating specific technologies. And this type of courses is taught now not just in the US, but also in Europe and in several universities worldwide. They were usually taught using philosophical textbooks, which proved to be a bit too abstract for technology students, so more and more professors and teachers are using classical science fiction readings in these courses.

---

[1] https://www.europarl.europa.eu/RegData/etudes/STUD/2016/571379/IPOL_STU (2016)571379_EN.pdf.

[2] https://data.europa.eu/doi/10.2759/346720.

[3] https://standards.ieee.org/wp-content/uploads/import/documents/other/ead_v2.pdf.

[4] https://www.acm.org/binaries/content/assets/education/curricula-recommendations/cc2020.pdf.

6   Science Fiction Narrative Engages Technology Students

Neal Stephenson, whom we mentioned earlier, advocates for the use of science fiction to anticipate future scenarios with ethics implications, and he says that "what science fiction stories can do better than almost anything else is to provide not just an idea for some specific technical innovation, but also to supply a coherent picture of that innovation being integrated into a society, into an economy, and into people's lives" [3], therefore drawing scenarios that permit imagining and discussing about the good and bad aspects of these new technologies.

Judy Goldsmith, who is a professor of computer science at Kentucky University, has been teaching a techno-ethics course using science fiction for seven years already, and she collected her experiences in a very nice paper [12]. One of her conclusions is that "using science fiction to teach ethics allows students to safely discuss and reason about difficult and emotionally charged issues without making the discussion personal".

Then, what type of classic science fiction stories is she and other professors using? Basically, classical works by Isaac Asimov, that anticipated robot nannies, by Philip K. Dick and Mary Shelley, anticipating androids, humanoid robots, and E.T.A. Hoffman, anticipating robot companions, robot nannies, and so on. But these are works from the last century, and nowadays teachers are progressively using more up-to-date, recent science fiction novels and short stories to exemplify future situations, since those depicted in last-century narrative are almost present, if not already past.

Next we mention some novels that we like and recommend, which raise a lot of questions that can foster debate on techno-ethics (Fig. 1). One is *The Windup Girl* by Paolo Bacigalupi, in which a robot that has been designed to serve, when she (because it's a female robot) is worn out and discarded, becomes aware of her having been designed specifically for this purpose and reflects on the issues this raises for and around her.

Ian McEwan, a very renowned writer, recently wrote the novel *Machines Like Me*. Observe the ambiguity of the title, it can be that machines like the person or that machines are like the person. This book raises some issues that are very up to date; for example, who is allowed to initially configure a robot or a learning application for their own purposes, in this case at home. There are several members in the family and each has their own goals and preferences, some of which might be conflicting. Another question is who is entitled to shut the robot or program down when it does something that the current user or someone else doesn't like.

The short-story writer Ted Chiang has become very famous after publishing just two compilations of stories, namely *The Story of Your Life* and *Exhalation*. One of the stories included in the latter is *The Life Cycle of Software Objects*, that deals with software pets, their evolution and the relationship between these pets and their users. Without going into details for each of the books in Fig. 1, we suggest that you have a look at them because their stories deal also with this type of topics.

Modern Science Fiction related to Ethics in Robotics & AI

Carme Torras @ ACAI 2021   28/65

Fig. 1. Examples of fiction narrative that can be used to trigger debate on techno-ethics.

As mentioned earlier, MIT press is becoming very interested in publishing science fiction narrative that helps teach courses on techno-ethics, because there is a shortage of that type of materials. For instance, not long ago they published *Robot Futures* by Illah Nourbakhsh, who is a professor in computer science at Carnegie-Mellon University, and he teaches a course based on these short stories. Along this line, MIT Press offered to translate my novel, originally written in Catalan and entitled *La Mutació Sentimental* (whose literal English translation would be "The Sentimental Mutation") and published it with the title *The Vestigial Heart*, together with ancillary materials to teach a course on "Ethics in social robotics and AI.

This course and materials will be described in the second part of the tutorial, but before let us open for questions, comments and a bit of debate.

7   Question Answering - First Round

Question from Audience: *I have the feeling that sometimes series like 'Black Mirror', for example, instead of making people think about some issues, in some way they normalize some dystopian future, and I don't know if you have some thoughts on this or some hints.*

Carme's Answer: This is a very nice and relevant question, since it is true that most science fiction narratives are dystopias, not precisely utopias. But I would say that authors who write these dystopias do it because they are optimistic. Why are they optimistic? Because they raise these issues to make people aware of what may happen, and they are optimistic in the sense that they think people can manage to change the course of history towards more utopian futures, so that they can somehow take measures to avoid bad uses of technology and head towards good futures instead. You may say this is turning things upside down somehow, but not, I really believe this, I myself wrote this book, *The Vestigial Heart*, which you can interpret that is a dystopia.

I will say a bit about the plot because it will come out in the second part of the tutorial. It's about a 13 years old girl, from our times, who has a terminal illness and her parents decide to 'cryogenize' her, meaning to frozen her somehow. She wakes up 100 years from now and is adopted by a mother of that future, where each person has a personal assistant, that is a robot, and where several things in the minds of people have changed, have evolved, for instance some feelings, some emotions have dried out, have disappeared, and other capacities have emerged. This girl of course remembers very well her biological parents, her teachers, everyone in her past life, and it's a big contrast for her in face of the new society, with her new mother and teachers, and so on. So, you can think that this is a dystopia, and it is, because she has a bad time at the beginning in this future society until other things happen as the plot develops. But I wrote it precisely because I'm optimistic, and I think we can orient our research towards what can be more beneficial to society. I think in general the research community is oriented to try to increase the well-being of people, to remove or avoid discrimination, to try to close digital gaps, and so on, but sometimes they are not aware of the implications.

Thus, I wrote that novel, about 13 years ago, and also other novels afterwards, first to reflect myself on what type of research I would like to pursue with my group. We have group discussions regularly, once a month, about what type of projects we would like to develop. And I hope that science fiction and these dystopias can be useful in this way of picturing and making people aware that the technology they are devising will shape humanity, will shape the way we will become, and in this sense I think dystopias are written by optimists, as I mentioned. But it's very important to accompany, not just leave students or general public watch and greet these dystopias without reflecting together with them about the consequences. I really like to use science fiction narrative to raise awareness, not just as an entertainment and to give scary views of what the future may look like.

I hope to have answered your question, which is very pertinent, since it is true that this type of dystopias attracts people, readers and movie watchers more than happy utopias, which are perhaps less exciting, but this is something we have to go with, that we cannot remedy, and the media sometimes amplify these dangerous futures to get larger audiences.

Question from Audience: *I just read the 'I, Robot' series and a lot of these stories that take place in those far away space stations or something that's clearly not possible today, so do you think it is more complicated to read those as an ethical exercise and then transfer them to the world as it is today? Does the fact that the setting is so far in the future make it more complicated to actually use it as a useful exercise rather than just some story in the future, especially in teaching, if you're using it as teaching material?*

Carme's Answer: Well, I like better the type of science fiction that amplifies the problems we have in the current society, in the current world. Not so much these space operas that do not have much contact with our reality. I'm more in favor of social science fiction, like this *Black Mirror* series I was mentioning, which takes a technology that is available today and maybe enhances it a lot to extremes, but that amplifies essentially problems that are now embryonic, that are really in a seed nowadays. Anyway, I will later explain an experience I had recently in which several writers were contacted by a publisher to write some short stories based on Mars. Well, now there are people that go to the space for tourism and things like that, and we were writing stories based on Mars, but stories that could happen in a new settlement today and deal with the needs these people would have. For instance, I wrote about robot companions in Mars, and this is not space opera, it is another type of amplification, as I mentioned, of things that happen here on Earth, but in another society that is starting from scratch, so with new politics, new social organization, new everything. This permits imagining other worlds, another type of relations with technology. I'm in favor of this, it is not many years into the future, but just now going to the Moon and setting up a new society. I like very much these simulation strategies within groups to hypothesize futures that could happen, those that we would like to happen and others that we would like to avoid. But I agree that some of these stories in the very distant future are not really very relevant to the problems ethics today wants to address and tackle. So, we have to choose somehow.

Question from Audience: *my question is about user acceptance, how do you implement that? Based on your research on assistive robotics and the way science fiction has amplified possible risks, how do you consider user acceptance in this context?*

Carme's Answer: Well, this is one of the topics of the materials I have developed, acceptance of robots by people, and it is very important for the type of research we are doing. As you saw, we do a lot of human-robot interaction and sometimes with people with disabilities. For instance, this experience I told before about a robot supplying cognitive training to people with mild cognitive disabilities, that we performed during the pandemic, taught us a lot about this acceptance. We were a bit hesitant that our robots could scare these people, or that they would just refuse to interact with them because they were strange or things that they were not used to interact with. And they were elderly people, more than 70 years old with mild disability. So, it was something we thought could be difficult, and it was just the other way around. Actually, we really struggled to make those robots very friendly, they have a face with cartoon-like traits and have a repertoire of expressions of consent, engagement, happiness, and so on. We tried to make them as engaging as possible and it was a success in the sense that the patients wanted to interact more and they were not scared at all. Maybe this was favored because they had been confined for several months, not interacting, and this was an activity that attracted them a lot when they could get out and go to the Alzheimer Foundation and interact with these robots. Thus, we think that if we struggle to make these robots friendly and very respectful to people, the acceptance would be high. But, as I said, it is an important topic many studies have been touching upon, as will appear in the next section.

8   Plotting, Writing and Teaching with *The Vestigial Heart*

Now let's come to the second part of the tutorial, in which we will explain how to teach ethics using science fiction, and in particular with the book *The Vestigial Heart*, as well as some lessons we have learned and suggestions for future initiatives.

The Catalan version of the book appeared 13 years ago, then it was translated into Spanish, and finally, three years ago, it was translated into English by MIT Press, as already mentioned. The leitmotif of this novel is "it is the relationships that we have constructed which in turn shape us". This was said by the philosopher Robert Solomon in his book *The Passions*. He said so in relation to people, namely our relationships with our parents, with our friends, with our teachers, with our children, with everyone, shape the way we are. We would be different if we had interacted with other people, different persons. Then, since we have so much interaction with technology nowadays, it is very important that we think very deeply what technology we would like to develop, because it will shape the way we will be and especially future generations. Therefore, we have a tremendous responsibility in the type of technology we are developing.

So, what is the techno-ethics course based on *The Vestigial Heart* about? The book includes the novel, an appendix with 24 ethics questions raised by scenes in the novel, and some hints for a debate. These are all contained in the physical book, the paper book. And then there are online ancillary materials: a guide for teaching 8 sessions on ethics in social robotics and AI, following the chapters in the novel and including references for further reading; and there is also a hundred-slide presentation that teachers can adapt, extend and use as they wish (Fig. 2). These materials are being used in several universities in the USA, in Europe and also in Australia. They can be downloaded from this address [1] free of charge, by just filling up a form with some data on the envisaged usage. These materials have also been translated into Catalan and Spanish, as well as adapted to high-school by Pagès Editors [13].

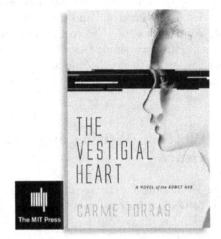

Course on Ethics in Social Robotics and AI

Four items:

- A **novel** about a future society in which people rely on personal-assistant robots to navigate daily life.

- An **appendix** with 24 ethics questions raised by the novel, as well as hints to trigger a debate.

- An **online teacher's guide** for 6-8 sessions on "Ethics in Social Robotics and AI" following the chapters in the novel and including scholarly references for further reading.

- A **100-slide presentation** that teachers can use and extend as desired.

https://mitpress.mit.edu/books/vestigial-heart

Carme Torras @ ACAI 2021   32/65

Fig. 2. Techno-ethics course materials.

There are six main chapters in these materials: Designing the 'perfect' assistant; Robot appearance and emotion; Robots in the workplace; Robots in education; Human-robot interaction and human dignity; and Social responsibility and robot morality; and they are wrapped up with an introductory and a concluding chapter.

Starting with the introductory one, first there is a quick overview of several ethical theories from the history of human ethics that can be applied to robotics. There are many quite diverse theories, like utilitarianism, deontologism, virtue ethics, social justice, common goods, religious ethics, information ethics, and many of them are somehow contradictory. Since no single theory is appropriate for addressing all the issues (specially the new ones), along the materials, a pragmatic option is taken, which has been termed 'hybrid ethics' and is advocated by Wallach and Allen in their book [14]. It entails combining top-down theories, those applying rational principles to derive norms, like virtue ethics for instance, with bottom-up theories, which infer general guidelines from a specific situation. This pragmatic option is very common nowadays and, along this line, since there are different cultures, countries and values for each of them, the general theories need to be applied and instantiated for different cultures, values and circumstances.

We will give a glimpse of the chapters and the issues addressed in each of them. More details can be found in the tutorial slides [15]. All chapters have the same structure (Fig. 3). They start with some highlights from the novel, then some ethical background is provided and 4 questions are posed to students. Next, hints for a discussion are provided mainly for the teacher to foster a debate on each question. In later chapters, there are revisited issues that reappear from different viewpoints, and finally many scholarly references for further reading and for suggesting projects to students are provided.

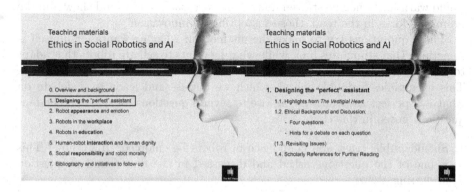

Fig. 3. Chapters and structure.

Before entering the six main chapters, let us summarize the plot of the novel. Celia, a-thirteen-year-old girl cryogenically frozen because of her terminal illness, is cured and brought back to life 100 years later in order to be adopted. Aside from her memories, she brings something else from the past: feelings and emotions that are no longer in existence. These are what most attract Silvana, a middle-aged woman who works as an emotional masseuse trying to recover the sensations humans have lost. Celia's feelings are also precious research material for Leo, a bioengineer who is designing a creativity prosthesis for the mysterious Doctor Craft, owner of the leading robotics company, CraftER.

8.1 Designing the 'Perfect' Assistant

Doctor Craft at the beginning of the book is very obsessed in getting the prosthesis because he is getting old, he was very creative in the past, and now he wants his creativity to be stimulated. He makes this reflection: "... A good choice of stimuli, that's the secret to wellbeing. [...] we can't change man or turn his brain upside down, we can't modify even the smallest reaction. The only option is to control his surroundings, control what he feels through the stimuli he receives. A key idea, but when he presented it as the leitmotif of the new line of robots, no one gave it a bit's worth of notice". Note that he is the owner of the company and the main chief that provides ideas. "Too simple, they said. How short-sighted! [...] they couldn't tailor-make a ROB for everyone; they had to come up with a generic ROB that was highly adaptable and, most important of all, one that could achieve a very fast adaptation. If it took one week for a ROB to work out how to wake up its PROP", its PROP is its user, "or how much sugar to put in his coffee, the whole idea would go down the drain". Thus, he is advocating for having very personalized robots that adapt to the user immediately. And, as mentioned, he is obsessed with having a creativity prosthesis for him. And the quotation continues: "what he [Doctor Craft] wants is a creativity prosthesis. Or an assistant [...]; something that would stimulate him to think differently, that would warn him when he started down well-worn paths and would show him the promising forks in the road, those susceptible to innovation".

These quotations try to make the distinction: what he wants for himself is something that stimulates him, while what he wants to sell are robots that adapt to people, and give them what they want, without having to think or do much. This exemplifies a double moral, which we discuss and leads to a debate on what is a perfect assistant, giving rise to several questions for debate. The four questions posed in this chapter are:

1. Should public trust and confidence in robots be enforced? If so, how? This is one of the questions asked and discussed in the first round of question answering above.
2. Is it admissible that robots/applications be designed to generate addiction? Because you know that apps are sometimes designed to generate addiction, especially from young people.
3. Should the possibility of deception be actively excluded at design time?
4. Could robots be used to control people?

When giving a course, these questions are raised and then, as already said, in the teacher's guide there are some hints for a debate, but here we will continue to other chapters. We cannot go over the eight sessions in just one hour!

8.2   Robot Appearance and Emotion

In the second chapter, which is about robot appearance and simulating emotions, some highlights are as follows: "as a birthday present, Lu [who is the adoptive mother] gave me [Celia] a robot. [...] it has a kind of head with no nose, mouth or ears, it just has two cameras, and a screen embedded in its chest. It's called ROBbie." In another scene: "Celia, touched by the words, looks for his eyes: no friend had ever sworn their loyalty so convincingly, but two black holes bring her back down to earth. Though not entirely, [...] she watches the robot out of the corner of her eye and it pleases her to see his dignified posture, gently swinging his strong, shiny arms. It feels good to walk along beside him, she feels protected, she can trust him. What does it matter that he doesn't have eyes, people don't look at each other anymore anyway." This is about trust generation by robots, and also the contrast with the society of the times, 100 years from now, in which people don't look at each other, they are so little empathetic that they don't really relate. This topic usually provokes strong debates.

The questions triggered by these and other highlights (Fig. 4) are:

1. How does robot appearance influence public acceptance?
2. What are the advantages and dangers of robot simulating emotions? This is another big topic: robots simulating emotions and people getting cheated or getting deceived because of this; ethics regulations and education should try to avoid this confusion in grown-ups and, especially, in children.
3. Have you heard of/experienced the "uncanny valley" effect? This effect is that people get more attached to robots, or to artificial creatures, the more anthropomorphic they are. For instance, the robot in the movie Wall-E has a kind of head with eyes and two things similar to arms, wheels that resemble legs, so it has a kind of anthropomorphic cartoon-like appearance. As robots get more and more anthropomorphic, both physically and also cognitively, people get more attached to them because we empathize more somehow. The empathy and the attachment increases up to a point in which an extreme similarity to people, but with an strange look, provokes repulsion. The growing acceptance curve suddenly goes down abruptly, this is the uncanny valley effect. This has to be taken into account by robot designers, and it is the reason why robots often have a cartoon-like face, because this engages people without cheating.
4. Should emotional attachment to robots be encouraged? Well, this depends on the situation, so it is discussed at length in the materials.

8.3   Robots in the Workplace

Here we will just highlight one passage from the novel. In the materials, more quotations are included for each chapter, and everything is well specified for instructors to be comfortable and ease their teaching. The high says "Leo looks up at the ever-watching electronic eyes [in his workplace] and thinks how lucky he is that they can't read his mind." This is anticipating that if, in the future, we wear implants, our boss may be able to read what we are thinking. And this poses questions of privacy, and also of property rights. "ROBco [which is Leo's robot] is waiting expectantly next to him, ready to act as his assistant." And Leo says: "I can't turn off and back on again and pick up where I left off, like you do [because robots are very quick at changing the context], see if you can finally build that into your model". They are cooperating at work and, of course, robots have to have a model of their user in order to be useful, so this raises many questions also of human-robot cooperation and these are discussed.

A theme to debate is how to define the boundaries between human and robot labor in a shared task, so that not only throughput is maximized, which is what the owner of the company wants, but, more importantly, the rights and dignity of

2.1. Highlights from *The Vestigial Heart*

Chapters 9/12 - Celia

As a birthday present, Lu [adoptive mother] gave me a robot. [..] it has a kind of <u>head with no nose, mouth or ears, it just has two cameras</u>, and a screen embedded in its chest. It's called ROBbie.

[..] Celia, touched by the words, looks for his eyes: no friend had ever sworn their loyalty so convincingly, but <u>two black holes bring her back down to earth. Though not entirely.</u>

[..] she watches the robot out of the corner of her eye and it pleases her to see his dignified posture, gently swinging his strong, shiny arms. It feels good to walk along beside him, she feels protected, she can trust him. <u>What does it matter that he doesn't have eyes, people don't look at each other anymore anyway.</u>"

At the Disasters stand, Leo is puzzled by a realistic <u>mechanical baby</u>. [..] What woman could resist the charm of a baby that smiles when she coos at it, that she can cuddle at will while watching her favorite program, that recognizes her voice and crawls along behind her, flattering her with sweet noises? Well no sir, the product didn't take off, almost certainly because it's too much like the real thing, déjà vu.

"Ethics in Social Robotics and AI" based on *The Vestigial Heart* @ MIT Press, 2018   /104

Fig. 4. Highlights to discuss about robot appearance and emotion.

professionals are preserved. This relates to some passages in which Leo struggles on two fronts: his privacy and intellectual property rights may be violated by the device they have that can somehow read his mind; and he struggles also to make his robot "understand" that they have different skills and, to optimize collaboration, they need to do what each does best and communicate on common grounds. This is trying to get to the utopia that robots and people collaborate using the best of themselves. The questions for this chapter are as follows.

1. Would robots primarily create or destroy jobs? This is the million-Euro question, that since the industrial revolution the media raises constantly, now concerning robots and AI, so this is discussed at length in the materials.
2. How should work be organized to optimize human-robot collaboration?
3. Do experiments on human-robot interaction require specific oversight? This is so, there are specific rules and guidelines to perform experiments with humans, in particular in EU projects. All these ethics issues need to be taken into account and, for example, consent forms and information sheets must be supplied to participants in experiments.
4. Do intellectual property laws need to be adapted to human-robot collaborations? Of course, yes, so these are discussed.

Just a glimpse on some data provided in the materials. In a wide survey performed by Frey and Osborne already in 2013 [16], about 47% of the total US employment was then at risk of being automated. And high wages and educational attainment have negative correlation with such risk, since the tasks that are being mechanized or automated are usually those that have low quality value. Three features that preserve jobs for humans are: (i) requiring negotiation, since humans are very good at this and the required capacities are difficult to be automated; (ii) needing creative solutions in front of unknown problems, unexpected situations, for instance doing maintenance of facilities that have broken down; and (iii) entailing empathizing with the situation of other people. Thus, jobs related to community and social services have the lowest percentage chances of being automated, whereas telemarketing has the highest percentage, this is the conclusion of that survey.

In another study, McKinsey & Company [17] plotted several jobs and, after interviewing many people, came up with an ordered list of jobs from the easiest to the hardest to be automated (Fig. 5). Among the hardest is education because teachers need to empathize with the students, motivate them, and transmit the life experience they have and their passion for knowledge.

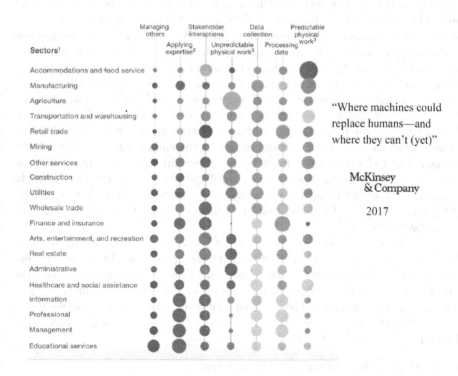

Fig. 5. Adapted from [17].

It is worth pointing out that what is susceptible of being automated are tasks, rather than entire jobs. A job description consists of several tasks, those most repetitive and predictable can be automated easily, but jobs often also entail other tasks that require intuition, creativity and empathy, the three human traits that were highlighted as the most difficult to be automated. This is well aligned with what happens in the novel, thus providing good examples and favoring the discussion of these issues.

Another conclusion from a related study is that "the best solutions are always going to come from minds and machines working together", thus taking the best of both type of agents. And the challenge is, of course, not to fall into complete technological dependency. There is a big risk of being so dependent on machines that if there were a blowout we could not recover, so it's important to retain human autonomy and avoid this dependency.

8.4 Robots in Education

Celia goes to a school in which teachers do not know anything, they just search and help students to search because the net, called EDUsys, which is more sophisticated than ours, has all the knowledge, so that students do not have to learn to think, they just learn to search. In a passage from the novel, we are told that the teacher has labeled Celia a rebel because, ignoring his advice, she insists on competing with machines. Why? Because apparently she has not understood the net's search mechanisms and, faced with a question, she stops and thinks about it, trying to make up an answer. Therefore, Celia gets very bad grades and is questioned all the time, just because, when faced with a problem, she tries to solve it by herself, not through search mechanisms. Since she does badly at school, her mother puts her a home teacher, Silvana, who is another big character in the novel. Silvana will have to work hand in hand with ROBbie, Celia's robot, because everyone knows that if the child turns out to be a rule-breaker, like Celia, the robot must learn to restrain them, to counteract their impulses to break rules. Robots are customizable for a reason, they have to complement their PROPs to make a good team user-robot, but that is the last thing Silvana expected to hear, that she will have to train a robot, because she is against technology.

In the novel there are the "pro-techno's", who are pro-technology, like Leo, Doctor Craft and all the people that work devising robots and technology in general, and the "anti-techno's", like Silvana, who form a community called "the ComU", in which they refuse to be assisted by robots, they want to be just fully autonomous humans. The confrontation between them permits exemplifying many of the ethical issues that are raised by digital technologies nowadays. The questions raised in this chapter are as follows:

1. Are there limits to what a robot can teach?
2. Where is the boundary between helping and creating dependency?
3. Who should define the values robot teachers would transmit and encourage?
4. What should the relationship be between robot teachers and human teachers?

8.5   Human-Robot Interaction and Human Dignity

The confrontation between pro and anti-technology perspectives can be observed in some dialogues between Silvana and Leo, who often get into this fight. In a passage from the novel Silvana says: "machines that augment human capabilities seem like a great idea to me: without remote manipulators surgeons couldn't operate on a microscopic scale and, without INFerrers, we'd take too long overthinking the consequences of our decisions ... it's ROBs that I reject, and the personal link that is established between them and their PROPs [their users] that ends up hogging people's most intimate time and space. You said it yourself [Leo]: you don't need anything else ... and, in the end, you become wooden like them."

In another passage Leo is discussing with her and he says: "I don't understand [what you say]. All ROBs are developed to serve people.", and Silvana answers: "Exactly. It's just that the service is often poisoned. Why do you think we are against those mechanical contraptions? [...] Because we're snobs? Well, no. [...] Overprotective robots produce spoiled people, slaves produced despots, and entertainers brainwash their own PROPs. And worst of all you people don't care what happens to the rest of us as long as they [the robots] sell".

The questions for this chapter are as follows:

1. Could robot decision-making undermine human freedom and dignity? Of course, this is a big risk and we, who are working in this field of human-robot interaction, especially in the assistive context, are very aware of it and discuss it often.
2. Is it acceptable for robots to behave as emotional surrogates? If so, in what cases? It could be cases in which faking emotions can be helpful, for instance, as we said, to engage people, as long as people are aware that they are interacting just with a machine. Machines showing happiness or sadness in particular circumstances can facilitate a friendly interaction. In some cases, like in emergency situations, a robot showing emotions can be more convincing to warn or guide people than an expressionless robot. But these are very specific circumstances, in general faking emotions, we think, should be avoided or used very cautiously.
3. Could robots be used as therapists for the mentally disabled? It depends on the circumstances and, of course, it has to be under human therapist control.
4. How adaptive/tunable should robots be? Are there limits to human enhancement by technological means? This will be briefly addressed in the Conclusion section.

8.6   Social Responsibility and Robot Morality

This is the subject of the last chapters in the novel, but we did not include any highlights from them to avoid making spoilers in case some readers want to read the novel with some intrigue. The questions for this chapter are as follows:

1. Can reliability/safety be guaranteed? This is a main issue. How can hacking/vandalism be prevented? Think of autonomous vehicles, for example.
2. Who is responsible for the actions of robots, of vehicles, of programs, of everything? Should moral behavior be modifiable in robots, machines, programs?
3. When should a society's well-being prevail over the privacy of personal data?
4. What digital divides may robotics, artificial intelligence, etc., cause?

9   Concluding Remarks and Other Writing Initiatives

We would like to end this chapter by proposing and showing two experiences in collective writing. One of them was already mentioned, and we will explain another one that is related to a question we posed in Sect. 8.5: are there limits to human enhancement by technological means? Actually, this is a question in posthumanism which now is raising a lot of discussion in the media, and there is a debate between bioconservatists, transhumanists and posthumanists on whether this human enhancement is ethical, in what circumstances, and what social implications it would have.

Thus, there was an experiment during the pandemic in which nine writers, Carme among them, were asked to picture the Barcelona of 2059. In particular, we did a lot of worldbuilding by virtually getting together and trying to imagine what would happen in Barcelona in that year, and we pictured a dystopian Barcelona city that had degenerated a lot in all fronts (sustainability, poverty, discriminations). But there was an island in the seafront, on a platform, that we called Neo Icària, in which there was a utopian society whose members had to sign a contract with a company that ruled the island. The contract guaranteed them free heatlhcare, jobs that they liked and everything else they needed, but they had to give up their privacy, accepting to take an implant (chosen among three options) yearly, which was used for the company to monitor their behavior all the time, physically and psychically. Some people signed, whereas others chose not to. And some of the problems this entails are explored in the book, which has been very successful and has been generating many discussions. It was a very nice experience of writing together with other authors and getting into this discussion on bioconservatism, transhumanism, and posthumanism (Fig. 6).

One of the issues that were raised in the plot is related to people with disabilities, who wanted to enter the island even if they were monitored. But implants can not only palliate disabilities, but also provide new capacities, like more strength, exoskeletons, night vision, etc., which could, for instance, be used for military purposes. Another distinction worth making is whether this technology is invasive, i.e. connected to the nervous system, or not. But even when it is not connected to the nervous system, it has implications in our brain, because our brain is plastic. For instance, there was a real experiment of putting a sixth finger in a hand, which could be handy for playing guitar or for doing some works at home. The extra finger was activated by the muscles in the forearm but not connected to the nervous system. In the motor-cortex we have a mirror of our five fingers, but the brain is so plastic that after continuous usage of that sixth finger, it was also mirrored in the motor-cortex. This tells us that we should be

Are there limits to human enhancement by technological means?
Bioconservatism / Transhumanism / Posthumanism

Some distinctions:
- Alleviate disability / Improve capacities / New capacities
- No connection / with connection to the nervous system (peripheral / central)

 ■CSIC ● Carme Torras @ ACAI 2021   62/65

Fig. 6. Some distinctions on technology-based human enhancement.

very careful of what technology we are using, because it is really shaping not just our way of behaving, but also our brain and nervous system.

Another collective experience was the one we mentioned earlier of imagining that now it was possible to travel to Mars and establish a new society. This was open to utopia, to make a society that was more egalitarian, guaranteeing well-being to everyone, without discrimination, without any of the issues we handle here on Earth nowadays. We got together for worldbuilding and it was a very nice experience again. While some authors wrote about politics in Mars, the health system, etc., Carme wrote a short story about a moral robot, which has some embedded values, is adaptable to the user, reconfigurable, and particularly handy in Mars, with all its peculiarities. Actually, the story is very optimistic and robots are very helpful to the first inhabitants of Mars, which concludes this chapter in a positive way by suggesting that, although technology poses many challenges, it can also be very helpful and lead us to a better, more egalitarian future. So, the question we leave open is "what role should the human being and the machine play in this *pas de deux* in which we are irrevocably engaged?"

9.1   Further Reading

As supplementary materials and readings, some suggestions follow. On the topic of the role of science fiction, we recommend Stephenson's *Innovation Starvation*

[3] and Torras' *Science fiction: A mirror for the future of humankind* [18]. On ethics education initiatives in the digital age, we recommend the aforementioned articles [12] and [5] as well as a lesson plan for robot ethics from the website Teach with Movies [19] based on the film *Robot and Frank*. And finally, as already indicated, the novel *The Vestigial Heart* and its associated teaching materials can be found on the MIT Press website [1].

10   Question Answering - Second Round

Question from Audience: *hi, thank you for your talk. I was wondering if you think there is an issue with the fact that most people actually get their information from social media, from newspapers, from these books, but not directly from actual science articles about the development of robots or AI that is currently going on. Especially considering that we have a bit of an iffy time with people's trust in science, more so lately with the pandemic when there has also been a misinformation time going on at the same time. So, just as a scientist, what is our responsibility in this case? How do we make sure that the information that people actually get is consistent with what is going on in science? And also, because of this disconnection between science and science fiction, how do we make sure that science fiction doesn't villainize science in a way that we are somehow endorsing these dystopic futures that are presented in novels? Even if they are only a science personal inspiration or most of the time, as you mentioned, they are rather what not to do than what to do. Yeah, this was quite a lengthy question, but I hope I was clear in my concerns about it.*

Carme's Answer: yes, you were very clear and these are very important concerns, especially for us working on AI, robotics, and this type of human-machine interaction that is growing fast, especially because we interact with mobiles every day. I have many answers to your questions. One is that we have a responsibility, as scientists, to disseminate correct views of what are the benefits and risks of technology. Because sometimes there is a lot of hype going on saying that technology can do a lot more than it can, both in the positive way and in the negative way. For instance, the idea that machines will get conscious, more intelligent than humans, so they will take over and humans will be extinguished. I don't think machines will get conscious, at least not in the next 50 years, as some are foreseeing. Thus, we should be very rigorous in the information we supply to the media not to hype in any of the two directions. Another answer is that we should promote techno-ethics education at all levels. I was advocating especially for the designers of this technology: engineers, computer scientists, university students in technological degrees, and so on. But also I would like to enforce such education in high school, as I did, and in primary school, because from the very beginning children need to know about how to use technology for their own benefit, not for the benefit of companies and not to get addicted and fall in the traps that these big corporations are setting, which make us click constantly and be dependent on technology.

Therefore, I am enforcing in my local context that primary schools have also this type of courses and education in ethics in technology. But sometimes the main barrier are teachers that are not very familiar with technology, and they themselves are somehow afraid that children will know more about apps than them. There are some experiences in which children teach teachers how to manage these apps, how to deal with technology, because they know better. And teachers give them clear criteria on how to use this technology for their benefit and advise them about the risks also. In this way, there is a mutual interchange of information and values, which I think is very positive. And the same for the general public, I am constantly accepting to participate in all types of forums and outreach activities to disseminate this need for ethics and to accompany all this science fiction narrative and all this science and technology dissemination with these values and these ethics guidelines.

Finally, I am also enforcing a lot the confluence of technology and humanities, this being why I am organizing forums on this confluence at conferences and also in all types of contexts. My university, the Technical University of Catalonia, only has technology degrees, so there are no humanities, no medical degrees being taught there. Thus, for students to take humanities subjects, an agreement has been made with another university that teaches humanities, so that students in engineering can take credits in humanities for their degrees. In sum, I think it is important to enforce this confluence at all education levels.

References

1. Torras, C.: The Vestigial Heart, together with instructor resources. https://mitpress.mit.edu/books/vestigial-heart. Accessed 12 Jan 2022
2. Many Worlds. Nature **448**(7149), 1–104 (2007)
3. Stephenson, N.: Innovation starvation. World Policy J. **28**(3), 11–16 (2011)
4. Center for Science and the Imagination. https://csi.asu.edu/. Accessed 12 Jan 2022
5. Torras, C.: Assistive robotics: research challenges and ethics education initiatives. DILEMATA Int. J. Appl. Ethics **30**, 63–77 (2019)
6. Web 2.0 Suicide Machine. http://suicidemachine.org/. Accessed 12 Jan 2022
7. ETER9. https://www.eter9.com/. Accessed 12 Jan 2022
8. HereAfter. https://www.hereafter.ai/. Accessed 12 Jan 2022
9. Replika. https://replika.ai/. Accessed 12 Jan 2022
10. Legathum. https://legathum.com/. Accessed 12 Jan 2022
11. Grosz, B.J., et al.: Embedded ethics: integrating ethics across CS education. Commun. ACM **62**(8), 54–61 (2019)
12. Burton, E., Goldsmith, J., Mattei, N.: How to teach computer ethics through science fiction. Commun. ACM **61**(8), 54–64 (2018)
13. Torras, C.: La Mutació Sentimental. https://www.pageseditors.cat/ca/guia-didactica-la-mutacio-sentimental.html. Accessed 12 Jan 2022
14. Wallach, W., Allen, C.: Moral Machines: Teaching Robots Right from Wrong. Oxford University Press, Oxford (2008)
15. Torras, C.: Writing Science Fiction ACAI Tutorial. https://www.iri.upc.edu/people/torras/2021-10-14_ACAI-Tutorial_CarmeTorras.pdf. Accessed 12 Jan 2022
16. Frey, C.B., Osborne, M.: The future of employment (2013)

17. McKinsey & Company: Jobs lost, jobs gained: What the future of work will mean for jobs, skills, and wages. https://www.mckinsey.com/featured-insights/future-of-work/jobs-lost-jobs-gained-what-the-future-of-work-will-mean-for-jobs-skills-and-wages. Accessed 12 Jan 2022

18. Torras, C.: Science-fiction: a mirror for the future of humankind. IDEES **48**, 1–11 (2020)

19. Teach with Movies: Robot and Frank. https://teachwithmovies.org/robot-and-frank/. Accessed 14 Jan 2022

Argumentation

Argumentation in AI

Bettina Fazzinga[1,2](✉) [ID] and René Mellema[3] [ID]

[1] DICES, University of Calabria, Rende, Italy
bettina.fazzinga@unical.it
[2] ICAR-CNR, Rende, Italy
[3] Umeå University, Umeå, Sweden
rene.mellema@cs.umu.se

1 Learning Objectives

In this chapter, we focus on abstract argumentation and probabilistic abstract argumentation. In particular, we aim at providing the reader with a proper knowledge of how dialogues and disputes are modeled as abstract argumentation graphs and how analysts reason over them. We illustrate the concepts of arguments and attacks, and the most popular semantics, that are properties defined over graphs. We discuss the fundamental problems arising when reasoning over argumentation graphs and some probabilistic ways of encoding uncertainty about the occurrence of arguments and/or attacks.

2 Introduction

The classical definition of argumentation is that it is a verbal, social, and rational activity aimed at convincing a reasonable critic of the acceptability of a standpoint. In fact, argumentation it is related to philosophy and law, but it has become very popular in AI due to its capability of dealing with uncertainty and providing explanations.

Argumentation-based techniques model disputes and dialogues as graphs of arguments (nodes) and attacks (edges). The nodes of the graph encode the arguments, that are what is said by the agents participating the disputes, while the edges of the graph encode the contradictions/contrasts between arguments. To show this, we will use the following example, taken from [6].

Example 1. Assume we have two people talking about weather forecasts, with different points of view, that generate the following dispute with the two conflicting arguments a and b:

a = 'Tomorrow it will rain because the national weather forecast says so.'

b = 'Tomorrow it will not rain because the regional weather forecast says so.'

How can we model this dispute? We have two possibilities. In the case that we have some reason to believe that one forecast is more reliable than the other, for example if we believe that the regional forecast might be more reliable than

© Springer Nature Switzerland AG 2023
M. Chetouani et al. (Eds.): ACAI 2021, LNAI 13500, pp. 347–362, 2023.
https://doi.org/10.1007/978-3-031-24349-3_18

the national one, we can model the dispute by putting an attack from b to a, that can be depicted as follows:

However, if we do not believe that the regional forecast is more reliable than the national one, we can model the situation as a mutual attack:

We will also consider a second example, also taken from [6].

Example 2. Assume we have a suspect for some crime, and an eyewitness, leading to a dispute with the following arguments:

a = 'The suspect is guilty because an eyewitness, Mr. Smith, says so'

b = 'Mr. Smith is notoriously alcohol-addicted and it is proven that he was completely drunk the night of the crime, therefore his testimony should not be taken into account'

In this case, a and b are not incompatible with one another, since the fact that Mr. Smith was drunk is not in contrast with the fact that the suspect is guilty. However, the fact that Mr. Smith was drunk affects the reason why the suspect should be believe to be guilty, and therefore we can model this situation as b attacks a (and not vice-versa). This means we get the following graph:

What is important to note from these examples is that the attack relations do not always correspond to conflicts in a strict logical sense. Instead, the attack relations are defined based on what is "reasonable". This is done by the analyst modelling the dispute based on their perspective of the situation and the strength of the arguments.

The general framework that we will be discussing in this tutorial is *abstract argumentation*.

3   Abstract Argumentation

The abstract argumentation framework was first proposed by [13]. The framework is called abstract, since the construction of the arguments and the reasons why arguments attack each other and the motivation that led to the graph at hand are completely ignored, and all the focus is on reasoning over the graph. The definition of an *abstract argumentation framework* is as follows:

Definition 1. *An abstract argumentation framework (AAF) is a pair $AF = \langle A, D \rangle$ consisting of a set A of arguments, and a binary relation $D \subseteq A \times A$, called the defeat (or, equivalently, attack) relation.*

Here the relationship D indicates which arguments attack other arguments, so if $(a, b) \in D$, then we say that argument a attacks b. The arguments themselves represent abstract entities that can be attacked and/or be attacked by other arguments. The abstract argumentation frameworks are drawn as graphs, with the direction of the arrows indicating the direction of the attack. This is the same style as we used in Example 1 and Example 2.

Since there are attacks between the arguments of an AAF, it is clear that the arguments cannot all be considered *reasonable* at the same time. This means that their status is subject to evaluation, and we are particularly interested in the *justification state* of the arguments. Intuitively, we can think that an argument is justified if it has some way to survive the attacks that it receives, and as not justified otherwise. The process of determining the justification state of an argument based on an AAF is called *argument evaluation*.

There are multiple ways to do argument evaluation, which are called argumentation *semantics* [6,8,13,14]. These semantics tell us how to derive a set of *extensions* from an argumentation framework F, where an extension E is a subset of A, which intuitively represents that the arguments in E can "survive together", or in other words, are "collectively acceptable". The different semantics basically define different properties on the set E, for different notions of surviving together and being collectively acceptable.

Different semantics for abstract argumentation have been defined over the years, but we will focus on the most popular ones, which are admissible, complete, grounded, preferred, and stable. All of these semantics are based on the concept of conflict-freeness. An overview of how these semantics relate can be seen in Fig. 1.

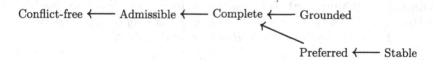

Fig. 1. An overview of how the different types of semantics relate. An arrow between two semantics means that the semantics on the right side is at least as restrictive as the one on the left. So every set that is admissible is also conflict-free, etc.

We now will see the definitions of the most popular semantics and some examples to better understand their meaning.

The idea behind conflict-freeness is that this property holds in a set of arguments that can "stand together". This means that the arguments cannot attack each other in any way.

Definition 2 (Conflict-free). *Given an abstract argumentation framework* $AF = \langle A, D \rangle$, *a set* $S \subseteq A$ *is conflict-free if and only if there is no pair of arguments* $a, b \in S$ *such that* a *attacks* b, *i.e., there is no pair* $a, b \in S$ *s.t.* $(a, b) \in D$.

A further requirement corresponds to the idea that an extension is a set of arguments which *can stand on its own*, namely is able to withstand the attacks it receives from other arguments by 'replying' with other attacks: a set is an admissible extension iff defends itself against attacks and is conflict free. Before formalizing the concept of admissible extension, we need to introduce the concept of *acceptable* argument: an argument a is acceptable w.r.t. (or, equivalently, defended by) a set S if S "counterattacks" all the attackers of a.

Definition 3 (Admissible). *Given an abstract argumentation framework $AF = \langle A, D \rangle$, a set $S \subseteq A$ is an admissible extension if and only if S is conflict-free and, $\forall a \in S$, a is acceptable w.r.t. S.*

The empty set is always admissible and conflict free.

Example 3. Consider the following argumentation framework $AF = \langle A, D \rangle$, where $A = \{a, b, c, d, e\}$ and $D = \{(a, b), (b, c), (b, d), (d, e)\}$, depicted in the figure below. It is easy to see that $S_1 = \{a, b, d\}$ is not conflict-free, set $S_2 = \{a, d\}$ is both conflict-free and admissible, set $S_3 = \{c, d\}$ is conflict-free but not admissible as no argument in it defends c and d from their attacks, and set $S_4 = \{a, c, d\}$ is both conflict-free and admissible.

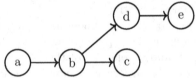

Now, we will recall the notion of complete extension.

Definition 4 (Complete). *Given an abstract argumentation framework $AF = \langle A, D \rangle$, a set $S \subseteq A$ is a complete extension if and only if S is admissible and, $\forall a \in A$ s.t. a is acceptable w.r.t. S, it must hold that $a \in S$.*

Basically, a set is a complete extension if the set is admissible and it contains every argument which is acceptable with respect to itself.

Example 4. Consider the following argumentation framework $AF = \langle A, D \rangle$, where $A = \{a, b\}$ and $D = \{(b, a)\}$. In this case, we have only one complete extension: $\{b\}$. The empty set is admissible, but not complete.

Consider now $AF_1 = \langle A_1, D_1 \rangle$, where $A_1 = \{a, b\}$ and $D_1 = \{(a, b), (b, a)\}$. In this case, we have three complete extensions: $\{a\}$, $\{b\}$ and $\emptyset$.

We denote as $IN(AF)$ the set of *initial* arguments of an argumentation framework AF, that are arguments that have no incoming attacks. It is easy to see that when there are no initial arguments, the empty set is complete. A complete extension must contain all the initial arguments, and the arguments defended by them, and so on. If there are multiple unconnected components in a graph, then we need to include all the initial arguments in a set to be complete, as show in the following example.

Example 5. Consider again the argumentation framework $AF = \langle A, D \rangle$, where $A = \{a, b, c, d, e\}$ and $D = \{(a, b), (b, c), (b, d), (b.e)\}$, shown in Example 3. It is easy to see that $S_5 = \{a, c\}$ is not complete, while $S_4 = \{a, c, d\}$ is complete.

Consider now the argumentation framework $AF_2 = \langle A_2, D_2 \rangle$, where $A_2 = \{a, b, c, d, e, f, g, h\}$ and $D_2 = \{(a, b), (b, c), (b, d), (d, e), (f, g), (g, f), (g, h)\}$, shown in the figure below. In this case, we have that $S_1 = \{a, c, d\}$ is complete, set $S_2 = \{f, h\}$ is not complete and set $S_3 = \{a, c, d, f, h\}$ is also complete. In fact, we have that a is acceptable w.r.t. S_2, but f is not acceptable w.r.t. S_1.

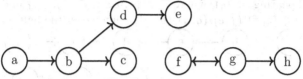

Consider now the argumentation framework $AF_3 = \langle A_3, D_3 \rangle$, where $A_3 = A_2 = \{a, b, c, d, e, f, g, h\}$ and $D_3 = \{(a, b), (b, c), (b, d), (d, e), (f, g), (g, h)\}$, depicted in the figure below. In this case, we have that $S_3 = \{a, c, d, f, h\}$ is the unique complete extension.

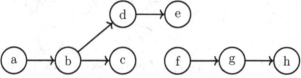

Finally, consider the argumentation framework $AF_4 = \langle A_4, D_4 \rangle$, where $A_4 = A_3 = \{a, b, c, d, e, f, g, h\}$ and $D_4 = \{(a, b), (b, a), (b, c), (b, d), (d, e), (f, g), (g, f), (g, h)\}$, depicted in the figure below. In this case, we have four complete extensions: $\{a, c, d\}, \{f, h\}, \{g\}$ and the empty set.

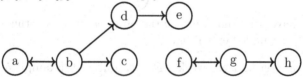

Let's now recall the definition of the grounded semantics.

Definition 5 (Grounded). *Given an abstract argumentation framework $AF = \langle A, D \rangle$, a set $S \subseteq A$ is a grounded extension if and only if S a is minimal (wrt $\subseteq$) complete set of arguments.*

Every argumentation framework admits only one grounded extension. Another way of defining the grounded extension is based on the characteristic function F: given a set $S \subseteq A$, $F : 2^A \to 2^A$ returns the set of the acceptable arguments w.r.t. S. The grounded extension of an argumentation framework AF, denoted as $GE(AF)$, is the least fixed point of its characteristic function F initially applied to the empty set. The basic idea is that the (unique) grounded extension can be built incrementally starting from the initial (unattacked) arguments (that are returned by the characteristic function applied to the empty set). Then a deletion step is performed: the arguments attacked by these initial arguments are suppressed, resulting in a modified argumentation framework where, possibly, the set of initial arguments is larger. In turn the arguments attacked by the 'new' initial arguments are suppressed, and so on. The process stops when no new initial arguments arise after a deletion step: the set of all initial arguments identified so far is the grounded extension.

Example 6. Consider the argumentation framework $AF = \langle A, D \rangle$ (inspired by an example appearing in [6]), where $A = \{a, b, c, d, e, f, g, h, i\}$ and $D = \{(a, b), (b, c), (c, d), (d, e), (e, f), (f, e), (g, h), (h, i)\}$, depicted in the figure below.

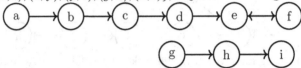

At the first step of the process, the set of initial arguments $IN(AF)$ is $\{a, g\}$, and after the first deletion step the graph becomes:

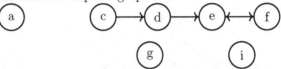

Then, now $IN(AF) = \{a, c, g, i\}$. After the second deletion step, the graph becomes:

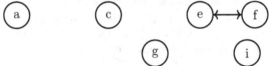

Then, we have that no more initial arguments arise, thus $IN(AF) = \{a, c, g, i\}$ is the grounded extension.

Example 7. Considering framework AF_2 introduced in Example 5, it is easy to see that set $\{a, c, d\}$ is the grounded extension. In framework AF_4, instead, the empty set is the grounded extension.

Let's now recall the preferred extension and the stable extension.

Definition 6 (Preferred). *Given an abstract argumentation framework $AF = \langle A, D \rangle$, a set $S \subseteq A$ is a preferred extension if and only if S is a maximal set (wrt $\subseteq$) complete set of arguments.*

This means that a preferred extension may be a superset of multiple complete extensions.

Example 8. Consider framework AF_2: set $\{a, c, d, f, h\}$ is a preferred extension. Consider now the framework $\langle \{f, h\}, \{(f, h), (h, f)\} \rangle$: both $\{f\}$ and $\{h\}$ are preferred extensions.

Definition 7 (Stable). *Given an abstract argumentation framework AF =* $\langle A, D \rangle$, *a set* $S \subseteq A$ *is a stable extension if and only if* S *is conflict-free and* S *attacks all the arguments in* $A \setminus S$

A set is a stable extension if it is conflict free and attacks all the arguments not in the set.

Example 9. Consider again framework AF_2. We have that set $\{a, c, d, f\}$ is not a stable extension, while set $\{a, c, d, g\}$ is stable. Consider now the framework $\langle \{a, b, c\}, \{(a, b), (b, a), (a, c), (c, a), (b, c), (c, b)\} \rangle$: we have the three stable extensions: $\{a\}$, $\{b\}$ and $\{c\}$.

According to the extension-based semantics the justification state of an argument is linked to the membership of the argument to an extension. We have two forms of justification: the one based on the skeptical semantics and the one based on the credulous semantics.

Definition 8 (Justification state). *Given a semantics sem and an abstract argumentation framework* $AF = \langle A, D \rangle$, *whose set of extensions according to sem is* $EXT(AF)_{sem}$, *an argument is:*
skeptically *justified under sem if and only if* $\forall E \in EXT(AF)_{sem}$ *it holds that* $a \in E$, *while*
it is credulously *justified under sem if and only if* $\exists E \in EXT(AF)_{sem}$ *such that* $a \in E$.

Example 10. Consider again framework AF_2 of above. We have that argument d is skeptically justified under the complete semantics as it belongs to all the three complete extensions $\{a, c, d\}$, $\{a, c, d, f, h\}$, and $\{a, c, d, g\}$, while argument h is skeptically justified under the complete semantics.

Basically, evaluating the justification status of an argument a is a way of verifying whether a can be considered reasonable and how much it can be considered reasonable. The membership of a to any (resp., all) extensions means that a has a chance (resp., very good chances) of representing, collectively with other arguments, is a good point of view in a dispute.

3.1 Complexity of Verifying Extensions

Now, let's take a look at how much effort is needed for verifying that a set is an extension, in terms of computational complexity. The characterization of the complexity of the problem $\mathrm{Ver}^{sem}(S)$ of verifying whether a set S is an extension according to a semantics *sem* in an AAF has been mainly done in [10, 17].

We can see in the table that $\mathrm{Ver}^{sem}(S)$ is polynomial, except for the preferred semantics.

Table 1. Complexity for the verification of extensions for the various semantics

Semantics	Ver$^{\text{sem}}(S)$
Admissible	P
Stable	P
Grounded	P
Complete	P
Preferred	coNP-complete

4   Uncertainty in Argumentation

In this section, we will deal with handling the uncertainty in abstract argumentation. In fact, when constructing an argument graph from informal arguments there is often uncertainty about whether some of the attacks hold, as shown in the following.

Example 11. Assume some people broke into a bank and two suspects, John and Peter, have been arrested based on the testimony of a witness, Harry. They make the following arguments:

a = 'John says he was not in town when the robbery took place, and therefore denies being involved in the robbery.'
b = 'Peter says he was at home watching TV when the robbery took place, and therefore denies being involved in the robbery.'
c = 'Harry says that he is certain that he saw John outside the bank just before the robbery took place, and he also thinks that possibly he saw Peter there too.'

In this case, it is clear that c attacks a, but there is uncertainty whether or not c also attack b. This means that we can get two possible argumentation frameworks out of this, depending on how much we trust Harry. If we do trust him, we get:

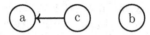

However, if we do not think that we can believe Harry about seeing Peter, we get the following:

$$a \longleftarrow c \qquad b$$

Uncertainty can be also over arguments: when modelling a dispute, we could be uncertain about the occurrence of some argument. In fact, it is not guaranteed that an argument will be actually presented, or that an argument would be accepted by the referee of the dispute.

Several state-of-the-art approaches for handling uncertainty in AAFs rely on probability theory. Mainly, these approaches can be classified in two categories, based on the way they interpret the probabilities of the arguments: those adopting the classical constellations approach [11,12,15,18,19,21–25,27,30,32] and those adopting the recent epistemic one [28,29,33]. We will focus on the former, and will see two forms of probabilistic frameworks that we call *IND* and *EX*.

4.1 Probabilistic Abstract Argumentation Framework of Form *IND*

One important framework proposed in [30] and further investigated in [21–24] is that defined below. We call this framework of form *IND* to recall and highlight the independence assumption that is the core of the approach. In fact, *IND* requires probabilities to be specified over arguments and attacks, that are assumed to the independent from one another.

Definition 9 (*IND*). *A probabilistic abstract argumentation framework (PAF) of form IND is a tuple (A, D, P_A, P_D) where A and D are as before and P_A and P_D are probability functions assigning a non-zero probability to each argument and defeat in D.*

The meaning of a PAF is given in terms of possible worlds, each representing a scenario that may occur in reality.

Given a PAF, a possible world w is an AAF such that its arguments and defeats are subsets of A and D, respectively. More formally:

Definition 10 (Possible world). *Given a PAF $F = \langle A, D, P_A, P_D \rangle$, a possible world w of F is an AAF $\langle A', D' \rangle$ such that $A' \subseteq A$ and $D' \subseteq D \cap (A' \times A')$.*

The set of all the possible worlds of F will be denoted as $PW(F)$.

We point out that certain arguments (i.e., having probability 1) are always included in every possible world.

Example 12. Consider the probabilistic argumentation framework $AF = \langle A, D, P_A, P_D \rangle$, where $A = \{a, b, c\}$, $D = \{(c, a), (c, b)\}$, $P_A(a) = 0.8$, $P_A(b) = 1$, $P_A(c) = 0.8$, $P_D((c, a)) = 0.6$, and $P_D((c, b)) = 1$, depicted in the figure below.

In this case, since $P_A(b) = 1$, b is included in every possible world. Furthermore, if $c \in A'$, then $(c, b) \in D'$, since $P_D((c, b)) = 1$. However, if c is not included, then (c, b) must also not be included. This means we get the following five possible worlds:

$$W_1 = \langle b, \emptyset \rangle \qquad\qquad W_2 = \langle \{b, c\}, \{(c, b)\} \rangle$$

$$W_3 = \langle \{a, b, c\}, \{(c, b)\} \rangle \qquad W_4 = \langle \{a, b, c\}, \{(c, a), (c, b)\} \rangle$$

$$W_5 = \langle \{a, b\}, \emptyset \rangle$$

$$\text{(a)} \quad \text{(b)}$$

An interpretation for a PAF is a probability distribution function I over the set PW(F). In the framework *IND*, the independence assumption holds (this is the reason why we call the framework *IND*): arguments represent pairwise independent events, and each defeat represents an event conditioned only by the occurrence of its argument events but independent from any other event. Thus, in the framework *IND*, we compute the probability of a possible world W as:

$$I(w) = \prod_{a \in A'} P_A(a) \cdot \prod_{a \in A \setminus A'} (1 - P_A(a)) \cdot \prod_{\delta \in D'} P_D(\delta) \cdot \prod_{\delta \in (D \cap (A' \times A')) \setminus D'} (1 - P_D(\delta))$$

Example 13. Continuing the previous example, we have that:
$I(W_1) = P_A(b) \times (1 - P_A(a)) \times (1 - P_A(c)) = 1 \times 0.2 \times 0.2 = 0.04$
$I(W_2) = P_A(b) \times P_A(c) \times (1 - P_A(a)) \times P_D(c, b) = 1 \times 0.8 \times 0.2 \times 1 = 0.16$
$I(W_3) = P_A(a) \times P_A(b) \times P_A(c) \times P_D(c, b) \times (1 - P_D(c, a)) = 0.8 \times 0.8 \times 1 \times 1 \times 0.4 = 0.256$
$I(W_4) = P_A(a) \times P_A(b) \times P_A(c) \times P_D(c, b) \times P_D(c, a) = 0.8 \times 0.8 \times 1 \times 1 \times 0.6 = 0.384$
$I(W_5) = P_A(a) \times P_A(b) \times (1 - P_A(c)) = 0.8 \times 1 \times 0.2 = 0.16$

Basically, each possible world is assigned the probability of being the 'real' one, that is the one that occurs in the reality, on the basis of the probabilities of arguments and defeats. Note that the probabilities of all possible worlds sum to one.

Now, let's see what happens to the extensions. When considering the probabilities, the problem of verifying whether a set is an extension makes no sense as a set could be an extension over a possible world and could not be so over another possible world. In fact, the problem now becomes: *Given a semantics, what is the probability that a set is an extension according to this semantics?.*

To compute the probability for a set of being extension, we have to sum the probabilities of all the possible worlds where the set is an extension over it.

Definition 11 ($P^{sem}(S)$). *Given a probabilistic abstract argumentation framework F, a set S and a semantics sem, the probability that S is an extension according to sem is given by:*

$$P^{sem}(S) = \sum_{W \in PW(F) \wedge ext(W, sem, S)} I(W)$$

where ext(W, sem, S) evaluates to true iff S is extension according to sem over W.

Example 14. Continuing the previous example, the probability $P^{ad}(\{a, b\})$, that is the probability for the set $\{a, b\}$ to be an admissible extension over F, is given by $I(W_5) = 0.16$, as $\{a, b\}$ is admissible only in W_5.

Also we need to revisit the concepts of credulous and skeptical justification by considering the probabilities: now an argument is justified with probability $P^{sem}_{cred/skep}(a)$, obtained by summing the probabilities of all possible worlds where a is cred/skep justified.

Definition 12. *Given a probabilistic abstract argumentation framework F, an argument a and a semantics sem, the probability that a is justified according to sem is given by:*

$$P^{sem}_{cred/skep}(a) = \sum_{W \in PW(F) \wedge acc(W,sem,a,cred/skep)} I(W)$$

where $acc(W, sem, a, cred/skep)$ evaluates to true iff a is cred/skep justified according to sem over W.

Example 15. Continuing the previous example, we have that the probability for a of being credulously justified according to the admissible semantics is $P^{ad}_{cred}(a) = \sum_{W \in PW(F) \wedge acc(W,ad,a,cred)} I(W) = I(W_3) + I(W_5)$, as a is credulously justified under the admissible semantics only in W_3 and W_5: in those possible worlds, indeed, a belongs to at least one admissible extension.

4.2   Probabilistic Abstract Argumentation Framework of Form EX

Another important probabilistic framework is that proposed in [12,15,32]. We call this framework of form EX to indicate that is 'extensive', in the sense that the probabilities must be specified for all the possible worlds. In fact, the probabilities are assigned to the possible worlds and not to the arguments/defeats, and there is no independence assumption.

Definition 13. *A probabilistic abstract argumentation framework F of form EX is a triple $\langle A, D, P \rangle$, where A and D are as before and P is a probability distribution function over the set of possible worlds $PW(F)$.*

We can use the form EX to force some correlations between arguments by making as 'possible' (i.e., by assigning a probability greater than zero) only the scenarios where the correlation is satisfied.

Example 16. Consider framework F of form EX where the set of arguments is $A = \{a, b, c\}$ and the set of defeats is $D = \{(c, a), (c, b)\}$. If we want to force the correlation between the occurrence of a and b, we could assign 0 to all the possible worlds W where a and b do not appear together and a uniform probability to all the others: $I(\langle \{a, b\}, \emptyset \rangle) = 0.2$, $I(\langle \{c\}, \emptyset \rangle) = 0.2$, $I(\langle \{a, b, c\}, \{(c, a)\} \rangle) = 0.2$, $I(\langle \{a, b, c\}, \{(c, b)\} \rangle) = 0.2$, $I(\langle \{a, b, c\}, \{(c, a), (c, b)\} \rangle) = 0.2$.

Probabilities of extensions and justification status of arguments are as before.

4.3   Comparison Between *IND* and *EX*

The main difference between the two probabilistic frameworks are summarized here: *IND* is compact, as we only need to specify probabilities for each argument and attack, whose number is typically less than the number of scenarios, but it relies on the independence assumption, thus no correlation can be enforced. *EX* allows correlations to be expressed, but the analyst needs to specify a very large number of probabilities: the number of scenarios is exponential w.r.t. the size of set of arguments/defeats. In Table 2, we report the complexity of the problem of computing the probability that a set is an extension under the various semantics.

Table 2. Complexity for the computation of the probability of extensions for the various (probabilistic) semantics

Semantics	$Ver^{sem}(S)$	$P^{sem}(S)$ – IND	$P^{sem}(S)$ – EX
Admissible	P	FP	FP
Stable	P	FP	FP
Grounded	P	$FP^{\#P}$-complete	FP
Complete	P	$FP^{\#P}$-complete	FP
Preferred	coNP-complete	$FP^{\#P}$-complete	$FP^{\|\|NP}$-complete

We recall that FP is the class of the function problems that can be solved by a deterministic Turing machine in polynomial time (w.r.t. the size of the input of the problem). $FP^{\#P}$ is the class of functions computable by a polynomial-time Turing machine with a $\#P$ oracle. $\#P$ is the complexity class of the functions f such that f counts the number of accepting paths of a nondeterministic polynomial-time Turing machine [34]. Analogously, $FP^{\|\|NP}$ is the class of functions computable by a polynomial-time Turing machine with access to an NP oracle, whose calls are non-adaptive (as explained above, this is equivalent to saying that the oracle invocations take place in parallel).

Note that even if the complexity seems to be lower when dealing with *EX*, it should be considered that the input of the two frameworks is different and, in the case of *EX*, is it exponential w.r.t. the size of set of arguments/defeats. A detailed characterization of the problem of computing the probabilities has been done in [20], where also a new framework has been proposed, that is called *GEN*. In *GEN*, the probability distribution function (pdf) over the possible scenarios is encoded using the paradigm of world-set descriptors and this results in a framework that is intermediate between *EX* and *IND*, as it has the same expressiveness as the form *EX* (since it allows any pdf to be encoded, thus allowing any correlation to be expressed), but is more compact, as its encoding does not require the explicit enumeration of the scenarios with non-zero probability.

4.4   Other Options for Handling Uncertainty

As mentioned before, another way of handling uncertainty in AAFs is the epistemic approach, that also relies on probability theory. In this approach, probabilities and extensions have a different semantics, compared with the constellations approach. Specifically, the probability of an argument represents the degree of belief in the argument (the higher the probability, the more the argument is believed), and a key concept is the 'rational' probability distribution, that requires that if the belief in an argument is high, then the belief in the arguments attacked by it is low. In this approach, epistemic extensions are considered rather than Dung's extensions, where an epistemic extension is the set of arguments that are believed to be true to some degree. The interested reader can find a more detailed comparative description of the two categories in [26].

Besides the approaches that model uncertainty in AAFs by relying on probability theory, many proposals have been made where uncertainty is represented by exploiting weights or preferences on arguments and/or defeats [3,5,7,9,16,31]. Another interesting approach to represent uncertainty in argumentation is that based on using possibility theory, as done in [1,2,4]. Although the approaches based on weights, preferences, possibilities, or probabilities to model uncertainty have been proved to be effective in different contexts, there is no common agreement on what kind of approach should be used in general. In this regard, [25,26] observed that the probability-based approaches may take advantage from relying on a well-established and well-founded theory, whereas the approaches based on weights or preferences do not conform to well-established theories yet.

5   Conclusion

In this tutorial, we have dealt with the basic notions of abstract argumentation, and with some frameworks relying on probability theory for handling uncertainty in abstract argumentation. This tutorial is naturally linked to the tutorial *Computational Argumentation and Cognitive AI* of ACAI 2021, where dialectic argumentation is addressed and argumentation-based explainable real-life AI applications are presented.

The reader interested further in abstract argumentation and in probabilistic abstract argumentation is encouraged to take a look at the articles [6,13,20,25, 30].

References

1. Alsinet, T., Chesñevar, C.I., Godo, L., Sandri, S.A., Simari, G.R.: Formalizing argumentative reasoning in a possibilistic logic programming setting with fuzzy unification. Int. J. Approx. Reasoning **48**(3), 711–729 (2008). https://doi.org/10.1016/j.ijar.2007.07.004
2. Alsinet, T., Chesñevar, C.I., Godo, L., Simari, G.R.: A logic programming framework for possibilistic argumentation: Formalization and logical properties. Fuzzy Sets Syst. **159**(10), 1208–1228 (2008). https://doi.org/10.1016/j.fss.2007.12.013

3. Amgoud, L., Cayrol, C.: A reasoning model based on the production of acceptable arguments. Ann. Math. Artif. Intell. **34**(1–3), 197–215 (2002). https://doi.org/10. 1023/A:1014490210693

4. Amgoud, L., Prade, H.: Reaching agreement through argumentation: a possibilistic approach. In: Proceedings of Principles of Knowledge Representation and Reasoning: KR, Whistler, Canada, 2–5 June, pp. 175–182 (2004)

5. Amgoud, L., Vesic, S.: A new approach for preference-based argumentation frameworks. Ann. Math. Artif. Intell. **63**(2), 149–183 (2011). https://doi.org/10.1007/ s10472-011-9271-9

6. Baroni, P., Giacomin, M.: Semantics of abstract argument systems. In: Simari, G., Rahwan, I. (eds.) Argumentation in Artificial Intelligence. Springer, Boston (2009). https://doi.org/10.1007/978-0-387-98197-0_2

7. Bench-Capon, T.J.M.: Persuasion in practical argument using value-based argumentation frameworks. J. Log. Comput. **13**(3), 429–448 (2003). https://doi.org/ 10.1093/logcom/13.3.429

8. Caminada, M.: Semi-stable semantics. In: Proceedings of Computational Models of Argument: COMMA, 11–12 September, Liverpool, UK, pp. 121–130 (2006)

9. Coste-Marquis, S., Konieczny, S., Marquis, P., Ouali, M.A.: Weighted attacks in argumentation frameworks. In: Proceedings of Principles of Knowledge Representation and Reasoning: KR, Rome, Italy, 10–14 June (2012)

10. Dimopoulos, Y., Nebel, B., Toni, F.: Preferred arguments are harder to compute than stable extension. In: Dean, T. (ed.) Proceedings of the 16th International Joint Conference on Artificial Intelligence, IJCAI 99, Stockholm, Sweden, 31 July - 6 August 1999, 2 volumes, 1450 p, pp. 36–43. Morgan Kaufmann (1999), http:// ijcai.org/Proceedings/99-1/Papers/006.pdf

11. Doder, D., Woltran, S.: Probabilistic argumentation frameworks – a logical approach. In: Straccia, U., Calì, A. (eds.) SUM 2014. LNCS (LNAI), vol. 8720, pp. 134–147. Springer, Cham (2014). https://doi.org/10.1007/978-3-319-11508-5_12

12. Dondio, P.: Toward a computational analysis of probabilistic argumentation frameworks. Cybern. Syst. **45**(3), 254–278 (2014). https://doi.org/10.1080/01969722. 2014.894854

13. Dung, P.M.: On the acceptability of arguments and its fundamental role in nonmonotonic reasoning, logic programming and n-person games. Artif. Intell. **77**, 321–358 (1995)

14. Dung, P.M., Mancarella, P., Toni, F.: Computing ideal sceptical argumentation. Artif. Intell. **171**(10–15), 642–674 (2007). https://doi.org/10.1016/j.artint.2007.05. 003

15. Dung, P.M., Thang, P.M.: Towards (probabilistic) argumentation for jury-based dispute resolution. In: Proceedings of Computational Models of Argument: COMMA, Desenzano del Garda, Italy, 8–10 September, pp. 171–182 (2010). https://doi.org/10.3233/978-1-60750-619-5-171

16. Dunne, P.E., Hunter, A., McBurney, P., Parsons, S., Wooldridge, M.: Weighted argument systems: basic definitions, algorithms, and complexity results. Artif. Intell. **175**(2), 457–486 (2011). https://doi.org/10.1016/j.artint.2010.09.005

17. Dunne, P.E., Wooldridge, M.: Complexity of abstract argumentation. In: Simari, G., Rahwan, I. (eds.) Argumentation in Artificial Intelligence, pp. 85–104. Springer, Boston (2009). https://doi.org/10.1007/978-0-387-98197-0_5

18. Fazzinga, B., Flesca, S., Furfaro, F.: Computing extensions' probabilities in probabilistic abstract argumentation: beyond independence. In: Proceedings of ECAI - 22nd European Conference on Artificial Intelligence, 29 August-2 September, The

Hague, The Netherlands - Including Prestigious Applications of Artificial Intelligence (PAIS), pp. 1588–1589 (2016). https://doi.org/10.3233/978-1-61499-672-9-1588

19. Fazzinga, B., Flesca, S., Furfaro, F.: Credulous acceptability in probabilistic abstract argumentation: Complexity results. In: Proceedings of the 1st Workshop on Advances in Argumentation in Artificial Intelligence Co-located with XVI International Conference of the Italian Association for Artificial Intelligence (AI*IA), Bari, Italy, 16–17 November, pp. 43–57 (2017)

20. Fazzinga, B., Flesca, S., Furfaro, F.: Complexity of fundamental problems in probabilistic abstract argumentation: beyond independence. Artif. Intell. **268**, 1–29 (2019). https://doi.org/10.1016/j.artint.2018.11.003

21. Fazzinga, B., Flesca, S., Parisi, F.: Efficiently estimating the probability of extensions in abstract argumentation. In: Liu, W., Subrahmanian, V.S., Wijsen, J. (eds.) SUM 2013. LNCS (LNAI), vol. 8078, pp. 106–119. Springer, Heidelberg (2013). https://doi.org/10.1007/978-3-642-40381-1_9

22. Fazzinga, B., Flesca, S., Parisi, F.: On the complexity of probabilistic abstract argumentation. In: Proceedings of the 23rd International Joint Conference on Artificial Intelligence (IJCAI), Beijing, China, 3–9, August, pp. 898–904 (2013)

23. Fazzinga, B., Flesca, S., Parisi, F.: On the complexity of probabilistic abstract argumentation frameworks. ACM Trans. Comput. Log. **16**(3), 22:1-22:39 (2015). https://doi.org/10.1145/2749463

24. Fazzinga, B., Flesca, S., Parisi, F.: On efficiently estimating the probability of extensions in abstract argumentation frameworks. Int. J. Approx. Reasoning **69**, 106–132 (2016). https://doi.org/10.1016/j.ijar.2015.11.009

25. Hunter, A.: Some Foundations for Probabilistic Abstract Argumentation. In: Proceedings of Computational Models of Argument: COMMA, Vienna, Austria, 10–12 September, pp. 117–128 (2012). https://doi.org/10.3233/978-1-61499-111-3-117

26. Hunter, A.: A probabilistic approach to modelling uncertain logical arguments. Int. J. Approx. Reasoning **54**(1), 47–81 (2013). https://doi.org/10.1016/j.ijar.2012.08.003

27. Hunter, A.: Probabilistic qualification of attack in abstract argumentation. Int. J. Approx. Reasoning **55**(2), 607–638 (2014). https://doi.org/10.1016/j.ijar.2013.09.002

28. Hunter, A., Thimm, M.: Probabilistic argumentation with epistemic extensions. In: Proceedings of the International Workshop on Defeasible and Ampliative Reasoning, DARe@ECAI, Co-located with the 21st European Conference on Artificial Intelligence (ECAI), Prague, Czech Republic, 19 August (2014)

29. Hunter, A., Thimm, M.: Probabilistic argumentation with incomplete information. In: Proceedings of the 21st European Conference on Artificial Intelligence (ECAI), 18–22 August, Prague, Czech Republic. Including Prestigious Applications of Intelligent Systems (PAIS), pp. 1033–1034 (2014). https://doi.org/10.3233/978-1-61499-419-0-1033

30. Li, H., Oren, N., Norman, T.J.: Probabilistic argumentation frameworks. In: Modgil, S., Oren, N., Toni, F. (eds.) TAFA 2011. LNCS (LNAI), vol. 7132, pp. 1–16. Springer, Heidelberg (2012). https://doi.org/10.1007/978-3-642-29184-5_1

31. Modgil, S.: Reasoning about preferences in argumentation frameworks. Artif. Intell. **173**(9–10), 901–934 (2009). https://doi.org/10.1016/j.artint.2009.02.001

32. Rienstra, T.: Towards a probabilistic dung-style argumentation system. In: Proceedings of the First International Conference on Agreement Technologies, AT 2012, Dubrovnik, Croatia, 15–16 October, pp. 138–152 (2012)

33. Thimm, M.: A probabilistic semantics for abstract argumentation. In: Proceedings of the 20th European Conference on Artificial Intelligence (ECAI). Including Prestigious Applications of Artificial Intelligence (PAIS) System Demonstrations Track, Montpellier, France, 27–31 August, pp. 750–755 (2012). https://doi.org/10.3233/978-1-61499-098-7-750
34. Valiant, L.G.: The complexity of computing the permanent. Theor. Comput. Sci. 8, 189–201 (1979). https://doi.org/10.1016/0304-3975(79)90044-6

Computational Argumentation & Cognitive AI

Emmanuelle Dietz[1(✉)], Antonis Kakas[2], and Loizos Michael[3,4]

[1] TU Dresden/Airbus Central R&T, Dresden, Germany
emmanuelle.dietz@airbus.com
[2] University of Cyprus, Nicosia, Cyprus
[3] Open University of Cyprus, Latsia, Cyprus
[4] CYENS Center of Excellence, Nicosia, Cyprus

Abstract. This tutorial examines the role of Computational Argumentation at the theoretical and practical level of Human-centric AI. It rests on the central role that argumentation has in human cognition rendering argumentation as a possible foundation for the two basic elements of intelligence, namely learning and reasoning, in a way that is suitable for human-centric AI. The tutorial examines argumentation as a basis for cognitive technologies of Learning and Explainable Inference or Decision Making and their application in today's AI.

Keywords: Argumentation · Human-centric AI · Learning and reasoning in argumentation · Cognitive modeling

1 Introduction

This tutorial follows a first tutorial, "Argumentation in AI" on Abstract Argumentation in AI, given at the same ACAI 2021 school. The purpose of the current tutorial is to connect argumentation with Human-centric AI by examining the natural link of argumentation with human cognition and the two basic elements of intelligence, learning and reasoning. The main **learning objective** of the tutorial is for participants to appreciate the potential central role of argumentation for Human-centric AI and how this can form the basis for developing real-life applications. The tutorial is structured into four parts, as follows:

- **Section 2: Structured Argumentation**, presenting a general review of structured argumentation as the underlying framework on which applications of (explainable) Human-centric AI can be build. These general ideas are illustrated within the concrete structured argumentation framework of *Gorgias* and its associated system, available at **Cloud Gorgias.**[1]

---

[1] http://gorgiasb.tuc.gr/GorgiasCloud.html.

Tutorial at the HUMANE-AI NET advanced course 2021 on Human Centered AI.

© Springer Nature Switzerland AG 2023
M. Chetouani et al. (Eds.): ACAI 2021, LNAI 13500, pp. 363–388, 2023.
https://doi.org/10.1007/978-3-031-24349-3_19

- **Section 3: Cognitive Argumentation**, examining the natural link between human reasoning and argumentation. The COGNICA system[2] implements such a Cognitive Argumentation framework. Also the link of argumentation to existing Cognitive Architectures, such as ACT-R, is examined.
- **Section 4: Argumentation for Learning**, introducing the features of argumentation that make it a fitting target language for learning and explanations. It showcases this natural fit by presenting two protocols that learn and represent knowledge in the language of argumentation.
- **Section 5: Real-life Applications of Argumentation**, presenting an argumentation-based software development methodology for acquiring the knowledge required for building systems under a general "mind-like" architecture. This methodology is illustrated through a series of real-life application systems and the major challenges it poses.

In the tutorial repository[3] one can find further details on all parts of the tutorial, e.g., extended presentations of examples or other illustrative applications. Note also that for each section of this tutorial, a general bibliography is listed separately at the end, without explicit citations in the text. For a more complete bibliography the reader can consult the tutorial repository.

2   Structured Argumentation

In contrast to Abstract Argumentation, **Structured Argumentation** puts the emphasis in providing argumentation frameworks that can be used to model and develop applications of argumentation. They provide the necessary scaffolding for dialectic argumentative reasoning (or inference) to be mapped into, and applications to be build on top of this.

At a general and abstract level a structured argumentation framework consists of a triple $\langle \mathcal{A}rgs, \mathcal{A}tt, \mathcal{D}ef \rangle$ where $\mathcal{A}rgs$ is a set of arguments, $\mathcal{A}tt$ an attack relation between arguments and $\mathcal{D}ef$ a defense relation between arguments. Typically, the defense relation $\mathcal{D}ef$ is a subset of the attack relation $\mathcal{A}tt$ and relates to the relative strength between arguments.[4] Informally, $(a, b) \in \mathcal{D}ef$ means that argument a is at least as strong as b, and can thus provide a defense against b.

In Structured Argumentation, like in abstract argumentation, we can give an underlying dialectical semantics for the acceptability of arguments. For example, a subset of arguments Δ **is admissible** iff (a) it is not self-attacking, i.e., there are no arguments a, b in Δ such that $(a, b) \in \mathcal{A}tt$ and (b) for any counterargument c against Δ, i.e., $(c, a) \in \mathcal{A}tt$ holds for some argument a in Δ, Δ defends against c, i.e., $(d, c) \in \mathcal{D}ef$ for some d in Δ. This then maps directly into a dialectic process of inference of recursively considering attacks against an argument supporting a desired conclusion and defending against these attacks

---

[2] http://cognica.cs.ucy.ac.cy/COGNICAb/index.php.

[3] https://cognition.ouc.ac.cy/argument.

[4] Alternatively, the notion or terminology of a *defeating attack* is used instead to express that an attack is strong enough to defeat the argument that it is attacking.

with possibly the help of other arguments thus building an admissible Δ. We call such an admissible set Δ a **case** for the inferred conclusion.

In practice, structured argumentation frameworks are realized in an application domain via triples of $\langle \mathcal{A}s, \mathcal{C}, \succ \rangle$ where $\mathcal{A}s$ is a set of (parameterized) argument schemes, instances of which form arguments, $\mathcal{C}$ is a conflict relation between the argument schemes and the arguments constructed from these schemes and $\succ$ is a priority or preference relation again between the argument schemes and their arguments. **Argument schemes** are parameterized named statements of association AS = (Premises ▷ Position) between some information called Premises and another statement called the Position or Claim.

The conflict relation $\mathcal{C}$ is typically defined through the language of the application domain, e.g., through some global notion of incompatibility between statements in the language, possibly also augmented with a direct expression of conflict between two argument schemes and/or particular instances of these. Given such a conflict relation we can build the attack relation between arguments by identifying three different types of attacks, called **rebuttal, undermining or undercutting attacks**. The first type results when the claim of the attacking argument conflicts with the claim of the argument attacked, the second type when it conflicts with a premise of the argument attacked and the third type when the two arguments have been declared as conflicting — the conflict is on the link of the argument that it is attacked.

Example 1. Consider argument $arg_1 : Arrival\_of\_Ambulance \,\triangleright\, Pick\_up\_Patient$, i.e., the arrival of an ambulance supports the claim that it will pick up a patient (from the place of arrival). A rebuttal attack against this is given by the argument $arg_2 : No\_Ambulance\_Siren \,\triangleright\, Not\_Pick\_up\_Patient$, i.e., the argument supporting the opposite claim when there is no ambulance (arriving) with its siren on, whereas the argument $arg_3 : Broken\_Ambulance \,\triangleright\, Not\_Arrival\_of\_Ambulance$ supporting the claim that an ambulance cannot arrive based on the premise that it is broken is an undermining attack on arg_1. Finally, the argument $arg_4 : Arrival\_of\_Ambulance \,\triangleright\, Pick\_up\_Nurse$ is an undercutting attack against arg_1 as this goes against the actual link of the argument: arg_1 claims that the reason it has arrived is to pick up a patient whereas arg_4 claims it is to pick up a nurse.

The third component, the priority or strength relation $\succ$ between arguments, is used to build the defense relation of an application argumentation framework. Informally, in most frameworks arg_1 defends against arg_2 iff arg_1 conflicts with arg_2 and arg_1 is not of lower priority than arg_2, i.e., $arg_1 \not\prec arg_2$. In contrast to the conflict relation which is static the priority relation is not so, but can be highly *context-sensitive* depending crucially on (how we perceive) the current state of the application environment.

To illustrate the process of how an argumentation framework is built dynamically through a changing current environment, let us consider the following example from the domain of common-sense temporal reasoning.

Example 2. Suppose we read the following piece of text: "Bob came home and found the house in darkness. He turned on the light switch in the hall." Consider the question "Is the hall still in darkness?". Can we explain[5] how (most) people reach the conclusion or explain why "the hall now is illuminated"?

One way to do this within an argumentation perspective is as follows.

- From the information $Room\_in\_darkness\_at\_T$ using the general argument schema that properties *persist* in time we have the argument $arg_1 : \{ Room\_in\_darkness\_at\_T \rhd Room\_in\_darkness\_at\_T^+ \}$ supporting the claim that the hall is still in darkness at some time T^+ after T.
- From the information $Turn\_on\_switch\_at\_T$ using the common sense knowledge that turning on the light switch *causes* the light to come on, we have the argument: $arg_2 : \{ Turn\_on\_switch\_at\_T \rhd Room\_illuminated\_at\_T^+ \}$ supporting the claim that the hall is illuminated at T^+.

These two arguments are counter-arguments of each other as their claims are in conflict: in our common-sense language a room in darkness is the opposite of a room illuminated and vice-versa. Furthermore, in our common sense temporal reasoning we consider causal information stronger than the persistence of properties (when the causal action occurs at least as late as the time of the observed property that we are persisting from into the future). This gives a priority or strength to causal arguments over persistence arguments and hence to arg_2 over arg_1, i.e., $arg_2 \succ arg_1$. This in turn means that arg_2 can defend against arg_1 but not vice versa.

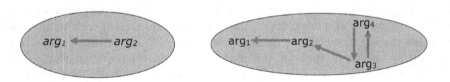

Fig. 1. The argumentation arena for the two narratives of Example 2.

We thus have an argumentation arena depicted by the left part of Fig. 1. In this figure, we have equated the defence relation with the attack relation so that we only show the non-weak attacks. From this we can see that $\{ arg_2 \}$ is an acceptable/admissible set of arguments forming a case supporting the conclusion $Room\_illuminated\_at\_T^+$ and that there is no case supporting the opposite conclusion as $\{ arg_1 \}$ is not acceptable/admissible. Hence we are "confident" about deriving the inference that the room is not in darkness after Bob has turned on the light switch.

---

[5] We are not looking here for an explanation of the subconscious operation of the brain to reach this conclusion, but for an explanation at a high cognitive level that would also be helpful to some other process that would act on our conclusion.

Example 3. Consider now a more complex case by changing slightly the narrative: "The power cut had turned the house in darkness. Bob came home and turned on the light switch in the hall." Now some people may not feel confident that the hall will be illuminated after turning on the light switch. This can be attributed to two things: (1) the text now alerts us to the fact that electricity is needed for the light to come on, and (2) it is not clear if the power cut has ended before or after Bob came home. From an argumentation point of view new arguments come into the arena:

– From the statement about a power cut we can build the following argument: $arg_3 : \{Power\_cut\_at\_T \triangleright No\_electricity\_at\_T\}$ which conflicts with argument arg_2. This is an undercutting[6] attack against arg_2 and it is, according to our common-sense knowledge, a stronger argument than arg_2. Hence arg_3 cannot be defended back by arg_2, or arg_3 is a defeating attack against arg_2. But to enable arg_3 we need to have an argument supporting its premise. We can thus extend argument arg_3 to: $\{\mathsf{hyp}(Power\_cut\_at\_T)); Power\_cut\_at\_T \triangleright No\_electricity\_at\_T\}$ where $\mathsf{hyp}(Power\_cut\_at\_T)$ is a hypothetical argument supporting that the power cut holds at the time of turning on the switch. This then means that now arg_3 can be attacked by the opposite hypothetical argument supporting that the power cut did not last until time T, i.e., we have a fourth argument in the arena: $arg_4 : \{\mathsf{hyp}(No\_power\_cut\_at\_T)\}$. This argument is in conflict with arg_3 on its weak premise and thus forms an (undermining) attack on it. Importantly, it is non-comparable in strength with arg_3. Hence arg_3 and arg_4 attack and defend against each other.

Given the above we now have a new argumentation arena depicted by the right part of Fig. 1. From this we now have two acceptable/admissible subsets of arguments: $\{arg_2, arg_4\}$ forming a case supporting $Room\_illuminated\_at\_T^+$ and the case of $\{arg_1, arg_3\}$ for the opposite conclusion of $Room\_in\_darkness\_at\_T^+$. We have a **dilemma** and hence we cannot be sure either way that the room is in darkness or not after turning on the switch. This then reflects the variability in answers given by different people (see more on this in Sect. 3).

There are several Structured Argumentation frameworks in the literature and although these may appear different they share a very similar theoretical underpinning. One of the earliest such frameworks is that of the GORGIAS framework, named after the ancient Greek philosopher of dialectics, on which we will concentrate.

2.1 The **GORGIAS** Argumentation Framework

GORGIAS is a structured argumentation framework where arguments are constructed using a basic (content independent) scheme of **argument rules**,

---

[6] Indeed, this attacks the link of arg_2 not its claim or premises. There is no general conflict between $No\_electricity\_at\_T$ and $Room\_illuminated\_at\_T$ as the room can be illuminated in other ways.

denoted by Premises ▷ Claim. The Premises and Claim are literals in the syntax of Extended Logic Programming, but where negation as failure is excluded from the language[7]. An important element of the GORGIAS framework is that it allows a special class of argument rules, called **priority argument rules** that are used to express a context-sensitive relative strength between (other) argument rules. They have the same syntactic form as argument rules, but now the Claim is of a special type, $a_1 > a_2$, where a_1 and a_2 are (the names of) any two other individual argument rules. When the claim of an argument rule is not a priority statement, i.e., it is a literal in the language, this is called an **object-level** argument rule.

The purpose of priority arguments, constructed from priority argument rules, is to provide the defense relation between arguments. They are combined with other (e.g., object-level) arguments to give them strength. A **composite argument** in the framework is then a (minimal and closed) set of (instantiated) argument rules, $\Delta = (A_1, A_P)$, where, A_1, is a subset of object level argument rules and A_P is a subset of priority argument rules, referring to the other arguments in Δ. Then, informally, a composite argument, Δ_1, defends against another composite argument, Δ_2, whenever they are in conflict, and the arguments in Δ_1 are rendered by the priority arguments that it contains at least as strong as the arguments contained in Δ_2.

The GORGIAS System. The GORGIAS system allows us to code argumentation theories of the form described above and subsequently query the system to find out if there is an admissible (composite) argument that supports the query. GORGIAS has been publicly available since 2003 and has been used by several research groups to develop prototype real-life applications of argumentation in a variety of application domains. Today the GORGIAS system is available as a service over the internet in **Cloud Gorgias** at http://gorgiasb.tuc.gr/GorgiasCloud.html.

Let us illustrate the GORGIAS argumentation framework and the dialectic computational model of the GORGIAS system through a simple example. This is written below in the internal GORGIAS system language.[8] This language is build on top of Prolog where an argument rule has the form:

$$rule(\mathit{arg\_name}, \mathsf{Claim}, \mathit{defeasible\_premises}]) : -\mathit{non\_defeasible\_premises}.$$

$\mathit{arg\_name}$ is a Prolog term with which we name the arguments expressed by this rule, $\mathit{non\_defeasible\_premises}$ can be any conjunction of Prolog conditions and are executed under ??? and $\mathit{defeasible\_premises}$ are conjunctions of literals executed under GORGIAS using argument rules relating to them. Priority argument rules have exactly the same form, but now Claim is $prefer(\mathit{arg\_name}_1, \mathit{arg\_name}_2)$ where $\mathit{arg\_name}_1$ and $\mathit{arg\_name}_2$ name two other different argument rules.

---

[7] Initially, the framework of GORGIAS had the name $LPwNF$: Logic Programming without Negation as failure.

[8] As we will see in Sect. 5 of the tutorial, it is not necessary to work at this internal level of GORGIAS when developing applications.

Example 4 (Commonsense Reasoning). The following argument rules express a common sense knowledge about birds (b), in particular penguins (p), flying (f) or not. We assume that we have sensors that can recognize clearly objects that are birds. They are unable to recognize directly penguins, but instead can recognize if an object walks like a penguin, how tall it is, and how far away it is.

$$rule(r_1(X), f(X), []) : -b(X).$$
$$rule(r_3(X), p(X), []) : -walks\_like\_p(X).$$
$$rule(r_2(X), neg(f(X)), [p(X)]).$$
$$rule(r_4(X)neg(p(X)), []) : -over\_a\_meter(X).$$
$$rule(p_1(X), prefer(r_2(X), r_1(X)), []).$$
$$rule(p_2(X), prefer(r_4(X), r_3(X)), []) : -1m\_dist.$$

Suppose our sensors have given us the following trusted information about a particular object with identifier obj_1: $b(obj_1)$, $walks\_like\_p(obj_1)$, $over\_a\_meter(obj_1)$. Can we infer that obj_1 (possibly) flies or not, i.e., can $f(obj_1)$ or $neg(f(obj_1))$ be supported by admissible arguments or not?

GORGIAS will try to build a (composite) argument Δ supporting $f(obj_1)$ starting with the argument rule $r_1(obj_1)$ which supports $f(obj_1)$ based on the premise of $b(obj_1)$. This is attacked by the argument $A = \{r_2(obj_1), r_3(obj_1)\}$ on the claim of $f(obj_1)$ of Δ. Δ itself forms a defense against this as they are equally strong. But this attacking argument can by strengthened by including in it the priority argument $p_1(obj_1)$. Now Δ as it currently stands cannot defend against this strengthened composite attacking argument. It therefore needs to look for other arguments to help it do so, and so it adds in Δ the argument $r_4(obj_1)$. This is in conflict with the attack A on the claim of $p(obj_1)$ and (in the absence of any information of how close we are to the object) these conflicting arguments of A and $r_4(obj_1)$ are of non-comparable (or equal) strength and so the latter can form a defense against the former. Thus the extended $\Delta = \{r_1(obj_1), r_4(obj_1)\}$ forms an admissible argument supporting $f(obj_1)$. Note that $A = \{r_2(obj_1), r_3(obj_1)\}$ supporting $neg(f(obj_1))$ is also admissible.

Suppose now that we also have that $1m\_dist$ holds. When we are looking for a defense against the counter-argument A, GORGIAS can now use a stronger (than above) defense by including also the priority argument $p_2(obj_1)$ resulting in a final $\Delta = \{r_1(obj_1), r_4(obj_1), p_2(obj_1)\}$. In addition, now we cannot build an admissible argument supporting $neg(f(obj_1))$. Argument $A = \{r_2(obj_1), r_3(obj_1)\}$ is attacked strongly (i.e. it cannot defend back at this) by $\{r_4(obj_1), p_2(obj_1)\}$ and there is no other argument strong enough to defend against this.

An important feature of the GORGIAS generated admissible composite argument Δ supporting a claim is that this serves as an **explanation** for the possible adoption of the claim. This explanation at the internal level of the GORGIAS framework can be naturally translated into an **application level explanation** exhibiting the desired characteristics of being **attributive, contrastive and actionable** as follows:.

- **Attributive:** Extracted from the object-level argument rules in Δ.
- **Contrastive:** Extracted from the priority argument rules in Δ.
- **Actionable:** Extracted from the hypothetical[9] arguments in Δ.

From the internal GORGIAS explanation of $\Delta = \{r_1(obj_1), r_4(obj_1), p_2(obj_1)\}$ of Example 4 we automatically generate the application level explanation:

- The statement "$f(obj_1)$" is supported by: — $b(obj_1)$ and $neg(p(obj_1))$.
- This support is strengthened: — (against $p(obj_1)))$ by: "$1m\_dist$."

3   Cognitive Argumentation

In what follows, the natural link between human reasoning and argumentation will be exposed. It will present how *cognitive principles* drawn from Cognitive Psychology, Social Sciences and Philosophy can help develop an argumentation framework, called *Cognitive Argumentation*, as a case of structured argumentation, $\langle As, \mathcal{C}, \succ \rangle$, that is customized according to these cognitive principles. These principles would help us capture the context sensitive and adaptive nature of human reasoning as well as other computational features such as the "on demand" or "lazy process" of human reasoning. The framework of Cognitive Argumentation will be illustrated by discussing in detail the particular case of the *suppression task* as studied in Cognitive Psychology to understand the nature of human reasoning.

3.1   The Suppression Task

In the psychological study of the *suppression task* three groups of participants were asked to derive conclusions given variations of a set of premises. Group I was given the following two premises: *If she has an essay to finish, then she will study late in the library. ($e \rightsquigarrow \ell$). She has an essay to finish. (e).* The participants were asked what **necessarily** follows from the above two premises. They could choose between the following three answers: *She will study late in the library. (ℓ) She will not study late in the library. ($\overline{\ell}$)* and *She may or may not study late in the library. (ℓ or $\overline{\ell}$)* In group I, 96% of the participants concluded: *She will study late in the library.*

In addition to the above two premises for Group I, Group II was given the following premise: *If she has a textbook to read, then she will study late in the library. ($t \rightsquigarrow \ell$)* Still, 96% of the participants concluded that *She will study late in the library.* Finally, Group III received, together with the two premises of Group I, additionally the following premise: *If the library stays open, then she will study late in the library. ($o \rightsquigarrow \ell$)* In this group only 38% concluded that *She will study late in the library:* The conclusion drawn in the previous groups was *suppressed* in Group III.

---

[9] These are arguments whose premises are empty but are generally weaker than any conflicting argument grounded on some given premises.

Cognitive Principles. Humans make assumptions while reasoning, many of which are not necessarily valid under formal (classical) logic. Yet, humans are pretty good in explaining plausibly why they make these assumptions. Let us consider some such (typically) non-formal or extra-logical properties and formalize them as cognitive principles.

According to Grice, human communicate according to the *maxim of quality*, implying that humans try to be truthful. Applied to the suppression task this implies the following: When the experimenter states *She has an essay to finish*, then participants believe this information to be true. To reflect this principle, we establish (strong) factual argument schemes. Further, following Grice's *maxim of relevance*, mentioned information is assumed to be relevant. Even though mentioned information is not necessarily factual (e.g., *if the library stays open*), humans can still construct various context-dependent hypotheses supporting statements concerning this information. For this purpose we establish (weak) hypothesis argument schemes.

Consider again the conditional $(e \rightsquigarrow \ell)$: *She has an essay to finish* is sufficient support for *She will study late in the library*. Thus we say that e in $(e \rightsquigarrow \ell)$ is a sufficient condition. Similarly, t is a sufficient condition in $(t \rightsquigarrow \ell)$ Yet, *the library stays open* is not sufficient support for *She will study late in the library* in conditional $(o \rightsquigarrow \ell)$. However, *the library is not open* plausibly explains *She will not study late in the library*. Here, o in $(o \rightsquigarrow \ell)$ is a necessary condition. Conditionals with sufficient condition and conditionals with necessary condition will be denoted by $\overset{s}{\rightsquigarrow}$ and $\overset{n}{\rightsquigarrow}$, respectively. Further, we establish two types of argument schemes for both types of conditionals.

The following cognitively motivated relative strength relation among schemes will apply for the dialectic argumentation process: Fact schemes are the strongest schemes, whereas hypotheses schemes are the weakest schemes, and necessary schemes are stronger than sufficient schemes.

The Suppression Task in Argumentation. Given the above principles we can build an argumentation framework, $\langle As, \mathcal{C}, \succ \rangle$, where As contains argument schemes drawn from the cognitive principles. To do so we assume that we have a cognitive state $\mathcal{S} = \langle \mathcal{F}, \mathcal{A} \rangle$ where $\mathcal{F}$ is the set of facts, and $\mathcal{A}$ is the set of relevance, namely $\mathcal{A}$ includes all concepts that we are made aware of by the external environment. Then the *maxim of quality* principle gives a **fact scheme**: $\mathsf{fact}(L) = (\emptyset \rhd L) \in As$, applied for any statement $L \in \mathcal{F}$ of the current cognitive state $\mathcal{S} = (\mathcal{F}, \mathcal{A})$. Similarly, the *maxim of relevance* principle gives a **hypothesis scheme**: $\mathsf{hyp}(A) = (\emptyset \rhd A) \in As$ and $\mathsf{hyp}(\overline{A}) = (\emptyset \rhd \overline{A}) \in As$, applied for any proposition, $A \in \mathcal{A}$ of the current cognitive state $\mathcal{S} = (\mathcal{F}, \mathcal{A})$. The two different types of a condition P in relation to a consequent Q, each give a **conditional** argument schemes: When P **is sufficient**: $\mathsf{suff}(P \rightsquigarrow Q) = (P \rhd Q)$ and when P **is necessary**: $\mathsf{necc}(\overline{P} \rightsquigarrow \overline{Q}) = (\overline{P} \rhd \overline{Q})$. Finally, the conflict relation $\mathcal{C}$ is simply that of negation, and the strength relation $\succ$ among the argument schemes is that given above in the cognitive principles.

We will then see that human reasoning in the suppression task can be understood through the dialectic process of argumentation to build acceptable (or admissible) arguments supporting the statement of the question and its

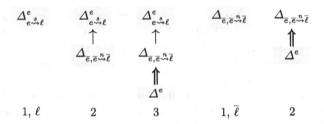

$$\Delta^e_{e\rightsquigarrow \ell} \qquad \Delta^e_{e\rightsquigarrow \ell} \qquad \Delta^e_{e\rightsquigarrow \ell} \qquad \Delta_{\bar{e},\bar{e}\rightsquigarrow^n \bar{\ell}} \qquad \Delta_{\bar{e},\bar{e}\rightsquigarrow^n \bar{\ell}}$$

$$\uparrow \qquad\qquad \uparrow \qquad\qquad \Uparrow$$

$$\Delta_{\bar{e},\bar{e}\rightsquigarrow^n \bar{\ell}} \qquad \Delta_{\bar{e},\bar{e}\rightsquigarrow^n \bar{\ell}} \qquad \Delta^e$$

$$\Uparrow$$

$$\Delta^e$$

$$1, \ell \qquad\qquad 2 \qquad\qquad 3 \qquad\qquad 1, \bar{\ell} \qquad\qquad 2$$

Fig. 2. Argumentation process for ℓ and $\bar{\ell}$ in Group I. Only ℓ is acceptable.

negation. Figures 2 and 3 show this for Group I and Group III in terms of the following **dialectic argumentation** process:

Step 1 construct a root argument supporting a conclusion of interest,
Step 2 consider a counterargument against the root argument,
Step 3 find a defense argument against the counterargument,
Step 4 check if this defense argument is not in conflict with the root argument,
Step 5 add this defense argument to the root argument,
Repeat from **Step 2**, with the extended root argument.

Carrying out the process until there are no other counterarguments in **Step 2** that have not already being considered, clearly results in an extended root argument that is an acceptable argument supporting the conclusion of interest.

Figure 2 shows this process to build an argument for ℓ (for Group I) starting with the relatively strong argument of $\Delta^e_{e\rightsquigarrow \ell} = \{\mathsf{fact}(e), \mathsf{suff}(e \rightsquigarrow \ell)\}$ (Fig. 2.1, ℓ). This is attacked by the argument $\Delta_{\bar{e},\bar{e}\rightsquigarrow^n \bar{\ell}} = \{\mathsf{hyp}(\bar{e}), \mathsf{necc}(\bar{e} \rightsquigarrow \bar{\ell})\}$ supporting $\bar{\ell}$ (Fig. 2.2) but this immediately defended against (or defeated) by $\Delta^e = \{\mathsf{fact}(e)\}$ (Fig. 2.3) which attacks $\Delta_{\bar{e},\bar{e}\rightsquigarrow^n \bar{\ell}}$ on the hypothesis part it contains. This strong attack by Δ^e which cannot be defended against is the reason why we cannot build an acceptable argument supporting $\bar{\ell}$, as we see in the right part of Fig. 2. Hence, on the one hand $\Delta^e_{e\rightsquigarrow \ell}$ acceptably supports ℓ while there is no acceptable support for $\bar{\ell}$. Consequently, ℓ is a definite conclusion. This conforms with the empirical observation of an overwhelming majority of responses for *She will study late in the library* in this first group (96%).

In contrast, for Group III, Fig. 3 shows how we can build acceptable arguments for either ℓ (left part of the figure) or $\bar{\ell}$ (right part of the figure) using the new argument $\Delta_{\bar{o},\bar{o}\rightsquigarrow^n \bar{\ell}} = \{\mathsf{hyp}(\bar{o}), \mathsf{necc}(\bar{o} \rightsquigarrow \bar{\ell})\}$ that is enabled by the awareness, in Group III, of the concept of open and conditional schemes involving this. Hence in Group III both ℓ and $\bar{\ell}$ are acceptably supported and hence are only plausible (credulous) conclusions. This then accounts for the observed suppression effect, where only 38% responded that definitely *She will study late in the library*. Those participants who considered the possibility of the library being not open could support that she did not study in the library and so did not answer that ℓ definitely holds. All twelve cases of the suppression task, where empirical data is collected, can similarly be accounted for in Cognitive Argumentation.

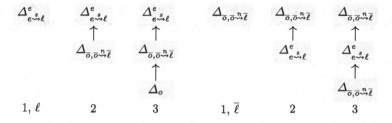

Fig. 3. Argumentation process for ℓ and $\bar{\ell}$ in Group III. Both ℓ and $\bar{\ell}$ are acceptable.

3.2 The COGNICA System

COGNICA[10] is a system, built on top of the GORGIAS system, that implements the framework of Cognitive Argumentation with emphasis on conditional reasoning. It is based on the particular work of Johnson-Laird and Byrne, "Conditionals: A Theory of Meaning, Pragmatics, and Inference" and the mental models theory that underlies this work. It has a simple interface of a Controlled Natural Language for expressing different types of conditional sentences which are automatically translated into the GORGIAS argumentation framework by adapting and extending the mental models interpretation from a theory on individual conditionals to sets of conditionals and their interaction.

The controlled natural language of COGNICA allows one to enter conditionals in these different types as *foreground knowledge*, i.e., particular knowledge that the system would reason about. Any relevant *background knowledge* is entered in the system, alongside the foreground knowledge, using exactly the same conditional form of controlled natural language.

Example 5 (Foreground Knowledge). Consider the ethics example of "Hal vs Carla" introduced in the tutorial on Argumentation and AI in this school.[11] Its specific foreground knowledge can be captured as:

If use someone's resource **then** compensate.
If justified use of someone's resource **then** not compensate.
If in life threatening situation **then** justified use of someone's resource.
If have alternatives **then** not justified use of someone's resource.

Then given a certain case where the following facts hold, "use of someone's resource", "in life threatening situation" and "have alternatives", the COGNICA system will reply "Maybe" to the query of whether "compensate" holds or not.

COGNICA provides explanations in verbal and graphical form for its answers. Figure 4 shows the graphical explanation for the above answer "Maybe". These

---

[10] http://cognica.cs.ucy.ac.cy/COGNICAb/login.php.
[11] "Hal, a diabetic, loses his insulin in an accident through no fault of his own. Before collapsing into a coma he rushes to the house of Carla, another diabetic. She is not at home, but Hal enters her house and uses some of her insulin. Was Hal justified, and does Carla have a right to compensation?".

graphical explanations present the argumentative dialectic nature of reasoning by COGNICA as *"reasoning pathways"* of the "mind" of the COGNICA system.

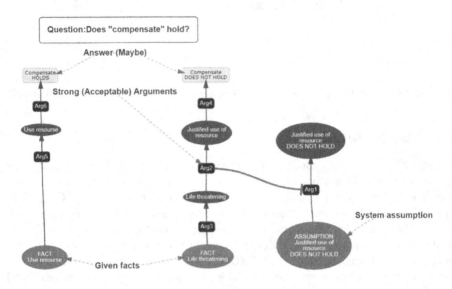

Fig. 4. Visual explanation of COGNICA for the "Hal vs Carla" example.

A first evaluation experiment has been set up to evaluate both the "naturality" of the system's conclusions and the possible effect of the system's explanations on the human reasoning. The main part of the experiment consists of each participant shown a short piece of text about a common everyday situation and asked to answer questions on whether a statement holds. The human participant is then shown the answer of COGNICA with its explanations and asked to reconsider her/his answer after seeing these. The initial results of this experiment have shown 70% agreement between human participants and COGNICA on the answers which increases to 85% agreement after seeing the explanation of COGNICA. The change of human's answers occurred mainly when the COGNICA answer was "maybe", and there is a "drift" to more "careful or intense reasoning" by the human participants as they continue. The exercise is open to anyone and can be found at http://cognica.cs.ucy.ac.cy/cognica_evaluation/index.html.

3.3 Argumentation and Cognitive Architectures

The cognitive architecture ACT-R is a theory about how human cognition works. Cognitive functions are represented by modules that communicate with others through buffers. Simulations of these modules and their interactions aim at better understanding processes in human cognition. One strength of ACT-R is that is allows the representation of knowledge symbolically while including sub-symbolic components. Here, we will sketch how cognitive argumentation can be guided by some functionalities in ACT-R. In particular, we discuss the declarative memory, the procedural module, and spreading activation.

Declarative Memory. Declarative memory stores knowledge as chunks, each of them having a name (used for reference) and possibly containing a set of named slots with single values. Consider the following two examples:

```
(ESSAY-SUF isa meaning word "essay" context SUFFICIENT)
(ARGUMENT-FOR-L isa argument fact "essay" position "library"
                opposite-pos "not library" context SUFFICIENT)
```

The chunk named `ESSAY-SUF` is of type `meaning` and has two slots: `word` has the (string) value `"essay"`, whereas `context` has the value `SUFFICIENT`, which is yet another chunk. The chunk `ARGUMENT-FOR-L` is of type `argument` and has four slots: `fact`, `position`, and `opposite-pos` have the (string) value `"essay"`, `"library"` and `"not library"`, respectively, whereas the slot `context` has as value the chunk `SUFFICIENT`.

```
(p retrieve-word-semantics        (p retrieve-counter-argument
   =imaginal>                        =goal>
      word       =word                  state       retrieve-counter
==>                                   =retrieval>
   +retrieval>                          fact        =fact
   isa meaning                          position    =position
   word       =word)                    opposite-pos =opposite-pos
                                      ==>
                                      +retrieval>
                                         fact        =fact
                                         position    =opposite-pos
                                      =goal>
                                         state       choose-strongest)
```

Fig. 5. Two simple examples of production rules in ACT-R.

Procedural Module. The procedural module synchronizes the different functionalities in ACT-R and modifies the model's state through the execution of rules. Consider the production rule `retrieve-word-semantics` in Fig. 5 (left): This production rule is only considered if the left hand side (everything before the `==>` sign) is true: there needs to be a slot called `word` in the imaginal buffer with a certain value represented as the variable `=word`. Note that the imaginal buffer can be understood as a place where context information is represented internally. If this rule fires, then the right hand side applies (everything after the `==>` sign): the cognitive model requests a chunk from the `retrieval` buffer, which needs to be of type `meaning` with the slot `word` and has the value `=word`, as defined in the imaginal buffer. Assume that the cognitive model reads the string "essay" which then will be represented internally in its imaginal buffer. If this rule is fired and ESSAY-SUF is in the declarative memory, then ESSAY-SUF matches the request and might be retrieved.

The production rule retrieve-counter-argument in Fig. 5 (right) only applies if the state of the goal buffer is retrieve-counter and the retrieval buffer on the left hand side (everything before ==>) contains a chunk with slots fact, position and opposite-pos. If this rule fires, a new retrieval request will be made, i.e., a chunk is requested to the declarative memory constraint by the following properties: The new retrieval needs to have (1) the same value in the slot fact as the current chunk in the retrieval buffer, and (2) the same value in the slot position as the current chunk in the retrieval buffer has in its opposite-pos slot.

Argument Retrieval Guided by Chunk Activation. Recall the dialectic argumentation process (Steps 1–5 on page 9) described in the previous section: This procedure is computationally intensive because in all the main steps, **Steps 1–3**, a choice is required and all counter arguments need to be considered. Yet, exhaustively searching for arguments does not seem to be cognitively plausible. It is more likely that humans consider only a few arguments, possibly only the most ubiquitous ones. Yet, how to determine these arguments? One possible assumption is that this choice is guided by the context, which in ACT-R can be modeled through the activation of chunks: The activation of a chunk in ACT-R is a numerical value based on the recency and frequency this chunk was previously used, a noise parameter and the spreading activation, i.e., in how far the chunk is related to other chunks in the current context.[12] The chunk's activation determines whether that chunk will be chosen upon retrieval.

In the current ACT-R implementation, the main arguments are represented as whole chunks. The retrieval of arguments depends on their activation, which is determined by whether the given contexts will rather activate the NECESSARY or SUFFICIENT chunks. Consider the production rule retrieve-counter-argument on page 13: The counter argument with the highest activation will be chosen, and this activation in turn, is determined by the parameters above. For instance, if the chunk SUFFICIENT has a higher activation than the chunk NECESSARY, arguments with the value SUFFICIENT in their context slot (see argument ARGUMENT-FOR-L on page 13) are more likely to be retrieved than arguments with the same slot values for fact and position but where context has the chunk value NECESSARY.

4   Argumentation for Learning

We now continue to discuss the fundamental role of argumentation in the backdrop of the emergent need for Explainable ML, and how argumentation supports

---

[12] For more information on the activation function see e.g., http://act-r.psy.cmu.edu/wordpress/wp-content/themes/ACT-R/tutorials/unit5.htm.

this role by: *(i)* acknowledging the need to deal with data that is uncertain, incomplete, and inconsistent (with any classical logical theory); *(ii)* offering a target language (syntax and semantics) for learned knowledge that is compatible with human cognition; and *(iii)* supporting a flexible prediction and coverage mechanism for learning that can feed back and guide the learning process.

4.1   What Should a Language of Learning Be Like?

Modern machine learning is typically viewed as a process of turning data into a model that can accurately predict the labels of future data. Increasingly, this focus on predictive accuracy is deemed insufficient as a metric of success, and the ability to explain the reasons behind these predictions is also emphasized.

What counts as an acceptable explanation ultimately boils down to what the purpose of learning is. Learning does not exist, nor carried out, in vacuum, but always takes place in the context of facilitating the informed decision-making of some agent. Learning is coupled with the eventual use of the learned model by the agent, by having each of the two processes guiding and restricting the other. Thus, for example, in situations where a learned model will be used to guide the taking of actions, the coupling implies that learning cannot be done passively.

Learning a model is, thus, not an end but a means to its eventual use. Explanations act as proxy translations of the model into a cognitively-compatible form for the decision-making agent to: *(i)* understand, and adopt or contest, the model's predictions; *(ii)* use predictions and prior knowledge to reach a conclusion; or *(iii)* assimilate the model with prior knowledge in a coherent way.

The importance of explanations as proxy translations becomes more apparent in cases of a dilemma: *(i)* on competing predictions of the learned model; *(ii)* on whether we can trust the prediction from a black box; or *(iii)* on how to best utilize or go forward from the prediction. The learned model by itself can not help the decision-making agent to resolve such types of dilemmas, and explanations, then, in support or against the various choices at hand, can help to do so.

The desired characteristics for a language of explanations are none others than those needed to support the role of learning as a facilitator of decision-making: flexibility, adaptability, and ability to recognize and accommodate the inadequacy of the learned model (and the learning process and data) to capture fully the phenomena that produce the data; ability to place the learned model in the cognitive sphere of the decision-making agent; and ability of linking back to the learning process to guide it towards improving the learned model's adequacy.

4.2   Argumentation as a Language of Learning

Below we demonstrate how argumentation can undertake the role for a language of learning and explanations through Pierce's "Beans from a Bag" scenario.

We draw beans from a given bag. Observing that all the drawn beans so far are white, we learn the induced argument arg(W): "beans in this bag are white". If, however, we happen to draw a black bean b1 from the bag, our learned model

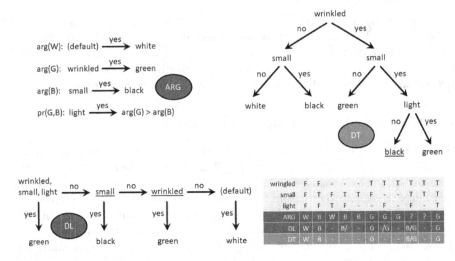

Fig. 6. Representations of a model learned following the "Beans from a Bag" scenario based on argumentation (ARG), decision trees (DT), or decision lists (DL). Underlined nodes are choices made during learning despite lack of evidence in the training data. The table shows the predictions of the three models on selected data points, where '?' is a dilemma, '-' is an abstention due to missing information in a data point, and pairs of predictions show a dependence on the choices of underlined nodes in learned models.

does not collapse, but is gracefully extended with the observational argument arg(b1): "this particular bean is black". By its nature, an observational argument is stronger than an induced one, naturally accommodating the specific exception or anomaly, while maintaining that all other beans in the bag are white.

As we continue drawing beans from the bag, we might encounter additional non-white beans and learn the induced arguments arg(B): "small beans in this bag are black" and arg(G): "wrinkled beans in this bag are green". Having more specific conditions than arg(W), these two induced arguments are stronger than the latter. So, if we draw again a small bean, then arg(B) will defeat arg(W), and will explain its predictions by *attributing* it to the size of the bean.

The two induced arguments are incomparable, and produce a dilemma in cases of a small wrinkled bean, suggesting that learning needs more such beans to resolve the ambiguity. By drawing additional beans, we might end up learning the priority argument arg(G) > arg(B) if light: "if light bean then green", which does not make prediction per se, but resolves the dilemma by offering a *contrastive* explanation of why a small wrinkled bean should be green rather than black.

One could posit that other typical white-box representations with some form of prioritization could equally-well take on the role of a language of learning or explanations. Figure 6 shows possible learned models for the scenario above, using argumentation, decision trees, and decision lists, which we compare next.

First, in terms of the representation structure, the conflict resolution process in argumentation is learnable and expressible in a layered fashion. This yields a more compact representation, and avoids imposing a total order or mutual exclusion between conditions. Argumentation does not necessitate access to full information, or even negative information in some cases, and is not over-committed to always reach a prediction if not supported by the statistical evidence from the data. Argumentation can still abstain if the information in any given data point is insufficient, and it will cleanly distinguish an abstention from a dilemma.

Second, in terms of cognitive compatibility, argumentation does not confound the attributive (object-level) explanations from the contrastive (meta-level) ones that defeat conflicting decisions. Argumentation also supports actionable explanations through the elaboration-tolerant amendment of the learned model.

Third, in terms of learning flexibility, argumentation supports the integration of other models/new knowledge, its lack of insistence to firmly predict if not supported by statistical evidence allows it to identify learning gaps for further training, and its natural handling of missing information allows it to encode knowledge and engage in conflict resolution from visible data only.

Despite the natural connection between argumentation and learning, and the diverse ways in which past learning work has used argumentation, this connection remains largely under-explored. This is particularly so in the context of neural-symbolic systems, where conflicts between signals from multiple neural modules could be resolved by an argumentation theory, offering a cognitively-compatible decision-support layer on top of the opaque perception layer, which could help guide the latter's training in a modular and compositional fashion.

To further appreciate how argumentation and learning can fruitfully interact, we will present two cases of learning with ex ante explainability in mind, where arguments are used natively to represent the learned model and/or data.

4.3   Case Study 1: Autodidactic Learning of Arguments

The first case study that we consider is that of autodidactic (or self-supervised) learning of arguments from partial data, treated as an appearance of some underlying reality, whose commonsense regularities one wishes to learn. These appearances, or observations, are represented as sets of literals; cf. Fig. 8.

The learning mechanism that we consider is called NERD, standing for Never-Ending Rule Discovery. NERD operates in an online/streaming fashion, and passively processes received observations, seeking to identify associations between literals. Confidence in learned rules increases or decreases every time they are satisfied or falsified by an observation. Rules start by being provisional, and become active when their associated confidence exceeds a prescribed threshold.

To resolve conflicts between rules, NERD prioritizes rules based on the order in which they became active, the intuition being that a rule with fewer exceptions (e.g., that penguins cannot fly) will have stronger statistical support from the data, and will become active earlier than a rule with more exceptions (e.g., that birds can fly). Accordingly, when the former rule becomes active, it explains away some of the counter-examples of the latter rule (e.g., observations where birds are also penguins do not count as negative evidence for the latter rule), supporting the latter rule further to gain confidence; see Fig. 7.

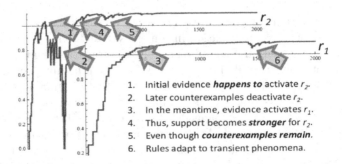

1. Initial evidence *happens to* activate r_2.
2. Later counterexamples deactivate r_2.
3. In the meantime, evidence activates r_1.
4. Thus, support becomes *stronger* for r_2.
5. Even though *counterexamples remain*.
6. Rules adapt to transient phenomena.

Fig. 7. Updating of the confidence of two learned rules as observations are processed by NERD. The horizontal line in each graph indicates the threshold above which rules are considered active. The arrows show key points of the learning process.

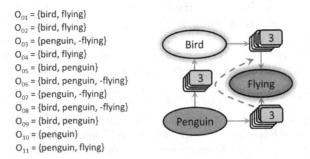

O_{01} = {bird, flying}
O_{02} = {bird, flying}
O_{03} = {penguin, -flying}
O_{04} = {bird, flying}
O_{05} = {bird, penguin}
O_{06} = {bird, penguin, -flying}
O_{07} = {penguin, -flying}
O_{08} = {bird, penguin, -flying}
O_{09} = {bird, penguin}
O_{10} = {penguin}
O_{11} = {penguin, flying}

Fig. 8. Observations (left) are iteratively processed by the NERD algorithm to produce the learned model (right). During the last iteration, "penguin" and "flying" are observed (green filled ovals), "bird" and "-flying" are inferred (green and red glowing ovals) by applying the corresponding active rules, and the confidence of the rules "penguin implies not flying" and "bird implies flying" is, respectively, demoted and promoted. The latter rule becomes active (having previously been deactivated from an earlier active state), and is given lower priority than the currently active former rule. (Color figure online)

The interaction between rules happens naturally by simply reasoning with active rules — chaining them together to form arguments, whose strengths come from rule priorities — before each observation is utilized for learning. This approach fully aligns with the coupling of learning with the eventual use of knowledge learned from partial data, as this knowledge is to be used to comprehend observations by completing their missing parts. As NERD proceeds, the learned model increases its coverage with additional (active) rules; see Fig. 8.

4.4 Case Study 2: eXplanations In, eXplanations Out

The second case study that we consider is that of learning by engaging with a user who offers advice to the learner, and from which one wishes to learn a user-specific policy. A learning algorithm processes the feedback coming from a user

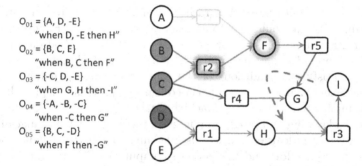

$O_{01} = \{A, D, -E\}$
    "when D, -E then H"
$O_{02} = \{B, C, E\}$
    "when B, C then F"
$O_{03} = \{-C, D, -E\}$
    "when G, H then -I"
$O_{04} = \{-A, -B, -C\}$
    "when -C then G"
$O_{05} = \{B, C, -D\}$
    "when F then -G"

Fig. 9. Contexts and corresponding user reactions (left) are iteratively processed by the Machine Coaching protocol to produce the learned model (right). During the last iteration, "B", "C", and "not D" are observed (green and red filled circles), and "F" is inferred (green glowing circle) by applying the corresponding rule. Following the user's reaction, a new rule $r5$ is added, and is given higher priority than the existing rule $r4$. (Color figure online)

following the eXplanations In, eXplanations Out (XIXO) principle: if we expect to learn a model able to offer explanations that are cognitively compatible with, and acceptable to, a given user, then the same type of explanations should be offered during the learning phase as training material to the learner.

The learning mechanism that we consider is called Machine Coaching, emphasizing the active interaction of the learner with a coach. Machine Coaching operates in an online/streaming fashion, and passively processes received observations. Unlike in the first case study, these observations are not meant to correspond to experiences from which one learns, but rather statements that provide the context within which learning takes place. Given such a context, Machine Coaching proceeds to reason with its existing learned model — following the approach of chaining rules to form arguments from the first case study, and aligning with the coupling of learning — to draw an inference, which it presents to the user along with the arguments in support of that inference.

The user reacts to the inference and the associated explanation of the learned model by offering a counter-argument explaining why the learned model's inference or explanation is not acceptable. Machine Coaching revises the learned model by integrating the user's explanation. This integration happens naturally by virtue of the learned model being represented in the language of argumentation, so that the simple addition of the counter-argument with higher strength than existing conflicting arguments suffices; see Fig. 9. This approach fully aligns with the XIXO principle and the coupling of learning.

Unlike typical online learning, in Machine Coaching the supervision signal is not the label of a data point, nor a reaction to whether the prediction of the current learned model is correct, but rather a reaction to whether the explanation of the learned model is acceptable to the user. On the other hand, the goal of the learned model is not to anticipate what supervision signal it would have gotten on a future data point, but rather to make a prediction and an associated explanation that would lead to no reaction from the user. Finally, note that each supervision signal offers information beyond the individual data point, as it proactively provides information on the labels of multiple future data points (those that satisfy the conditions of the counter-argument), making the process more efficient than a typical supervised learning process. Despite ultimately being a form of machine learning, Machine Coaching can be best understood as lying between learning and programming, with the dialectical exchange of explanations between the learner and the user leading to a better balance between the user's cognitive effort and the learner's computational burden, compared to what one would get at either of the extreme cases of learning and programming.

5   Applications of Argumentation

In this final section we will see how to develop real-life, large scale applications of argumentation based on the theory and methods presented in the earlier parts of the tutorial. We will examine a general methodology for developing argumentation-based systems within a simple high-level architecture and illustrate this with several example applications from various domains. These AI systems are designed with an emphasis on their (**soft**) **embodiment** within an external dynamic environment with a two-way continual interaction with the environment that includes the "human in the loop". To realize such human-centric AI systems we can follow a human, "mind-like" architecture, as in Fig. 10.

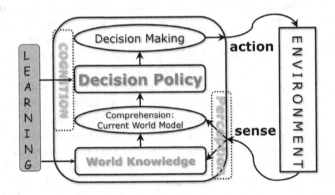

Fig. 10. High-level architecture for Cognitive AI Systems.

In this architecture there are two levels of knowledge that the system utilizes. At the top we have the decision policy containing the specific **application knowledge** of the requirements which regulate the decision making process. This is expressed in terms of high-level concepts about the current state of affairs under which a decision has to be taken and depends on the high-level understanding of the current external environment based on the sensory information that the system has (just) received. Recognizing the information received through the sensors and comprehending this in terms of the higher-level application language is based on **world knowledge**. This knowledge associates the lower-level information from the environment to increasingly higher-levels of generalization or abstraction required by the top application knowledge.

The central task of developing these system rests in acquiring or learning these two pieces of knowledge. This poses two **major challenges**:

- **Acquisition of Application Knowledge** What is an appropriate language level that would facilitate capturing the application knowledge either from the application expert and/or the application data? What is the appropriate cognitive-level of this language?
- **Middleware from Sensory Information to High-level Application Concepts** What are effective ways of comprehending the relevant part of the current application environment? How do we recognize the current state of affairs and the particular decision context in which the system finds itself?

5.1   SoDA: Software Development Through Argumentation

Motivated by the above challenges we can adopt a knowledge representation approach where knowledge is captured in terms of a structure called **Scenario-Based Preference (SBP)**. This is a high-level structure that allows us to represent knowledge directly at the application level in terms of the application language. It can be translated automatically into an executable *Gorgias* argumentation theory thus implementing the decision policy and comprehension modules of our Cognitive AI system.

Scenario-based preferences are triplets, $\langle Id, Scenario, POptions \rangle$ where Id is a unique identifier of the triplet, *Scenario* is a set of conditions that partially describe a possible subset of states or scenarios of the application environment and *POptions* is a subset of decision options that are preferred in any state where the *Scenario* conditions hold. As we will see below it is very useful to group these scenarios in hierarchies of increasing specificity. Essentially, scenario-based preferences are a formal structure that allows us to capture knowledge of the general cognitive form:

"Generally, when [SITUATION] prefer O_i, but in the more particular [CONTEXT], prefer O_j"

where O_i and O_j are subsets of options and SITUATION, CONTEXT are subsets of scenario conditions with CONTEXT describing a more specific situation.

Let us illustrate, through a simple example, SBPs and a methodology, called *SoDA: Software Development through Argumentation*, for acquiring and building the application knowledge as a set of hierarchies of SBPs.

Example 6 (Study Assistant). Consider the problem of deciding where to study with three possible options, study at the *Library*, *Home* or *Cafe*. Assume that we are given or learned the decision guidelines:

"When [Have Homework] prefer to study at *Home*, *Cafe*, but if [Late], prefer to study at *Home* or when [Need Sources] prefer to study at *Library*."

This is captured by following hierarchy of scenario-based preferences:

$$\langle 1, \{Homework\}, \{Home, Cafe\}\rangle \quad \begin{array}{l} \langle 11, \{Homework, Late\}, \{Home\}\rangle \\ \langle 12, \{Homework, Need\_Sources\}, \{Library\}\rangle \end{array}$$

Here each of 11 and 12 form **refinements** of the root scenario-based preference 1 resulting into two the hierarchies of (1,11) and (1,12).

Together with the operation of refinement, we have a second operation of **combination**, where we consider the union of scenario conditions from two SBPs. From Example 6 consider the combination of scenarios in 11 and 12 to generate the interim new SBP of: $\langle 11|12i, Homework, Late, Need\_Sources\}$, $\{Home, Library\}\rangle$.

We can then return to the decision policy, e.g., ask or learn from the application owner or user, for possible preferences in the combined scenario and generate SBPs refining the interim SBP. For example, we may learn a preference to *Library* and so have: $\langle 11|12, \{Homework, Late, Need\_Sources\}, \{Library\}\rangle$.

The *SoDA* methodology provides guidelines for carrying out this process of knowledge engineering of scenario-based preferences. An associated tool, called **Gorgias-B**[13], supports the methodology by providing a framework to build contextual refinements of SBPs and to consider appropriate combinations of these. This tool also carries out an automatic generation, from the SBPs, of an argumentation theory in the *Gorgias* framework and an interface to execute this under the GORGIAS system. This has now evolved into a professional platform tool, called *rAIson*, developed by a new company, called *Argument Theory*[14].

5.2   Application Language Levels: Example Applications

The language that we use to specify the decision policy of an application can vary according to the nature of the application. Ideally, the level of the application language should be as close as possible to natural language or some form of structured natural language. Given a language level the task for translating a decision policy into scenario-based preferences differs in the degree of manual effort required. The following is a list of different application language levels each together with a typical real-life application domain.

– **Free Text in Structured Natural Language**.
   An example case is that where the policy is given in a **Legal Document**. Such documents are highly structured and are already in a scenario-based preference and argumentation form. The translation into a scenario-based preference form is carried out manually but this is direct and it is easily

---

[13] http://gorgiasb.tuc.gr/.
[14] https://www.argument-theory.com/en/.

carried out. We can then automate the task of **compliance** with the legal requirements providing explanations of why an action is compliant or not and if not how it can become compliant. An example of such application is MEDICA[15] a system for granting the appropriate level of access to the electronic patient record, as specified by the European law.

- **Controlled Natural Language in a Restricted Vocabulary**
  This language level is appropriate for **Cognitive Assistant** applications where these systems provide services in a restricted domain of interest. Examples of such cognitive assistants are Call Assistant, Tourist Assistant, Care Assistant, Calendar Assistant, Investor Assistant and Social Media Assistant. These systems can start with a minimal vocabulary and gradually expand it as the systems are starting to be deployed. The policy guidelines are given in a controlled form of natural language customized to the vocabulary and particular features of the domain of application.
  Let us consider the example of a Social Media assistant. This is a system that monitors the user's social media feed and helps a user manage the information overload by explainably "re-arranging", according to the user's liking, the information pieces, e.g., posts, that she/he receives. For example, for each post the assistant would decide amongst highlighting this at the top or even notifying the user, demoting it to the bottom or hiding it completely and other such actions. A user can express her/his personal policy guidelines at a high level using controlled natural language. For example:

  I like sports, particularly tennis and basketball. I love drama and comedy movies especially if produced in the UK. I like to know what my closest friends are doing and to stay in touch with current popular news. But I hate politics except when related to climate change.

  Representing this in scenario-based preferences we take into consideration two types of information conveyed in this type of policies: (1) the high-level concepts that act as decision criteria, e.g., "sports", "drama movies", "produced in the UK", "closest friends", "popular news", ..., that form the scenario conditions and (2) the implicit preferences conveyed by various keywords used, e.g., "like", "love", "particularly" "stay in touch", "hate", "except", ..., used to fill in the preferred options in scenario-based preferences and to form refinements of these. The sensory information received by the social media assistant is the low-level data on each post that the user receives on a social media platform, such as who posted it, its content, its popularity figures, etc. We can then build *middleware* based on different technologies to decide on the description of the post in terms of the high-level concepts referred to in the decision policy. The output of the assistant is a presentation of the user's posts based on which classification and related action can be supported acceptably by the underlying *Gorgias* argumentation theory. The classification is shown next to the post together with its supporting explanation when the user wishes to see it. A typical example explanation, that highlights their contrasting nature is:

---

[15] http://medica.cs.ucy.ac.cy/.

"Even though this post is not (very) interesting to you it was made from a close friend."

– **Structured Tables of Scenario Hierarchies**

For applications that are based on expert knowledge, e.g., **Decision Support Assistants,** we need a more structured language to capture large scale amounts of expert knowledge. A suitable such structure is that of *structured tables* where each row essentially corresponds to a scenario-based preference. The first column of the table contains the scenario conditions and each of the other columns corresponds to a single option which is marked or not in each row as one of the preferred options in the scenario of the row.

In the medical domain, where this has been mostly applied, the doctors use their familiar medical language for constructing/filling these tables. Also they are already familiar, from Evidence Medicine, with the notions of supporting and differential evidence, which are directly used in the construction of these tables. This method for knowledge acquisition has been applied to two particular cases of medical decision support, in ophthalmology and in the much larger domain of gynecology. The purpose of the first system of *OPHTALMOLOGICA,* is to understand the level of severity of the possible disease(s) so that a scheduling appointment system (or the receptionist) can give an appropriate priority to the patient. The second system of *GAID: Gynecological AI Diagnostic Assistant* has its overall aim to:

"*Support clinicians feel more confident in decision, helping to avoid over-diagnosis of common diseases and to ensure that emergency cases are not missed out.*"

It covers fully the area of gynecology with over 140 diseases (i.e., options) and over a thousand different parameters (current symptoms, patient record, clinical examination findings and laboratory tests) that can affect the diagnosis. The system generates a set of suspicious diseases every time some new information about a patient is received (during a clinical visit to the doctor). All suspicious diseases come with an explanation, generated automatically from the *Gorgias* object-level and priority arguments that support the suspicion of the disease. A typical example of an explanation is:

"Under the information *Vaginal Burning* it is **recommended** that you investigate *Vulva Candidiasis.* This is also **supported** by *Post-Coital Bleeding* and further **strengthened** by *Vaginal Discharge.* A negative test for *Vaginal Secretions* would **exclude** this disease."

The GAID system is under a pilot clinical trial to evaluate both the accuracy of its suggested suspicious diseases as well as its guidance to (junior) clinicians to collect relevant information that would help focus the diagnosis.

5.3   Machine Learning Assisted Policy Formation

Machine Learning offers the possibility to automatically acquire (at least partly) the knowledge for Cognitive AI systems with the high-level architecture of

Fig. 10. As presented in Sect. 4, treating learned associations as object-level arguments we can continue the learning process to construct priority arguments over these thus improving the predictive power of our learned theory and providing more informed explanations. Importantly, by adopting this argumentation perspective on learning we can then integrate together with the machine learned knowledge other knowledge that is already known by experts (e.g., medical or clinical knowledge) and thus have a hybrid approach in generating and updating the knowledge of our application. Machine learning is thus integrated with knowledge elicitation methods directly from the "policy source/owner" as we saw above. Indeed in many expert application cases, but also in other application domains, we can have domain expert knowledge, or a company's business policy or a legal requirement, that it would be futile to insist to learn again through machine learning on a large data corpus of example cases.

Examples of applications where we have machine learning assisted knowledge generation or acquisition have been developed in the area of medical decision support area based on real-life data sets in the area of risk assessment of Stroke and the area of deciding on the possible development of Alzheimer. These systems act as *peer companions* to the doctors to offer a second opinion on a new case. This is done through **"peer explanations"** at the cognitive level of the specialists, e.g., the radiologist or doctor, offered by the system. An example of such a "peer explanation" for the domain of Stroke is:

"This patient is judged to be *asymptotic* **because** Log(GSM+40) is in the range [4.28, 5.17] and has no history of contralateral TIAs or Stroke. **Although** the patient has (Plaque Area)1/3 in the range [3.47, 6.78] and Discrete White Areas in the plaque, suggesting a risk for *stroke*, the first symptoms are **more significant when** the patient has (Plaque Area)1/3 less than 3.9."

Finally, we mention the area of **argument mining** which in effect uses machine learning to extract arguments (mostly from text) to construct knowledge in the form of argument graphs. This is particularly appropriate for learning the world knowledge on which we base the middle-ware of an application that links sensory information to high-level cognitive concepts on which the decision policy is formed. Argument mining is not covered in this tutorial but it is very important and the reader is urged to consult the many references on this topic.

References

1. Besnard, P., et al.: Tutorials on structured argumentation. Argument Comput. **5**(1), 1–4 (2014)
2. Kakas, A.C., Moraitis, P.: Argumentation based decision making for autonomous agents. In: Proceedings of 2nd International Joint Conference on Autonomous Agents & Multiagent Systems, AAMAS, pp. 883–890. ACM (2003)
3. Prakken, H.: An abstract framework for argumentation with structured arguments. Argument Comput. **1**(2), 93–124 (2010)
4. Anderson, J.R.: How Can the Human Mind Occur in the Physical Universe? Oxford University Press, Oxford (2007)

5. Byrne, R.: Suppressing valid inferences with conditionals. Cognition **31**, 61–83 (1989)
6. Dietz, E., Kakas, A.C.: Cognitive argumentation and the suppression task. CoRR abs/2002.10149 (2020). https://arxiv.org/abs/2002.10149
7. Michael, L.: Autodidactic learning and reasoning. doctoral dissertation. Harvard University, Cambridge (2008)
8. Michael, L.: Cognitive reasoning and learning mechanisms. In: Proceedings 4th BICA International Workshop on Artificial Intelligence and Cognition, pp. 2–23 (2016)
9. Michael, L.: Machine coaching. In: Proceedings 2019 IJCAI Workshop on Explainable Artificial Intelligence, pp. 80–86 (2019)
10. Almpani, S., Kiouvrekis, Y., Stefaneas, P.: Modeling of medical devices classification with computational argumentation. In: 2021 12th International Conference on Information, Intelligence, Systems Applications (IISA), pp. 1–6 (2021)
11. Kakas, A.C., Moraitis, P., Spanoudakis, N.: Gorgias: applying argumentation. Argument Comput. **10**(1), 55–81 (2019)

Social Simulation

Agent-Based Social Simulation for Policy Making

Fabian Lorig[1]($\boxtimes$), Loïs Vanhée[2], and Frank Dignum[2]

[1] Department of Computer Science and Media Technology, Internet of Things
and People Research Center, Malmö University, Malmö, Sweden
fabian.lorig@mau.se
[2] Department of Computing Science, Umeå University, Umeå, Sweden
{lois.vanhee,frank.dignum}@umu.se

Abstract. In agent-based social simulations (ABSS), an artificial population of intelligent agents that imitate human behavior is used to investigate complex phenomena within social systems. This is particularly useful for decision makers, where ABSS can provide a sandpit for investigating the effects of policies prior to their implementation. During the Covid-19 pandemic, for instance, sophisticated models of human behavior enable the investigation of the effects different interventions can have and even allow for analyzing why a certain situation occurred or why a specific behavior can be observed. In contrast to other applications of simulation, the use for policy making significantly alters the process of model building and assessment, and requires the modelers to follow different paradigms. In this chapter, we report on a tutorial that was organized as part of the ACAI 2021 summer school on AI in Berlin, with the goal of introducing agent-based social simulation as a method for facilitating policy making. The tutorial pursued six Intended Learning Outcomes (ILOs), which are accomplished by three sessions, each of which consists of both a conceptual and a practical part. We observed that the PhD students participating in this tutorial came from a variety of different disciplines, where ABSS is mostly applied as a research method. Thus, they do often not have the possibility to discuss their approaches with ABSS experts. Tutorials like this one provide them with a valuable platform to discuss their approaches, to get feedback on their models and architectures, and to get impulses for further research.

Keywords: Agent-based modeling · Simulation for crisis situations · Sophisticated agent architectures · Analysis of simulation outputs · Interaction with stakeholders · NetLogo

1 Introduction

The ongoing Covid-19 pandemic has impressively shown the field of tensions in which policy makers, e.g., politicians, public health agencies, and regional authorities, find themselves. There are expectations from the society, that critical

© Springer Nature Switzerland AG 2023
M. Chetouani et al. (Eds.): ACAI 2021, LNAI 13500, pp. 391–414, 2023.
https://doi.org/10.1007/978-3-031-24349-3_20

decisions should be made based on clear facts and reliable data, such that they are transparent for everyone. However, especially during pandemics and other crisis situations, decision makers are often facing challenges related to incomplete data, contradicting information, as well as rapid developments and changes of the situation, which results in a high degree of uncertainty. This makes it difficult to predict the effects of actions in advance and to identify the most suitable policies for a new situation. To take uncertainty into consideration when making decisions, different sources of data and evidence need to be taken into account and weighed against each other, to make a sound decision that ultimately results in the desired outcome.

A method that is particularly well-suited for assessing uncertainty is computer simulation [14]. Simulations provide a testbed that allows for efficiently conducing *what-if* analyses. It enables the observation of a system's behavior under different circumstances and the investigation of the effects of different actions without actually interfering with the system that shall be analyzed. This is achieved by developing and executing a model of the target system, which allows for conducting more time- and cost-efficient experiments without the risk of jeopardizing the target system itself. Especially with respect to the Covid-19 pandemic, simulations provide a valuable alternative to real-world experiments, which might take too long time in critical situations or which might be unethical as humans might be harmed. An example is the investigation of the effects different interventions might have on the spread of the virus, whose testing in the real world could cost human lives [10].

When investigating the effects and success of different policies, a major factor that needs to be taken into consideration is the behavior of the individuals that are affected by this policy. When, for instance, investigating the effects of interventions for containing epidemics (e.g., lockdowns, social distancing, or facemasks), it is crucial to consider that individuals (because of different reasons) may not always comply with restrictions or recommendations, which might lead to an undesired outcome. To this end, agent-based social simulations (ABSS) are a promising tool for decision makers as they, among other things, allow for investigating the effects different policies have on an artificial population consisting of so called *agents* [5,15]. In ABSS, each agent is characterized by a number of attributes, e.g., age, gender, or occupation, and reacts to its environment by imitating human behavior using AI. This allows for investigating the effects different policies might have before actually implementing them.

Discussing how ABSS can be used to facilitate policy making was the goal of the *"Social Simulation for Policy Making"* tutorial that was part of the *Advances Course on AI on Human Centered AI* (ACAI 2021), which took place in Berlin, Germany on October 11–14, 2021. ACAI[1] is the bi-yearly European summer school on AI, that was first organized in 1985.

The tutorial aimed at introducing the concept of ABSS as well as to discuss its applications to facilitate policy making by enabling the investigation of the

---

[1] https://eurai.org/activities/ACAI_courses (accessed Jun 2022).

potential effects of policies in advance. The Intended Learning Outcomes (ILO) [3] of the tutorial include that the students are able:

ILO-1: to describe and relate the principles of ABSS, including fundamental ABSS approaches and techniques as well as applications of ABSS to real-world problems

ILO-2: to conduct and analyze experiments using an existing ABSS model and a well-established ABSS simulator (NetLogo)

ILO-3: to identify and relate the key cognitive components in advanced ABSS models, to explain the main reasons for using cognitive models, and to identify the need for such models on a real-world problem

ILO-4: to explain and specify how an existing agent architecture in an ABSS model can be extended for facilitating the investigation of new policies

ILO-5: to explain how using ABSS for policy making alters the ABSS-making activities and to relate these activities to concrete deliverables

ILO-6: to analytically discover the origin of a complex emerging phenomena, based on extensive raw multidimensional ABSS output

The ILOs are structured in pairs of theoretical knowledge (Bloom's cognitive levels) and practical skills using action verbs (e.g., apply, analyse, evaluate, create) [1]. This enables the students to learn about the (intrinsically conceptual) cutting-edge research while still developing concrete first-person experience of practical skills through active learning [3].

The learning activities have been structured in three main sessions of around 90 min each, each session covering one conceptual and one practical ILO (Session 1 covering ILO-1 and ILO-2; Session 2 covering ILO-3 and ILO-4; Session 3 covering ILO-5 and ILO-6). Each session is dedicated to a particular topic, building upon and specifying the topics covered by the previous sessions. The conceptual activity was covered as an open lecture (lecture with on-the-fly questions and discussions). The practical activities differ for every session but involve student-centered tasks seeking to develop a core practical skill introduced by the conceptual part and required for effective use of the skill in practice.

The first session provides an introduction to ABSS as well as to the ASSOCC model for simulating interventions during the Covid-19 pandemic. The second session picks up on this and introduces why more advanced agent architectures are required to model more sophisticated policies. Finally, in the third session, the focus lies more on the stakeholders, what challenges are associated with using ABSS for policy making, and how simulation results can be analyzed and interpreted to provide policy makers with the information and data they need for making sound decisions. The tutorial was organized by Frank Dignum, Fabian Lorig, and Loïs Vanhée.

Besides the sessions, the course material included the following reading list:

- Gilbert, N., & Troitzsch, K. (2005). Simulation for the social scientist. McGraw-Hill Education (UK).
- Dignum, F. (2021). Foundations of Social Simulations for Crisis Situations. In Social Simulation for a Crisis (pp. 15–37). Springer, Cham.
- Edmonds, B., & Meyer, R. (2015). Simulating social complexity. Cham, Switzerland: Springer.

- Verhagen, H., Borit, M., Bravo, G., & Wijermans, N. (Eds.). (2020). Advances in Social Simulation: Looking in the Mirror. Springer Nature.
- Lorig, F., Johansson, E., & Davidsson, P. (2021). Agent-based social simulation of the covid-19 pandemic: A systematic review. JASSS: Journal of Artificial Societies and Social Simulation, 24(3).

2   Session 1: Agent-Based Social Simulation

We do not assume that the participants of this tutorial have previous experiences with modeling and simulation, i.e., with using simulation frameworks, parametrizing models, or executing experiments. Hence, we start the tutorial with an introduction to the most central concepts of modeling and simulation. In particular, this tutorial provides an introduction to agent-based simulations, where the behavior of single individual is modeled, and how such simulations can be applied to investigate social phenomena. This is to achieve the first learning outcome:

ILO-1: *Students are able to describe and relate the principles of ABSS, including fundamental ABSS approaches and techniques as well as applications of ABSS to real-world problems.*

2.1   Foundations of Modeling and Simulation

When hearing about simulations, most people might intuitively first think of flight simulators or crash tests, where realistic situations are re-created in an artificial and controlled environment, to educate pilots or to investigate the safety of motor vehicles. It is obvious for us that emergency situations such as engine failures should not be trained using a real airplane and that the consequences of car accidents should not be investigated using human drivers and real pedestrians. However, it is of great importance for our safety that pilots have been thoroughly trained for all potential emergency situations and that the safety of cars in case of a crash has been proven in advance.

To this end, the use of simulators provides a variety of benefits compared to real-world testing, e.g., not harming people, not jeopardizing expensive objects such as airplanes, more time-efficient and economical, and the possibility to generate situations or circumstances that might rarely occur in reality [9]. Imitating the real world provides us with new possibilities to investigate different phenomena or the behavior of a system under certain conditions. In case of the flight simulator, pilots can repeatedly undergo the same emergency situation and experience how different responses but also how different circumstances (e.g., bad weather) might affect the outcome of the situation. Simulations allow us to conduct *what-if* analyses to help us gain a better understanding of how the system we investigate works and to investigate the behavior in certain situations.

However, simulations are not only limited to practical applications. Also in science, simulations are widely used to model and imitate real-world systems and to gain new insights into how these systems work or how they behave under certain circumstances. This does not only include technical disciplines such as computer science, engineering, and physics but also biology, economics, sociology, medicine, and others [2].

"Simulation is the imitation of the operation of a real-world process or system over time."

(Banks, 2000, p. 9 [2])

The term *simulation* can be used in different contexts, which makes it difficult to provide a clear definition. Yet, the definition of Banks summarizes the most important aspect, namely that a system's operation (behavior) is explored over time. For this purpose, a simplified *simulation model* is developed, which approximates the underlying mechanisms of a target system in a logical way, to imitate its behavior. The target system might be an existing system from the real world but also a hypothetical system. Either way, the model represents a state of the target system at a given point in time and is able to calculate the next state at the following point in time, taking into consideration all relevant influencing factors. This is achieved by a series of model inputs (*parameters*) that define the circumstances or environment of the system, to observe a series of *model outputs*, that describe the behavior.

Figure 1 shows the process of model building and simulation [7]. Instead of conducting experiments with the target system itself, a model is developed, which describes the relevant parts of the target system in an abstract and simplified way. As not all mechanisms of the underlying system might be known, assumptions must be made to formalize the system's behavior. In the next step, the developed model can be executed to imitate the behavior of the target system. Through this, an artificial system is created that can be used as a sandpit for conducting experiments, e.g., to analyze what effects different changes in the environment or in the assumptions of the model might affect the behavior of the system. The observations made in simulations can then be used to draw conclusions regarding mechanics of the target system.

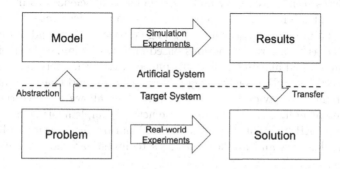

Fig. 1. Relationship between target system and simulation model (based on [7]).

2.2   Modeling Human Behavior

A major challenge in simulation studies is to develop a realistic model that adequately represents the target system and that provides a sufficient level of detail making it suitable for its intended purpose. In terms of the Covid-19 pandemic, for instance, decision makers might want to analyze and compare the effects of different interventions against the spread of the virus. Obviously, this requires the modelling of transmission and disease processes. However, the success of different interventions also strongly depends on the compliance of the individuals as well as on their personal routines and conditions. The effects of school closures might depend on household structures, the fact whether or not parents also work from home, and whether children decide to meet anyway.

Simpler epidemiological simulation models often consist of homogeneous individuals with identical behavior, whose policy obedience is assumed unconditionally or based on a stochastic model. An example are SIR compartment models, where individuals of a population are assigned to compartments according to their disease state, e.g., *susceptible*, *infectious*, or *recovered* [8]. The progress of the disease is modeled via transition probabilities between the states. Such models allow for analyzing the dynamics of an entire population, however, more in-depth analyses of infection routes or of more advanced interventions are not possible. Instead, the effects and success of interventions is indirectly modelled through changed transition probabilities.

The Covid-19 pandemic has shown that rules and recommendations do not have the same effects in different countries and are violated due to different reasons. Hence, simulating the effects of different interventions on the spread of the virus also requires more sophisticated models that take into consideration human behavior, individual actions, and personal characteristics. This includes individual daily routines, e.g., working, leisure activities, or shopping, but also personality traits and socio-demographic attributes, e.g., age, family, and household structures, or the degree of extroversion with respect to meeting other people. To achieve this, a more sophisticated simulation paradigm is required.

Agent-based Social Simulation (ABSS) makes use of AI as well as of different theories from psychology and other behavioral sciences to model human behavior [15]. Each individual is represented by an *intelligent agent*, that is characterized by a number of attributes, e.g., age or occupation, and autonomously makes decisions and performs actions based on its environment, personal situation, and individual attributes. For this purpose, ABSS models make use of, for instance, needs models, socio-demographic attributes, and character attributes, to model human behavior in a realistic way. This allows for investigating the effects different policies might have before actually implementing them.

The use of ABSS is not limited to crisis scenarios. Instead, it can be applied in different domains and application areas to investigate how a social system behaves in or reacts to specific situations. To this end, ABSS can be used to derive or review theories, to verify assumptions, or to generate data on a particular phenomena.

2.3   ASSOCC - A Simulation Model of the Covid-19 Pandemic

To goal of this tutorial is not only to provide the students with a theoretical introduction to ABSS. With respect to their active learning process, we combine theoretical lectures and practical exercises, such that the students can apply the introduced methods and approaches to discover new details, to develop a deeper understanding, and to transform theories into concrete skills.

We have chosen the $ASSOCC^2$ simulation model of the Covid-19 pandemic as framework for the practical exercises [6]. The development of the ASSOCC model has started in march 2020 and was driven by a group of about 15 researchers from Sweden, Netherlands, and France. The ASSOCC model has been developed using NetLogo, a simplistic yet powerful simulation framework that is free-to-use, making it well suited for educational purposes. The behavior of the individuals in the model is based on needs (inspired by Maslow's hierarchy of needs) and the satisfaction of these needs promotes certain values (Schwartz basic value theory).

The model allows for specifying different countries, cultures, and household structures, to adequately specify the region that shall be investigated. To model daily routines more realistically, there are four different types of individuals, i.e., children, students, adults, and pensioners, each of which behaves differently. Children, for instance, live with their parents, who will go to work after bringing them to school. Pensioners, in contrast, do live with other pensioners, and their daily routines do not include going to schools or work.

To model disease progress, ASSOCC implements an epidemiological extension of an SIR compartment model, which is calibrated to the typical progress of Covid-19. In contrast to solely using SIR models for the simulation of pandemics, the SIR model is only one of many components of the ASSOCC model. There is one instance of this epidemiological model for each individual, which allows for reproducing when and where an infection occurred. Moreover, transition probabilities depend on the type of agent and the infection probability is determined based on the specific situation in which the agent meets other agents taking into consideration crucial factors that potentially promote an infection, e.g., being indoors or outdoors, the number of individuals one is meeting, or the individual health condition. An overview of all modules and sub-models that are included in the ASSOCC framework is shown in Fig. 2.

---

[2] https://simassocc.org/ (accessed Jun 2022).

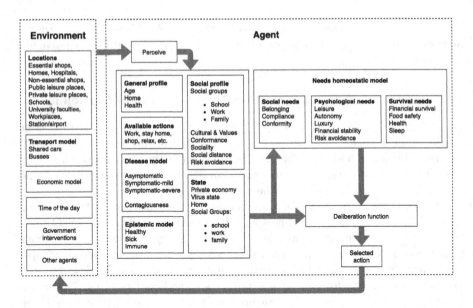

Fig. 2. Overview of the components of the ASSOCC model and their interconnections.

2.4   Practical Exercise: Experimenting with the ASSOCC Model

ILO-2: *Students are able to conduct and analyze experiments using an existing ABSS model and a well-established ABSS simulator (NetLogo).*

The purpose of the first practical exercise is to introduce the students to the NetLogo simulator, which is particularly well-suited for both novice but also more advanced ABSS modellers. Moreover, the first exercise aims to make the students familiar with the ASSOCC model, which we will also use for the other exercises. For this tutorial, we assume that all students have basic technical understanding, however, we do not assume previous experiences with modeling and simulation, i.e., with using simulation frameworks, parametrizing models, or executing experiments.

As model building is a complex task, it is not uncommon that analysts make use of existing models. Hence, the second ILO aims at gaining experience with the use of existing simulation models, i.e., how to parametrize it in accordance with the circumstances that shall be investigated as well as to generate and to analyze the output data.

To get started, we invite the students prior to the tutorial to download and install NetLogo[3] version 6.1.1 or newer, which is required to open and execute the ASSOCC model. To be optimally prepared, we recommend working with the tutorials that are provided by the NetLogo developers as part of the official documentation[4], especially the first tutorial on models. The latest version of

---

[3] https://ccl.northwestern.edu/netlogo/download.shtml (accessed Jun 2022).

[4] https://ccl.northwestern.edu/netlogo/docs/ (accessed Jun 2022).

the ASSOCC model can be downloaded via github[5]. After opening the model in NetLogo, the interface of the model appears, which can be used for configuration, execution, and analysis (see Fig. 3).

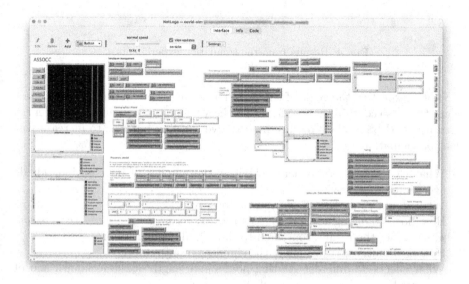

Fig. 3. NetLogo interface of the ASSOCC model.

As a first step towards using ABSS for policy making, we make use of the standard scenarios that are already included in the ASSOCC model. To be able to compare the effects of different measures, a baseline needs to be defined, which can be used as a reference for all possible scenarios that are investigated. For this exercise, the students initialize the model with the so called "scenario 1 zero action" settings, which contain the default configuration of the model, in which no interventions are applied. Additionally, the *household-profile* is set to "Sweden", which, for instance, affects the composition of households and the cultural properties of the population. To get an impression of the course of the pandemic, the model then needs to be executed for at least 480 ticks, which corresponds to four months. The number of individuals grouped by their health state over time is shown in Fig. 4.

---

[5] https://github.com/lvanhee/COVID-sim (accessed Jun 2022).

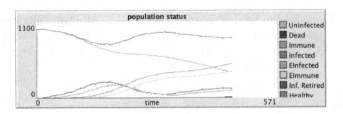

Fig. 4. Results from the simulation experiments.

With respect to the goals of this tutorial, we use the following guiding questions, that also contain tasks to facilitate the students' first practical experiences with using ABSS. This is to encourage active learning but also to increase student participation.

– What can you observe when looking at the number of infected individuals over time?
– What might cause the effects you can observe?
– How does changing the preset scenario to *"scenario 1 closing schools and univ"* affect the results compared to the initial configuration?
– How do country settings affect the simulation outputs?
– What effects do different starting points and length of the lockdown and of closures have on the dynamics of the pandemic?

2.5   Activity Outcome

To emphasize the interactive character of this tutorial and to benefit from the smaller group size compared to classical lectures, we explicitly motivated the students to ask questions at any time during the sessions. This is to promote discussions, to be able to enlarge upon specific topics or questions that the students find relevant, and to provide further examples, which can be beneficial for the learning process of all participants.

Throughout all sessions, the students were actively participating, asking relevant questions, and even discussed approaches and thoughts among each other. Overall, the tutorial was remarkably interactive and already during this first session, the curiosity and preparedness of the students was noticeable. Many of them had thought of specific questions, most likely originating from their individual PhD projects, which they wanted to discuss during the lecture. Due to the flexibility that is associated with tutorial like this one, we were able to respond to these questions and to expand the planned schedule. A take away for future tutorials with a similar topic is, thus, to ask the participants already when registering or prior to the event to submit their questions and expectations regarding the subjects that are valuable for them and that they would like to be covered. This allows us as organizers to prepare respective slides and to shift the focus of the tutorial and to maximize the benefits the participants get from the tutorial.

3   Session 2: Advanced Agent Architectures for Modeling Policies

During the first session, the participants were introduced to the concept of ABSS and gained first experiences on how simulations can be used to support and facilitate decision making processes. Policies, however, can quickly become complex and the question arises how complex simulation models need to be in order to adequately cope with more sophisticated policies. To simulate curfews or lockdowns, for instance, it might be sufficient to model spatiality on a location-based level, i.e., to represent whether an individual is at home, at work, or at school. When simulating social distancing, however, a more accurate and detailed representation of the individuals' locations is required to be able to measure distances between them and to determine the probability of infecting one another. To address this issue, and with respect to ILO 3, different approaches are discussed in this session that enable the building of more sophisticated models of human behavior, which ultimately also allows for simulating more complex policies.

ILO-3: *Students are able to identify and relate the key cognitive components in advanced ABSS models, to explain the main reasons for using cognitive models, and to identify the need for such models on a real-world problem.*

3.1   Human Behavior as Key for Simulation Policies

Developing simulation models that can be used for policy making can be compared to sandpits, where decision makers can play with different ideas or scenarios. This allows them to get an impression of potential effects and interdependencies, which one might not have thought of in the first place. This also makes model building for policy making different from developing simulations of a specific situation or use case. Simpler models are often limited with respect to how they can be parametrized and, thus, to not provide the same variety of scenarios that can be investigated. Policy makers, instead, rather need a "scenario builder", which enables them to instantiate the model in different ways. To build a variety of scenarios, different concepts need to be integrated in the model, which makes the model itself more complex.

Another challenge in building simulation models for policy making is the fact that it is not sufficient to only show that certain effects happen in certain scenarios. Instead, policy makers want to know *why* a certain situation occurred or *why* a certain behavior can be observed. It is also more likely that findings from simulation are used as part of the decision making process if they seem logical and can be explained. This is also because policy decisions will affect other people, which demands that decisions should be based on reliable and transparent information.

Because of the same reason, political decision makers tend to consult epidemiologist and not computer scientists for analyzing the effects of different interventions in the current pandemic. They follow epidemiological models because they trust these models. Yet, the effects and success of policies is always about the behavior of the people to who this policy applies rather than the transmission dynamics itself, which of course still plays an important role. Hence, it is the behavior of the individuals that needs to be in the center of the simulation.

With respect to the Covid-19 pandemic, there are three systems that need to be considered: the *economical* system, the *social* system, and the *epidemiological* system (see Fig. 5). Each of these three systems consists of its own feedback loop, with the human in the center. This is because the behavior of each individual influences society around the individual in these three aspects and reversely the individual is influenced by all of these three systems. Hence, the feedback loops are required in order to catch interdependencies between the three systems. The economical system, for instance, drives people, as money is a crucial pillar of our society. People need money for living and want to spend their money on their well-being. Tourism is an example of a part of the economic system, which affects people as they are incentivized to travel, to generate revenue. At the same time, the risk-aversion of individuals might affect tourism, as tourists staying at home will result in drawbacks for those working within this sector. Still, these systems might need to be extended or exchanged for simulating other effects. For investigating sustainability, as an example, a cycle for *ecology* might need to be added.

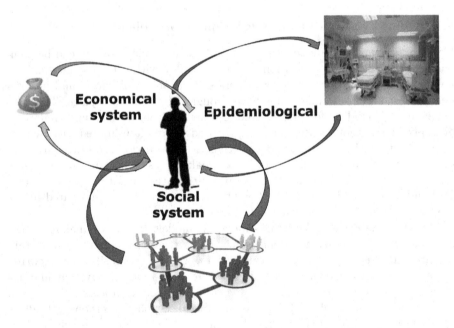

Fig. 5. The human in the center of the economical, social, and epidemiological system.

Modeling human behavior based on different systems, e.g., economics, sociality, and health, is challenging. Usually, when modeling human behavior, historical data is collected and projected into the future. This, however, does not cover unexpected events such as the crisis in which we currently find ourselves. We cannot use data from a different setting, i.e., the pre-pandemic situation, to simulate how people will behave once the circumstances change so drastically. For this purpose, advanced agent-based behavior models make use of common factors that people share, to develop a motivational model of agent behavior in different situations. These factors are of course different between different individuals or cultures, however, they are still structurally the same (contain the same aspects).

3.2   Modeling Human Values, Motivations, and Needs

A main driver of peoples' behavior are their *values*, which are more or less stable over lifetime. Examples of basic human values are security (i.e., aspiration after harmony and stable relationships) or achievement (i.e., in showing personal competence and success). Yet, there are different steps that link different values to specific actions of individuals. Mostly, these actions are highly dependent on the environment or context the individuals are in, which is a result of personal or social rules (e.g., norms, conventions, and practices). While it might be a sign of politeness to talk in one setting, e.g., when meeting a good friend as a sign of interest and attachment, it might be highly inappropriate to talk in another context, e.g., when listing to a presentation, where talking would be considered rude.

Schwartz's *Theory of Basic Human values* defines 10 universal values that are recognized in most cultures and which are the ultimate drivers of people (see Fig. 6) [13]. The importance of different values varies across cultures and how they lead to specific actions is strongly influenced by individual motives. This includes achievements, affiliation, power, or avoidance, in accordance with McClelland's human motivation theory [12]. Yet, not all actions are feasible in every situation, which is why affordances also play an important role, i.e., what actions the current environment of an individual admits. This is the reason why individuals sometimes go to specific environments for being able to do certain actions, e.g., children go to school to learn, we go to shops to buy food, etc.

The resulting value system, where specific values guide behavior in different ways depending on the context, can be used to model actions of individuals. Based on the current situation, the agent's impulse to act is the result of different motivations, personal skills, and the importance of the action's result. The importance of an action is determined by a needs model (*homeostatic model*), which is inspired by combining Maslow's hierarchy of needs [11], the Schwartz basic value system, and McClellands human motivation theory.

In the homeostatic needs model, each need is seen as an individual container, from which fluid leaks with a certain rate. For each container, a personal threshold exists that represents the importance of that particular need. The further the fluid level falls under this threshold, the more important it gets for the individual to "fill up" this need by taking respective actions. Through this, agents don't need to make advanced plans to determine their most suitable action. Instead,

Fig. 6. Schwartz's basic human values [13].

their behavior is determined by taking actions that meet their strongest needs depending on the opportunities the current environment offers. Using this needs model, the adaptation to changing environments is achieved as agents agent get different opportunities to fulfill their needs. A list of needs we used in the ASSOCC model is provided in Table 1.

With respect to the decision model of the agents, we define different locations, that represent different environments where agents can fulfill their needs. For shops and leisure places, there exists two types of locations. In case of the shops, the model distinguishes between non-essential shops, e.g., clothing stores or building supplies store, that will be closed during a lockdown, and essential shops, e.g., grocery stores or pharmacies, that will remain open in case of a lockdown. Considering leisure places, there are private leisure places, i.e., where people meet with friends or relatives, and public leisure places, i.e., where people meet with strangers. An overview of the locations is provided in Table 2.

3.3 Opportunities of Social Simulations

Considering how locations are modeled and how agents decide where to go and what to do, one major difference between traditional epistemological models and agent-based models can be observed. In classical mathematical transmission models, the number of contacts with other individuals, and thus also the number of occasions where infections can occur, is a parameter, which is often identical for all individuals of the population or predetermined by static contact networks. Accordingly, these models can not simulate the individuals' adaptation

Table 1. The needs of the agents in the ASSOCC model.

Need	Description
autonomy	The need for autonomy and self-direction. This freedom of choice can be limited by government interventions
belonging	The belonging need, i.e. meeting friends and relatives
compliance	The need for complying with formal instructions, notably arising from the government and contractual obligations (e.g. work)
conformity	The need for conformity with regards to one's social network. Or in other words the social need of choosing an action that the majority of agents in its network has previously chosen
fin_stability	Represents the need for financial stability, with an income matching the expenses
fin_survival	The need of having enough money to buy food and other essentials to survive
food_safety	The need of having enough food at home, with decreasing reward as we narrow two weeks
health	The need for being in good health. When agents believe that they are infected, they want to either stay home or go to the hospital
leisure	The need of agents to have leisure time and relaxing. Resting at home is possible as well, but gives less satisfaction when compared to relaxing at a different location
luxury	The need for acquiring luxury goods
risk_avoidance	The need for avoiding taking risks. The satisfaction of this need depends on the contagion status of the agent and the amount of agents at a gathering point. Furthermore, social-distancing is taken into account
sleep	The need of an agent to sleep, which is satisfied every night by sleeping. Furthermore, it is modelled that sleep when being sick is not as restful as when being healthy

to new situations and differences in behavior between individuals. In agent-based models, the number of contacts per agent is an output of the model, that depends on many different personal factors, the individual circumstances, as well as on the scenario that is simulated.

A detailed representation of each individual, its needs, and its behavior also enables more in-depth analyses of the dynamics of the model. In particular, it enables the analysis of *why* certain effects and phenomena occur. One example is the reconstruction of infection networks, i.e., who has infected whom, when the infection happened, and at which location the critical interaction occurred. This might be particularly relevant for identifying how and when people might become super-spreaders, individuals, that infect a great number of other individuals. Moreover, due to the strong connection between the different systems,

Table 2. The locations of the agents.

Location type	N	Description
Essential shops*	10	This is the place where agents buy food, they have to do this every once in a while
Homes*	391	The agents live in their homes, they are always at home during the night to sleep. The homes can be used as a workplace if the agent has to be in quarantine
Hospitals*	4	The hospital has some workers and treats agents who get severely infected, if they have enough capacity (number of beds)
Non-essential shops*	10	With non-essential shopping agents can satisfy the need for luxury
Private leisure places	60	These are places where agents can meet with their friends
Public leisure places	20	The public leisure places represent places such as parks where everyone can go to. The needs Self-Esteem, compliance are satisfied by going there. However risk-avoidance and safety depletes
Schools*	12	The youth go to school during working days. Needs such as compliance and autonomy are satisfied here
University faculties*	4	The students go to the university and can also satisfy autonomy and compliance here
Workplaces*	25	Where most of the worker agents work. Many needs can be satisfied through going to work
Station/airport (away)	-	This represents agents travelling outside of the city

agent-based models allow for investigating dependencies between health, socio-psychological, and economic aspects.

Sophisticated models of human decision-making can facilitate decision making as they can be used to simulate different scenarios, to assess the potential effects of policies. Starting from a principled agent-based approach is feasible, however, agents require an internal state representation to be able to balance different influences. Besides these advanced agent architectures, a series of tools is required to make the models usable for decision makers. This includes tools to design scenarios, to generate a realistic agent population (e.g., in terms of socio-demographic attributes, needs, possible actions), and to analyze the results of the simulation experiments.

Finally, the computational efforts required to execute more sophisticated agent-based models are considerably higher than those of models with more simple and homogeneous agents. To this end, the use of more "user friendly" frameworks like NetLogo is limited. To facilitate the scalability of such models, more specialized simulation frameworks need to be used, which imply other drawbacks.

3.4 Practical Exercise: Extending Models to Simulate Policies

ILO-4: *Students are able to explain and specify how an existing agent architecture in an ABSS model can be extended for facilitating the investigation of new policies.*

The level of detail of agent architectures is a result from the purpose of the simulation model. The agents should be kept as simple as possible but as complex as required for the questions and scenarios that shall be investigated. Overloading the agents with too many aspects will make them impractical to calibrate. Hence, the used agent architecture determines what policies and scenarios can be simulated and investigated. To this end, the fourth ILO addresses the challenge of understanding the possibilities and limitations of specific agent architectures and to identify how they need to be extended to conduct certain investigations.

As part of this second practical exercise, the students will work with the extension of an existing simulation model such that new policies can be simulated. This includes the discussion of the limitations of the existing architecture, an abstract and more formal description of the new policy, as well as the identification of requirements, in which regard the model needs to be extended and adapted.

An intervention which can not yet be simulated using the ASSOCC model is *social distancing*. The goal of this intervention is to urge people to keep a minimum distance to other people to reduce the likelihood of infecting each other. Currently, the location of individuals in the model is defined by the building where they stay. Yet, these locations do not have a sufficiently granularity to determine the exact distance between the individuals. For simulating *social distancing*, an example of an aspect of the model that needs to be adapted is the spatial representation of agents.

Guiding questions that can support the students in discussing how the model needs to be extended include:

– How do we need to extend the model to simulate *social distancing*?
– What are the shortcomings of the current spatial representation of agents and how does it have to be extended?
– Is the transmission model sufficient for this new intervention?
– How do other simulations model social distancing?

3.5 Activity Outcome

Very similar to the first session, the students were very actively participating in the session, asking relevant and interesting questions, promoting the discussion of different aspects related to the modeling of advanced human behavior. Yet, in contrast to the first sessions, the discussions were more focused on specific applications of the presented theories and architectures as well as on specific design decisions. Whereas agent deliberation and decision making models usually tend to be rather abstract, it was positively pointed out by the participants that providing specific examples such as the water tank model that was used in the ASSOCC model was very insightful.

4   Session 3: Simulating for Policy Makers

4.1   Conceptual Activity

ILO-5: *Students are able to explain how using ABSS for policy making alters the ABSS-making activities and relate these activities to concrete deliverables.*

The purpose of the activity is dedicated to have the learners sensitivized about how designing ABSS for policy makers fundamentally affects the activity as a model builder. The first part of this activity has been built around the keyframes depicted in Fig. 7, which recalls the main concerns of scientific ABSS design introduced in previous sessions and shows whether and how the importance of these concerns is turned over when working for policy making. The rest of the presentation then reviewed the three major angles of approach for covering the main policy-making-driven concerns (i.e., adequate models, implementations, and public relations management) and then, for each angle, a set of key resources that was used during the ASSOCC project for collaborating and supporting policy-makers. The model part insisted on the value of the key modelling elements formerly introduced in Session 2 for interacting with stakeholders; the implementation part focused on implementation features dedicated to support trustworthy interaction with stakeholders, such as qualitative interfaces presented in Fig. 8a; the public relations reviewed of the actual slides used to interact with policy makers and a review of their core structural elements. The underlying conceptual message is as follows.

There are a variety of purposes for which simulations can be used. This includes, simulations for education or training, where the purpose is to communicate knowledge or to represent information. An example would be when using simulations to demonstrate phenomena to students or serious games, where students can perform experiments to learn about the effects of different changes of a system. Simulations can also be used for engineering purposes, i.e., to better understand a system or to investigate the suitability of different system configurations. Finally, simulations can be used for discovering and predicting system behavior.

Considering the requirements that are placed on the models, these purposes of simulations differ strongly from doing simulations for decision makers. Scientific simulation models are more technique-driven and there are high expectations on developing an accurate model. When building models that have to facilitate decision-making processes, the entire modeling process is more society-driven as the goal is to engage with policy makers and to contribute to a social debate.

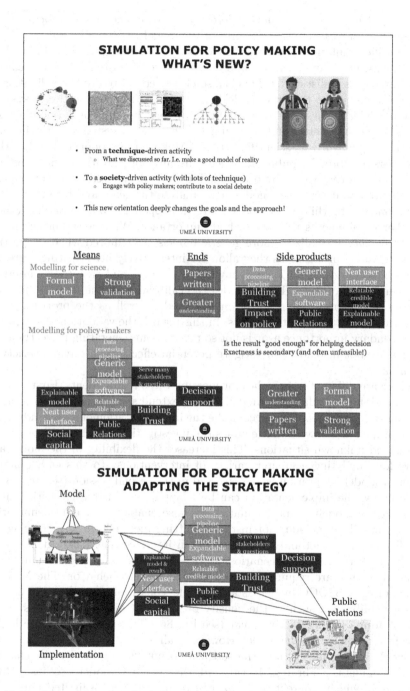

Fig. 7. Keyframes stressing the influence of policy-making on the relative importance of ABSS design concerns

Hence, modellers need to follow different paradigms and put the focus of the development process on other features of the model.

Scientific simulations have a strong focus on the formal model itself, i.e., how mechanisms, inter-dependencies, and circumstances from the real world can be represented in a realistic way. This is also closely connected to the validation of the model, to ensure that the model adequately represents the target system, whose behavior it tries to replicate. Often, the primary goal of developing such models is to gain a better understanding of the modeled system and the insights are usually published as scientific articles. Making the model usable by other researchers or a broader public audience is usually not prioritized and interfaces of the model, if they exist, are overloaded, making it impossible for non-experts to configure and execute the model or to analyze the generated results.

In contrast to this, when models are developed for policy making, there are other requirements that are of high importance. Whereas scientific models tend to be very specialized, more generic models are required when supporting decision-making processes as they allow for interactively investigating a greater variety of scenarios. Additionally, having an intuitive and easy-to-use interface is of utmost importance. This includes the calibration of the model, the specification of scenarios that shall be investigated, as well as the processing and visualization of the generated results. In this regard, the validation of the model is of secondary importance as it is not so much about generating perfectly accurate results but instead to investigate potential effects for a greater variety of scenarios.

There are different approaches for meeting these requirements. Firstly, there is the possibility to adapt the model, e.g., to extend specialized models to make them more generic. As example could be the implementation of a more advanced model of human behavior that enables the investigation of individuals adapting to new and unknown situations. This increases the flexibility of the model and allows for simulating a greater variety of interventions. To this end, different means of model adaptation were discussed in the second session (see Sect. 3).

Secondly, the implementation can be adapted such that users with limited experience in modeling and simulation are also enabled to conduct simulation experiments. This includes, for instance, putting more efforts in increasing the usability of the model and by developing an interface that makes it easier for decision makers to specify scenarios. Models often consist of a great number of parameters, that are required to calibrate the model's behavior. The NetLogo version of the ASSOCC model, as an example, consist of more than 170 parameters for calibration such as the density of people at different locations or the ratio of adults having a private car (see Fig. 8a). These parameters are highly relevant for calibrating the model. However, calibration is done by the modeler, not by the policy maker, and the settings do not usually need to be changed once the model is calibrated. To this end, the ASSOCC model also has a Unity interface, in which different scenarios can be defined with a limited number of parameters and which provides a 3D visualization of the simulation, to facilitate the understanding of the results (see Fig. 8b).

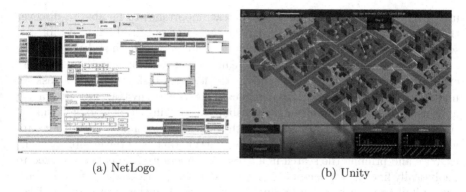

(a) NetLogo

(b) Unity

Fig. 8. Interfaces of the ASSOCC model. The left interface (*"backend"*) is for developers only, with all parameters and code easily accessible but requiring expert-knowledge for setup and result processing; the right interface (*"frontend"*) is for interaction with stakeholders, with simplified and more friendly display that is suited for a novice observer to understand the many concepts at play in the simulation and relate them with real-world issues.

Finally, a greater emphasis can be placed on working on public relations, i.e., to raise awareness for the existence of simulations that can be used to generate valuable insights for decision makers. One the one hand, this can be achieved by increased personal and institutional visibility of the modelers such that policy makers take notice of their existence. There is still a lack of information that causes that policy makers often are not aware of both the existence and the benefits of simulations. On the other hand, researchers also need to reach out to practitioners and decision makers, to establish collaborations and to build models that are more oriented towards practical needs. In general, the communication between modelers and stakeholders is challenging with respect to expectations and requirements.

Modellers often do not know how to work together with policy makers. Hence, their approaches might not always be aligned with the requirements of the stakeholders. Working together with decision makers also creates a new dynamics for the development of the simulations. Early results might not be sufficiently mature and should not be used to create policies whereas late results might be too late to be of value.

4.2   Practical Activity: Data to Factors

ILO-6: *Students are able to analytically discover the origin of a complex emerging phenomena, based on extensive raw multidimensional ABSS output.*

ABSS for policy making is often used for putting forward what are the key factors at play in the emergence of complex phenomena. However, determining these factors involves a careful analysis of the output of the ABSS. In terms of ASSOCC, the challenge was to get from extensive (150+) curves and 80 pages of graphs, charts, and plots down to a few core explanations. With respect to the use of ABSS in policy making, it is of great importance to be able to discover the origin of the observed effects from the generated output data, to establish a solid argument, which is required for trusted interactions with stakeholders.

As a matter of making the exercise realistic and allowing us to have the best expert knowledge to guide the students, the learning task is built on a task we undertook ourselves during the pandemic: to determine why tracking and tracing apps will likely fail to significantly contribute to reducing the spread of Covid-19. As resource, students are provided with the multifactorial simulation output data we relied on for building our own analysis (thus guaranteeing the feasibility of the exercise and priming the search in a workable direction). Students are tasked to analytically find the key factors at play based on the provided data. The students are invited to work in small groups, which is eased as they can split the large quantity of data they are offered to process and collaboratively provide elements of answer to each other. At the end of the session, each subgroup is invited to share its findings with the rest of the group and try to figure out an answer to the question.

As means for ensuring an overall harmony of progression, an array of pedagogic strategies was available for bending the difficulty curve in both directions. For easing the activity, indirect and then direct hints on some set of variables to consider and on the factors to be found could be given; for increasing the challenge. Faster students could be given the additional task to 1) develop an argument for convincing the reviewers; 2) what additional data they would require to gather out of the model; 3) what other questions stakeholder might have; thus inviting the students to further engage with the public-relation materials introduced during the related theoretical activity (i.e. ILO-5) and, for the fastest, into the whole process of developing ABSS features for supporting policy-makers.

Besides the goal set by the ILO, i.e., acquiring a first-person experience and expertise with multifactorial analytic skills, the task was set as to enable students to develop a postformal thinking ability regarding analysis [4], through experiencing that different groups can have different explanations and, if so, to learn to assess the relative insights, validity, and complementarity of various explanations. Such postformal thinking ability is rare and highly valuable given how conflicting can be short-sighted analytical interpretations of the many sources of information of our world, being actually a critical skill for PhDs-in-training to develop a comprehensive understanding of our world and of other fields of research.

4.3   Activity Outcome

Due to time limitation, only a part of the lecturing activity could be undertaken. This outcome was expected and actually desired as it shows the success of the previous two sessions in instilling questions and discussions among the student cohort. Despite the short amount of time for exposition and activity, informal discussions a posteriori suggest that the core of the message was received (i.e., policy-making involves significantly different modelling, implementation, and communication approaches).

5   Conclusions

In this tutorial, we provided students with an introduction to using agent-based social simulation to facilitate policy making. Based on 6 relevant ILOs, we structured the tutorial in three main sessions, each of which was dedicated to a specific topic and consisted of a theoretical knowledge part (with focus on concepts) and a practical skill part (with focus on the application of these concepts to real-world problems). The outcome of the three sessions showed us that we were able to achieve the ILOs and that the participants found the tutorial very insightful and helpful with regard to their PhD projects.

Compared to the "traditional" application of simulation, it is important to note that modelling and simulation for policy making dramatically alters the purpose of the activity. Accordingly, this new purpose requires a very different approach towards modeling and simulation. This includes more explainable, demonstrable, and relatable models, more solid implementation (combined generic basis and ease for specification), as well as the ability for engaging with stakeholders and offering complementary perspectives. To this end, this tutorial helps the participants to gain an understanding of how ABSS can be applied to facilitate policy making.

The PhD students that participated in the tutorial came from a variety of different disciplines and cultures. Already at the beginning of the tutorial, it became apparent that most participants have chosen to attend this tutorial to gain more practical insights into the application of ABSS. Most of the participants use ABSS as method in their PhD studies, however, find that the (sparsely) existing literature does not sufficiently provide guidelines on how to practically apply ABSS and how to develop suitable models. To this end, the participants appreciated the use of examples and best practices from the ASSOCC project to illustrate the practical implementation of different theoretical concepts and approaches. This also led to fruitful discussions on challenges that are associated with building ABSS models for policy making purposes as well as creative solutions on how these challenges can be addressed.

To further improve the benefits the participants get from the tutorial, we recommend asking them to submit their questions, expectations, and requests regarding the structure and thematic focus of the workshop as part of their registration or some weeks in advance to the tutorial taking place. This allows organizers to plan the tutorial according to the participants' needs and to prepare respective material. It also enables the organizers to plan the schedule of the tutorial according to the demand of the participants. In the case of this tutorial on *Social simulation for policy making*, many participating PhD students were not primarily working in research groups with strong focus on ABSS but instead apply ABSS as a method for addressing and investigating research challenges in a great variety of disciplines. Hence, tutorials like this one are crucial for PhD students working with ABSS as it allows them to discuss their approaches with others. This makes the tutorial to more than a series of lectures but also to a platform for discussing ABSS approaches with other PhD students working with the same method, to get feedback on own models and architectures from experts in the field, and to get impulses for further research. Facilitating and promoting this exchange is, thus, also an important task of the organizers of the tutorial.

Acknowledgement. This tutorial was partially supported by the Wallenberg AI, Autonomous Systems and Software Program (WASP) and the Wallenberg AI, Autonomous Systems and Software Program - Humanities and Society (WASP-HS) research program funded by the Marianne and Marcus Wallenberg Foundation, the Marcus and Amalia Wallenberg Foundation, and the Knut and Alice Wallenberg Foundation (no. 570080103). The simulations were enabled by resources provided by the Swedish National Infrastructure for Computing (SNIC), partially funded by the Swedish Research Council through grant agreement no. 2018-05973.

References

1. Anderson, L.W., et al.: A Taxonomy for Learning, Teaching, and Assessing: A Revision of Bloom's Taxonomy of Educational Objectives, Abridged Edition, vol. 5, no. 1. Longman, White Plains (2001)
2. Banks, J.: Introduction to simulation. In: 2000 Proceedings of the Winter Simulation Conference, vol. 1, pp. 9–16. IEEE (2000)
3. Biggs, J., Tang, C.: Teaching for Quality Learning at University. McGraw-hill education (UK), New York (2011)
4. Commons, M.L., Richards, F.A.: Four postformal stages. In: Demick, J., Andreoletti, C., (eds) Handbook of adult development. The Springer Series in Adult Development and Aging, pp. 199–219. Springer, Boston (2002). https://doi.org/10.1007/978-1-4615-0617-1_11
5. Davidsson, P.: Agent based social simulation: a computer science view. J. Artif. Soc. Soc. Simul. **5**(1) (2002)
6. Dignum, F.: Social Simulation for a Crisis: Results and Lessons from Simulating the COVID-19 Crisis. Springer, Cham (2021)
7. Gilbert, N., Troitzsch, K.: Simulation for the Social Scientist. McGraw-Hill Education (UK), New York (2005)
8. Kermack, W.O., McKendrick, A.G.: A contribution to the mathematical theory of epidemics. Proc. Roy. Soc. London. Ser. A, Containing Pap. Math. Phys. Charact. **115**(772), 700–721 (1927)
9. Law, A.M.: Simulation Modeling and Analysis, vol. 5. McGraw-Hill, New York (2014)
10. Lorig, F., Johansson, E., Davidsson, P.: Agent-based social simulation of the covid-19 pandemic: a systematic review. JASSS: J. Artif. Soc. Soc. Simul. **24**(3) (2021)
11. Maslow, A., Lewis, K.: Maslow's hierarchy of needs. Salenger Incorporated **14**(17), 987–990 (1987)
12. McClelland, D.C.: Human Motivation. CUP Archive (1987)
13. Schwartz, S.H.: An overview of the schwartz theory of basic values. Online Readings Psychol. Cult. **2**(1), 2307–2919 (2012)
14. Sokolowski, J.A., Banks, C.M.: Principles of Modeling and Simulation: A Multidisciplinary Approach. John Wiley, Hoboken (2011)
15. Squazzoni, F., Jager, W., Edmonds, B.: Social simulation in the social sciences: a brief overview. Soc. Sci. Comput. Rev. **32**(3), 279–294 (2014)

Towards a Social Artificial Intelligence

Dino Pedreschi[2], Frank Dignum[1], Virginia Morini[2,4(✉)],
Valentina Pansanella[3,4], and Giuliano Cornacchia[2,4]

[1] Umeå University, Umeå, Sweden
dignum@cs.umu.se
[2] University of Pisa, Pisa, Italy
dino.pedreschi@unipi.it,
{giuliano.cornacchia,virginia.morini}@phd.unipi.it
[3] Scuola Normale Superiore, Pisa, Italy
valentina.pansanella@sns.it
[4] KDD Lab ISTI-CNR, Pisa, Italy

Abstract. Artificial Intelligence can both empower individuals to face complex societal challenges and exacerbate problems and vulnerabilities, such as bias, inequalities, and polarization. For scientists, an open challenge is how to shape and regulate human-centered Artificial Intelligence ecosystems that help mitigate harms and foster beneficial outcomes oriented at the social good. In this tutorial, we discuss such an issue from two sides. First, we explore the network effects of Artificial Intelligence and their impact on society by investigating its role in social media, mobility, and economic scenarios. We further provide different strategies that can be used to model, characterize and mitigate the network effects of particular Artificial Intelligence driven individual behavior. Secondly, we promote the use of behavioral models as an addition to the data-based approach to get a further grip on emerging phenomena in society that depend on physical events for which no data are readily available. An example of this is tracking extremist behavior in order to prevent violent events. In the end, we illustrate some case studies in-depth and provide the appropriate tools to get familiar with these concepts.

Keywords: Human-centered AI · Complex systems · Multi-agent models · Social networks · Mobility networks · Financial networks

1 Introduction

Nowadays, given the ubiquity of increasingly complex socio-technical systems - made of interacting people, algorithms, and machines, - the social dimension of Artificial Intelligence (AI) started emerging in our everyday lives. Examples range from urban mobility, with travellers helped by smart assistants, to the public discourse and economic markets, where decisions on what to see or buy are shaped by AI tools, like recommendation and filtering algorithms.

While at the individual level AI outputs could be beneficial, from a societal perspective they can lead to alarming phenomena such as traffic congestion

© Springer Nature Switzerland AG 2023
M. Chetouani et al. (Eds.): ACAI 2021, LNAI 13500, pp. 415–428, 2023.
https://doi.org/10.1007/978-3-031-24349-3_21

[1], radicalisation of opinions [2,3], and oligopolistic markets [4]. The current use of AI systems is often based on the hypothesis that a crowd of individuals that make "intelligent" choices would result in an intelligent crowd. However, this may be too optimistic. There are many examples of such systems giving rise to alarming phenomena at the aggregate and societal level. This tendency is well represented by the model of ethnic segregation theorized by Schelling [5]. The American economist defined an agent-based model for ethnic segregation that shows that, even when individuals are relatively open-minded and do not mind being surrounded by some people of a different ethnicity or economic background, they will still end up in segregated communities in the long run.

Therefore, to reach the goal of a human-centred AI that supports society in a positive way, there is a need to gain a better understanding of how AI can both support and affect emerging social behaviours. If we can better understand how AI interacts with social phenomena, we can employ it to help mitigate harms and to foster beneficial outcomes, oriented to social goods.

In this tutorial - part of the social simulation chapter with [6] - we approach this challenge from two sides. First, we discuss how complex human systems may experience negative consequences due to their intrinsic nature and under what circumstances Artificial Intelligence may positively or negatively impact such systems. Then, we look at the use of behavioural models as an alternative solution with respect to the data-based approach in scenarios where the human behaviour plays a key role, in order to get a further grip on emerging phenomena in society.

The **learning objectives** of this tutorial are *i)* understand and approach the emergent properties of real networks as well as their possible harmful effects on society; *ii)* leverage agent-based models to understand phenomena where human behaviour play a key role; *iii)* familiarize with the previously illustrated concepts through python libraries and tailored notebooks.

The rest of this tutorial is structured as follows. In Sect. 2, we start by introducing network effects on society and the impact of AI, providing various examples in the urban mobility, public discourse, and market domains. Then, in Sect. 3 we approach the problem of going beyond data-driven approaches – when these are not a suitable solution – in favour of behavioural models to tackle complex challenges like detecting radicalisation or predicting the overall effects of a pandemic. In Sect. 4, we describe a fully reproducible hands-on tutorial to familiarize oneself with the concepts introduced in the tutorial. In Sect. 5 we conclude by discussing limitations of the current approaches in the field of Social AI as well as setting relevant research directions.

2   Network Effects of AI and Their Impact on Society

In the following section, we explore some examples of how Artificial Intelligence may amplify intrinsic and alarming properties of real networks and worsen the wellness of society as a whole. Further, we discuss how AI can be used to better understand these phenomena and find possible solutions.

To tackle this goal, we start by describing real networks and some of the main emerging properties reported by network science literature, followed by three concrete examples of this interconnection of AI and network science.

2.1 Emergent Properties of Real Networks

The earth's climate, the human brain, an organism, a population, an economic organization are all examples of complex systems. Complex systems can be made of different constituents, but they display similar behavioural phenomena at the aggregate level, which are normally called emergent behaviours. According to complex systems theory, these emergent behaviours cannot be explained by analysing the single constituents and need a new approach to understand how they emerge.

Traditionally, social scientists tried to understand how groups of individuals behave by focusing on simple attributes. Understanding emergent behaviours, such as how a population reaches consensus around a specific topic or how a language prevails within a territory, cannot be done by focusing on the individual agents, but instead, the problem needs to be approached in terms of interaction between them. In recent years, this change of approach happened both with the advent of complex systems and network science theory, but also thanks to the availability of a huge amount of data that allow studying individual and higher-order properties of the system. Behind each complex system, there is - in fact - a network that defines the interactions between the system's components. Hence, to understand complex systems, we need to map out and explore the networks behind them. For example, in the field of disease spreading it is nearly impossible to understand how a population reaches the epidemic state without considering the very complex structure of connections between individuals.

In the remainder of this section, we are going to briefly describe some of the emerging properties that characterize many real networks and have a direct impact on real-world phenomena: connectedness, "small-world" property, hubs, and high clustering.

Connectedness. A network is said to be connected if there exists a path between any two pairs of nodes. This may not be surprising in some domains, since connectedness is essential to the correct functioning of the service built on top of the network. For example, if communication networks were not connected we could not call any valid phone number or we would not be able to send an email to any address. However, this property surprisingly emerges also in other domains. For example, online social networks, despite being very large and very sparse, present a giant connected component and any two users are very likely to belong to this component.

According to Erdős-Rényi random network model [7], the necessary and sufficient condition for the emergence of a giant connected component is that the average degree of the network (the number of arcs going out of a node) $\langle k \rangle = 1$. This critical point separates a situation where there is not yet one giant component from the situation where there is one. If the average degree $\langle k \rangle > 1$ the giant component absorbs all nodes and components and the network becomes connected.

Small-World. In real networks it holds not just that everybody is connected to everybody else, but the length of the path to get from one person to a random other person is on average very small. This property is known as "small-world phenomenon".

In the language of network science, the small world phenomenon implies that the distance between two randomly chosen nodes in a network is short, i.e. the average path length or the diameter depends logarithmically on the system size. Hence, "small" means that the average distance is proportional to $\log N$, rather than N or some power of N. In practice this means that in a town of around 100.000 people any person is connected to any other person in 3 or 4 steps. While discovered in the context of social systems, the small-world property applies beyond social networks.

Hubs. Another property that emerges in real networks is the presence of hubs. According to the Erdős-Rényi random network model [7] every node has on average the same number of links. In real-world networks, instead, the degree distribution follows a power-law, i.e. it is scale-free, meaning that there will be very few nodes that are order of magnitudes more connected than the remaining part of the nodes, namely, the hubs. In the known Barabási-Albert model [8] two factors are included to explain the presence of hubs: first, the number of nodes in the network is not fixed, but networks grow; second, there is a so-called "preferential attachment", i.e. the higher the degree of a node, the higher its attractive power to the new nodes entering the network. This second phenomenon can inevitably bring about inequalities in the distribution of resources in the system and this holds for e.g. popularity in social media or for success in the market, but also in protein-to-protein interaction networks. In socio-economical settings, this may cause an excessive amount of inequalities, unsustainable for the social outcomes that, as a society, we would like to pursue.

Clustering. The last emerging property discussed here is network clustering. To measure the degree of clustering in a network we use the local clustering coefficient C, which measures the density of links in a node's immediate neighbourhood. If $C = 0$ it means that there are no links between the node's neighbours, while if $C = 1$ each of the node's neighbours link to each other, i.e. the clustering coefficient is given by the number of triplets in the network that are closed. In real networks there is a higher clustering coefficient than expected according to the Erdős-Rényi random network model [7]. An extension of this model, proposed by Watts and Strogatz [9], addresses the coexistence of a high average clustering coefficient and the small-world property, reconciling the fact that everybody is connected and close to everybody else with the presence of segregation and communities. However, the model fails to predict the scale-free degree distribution seen in real networks mentioned in the previous paragraph.

2.2 AI Pitfalls on Real Networks

We have just seen in Sect. 2.1 that there exists an endogenous tendency of real networks to polarize and segregate that is well represented by their peculiar properties, such as the presence of hubs and the emergence of clustered communities.

In digital environments, such a tendency is further exacerbated by AI-powered tools that, using big data as fuel, make personalized suggestions to every user to make them feel comfortable and, in the end, maximize their engagement [2]. Even if, at the individual level, this kind of suggestion can be beneficial for a user, from a societal point of view it can lead to alarming phenomena in a wide range of domains. Some examples are the polarization and radicalization of public debate in social networks, congestion in mobility networks, or the "rich get richer effect" in economic and financial networks.

In the following, we discuss in detail these three different types of AI pitfalls on real networks, as concerns both their causes and effects.

Polarization, Echo Chamber and Filter Bubble on Social Networks. The rise of online social media and social networking services has drastically changed how people interact, communicate, and access information. In these virtual realms, users have to juggle a continuous, instantaneous, and heterogeneous flow of information from a wide variety of platforms and sources.

From a user perspective, several psychological studies [10,11] have observed that people, both in the online and offline world, feel discomfort when encountering opinions and ideas that contradict their existing beliefs (i.e., Cognitive Dissonance [12]). To avoid such discomfort, as stated by Selective Exposure theories, people tend to select and share contents that reinforce their opinion avoiding conflicting ones [13]. This human tendency to mainly interact with like-minded information and individuals is further strengthened by social media services. Indeed, recommendation and filtering systems play a key role in leveraging users' demographic information and past behaviors to provide personalized news, services, products, and even friends. Despite their success in maximizing user satisfaction, several studies [2,14,15] showed that such systems might lead to a self-reinforcing loop giving rise to the alarming *Filter Bubble* and *Echo Chamber* phenomena.

Even if the discussion about their definitions is still active, traditionally the term Filter Bubble (coined by Parisier [2]) refers to the ecosystem of information to which each online user is exposed, and that is driven by the recommendation algorithms of digital platforms. Similarly, but at an aggregated level, the term Echo Chamber refers to the phenomenon in which beliefs are amplified or reinforced by communication repetition inside a closed system and insulated from rebuttal [3]. In recent years, there is strong concern that such phenomena might prevent the dialectic process of "thesis-antithesis-synthesis" that stands at the basis of a democratic flow of opinions, fostering several related alarming episodes (e.g., hate speech, misinformation, and ethnic stigmatization). In this context, there is both a need for data-driven approaches to identify and analyse real situations where these phenomena take place, but also for tools to investigate causes and effects of different factors on polarizing phenomena on online and offline social networks, as well as mitigation strategies.

Congestion in Mobility Networks. Traffic congestion can cause undesired effects on a transportation network such as waste of time, economic losses to drivers, waste of energy and increasing air pollution, increased reaction time to emergencies, and dissatisfaction of the well-being of people in the urban environment [1]. To avoid such negative effects, congestion prevention is crucial to improve the overall transportation system's sustainability.

Congestion happens due to demand-supply imbalance in the road network, which can be exacerbated by AI navigation systems' advice. Indeed, while these recommendations make sense at the individual level, they can lead to collective dissatisfaction, when the same advice is given to many different drivers (e.g., the navigators suggest to all vehicles to travel across the same road to reach a certain destination) because the road links will saturate and congestions emerge.

A naive solution for traffic congestion prevention, i.e. adding an extra road to redistribute the traffic, can instead lead to the opposite effect, as stated in Braess's paradox [16]. The paradox occurs because each driver chooses whatever route minimizes their personal travel time (selfish choice). When people share a common public resource - like the road network - the lack of cooperation along with selfish behavior might lead to a stable state with a social value that is far from the social optimum, as claimed by John Nash.

In the problem of traffic congestion avoidance, there is a need for coordination, cooperation, and diversification of routes. In the very same way that we need diversification of opinions to have democracy work in our societies, we need diversification of behavior for having a better ability to travel in our cities. Therefore, we need AI systems that can forecast where a traffic congestion will occur to avoid its formation.

Disparity in Economic Networks. In just about a decade, a handful of companies have contributed to an increasingly centralized World Wide Web, contradicting the Internet's original slogan of net neutrality [17]. This is the first time in history that technology companies (e.g., Apple, Google, Microsoft, Amazon, and Facebook) have dominated the stock market, being the most valuable public businesses in the world by market capitalization [18].

However, dominance on the Internet is not limited to the digital realm, but transcends the economy as a whole, such as digital advertising and e-commerce.

Economic and financial networks are deeply characterized by the so-called *winner-takes-all markets* (WAT). This terminology refers to an economy in which the best performers can capture a considerable share of the available rewards, while the remaining competitors are left with very little [4]. Such a behavior, also known as the "rich get richer effect", is well reflected in the topology of real networks with the presence of hubs due to the law of preferential attachment that states that the growth rate is proportional to the size of the nodes [8].

As we can imagine, the prevalence of "winner-takes-all" phenomena in markets increases wealth inequalities because a selected few can capture increasing amounts of income that would otherwise be more evenly distributed throughout the population of companies [19]. Accordingly, such kind of economic polarization strongly limits the possibility of small companies emerging.

2.3   Addressing AI Pitfalls

In literature, the AI drawbacks described in the previous section have been tackled from three main perspectives: *i)* designing models to capture their dynamics and behaviors; *ii)* analyzing their emergence in real-world scenario via empirical data; *iii)* mitigating their effect through ad-hoc prevention strategies. In the following, we explore an exemplifying case study related to Polarization, Congestion, and WAT phenomena for each of these approaches.

Modeling. *How is it possible to model how opinions evolve within a population as a result of peer-to-peer interactions among people?* This kind of question can be investigated through the tools of **opinion dynamics**. Opinion dynamics models aim at understanding how opinions evolve within a population, simulating interactions between agents of the population, in a process governed by mathematical equations incorporating sociological rules of opinion formation. The perks of opinion dynamics models - and agent-based models in general - is that they allow for "what-if" scenarios analyses and to track the cause-consequence link to understand the drivers of a certain state.

In the following, we describe an opinion dynamics model that incorporates cognitive biases and explores the effects that a recommender system - creating an algorithmic bias - may have on the resulting dynamics.

Algorithmic Bias Model. The so-called *bounded confidence models* constitute a broad family of models where agents are influenced only by neighbours in the social network having an opinion sufficiently close to theirs. Specifically, the DW model [20] considers a population of N agents, where each agent i has a continuous opinion $x_i \in [0,1]$. At every discrete time step the model randomly selects a pair (i,j), and, if their opinion distance is lower than a threshold ϵ_{DW}, $|x_i - x_j| \le \epsilon_{DW}$, then the two agents change their opinion taking the average. The AB model [21], which extends the DW one, introduces a bias towards similar individuals in the interaction partner's choice adding another parameter to model the algorithmic bias: $\gamma \ge 0$. This parameter represents the filtering power of a generic recommendation algorithm: if it is close to 0, the agent has the same probability of interacting with all of its peers. As γ grows, so does the probability of interacting with agents holding similar opinions, while the probability of interacting with those who hold distant opinions decreases. The introduction of stronger bias causes more fragmentation, more polarization, and more instability. Fragmentation is interpreted as an increased number of clusters, while polarization is interpreted as an increasing pairwise distance among opinions and instability means a slowdown of time to convergence with a large number of opinion clusters that coexist for a certain period.

Characterizing. *How is it possible to detect and prevent congestion in mobility networks?* The detection and prediction of traffic congestions across road networks are crucial for several reasons, such as the reduction of air pollution, reduction of the travel time for the drivers, and the increase of security along roads. According to [22], the congestion detection problem requires data-driven approaches. In fact, several works use empirical data to perform their study on traffic congestion.

The pervasive presence of vehicles equipped with GPS localization systems provides a precise way to sense their movements on the road; vehicles equipped with GPS can act as mobile sensors that sense information regarding traffic conditions as well as providing a characterization of drivers' behavior that can be an indicator of congestion happening.

With proper analysis, GPS trajectories can be used for detecting and/or predicting traffic jam conditions [23] as it is possible to recognize some patterns that indicate if a driver is stuck in a traffic jam, e.g. if their speed is significantly lower than the speed allowed in that particular road and their trajectory is characterized by sudden speed changes indicating close (both in time and space) starts and braking. Vaqar et al. [23], propose a methodology that detects traffic congestion using pattern recognition.

Recently, AI models were used in the traffic congestion detection/prediction task. As an example, in [22] the authors use both Deep Learning as well as conventional Machine Learning models, trained with real vehicular GPS data, to predict the traffic congestion level. According to their results, Deep Learning models obtain higher accuracy in traffic congestion prediction compared to conventional Machine Learning models.

Mitigating. *How is it possible to mitigate the winner-takes-all effect on economic networks?* Traditionally, progressive taxes, antitrust laws, and similar legislation are typical countermeasures against centralization. However, Lera and colleagues [17] recently found that the mere limitation of the power of most dominant agents may be ineffective because it addresses only the symptoms rather than the underlying cause, i.e. an imbalanced system that catalyzes such dominance.

Following such reasoning, they designed an early warning system and then an optimal intervention policy to prevent and mitigate the rise of the WAT effect in growing complex networks. First, they mathematically defined a system of interacting agents, where the rate at which an agent establishes connections to others is proportional to its already existing number of connections and its intrinsic fitness (i.e., growth rate). Then, they found that by calibrating the system's parameters with maximum likelihood, they can monitor in real-time its distance from a WAT state. Therefore, if the system is close to a WAT state, they increase the fitness of the other economic actors of the networks.

In such a way, they have shown how to efficiently drive the system back into a more stable state in terms of the fitness distribution of all the actors involved.

3   Beyond Data-Driven Approaches: Behavioural Models to Understand Societal Phenomena

There are phenomena depending on physical events for which not all data is readily available that lead to real-world effects. One example comes from our recent experience with the Covid-19 pandemics. For example, we may imagine that after restrictions are lifted people will spend more in shops, but how can we know how much or when will this happen? How can we answer very specific questions like: will a souvenir shop survive? Surely, we need data to answer these questions, but data themselves are not enough if they are not contextualised into an underlying model. Hence, in this uncertain situation, we need models that include human behaviour to support decisions, since data-based predictions are insufficient if we want to predict human behaviour based on sociality, economics and health.

In the remainder of this section, we describe some case studies in-depth and discuss approaches to analyse them with appropriate tools to try to answer the question of how data and models can be connected.

3.1   Tracking Online Extremism that Leads to Offline Extremist Behaviours

The concept of radicalisation is by no means solid and clear, and also, when it comes to radical behaviours like terrorism, there is no universally accepted definition. Such a lack of definition inevitably makes it harder to understand the process that brings people on the path towards radicalisation and how and if people can be de-radicalised.

Theory of Radicalisation. According to Kruglanski et al. [24] the radicalisation process involves an individual moving toward believing and engaging in activities that violate important social norms, mainly because radicalised individuals are focused on only one personal goal, undermining everything else that may be important to other people, seeing radicalism as motivational imbalance. The model developed by Kruglanski et al. [24] identifies three crucial components - both personal and social - that lead to the extreme commitment to a certain goal that we can find in radicalised individuals:

1. The need for significance: the motivational component that identifies the goal to which the individual is highly committed
2. Ideology: the cultural component that defines the role of group ideologies in identifying violent means as appropriate in goal pursuit
3. The social component identifies the group dynamics through which the individual comes to endorse the group ideology. Commitment to ideology is fostered through social connections and the considerable group pressure placed on the individual when those surrounding him espouse his ideological views.

Having this (still very crude) model of extremism can support us in finding out extremist behavior on social media. We can start looking for expressions on social media platforms where people make extreme remarks just to get attention. One can also check whether people reinforce each other ideas and all these ideas can be linked to the same ideology.

Extremism on Online Social Networks. A social media platform is a powerful tool for the formation and maintenance of social groups. Crucially, social media platforms let users actively participate in groups through several mechanisms explicitly designed for the purpose. In the case of radicalisation outlined above, active participation in groups plays a crucial role: people first identify themselves as belonging to a group, and then through various types of active participation, identify increasingly closely with that group, discriminate increasingly strongly against out-groups, and eventually participate in practices that isolate the group, and instil fear of external groups. Of course, the vast majority of the time, these mechanisms help users create socially beneficial groups, and help people find, join, and participate in these groups. Nonetheless, social media systems also have minor effects in encouraging users to move along the pathway towards radicalisation alongside these socially beneficial functions.

The goal is to capture the early signals of radicalisation (on social networks) and understand the path towards such behaviour to prevent extremist behaviour in real life. We need to bridge the gap between data and models to tackle this goal.

Identify Extremism on Online Social Networks. Identifying extremist-associated conversations on Online Social Networks (OSN) is an open problem. Extremist groups have been leveraging OSN (1) to spread their message and (2) gain recruits. To determine whether a particular user engages in extremist conversation, one can explore different metrics as proxies for misbehaviour, including the sentiment of the user's published posts, the polarity of the user's ego network, and user mentions. In [25] they find that - on a Twitter dataset - combining all these features and then using different known classifiers leads to the highest accuracy. However, the recent events of the Capitol Hill riot showed how one cannot assume anything on extremist behaviours by only looking at one social network data. In fact, after the start of the Capitol Hill riot, related posts started to trend on social media. A study by Hitkul et al. [26] analysing trending traffic from Twitter and Parler showed that a considerable proportion of Parler activity was in support of undermining the validity of the 2020 US Presidential elections, while the Twitter conversation disapproved of Trump. From this simple example, one can understand that while in one social media we may not see pathways towards radicalisation, these may emerge by changing social media, so the data we need to analyse the collective behaviour is scattered between several platforms, and we need to look at the right one if we want to identify the characteristics of the phenomena. So if we want to understand radicalisation, we need to ask ourselves what is the right data for the task, whether this can be retrieved and, eventually, what is the connection between the data and reality.

A Model of Radicalisation. In order to answer the question of how people radicalise and if we can find pathways towards radicalisation, we need a model of human behaviour. The purpose of the model by Hurk and Dignum [27] - based on the theoretical framework by Kruglanski et al. [24] - is to show that the combination of a high need for significance, a radical ideology and a social group acting according to that ideology can start the process of radicalisation. Agents - connected in a social network - live in a world where the goal is to keep their significance level as high as possible. They can gain significance by performing actions and getting acknowledged by their social surrounding. How actions can increase significance is defined in two different ideologies. Every agent belongs to a group that acts according to an ideology. In extreme cases, the agent can switch to the other group with the other ideology. In this context, radical behaviour means agents that perform actions that give them a significant gain in significance, but others reject those actions. Furthermore, the population of agents will split into groups, where agents will be surrounded mainly by other agents belonging to the same group. The results show that groups of radical agents emerge, where radicalising individuals form isolated social bubbles. It shows the importance of social surroundings in order to start radicalising. Furthermore, the agent's circumstances seem to be important because not all agents with a low level of significance can gain it back. These results support understanding the radicalisation process, but they can also give insights into why de-radicalisation is not straightforward as long as one cannot escape his social group.

3.2 Multi-agent Behavioural Models for Epidemic Spreading: From Model to Data in the Covid-19 Crisis

During the Covid-19 crisis, policymakers had to make many difficult decisions with the help of models for epidemic spreading. However, classical epidemiological models do not directly translate into the interventions that can be taken to limit the spread of the virus, neither these models include economic/social consequences of these interventions. Policies may impact epidemics, economics and societies differently, and a policy that can be beneficial from one perspective can have negative consequences from another. In order to make good decisions, policymakers need to be aware of the combined consequences of the policies. There is a need for tools to support this decision-making process that enable the design and analysis of many what-if scenarios and potential outcomes. Tools should thus facilitate the investigation of alternatives and highlight the fundamental choices to be made rather than giving one solution.

Agent-Based Social Simulation for Covid-19 Crisis. The consequences of a pandemic can be addressed from different points of view, that all have some limitations when considered separately: (1) classical epidemiological models do not consider human behaviour or consequences of interventions on actions of people or - if they incorporate such things into the model parameters - they lose the cause-effect links and causes cannot be easily identified and adjusted; (2) also economic models fail to capture human behaviour always assuming perfect rationality; (3) social network theory does not say anything on how the social network will change and how people will react to a new policy. The proposed solution by Dignum et al. is to make human behaviour central and use it as a link to connect epidemics, economics, and society. ASSOCC, a model by Dignum et al. proposed in [28] is an agent-based social simulation tool that supports decision-makers gain insights on the possible effects of policies by showing their interdependencies, and as such, making clear which are the underlying dilemmas that have to be addressed. Such understanding can lead to more acceptable solutions, adapted to the situation of each country and its current socio-economic state, and that is sustainable from a long-term perspective. In this model - implemented in Netlogo - the main components are agents, places, global functions, and policies. Agents take decisions based on the container model of needs: needs are satisfied by activities and decay over time. The basic needs included in the Covid-19 simulation model are safety, belonging, self-esteem, autonomy, and survival. These needs combine health, wealth, and social well-being in the same simulation model. Agents are organised along a grid and the environment can pose constraints to physical actions and impose norms and regulations, while when interacting, agents can take other agents' characteristics (e.g., being infected).

One of the advantages of using such model is that instead of providing a single prediction, it gives support to investigate the consequences of different scenarios. Due to its agent based nature, it is also possible to explain where results come from; it allows for more fine grained analysis on the impact of interventions, and it can be used in combination with domain specific models. Having a good insight into these dependencies can provide the domain-specific models with better information to make specific optimisations or predictions for that intervention's effect. Thus, the strength of the different types of models can be combined rather than seen as competing.

4   Hands-on Tutorial

In this lecture, we also provided a three-part tutorial[1], explaining how to use different tools to simulate the effects on networks treated within this manuscript.

For this practical part of the tutorial, we employed two Python libraries: scikit-mobility [29] for the study and analysis of human mobility and NDlib [30] for the simulation and study of spreading phenomena on networks.

The first part of the tutorial introduces the fundamental concepts of human mobility and explains how to create a mobility network that describes the movements of individuals. In the second part of the tutorial, diffusion phenomena are simulated on a real network with different state-of-the-art algorithms. In the last section, state-of-the-art opinion dynamics algorithms are simulated over a real social network.

5   Conclusions

In this tutorial, we have discussed the social dimension of Artificial Intelligence in terms of how AI technologies can support or affect emerging social challenges.

---

[1] https://github.com/GiulianoCornacchia/ACAL_SAI_Tutorial.

On the one hand, the goal of this tutorial was to consider the network effects of AI and their impact on society. On the other hand, we wanted to introduce strategies, both data-driven and not, to model, characterise and mitigate AI societal pitfalls. Here we conclude by pointing out some limitations of the existing approaches and the research directions that should be addressed in the future.

First, both empirical and modelling works consider AI drawbacks too simplistically, often relying on unrealistic assumptions that do not reflect real-world phenomena' complexity. For such a reason, we claim the urgency of starting cooperation with digital platforms to understand better whether AI-powered tools exacerbate endogenous features of human beings. In this direction, ongoing projects such as the Global Partnership of Artificial Intelligence (GPAI[2]) are trying to collaborate with social media platforms in order to study, from the inside, the effects of recommendation systems on users.

Secondly, we want to stress the importance of designing AI systems that pursue goals both at the individual level and considering the whole population involved. Indeed, most harmful phenomena analysed in this tutorial emerge as group phenomena. For instance, congestion in mobility networks happens because every individual is given the same suggestion, or echo chambers emerge because recommendation systems cluster together like-minded individuals.

In conclusion, towards social AI ecosystems, we encourage readers to design AI tools that foster collective interests rather than individual needs.

References

1. Afrin, T., Yodo, N.: A survey of road traffic congestion measures towards a sustainable and resilient transportation system. Sustainability **12**(11), 4660 (2020)
2. Pariser, E.: The Filter Bubble: What the Internet is Hiding From You. Penguin UK, Westminster (2011)
3. Sunstein, C.R.: Republic. com. Princeton University Press, Princeton (2001)
4. Rycroft, R.S.: The Economics of Inequality, Discrimination, Poverty, and Mobility. Routledge, Milton Park (2017)
5. Schelling, T.C.: Models of segregation. Am. Econ. Rev. **59**(2), 488–493 (1969)
6. Lorig, F., Vanhée, L., Dignum, F.: Agent-based social simulation for policy making (2022)
7. Erdős P., Rényi, A.: On random graphs. i. Publicationes Math. **6**, 290–297 (1959)
8. Barabási, A.-L., Albert, R.: Emergence of scaling in random networks. Science **286**(5439), 509–512 (1999)
9. Watts, D.J., Strogatz, S.H.: Collective dynamics of 'small-world' networks. Nature **393**, 440–442 (1998)
10. Jean Tsang, S.: Cognitive discrepancy, dissonance, and selective exposure. Media Psychol. **22**(3), 394–417 (2019)
11. Jeong, M., Zo, H., Lee, C.H., Ceran, Y.: Feeling displeasure from online social media postings: a study using cognitive dissonance theory. Comput. Hum. Behav. **97**, 231–240 (2019)
12. Festinger, L.: A Theory of Cognitive Dissonance, vol. 2. Stanford University Press, Redwood City (1957)

---

[2] https://gpai.ai/.

13. Borah, P., Thorson, K., Hwang, H.: Causes and consequences of selective exposure among political blog readers: the role of hostile media perception in motivated media use and expressive participation. J. Inf. Technol. Polit. **12**(2), 186–199 (2015)
14. Bozdag, E.: Bias in algorithmic filtering and personalization. Ethics Inf. Technol. **15**(3), 209–227 (2013)
15. Ge, Y., et al.: Understanding echo chambers in e-commerce recommender systems. In: Proceedings of the 43rd International ACM SIGIR Conference on Research and Development in Information Retrieval, pp. 2261–2270 (2020)
16. Braess, D.: Über ein paradoxon aus der verkehrsplanung. Unternehmensforschung **12**, 258–268 (1968)
17. Lera, S.C., Pentland, A., Sornette, D.: Prediction and prevention of disproportionally dominant agents in complex networks. Proc. Natl. Acad. Sci. **117**(44), 27090–27095 (2020)
18. Moore, M., Tambini, D.: Digital dominance: the power of Google. Facebook, and Apple. Oxford University Press, Amazon (2018)
19. Cook, P.J., Frank, R.H.: The winner-Take-all Society: Why the Few at the Top Get So Much More Than the Rest of Us. Random House, New York (2010)
20. Deffuant, G., Neau, D., Amblard, F., Weisbuch, G.: Mixing beliefs among interacting agents. Adv. Complex Syst. **3**, 87–98 (2000)
21. Sîrbu, A., Pedreschi, D., Giannotti, F., Kertész, J.: Algorithmic bias amplifies opinion fragmentation and polarization: a bounded confidence model. PLoS ONE **14**(3), e0213246 (2019)
22. Sun, S., Chen, J., Sun, J.: Congestion prediction based on GPS trajectory data. Int. J. Distrib. Sens. Netw. **15**, 155014771984744 (2019)
23. Vaqar, S.A., Basir, O.: Traffic pattern detection in a partially deployed vehicular ad hoc network of vehicles. IEEE Wireless Commun. **16**(6), 40–46 (2009)
24. Kruglanski, A.W., Gelfand, M.J., Bélanger, J.J., Sheveland, A., Hetiarachchi, M., Gunaratna, R.K.: The psychology of radicalization and deradicalization: How significance quest impacts violent extremism. Polit. Psychol. **35**, 69–93 (2014)
25. Wei, Y., Singh, L., Martin, S.: Identification of extremism on Twitter. In: 2016 IEEE/ACM International Conference on Advances in Social Networks Analysis and Mining (ASONAM), pp. 1251–1255. IEEE (2016)
26. Prabhu, A., et al.: Capitol (pat) riots: a comparative study of Twitter and parler. arXiv preprint arXiv:2101.06914 (2021)
27. van den Hurk, M., Dignum, F.: Towards fundamental models of radicalization. In: ESSA (2019)
28. Dignum, F., et al.: Analysing the combined health, social and economic impacts of the corovanvirus pandemic using agent-based social simulation. Minds Mach. **30**(2), 177–194 (2020). https://doi.org/10.1007/s11023-020-09527-6
29. Pappalardo, L., Simini, F., Barlacchi, G., Pellungrini, R.: Scikit-mobility: a Python library for the analysis, generation and risk assessment of mobility data. arXiv preprint arXiv:1907.07062 (2019)
30. Rossetti, G., Milli, L., Rinzivillo, S., Sîrbu, A., Pedreschi, D., Giannotti, F.: Ndlib: a python library to model and analyze diffusion processes over complex networks. Int. J. Data Sci. Anal. **5**(1), 61–79 (2018)

Author Index

Printed in the United States
by Baker & Taylor Publisher Services